MW00616399

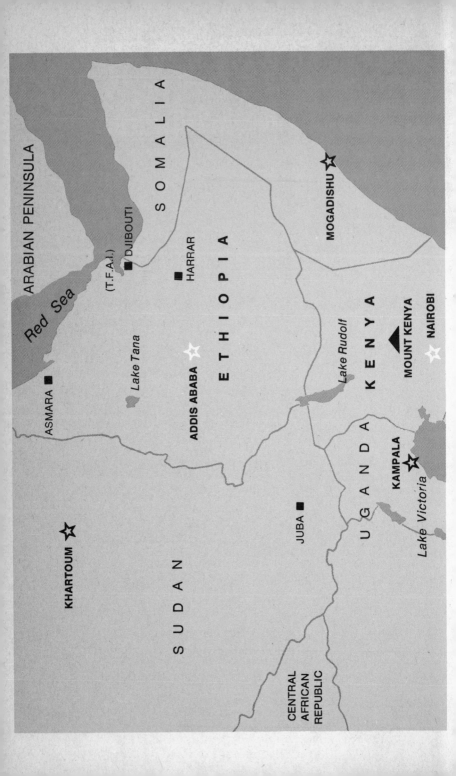

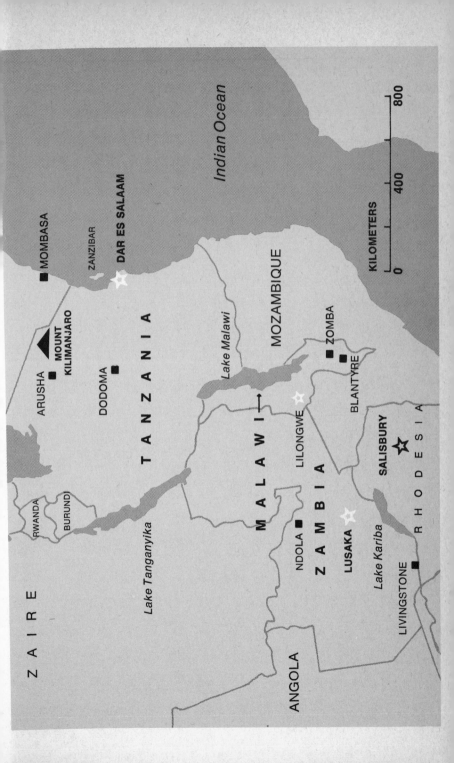

EAST AFRICA

EAST AFRICA

A TRAVEL GUIDE

Alan Magary and Kerstin Fraser Magary

HARPER & ROW, PUBLISHERS

New York, Evanston, San Francisco, London

FIRST EDITION

Maps by *Clifford Line*
Drawings by *Rena Fennessy*

Designed by *Sidney Feinberg*

Library of Congress Cataloging in Publication Data

Magary, Alan.
  East Africa: a travel guide.
   1. Africa, Eastern—Description and travel—Tours.
I. Magary, Kerstin Fraser, joint author. II. Title.
DT365.2.M33 1974   916.7′04   74–1836
ISBN 0–06–012792–9

To the peoples and wildlife
of Eastern Africa

CONTENTS

Preface, xiii

How to Use This Book, xvii

Hotel Rating System, xviii. Abbreviations, Terms, and Symbols, xix. Quick Metric Conversion Table, xxi. Quick Currency Conversion Table, xxi.

INTRODUCTION: *Plans and Preparations,* 1

Planning a Trip to Eastern Africa, 1. Traveling to and around Eastern Africa, 13. Before You Go, 54. General Information, 63.

KENYA: *Beauty and the Beasts,* 77

Planning a Trip, 83. Entry Requirements, 92. Getting to Kenya, 95. Getting around Kenya, 99. General Information, 123. Nairobi, 142. Mombasa, 174.
Driving Routes:
  K-1: Nairobi–Mombasa, 188.
  K-2: Mombasa–North Coast–Malindi–Lamu, 201.
  K-3: Mombasa–South Coast, 219.
  K-4: Taveta–Taita Hills–Voi, 224.
  K-5: Namanga–Amboseli–Kajiado–Nairobi, 225.
  K-6: Nairobi–Masai Mara, 229.
  K-7: Nairobi–Nyeri–Nanyuki–Isiolo–Marsabit–Ethiopia, 234.

K-8: Murang'a–Embu–Meru–Isiolo (East Side of Mount Kenya), 259.

K-9: Nanyuki–Nyahururu (Thomson's Falls)–Nakuru, 263.

K-10: Nairobi–Naivasha–Nakuru–Eldoret–Uganda, 269.

K-11: Western Kenya Circuit from Nakuru, 284.

K-12: Limuru High Country–Kikuyu Escarpment Excursion from Nairobi, 292.

K-13: Karen–Ngong Hills Excursion from Nairobi, 295.

K-14: Nairobi National Park–Olorgesailie–Lake Magadi Excursion from Nairobi, 298.

TANZANIA: *Socialism and Tourism,* 306

Planning a Trip, 312. Entry Requirements, 319. Getting to Tanzania, 322. Getting around Tanzania, 326. General Information, 334. Dar es Salaam, 342. Zanzibar, 356.

Driving Routes:

T-1: Serengeti–Ngorongoro Crater–Lake Manyara–Arusha, 362.

T-2: Arusha–Namanga, Kenya, 384.

T-3: Arusha–Moshi–Dar es Salaam, 385.

T-4: Moshi–Kilimanjaro (Marangu)–Taveta, Kenya, 395.

T-5: Lunga Lunga, Kenya–Tanga–Junction with Arusha–Dar es Salaam Highway, 403.

T-6: Dar es Salaam–Mikumi National Park–Iringa–Mbeya–Tunduma–Zambia, 406.

T-7: Dar es Salaam–Beach Hotels–Bagamoyo, 414.

T-8: Arusha–Tarangire National Park–Dodoma–Iringa, 420.

T-9: Seronera, Serengeti–Fort Ikoma–Lake Victoria–Lake Tanganyika–Gombe Stream National Park, 428.

Kilwa Ruins, 436.

Mafia Island, 438.

ETHIOPIA: *The Hidden Empire,* 441

Planning a Trip, 446. Entry Requirements, 450. Getting to Ethiopia, 452. Getting around Ethiopia, 455. General Information,

464. Addis Ababa, 474. Historic Route, 489. Asmara, 518. Other Destinations, 525.

ZAMBIA IN THE SUN, 536

Planning a Trip, 541. Entry Requirements, 545. Getting to Zambia, 547. Getting around Zambia, 550. General Information, 556. Lusaka, 562. Livingstone and Victoria Falls, 571.
Driving Routes:
Z-1: (Great North Road): Tunduma, Tanzania–Mpika–Kapiri Mposhi–Kabwe–Lusaka–Chirundu, Rhodesia, 584.
Z-2: (Great East Road): Lusaka–Luangwa Valley–Chipata–Malawi, 591.
Z-3: Lusaka–Livingstone–Victoria Falls, 598.
Z-4: Lusaka–Blue Lagoon–Kafue National Park–Mongu, 601.
Z-5: Lusaka–Copperbelt–Zaire, 606.
Z-6: Lusaka–Siavonga–Kariba Dam–Rhodesia, 614.
Z-7: Tunduma, Tanzania–Mbala–Lake Tanganyika–Kalambo Falls, 617.

MALAWI: *Land of the Lake,* 621

Planning a Trip, 625. Entry Requirements, 629. Getting to Malawi, 630. Getting around Malawi, 633. General Information, 638. Blantyre, 644.
Driving Routes:
Q-1: Nyala, Zambia–Rumphi–Lilongwe–Zomba–Limbe (Blantyre)–Thyolo–Mulanje–Milanje, Mozambique, 652.
Q-2: Blantyre–Lengwe National Park–Chiromo–Thyolo, 666.
Q-3: Liwonde Barrage–Mangochi–Monkey Bay–Salima, 669.
Q-4: Salima–Nkhotakota, 677.
Q-5: Mzimba–Vipya Plateau–Mzuzu–Nkhata Bay, 680.
Q-6: Rumphi–Livingstonia–Karonga–Chitipa–Nyala, Zambia, 682.

Acknowledgments, 687
Index, 689

MAPS

Nairobi, 144–145
Mombasa, 176–177
Kenya Driving Routes
    K-1, K-4, and K-5, 189
    K-2, 202
    K-3, 220
    K-6, 230
    K-7, K-8, and K-9, 235
    K-10, 270
    K-11, 285
    K-12 and K-13, 293
    K-14, 298
Dar es Salaam, 343
Tanzania Driving Routes
    T-1 and T-2, 363

T-3, T-4, and T-5, 386
T-6, 407
T-7, 415
T-8, 421
T-9, 429
Ethiopia, 440
Addis Ababa, 475
Lusaka, 564–565
Zambia Driving Routes
    Z-1 through Z-7, 585
Blantyre, 646–647
Malawi Driving Routes
    Q-1, Q-2, and Q-3, 653
    Q-1, Q-4, Q-5, and Q-6, 678

City-to-city distance charts, 35-37

PREFACE

Safari. East Africa. Even these days, to millions of blasé jet travelers the words sound romantic beyond all measure. There in the mind's eye is a thundering, lowing herd of wildebeest on the infinitely large Serengeti, stretching across the horizon against a big orange African sun. In Amboseli, with grand Kilimanjaro as a backdrop, a lion stalks and kills a zebra. A herd of elephant takes a red-dust bath in Tsavo. You are there, rolling across the savanna in a Land-Rover, sitting out the heat of the day near thornscrub wild with the raucous chatter of weaverbirds, going to sleep at night as a million crickets celebrate the perfect starry sky. And somewhere, of course, there are drums and dancing in an African village.

That is just *one* safari, and that is just *one* Eastern Africa. First, the Swahili word *safari* means just about any journey anyone makes. It is by no means only a hunting expedition with the traditional (and outmoded) line of porters with boxes on their heads. A safari these days for increasing thousands of travelers is a trip taken in a zebra-striped minibus through half a dozen national parks, with each day's destination a modern game lodge. This safari perhaps includes a tour of Ethiopia's historic places and a flight to Victoria Falls, a few nights under canvas in Kenya's Northern Frontier District and a day or two on an Indian Ocean beach. That's the modern safari.

And Eastern Africa is more than game parks. Eastern Africa is people: fine-featured Ethiopians with their ancient Christianity; tall, spear-carrying Masai herdsmen, clinging to a pastoral life; Malawian youth in the Young Pioneers, learning how to be "agricultural missionaries"; busy Kikuyu, Luo, and Kamba businessmen and politicians in East Africa's metropolis, Nairobi; Zambian long-haul truckdrivers driving enormous Fiat trucks up the monotonous "Hell Run" to Dar es Salaam; Africans of all kinds and descriptions, going about the business of developing their countries.

And Africa is more than a 200-mm telephoto view of a wealth of wildlife. Try climbing the highest and second-highest mountains in Africa—19,340-foot Kilimanjaro and 17,058-foot Mount Kenya; you can do both easily on a three-week vacation. Try goggling on Kenya's coral reefs. Try going after a mako shark in the Indian Ocean or a fighting tigerfish in Lake Rudolf, Lake Kariba, or Lake Tanganyika. Try golfing at the Commonwealth's highest golf course—Molo, Kenya. Take a first-class steamer cruise on Lake Victoria or Lake Malawi.

So welcome to Eastern Africa.

This book, the product of sixteen months of traveling and writing, is the first comprehensive, *practical* guidebook to Eastern Africa—Kenya, Tanzania, Ethiopia, Zambia, and Malawi. Intending to open up Eastern Africa, we wrote this book for all manner of travelers—not only people with lots of money but people with very little. We describe package tours and big international-class hotels, but we also put in information about local bus travel and cheap places to stay. You can find the descriptions of a klipspringer and a white rhino in this book, and you can find out the best place to camp in Samburu, four different ways (and prices) up Kilimanjaro, and where to find African food in Nairobi (no easy trick!). We tell you about package tours from the U.S., if that's what you want, and we tell you about deluxe photo safaris, but we also tell you how to make your own self-drive camping safari for only $20 per person per day (car-camping in East Africa is not only possible but it's grand fun, and we encourage it). We try to stress the how-to's of travel in Eastern Africa today, and that includes what things cost, everything from the price of a lucky elephant-hair bracelet (bargain down from 10/–) to the cost of a double room at the Addis Ababa Hilton (US $23–25).

Uganda has not been included in this guide, despite the fact that it is part of a socioeconomic-political unit called East Africa, with Kenya and Tanzania. The reason for its exclusion is that we could not go there, since General Idi Amin had closed Uganda to tourism from fall 1972 to fall 1973. During the period of turbulence, the tourist industry was reorganized, and as of this writing we not only had no firsthand information about Uganda tourism but no reliable secondhand information. Tour operators are still (1974) steering clear of the country.

A guidebook is valueless without prices, but prices do change. Those quoted in this guidebook are mainly 1973, with major hotel rates and air fares as of mid-1974. Prices actually had not changed much from 1973 and were not expected to change much in 1974 (gasoline may be the exception). We have noted all prices in the local currency. We did this because local prices did not change while the U.S. dollar was being periodically devalued, changing its relationship to the Ethiopian, Zambian, and Malawian currencies and, in mid-1973, with the three East African shilling currencies.

Inevitably in a book of this size and scope, there are errors and mistaken opinions. We ask for your forgiveness and for your help in correcting them. If you travel to any of the countries described in this book, send us reports on new prices and new hotels, and give us your criticisms, not only of this book but also of the hotels you stayed in and tour operators you used. If no one else will entertain your travel gripes, we will. We'll appreciate brochures, hotel tariff sheets, etc.

Please send letters to: East Africa Guide, c/o Harper & Row, 10 East 53d St., New York, N.Y. 10022. The authors intend to prepare, for interested readers, periodic updating sheets, probably mimeographed, and the more readers who write to us, the better.

The photographs appearing in this guide have been taken with GAF color and black and white film and have been processed by the GAF Photo Service.

HOW TO USE THIS BOOK

Practical information in this guide is easily found—each bit of information, such as "Weights and Measures" or "Vehicle Documents," is in its own small section in each country chapter. See the table of contents and index. Tourist attractions and other places, however, fall in no neat order. What we have done is to divide each country (except Ethiopia) into road routes, e.g. "Route K-1, Nairobi–Mombasa." Kenya, well covered by roads and tourists and hotels, is handled in fourteen routes, ten of them reasonably straight A-to-B routes, three of them excursions from Nairobi, and one a long circuit around western Kenya. If a place is not on the road itself, it is listed (and so described) as a turnoff from the main road. In this fashion, "Route K-9, Nanyuki–Nyahururu (Thomson's Falls)–Nakuru," includes Lake Rudolf, because the main-traveled road to the lake starts at Thomson's Falls.

All routes are annotated in *kilometers* (abbreviated *km*) because road signs and car odometers are marked in kilometers (1 km equals .6 of a mile; 1 mile equals 1.6 km). "Km 300" is a location; "300 km" is a distance. By this method, "Route K-10, Km 0" is the beginning of that route in Nairobi, while "Km 40" is the Kikuyu Escarpment viewpoint over the Rift Valley, "Km 83" the turnoff to Lake Naivasha, "Km 154" the road to Lake Nakuru. By subtracting, you can follow the route in reverse, from Nakuru to Nairobi, and you can determine intermediate distances—it is 43 km from the Escarpment to Lake Naivasha.

The system of route numbering is our own: "K" is for Kenya routes, "T" for Tanzania, "Z" for Zambia, and "Q" for Malawi ("Q" because the Malawi road system already has M-1, M-2, etc., designations as trunk routes). For the most part, our country routes connect to one another. Where possible, we note local highway numbers, though many do not yet appear on road signs.

We flew around Ethiopia, so fewer tourist attractions are described. Flying is the best method of traveling in Ethiopia and Zambia, while driving is by far the best way in East Africa and Malawi.

To find the description of a specific place, refer to the index.

Rather than describe all of Africa's animals in one section (a job better done by a wildlife guide—see p. 10), we have dispersed them through the game parks, so you can read about the white rhino where you are most likely to see one—in Meru National Park, Kenya. See the index under the type of animal to find the description and picture.

Hotel Rating System. There exists no area-wide rating system for hotels. Zambia has a system of one to four stars and "ungraded." Kenya's system, covering 132 hotels, puts lodging on six levels, from A* down to D. Ethiopia is coming up with a star system. We have imposed our own rating system. It is a *relative* system; the very top hotels in Kenya, for instance, may be a couple of notches below the very best in Europe, but they are top of the heap in East Africa, so we have called them *"1st-class international."* Hotels that are generally new, modern, very clean, and entirely adequate for today's international tourist, but lack the style, class, personality, and perhaps prices of the top hotels, are *"2d-class international."* All other hotels fall into a *local* category—1st, 2d, or 3d. *1st-class local* hotels are those which are generally older and show their age and for one reason or another can't rate with international hotels; but they are all quite clean, comfortable, generally well-managed hotels that the tourist should be happy in. *2d-class local* hotels are definitely a step down; they are inadequate in a number of respects but may be suitable for economy travelers. *3d-class local* hotels are substandard, and even low-budgeters had better look before they book.

In addition to this somewhat objective five-level system, we give some hotels one, two, or three stars. This may have nothing to do with the rating, but indicates the hotel is *special* in some way—it has a great location, or an especially nice personality, or superb management. This is a more personal rating system. Not all 1st-class international hotels get a star; in fact, most don't. Some 1st-class local hotels get stars; but this does not mean they are superior in all ways to other hotels.

Unless otherwise stated, room rates (called "tariff" in Eastern Africa) include private bath or shower. The note "w/o bath" means the bathroom is not in your room and is shared. Though a hotel may offer a variety of room rates, we have listed the least expensive plan— usually "B&B," which means you pay for bed and breakfast. "DB&B" is dinner, bed, and breakfast; "FB" is full board (three meals); "bed only" means you pay for room only, though it doesn't mean meals aren't available. The hotel without a dining room is rare, but table d'hôte meals (menu changed every day) are the rule. In the capital cities, Asmara, Mombasa, and on the Kenya coast, we'd advise not paying for DB&B or full board at the hotel; restaurants or other hotel dining rooms are worth trying.

Banda, rondavel, cottage, and *chalet* are somewhat interchangeable terms used in East Africa to refer to a room, usually with bath, in its own small building. A rondavel is round, whereas the others are not necessarily. Hotels with bandas, rondavels, cottages, or chalets of course have a main building with dining room, lobby, and so forth.

Air-conditioning: The very top hotels are air-conditioned, and most coast hotels are, also. Elsewhere, a-c is not necessary.

Abbreviations, Terms, and Symbols. Following is a summary list of abbreviations, terms, and symbols, some of which are explained in more detail elsewhere.

a-c	air-conditioned
AE	American Express credit card accepted
BA	BankAmericard/Barclaycard accepted
B&B	bed and breakfast hotel rates
bed only	no meals included in hotel rates
DB&B	dinner, bed, and breakfast hotel rates
dbl	double room (with twin beds or double bed) or the rate applying to two persons in one room
DC	Diners Club card accepted; also District Commissioner
EP	Ethiopia Package tour (used in listings)
FB	full board—all three meals included in hotel rates
FIT	Foreign Individual Tour (independent; agent-arranged)
GIT	Group Inclusive Tour—cheapest commercial airfare generally available on a route, sold only with land arrangements (a package tour)
GPO	General Post Office
G.R.	Game Reserve (on maps)
H.S.I.	Haile Selassie I
incl	including

km	kilometer(s)
KP	Kenya Package tour (used in listings)
(L)	left
MP	Malawi Package tour (used in listings)
mpg	miles per gallon
NFD	Northern Frontier District, former official name of northern part of Kenya, still in use
N.P.	National Park (on maps)
N.R.	National Reserve (on maps)
opp.	opposite
pax	passengers
PC	private car—used in reference to a nongroup package tour (see p. 114)
qdrpl	quadruple (room for four persons)
(R)	right
rm(s)	room(s)
sgl	single room or the single occupancy rate applying to one person in a room, whether one-bed or two-bed room
SIC	seat-in-car (as opposed to PC—private car)—used in reference to a package tour in which seats in a car are individually sold and the tour run on a group basis (see p. 114)
tel.	telephone
TFAI	French abbreviation for French Territory of the Afars and the Issas, formerly French Somaliland (Djibouti)
TP	Tanzania Package tour (used in listings)
trpl	triple (room for three persons, usually a double with space for another bed)
w/bath	with private bathroom (all facilities including bathtub, possibly shower as well)
w/o bath	without private bathroom (room shares facilities elsewhere on the floor, but room usually has a washbasin)
ZP	Zambia Package tour (used in listings)
★	one star, given to a hotel that, in the personal opinion of the authors, is absolutely outstanding in at least one way (management, cuisine, location, atmosphere, character, comfort . . .)
★★	two stars, given to a hotel excelling in two or three ways
★★★	three stars, given to a hotel excelling in four or five ways. Details on this system on p. xviii

H   map symbol for hotel or other accommodation, with and
                   without dining rooms
1Xwk, 2Xwk, etc.   Once a week, twice a week, etc., in reference to
                   frequency of flights, departures, etc.

Quick Metric Conversion Table. Below are a few metric equivalents.
Inside the back cover is a detailed mile-kilometer conversion chart.

> 1 inch = 2.54 centimeters
> 1 yard = .914 meters
> 1 meter = 39.37 inches
> 1 mile = 1.609 kilometers
> 1 kilometer = .621 miles
> 1 pound = .453 kilograms (kilos)
> 1 kilo = 2.2 pounds
> 1 U.S. gallon = .833 Imperial gallons = 3.785 liters
> 1 liter = 1.05 quarts = .26 U.S. gallons = .22 Imperial gallons
> (1 Imperial gallon = 1.2 U.S. gallons)
> 1 square mile = 2.59 square kilometers = 259 hectares
> 1 square kilometer = .3861 square miles = 247.1 acres

Gasoline (petrol) consumption is usually measured in liters per 100
kilometers. 15 mpg works out to 15.5 liters per 100 km; 20 mpg to
11.8 liters per 100 km; 25 mpg to 9.4 liters per 100 km; 30 mpg to 7.8
liters per 100 km.

Temperatures are often quoted on the Centigrade scale: 0°C is
freezing (32°F), and 100°C is boiling (212°F). To convert to Fahren-
heit, multiply Centigrade by 1.8 and add 32. To convert to Centigrade,
subtract 32 and divide by 1.8.

Quick Currency Conversion Table. Detailed currency conversion
tables will be found in each country chapter.

Kenya
Tanzania
Uganda: $1 = 7/14 (7 shillings, 14 cents)
            1/– = $.14
Ethiopia: US$1 = E$2.07 (2 Ethiopian dollars, 7 cents)
            E$1 = US$.48
Zambia: $1 = K.64 (.64 of a Zambian kwacha, or 64 ngwee)
            K1 = $1.56
Malawi: $1 = K.82 (.82 of a Malawian kwacha, or 82 tambala)
            K1 = $1.21

The Zambian kwacha and the Malawian kwacha are not the same
currency. The three East African shilling currencies are separate, of-

ficially equal, but not readily convertible to one another. Finally, the Ethiopian dollar bears no resemblance to its U.S. namesake. The Rhodesian dollar (referred to in the Zambia chapter) is worth about US $1.70.

INTRODUCTION

PLANS AND PREPARATIONS

Planning a Trip to Eastern Africa

Where to Go—Highlights of Eastern Africa

As a guide to itinerary planning, here are the top tourist destinations of the six countries. More details are found under "What to See and Do" in the country chapters.

Kenya, a thriving capitalist country with bustling, skyscrapered Nairobi the travel center of Eastern Africa. Kenya is the land of sun, sea, savanna, and safari. Its main game parks: sprawling Tsavo; Amboseli, dominated by Kilimanjaro in the background; gently rolling Masai Mara; Lake Nakuru with its million flamingos. Tourists rarely miss shopping days in Nairobi or an overnight at a Mount Kenya or Aberdare game-viewing lodge like Treetops or The Ark. Other attractions: Lake Rudolf, Lake Naivasha, Mount Kenya, Meru, Marsabit, and Samburu game parks, Mombasa, Malindi, Lamu, and the marine parks.

Tanzania: With fantastic game parks and Kilimanjaro, Africa's highest mountain, diverse Tanzania is also a laboratory of African socialism. Main destinations: the Serengeti, "kingdom of predators" and teeming with huge herds of zebra and wildebeest; Ngorongoro Crater, a natural zoo within a volcanic caldera; Olduvai Gorge, the world's most famous prehistoric site; Lake Manyara, with its tree-climbing lions. The seaport-capital of Dar es Salaam, opposite the clove-and-arabesque island of Zanzibar, also attracts travelers. Other destinations: Arusha and its mountain-and-lake game park, Tarangire, Ruaha, Mikumi, and Selous game parks, and, of course, Kilimanjaro.

Ethiopia, an ancient Christian kingdom hidden and protected for centuries in its fortress of mountains, has the visible history the other countries lack: Gondar, with 16th-century castles and churches; Lalibela, a high, isolated mountain village with a dozen 12th-century churches hand-hewn out of solid rock; Axum, traditional capital of the Queen of Sheba, with stelae, tombs, and ruins from the 4th century. Bahar Dar, also on the "Historic Route," is the jumping-off point for the Blue Nile Falls and the island monasteries of Lake Tana. Other destinations: Massawa on the Red Sea, Asmara, Harrar, Dire Dawa, Makalle, the Rift Valley lakes, Semyen Mountains, and, naturally, Addis Ababa.

Zambia, a copper-rich nation also wealthy in wildlife, shares Africa's greatest geographical spectacle, Victoria Falls, with its bitterest enemy, Rhodesia. Unique to Zambia are walking safaris—at very reasonable cost—in lush Luangwa Valley and in Eastern Africa's biggest national park, Kafue. Other destinations: Lusaka, Kasaba Bay on Lake Tanganyika, Kariba Dam, and Lake Kariba.

Malawi, a slender, mountainous country hugging a long, blue lake, and wedged between black and white Africa, does not draw the tourists the other countries do. Its attractions for off-the-trodden-track travelers are the beautiful swimmable lake and the high, rolling Nyika Plateau and other forested highlands, Vipya and Zomba plateaus, and the new capital, Lilongwe.

What Kind of Trip for You?

There are a multitude of ways to get to and around Eastern Africa. Briefly, these are (1) the group package tour, (2) travel-agent-arranged Foreign Individual Tour, or FIT, (3) the expensive, luxury safari, (4) low-budget free-lancing, and (5) the U.S.-style car vacation (camping or lodging).

The easiest way to plan a trip is to walk into a travel agency, select a package tour and—presto! there's your trip. All you have to do is get visas and shots and then pack. That's the way most Americans go to East Africa, and there are advantages, such as cheaper GIT air fares and somebody's taking care of all your arrangements. On the other hand, group package tours are notorious for regimentation and inflexibility. And you will often whiz by or through far more than you can appreciate, winding up tired rather than enlightened.

The alternatives are generally more expensive. The FIT (a travel-trade term) is arranged to suit you, and you exercise great control over your travel arrangements. After reading this book, you would, for example, go to your travel agent and say, "I want to stay four days in Nairobi, two days in Dar es Salaam, two days each in Tsavo, Amboseli, Serengeti, and Ngorongoro Crater, and a day at Lake Nakuru, and I want to go on Ethiopia's Historic Route, take a three-day Zambia walking safari, and climb up Kilimanjaro." You'll probably pay higher air fares, you won't share in the group rates that many hotels give package tours, you'll have to pay the full cost of transport rather than, say, one-eighth share in a minibus, and so forth. The skillful travel agent, though, can find short package tours and tie them together, saving money. But if you have money, FITs are the way to go. Your local travel agent should be able to arrange everything; otherwise you can make arrangements by mail with a travel agency or tour operator in Africa (Nairobi makes the best tour center) and have access to his wider sources of information and more intimate knowledge of the area.

The East African version of a super-deluxe FIT is the luxury safari, as individually tailored as an Ahamed Brothers safari suit. A safari is literally any journey, but in the East Africa tourist industry it refers to a tourist's bush adventure, accompanied by professional hunter or guide, with nights spent in a luxury tented camp. Safari firms generally take you off the tourist circuit, and bend over backwards to cater to your whims. If you want to search for the black-faced rufous warbler, or take a canoe or camel safari, or simply see all the parks in style, the safari firm will arrange it for you—at a handsome price.

A fourth way to travel is the free-lance method, where you collect the information (which can be found mostly in this guidebook) and make your own arrangements as you go along. This is the preferred means for low-budget travelers, but you have to have time and patience.

Similar in spirit is the travel means we wholeheartedly endorse: U.S.-style car camping. At the risk of scandalizing Nairobi tour operators and safari firms, we say that any American who has more or less roughed it on a U.S. vacation can do the same in East Africa for three weeks and have the time of his life, at a moderate cost, too—about $20 per person per day, versus the full-fledged luxury safari's $250 a day for a couple, the package tour's $50 per person a day, the FIT's $75-plus a day, the low-budget free lance's $5 to $10 a day. (These figures don't include air fare and are highly approximate, but do indicate relative costs.) Don't forget you can always drive yourself and stay in lodges and hotels.

There are in-between variations. There is no reason why you can't take a two-week package tour around East Africa's best game parks, then have a week-long luxury-tented-camp safari in some remote, exotic place. Or how about an eight-day walking safari in Zambia, a couple of days in Nairobi, then eight days among hand-carved rock churches and 16th-century castles in Ethiopia? There is no reason, on *your* vacation, why you should have to return home feeling guilty that you didn't see 21 game parks in 21 days.

In this general introduction are sections with more details on ways and means of travel.

What Not to Worry About

Tell somebody you're going to Africa and he'll suggest, with great originality, that you watch out for lions, tigers, and cannibals. Many people seem to think Africa hasn't changed much from the days of Stanley and Livingstone, that it is still the Dark Continent. Only in the minds of those who haven't been.

There are no cannibals. There are no tigers. Lions there are, but not to be afraid of. All the lions you see (from within a vehicle) will probably be lying down, either asleep or half-asleep. They'll ignore you completely. But you don't want to encourage them. There are many snakes in Africa, but just about every one will slither away very quickly if it hears something coming. In a year of traveling we saw not more than four snakes, all slithering rapidly across the road in front of our car.

Take ordinary precautions—get inoculations, take malaria pills, don't wade or swim in still water—and you probably won't get sick. There are enough doctors and hospitals, even the Flying Doctor Service.

Don't worry about getting caught up in political turmoil. The Africa of Ruark's *Something of Value* and *Uhuru* is in the past. What turmoil there is you will certainly get notice of before you get anywhere near it.

There are lots of good roads and good hotels. There are lots of people who speak English. The food in restaurants is safe to eat. Murderers do not roam the streets. Do watch out, as you would in New York, for con men and purse snatchers, and do lock your car and don't leave valuable things lying around in view.

If you left something at home, don't worry about it. There are shops, grocery stores, markets, drugstores, department stores, five-and-dimes, hotel sundry shops, and *dukas* (general stores) nearly everywhere. Nairobi seems to have everything.

Accommodations in Eastern Africa

Tourists accustomed to comfort, cleanliness, and amenities need not fear they will have to stay in jungle huts or fleabags because they can't imagine Africa's having anything else. While the region doesn't generally have the hotel standards of the U.S. or Western Europe, it has many new and old hotels that are perfectly clean, decent, even stylish.

The problem is mainly lack of choice. Kenya has a wide range—Tsavo National Park, for instance, has three first-class game lodges, a modern motel and two middle-budget hotels outside the park, three self-service lodges (you bring the food, prepare it yourself), and campgrounds. But in Tanzania's Serengeti and Lake Manyara, you stay in the first-class game lodge—or you camp. At three of Ethiopa's Historic Route stops, there is now only one tourist-class hotel; four Hilton lodges open in 1975. And there are only scattered luxury establishments for the well-to-do and the picky—the Mount Kenya Safari Club being the most famous. The hotelkeeping is generally better than the cooking.

In this book we have at least listed the name of *every accommodation that is acceptable to American travelers.* We list and describe nearly all the tourist-class hotels and in addition list many suitable for low-budget travelers. We have also noted campsites, rest houses, and self-service lodges that can be used by those with their own cars. A glance at this book will show there are far more places to stay than is generally believed.

For notes on how we rate hotels, see "How to Use This Book."

Bringing Children to Africa

Africa is a fantastic place for children, and there's no reason why you can't bring them if you think they'll appreciate the animals, the scenery, the people, the experience. Nothing seems to stop European families residing in Africa from going on a camping safari even with babies (though traveling anywhere with infants can be more trying than it's worth). Restaurant and hotel dining room food is standard Western food (no fried caterpillars). Medical attention for tourists is readily available. Game parks are no more dangerous for children than for anyone else.

In fact, the only difficulty we can think of is finding a babysitter should you want to step out on the town or spend a night at Treetops, The Ark, or other game-viewing lodge where generally children under

12 or 8 are not allowed. Tour escorts and big hotels may be able to help you, but make sure the babysitter knows exactly what's expected.

Weather or Not to Travel

Here are the best times and rainy times in the five countries:

Kenya: Best—mid-December–March, August–October. Rainy—April–June, November–mid-December.

Tanzania: Best—mid-December–February, June–September. Rainy—mid-March–May, November–mid-December.

Ethiopia: Best—October–mid-February, May–mid-June. Rainy—mid-June–September, mid-February–April.

Zambia: Best—May–August, September–November. Rainy—December–April.

Malawi: Best—May–October. Rainy—November–April.

Can you travel in the rainy season? For the most part, yes. Ethiopia's Lalibela, Zambia's game parks, and various hotels in East Africa are closed during the long or big rains. Some roads become passably muddy, others impassable. But there are many tourists anyway, and local travelers do not stop traveling. Additionally, rainy seasons in East Africa are notoriously unpredictable. The long or short rains in Kenya, for instance, may fail altogether; anyway, it usually rains less than it does in any U.S. state picked at random. For game viewing, the dry seasons are preferable, for the animals are more concentrated at waterholes and rivers. However, it can be financially worthwhile traveling in off-seasons; United Touring Company and many hotels offer reductions.

So weather or not to travel is a series of buts, ifs, and howevers. *But* one thing is certain—weather is less likely to be a problem if you come during the good seasons. More details are under "When to Go" in the country chapters.

Calendar of Events

Africa does not have pageants and festivals and big wingdings like the U.S. and Europe. Other than Ethiopian religious celebrations, such as Timkat and Maskal, and perhaps the movable Moslem celebrations of Id-ul-Fitr, Id-ul-Azha, and Maulidi (Kenya and Tanzania coasts), there are no other events worth changing your itinerary for.

Meeting the People

Package tourists may get to know the tour courier (minibus driver-guide) but will actually meet hardly any other Africans. This is true anywhere—the tourist is a stranger who shuffles in and out too quickly. But even longer-term travelers will have difficulty.

There are, first, no government-sponsored "meet the people" programs, such as in certain European countries. The best alternative would seem to be clubs and associations, but this depends. In Nairobi it is mostly resident Europeans who turn out for Natural History Society birdwalks or Film Society showings. But there are many clubs, societies and associations in Kenya; the Nairobi Tourist Information Bureau (p. 169) has details. Professional people can more easily meet their counterparts; Yellow Bird Safaris (p. 114) helps arrange this.

There are "meet the people" tours (all, please note, in Kenya), run by Yellow Bird and Kenya Mystery Tours to Kikuyu coffee farms, an alleged "Masai *manyatta*," a Kamba nightclub (Small World Country Club); see pp. 115–116.

Many travelers have found it easier to meet people in Ethiopia, because it was never colonized like the other four countries and there is no historic social barrier between Africans and "Europeans" (the universal synonym for whites).

As usual, it is low-budget travelers, who hitchhike, take the bus and train (second or third class), and stay in inexpensive accommodations, who meet the *wananchi* (ordinary folk). Those with time to spare might consider participating in a Kenya Voluntary Development Association workcamp (April, July–August and December); inquiries to Secretary KVDA, Consulate Chambers, Racecourse Road, Box 48902, Nairobi; tel. 25379.

An American-church-sponsored organization called SERVAS (475 Riverside Drive, Room 665, New York, N.Y. 10027) specializes in getting people together; you have to be interviewed and "approved" before they'll give you any names, and there is a service charge.

Any scholarly or journalistic plan to study or live with a remote tribe, at least in Kenya, has to be sanctioned by the government (the Office of the President, Box 30510, Nairobi; tel. 27411, handles research permit applications).

Things to Do in Eastern Africa

If you take a package tour, Eastern Africa will mainly be viewed from the window seat of a minibus. If you want to get out and *do* something, you should not take a package tour.

Hunting: Mainly Kenya (where the hunting safari industry is based), but also some in Zambia and Ethiopia.

Fishing: Deep-sea fishing off the Kenya coast, to a lesser extent off Tanzania and Ethiopia. Fresh-water fishing in Lake Malawi and Rift Valley lakes (including Lake Rudolf), and mountain streams all over.

Mountain climbing: Very popular on Kilimanjaro (summit can be achieved by the moderately fit and unskilled) and Mount Kenya (third-highest peak can easily be walked up), also Mount Meru in Tanzania, and Mount Mulanje in Malawi.

Water sports: Kenya coast is most popular, then Tanzania coast and the Red Sea at Massawa; also Lake Malawi.

Golf: Easy to participate in at several fine Kenya greens.

Walking safaris: In Zambia's Luangwa and Kafue national parks, also near Isiolo in Kenya.

Mule trips: In Ethiopia into the Semyen and Bale mountains, also into and around Lalibela. Horse, camel, and zebroid treks on Mount Kenya and in the Northern Frontier District. Riding near Nairobi Park and the Ngong Hills.

Birdwatching: Everywhere, especially Kenya's Lakes Nakuru and Naivasha. Go on one of the East Africa Natural History Society's naturalist outings.

Boat cruises: Five days around Lake Victoria, eight days up and down Lake Malawi.

Visiting nontourist places: Brooke Bond tea estates and factory at Kericho or Limuru, Kenya; College of African Wildlife Management, Mweka, Tanzania; National Arts of Tanzania Makonde sculpture workshop, Dar es Salaam; Fisheries Research Unit, Monkey Bay, Malawi; diamond mine or sisal estate in Tanzania; coffee auction in Nairobi; tea auction in Blantyre.

Canoeing: On Tana River in Kenya, on Omo River (whitewater) in Ethiopia.

Trains: Nairobi–Mombasa; from Nairobi down Escarpment to Nakuru; Asmara–Massawa; Lusaka–Livingstone; soon, Tan-Zam Railway.

Exotic things: Participate in a game count in Nairobi National Park. Make a hiking, mulepacking, and rock-climbing tour of Ethiopian rock-hewn churches around Makalle. Take a dhow between the Persian Gulf and East African coast. Go spelunking in East Africa.

Sources of Information

Under each country we have listed maps, books, newspapers, and other sources of information, such as chambers of commerce.

The serious road traveler will have a difficult time getting the information he needs (or thinks he needs); see pp. 43–45.

New York consulates, U.N. missions, embassies, and tourist offices aren't as helpful as they could be; the tourist authorities don't give them enough information to hand out. Some tourism ministries and/or official tourist organizations are generally helpful to the common tourist—Zambia, Malawi, Ethiopia; some are less helpful—Kenya, Tanzania.

Commercial enterprises in Eastern Africa can often be unreliable correspondents; some tour operators didn't seem to realize it was in their economic self-interest to reply to *our* letters. So don't be too hopeful about getting all the car-hire rate sheets and tour price lists from the firms you write to.

Whatever you do, be sure to ask *specific* questions. Letters asking about, say, "road travel in Kenya" will certainly go unanswered.

Finally, you will find most travel agencies in the U.S. not very well informed about Africa—except about the few package tours they want to sell. But travel agencies usually have better means of locating information than you or I.

Be sure to address your Africa inquires to the P.O. box, *not* the street address.

Maps

We've included a section in each country chapter on the best maps available of the country, cities, game parks. Here are some of the regional maps, and places you can buy maps.

Eastern Africa: All but Ethiopia are covered quite well in the handsome Michelin No. 155, East, Central, and Southern Africa, revised biannually. Ethiopia (also Somalia, Sudan, and Egypt) are in No. 154. Scale is 1:4 million (1 inch = 63 miles). Maps cost $1.40 each from French & European Publications Inc., 610 Fifth Ave., New York 10020; or the sources below.

Kenya, Tanzania, Uganda: BP map (1:2 million), available for about $1.50 from Automobile Association of East Africa (p. 107), perhaps other sources. Kenya and Northern Tanzania best covered in the Kenya Shell 1:1 million map ($1).

Topographical maps: The U.S. and British military survey maps of Series 2201 cover Africa in 36 sheets, scale 1:2 million. They are not very detailed, and they are not useful for tourists or drivers. The Y-401 series (1:500,000) is old, with World War II data. 1:1 million mapping has been discontinued. See topographical maps available under country listings.

Map sources: Edward Stanford Ltd., 12–14 Long Acre, London WC2E 9LP. *The Map Store,* 595 Broad Ave., Ridgefield, N.J. 07657. *Rand McNally,* 10 East 53d St., New York 10022. Those planning to drive should write to the auto clubs of East Africa and Zambia for the latest of what's available.

General Bibliography

In each country chapter we have listed books to read about that country, and in the case of the Kenya list, books on East African history. A few general books, necessarily the authors' selection, are listed here:

Bates, Joseph D., Jr. *The Outdoor Cook's Bible.* New York: Doubleday, 1963.

Bohannan, Paul, and Curtin, Philip. *Africa and Africans.* Rev. ed. Garden City, N.Y.: The Natural History Press (Doubleday) paperback, 1971.

Cartey, Wilfred, and Kilson, Martin, eds. *The Africa Reader: Colonial Africa* and *Independent Africa.* 2 vols. New York: Vintage Books paperback, 1970.

Dathorne, O. R., and Feuser, Willfried, eds. *Africa in Prose.* Baltimore: Penguin Books paperback, 1969.

Dorst, Jean. *A Field Guide to the Larger Mammals of Africa.* Illus. by Pierre Dandelot. Boston: Houghton Mifflin, 1970. Has more comprehensive and broader descriptions than Williams' *National Parks* guide (below).

Fagg, William, and Plass, Margaret. *African Sculpture: An Anthology.* London and New York: Studio Vista/Dutton paperback, 1964.

Feldman, Susan, ed. *African Myths and Tales.* New York: Dell, 1970.

Greenbank, Anthony. *The Book of Survival.* New York: New American Library paperback, 1968. Possibly of interest to expeditions.

Hargreaves, Dorothy and Bob. *African Blossoms* and *African Trees.* Kailua, Hawaii: Hargreaves Co., 1972 (paperback). Both for $4 postpaid, Box 895, Kailua, Hawaii 96734; these well-illustrated books are valuable for the tourist with an ordinary interest in flame trees, baobabs, bougainvillaea, etc.

Kaplan, Irwin *et al. Area Handbook for Kenya.* Washington, D.C.:

Government Printing Office, 1967. Also *Tanzania* (1968), Ethiopia (1971), and Zambia (1969).

Kenya Shell Ltd. *Shell Guide to the Water's Edge. Guide to Some of East Africa's Flowering Trees and Shrubs. Guide to Some of East Africa's Upland Flowers. Shell Guide to East African Birds. Shell Guide to Wild Life*. Obtainable from AA of East Africa, 3/- or 5/- each.

Kjellstrom, Bjorn. *Be Expert with Map and Compass: The "Orienteering" Handbook*. Harrisburg, Pa.: Stackpole Books, 1967 (also in paperback). For expeditions.

Klinger, Herb and Judy. *Knapsacking Abroad*. Harrisburg, Pa.: Stackpole Books paperback, 1967.

Nesbitt, Paul H., Pond, Alonzo W., and Allen, William H. *The Survival Book*. New York: Funk & Wagnalls paperback, 1968. Desert chapter may interest trans-Africa groups.

Radin, Paul, ed. *African Folktales*. Princeton, N.J.: Princeton University Press/Bollingen Series paperback, 1970.

Saint Andrew's Church Women's Guild, Nairobi. *The Kenya Cookery Book and Household Guide*. 13th ed. Nairobi: Heineman Educational Books paperback, 1970.

Schofield, Miles, and others. *Motor Trend Basic Auto Repair Manual No. 3*. Los Angeles: Petersen Publishing paperback, 1971. Available from publisher, 8490 Sunset Blvd., Los Angeles, Calif. 90069.

Wiedner, Donald L. *A History of Africa South of the Sahara*. New York: Vintage Books paperback, 1962.

Willet, Frank. *African Art: An Introduction*. New York: Praeger, 1971.

Williams, John G. *A Field Guide to the National Parks of East Africa*. Illus. by Rena Fennessy. Boston: Houghton Mifflin, 1968; London: Collins, 1967. *A Field Guide to the Birds of East and Central Africa*. Illus. by author and Rena Fennessy. Boston: Houghton Mifflin, 1964; London: Collins, 1963.

Zell, Hans M., and Silver, Helene, comp. and ed. *A Reader's Guide to African Literature*. New York: Africana Publishing Corp. paperback, 1971.

Visiting Neighboring Countries

This book was purposely limited to comprehensive coverage of five countries. For information about adjacent countries, contact the tourism authorities and diplomatic missions listed below.

Botswana: Tourism Division, Ministry of Commerce, Industry, and Water Affairs, Private Bag 4, Gaberone, Botswana, Southern Africa. Chief Game Warden, Department of Wildlife and National Parks, Box 131, Gaberone. Embassy of Botswana, 1825 Connecticut Ave., N.W., Washington, D.C. 20009; tel. (202) 332-4994. U.N. Mission of Botswana, 866 U.N. Plaza, New York, 10017; tel. (212) 759-6587.

Burundi: Embassy of Burundi, 2717 Connecticut Ave., N.W., Washington, D.C. 20008; tel. (202) 387-4477. U.N. Mission of Burundi, 305 East 45th St., New York 10017; tel. (212) 689-7090.

Madagascar (Malagasy Republic): Commissariat au Tourisme et aux Arts Traditionnels, Tananarive, Malagasy Republic, Indian Ocean. Embassy, 2374 Massachusetts Ave., N.W., Washington, D.C. 20008; tel. (202) 265-5525.

Mauritius: Mauritius Government Tourist Office, Cerné House, La Chaussée, Port Louis, Mauritius, Indian Ocean. Embassy, 2308 Wyoming Ave., N.W., Washington, D.C. 20008; tel. (202) 234-5436.

Mozambique: Centro de Informacão e Turismo, Caixa Postal 614, Lourenço Marques, Mozambique, Southern Africa. Casa de Portugal, 570 Fifth Ave., New York 10036; tel. (212) 581-2450. Embassy of Portugal, 2125 Kalorama Road, N.W., Washington, D.C. 20008; tel. (202) 265-1643.

Rhodesia: Rhodesia National Tourist Board, Box 8052, Causeway, Salisbury, Rhodesia.

Rwanda: Départment du Tourisme, B.P. 83, Kigali, Rwanda, Central Africa. Embassy, 1714 New Hampshire Ave., N.W., Washington, D.C. 20009; tel. (202) 232-2882.

Seychelles: Director of Tourism, Box 92, Victoria, Seychelles, Indian Ocean. British embassies, consulates, information offices.

Somalia: Ministry of Tourism and National Parks, Mogadishu, Somalia, East Africa. Embassy of Somali Democratic Republic, 1875 Connecticut Ave., N.W., Washington, D.C. 20009; tel. (202) 234-3261.

South Africa: South Africa Tourist Corp. (SATOUR), Private Bag 164, Pretoria, South Africa; also 610 Fifth Ave., New York 10020; tel. (212) 245-3720. Consulate-General and Information Service, 655 Madison Ave., New York 10021; tel. (212) 838-1700.

Sudan: Tourism Department, Ministry of Communications and Tourism, Box 2424, Khartoum, Sudan. Embassy, 3421 Massachusetts Ave., N.W., Washington, D.C. 20019; tel. (202) 338-8565.

TFAI (*Djibouti*): Office de Développement du Tourisme, Box 32, Djibouti, Territoire Française des Afars et des Issas (TFAI), East Africa. French embassies, consulates, information offices.

Uganda: Uganda Tourist Board, Box 4241, Kampala. Embassy, 5909 16th St., N.W., Washington, D.C. 20011; tel. (202) 726-7100.

Zaire: Commissariat General au Tourisme, B.P. 9502, Kinshasa, Zaire, Central Africa. Embassy, 1800 New Hampshire Ave., N.W., Washington, D.C. 20009; tel. (202) 234-7690.

For basic information on these and other African countries, see Allen and Segal, *The Traveler's Africa* (New York: Hopkinson & Blake, 1973), $12.95.

Traveling to and around Eastern Africa

Some Planning Tips

For purposes of comparing one means of travel to another, here are some rough per-person-per-day costs: pretty low budget (hitchhiker or bus traveler)—$5–10; do-it-yourself driving-and-camping trip—$20–25; group package minibus tour—$50–55; individually arranged FIT tour—$75; cheap tenting safari with some do-it-yourselfing (student groups)—$60–65; large group tenting safari with some comforts (scientific groups, nature tours)—$70–90; luxury camping safari/photo safari—$230–250 for two persons (double the money for four persons).

The most important consideration in planning and preparing a trip is to *allow sufficient time to make arrangements.* To take a luxury hunting or photographic safari, you *must* book a year or more ahead. East Africa's game lodges are sometimes booked solid a year or more in advance by tour packagers, which usually results in a fair number of empty rooms each night of the busy season. But you should still reserve ahead, if possible. Rent-a-cars should be reserved at least four months in advance so that you are certain of getting the model you want the day you want it. Package tours from the U.S. should be booked three to six months beforehand. Local package tours (say, from Nairobi or Addis Ababa) cannot be arranged instantly except for the popular, short-duration tours (say, to Nairobi National Park or Treetops) that have daily departures. Generally speaking, the longer the tour you contemplate, the further in advance you must start making arrangements with a travel agency. (The only way to gain freedom from the tyranny of booking tours and making hotel reservations is to hire a car and then camp out, or at least be prepared to camp.)

Allow a week for airmail letters to go to and from Africa, even if all concerned answer promptly.

Generally speaking, the tourist high seasons in East Africa are December–February and July–October.

In writing query letters to car-hire firms, tour operators, safari firms, and travel agencies, *ask specific questions,* such as, "What rate will you charge on a Toyota Corona for 19 days, driving 2,000 miles?" and ask for the brochure-tariff sheet to get the rest of the rates. If you are stringing short package tours together, always find out the frequency, days, and times of *departures* so you can plan the itinerary properly.

Always find out what a certain price includes. Tour brochures sometimes neglect to say that a tour price doesn't include air fare, though it may say "all-inclusive price."

Finally, save all your correspondence with hotels, travel agencies, car-hire firms, and tour operators—and be ready to produce it when you arrive to check into your room or pick up the rent-a-car. Take with you the brochure of the package tour you're on. You are otherwise at the mercy of new employees, sloppy filing systems, poor memories, and unscrupulous people who would change prices and conditions.

Package Tours from the U.S.

The traveler seeking an all-inclusive package tour to Eastern Africa can easily find one—and that's about it, one basic tour. Tour packagers don't offer anything that different from the competition. The language of colorful glossy brochures aside, few tours include anything other than a selection of only 25 destinations—nine in Kenya, six in Tanzania, three in Uganda (when it's open to tourists), six in Ethiopia, one in Zambia. (This selection will even be more limited if the tour includes Southern Africa or more.) Now, there is no doubt these places *are* the highlights of Eastern Africa, and the first-time visitor *will* like those places he visits. But the tourist going to the area for the second time will be on the same merry-go-round, unless he chooses a fairly unusual tour such as a camping safari.

First-timers, meanwhile, can select what appeals to them from our list of 70 or so (early 1974) tours, listed below by tour operator. The name of the tour, as advertised in the *current* brochure, is followed by the IT (International Tour) number, the number of days, and countries visited. We describe the itinerary for some tours, with the number of nights spent at various destinations in parentheses. Following that is the so-called land cost, which is the price of all arrangements except for international air fares. Air fares quoted below are, frankly, out of date by the time you read this, and we give them only as an indication.

Daytime or overnight accommodations in London, Paris, Athens, or elsewhere are common elements in African tours. Very common is the triangular "three continents" tour that includes Brazil, sometimes Argentina as well, before going on to South Africa. Almost every package below is a group tour with escort, sometimes from New York, most times from Nairobi. Groups are groups are groups, and if you don't like them, book an FIT (Foreign Independent Tour). Prices are inclusive of nearly everything but lunch and dinner in European and African cities, passport and visas, laundry, tips, etc. Tour prices are quoted on a double-occupancy basis—e.g., "Land cost—$1,320" means $1,320 each of two persons; single occupancy (where possible) can cost a couple of hundred dollars more. To figure per-day cost, divide days into land cost, then compare with other tours. Departures are from New York unless otherwise stated.

Big-gun tour operators are American Express, Four Winds, General Tours, Kuoni, Lindblad, Maupintour, Olson's, Percival, SITA, Travcoa, and Travelworld.

Fairly unusual tours are offered by African Safari Club (beach holidays), Club Tours (one includes a camel trek), East African Travel Consultants (basic arrangements only—you get free periods), Globe Star (a horse safari), Hemphill (inexpensive luxury tented camp safari), Henkle (Kilimanjaro climb, inexpensive camping safari), Kimbla (cheap camping safari), Lindblad (air safari), Mountain Travel (hiking and climbing trips), *Oceans Magazine* (coast and island nature tour), Penn Overland (Nairobi-Johannesburg overland trip), Swans and African Explorers (thorough Ethiopia tours), Thru the Lens (rugged safari in Kenya's NFD), United Touring (many special interest ideas), and Wilderness Expeditions (Bale Mountains mule-trekking).

Most tours offered are too hurried—East African versions of the "if it's Tuesday this must be Belgium" European package tour hustle. If you don't want your African experience to be blurred *and* tiring, pick a tour where you stay two nights (not one) in most places, and choose one that doesn't rush you madly from one country to another.

Your local travel agency really should have information on most of these tours, or more current ones. If not, write the addresses listed, but remember that many tour packagers deal with travel agents, not with the general public.

Adventures Unlimited (Abercrombie & Fitch), 19 East 45th St., New York 10017. Operates FITs mainly but does sell a couple of expensive packages. *"Invitational Safari"* is a 21-day luxury-camping photo safari, limited to 12 persons, sometimes guided by ornithologist John Williams. NYC, Athens (1), Nairobi (Norfolk—2), Samburu (camp—2), Lake Nakuru, Kericho (Tea Hotel—1), Masai Mara (camp—4), Lake Naivasha (Lake Hotel—2), Amboseli/Tsavo area (Kimana Camp—4), Nairobi (1), Athens, NYC. Kenya arrangements by Safari Air Services. Departs about 7Xyear. Land—$2,440. Approx. air fare—$927–1,000. *"Headquarters Safari"* (IT2PA1HQSA), 22 days to Kenya and Tanzania. Air and road safari in and out of Nairobi to Masai Mara, Serengeti, Treetops, Mount Kenya Safari Club, Lakes Nakuru and Naivasha, Ngorongoro, Amboseli, Tsavo, Lamu, Lake Baringo, Samburu. Brochure suggests you may want to use up the rest of the 45-day excursion fare, and adds some info about Zambia's walking safaris. Headquarters Safari land cost—$2,095. Approx. air fare—$763–838. Departs about 6Xyear.

African Explorers, Professional Bldg., Route 9, Parlin, N.J. 08859. *"South of Asmara"* (IT1AF1A510), 18 days in Ethiopia. NYC, Paris (1), Asmara (1), by train to Massawa (1), by train or bus to Asmara (1), by road to Matara, Senafe (1), Negash Pass, Wogro, Simkata, Makalle (1), Yeha, Adowa, Axum (1), by air to Lalibela (1) and Gondar (1) and Bahar Dar (1), Tissisat Falls, by air to Addis Ababa (2), by road to Debre Zeit, Koka Dam, Nazareth; by train to Djibouti (2), Paris, NYC. Extensions to other parts of Africa can be arranged. Monthly departures. Independent or group. Land cost—$699. Approx. air fare—$871–959.

African Safari Club, c/o African Explorers (address above). European address is: Baslerstrasse 275, CH-4122 Neuallschwil/Bâle, Switzerland. European operation has own prop-jet with inexpensive flights from Basel, and a chain of Kenya hotels—two near Tsavo Park, five on the coast (see p. 87). Safaris are beach-based (lots of water sports, other activity), with game-viewing tours secondary, bookable on arrival (sample: 3 days to Tsavo East and West and Amboseli—820/–). Many prices; sample: 17 days to Kenya and Tanzania, starting from Basel, main accommodation at Dolphin Hotel (North Coast)—2,335 Swiss francs (about $600), incl air fare from Basel.

AITS, Inc., 210 Boylston St., Chestnut Hill, Mass. 02167. *"African Carnival"* (IT3SN1024), 14 days in Kenya. NYC, Brussels, Nairobi, Hunter's Lodge (2), Diani Beach (Trade Winds—3), Tsavo (Kilaguni—1), Amboseli (Namanga Hotel—1), Lake Nakuru (Stag's Head—1), Mountain Lodge (1), Nairobi (680 Hotel—1), Brussels (1), NYC. Thursday departures. Air and land cost—$1,098.

American Express, 65 Broadway, New York 10006 (many U.S. offices). *"African Safari Plus Rio"* (IT3PA1AX52), 22 days in Kenya, Tanzania, South Africa, and Brazil. Fully escorted. Saturday departures 21Xyear. Land cost—$1,127–1,197; approx. air fare—$768–832.

American Institute for Foreign Study, 102 Greenwich Ave., Greenwich, Conn. 06830. *"Wildlife Safari Program in East Africa"* (IT3BA-17700), 16 days. NYC, London (1), Nairobi (Brunners—2), Masai *manyatta,* Masai Mara (1), Serengeti (lodge—1, Ndutu Camp—1), Olduvai, Ngorongoro (1), Arusha (1), Tsavo (1), North Coast (Bamburi Beach Hotel—3), Mombasa, Nairobi, London, NYC. Incl 6 lectures (big game and antelope; Masai; Serengeti migrations; Olduvai and prehistory; game rangers; cattle vs. wildlife), visits to Serengeti Research Institute and College of African Wildlife Management in Tanzania. Departures every Friday. Air and land cost—$1,434–1,489.

Archer's Tours, 1440 South State College Blvd., Anaheim, Calif. 92806. *"Lion Safari"* (IT3BR2AT001), 24 days to Kenya and Tanzania, and *"Leopard Safari"* (IT3BR2AT002), 17 days to Kenya and Tanzania. Longer tour does the usual, adds Kericho tea country (1) and Secret Valley (1). Weekly departures Friday. 24-day tour land cost—$690. 17-day tour land cost—$522. Approx. air fare—$808–887.

Brendan Tours, 650 South Grand, Los Angeles, Calif. *"First Class Tour G"* is 23 days to Kenya and Tanzania. The usual plus 2 days in Paris. Air transport is by Overseas National and Capitol charters. 9 departures June–Oct. from L.A., San Francisco, Denver. L.A. package cost—$1,578.

Club Tours Inc., 25 West 43rd St., New York 10036. Club Tours arranges two field trips for the National Parks and Conservation Association. *"East Africa Field Trip by Road"* (IT3SN1077), 23 days to Kenya and Tanzania. NYC, Amsterdam (1), Nairobi (New Stanley —1), Hunter's Lodge (1), Amboseli (Namanga Hotel—1), Nairobi (New Stanley—2), Rioki Coffee Estate, Mountain Lodge (1), Lakes Nakuru and Naivasha (Safariland Lodge—1), Masai Mara (2), Serengeti (Fort Ikoma Lodge or Grumeti Safari Camp—2), Olduvai, Ngorongoro (2), Lake Manyara, Arusha (1), College of African

Wildlife Management, Mombasa, Kilifi (Mnarani Club—2), Tamarind Restaurant lunch, Tsavo (Kilaguni—2), Nairobi (1), Brussels, NYC. About 30 Tuesday departures. Land cost—$1,095. Approx. air fare— $731–786. *"East Africa Field Trip by Air"* (IT3SN1078), 25 days to Kenya and Tanzania. Less strenuous tour (9 persons maximum) by 6-pax Beechcraft Baron, VW bus and Land Cruiser. NYC, Brussels, Nairobi (3), Masai Mara (1), Serengeti (Grumeti Camp—2), air to Lake Manyara, road to Ngorongoro (1), air to Tsavo (Kilaguni—2), Diani Beach (Trade Winds—3), Zanzibar excursion, Mombasa, air to Samburu (1), Lake Rudolf (Eliye Springs—2), Nairobi (2), Mountain Lodge (1), Amber May Camel Trek (2 overnights at safari camps), Mount Kenya Safari Club (1), Nairobi, Brussels, NYC. About 24 departures Tuesdays. Africa cost—$1,880. Approx. air fare—$930– 1,003. 8-day Ethiopian extension available with air field trip, visiting Addis Ababa (2), by air around Historic Route: Bahar Dar (1), Gondar (1), Lalibela or Makalle (1), Axum (1), Asmara (1). Land cost —$215. Approx. extra air fare (if you flew GIT from U.S.)—$178– 207.

Club Universe (Unitours Inc.), 1671 Wilshire Blvd., Los Angeles, Calif. 90017. *"East Africa Safari"* (IT3AF140BD), 23 days to Kenya and Tanzania. Los Angeles/San Francisco departures to the usual game parks plus 2 days in Paris. Package cost—$1,495 (club membership is $5; couple—$8).

Continental Express Inc., 144 South Beverly Dr., Beverly Hills, Calif. 90212. *"East African Safari"* (IT2BR1051CE), 21 days to Kenya and Tanzania, incl London (4), East African milk run with Tarangire (1). 14 high-season (Oct.–Apr.) departures from West Coast. Package cost—$1,195–1,225.

East African Travel Consultants, 55 Bloor St., E., Suite 300, Toronto, Ont., Canada M4W 1A9. Canadian tour packager has several itineraries from Montreal (other cities in Canada for extra air fare) to East Africa with stopover in Brussels. *"The Beach Safari"* (IT4SN1C12), 19 days to Kenya, with days 4–16 at a coast hotel. Land cost—$275–350. *"The Lion Safari"* (IT4SN1C13) is the same, with days 3 to 16 in Nairobi, leaving you free to make your own arrangements (mini-tours are optional, if you like). Land cost—$290. *"The Elephant Safari"* (IT4SN1C14), also 19 days, is a combination of *"Lion"* and *"Beach,"* with days 3–7 in Nairobi, then Tsavo, then days 9–14 in Mombasa, 15– 17 in Nairobi. Land cost—$460. Approx. air fare on these packages—

$900–974. Departures 2Xmonth. *"On Safari"* (IT4SN1C10), 23 days to Kenya, Tanzania, Ethiopia, incl Vienna, Athens, and Brussels stopovers, and tree hotel, Nakuru, Masai Mara, Serengeti, Ngorongoro, Lake Manyara, Amboseli, Mombasa, Nairobi, Addis Ababa, Lalibela, Axum, Asmara. Departs weekly. Land cost—$1,085. Approx. air fare —$830–914. Note: Be sure to ask which hotels you stay in—and then look at our comments.

Foreign Tours Inc., 1140 Avenue of Americas, New York 10036. Has two Israel and East Africa safaris, of 16 days ($1,489–1,544) and 22 days ($1,809–1,864). Prices too high, we think.

Four Winds Travel Inc., 175 Fifth Ave., New York 10010. Several fully escorted group tours: *"Kilimanjaro"* (IT3AF1FWAK), 22 days to South Africa, Rhodesia, Malawi, Kenya, Tanzania, Ethiopia. Friday departures from NYC. Land cost—$1,345. Approx. air fare—$893– 949. *"Safari"* (IT3AF1FWAS), 16 days to Ethiopia, Kenya, Tanzania, or 27 days to same plus Nigeria, Ghana, Ivory Coast, Mali, and Senegal. 16-day land cost—$895. Approx. air fare—$682–737. 27-day land cost—$1,745. Approx. air fare—$898–982.

Gateway Holidays/Globus Tours, 8 South Michigan Ave., Chicago, Ill. 60603. Mammoth tour operator now has *"Gateway Escorted Tour E—East African Safari"* (IT4BR1G102GH), 19 days to Kenya and Tanzania. Package cost from NYC—$1,426–1,448; from London— $1,125–1,190.

General Tours Inc., 49 West 57th St., New York 10019. Several fully escorted tours. *"Africa I"* (IT4PA1A134), 18 days to Kenya, Tanzania, Ethiopia. Departs Saturdays about 2Xmonth. Land cost— $870. Approx. air fare—$728–783. *"Africa II"* (IT4PA1B134), 16 days to Kenya and Tanzania. Incl 3 days on Kenya coast. Departs Saturdays about 2Xmonth. Land cost—$710. Approx. air fare—$738– 794. For doctors, General Tours has *"International Medical Journey"* to Kenya and Tanzania (IT4PA1E488), 16 days, visiting game parks and Kenyatta National Hospital and Aga Khan Hospital in Nairobi. Departs Saturdays about 6Xyear. Land cost—$765. Approx. air fare —$679–734 (GIT).

Globe Star Inc., 120 East 56th St., New York 10022. With Nairobi's Safaris Unlimited, Globe Star is putting on *"The Kenya Saddle Safari"* (IT3SN1085), 25 days combining a few riding excursions with luxury tented camping and air safaris. Riding is in area around Loita near

Masai Mara, and around Maralal, north of Thomson's Falls. Amboseli and, optionally, Lake Rudolf and Ngorongoro Crater are visited by air, and there's a tour by Land Cruiser Nairobi-Loita Camp-Masai Mara-Kericho-Nakuru-Ngobit-Treetops-Maralal-Samburu-Mount Kenya Safari Club-Nairobi. Planned for 18 departures a year. Other activities planned for non-riding spouse, and riders themselves can be complete amateurs. Land cost—$1,835. Approx. air fare—$857–902. Slightly shorter 23-day itinerary also available.

Hemphill World Air Cruises (Hemphill Travel Service Inc.), Box 17444, Los Angeles, Calif. 90017. *"East African Tent Safari"* (IT4AZ-1LAO2), 22 days, is an Abercrombie & Kent-arranged packaged luxury camping safari, for a group of 20 maximum. NYC, Rome, Nairobi (Hilton—2), Tsavo/Amboseli (Kimana Camp—2), Tsavo West (Royal Little Camp—2), Arusha (New Arusha—1), Lake Manyara (Lake Manyara Camp—2), Ngorongoro (Wildlife Lodge—1), Serengeti (Serengeti Camp—3), Masai Mara (Talek Camp—2), Lake Naivasha (Lake Naivasha Hotel—2), Lake Nakuru, Nairobi (1), Rome, NYC. From Nairobi, fully escorted. Departs 2–3Xmonth. Land cost—$1,697. Approx. air fare—$679–734.

Henderson Travel Service Inc., 66 Luckie St., N.W., Suite 304, Atlanta, Ga. 30303. Black-owned Henderson Travel has many West Africa tours, a few East Africa, including: *"Ethiopian and East African Images"* (IT3SN1023), 22 days to Tanzania, Kenya, Ethiopia. NYC, Brussels, Dar es Salaam (Bahari Beach Hotel—3; $42 optional day tour to Zanzibar available), by road to Arusha, Ngorongoro (1), Lake Manyara (1), Arusha, fly to Nairobi (680 or Hilton—5; $65 optional tour to Mountain Lodge or $79 tour to Treetops available), fly to Addis Ababa (Hilton—3; $25 optional tour to Koka Dam and Hippo Pool available), fly Historic Route (4), Asmara (1), Athens (1), Brussels, NYC. Departs Saturday about 1Xmonth. Deluxe version land cost—$790; economy version—$690. Approx. air fare—$708–765.

J. W. Henkle Presents, Inc. (*Africa Unlimited*), 647 Los Mares, Suite 202, San Clemente, Calif. 92672. Two very interesting tours, one including an optional climb up Kilimanjaro. *"Family Safari"* (IT4SN1019), 22 days to Kenya and Tanzania. NYC, Brussels, Nairobi (Norfolk or Safari Park—2), Nanyuki, Meru (Mulika Lodge —3), Samburu (2), Mountain Lodge (1), Nairobi (1), Lake Nakuru, Lake Naivasha (Safariland—1), Masai Mara (Governor's Camp—2, incl foot safari, Mara River rafting), Serengeti (Ndutu Camp—1),

Olduvai, Ngorongoro (Crater Lodge—1), Arusha (1), then either Kili-
manjaro climb with guide and porters (5 nights) *or* Arusha National
Park (Tanzanite Hotel—2) and Amboseli (Serena Lodge—2); then
Nairobi, Brussels, NYC. Land cost—$1,275. Approx. air fare—$783.
"Tent-Lodge Safari" (IT4SN1018), 22 days to Kenya and Tanzania.
Roughly the same itinerary but no Kilimanjaro climb. Tented camping
is in Meru (3), Samburu (2), Masai Mara (3), Serengeti (Ndutu—1),
also overnights at Mountain Lodge, Ngobit Fishing Lodge, Safariland
Lodge at Naivasha, Ngorongoro Crater Lodge (2), Amboseli Serena
Lodge (2). Land cost—$1,495. Approx. air fare—$728–783.

Ideal Tours Inc., 48 West 48th St., New York 10036. Runs 2
"Kosher Safaris"—*"The Gazelle"* (IT3LY10346), 15 days to Kenya
and Israel; and *"The Antelope"* (IT3LY10348), 22 days to Israel,
Kenya, Ethiopia. Package costs: 15 days—$1,249; 22 days—$1,499.

Kimbla Travel (U.K.) Ltd., c/o U.S. Student Travel Service, Inc.,
866 Second Ave., New York 10017. South Africa-based overland firm
offers a 21-day camping safari around Kenya using a custom-built
safari bus, with 2 cooks preparing 3 meals a day, accommodations in
2-man tents. Itinerary: Nairobi-Nakuru-Thomson's Falls-Samburu-
Nanyuki-Thika-Amboseli-Tsavo West-Mombasa-Malindi-Tsavo East-
Nairobi. Runs about 12Xyear. Land cost—$324. Land plus air from
London—$636. A longer (30 days) Kimbla trip is similar to Penn
Overland's (below) except route goes through Zambia instead of
Malawi. Departs about 9Xyear. Land only from Nairobi—$576, not
incl park fees and Ngorongoro tour. Land and air from London—$756.
With 8-day Egypt extension, package from London—$852.

Kuoni Travel Inc., 11 East 44th St., New York 10017. *"Africa Call"*
(IT4BA17440), 22 days to South Africa, Rhodesia, Kenya, Tanzania.
Fully escorted. Land—$1,397. Approx. air fare—$738–774 (GIT).

K.U.T. Tours Inc. (Pan Universal Inc.), 1440 South State College
Blvd., 4–C, Anaheim, Calif. 92806. Low-cost 17- and 22-day safaris,
flights on Olympic with 3-day layovers in Athens on the 22-day tours.

Lindblad Travel Inc., 133 East 55th St., New York 10022. *"East
African Wing Safari"* (IT2BA16500), 23 days in Kenya and Tan-
zania. New York, London, Nairobi (Hilton—1), by air to Lake
Baringo (Lake Baringo Lodge—2), Masai Mara (Mara Serena Lodge
—2), Serengeti (Fort Ikoma Lodge—2), Amboseli (Amboseli Serena
Lodge—2), Nairobi (Masai Lodge—1), Tsavo East (Tsavo Tsafaris—
2), Lamu (Peponi Hotel—2), Tana River Camp (2), Samburu (2),
Nairobi (Hilton—1), London, New York. Group of 10 (maximum).

Deservedly popular but expensive "Wing Safari" has 99 New York departures, mostly in Jan., Feb., June, July, Aug., Sept., Oct. Africa airland arrangements—$1,800. Approx. air fare—$808–887. *"Lindblad Safari"* (IT3RG15200), 24 days to Brazil, South Africa, Rhodesia, Botswana, Zambia, Kenya, Tanzania. Road safari incl. both sides of Victoria Falls (3 nights), Ark (1), milk run. 29 departures. Land cost —$1,250. Approx. air fare—$808–887.

Lislind International, 5 World Trade Center, New York 10048. Has a 26-day tour to South Africa, Rhodesia, Kenya, Tanzania, Ethiopia, for $1,595 land plus $1,136 air. Pretty expensive.

Maupintour, 900 Massachusetts St., Lawrence, Kan. 66044. Fully escorted tours. *"East Africa Wildlife"* (IT3SN1MAEW), 20 days to Kenya and Tanzania. Air and road safari to Treetops or Mountain Lodge (1), Mount Kenya Safari Club (1), air to Tsavo (Kilaguni—2), road to Amboseli (Serena Lodge—1), Ngurdoto Crater, Arusha National Park, Lake Manyara (2), Ngorongoro (1), Serengeti (Seronera —2), Masai Mara (Serena Lodge—2), Nairobi (2) and flight over Rift Valley; Brussels, New York. 16 departures. Land—$1,519. Approx. air fare—$682–737.

Merriman & Finnerty Associates (Brien Merriman's Africa), 15 East 48th St., New York 10017. Escorted or independent tours: *"Safari in Three Lands"* (IT3BR1MF01), 22 days to Brazil, South Africa, Kenya, Tanzania. Land—$1,020–1,035. *"Safari and Sea"* (IT3BR1-MFO2), 22 days to Kenya and Tanzania. Land—$975–990. *"The King of Beasts and the Queen of Sheba"* (IT3PA1MFA3), 22 days to Kenya, Tanzania, Ethiopia. Land—$940–960. Approx. air fare for above 3 tours—$679–734 (GIT) or $857–941 (excursion—independent travel). Each tour departs 7Xyear.

Mountain Travel Inc., 1398 Solano Ave., Albany, Calif. 94706. Runs back-country wilderness trips all over the world, including East Africa. These were run in 1974, may be repeated: *"Northern Frontier District"* (IT3PA1SFFN), 30 days in Kenya. Incl Mount Kenya climb, Masai Mara, Lake Nakuru, Maralal, Lake Rudolf, Marsabit, Samburu. Package cost—$2,288, from New York. *"East Africa Climbing"* (IT3PA-1SFFJ), 23 days to Kenya and Tanzania. Itinerary includes climb up Point Lenana on Mount Kenya (Batian if experience of tour members warrants it), break in Amboseli, then climb up Kilimanjaro, then rest-up on coast. Basic mountaineering experience required. Package cost —$2,242, from New York. *"Omo River, Ethiopia"* (IT3PA1SFFR),

34–35 days to Ethiopia, mostly spent in rafting on the whitewater Omo River. Designed for those with some endurance. Package cost—$2,827, from New York. Also an East African game-viewing package of 27 days for $2,342.

Nilestar Tours (Africa) Ltd., Pan Am Bldg. east mezzanine, 200 Park Ave., New York 10017. A number of 16-day tours, departures from London, Frankfurt, Paris.

Oceans Magazine, 125 Independence Dr., Menlo Park, Calif. 94025. In 1974 *Oceans* sponsored a 22-day educational expedition to the Kenya coast and the Seychelles to study marine biology, geology, birds, plants, peoples. Kenya naturalist Leslie Brown was one of the leaders. Magazine expects to run the trip in the future, to cost about $2,800, incl air fare from Los Angeles (a bit less from New York).

Olson Travel Organization Inc., 1 North LaSalle St., Chicago, Ill. 60602. Fully escorted. *"Olson's East African Adventure Safari"* (IT4-BA12341), 22 days to Uganda, Kenya, Tanzania. Incl Kampala (1), Queen Elizabeth/Ruwenzori National Park (Mweya Lodge—2), Fort Portal (Ruwenzori Tea Hotel—1), Murchison Falls/Kabalega Falls National Park (New Kateer or Paraa Lodge—2), Nairobi (Hilton—3), Tsavo (Ngulia—1), Lake Manyara (1), Ngorongoro (2), Serengeti (Seronera—1), Masai Mara (Serena Lodge—1), Lake Nakuru (Stag's Head—1), Mount Kenya Safari Club (1), Mountain Lodge or Ark (1), Nairobi (1). Departs 4Xyear. Package cost—$2,295–2,350.

Park East Tours Inc., 150 Fifth Ave., New York 10011. *"Royal Safari"* (IT3SN1147), 16 days to Kenya and Tanzania. Departs 9Xyear. Package cost—$1,395–1,450.

Penn Overland Tours Ltd., c/o University Travel, 44 Brattle St., Cambridge, Mass. 02138. Mainly long overland trips (see p. 46), also offers a 30-day camping trip in Bedford buses, *"South-East Africa"* (IT3BA18313) between Johannesburg and Nairobi, as an extension of its London-Algiers-Nairobi overland trip. Itinerary: Nairobi-Masai Mara, into Tanzania, Serengeti-Ngorongoro-Lake Manyara-Arusha-Korogwe-Dar es Salaam-Mikumi Park-Mbeya, cut across Zambia into Malawi, Karonga-Livingstonia-Nkhata Bay-Salima, then back to Zambia, Chipata-Lusaka-Victoria Falls, into Botswana, Rhodesia, ending Jo'burg. Departures 5Xyear about Jan., April, July, Sept., Dec. Basic tour cost is $610 plus minimum $165 for food, camping, park fees (or $610 plus $315 if you want to stay in hotels most nights). With air connections NYC-Nairobi, then Johannesburg-NYC, cost is $1,447–1,551 plus $165 or $315. A lodge-and-minibus tour is *"Masai,"* 16 days to Kenya and Tanzania; with Ethiopia, *"Masai-Sheba,"* 20 days. About 20Xyear. "Masai" package—$1,399–1,454. "Masai-Sheba" package—$1,674–1,729.

Percival Tours Inc., 5820 Wilshire Blvd., Los Angeles, Calif. 90036. Fully escorted tours. *"Highlight Tour"* (IT4PA1A106), 22 days to Senegal, Rhodesia, Zambia, Kenya, Tanzania, Ethiopia. Departs about 4Xmonth. Land—$1,260. Approx. air fare—$738–795. *"Adventure Tour"* (IT4PA1B106), 21 days to Tanzania, Kenya, Ethiopia. NYC, London (1), Nairobi, Dar es Salaam (Kunduchi Beach—2), Bagamoyo, Mombasa (Mombasa Beach Hotel—2) Tsavo East (Voi Lodge —2), Tsavo West (Ngulia—1), Nairobi (Inter-Continental—2), Masai Mara (Keekorok—1), Serengeti (Lobo—1), Olduvai, Ngorongoro (Wildlife Lodge—1), Lake Manyara (1), Amboseli (1), Mount Kenya Safari Club (1), Treetops or Ark (1), Nairobi (1), Addis (Hilton—1), NYC. Departs about 4Xmonth. Land—$1,360. Approx. air fare—$689–745. *"Enchantment Tour"* (IT4PA1D106), 22 days to Brazil, South Africa, Rhodesia, Botswana, Zambia, Kenya, Tanzania, Ethiopia. Departs 4Xmonth. Land—$1,428. Approx. air fare—$906–963.

Pierre C. T. Verheye's Adventureland Safaris, 733 North La Brea Ave., Hollywood, Calif. 90038. "Africarama Safaris" on several itineraries, escorted group or independent. *"No. 9"* (IT4AF140AI), 20 days to Ethiopia, Kenya, Tanzania, Egypt. NYC, Paris (1), Addis Ababa (Hilton—3), Debre Zeit, Nairobi (Hilton—2), Masai Mara (2), Serengeti (2), Olduvai, Ngorongoro (1), Lake Manyara (1), Nairobi (1), Cairo (3), Paris (1), NYC. Departs 22Xyear. Land—$1,001–1,302. Approx. air fare—$872. *"No. 11"* (IT4AF140AK), 31 days to Ethiopia, Kenya, Tanzania, Greece. Incl Historic Route, Athens (3). Departs 24Xyear. Land—$1,551–1,954. Approx. air fare—$872. *"No. 12"* (IT4AF140AL), 38 days to Ethiopia, Kenya, Tanzania, Rwanda, Zaire. Incl Kigali (1), Kagera National Park (2), Goma (2), Virunga National Park (1), Beni (1), Mount Hoyo (2), Goma (1), Bukavu (1·), Kinshasa (2), Paris (1), NYC. Independent basis only. Departs Saturdays except mid-March–late May. Land—$3,530. Approx. air fare—$878.

Questers Tours and Travels Inc., 257 Park Ave. South, New York 10010. Has nature tours all over world, will do East Africa itineraries 1975 and after.

Sierra Club, 220 Bush St., San Francisco, Calif. 94108, includes in its mammoth catalog of annual outings a couple to East Africa, with the only catch that you have to join the Sierra Club (very worthy organization) to go on the outing. Kenya tour in 1974 included canoeing on the Tana River.

Simba Safaris Inc., 1113 Union Blvd., Allentown, Pa. 18103. *"Simba Adventure Safari"* (IT3SN1163), 15 days to Kenya and Tanzania, extendable to 21 days, is one of the least expensive tours, at $1,098 from New York.

SITA World Travel Inc., 530 West 6th St., Los Angeles, Calif. 90014. *"Africa Odyssey"* (IT3LH1I4A), 16 days to Kenya and Tanzania. Departs 16Xyear. Land—$896. Approx. air fare—$679.

Special Tours & Travel Inc., 8 South Michigan Ave., Chicago, Ill. 60603. U.S. arranger of hunting and photo safaris has several Eastern Africa, including Zambia, itineraries.

Sundowner Tours Ltd., 207 Lakeshore Road, East Mississauga, Ontario, Canada L5G 1E1. *"Africa Under Canvas Safari"* (IT4BA10-872), 21 days to Kenya. USA, London, Nairobi (Masai Lodge—2), Lake Nakuru, Lake Naivasha (tented camp—2) with jaunt to Masai Mara (Keekorok—2); Nyeri, Nanyuki (tented camp—3, optional overnight at tree hotel) with jaunt to Mount Kenya Safari Club and Samburu; Embu (Izaak Walton Inn—1), Garissa (Elephant Camp—2), then fly to Lamu (Ras Kitau—3), Malindi, Mombasa, Tsavo West (Ngulia—1), Amboseli (1), Nairobi, London, USA. About 20Xyear. Land cost—$1,395. Approx. air fare from New York—$927–1,000.

W. F. & R. K. Swan (Hellenic) Ltd., c/o Esplanade Tours, 14 Newbury St., Boston, Mass. 02116. Swans, a British operator, has a British naturalist to accompany each group. *"Big Game and Birds Safari"* (IT3BA18350), 23 days to Kenya and Tanzania. NYC, London, Nairobi, Lake Naivasha (1), Lake Nakuru, Thomson's Falls (1), Samburu (2), Nairobi (Masai Lodge—1), Tsavo West (Kilaguni—2), Amboseli (Serena Lodge—2) , Lake Manyara, Ngorongoro (2), Olduvai, Serengeti (Fort Ikoma—1), Masai Mara (Keekorok—2), Nairobi (New Stanley—1; or optional $54 tour to Treetops or $43–96 tour to Coast), London (1), NYC. Departs 15Xyear. Package cost—$1,621 from NYC, $1,388 from London. *"Beach and Treetops Holiday"* is largely a relax-vacation. NYC, London, Nairobi, Kenya Coast (13), Nairobi (New Stanley—1), Outspan (1), Treetops (1), Nairobi (1), London (1), NYC. Costs (London-London) depend on coast hotel chosen: $799 for Seafarers (Malindi) up to $936 for Mnarani Club (Kilifi). *"Ethiopia"* (IT2BA16307), 19 days. NYC, London, Addis Ababa (Ghion—2), Harrar, Dire Dawa (Ras—1), Addis (1), Debre Zeit, Lakes Zwai, Abiata, Langano, Shalla, Awasa (Belle Vue du Lac —1), Wondo, Addis (2), excursion to Debre Libanos and Blue Nile, Bahar Dar (2), Gondar (1), Lalibela (1), Makalle (1), Axum, Massawa (Red Sea Hotel—2), Asmara (1), London (1), NYC. Departs 6Xyear. Package cost—$1,264, approx.

Thru the Lens Tours, Inc., 5301 Laurel Canyon Blvd., North Hollywood, Calif. 91607. Specializes in camera tours. *"Kenya's Northern Frontier"* (IT2BA1W075), 23 days to Kenya. NYC, London (1), Nairobi (Hilton—1), Treetops (1), Samburu (camp—3), Marsabit (camp—3), North Horr (camp—1), Loyengalani, Lake Rudolf (camp—3), Baragoi (camp—1), Thomson's Falls (Lodge—1), Lake Nakuru (Stag's Head—1), Masai Mara (camp—4), Nairobi, London, NYC. Rugged trip, only for the willing and able. Group of 9 only. January and August departures. Land cost—$2,175. Approx. air fare —$881–984. *"East Africa"* (IT3TW12634), 23 days to Uganda (when possible), Kenya, Tanzania. Limited to 3 pax per Land-Rover; group of 12 only. Lodge accommodations. February and July departures. Land cost—$2,075. Approx. air fare—$911–984. *"Across Africa"* (IT3PA1TLAF), 55 days to Morocco, Senegal, Mali, Niger, Dahomey, Nigeria, Uganda, Kenya, Ethiopia, Egypt. January departure. Land— $3,860. Approx. air fare—$1,320. 35 days, minus Ethiopia and Egypt: Land—$2,675. Approx. air fare—$1,000. *"Ethiopia and Egypt"* (IT3PA1TLET), 23 days. NYC, Paris, Addis Ababa (Hilton—2), Bahar Dar (2), Gondar (2), Falasha village, Lalibela (1), Axum (2), Asmara (2), Keren, on to Egypt. February departure. Land—$1,265. Approx. air fare—$860.

Travcoa, 111 North Wabash, Chicago, Ill. 60602. Large group-tour operator. Fully escorted tours. *"East Africa and Indian Ocean"* (IT4-PA1EATC), 33 days to Kenya, Tanzania, Comoro Islands, Madagascar, Reunion, Mauritius, Seychelles. Days 3–15 are in Kenya and Tanzania. Departs 11Xyear. Land cost—$1,895. Approx. air fare— $1,150. *"Classic Safari"* (IT4PA1CSTC), 22 days to Brazil, South Africa, Rhodesia, Kenya, Tanzania. Departs 20Xyear. Land—$1,250. Approx. air fare—$750–890. *"Cape to Kigali"* (IT4PA1CKTC), 39 days to Brazil, South Africa, Rhodesia, Tanzania, Kenya, Rwanda, Zaire. Departs 1Xmonth. Land—$2,295. Approx. air fare—$1,040.

"The Air Safari" (IT4PA1ASTC), 23 days to Kenya and Tanzania. NYC, Europe, Nairobi (2), Masai Mara (2), Serengeti (1), Lake Manyara (1), Ngorongoro (1), Lamu, Mombasa (2), Tsavo (Tsavo Tsafaris—2), Mount Kenya Safari Club (2), Treetops (1), Samburu (2), Lake Baringo (2), Nairobi (2), NYC. 13 departures. Land—$1,795. Approx. air fare—$910.

Travelworld Inc., 6922 Hollywood Blvd., Hollywood, Calif. 90028. *"East African Jet Trek"* (IT3SN1AJ1 to AJ48), 20 days to Kenya, Tanzania, Ethiopia. Departs 4Xmonth. Land—$998. Approx. air fare —$697–752.

United Touring International Ltd. (c/o local travel agents). Big wholesaler has drawn up some unique 14- and 21-day special interest tours and safaris in Kenya and Tanzania, starting from Nairobi, arrangeable for groups of 15 or more through travel agents. *"Archaeological Safari"* (KG465A), 14 days, incl Nairobi National Museum, Olorgesailie, Olduvai Gorge, Kariandusi, Hyrax Hill, Fort Jesus, Jumba la-Mtwana, Gedi ruins, Manda and Lamu islands, plus game parks; land cost from Nairobi—$618. *"Ornithological Safari"* (KG465B), 21 days, incl Nairobi National Museum and private aviary, Nairobi Park (more species than British Isles), Lake Naivasha (2), Crescent Island, Lake Nakuru (1), Samburu (2), Nairobi again, Arusha (1), Arusha Park, Tarangire (Safari Camp—2), Lake Manyara (2), Ngorongoro Crater, Taita Hills (1), Tsavo East, Malindi (3), Sokoke-Arabuko Forest, Mida Creek, Mombasa (1), Tsavo West (1), Nairobi; land cost—$924. *"Climbing Safari"* (KG465C), 14 days, incl Amboseli, Arusha Park, Tsavo West, climb up Kilimanjaro (Mount Kenya climb can be arranged); land cost—$568. *"Golfers Safari"* (KG465G), 21 days, incl golfing at Muthaiga, Sigona, Karen, Tigoni, Nakuru, Njoro, and Kericho golf clubs, plus game parks; land cost—$954. *"Deep-Sea Fishing Safari"* (KG465D), 14 days, incl Mombasa (Outrigger Club—3) and Kilifi (Mnarani Club—4); land cost—$663. *"Foot Safari"* (KG4-65F), 14 days, incl walking in Kitengela Game Conservation Area near Nairobi Park, Mount Kenya (3), Taita Hills (4); land cost—$498. *"Horse Riding Safari"* (KG465H), 14 days, incl 4 days riding; land cost—$655. *"Horticultural Safari"* (KS465K), 14 days, incl Bobs Harries Ltd. fruit plantation and cannery in Thika; Kericho tea estate and factory; Nairobi City Park and Arboretum; Marangu Hotel's 10-acre garden and Kilimanjaro lower slopes; Arusha Park; Kirchoffs Seed Merchants, Nairobi; land cost—$602. UTC also suggests safaris for entomology (40–50,000 species), lepidoptery (1,000 butterfly, thousands of moth species), ethnology, fresh-water fishing, railways, gambling, and the "Safari Rally Safari."

Wilderness Expeditions Inc., 230 Park Ave., New York 10017. *"Kenya's Outback"* (IT4PA1G919) is a Friends of the Earth tour run for 22 days in June 1974, perhaps to be repeated. Kenya arrangements by Swala Safaris. Itinerary: NYC, London, Nairobi (Norfolk—1), Mountain Lodge (1), Samburu (Lodge—2), Marsabit (tented camp—2), North Horr (camp—1), Loyengalani, Lake Rudolf (camp—2), Maralal (camp—1), Lake Nakuru (1), Masai Mara (Keekorok—2), Lake Naivasha (Safariland—1), horse safari in Rift Valley (camps—4), Nairobi (1), London, NYC. Land—$1,350. Approx. air fare—$734–941. Another 1974 Wilderness Expeditions trip was *"Ethiopia's Bale Mountains"* (IT4PA1L919), 21 days of mule-trekking, trout-fishing, and cave-exploring. Land—$985. Approx. air fare—$650–814. Both these tours were advertised for the fit and willing.

World Travel Consultants, Inc., 8111 Beverly Blvd., Los Angeles, Calif. 90048. *"East African Safari"* (IT3BR11018), 18 days to Kenya and Tanzania. L.A. or NYC, London, Nairobi (Hilton—2), Masai Mara (2), Serengeti (2), Olduvai, Ngorongoro (2), Lake Manyara, Arusha (1), Tsavo West (2), Nairobi (1), Treetops or Ark (1), Nairobi (1), London (1), NYC or L.A. Departs 2Xmonth. Land—$656. Approx. air fare from NYC—$679–734.

Planning an Individual Itinerary

It would take a couple of years to see every place mentioned in this book, and three weeks is little time to gain a comprehensive view of the region. Unless you have a special interest, such as history (Ethiopia), prehistory (Kenya, Tanzania), game (East Africa, Zambia), fishing (Kenya, Tanzania), hunting (Kenya), or birdwatching (anywhere), and you simply want an overall three-week view of what the region offers, we would say choose a package tour (from the U.S., p. 14; from Nairobi, p. 112). If tours are not your style, or if you have more than three weeks, read on.

Decide how much ground you can comfortably cover, keeping in mind that the more time in a place, the better. Here are some suggestions: Three weeks—Kenya, Tanzania, Ethiopia. Four weeks—same plus Uganda. Five weeks—East Africa, Ethiopia, and Zambia (Victoria Falls). Six weeks—all five countries plus perhaps Uganda. That is an average of a week in each country, though over six weeks, different activities will take up different amounts of time—a Kilimanjaro climb and a drive through Tanzania's northern circuit will be 8–10 days, while Malawi may call for a three-day stay, to visit the lake and recuperate from, say, your eight-day walking safari in Zambia's Luangwa Valley. Second-timers may wish to spend all their vacation in just one country—and we favor the idea.

We recommend that you *try* to plan each week to include at least two two-night stays in the same place; seven nights in seven different places is far too many. And in a trip of a month or more, plan several two-night stays in interesting places (like Lalibela and Gondar on Ethiopia's Historic Route) *and* a stay of three or four days in one place (Kenya coast, Lake Malawi, a mountain resort, or Rift Valley lake). It's your vacation, after all. Finally, after reading about the many game parks, you should schedule a stay of three or more days in just *one* game park; Tsavo, Serengeti, and Luangwa Valley are ideal for this purpose. If you rush through game parks at the rate of one a day, they will—guaranteed result—all look the same in the end.

Following are three itineraries—of 22, 31, and 49 days' duration—that we have drawn up as suggested rough programs. Airline and tour schedules would affect the exact itinerary, while the availability of short-duration package tours and the kind of accommodations desired affect the cost, so we cannot estimate costs here. The 22-day program is an orthodox one; the other two are definitely different. Travel is variably by air and road. Numerals in parentheses below refer to number of nights spent in each place.

Three weeks in Ethiopia, Kenya, and Tanzania: NYC, Rome, Asmara (1), Axum (1), Lalibela (1), Gondar (1), Addis Ababa (1), Nairobi (2), Masai Mara Game Reserve (2), Serengeti (2), Olduvai Gorge, Ngorongoro Crater (1), Arusha (1), Mombasa (1), Lamu (1), Mount Kenya Safari Club (1), The Ark (1), Lake Naivasha (1), Lake Nakuru, Rift Valley Escarpment, Nairobi (1), Europe, NYC.

Four weeks in Kenya, Tanzania, and Ethiopia, including a climb to the top of Kilimanjaro, goggling in Watamu Marine National Park, night train from Mombasa to Nairobi. NYC, Nairobi (2), Marangu (1), Kilimanjaro climb (4), Marangu (1), Arusha (1), Lake Manyara (1), Ngorongoro Crater (1), Serengeti (2), Masai Mara (1), Nairobi (1), Tsavo West (1), Taita Hills, Tsavo East (1), Malindi, Watamu (2), Gedi, Marine Park, Mombasa, night train (1), Nairobi (1), Addis Ababa (1), Bahar Dar (1), Lake Tana, Tissisat Falls, Gondar (1), Lalibela (1), Axum (1), Asmara (1), Europe, NYC.

Seven weeks in Eastern Africa, including the Historic Route, a round-the-peaks walking tour on Mount Kenya, a self-drive car trip (camping or lodging), night train Mombasa to Nairobi, 2 days in Africa's largest game park (Selous), a Luangwa Valley walking safari, 4 days in Malawi, stopover in Uganda (if open). NYC, Europe, Asmara (1), Axum (1), Lalibela (1), Gondar (1), Addis Ababa (1), Nairobi (2) (rent car, game view in Nairobi Park, drive to and walk on Ngong Hills), drive to Outspan, Naro Moru River Lodge (1), walking trip on Mount Kenya (3), Naro Moru, Aberdare Country Club (1), The Ark (1), drive on to Lake Nakuru and Lake Naivasha (1), Nairobi (1) (turn in rent-a-car), Malindi, Lamu (2), Malindi, Mombasa, night train (1), Nairobi (1), Masai Mara (2), Serengeti (2), Olduvai Gorge, Ngorongoro Crater (1), Arusha (1), Dar es Salaam (1), Selous Game Reserve (tented camp—2), Dar Beach Hotel (1), Lusaka, Livingstone, Victoria Falls (2), Livingstone, Mfuwe Lodge in South Luangwa National Park (1), 5-day walking safari (4), Mfuwe, Lusaka (1), Blantyre, Zomba Plateau (1), Lake Malawi resort (2), Blantyre (1), Nairobi (1), Entebbe, Kampala (1), Kabalega Falls (2), Kampala (1), Entebbe, London, NYC.

Luxury Safaris

The individually tailored, professionally guided safari is generally for the well-to-do, for who else can afford to lay out several thousand dollars for three weeks or a month? There are three types of safari—hunting, photo, and game viewing—costing about the same to operate (hunting and trophy fees are very high for that kind of safari). On photo safaris, you use a camera instead of a gun, but you go after animals with a serious intent, to snap close-ups of snarling lions and whatnot. If you take a game-viewing safari, you might take the Masai Mara–Serengeti–Ngorongoro–Lake Manyara–Amboseli circuit, but you'd stay in your own private tented camp—unless you want to stay in lodges.

Nairobi is undubitably the safari capital; safari firms there will do your bidding, but tend to operate only in Kenya and Tanzania. There are a couple safari outfitters in Ethiopia and Zambia, a few in Tanzania. For more details on safari organizing, see Kenya, p. 110.

Drive Yourself

For the American who always uses his car to get to work, to the store, on weekend trips, business trips, summer vacations—or just to drive around—there is a real alternative to (1) taking a zebra-striped minibus tour around East Africa's game parks, or (2) spending more money than you have on a full-scale, individually tailored safari. The alternative is a simple one: fly to Nairobi and rent a car or, if you're a long-term traveler, buy a car. If you like, you can stay in game lodges and hotels, or if you want a true African experience, you can camp out.

The advantages are many: you can go where you want when you want and at your own speed, especially if you camp. Learning how to drive on the left in four countries (Ethiopia is on the right) is easy. Other drivers are no more dangerous than anywhere else. Gasoline is not cheap, but it is available. Roads in the tourist areas are not bad, and most of the main roads in East Africa are paved—you can drive on two-lane blacktop all the way from Mount Kenya to Cape Town. Your route need not duplicate that of the East African Safari Rally. In Nairobi, which is the best safari center, you can rent a new car (European and Japanese models) in good condition from any of a dozen very reliable firms, or you can take a mechanical chance and rent a cheaper car. Nothing terrible will happen to you just because you're outside the precincts of a tour minibus. See p. 104 for Nairobi car-hire firms, p. 108 for addresses of new and used car dealers. Each country chapter has a section on driving with further details.

You need no special car. In fact, you can drive just about *any* model car—a VW Beetle or a big Land Cruiser, a tiny Fiat or a powerful Land-Rover, a Toyota Corolla or a Mercedes. The best cars—VW buses and four-wheel-drives—are generally the most expensive to rent, but there are few important places where you cannot drive in a small car —Lake Rudolf and Lalibela are the only main destinations for which four-wheel-drive vehicles are necessary. Adventurous sorts have driven VW Beetles all over Africa—across the Sahara, through Ethiopia's mountains to Addis, through Central Africa; very ordinary people with families go on safari in East Africa with their very ordinary town vehicles as a matter of course. You can do it too. This is not to say that four-wheel-drives don't have their uses—they can go off the road, wade a stream or plow through a mud hole, travel in the wet season, take mountain tracks. But the ordinary tourist doesn't need one to go through the Kenya–Northern Tanzania "milk run" without undue trouble; only to go down into Ngorongoro Crater, where a four-wheel-drive is mandatory, will you have to leave the small car at the hotel and rent a seat in a government Land-Rover.

˙ At most game parks you can hire an armed game ranger to accompany you. He will not only help you find and identify animals but will help you stay out of trouble. Fee is usually $1.50 or so.

Here are some tips for car hirers, particularly those renting in Nairobi:

• If planning a lengthy rent-a-car safari, make as many arrangements as possible by mail with the car-hire firm. Negotiate lower charges, ask for the model you want to be definitely reserved for you on a certain date, indicate that you'll be extremely happy to pick up a car that has been newly serviced (ask for proof of this when you pick it up), come to an understanding about who pays for nonaccident repairs and necessary servicing, and ask for a gasoline jerrycan, a second spare tire, a couple of water jerrycans to sweeten the deal.

• A second spare tire is a must. Cars have a tendency to lose two tires in quick succession. Of our ten flats (over the course of 30,000 km), we had two within half an hour, two within a day, then three within two days. With a second spare, we never had to take the tire off the rim and fix the tube; any garage will do this quickly for only 5/–. (Tubeless tires are rare in Africa.)

• Give the car a once-over before renting. Even if you aren't a mechanic, you can see if the radiator hoses, fan belt, or tires are worn. Listen to the motor. Take it out for a spin, go through the gears, test the brakes, see if the steering, alignment, and wheel balance are good.

• Don't rent a car with more than 50,000 km on it—just to be safe.

• Make sure the odometer registers mileage correctly; in Nairobi, take the vehicle a short distance south on the Mombasa highway, where there are kilometer stones every 2 km.

• Pin the car-hire firm down on how extensive the insurance coverage is, and what the deductible is. Many firms offer automatic coverage, but the deductible may be 1,000/– ($142) and the windshield might not be covered. You may get a better insurance deal for a flat 7/– or 10/– a day more.

• Find out what extra charges there might be for cleaning the car when you get back, whether it has to be returned with a full tank, and whether premium gasoline is required.

• Ask whether the rental vehicle has a Tanzania Foreign Commercial Vehicle License, which you need to enter that country. See p. 321.

• "Renting it here, leaving it there" is not common; only some firms have drop-off arrangements—Avis makes no charge to drop a car off in Mombasa, but Car Hire Services, for one, charges 500/–.

• You might consider hiring a chauffeur with the car. This is not expensive. Typically, rent-a-car firms charge –/15 to –/30 (U.S. 2¢– 3¢) per km, plus a driver's allowance of 30/– per night away from Nairobi, occasionally plus an extra flat daily charge of 10/– to 40/–, and gasoline is usually included in the deal. Alternatively, you can find some knowledgeable resident who will act as a chauffeur-guide-helper. The advantages of a chauffeur are manifest: he *may* know East Africa better than you do, will do all the driving while you relax and take pictures, is perhaps a better mechanic; for added monetary inducement, he may be willing to help set up camp, wash the dishes, etc. Come to an understanding before setting out.

• When renting, remember that in East Africa nearly everything is negotiable, and many firms charge a daily rate for only six days of the week, or drop the daily rate if you're taking the car on a long safari. Rental cars are available from firms in Nairobi, Mombasa, Malindi, Arusha, Dar es Salaam, Lusaka, Blantyre, Addis Ababa, and Asmara; chauffeured cars can be hired at most East African and Zambian game lodges, should you want to take a game-viewing or scenic drive by yourself.

Tips on Driving in Africa

Whether you drive a small car or a big four-wheel-drive, here are some car safari tips:

• Take it slow. Roads in Eastern Africa are, by American standards, "crowded" with pedestrians and bicyclists, cattle, sheep and goats, elephants, antelope, tortoises, dogs and cats.

• Before crossing a mud hole or stream of any size, get out and look at it. Take a stick and see how deep it is. You may profit by throwing some brush or sticks into the mud hole, or making sure the floor of the stream is clear of projections. On tourist routes, bridges are found everywhere, but there is the odd crossing you will have to wade, such as one in Samburu which is well used.

• Many muddy patches and sand patches, also short steep gradients, can be rushed. Back up a suitable distance, step on the accelerator, and let the momentum take you across or up. If you can't rush it, take it steadily in low gear, going up to second if it is all right. If your wheels start spinning in mud or sand, don't keep doing it—you'll just have more digging, jacking, and pushing to do.

• Chains are helpful over long muddy stretches. Over long distances in soft sand, deflate your tires, and try not to slow down.

• Far more common than mud and sand are corrugated roads. You will vibrate to pieces if you drive slowly, because the tires are going down and up every individual corrugation. So drive fast on straight sections; vibration eases considerably. Do slow down on curves, since the vibration can overpower the steering.

• Stay very alert on narrow paved roads. Buses and trucks have great difficulty on poorly engineered paved roads (or maybe any road) in staying in their own lane, and bicyclists are fond of riding on roads too. Pedestrians are everywhere, even in the middle of nowhere.

• Trucks and buses will generally flash the outside turn blinker if it's safe for you to pass, the inside blinker if there's something coming they can see but you can't.

• Should you get a flat tire or breakdown, try to pull off the road, though not if it puts the car at an awkward angle for jacking it up. The common method of alerting other drivers is to put branches or a few small piles of leaves at periodic intervals in the road 100 yards in front of and behind your car.

Overlanders and those doing much road traveling will quickly learn driving techniques. Four-wheelers may want to read *Rough Riding,* by Dick Cepek and Walt Wheelock (Glendale, Calif.: La Siesta Press, 1968; available from publishers, Box 406, Glendale), also Rover's "Guide to Land-Rover Expeditions" (see p. 44).

Road Distance Tables

Those planning car safaris, especially if they are renting a vehicle, can use the following tables to calculate rough distances. Adding the mile and kilometer figures on maps is also useful.

It is easier than you think to cover long distances in Africa. However, after more than a year of road travel in Eastern Africa, we would advise you to attempt no more than 250 to 300 miles a day on paved roads (not necessarily smooth riding), no more than 150 miles on dirt, no more than 200 miles on dirt and blacktop. Even short distances on pavement, such as between Nairobi and Lake Nakuru, can be utterly exhausting.

Figure each morning and afternoon game run in a game park as about 50 miles (80 km) in distance.

Kilometer Distances—Eastern Africa

ADDIS ABABA

2048	ARUSHA												
1083	3123	ASMARA											
4680	2640	5763	BLANTYRE										
3320	1834	4403	4473	BUJUMBURA, BURUNDI									
2774	639	3857	2124	2568	DAR ES SALAAM								
2428	942	3511	3582	892	1676	KAMPALA							
3024	1538	4107	4177	296	2272	596	KIGALI, RWANDA						
4322	2382	5405	358	4116	1766	3224	3820	LILONGWE					
4974	2934	6057	1585	4768	2418	3876	4472	1227	LIVINGSTONE				
4499	2459	5582	1110	4293	1943	3401	3997	752	475	LUSAKA			
1763	277	2846	2917	1577	1011	665	1261	2559	3211	2736	NAIROBI		
3450	1410	4533	1230	3243	894	2352	2947	872	1524	1049	1687	MBEYA	
2255	401	3338	3476	2049	570	1157	1753	3118	2770	2295	492	1355	MOMBASA

Kilometer Distances—Zambia

CHIPATA

916	CHUNGA CAMP, KAFUE N.P.														
741	314	KABWE													
1183	609	716	KASANE, BOTSWANA												
807	382	66	782	KAPIRI MPOSHI											
989	499	322	764	388	KARIBA DAM										
957	535	221	932	153	538	KITWE									
1077	424	610	73	676	544	826	LIVINGSTONE (VICTORIA FALLS)								
1144	721	407	1119	339	725	186	1013	LUBUMBASHI, ZAIRE							
604	314	137	579	203	185	353	473	540	LUSAKA						
1821	1379	1085	1802	1017	1408	1170	1696	1356	1223	MBALA					
130	1048	871	1313	937	919	1087	1207	1274	734	950	MFUWE, SOUTH LUANGWA N.P.				
1261	334	1205	407	716	842	869	382	1055	657	1713	1382	MONGU			
919	499	183	894	117	500	59	788	245	315	1134	1049	833	NDOLA		
626	1205	889	1605	823	1211	976	1499	1162	1022	194	756	1539	940	TUNDUMA	
734	446	271	850	337	140	487	520	674	134	1357	868	791	449	1156	CHIRUNDU

Kilometer Distances—Tanzania

ARUSHA

639	DAR ES SALAAM								
1136	1816	KIGOMA							
1016	499	1317	IRINGA						
1410	894	923	394	MBEYA					
277	1011	1413	1293	1687	NAIROBI				
108	747	1244	1124	1518	169	NAMANGA			
177	816	1024	1193	1587	454	285	NGORONGORO		
315	954	984	1331	1725	592	423	138	SERONERA, SERENGETI N.P.	
1523	1006	890	507	113	1800	1631	1700	1838	TUNDUMA

Kilometer Distances—Kenya

ELDORET

379	KEEKOROK, MASAI MARA G.R.												
134	245	KISUMU											
131	415	170	MALABA BRIDGE, UGANDA										
1022	864	966	1053	MALINDI									
690	811	732	821	1228	MARSABIT								
802	741	843	932	121	1107	MOMBASA							
1018	1138	1060	1149	1502	243	1381	MOYALE						
309	249	351	440	615	562	492	889	NAIROBI					
153	293	195	284	769	537	648	865	156	NAKURU				
478	418	420	609	728	731	607	1058	169	325	NAMANGA			
321	449	363	452	813	369	692	697	200	168	369	NANYUKI		
262	288	304	393	775	449	654	777	162	109	331	80	NYERI	
645	585	687	776	277	898	156	1225	336	492	441	536	498	VOI

Kilometer Distances—Malawi

BLANTYRE

917	CHELINDA CAMP, NYIKA N.P.									
1024	228	CHITIPA								
127	1044	1151	CHIROMO							
493	421	528	623	KASUNGU						
358	559	666	485	138	LILONGWE					
196	875	982	323	454	316	MANGOCHI				
472	673	780	599	252	114	430	MCHINJI			
748	184	290	875	264	390	706	504	MZUZU		
402	665	772	529	244	106	207	220	496	SALIMA	
68	849	956	195	425	290	128	404	680	334	ZOMBA

Kilometer Distances—Ethiopia

ADDIS ABABA

1083	ASMARA								
259	1352	AWASH							
1012	178	1271	AXUM						
578	721	837	543	BAHAR DAR					
748	551	1007	383	183	GONDAR				
537	1610	656	1541	1115	1285	HARRAR			
646	651	905	580	736	755	1183	LALIBELA		
1173	90	1432	268	811	641	1710	741	MASSAWA	
875	1958	616	1887	1453	1623	1272	1521	2050	MOYALE, KENYA

Camping

If you camp in the U.S. under semirugged conditions—that is, without electric appliances and contraptions and gadgets—then you can camp in East Africa, especially Kenya and Tanzania. You need nothing extraordinary in the way of equipment. Camping is allowed in almost every national park and game reserve in designated locations, and you need *not* fear wild animals barging into your tent (do put your food away in the car, however). More likely than not, there will be a few other campers at these game park campsites—mostly resident European families and overlanders—though your privacy will be well respected. Outside the game parks you can camp just about anywhere off the road, though if it looks like private property (say, along the Kenya coast), try to get permission from the owner. As for your safety, be prudent, as you would anywhere else in the world. Campsites in Africa usually have minimal facilities—latrine and garbage pit, perhaps, but rarely drinking water (though you won't have any trouble getting that), hardly ever a shower. The lack of facilities can heighten the wildness and the beauty, for if you camp here, your neighbor (if you have one) will not be in a big trailer or recreational vehicle with TV blaring, Chinese lanterns strung around his campsite, and a signboard, "The Joe Blows from Indianapolis," at the entrance.

Malawi has, conveniently spotted around the country, very nice rest houses, with hot baths, where you can camp for pennies, and have your meals prepared and served indoors by the cook. Kenya has a variation of these—self-service lodges, usually in the game parks. These are simply furnished bandas (cottages, rondavels) equipped with cooking equipment, utensils, stove and lantern, beds and bedding—all you do, generally, is bring the food and cook it yourself.

If you can afford the weight, bring from home as much as possible of the more expensive camping equipment items—tent (with sewn-in floor and netting at door and windows), warm sleeping bag, air mattress, stove (gasoline pressure stove or a midget propane stove)—and whatever light, inexpensive items you don't want to buy locally, such as knives, forks, spoons. Pots and pans are cheap and easily obtainable in Nairobi. Camp chairs, tables, and anything else can be purchased or rented (see p. 109), though not cheaply. In Kenya, fresh fruit, vegetables, and meat are good and inexpensive, and generally available throughout the country (though not north of Mount Kenya); good fresh food is less obtainable in Tanzania, Ethiopia, and Zambia. You can always find a shop (*duka*) selling some canned goods, however. Carry all the food you'll need for inside a game park, and all food between Masai Mara–Serengeti–Ngorongoro–Lake Manyara–Arusha, though there are *dukas* at Ngorongoro settlement. Take as many jerries with drinking water as your vehicle has room for.

You won't know how easy camping in East Africa is until you're actually doing it. Breaking camp in the morning is, as ever, the worst chore. Wild animals won't bother you, though bold vervet monkeys may run off with a sandwich. In fact, mosquitoes probably won't bother you much, either. Of the 130 days or so we spent camping, mosquitoes harassed us on only a few. More hazardous were moths and flying beetles—none biting—attracted by the light. To avoid bugs in the broth, we always tried to stop about 5 P.M., set up camp, and eat before dark (the sun sets about 6:20 P.M. every day). Another occasional hazard in camping is biting army ants, or *siafu*. They march in columns and, on the *off-chance* they come into your campsite, can be discouraged with pyrethrum powder or spray (Johnson's IT, produced in East Africa, is good); boiling water (in quantities) also does the trick, and a ring of ashes around your tent will be an effective barrier. And when camping outside game parks, watch for the occasional sneak thief.

You can't walk about in game parks except at campsites and designated spots, but in other places and, say, on Mount Kenya, animals will give you a wide berth if you make your presence known by whistling or clapping or walking noisily.

Well, then, are there *any* good reasons not to camp in East Africa? We have no qualms about saying there are no important deterrents—except you may not want to go home again. Camping out is a special thrill because you seem more one-with-nature, and you are both physically and spiritually closer to the wildlife than you would be if staying in a crowded game lodge.

Budgeting a Self-Drive Camping Safari: East Africa on $20 a Day

In this section we describe a 31-day Kenya–Tanzania self-drive do-it-yourself economy camping safari itinerary. The estimated budget, using 1973 figures, totals 8,350/– ($1,193). This includes renting a VW Beetle and driving it 2,500 miles (4,200 km), entry fees into 14 parks, accommodations (mainly camping) and food for two people (with quite a few meals in hotels), a four-day round-the-peaks walking safari on Mount Kenya, and minor equipment purchases in Nairobi. Per-day cost for the two people: $38, or $19 each—or call it $20 now that there's an oil shortage. In addition to this, you must count air fare from the U.S. to Nairobi; if you take charters New York–London, London–Nairobi, and back, this totals $1,160 for two people, round trip (excursion fares would total $1,854 to $2,000). Total cost for two people: $2,353. This compares with a total of $5,200 for two people on a 30-day group package tour.

Assumptions: That you are willing to drive 2,500 miles in a jam-packed Beetle, set up your own camp, and cook your own food (not quite as good as game-lodge food). That you are willing to hassle your own arrangements (which you wouldn't have to do on a package). That you are, in general, willing to rough it—but not much more than you would in the U.S. (you'll manage a shower at least every two days). That you have, or will buy, in the U.S. most backpacking/camping gear—44 pounds per person—and carry it over and back; this equipment should include some dried and freeze-dried food. (Details on Kenya camping, pp. 108–110.)

Here is the suggested itinerary:

Day 1. Arrive Nairobi. To Mayfair Hotel (annex double without private bath), recuperate. *Day 2*. Pick up VW Beetle at car-hire firm; try to borrow a couple of five-gallon water jerrycans; failing this, buy them, along with such things as an extra cooking pot, washbasin, breadboard, dish soap, laundry soap. Buy canned and fresh food. Check the car over, drive out to Westwood Park Country Club to camp—this is a milk run, to see what you're missing in the way of equipment. *Day 3*. Drive out to the Ngong Hills, take the circular road around them counterclockwise, coming out on the Magadi Road, which goes back toward Nairobi. Take a game-drive in Nairobi National Park. Camp second night at Westwood Park. *Day 4*. Drive north past Nyeri (tea at Outspan Hotel) to Naro Moru River Lodge, stay in self-service climbers' bunkhouse. *Days 5–8*. Mount Kenya walking tour, all arrangements made previously with the lodge. First day reach Mackinder's Camp, second day Kami Hut, third day top of Point Lenana (16,355 ft) and back to Mackinder's, fourth day down to roadhead and Naro Moru. Recuperate afternoon and evening. (If you don't want to climb, Days 5–8 can be spent at Samburu and/or Meru game parks.) *Day 9*. Drive Nyeri into Aberdare National Park (or, if closed, through Ngobit to Thomson's Falls). Camp by a waterfall in either case. *Day 10*. To Lake Naivasha, camp at Safariland Club. *Day 11*. To

Lake Nakuru (flamingo spectacle), camp beneath the fever trees. *Day 12*. To Molo, high (8,000 ft) in the Highlands. Camp near Highlands Hotel, have dinner and breakfast there. *Day 13*. To Kericho, tea country. Tour Brooke Bond estate and tea factory. Buy as much fresh food as possible—little available until Arusha. Camp at Mau Forest fishing camp (inquire in Kericho). *Day 14*. Press on to Masai Mara Game Reserve. Camping fee is high here (30/– per person), so try to camp just outside reserve. *Day 15*. In Masai Mara. Lunch at Keekorok or Mara Serena Lodge. *Day 16*. Across the Tanzania border into the Serengeti. Lunch at Lobo Lodge, architecturally delightful. Camp at Seronera. *Day 17*. In Serengeti, another night at Seronera. *Day 18*. Through the Serengeti Plains to Olduvai Gorge, onward up to Ngorongoro Crater rim, night at Simba Camp. *Day 19*. Leave VW, buy seats in Tanzania Tours Land-Rover for trip down into Ngorongoro Crater. Noon lunch at lodge on rim, then take VW on to Lake Manyara National Park. Camp there. *Day 20*. Game view, then drive on through Arusha (restock food chest) into Arusha National Park, camp. *Day 21*. To Marangu on Kilimanjaro's lower slope, camp at Marangu Hotel, eat dinner there. *Day 22*. Back into Kenya at Taveta, then north into Tsavo West National Park. Night at Kitani or Ngulia self-service lodge. *Day 23*. In Tsavo West—to Mzima Springs, Poacher's Lookout, Shaitani, and Roaring Rock, at all of which you can alight from the car. *Day 24*. Out Tsavo Gate, south to Voi. Excursion into Taita Hills, then back to Voi and into Tsavo East. Camp. *Day 25*. Game viewing, then head east along Galana River, out Sala Gate, and through the *nyika* (thornbush country) to Malindi on the coast. Recuperate at Driftwood Beach Club (bed and breakfast terms so you can sample other hotels' lunch and dinner). *Day 26*. Around Malindi—excursion to Gedi ruins, go goggling in Watamu Marine National Park. Driftwood Club overnight. *Day 27*. Down the coast highway to Mombasa (sightseeing at Fort Jesus, harbor cruise perhaps), cross Likoni Ferry and on to Twiga Lodge campground. *Day 28*. On South Coast—excursion into Shimba Hills National Reserve (sable antelope) early in the morning, then to Diani Beach for remainder of day, drive to Mombasa for Tamarind Restaurant dinner, then back to Twiga. *Day 29*. Leave the coast, take Nairobi road past Tsavo to Bushwhackers Camp. *Day 30*. Another 100 miles into Nairobi, turn in the car, recuperate by the Mayfair's pool. *Day 31*. Leave for home.

Summary: 19 nights of tent camping, 4 nights of self-service lodge camping, 2 nights in Nairobi hotel, 2 at coast hotel, 3 on Mount

Kenya. Of the 2,500 miles, nearly half is on paved road, the remainder on well-traveled dirt.

Here is the estimated budget for two people in dollars and shillings (Kenyan and Tanzanian):

	U.S. dollars	Shillings
VW rental—daily charge plus mileage for 30 days, 2,500 miles (4,200 km)	467	3,270/–
Gasoline (5/– per U.S. gallon; 20 mpg)	89	625/–
Park entry fees	113	790/–
Accommodations (mainly camping)	97	674/–
Mount Kenya Foot Safari (Naro Moru River Lodge—arranged package)	214	1,500/–
Game drive down into Ngorongoro Crater	26	180/–
Tanzania Foreign Commercial Vehicle License	3	22/–
Food (as outlined above with some hotel lunches, dinners)	97	674/–
Purchase or rental of miscellaneous (mainly bulky) camping gear in Nairobi	43	300/–
Miscellaneous (10/– per day)	44	310/–
Total land cost	$1,193	8,345/–

We would call this an economy-minded budget, but there are items you can save money on, such as the Mount Kenya walking trip. If you make your own arrangements (see p. 248), you can lower the price for two people more than 50 percent. By cooking all your own food, that item is cut by half. If you decide to get along without a camp table and stools (rented or purchased), and if you bring every item of camping gear you need, then the 300/– budget item can be knocked out. You can camp at Malindi and save 90/–, and by camping outside Masai Mara, you can save another 120/– on lodging. But consider the necessity of some comfort and some amenities, and reserve a sizable contingency fund, before you wield the financial razor.

We included the Mount Kenya climb because it was, for us, a particularly enjoyable four days. It is an extraordinary expense—but it is not extraordinary to do something special during an economical car-camping safari. Alternatives to Mount Kenya might be Kilimanjaro, a Lake Victoria cruise, a flight to Lamu, a couple nights at game-viewing lodges, a fishing trip to Lake Rudolf, and so forth. We bet it will still average out at $20 per person per day.

After air fares, the single most costly item is, of course, the rented VW. The 30-day, 4,200-km cost of 3,270/– is the average of four car-hire firms. The range was from a low of 2,500/– up to 3,690/–, indicating it's worthwhile to shop around.

If you want slightly more comfort, a Datsun 1600, a medium-size compact, is 4,281/– (three-firm average) for the same time and distance. This brings the daily cost up to $21 per person.

How much would it cost for a family of four to do the same thing in a VW bus? With the same assumptions, though substituting Samburu and Mount Kenya Safari Club day visit for the climb, and figuring the rent-a-car cost at 7,238/– (average of four firms; range from 5,880/– up to 7,875/–), the total land cost is 12,279/– or $1,754. This is a total of $56 per day, or only $14 per person.

Four unrelated adults, or two couples, going on the climb and driving a VW bus, would spend 16,547/– or $2,364. This is back to $19 a day. Each person would spend about $589 for the land cost of his month-long East African camping safari.

Inflation and the oil crisis will, naturally, affect all these estimates; see note, pp. 84–85.

Organizing Your Own Trans-African Expedition

It takes much time, money, energy, and patience—and a high frustration threshold—to organize an overland trek from Europe to East or South Africa. The trip includes two long, rough sections—across the Sahara and across Francophone Central Africa (Cameroon, Central African Republic, and Zaire)—before arriving in East Africa, which comparatively is a traveler's dream. A whole book can easily be written about overlanding, and we don't have the space to cover the subject adequately here. This short section, necessarily concise, consists mostly of guidelines and scattered advice based on our own experience and the experience of others.

You must, first of all, realistically examine your finances. Three people must be prepared to spend about $10,000 for a three- or four-month London–Nairobi journey in a new Land-Rover, perhaps a bit less in a VW microbus. You will always spend more than you contemplate. Forget about finding jobs en route (except in South Africa); further, you'll be very lucky if you can get anybody to give you money in advance for something you can do on the road—taking pictures, writing articles, testing equipment.

Organizing and then running an expedition is a challenge, and it is absolutely vital you go with the right people. If you can't agree and disagree properly, make decisions democratically, or even live together before the trip, forget it altogether. Three or four people is the right number, and they should be either all one sex or equally balanced in males and females. A family or two couples would work. Funds should be contributed equally.

In planning a rough itinerary, don't try to figure out a day-to-day, mile-by-mile schedule; it won't work. Settle for a week-by-week, country-by-country, itinerary. You might use the organized group itineraries (see p. 46) as a guide, ad-libbing as you travel. London makes the best starting point, and you should set off between September and March. Allow at least four months to organize before D-day; it can take a long time to get outfitted vehicle, equipment, personnel, supplies, and papers together.

Long-wheel-base Land-Rovers or VW buses are the two best bets. Most sedans aren't high enough off the ground. You can't get parts or servicing for American four-wheelers or pickups.

You cannot carry everything you *might* need; in fact, you can barely carry everything you *will* need. If in doubt, don't bring it. Think double-purpose or multipurpose in choosing equipment. Don't go overboard on buying tools. But do consider your minimum comfort needs; a trip can be hell if you don't have something comfortable to sleep on.

Readers interested in overlanding are invited to write to the authors (address, p. xv). Other sources of information:

Michelin maps No. 153, 154, and 155 for most route planning and traveling purposes; see p. 9.

"Guide to Land-Rover Expeditions" (5th ed., 1969), free 17-page guide from Public Relations Dept., The Rover Co. Ltd., Solihull, Warwickshire, England.

Brochures published by organized overland companies; see pp. 46–49.

Trail Finders Information Centre; see p. 48.

Royal Automobile Club, Foreign Touring Dept., Box 92, Croydon, Surrey ("Road Conditions and Information—North Africa"). The Automobile Association, Overseas Operations (Routes), The Marlborough Bldg., 383 Holloway Road, London N7 ("Travel Across the Sahara Desert" and "Africa—States and Main Routes").

Africa on Wheels: A Scrounger's Guide to Motoring in Africa, a 160-page paperback by John J. Byrne, is a good anecdotal guide to doing Africa overland (he used a VW camper), with section on picking partners, outfitting the car, camping out, even on using the black

market and forging travel documents (in a pinch). $4.95, from
Haessner Publishing, Inc., Newfoundland, N.J. 07435.

The Expedition Organizers Guide from the Scientific Exploration Society, c/o Daily Telegraph, 135 Fleet St., London EC4; costs about
50¢.

Handbook for Expeditions: A Planning Guide, published by the
Brathay Exploration Group and the *Geographical Magazine,* is
particularly good for scientific expeditions, and can be obtained for
$2 from the *Geographical,* 128 Long Acre, London WC2E 9QH.

Starting an Expedition in Nairobi

This idea has attractive possibilities. Why not carefully select 44
pounds of the more expensive or hard-to-get expedition items, catch a
charter flight to Nairobi, and there take advantage of the pool of experience of overlanders just in from London and all the other travelers
you'll find there? There are also secondhand expedition- or safari-
equipped vehicles and used equipment to be found (bargain rates are
possible), and anything missing can be purchased locally. You can
travel around Eastern Africa, then go across Central Africa and the
Sahara to Europe, perhaps selling the vehicle there.

Those contemplating the organizing of a *new* expedition in Nairobi
or any other place in Eastern Africa should think twice. New vehicles
are getting flabbergastingly expensive (in early 1974, a new Toyota
Land Cruiser station wagon cost $6,765, a standard VW microbus
$7,570, a Land-Rover-109 $6,977), and to outfit completely with new
equipment would cost a small fortune. A hire-purchase or guaranteed
repurchase plan (check with Cooper Motors, p. 108, on this) might be
economical—if you've money to spare. The alternative would be to
have a vehicle outfitted in England or Japan and get it imported into
Kenya, along with all your own equipment. This can cost a lot of
money and even more grief unless you're properly equipped with importation and other official papers. Perhaps a bit of money can be
saved by ordering from the factory a stripped-down vehicle (chassis,
engine, wheels, dashboard, and steering wheel), importing it to Kenya
and having a body shop build to your own specifications. Safari operators in Nairobi do this with Land Cruiser pickup models. Land
Cruiser models imported into Kenya cannot be introduced into the
U.S. because they don't have the right antipollution equipment. For
other reasons, the Land-Rover-109 is also prohibited from the U.S.

If this sounds like a bit too much, you can save a hassle by renting an expedition vehicle and bringing some equipment with you. But you can't drive very far or long before the rental cost approaches the purchase cost. Best bet, then: buy a used expedition vehicle in Nairobi, where you can always resell it. If you drove it back to Europe, it would still be worth something on resale.

Organized Group Overland Expeditions

Those with the urge to go overland but who lack the wherewithal, or don't like the incredible hassle of doing-it-yourself, can join an organized overland group catering to the under-thirties blue-jeans crowd. There are several of these based in England—the word is only beginning to spread to the U.S.

The groups that run overland treks are as follows:

Siafu Expeditions Ltd., 18 Dawes Road, Fulham, London SW6 7EH; tel. 01–381 1388; cable SIAFU (bookings to Trail Finders, address below). Siafu (Swahili—"safari ant") is the real veteran on the overland route, with the first trip done in 1966. Siafu route is London-Tangier by air, then by land Tangier-Kano-Bangui-Kigali-Nairobi, a 12-week journey operated each way 6 times a year. Siafu is switching from Land-Rovers to 15-passenger Bedford four-wheel-drive trucks. Passengers are 55 percent male, range in age from 17 to 45 (average is 28). Baggage limit is 30 lbs. Two meals a day included in cost; sleeping is in two-man tents. Southbound departures March, May, July, September, October, December. Cost: $1,080 (£450). Inexpensive connecting travel to India, Australia, New Zealand or wherever is easily arranged.

Encounter Overland Ltd., 1 Munro Terrace, London SW10; tel. 01–352 3702 (bookings to Trail Finders). Encounter Overland has been running its 16-passenger Bedfords from London to Johannesburg (and back) since 1970, operating the 13–14-week trip 3–4 times a year. Cost: $1,164 (£485).

Penn Overland, 122 Knightsbridge, London SW1X 7PG; tel. 01-589 0016; cable SEEWORLD (in U.S.: University Travel, 44 Brattle St., Cambridge, Mass. 02138; tel. (617) 864-7800; and Penn Tours, 330 Sutter St. 94108; tel. (415) 391-5728). Penn Overland, in business since 1957, has 9-week trips London-Nairobi 3–4 times a year, using Range-Rovers and "Afrikabuses." You fly London-Algiers, drive to Nairobi. Cost: $760–998, not including contribution of about $45 to food kitty.

Hughes Overland Ltd. (Jet-Trek; Asiaman), 14 **Exchange Way**, Chelmsford, Essex, England; tel. (0245) 65501 (bookings to **Trail** Finders). Hughes has much experience on the London-India **and other** runs, did its third trans-Africa trip in late 1974. 18-pax Bedfords **are** used on the 21-week journey to Johannesburg. Basic cost is $528 (£220) to Nairobi, $672 (£280) to Jo'burg, but all-inclusive **cost** raises it to about $888 (£370) to Nairobi, $1,076 (£490) **to** Jo'burg.

The Great African Adventure Co. Ltd., 34 St. Andrews Road, **Roch**ford, Essex, England; tel. (0702) 544819 (bookings to Trail **Finders**). This is a new company which Trail Finders is satisfied with. 2 **trips a** year to Johannesburg in 12-seater Land-Rovers. Cost: $828.

Kimbla Travel (U.K.) Ltd., 62 Kenway Road, London SW5 ORD; tel. 01–370 4011; cable KIMBLA (bookings to Trail Finders) in U.S.; Going Places, 422 S. Western Ave., Los Angeles 90005; tel. (213) 385-0012; and U.S. Student Travel Service Inc., 866 Second Ave., New York 10017; tel. (212) 421-6680. South Africa-based Kimbla has broadened its offerings, now operates the following trips: (1) London-Marrakech (air) then overland to Johannesburg, 14 weeks, run about twice a year—cost: $900 (£375) to Nairobi (limited places available), $1,020 (£425) to Jo'burg. (2) London-Cairo (air), 7 days touring in Egypt, to Nairobi (air), then by road around East Africa and south to Jo'burg, run about 9 times a year— cost: $756 (£315 for 30 days excluding Egypt; $852 (£355) for 38 days including Egypt. (3) Quite different overland trip through Egypt, Sudan, Ethiopia, East Africa to Johannesburg. Starts with a flight London-Cairo, touring to the pyramids, Luxor, Aswan, Abu Simbel, etc., then Nile steamer from Aswan to Wadi Halfa, then by train to Khartoum, then plane to Asmara, onward by Bedford safari truck: Asmara-Massawa-Axum-Gondar (optional by air to Lalibela)-Bahar Dar-Addis Ababa-Moyale-Marsabit-Samburu-Nairobi, at which point the route to Johannesburg is the same as (1) above. Operates about 2Xyear, runs both ways London and Johannesburg. London-Nairobi sector only— $924 (£385) or $972 (£405); London to Johannesburg, ending there—$1,088 (£495) or $1,236 (£515).

All these expedition costs are all-inclusive but do not include visas, personal equipment, insurance, accommodations other than camping except a couple of nights. No matter which way you go, these economy-minded organizations will help arrange onward transport by charter plane or cheap freighter.

You can save some postage in getting brochures by writing to: Trail Finders Ltd., 46-48 Earls Court Road, London W8 6EJ; tel. 01–937 9631; cable TRAILFIND. Offices also at 7825 159th St., Edmonton, Alberta T5R 2E1; 6725 Somerued Ave., Montreal 265, Quebec; and in Sydney and Melbourne. Ask for a copy of the *Trail Finder* newspaper and the brochures you want. Trail Finders also does expedition bookings and sells do-it-yourself overland information.

Hitchhiking and Other Low-Budget Travel

The traveler of slender means is sure to have an interesting time in Eastern Africa. As interesting as Ethiopia's ancient places, East Africa's game parks and, of course, The People are, the low-budget experience will be uncomfortable at times, and you should be reasonably equipped with time, energy, and fortitude.

Hitching is cheap but unpredictable. Compared with West and Central Africa, it is easy in East Africa; one thumb authority says you can average 150 to 200 miles per day in daylight, except in remote areas. Unfortunately, it may depend on what color you are: white and black drivers will stop for whites, but rarely for blacks. The main routes—the heavy red lines in the Michelin map—are the most easily hitched. If there's no private-car traffic there will certainly be trucks (make sure there's no charge) and buses. Bus travel is very cheap in Eastern Africa, with buses going anywhere there are people, though Addis Ababa–Nairobi is not completely covered. See "Getting To" and "Getting Around" in the country chapters.

Single women should not travel alone—at least, not without karate. Two thumbers—two boys or a girl and a boy—will have as easy a time as one.

Reception: Freaks are tolerated except in Uganda and Malawi, which frown on long hair and unkempt beards on men and trousers or short skirts on women. Lamu is getting stricter, Zanzibar looser, Tanzania gets rabid periodically on minis. All the countries want you to have adequate resources and onward transportation.

Information: Cheap travelers have a couple sources of up-to-date information. The Globetrotters Club (BCM/Roving, London WX1V 6XX) publishes *Globe,* chock-full of useful (also badly organized and badly written) information about hitching, public transport going anywhere, cheap accommodations. Membership of $4 a year gets you six issues of *Globe,* the club directory (help and info all over the world), advice; there's a monthly meeting in London. For an extra

$2.50 you can get the BIT Information & Help Service's 64-page mimeographed "Overland through Africa," full of poor spelling and horrible errors of fact, but still hip and useful. Likewise the 56-page Danish production "West Africa for the Hitchhiker," with some information on other parts; $1.50 (plus 25¢ postage) from TEJ Processing Center, 22 West Monroe, Chicago, Ill. 60603. Once you're on the road the Freak Information Network will tell you all about free or cheap accommodations, transport, money, pot, and experiences. Clearing house in Nairobi is the City Park Campground.

Charter flights: See next section.

Accommodations: Be prepared for the occasional night on the ground. You may get invitations from people to stay in their homes. Otherwise, cheap accommodations include campgrounds (Nairobi City Park, but few game parks without a car), university dorms (capital cities), YMCAs (in scattered cities; a bit expensive), government rest houses (Malawi, especially; also Kenya), Kenya Forest Dept. rest houses, Sikh temples (free, but obey the rules), youth hostels (Kenya—Nairobi, Naivasha, Kitale, Wundanyi in Taita Hills), and African hotels—in Swahili, *hoteli*. In these a bed may be only a couple shillings, but it may have bugs and fleas, too. Look before you book. And lock the door at night.

Budget: Free-market money (p. 72) aside, better plan on $3 to $6 a day on the average, even if you plan on scrimping, living on bananas, and sleeping outside. Seeing game parks can be expensive (try showing your student ID for perhaps 50 percent off in Tanzania), food will occasionally be expensive, and you'll fritter coins away.

Equipment: Rucksack, packframe, or easily carried dufflebag of some kind should contain, among other things, a warm sleeping bag (nights can be very cold), a few food items for when you get stranded, a small water container, halazone (water-purifying) tablets, an antidiarrheal agent (like Lomotil, but *not* Entero-Vioform), some kind of raingear, and sports coat or dress so you can look decent if the occasion demands. Shower clogs are necessities for bathing outdoors and in. Carry your papers on your body all the time.

Getting to East Africa by Air

The cost of getting to East Africa by air is, for many travelers, the most frightening aspect of the trip. In order to do this book, we tried to get to Nairobi and back without paying untold thousands to the commercial airlines, and we did manage to save about 45 percent. But at one point on the way back from Nairobi we found ourselves nervously impersonating members of a two-week package tour to Paris. This was rather illegal, and we wouldn't do it again.

Those deciding to buy a tour package don't have to worry about air fare differences. Our advice to readers wanting to travel independently is to take the 14/45-day excursion fare if six weeks *is* the longest you can stay and you don't have time to hassle other arrangements. Those staying longer either have the prospect of paying the flabbergastingly high regular economy fare or seeking less expensive flights on the U.S.– Europe and Europe–East Africa legs. This requires patience.

Following are details of the ways and means to fly, and the mid-1974 fares:

Group Inclusive Tours (GITs): Members of package tours of short duration almost always get the GIT air fare, currently a low $779 (winter) or $838 (summer) round-trip from New York (add $141 if you live on the West Coast). GIT departure dates aren't guaranteed if the group (of 10 or 15 persons) can't be put together. You can't get the GIT fare without buying the land arrangements (minimum $70 to $100). Few East Africa packages offer *only* minimum arrangements, but check around.

Excursion fare: Next up in cost is the 14/45-day excursion fare to East Africa. This is the most advantageous fare available for most independent travelers. You have to stay at least two weeks but can't stay more than six. Current 14/45-day excursion fare New York–Nairobi, round-trip, is $992 (September–May) or $1,070 (June–August); West Coast, add $195. Longer package tours usually use the 14/45-day fare.

Ordinary economy fare: The regular economy fare on scheduled airlines allows any number of stopovers (a New York–Nairobi ticket allows you to fly through South America and South Africa on the way), and the ticket is valid one year at the price you paid. Current round-trip economy fare New York–Nairobi is $1,374 (winter and shoulder seasons) or $1,482 (peak); for West Coast it's $1,676 or $1,784.

The other choices—including charter flights—are mainly available on the first leg of the trip, across the Atlantic. To fly on to East Africa you have to combine ways and means, which takes some effort if you want to save money.

Non-IATA airlines: Icelandic (from New York) and International Air Bahama (from Nassau) are not members of that price-fixing cartel, the International Air Transport Association, and so they offer a cut-price fare across the Atlantic: $252 (winter) to $363 (peak) 22/45-day round-trip excursion fare on Icelandic. It's a bargain—but catch-22 is that both airlines land only in Luxembourg.

Youth fares to Europe aren't possible in the U.S. any longer, but those between 12 and 23 can save money by flying out of Montreal, Toronto, Vancouver or Mexico City on any of several airlines. Right now there is a special half-price student fare on Sabena to Nairobi, available only in Brussels.

African Safari Club: This Swiss travel club (address, p. 16) has five hotels on the Kenya coast but, more importantly, has its own prop-jet with weekly flights from Basel to Mombasa. If you signed up for an April or May (low season) departure, round-trip fare would be $382 (1,070 Swiss francs); high season (July) fare is more like $500. With the flight you would get two weeks of full-board accommodation at one of the hotels. Maximum length of stay which can be arranged is six months. How do you get to Basel? Fly Icelandic to Luxembourg, then take the train for about $15 each way.

Skytrain: Britain's Laker Airways, if it clears the final government hurdles, intends to offer a no-reservation, no-frills, year-round $125 (one-way) service New York-London (Stansted Airport). You would pay at the gate, buy meals on board (unless you bring food). If Sky-train goes into operation, other airlines (TWA, for one) say they will follow.

Air Europe International, based in L.A., may have cheap flights Tiajuana to London.

Study-Group Charters are a possibility for students traveling together on a credit-producing trip.

Inclusive Tour Charters (ITCs): These inexpensive package tours, usually fairly short, aren't offered yet to East Africa.

Affinity group charters are the most common kind of charter flight. Almost all are strictly legitimate. Among others, the AAA, consumers' co-ops, labor unions, and student organizations have charter flights. All these are legal, but the catch for the would-be ticket-buyer is that you have to be a member for six months before the flight, and the organiza-tion (affinity group) must have been formed for purposes other than travel. Flight reservations usually have to be made quite far in ad-vance, but budgeters will find the savings make it worthwhile. Non-joiners may wish to join a big club called the *United European Ameri-can Club* (12229 Ventura Blvd., Studio City, Calif. 91604), which has several chapters and hundreds of inexpensive charters from various U.S. cities to Europe. This and similar associations are quite legitimate and have numerous social and recreational activities—which you don't have to participate in to fly somewhere. Another is the *British American Club* (4250 Williams Road, San Jose, Calif. 95129). These clubs have a yearly membership fee—United European's is $10 single, $15 family, with an initial $10 registration fee. The affinity charter flight to East Africa is rare, but you can at least get to Europe inexpensively.

Tour Group Charters (*TGCs*) are the latest wrinkle. Governed by somewhat complex CAB regulations, TGCs are point-to-point charters, with no land arrangements. You don't have to join anything. You do have to make a reservation and put down a $100 deposit 90 days beforehand. You're allowed a stay of 22 to 57 days.

Illegal charters: The illegality of these flights is in the organizing and ticket-selling process, not in air safety regulations or even the flight itself. Typically, a freelance promoter with a temporary office, staying a step ahead of the CAB, will sign you up as a member of long standing in a fictitious club, then sell you the cheapest possible ticket—perhaps $230 round-trip New York–London. Deal with these people at your own risk. While they've sent thousands of happy travelers to Europe and back without problems, sometimes a flight has been stopped by the CAB or a promoter has skipped town—either action leaves you stranded.

Europe–East Africa excursion fares, of interest to those who get to Europe by other means, do indeed exist, but the rules of the international airline game say that the excursion fares are neither quotable, promotable, nor salable in the U.S. So get someone in London to find out for you, and even buy your money-saving ticket, if necessary.

London–Nairobi charters are frequent. East African Airways' Simbair charter operation runs weekly, and we took it both ways without any problem, though a Pan Am ticket agent has since suggested the flight was somehow not cricket. But the flight is easily arranged in London (allow a few days' layover) or by mail beforehand. You can try *East African Travel Consultants,* 55 Bloor St. E., Suite 300, Toronto, Ontario; tel. (416) 967–0067; cable SAFARIS. This firm, the Canadian representative of the Kenya Tourist Office, sells EAA charter tickets for about $475 round-trip London–Nairobi. For London charter agents, check the travel classified ads in the *Observer* or the *Telegraph.* Two firms we know of are *Sun Sea & Safari Ltd.,* 62 Blandford St., London W1 (in Nairobi on Tubman Road, Box 20393), and *East*

African Holidays Ltd., 3d floor, Radnor House, 93 Regent St., London W1 (also a Nairobi office).

Some things to remember as you seek cheaper fares: Straight-through commercial fares are cheaper than each leg purchased separately. International air fares are complicated; always get a fare quotation from two airlines or two travel agents. Finally, don't needlessly enrich a big airline when it is easily possible to save several hundred dollars by shopping around.

Getting to East Africa by Boat

It isn't easy, in these days when everybody hops fast jets, to find a slow ship going somewhere you want to go. But passenger-carrying freighters, and one regular passenger line, still have service to East Africa from the U.S. and Europe, despite the 1967 closing of the Suez Canal. The one regular passenger line to Mombasa is Lloyd Triestino, whose *Asia* and *Victoria* operate out of Trieste, picking up passengers also in Venice, Brindisi, Marseilles, and Barcelona, making the trip around the Cape of Good Hope to Mombasa (22 days from Barcelona, 30 from Trieste), on to Bombay and Karachi. Tourist-class fares start at $390 February–June, $487 July–January; first-class fares start at $560 and $700 respectively. Average fare is $27 a day.

As for freighters, not all lines are willing to commit themselves on schedules, ports of call, fares, or anything. The following have freighter service to Mombasa 3 to 24 times a year from various ports, also to Dar es Salaam, and Southern Africa ports, perhaps Tanga, Zanzibar, Massawa: *Hellenic Lines,* 39 Broadway, New York 10006. Two sailings a month from U.S. to South, East African ports, and to Red Sea. Fare NYC–Mombasa, $850. *Farrell Lines,* 1 Whitehall St., New York 10004. Periodic sailings U.S. to South, East African ports. About 25 days to Mombasa, $800 to $850. *Lykes Line,* 1300 Commerce Bldg., New Orleans, La. 70112. From Gulf ports to South Africa, Dar es Salaam, Mombasa ($615). *East Africa National Shipping Line,* Box 3335, Dar es Salaam, Tanzania. Monthly from Far East to Mombasa, Zanzibar, Dar es Salaam; bimonthly from Britain. *Polish Ocean Lines,* c/o Gdynia America Line, 115 Broadway, New York 10006. Europe to Dar es Salaam once a month, to Mombasa twice a month, Massawa bimonthly. Fares: Dar es Salaam $435–453, Mombasa $446–464. *CMB Line* (Compagnie Maritime Belge S.A.), Pier 36, New York 10002. North Europe to Mombasa and elsewhere monthly, taking 25 days, $570 to Mombasa. *Moore McCormack Lines,* 2 Broadway, New York 10006. Three times a year U.S. to Mombasa, $815. Other lines which may operate occasionally are Christensen Canadian Africa Line, Hansa Line, Robin Line, German African Lines, Jadranska Slobodna Plovidba, Clan Line, and Royal Interocean Lines.

Travel agencies specializing in freighter travel include *Freighter Travel Service Ltd.,* 201 East 77th St., New York 10021; *Kirsten Air & Steamship Agency,* 3462 Main Highway, Coconut Grove, Miami, Fla. 33133; *Air & Marine Travel Service,* 501 Madison Ave., New York 10022 ("Trip Log" for $1); and *Pitt & Scott Ltd.,* 1/3 St. Paul's Churchyard, London EC4.

See *Ford's Freighter Travel Guide,* available for $3.95 from Box 505, Woodland Hills, Calif. 91364.

There is irregular freighter service from Aqaba, Israel, to Massawa, Ethiopia; cars can be shipped, too. The genuinely footloose can arrange dhow passage from the Persian Gulf to the East African coast (see p. 97).

Before You Go

What to Wear

These countries are fairly informal, and climatic considerations are more important than Emily Post's dictums. In general, we would say, wear the kind of informal clothes you would if you were on a car trip around New England or the Northwest. The coastal areas are hot and humid. Inland it may get dry-hot in the day, but it will be cool at night. However, don't bring anything too bright and flashy for game parks, because the animals will take notice and run. And women should not wear anything revealing or see-through; these new nations are moralistic about minis, especially Tanzania, Uganda, and Malawi, where very short skirts are forbidden. Men and women both should wear middle-of-the-road fashions, though in cosmopolitan Nairobi you can wear practically anything.

Men can wear shorts and slacks and open-neck, short-sleeve shirts most of the time, but should have one semiformal suit (ordinary summer-weight suit will do) for business meetings and evenings on the town. Women can wear spring or summer dresses around the city, shirt and slacks in the game parks, long or short dress or pantsuit at night. Hats are generally worn only in game parks and on the beach.

At "formal" occasions, men have a good compromise: the long-
or short-sleeve shirt with pants combinations (both the same color),
sometimes worn with cravat, made popular by Zambia's President
Kaunda; it is something like a safari suit and can be bought ready-
made in Nairobi.

Safari suits—usually a green or khaki pants and short combination
—can be bought ready made or individually tailored in Nairobi. The
jacket in particular is popular because its many pockets come in
handy for film, money, etc. Safari suits immediately identify you as a
tourist, though. Buying a safari suit in the U.S. is a terrible waste of
money.

What to Pack

Package tourist: Besides ordinary recreational clothing or business
clothing, you should bring a warm sweater or coat for the chill from
late afternoon through early morning. Do bring some ordinary medicines and an antidiarrhea agent (see following discussion on health),
favorite cosmetics, razor blades and toilet articles, tissues, a small bar
of soap, plug converter for electric razor, needle and thread, safety
pins, some plastic bags to wrap things in, a small clothesline if you
like to wash a few things in your hotel room. Binoculars we think
are a must. Our advice on how much to bring is this: you won't need
very much more than you would for Europe or most other vacation
spots. Don't bring 44 pounds of baggage; save some weight for purchases. Pack in light, dustproof suitcases—but no more containers
than you can carry yourself.

Independent travelers and campers: see sections on "Camping,"
"Budgeting a Self-Drive Camping Safari," and "Hitchhiking and
Other Low-Budget Travel."

Health Hazards and Precautions

Travelers' health is one of the most written-about subjects; it's
probably as popular a topic as, say, food. Ordinary tourists to Africa,
if basically healthy and reasonably experienced as travelers, have
little to worry about if they take the right precautions. Briefly, these
are:

• Get vaccinated. Yellow fever, smallpox, and cholera vaccinations
are required; polio, typhoid-paratyphoid, tetanus, typhus, and (perhaps) plague are variously recommended.

- Take malaria prophylactic pills and use a mosquito net at night.
- Be careful about drinking water, unpeeled and uncooked food, and dairy products.
- Do not swim or wade in most fresh slow-moving lake or river water.
- Stay clean.
- Bring a few basic medicines and insect repellent with you.
- Finally, if you have any special medical problem, talk to your doctor.

Inoculations: If you want all the necessary and recommended immunizations, totaling 13 shots, you can get them all in an 8-day period, but ending a week before departure so they are all valid as you board the plane. Doctors can administer all of them except yellow fever, given at several centers in each state (call your local health department to find out where). Cholera shots are good for 6 months, yellow fever for 10 years, smallpox for 3 years. All required shots have to be registered on the yellow WHO card, the International Certificate of Vaccination. In addition to the immunizations mentioned above, many travelers get a gamma globulin injection, helpful against hepatitis. Children should also be vaccinated for diphtheria and measles. An inoculation by a doctor in the U.S. typically costs $5. Ask around or bargain for a less expensive series at a clinic or hospital. Overlanders might consider getting shots with long validity (yellow fever, smallpox) anytime in the U.S., others *just before* leaving, to stretch the validity. If you're outfitting in England, you can get shots at the BOAC Air Terminal; the West London Designated Vaccinating Centre, 53 Great Cumberland Place, London W1 (only $2.50 each); or, possibly, the Hospital for Tropical Diseases, 4 St. Pancras Way, London NW1 (usually all booked up). Inoculations like cholera and plague, which have short validity, can be renewed in Nairobi (see p. 173).

Drinking water: Many medical authorities, including the U.S. Public Health Service, suggest that water from a hot-water tap, if hotter than your hand can bear, is safe to drink (let it cool in a clean container first). This is, in fact, preferable to drinking the water in the carafe in your hotel room. While all water (except bottled mineral water) in Ethiopia is suspect, you will find the water in many places— Nairobi, for instance—is safe to drink even out of the cold-water tap. But always solicit reliable advice—say, from resident Europeans, who have the same stomach you do—or stick to bottled water and drinks, hot tea and coffee. Of course, don't brush your teeth in doubtful water. And watch out for dirty ice cubes in clean soda pop.

Food: Eat food well cooked if you're leery at all. Food customarily served at tourist hotels in East Africa is the same as Americans are accustomed to. Pass up the salad, perhaps; avoid raw fruit and vegetables you can't peel; beware of dairy products. Again, if this seems like alarmist advice, ask locally; Kenya cheese on the postmeal cheeseboard shouldn't be missed.

Swimming: Don't swim anywhere but in chlorinated swimming pools, the ocean, and, after inquiring locally, in Lake Malawi. Crocodiles are one health hazard, but bilharziasis, a debilitating disease, can be contracted in lake or river water from parasites which live alternately in a certain snail and in man. (Don't be afraid of bath or shower water, however.)

Malaria pills: Malaria is widespread in Eastern Africa, found in some areas but not in others. It is not endemic in upland East Africa. All travelers should take a malaria prophylactic such as chloroquine phosphate (marketed as Aralen), two tablets once a week, starting two weeks before you arrive, ending four weeks after you get home. Try also to sleep under a mosquito net, which hotels in malarial areas usually have.

Diarrhea: Sometimes, no matter what water and food precautions are taken, you'll come down with diarrhea, Africa's revenge on the imperialists. Some people get diarrhea just by changing locale, getting overtired, nervous, or upset, or eating strange food; but diarrhea is more commonly caused by bacteria and viruses. Minor diarrhea can be treated with nonprescription drugs, but more severe cases should be treated with a codeine or opium antidiarrheal drug, usually sold by prescription only. Consumers Union suggests you ask your doctor to prescribe a small amount of codeine tablets, tincture of opium, paregoric, powdered opium in capsules, or Lomotil, all of which are good for relieving ordinary diarrhea somewhat quickly. Two warnings: a drug called Entero-Vioform, once widely used, should *not* be taken at all; recent evidence indicates that it has serious side effects, causing eye and nerve damage. If diarrhea persists, see a doctor, since diarrhea is sometimes a symptom of something more serious, like amoebic dysentery.

Sleeping sickness: This is not all that common (three cases in Kenya one recent year). It is spread by certain species of tsetse fly, not all members of which carry it, and tsetses are by no means found everywhere (we found them in southern Tanzania and Zambia). In infested areas, the best weapon is a rolled-up magazine; tsetses, with distinctive crossed wings, are stupid and easily swatted. Otherwise, they give a vicious bite in a soft place, like on the neck.

Mountain sickness: If you're planning on climbing Mount Kenya or Kilimanjaro, see p. 401.

Jet lag: East Africa is a long way from New York, even longer from the West Coast. If you can, break your journey in Europe. In any case, we would recommend you lie down for at least two or three hours on arrival in East Africa, and then take it easy for one or two days.

Medical attention in Eastern Africa: Tourists will have little difficulty in getting medical attention, especially if they are on tours. There are U.S.- and European-trained doctors in all the cities, also at many rural hospitals. The names of recommended doctors and dentists in the cities can be obtained from the U.S. embassies. Many tourists join the Flying Doctors' Society of Africa (Box 30125, Nairobi; tel. 27281) at inexpensive tourist rates ($2.50 or 15/– for up to a month) since the flying doctors provide members free emergency treatment and air transport (conditions permitting) to a medical center if the person gets sick or injured while on safari anywhere in East Africa (Kenya, Tanzania, Uganda). IAMAT, 350 Fifth Ave., Suite 5620, New York, N.Y. 10001, and Intermedic, 777 Third Ave., New York, N.Y. 10017, both can provide a directory of English-speaking doctors, who are very easy to find.

Before you leave home: Consider getting a checkup, especially a dental exam. This is especially important for those contemplating long expeditions to out-of-the-way places.

When you get home: It is a good idea, upon your return to the U.S., to have a stool examination for amoebic or other intestinal parasites, some of which can cause serious ailments months or years later.

Medical kit: Tourists can easily obtain common drugs such as aspirin and antacid pills, even though in Eastern Africa they are probably made in and imported from Europe. However, game parks do not have pharmacies, and it does no harm to carry a few aspirin, a stomach settler, your own laxative or whatever, and diarrhea pills. Into a small medical kit you might put a couple of Band-Aids, tweezers, an antiseptic, suntan lotion or cream, a good insect repellent, a clinical thermometer, an extra pair of glasses (or at least the lens prescription).

Medical history: Some authorities advise travelers to carry a short medical history with them in case of serious accident or illness abroad. The Medical Passport Foundation Inc. (Box 820, Deland, Fla. 32720) produces the "Medical Passport," a wallet-size medical record containing such information as drug sensitivity, allergies, etc. Cost $2.75 for adults, $3 for children.

Books, pamphlets: As indicated, travelers' health is a popular subject, and much has been written. Long-term and overland travelers should take along a medical guide such as Adam's *Traveller's Guide to Health* or the *Ship Captain's Medical Guide;* these have a lot of information you hope you never have to use, such as emergency extraction of teeth. Ordinary travelers wishing to pursue the subject of tourism and health might read Dr. Cahill's book or the one by Drs. Doyle and Banta. There's a certain hazard in reading doctors' books—you may be frightened away from Africa. Dr. Cahill, a bit zealously, advises a 25-item medical kit for travelers in the tropics; too much, we think. The books available:

Adam (Lieut. Col.), James M. *A Traveller's Guide to Health.* London: Hodder & Stoughton (for the Royal Geographical Society), 1966. Available for $2.50 from the RGS, Kensington Gore, London SW7.

Atkins, R. T., M.D., and J. M. *The World Traveler's Medical Guide.* New York: Simon & Schuster, 1958. $1.95.

Board of Trade. *The Ship Captain's Medical Guide.* 20th ed. London: Her Majesty's Stationery Office, 1967.

Cahill, Kevin M., M.D. *Medical Advice for the Traveler.* New York: Holt, Rinehart & Winston, 1970. $3.95.

Doyle, P. J., M.D., and Banta, J. E., M.D. *How to Travel the World and Stay Healthy.* Washington, D.C.: Acropolis Books, 1970. $4.95.

Henderson, John, M.D. *Emergency Medical Guide.* 2nd ed. New York: McGraw-Hill, 1969. $3.95.

Ross Institute. *The Preservation of Personal Health in Warm Climates.* London: London School of Tropical Medicine (Keppel St./Gower St., London WC1).

A final word: Not to worry too much. If you read too many books and take it all too seriously, you'll be afraid to travel, or you'll be carrying a drugstore and medical library in your suitcase.

Pets

If you want to trouble with inoculations, quarantines, transport difficulties, and paperwork, yes, you can bring your pet with you—but what for? For one thing, you can't have a pet inside a game park, and that should discourage you. As for bringing home a pet, see below under "U.S. Customs."

Insurance

When we were contemplating a two-year, sixty-country expedition, we also thought of all the terrible things that could happen: the horrible, dreadful diseases, the hordes of thieves who would descend on us and strip us of everything, the deep chasms and raging tropical rivers our vehicle would disappear into. So we tried to find some insurance. In the horrible diseases department, it took a year of correspondence to find an English insurance broker who could fix us up, but the premium for personal accident, sickness, and medical expenses alone was more than $400. We did without it—and met up with no dread diseases, and no hordes of thieves, yawning chasms, raging rivers, or anything else worth worrying about.

Ordinary tourists should, if already insured, find out if their existing policies cover them while traveling—whether their homeowner's policy protects their cameras, for instance.

Overland groups can often get a reasonably priced group policy written. Constitution Insurance Co. of Canada (2/3 Philpot Lane, London EC3) has a very comprehensive policy for members of Penn Overland trans-Africa groups for about $18 for 57 days. The Royal Insurance Co. covers Encounter Overland members for $42 for four months. U.S. insurance companies are not accustomed to insuring expeditions; try the British firms for this.

Other travelers have a few alternatives. The AAA has short-term (up to 180 days) comprehensive coverage that might suit ordinary tourists; ask your local motor club. Longer-term travelers should perhaps approach insurance brokers accustomed to insuring U.S. Foreign Service Officers and their families. We found Clements & Co. (Suite 1015, Cafritz Bldg., 1625 Eye St., N.W., Washington, D.C. 20006) had several reasonable plans covering baggage, cameras and valuables, and vehicles (all risks). Cameras, for instance, can be insured for a year for $1.50 to $3.00 per $100 of value. Auto insurance premiums vary.

A $3,000 auto can be covered for $125 to $170, but the premium on our $4,500 Land Cruiser cost $383 for a year for collision only.

Some U.S. brokers will offer liability coverage. This may be useful—but many African countries demand you buy local third-party insurance anyway. A British motor insurance broker accustomed to expedition inquiries is Slugocki, Norman & Co., Ltd., 110 Fenchurch St., London EC3.

Long-term health insurance is another question, and we can offer little advice. Lloyd's of London underwriters think international; we dealt with the Price Forbes Group, King William Street House, Arthur St., London EC4P 4HU, before deciding not to buy insurance because we weren't doing anything really unhealthful or dangerous. Another possibility might be the Travellers' Insurance Association Ltd., 82 Pall Mall, London SW1, which has a health insurance policy for about £10 ($25) for three months. Students and nonstudents can get a three-month policy for £6.50 ($16.25) from Isis Travel Insurance, a subsidiary of Britain's National Union of Students (NUS), Cranfield House, 97/107 Southhampton Row, London WC1.

Passport

We'll assume your trip to Africa is not the first time you've been overseas, and that you have a valid passport. If not, inquire at: Office of the Clerk of Federal, State, and probate courts; Passport Agency offices in eleven major U.S. cities; post offices in some states, including California, Massachusetts, Minnesota, and New York; and Passport Office, Department of State, 17th and H Sts., N.W., Washington, D.C. 20524. *Important:* If you're going to both black countries (such as Tanzania) and white countries in Africa (such as South Africa and Rhodesia), it may be wise to obtain a second passport valid in the white countries, thus avoiding telltale visa stamps in the passport you use to get into black countries, which may not otherwise let you in—Tanzania threatened this in 1973. The Passport Office can tell you how to obtain this second, restricted passport, which we think every independent traveler with ambitious plans should get.

Carnet

The Carnet de Passages en Douanes, also called a triptyque, is the document that gets your vehicle across international borders without paying customs duty. You do not need a carnet for rent-a-cars, and a vehicle registered in one East African country doesn't need it for the other two. In the U.S. you get a carnet from the AAA, Foreign Motoring Services, 1712 G St., N.W., Washington, D.C. 20006. The trick is you have to post a $2,000 returnable bond—generally in the form of a "clean credit" letter issued by a bank. AAA also requires a $135 service fee, up to $100 returnable. If you don't have this spare $2,000, and nobody you know is willing to put a lock on his savings account there is an alternative: ADAC, the German auto club (Allgemeiner Deutscher Automobil-Club e.V, Koeniginstrasse 9-11a, Munich 22, West Germany) may be able to provide a carnet for about $50, nonreturnable. You might try the British AA (p. 44), too.

Visas

All our countries except Malawi require Americans to have visas in order to enter. Ethiopia will sell you one when you arrive at the airport; get the others beforehand from embassies or U.N. missions (addresses in the country chapters).

The countries are fairly nosy. Tanzania wants to know "means at your disposal for proposed visit." Kenya asks for "references in Kenya" and "names and references in other countries to be visited." Zambia wants tourists and businessmen to provide names and addresses of firms or persons to be visited, also wants to know your final destination—if it's Rhodesia, South Africa, or a Portuguese area, don't say so.

There are two time periods related to a visa: one is how long a visit the visa authorizes (for instance, 30 days for Ethiopia, three months for Kenya); the second is the period of validity (usually a year) of the visa—the date beyond which you can't use it. Since this last is sometimes fairly short, don't start getting your visas until you know when you are traveling. For help in getting visas, see under "Visa Service" in the Yellow Pages.

Overlanders and low-budget travelers usually advise each other to get the cheapest (that is, shortest) visa and worry about its expiring once you're inside the country. It's just a matter of going to the immigration department in the capital and getting a renewal stamp (maybe for a fee) and a new visitor's pass stamp in your passport.

Travelers with cars may be asked for ownership papers (logbook in East Africa) before a visa or visitor's pass is renewed. Others will probably be asked to show an air ticket out of the country. Low-budgeters may find it convenient to have a Nairobi–London charter ticket or simply a commercial air ticket from whatever city they're in to the next country. There are currency control problems here, but tickets are always convertible to some kind of cash, usually local.

International Driving Permit

Your local motor club will issue an International Driving Permit, valid for a year, good everywhere in Africa, for $3; when you apply, bring your license and a passport photo. When driving in Africa, have your regular license with you also.

Documents for Low-Budget Travelers

The International Youth Hostel Card is of very limited value if you're doing just East Africa. The International Student Identity Card (credentials and $1.25 to Council on International Educational Exchange, 777 U.N. Plaza, New York 10017) is also of limited value in East Africa, though it may be good for a 50 percent reduction in Tanzania game parks. Nonstudents get the cards by other means: "Bits" (p. 49) has a list.

More necessary documents are a return air ticket ("onward transportation") and/or "proof of financial responsibility." Most often, a wad of traveler's checks will get you past the border official who wants proof. A handy item might be a letter from your bank simply stating the amount of money in your account on any one date.

See Byrne (p. 44) on the subject of papers.

General Information

Pronouncing "Kenya" and Other Difficult Words

The British colonial KEEN-*yuh* has given way to a new pronunciation —KEHN-*yuh*. There's another one loose—KAYN-*yuh*—but pay no attention to it. Tanzania, a coined combination of Tanganyika (still the name of the mainland) and Zanzibar (the semiautonomous island), is pronounced *tan-zuh*-NEE-*uh*. Zambia (coined from the Zambesi River) is pronounced with a soft *a*—ZAM-*bee-uh*. Malawi is often mispronounced by Americans. Properly (and with difficulty), the *w,* officially written with a circumflex accent (ŵ), is supposed to be pronounced sort of like a *v* and an *r,* but don't bother, since *muh*-LAU-*wee* is more common. Ethiopia is pronounced as it is spelled.

Malawi was the colonial Nyasaland (and Lake Nyasa is Lake Malawi in that country); Zambia was formerly Northern Rhodesia. Ethiopia hasn't been Abyssinia for years.

Finding Your Way Around

Street names, even to the use of "street," "road," and so forth, are in English in all five countries, except in Arusha, Tanzania, where *barabara* is used for "street." The European system for numbering floors in buildings is followed: street floor is *ground floor,* the first one up is the *first floor*. To cross streets safely, look *both* ways. At zebra crosswalks, pedestrians usually have the right of way *if* they're actually in the walk.

Briticisms

Just as a Californian who refers to a "chesterfield" (sofa) may not be understood by a New Yorker, so an American might not understand some of the confusing things an East African, whether white or black, says. One peculiarity of British English is that the government, corporations, and other groups are "they"—and so are referred to in the plural: "The Rover Company have announced . . ." The same with a committee or other group. This is changing.

Herewith some examples of Briticisms you may run into:

British	American
bathe, bathing	swim, swimming
bob (colloq.)	shilling
bonnet	hood (of car)
boot	trunk (of car)
chemist	drugstore
dam	lake behind dam
drift	ford, crossing
fillet	steak (fish or beef); filet mignon
House (e.g., Caltex House)	Building (offices)
lay-by	rest area on road, pull-off
lorry	truck
paraffin	kerosene
petrol	gasoline ("gas" in Kenya is propane-LP gas)
roundabout	traffic circle
scheme	plan, project, program
tariff	rates, charges, cost
tarmac	blacktop, asphalt, paved highway
WC, gents, ladies	the euphemism

Note: The term "European" refers to any white person. Animals are often referred to in the singular.

Cuisine

Thanks (or no thanks) to imperialism, Western tourists can eat Western food everywhere in Eastern Africa, with perhaps only road travelers in remote places unable to find a place serving that British staple—eggs, chips, and sausage. Tourist restaurants serve Reuben sandwiches, filet steaks, and lobster thermidor. Most Africans, meanwhile, are eating such typical dishes as *ugali* (*nsima* in Zambia and Malawi), which is basically *mealie* meal (corn meal, white cornstarch) mixed with water. In between is the African food you can sometimes find in places like the Nairobi Hilton's Kenya Coffee Shop—*ugali* spiced up with meat and vegetables, and priced up. Somewhat native to East Africa is Indian food, all very spicy.

Some dishes you will be able to find:

Ethiopia: Food here is either Italian and other Continental or Ethiopian. Many of the national dishes are based on hot red chilies (*berebere*) and called *wat*. Spicy food often comes with *injera,* the local millet bread that is like a limp, thin, holey, sourdough pancake. One *wat* dish is *dobo wat*, made with chicken and chili and green onions; other *wat* plates are made with lamb and cubed or chopped beef. The national drink is *tej,* a thin, pale-yellow, alcoholic honey drink that tastes remotely like fermented apple cider, drunk alone or with food. Addis Ababa and Asmara have Ethiopian national restaurants.

Kenya: Irio, a Kikuyu dish, is made with corn (maize), beans or dried chickpeas, and potatoes, all mashed and cooked together. *Githeri* is another corn and bean dish, and there's a vegetable dish called *sukuma wiki,* "sees you through." Go to the Panafric Hotel's Simba Grill and choose from Kenya dishes on the regular à la carte menu. There are Wednesday special lunches at the Simba Grill (*muteta* soup, *matoke*—Uganda banana dish, *githeri, sukuma wiki, mseto, ugali,* grilled leg of impala, and other meats) and at the Norfolk's Lord Delamere (12 of the tastiest Luo, Kikuyu, and Kamba dishes of fish, chicken, beef, game meat, and vegetables). Beer in its various forms is the national drink. Njohi Muratina is the African beer available in bottles; more Western brews are Allsopps Pilsner and Tusker.

Photography

This subject calls for an entire book, but this is already an entire book, so we must cover photography superficially.

Unless you are properly prepared, your camera-eye tour of East Africa's game parks could be a photographic disaster. Your picture of some impalas is poor because you can barely see the impalas against their woodland habitat; what's more, all you can see is their hind ends because they started moving off the second the minibus stopped. Your picture of zebras and wildebeests—all those thousands on the Serengeti —shows only two zebras and three wildebeests, a vast expanse of washed-out sky, and another vast expanse of brown grass, and the picture looks dusty because the dust trailing the minibus caught up when the minibus stopped. The picture of the lion hunting in Ngorongoro Crater is blurred—you must have been so excited that you jerked the shutter release button. In the Masai pictures that you paid 5/– each to shoot, their faces are so dark you can't see their features. And so on.

Some hints:

- A telephoto lens, 135 mm or 200 mm, is a must. A zoom lens— say, 85 mm to 210 mm—gives great flexibility but slightly less definition. A 100-mm lens is ideal for people pictures.
- The longer the lens, the steadier you must hold the camera. Brace the camera against the window frame (if the motor is off), or increase the shutter speed.
- Remember that depth of field tends to be shallower with a telephoto, so foreground and background are less likely to be in focus.
- It is better to wait for the right moment to shoot an animal than to shoot at first sight. Which is better, an elephant simply standing there sideways in a perfect, dull profile, or an elephant with his trunk raised high in your direction to catch your scent?
- Don't get so excited you forget what exposure the camera is set for, and do take time to focus properly.
- Make an effort to compose the picture. A zebra walking to the left should be given a bit of extra space to the left of the picture. The horizon should not bisect the picture but is better one-third from the top or bottom, or try to leave out the sky altogether. Try to get something else in the picture if it's only one wildebeest on a very flat plain. If taking a scenic panorama, get something—tree, vehicle, person—in the foreground.
- Try to take game pictures in early morning or late afternoon for the best lighting. Like animals, photographers should lie up during the noonday sun, between 10 A.M. and 3 P.M.
- Use a 1A (Skylight) filter all the time in shooting color; this re-

duces bluishness and is a cheap way of protecting your valuable lens. A yellow filter serves the same purpose if you're taking black and white pictures.

• Bring some very fast film—ASA 400 or 500—for taking pictures of woodland animals, also for use on dark days or at a game-viewing lodge. We found GAF 500 Color quite satisfactory. Shoot an experimental roll before leaving home.

• In taking pictures of dark-skinned Africans, you must generally compensate for the light meter reading by opening up the aperture one f/stop or more. Or get strong front lighting so the face of the Masai *moran* is well lighted, or use a fill-in flash. Or take a meter reading of the person's face.

• After you've taken ten pictures of animals running or walking away from you, stop. Ten is ten too many unless they're of gorillas, leopards, or, perhaps, almost extinct animals.

• Bring the film you like best with you. Film is generally available in tourist areas but is more expensive.

Note on taking people pictures: Most Africans are reluctant to have their picture taken, and will on occasion react violently if you take one without their consent. This is sometimes refused altogether, but is more often granted for a monetary consideration, anything from one shilling to a ridiculous amount. Members of photogenic tribes like the Masai and Samburu uniformly demand money. We never paid, but we don't have any Masai pictures either. Personally, we do not feel people should be paid picture fees unless they're asked to do something special, or to pose for a long time. What is certain, even if you try the friendly approach, with greetings in Swahili and gestures, is that candid pictures are nearly an impossibility.

Do not take photos of soldiers, policemen, or military places. In Kenya it is illegal to take a picture of the President or the flag.

Shopping—What's Best Where

Here are some of the best buys:

Kenya: Fabrics, safari clothes and shoes, contemporary crafts, paintings, prints and photos, soapstone carvings, jewelry, Zanzibar chests, traditional items (gourds, etc.).

Tanzania: Meerschaum pipes, Makonde sculpture, Masai beadwork, gemstones, fabrics, Zanzibar chests.

Ethiopia: Silver and gold crosses and jewelry, rugs, basketware, Solomon and Sheba and battle scene "comic strip" paintings, old Bibles and manuscripts, brass and wood hand crosses, *shammas* (traditional dress).

Zambia: Wooden sculpture (carvings), copperware, gemstones.

Malawi: Basketware, soapstone carvings, beadwork.

If you're on a short package tour, plan to shop in Nairobi, especially. It is virtually the department store of Eastern Africa, with everything available at prices Americans can afford (sellers know this!). Bargain hunters should go to the source—Makonde sculpture, for instance, is by far cheaper in Dar es Salaam, for the government's Makonde workshop is there. If you're traveling long and seriously by road, you'll find genuine African items—Samburu spears, Swahili *bao* boards, Ethiopian crosses. In the cities, at curio shops, you cannot be sure some items are genuine.

On the street, in the market and at small, out-of-the-way shops, bargaining is virtually the rule. Don't be afraid to bargain; the seller doesn't expect to sell the item at his price, and doesn't feel gypped if you dicker him down. If he quotes a soapstone lion at 30/–, don't answer, just scoff, and he'll drop to 15/–. Then you offer 5/–, and *he'll* scoff. So you raise it to 7/– and settle at 8/50. If the figures are close but he won't accept your offer, turn around and walk away; you won't get far before he changes his mind.

Art versus curios: Unless you're a collector with many contacts, you will not find any genuine, old, traditional African art—such as a genuine tribal mask—offered for sale anywhere. The good stuff has already been exported, or it's not available to tourists. What you will find in Eastern Africa, readily available, is a surfeit of curios—"airport art": either schlocky, sleek imitations of genuine West Africa–Congo Basin art and crafts, or touristy curios with African motifs and Western functions (such as a pair of salad servers decorated with what looks like a fertility god), or tourist versions of genuine items (such as miniature tribal drums), or, if you look hard enough for it, contemporary or modern art. Makonde sculpture falls in this last category, as does the odd carving here and there, such as a fine one-of-a-kind bust we picked out from a clutter of junk at Victoria Falls. Generally speaking, the cheaper something is, the more likely it was made purely for tourist consumption. Not that the item doesn't "look African," not that it wasn't hand-carved by a genuine African. But it was made for tourists on an assembly-line basis, thus falling into the same category as Statue of Liberty ashtrays. Before you buy any nonfunctional—i.e., "artistic"

—wooden carving, make the rounds of curio shops and sidewalk vendors; after seeing a hundred copies of it, decide whether or not to buy it.

If you want to save money, avoid hotel and airport curio shops, and shops on expensive shopping streets or in brand-new office buildings. In Nairobi, especially, go to the smaller side streets—Koinange, Muindi Mbingu— for better prices.

Shipping Things Home

Because of postal restrictions on value, size, and weight, you may find yourself having to ship something home. See "Travel Agents" and "Shops and Services" in the country chapters for the addresses of freight forwarders.

Almost all freight forwarders will attend to crating and packing, shipping, customs clearance, delivery. This does not mean a hassle-free trip for you. Kenya, for instance, requires completion of customs declaration CD-3, simple enough to fill out but a devil to get processed by the Central Bank Currency Control section (you have to show you brought in hard currency to pay for your purchases). Before you buy anything that you can't carry with you or send through the post office (22-pound weight limit), make sure either (a) the shop or the freight forwarder will take care of *all* export arrangements, or (b) you have the time to take care of the paperwork yourself.

If you have to ship expedition equipment from the U.S., here are a couple forwarders: *Baggage International Corp.,* 2 Penn Plaza, New York 10001; tel. (212) 868-2860. *International Sea & Air Shipping Corp.,* 60 Stone St., New York 10004; tel. (212) 422-2820.

U.S. Customs

As a resident returning to the U.S. you are entitled to a $100 customs exemption on foreign purchases physically with you on return to the U.S. (No more than one quart of liquor and 100 cigars, however.) This includes items purchased in duty-free shops (free of duty only so far as that country is concerned). Each member of a returning family gets the $100 exemption. You must declare the price you actually paid for each article; don't try to fool the customs inspector—he knows what things are worth. Keep receipts and they'll show what you paid for which items.

Customs duty is charged on articles in excess of $100. The only way to beat that is to send bona-fide gifts, each worth under $10, to friends and relatives. You can't send these $10 parcels to yourself, directly or indirectly. The gift recipient will get charged duty on more than $10 worth received at the customs mail office the same day.

Rates of duty vary, and not everything is dutiable. Samples: Antiques 100 years old or more and traditional ethnographic objects more than 50 years old—free. Leather hand bags—10 percent. Ivory beads— 10 percent. Books—free. Chess sets—10 percent. All hand-done drawings and paintings (original or copies), original sculpture in any form, of any material—free. Wood carvings—8 percent. Fur wearing apparel or other articles—8½ to 18½ percent. Ivory articles—6 percent. Jewelry—12 percent. Silver jewelry—27½ percent. Postage stamps—free. Cut, unset stones—free to 5 percent. Dolls, toys—17½ percent. Rattan, bamboo—12½ to 15 percent. Wearing apparel—very high rates.

Among prohibited articles are wild birds and feathers and eggs of wild birds; flamingo feather "corsages" seem to be okay. Seashells are okay. Plant seeds are admitted; live plants are restricted. Fully tanned skins are admitted. Rocks and minerals are admitted.

Importing a pet, especially a wild or formerly wild one, is tricky, with the number one requirement being that it is healthy and free of disease; permits are necessary. Information on U.S. Public Health Service regulations on dogs, cats, and monkeys can be obtained from: Center for Disease Control, USPHS, Atlanta, Ga. 30333 (Attn: Chief, Foreign Quarantine Program). For information on entry requirements (restrictions and prohibitions) of birds, fish, and animals (and agricultural items), write to: Veterinary Services, APHIS, USDA, Federal Center Bldg., Hyattsville, Md. 20782. Certain endangered species cannot be imported; inquiries to: Bureau of Sport Fisheries and Wildlife, Department of the Interior, Washington, D.C. 20240. Remember that if Kenya, say, bans the export of this or that, the U.S. will ban the import of it.

It is worthwhile to register items such as German or Japanese cameras with U.S. customs before you go—so you can bring them back into the U.S.

Among customs publications available: *Know Before You Go: Customs Hints for Returning U.S. Residents; Rates of Duty for Popular Tourist Items; Pets, Wildlife; U.S. Import Requirements* (if you want to import and sell African items). Publications from: Department of the Treasury, Bureau of Customs, Public Information Division, Washington, D.C. 20229. Inquiries: District Director of Customs, offices in 43 U.S. cities.

Sending and Receiving Mail

We never lost so much mail in all our lives as during our sixteen months in Africa. Savings passbook, a check, copies of part of the manuscript of this book, letters—lost or stolen in or between Nairobi and the U.S. Not much you send from East Africa can be insured, and not all of it can be registered—no registration between Kenya and Zambia, for instance. You take your chances on registration anyway; some say the red "R" sticker is like yelling, "There's something valuable in here!" The least that can happen to you is your airmail letters will be sent by slow ship.

The problem for the traveler is complicated by having no safe place to receive mail. Poste Restante (general delivery) in Nairobi, for example is a joke—anybody, with no identification, can riffle through the stack of envelopes and take what he likes; Poste Restante may be more reliable elsewhere. We've heard travelers complain about American Express in Nairobi losing their mail, and no Amex office will save mail for more than 30 days. The U.S. Embassy will no longer save Americans' mail in any country in Africa; it is sent automatically to Poste Restante.

American Express offices in the main cities (exact addresses listed under "Travel Agents" in the country sections) are as follows: Nairobi —ETCO Ltd. Mombasa—ETCO Ltd. Addis Ababa—ITCO Tourist & Travel Agency. None elsewhere. American Express service is for clients only—so buy yourself one $20 traveler's check and you're a client.

If you take Pan Am anywhere, you can use Pan Am offices, located as follows: Commerce House, Government Road, Box 30544, Nairobi. Dar es Salaam Airport, Box 1428, Dar es Salaam. H.S.I. Theatre Bldg., Churchill Road, Box 3331, Addis Ababa. Lufthansa also holds your mail.

General delivery mail should be addressed to you c/o Poste Restante, General Post Office, in the city or town in which you'll be.

You can also chance having mail addressed to you at the tour company you use, and at hotels.

In all cases, tell people who might be sending you letters (keep the list short) to note on the envelope something about your time of arrival, or duration of stay, or the tour group you're with.

MAIL, P.O. Box 907, El Sobrante, Calif. 94803, is a forwarding service that may be handy for you.

Sending mail to Africa: There is no home delivery of mail in these five countries. In addressing a letter, don't bother to put the street address, just the P.O. box number. If no box number is included, the letter probably won't get there.

Money

These countries have, compared with European countries, strict currency regulations, and the two most visited countries—Kenya and Tanzania—do not allow you to bring in the local currency.

The safest thing is to carry nearly all your money in traveler's checks —dollars or pounds sterling—along with a very few cash' dollars in small denominations. You'll need the cash to buy things at duty-free shops and on the airplane, to pay airport taxes if you've run out of local currency, and, finally, when you get back to the U.S.

We found Barclays traveler's checks, issued in the U.S., were quite satisfactory. Do not cash traveler's checks in hotels and shops if you can avoid it; you'll lose money because hotel conversion rates include a high service charge. Use banks.

Be sure to keep the list of check numbers separate from the checks, and don't keep all your checks in the same place.

Be sure to keep the bank currency-exchange slips until you leave. You will need at least one of them to reconvert any local money you haven't spent, also to show if you're shipping anything home.

The black market: Obviously we cannot advise you to deal on the black market. It's illegal. Lots of low-budget travelers do, because their money stretches much further. The black market exists to some degree in all five countries, with Kenya's the easiest to locate. Because they are a persecuted, well-to-do minority always teetering on the edge of being kicked out without a dime (Uganda, 1972), the Asians in East Africa are constantly illegally seeking high-denomination greenbacks and traveler's checks at a rate of 10/– and up to the U.S. dollar. You can be put into jail, fined, deported if caught.

Figuring in Foreign Currency

Figuring in shillings, kwachas, and Ethiopian dollars is confusing at first. It helps that Kenya and Tanzania both use the shilling, convertible at about 7/– to the U.S. dollar (1 shilling equals U.S. 14¢). The Zambia and Malawi kwachas, however, are not worth the same, and the Ethiopian dollar is certainly not the same as a greenback dollar.

If our country conversion tables aren't enough, the Peoria *Journal*

Star has invented an extremely handy converter. The Unicon Universal Money Converter costs $3.95 (10¢ postage), from PJS Enterprises, 1 News Plaza, Peoria, Ill. 61601. Another flexible one is the Money-verter, $1.95 from H. Lawson & Co., Box 34016, West Bethesda, Md. 20034.

If Deak, Perera, or U.S. banks can't tell you the latest currency quotation, check with Foreign Commerce Bank, 82 Bellariastrasse, CH-8038 Zurich, Switzerland, or an international edition of *Newsweek*.

Security

We were robbed twice in East Africa, both times while within a foot or two of our Land Cruiser. The first time a purse was stolen from the front seat, the second time a camera and two lenses. We did not learn until too late that *it pays to be paranoid*. In this case, we should have kept windows closed and doors locked every second we were not in the car.

Purse snatching is common in Nairobi. A man will jump out of a car, snatch a woman tourist's purse—usually reported to have contained a lot of money—then jump back in the car, which speeds off and is later found abandoned as a stolen car. Too bad for the tourist. Don't carry too much in your purse; if you don't trust your hotel, or you're not in one yet, or you're shopping and need the money, then try to keep a lot of it close to your person—a four-pocket safari jacket seems ideal for this purpose.

In the city, put anything remotely valuable in the trunk of the car, or carry it with you, or leave someone with the car (the practice of many overland groups, who are too often the prey of thieves). If you go camping, do not leave anything valuable in your tent while you're away from it.

Con men in East Africa don't have a New York repertoire of confidence tricks. The most common is highlighted in this short news story from a Nairobi paper: "Conrad Ferdinand, a tourist, has reported he was approached by three men in Koinange Street who said they were Government officials checking on foreign currency. They asked him to produce all the money he had on him, which was £270 10s. ($773) in Kenya and foreign currency. The bogus officials then disappeared with the money, police said." This happened to the No. 2 U.S. delegate to the 1973 World Bank–IMF Conference! Be suspicious of anyone who stops you in the street. Ask to see official identification

—real plainclothes Kenya police carry blue plastic-covered ID cards. Do not be fooled into accompanying any alleged officials to your hotel room or anywhere else. In fact, stay on the sidewalk and yell.

Peace Corps Volunteers and others have found a cotton-cloth money belt worn around the waist under the shirt, or a thin leather wallet attached to a cord around the neck, handy for keeping passport, papers, and money safe from would-be pickpockets and thieves.

All good hotels, of course, have safes where you can deposit your valuables. Be sure to get a receipt. If you'll be in a place a long time, a bank may maintain a security envelope for you for a small service fee.

Be sure to carry small change with you. If you go to pay for a –/60 newspaper with a 100/– note, someone may run off to get change for you, and not return.

Remember that you are in a land where a good wage is 5/– (72¢) a day, and no matter how poor you may regard yourself, you're actually a rich *mzungu* (foreigner).

Credit Card Travel

Because charging things is convenient, and because holders of credit cards are at an advantage during times of international monetary crises, we have noted, where possible, hotels and restaurants that accept various credit cards, specifically American Express (abbreviated AE), BankAmericard (same as Barclaycard overseas; abbreviated BA), and Diners Club (DC). DC has a special Africa program, so appears to be the most widely accepted, being recognized in Nairobi by about 20 hotels, 30 restaurants and nightclubs, 20 tour operators and travel agents, 120 shops, several garages, two cinemas, the Wild Life Society, and the Automobile Association. American Express is accepted at 9 hotels, 13 restaurants, 40 shops. BankAmericard is less recognized in this region—only one establishment outside Kenya, in fact.

We'd suggest you have at least one credit card for use in emergencies (this goes for overland groups as well). A credit card can make check-cashing easier, cash advances can be drawn, and airline tickets charged.

Tipping

Tipping is not the onerous problem in Eastern Africa it is in the U.S. For one thing, most hotels and restaurants add a service charge, making a tip strictly a gratuity for service well rendered.

Generally, tip 10 percent. Give a porter or taxi driver a shilling (or equivalent in the other countries) for helping with the luggage. Tour minibus drivers can be tipped 3/– per day per tourist. At a self-catering game camp or rest house where a cook prepares the food you bring (Zambia and Malawi have these), give the cook a tip when you leave. The rule of thumb in Ethiopia is "tip often and tip little"—about E10¢ to E25¢ for luggage, for instance.

Whatever you do, don't overtip; Eastern Africa isn't ruined yet.

Cost of Living

If relative cost-of-living statistics mean anything to you, here are the U.N.'s 1973 statistics for the five capitals (New York is the index at 100): Addis Ababa—91; Dar es Salaam—80; Nairobi—78; Lusaka—103; Zomba, Malawi—70. (Housing was not taken into account for the last two cities.)

The price of imported items, especially clothes, is high in all five countries, not only because of transport costs but also customs duty and import restrictions. Gasoline (petrol) costs are high—in Nairobi, where it is (February 1974) relatively cheap, regular gas is U.S.71–91¢ for the equivalent of a U.S. gallon. Fresh food is uniformly cheap. Imported canned food is expensive—perhaps double what it is in the U.S.; local canned food is reasonable. In Lusaka, a regular-size can of Right Guard is almost $2, a fifth of scotch about $20. Housing is variably expensive. A short-term Nairobi resident can find a three-room house or cottage in a nice neighborhood for $140 to $210 a month, which beats a hotel, though housing is getting tighter.

Generally, labor is cheap, goods are expensive.

Game Park Rules

Most national parks and game reserves have a few sensible regulations, generally posted at the main gate. They vary from park to park, but include the following:

• Don't annoy the animals in any way. Don't try to feed them, coax them forward, throw anything at them, yell, or honk. Near the animals, stay inside the vehicle; if you don't, the animals will react unfavorably by either running away, or in the case of a couple of species, running toward you. Be prepared to roll up your window in a hurry.

• Drive slowly—not more than 35 mph, though it depends on the park. If you drive fast, you won't see any animals, and you'll get dusty, too.

- If necessary, get out of the car only where it looks safe, and don't walk too far.
- Don't litter.
- Generally, no entry or exit before 6 A.M. or after 6 or 7 P.M., and no driving between dark and dawn.
- No pets are allowed in game parks.

KENYA

BEAUTY AND THE BEASTS

Imagine, say, Colorado. Imagine that it's in Africa, and that it has an Indian Ocean coastline with 380 miles of coral sand beaches and coconut palms. Imagine that this Colorado has a 17,000-foot glacier-capped mountain crossed at about 11,000 feet by the equator. Imagine that this beautiful country has a string of blue lakes, left over from earth-cracking geological events that created a huge Rift Valley with mile-high escarpments. Now, imagine under a limitless blue sky that there are millions of wild animals—elephants and zebras and antelope and lions and rhinos—and that there are more species of exotic, colorful birds than are known in all but one or two countries.

In short, imagine Kenya.

It is hard to write about Kenya without sounding like a government travel brochure. The Texas-sized country is a fabulous one for travelers, because in the wide-open spaces, in the vast wilderness with wildlife, in all the beauty untouched by superhighways and striding-Martian electricity transmission towers, it is possible for the traveler to be alone to enjoy nature. You can easily find yourself practically the only visitor in a game park, and even when a crowd materializes—say, when two Masai herdsmen appear out of nowhere to watch you cook a camp breakfast—you don't mind it much. And even the "crowds" of tourists at the height of the season (December to February) don't exactly fill the horizon in Tsavo National Park, which is the size of New Jersey.

There's lots of contrast, lots of variety. Lions stalk, kill, and feast on antelope only a few minutes away from Nairobi's skyscrapers, though this scarcely makes the city a dangerous place. The traffic on the Nairobi–Mombasa trunk highway (two lanes wide) must beware of elephants crossing the road. And there are less pleasant contrasts, such

§ 77

as the tin-and-cardboard hovels in the Mathare Valley five minutes from the deluxe Nairobi Hilton.

It is a terribly easy country to travel around in and see, for there are roads everywhere that can be traveled by small sedans, there is a good range of tourist accommodations—and if you can't find a good hotel, camping is probably better anyway. There are more tourist attractions than just game parks, which is just as well, for the tourist can tire of animals as quickly as he can of Europe's infinitude of museums and historic buildings.

For such a fascinating country, Kenya has a notable lack of history. Compared with neighboring Ethiopia, which had a civilization 500 years before Christ, which has old castles and rock churches, which was the scene of great events, Kenya has a short, very different, but somewhat dull history, becoming reasonably full of detail only at the appearance of the colonizers seven or eight decades ago. Indeed, the history must be divided into two parts: the history of the coast and the history of the interior. The former is coherent and has some drama, the latter is vague, shadowy, and only now being written down. The history of both is remarkable for lack of contact between coast and interior.

It is now evident that mankind was born in East Africa. The Leakeys' discoveries at Olduvai Gorge in northern Tanzania and more recently east of Lake Rudolf in Kenya have put man's origins far back, and East Africa has certainly replaced Asia as cradle of mankind. What is even more certain is that more discoveries are yet to come. But once born here, man did not develop very fast in this region, and was still very primitive when the descendants of those who had migrated north into the Nile Valley and elsewhere moved back to East Africa some 10,000 years ago, pushing out or absorbing the Bushmen and other groups. The region became peopled with Hamitic or Cushitic types such as the Somali and Galla; Nilo-Hamitic or Eastern Nilotic people such as the Masai, Kalenjin tribes, and Turkana; Nilotes—the Luo of Lake Victoria being the only representatives in Kenya; and, as the most populous, the Bantu tribes, including the Kikuyu, Kamba, Luhya, Kisii, Giriama, and Digo. Very little is known about the movements of these tribes into Kenya, since they kept no records, but a new kind of historian who uses analysis of oral history and various esoteric scientific techniques is beginning to retrieve some of this lost history. Some of the inland tribes began having sporadic contact with outsiders such as Arab traders in the 1700s, for some vague information about the interior—large lakes and snow-capped mountains—was known to Europe's mapmakers, who, as Jonathan Swift jibed, "placed elephants for want of towns."

The coast was known to the earliest traders, though the first documentary evidence comes from the 1st-century-A.D. Indian Ocean guidebook, *The Periplus of the Erythraean Sea,* which mentioned the places we know as Lamu, Mombasa, and Zanzibar. Arab, Persian, Indian, and Chinese traders came seeking "ivory, apes, peacocks, and gold," and the Chinese additionally wanted to find a unicorn (they got a giraffe).

Europeans first came on the scene in 1498 with the arrival in Mombasa and Malindi of Vasco da Gama. Within eight years the Portuguese had sent expeditions to subdue the coastal Arab and Swahili towns, except for their ally Malindi, and the Portuguese hold on the coast was strengthened with the building of Fort Jesus in Mombasa in 1593. The Ottoman Turks ventured into the area in the 1580s, roughly at the same time as the cannibalistic Zimba moved north up the coast. Those Turks who were not eaten at Mombasa were driven off by the Portuguese; the Zimba went on to be defeated at Malindi. The Portuguese dominion weakened as a new power appeared on the Indian Ocean, that of Oman on the Persian Gulf. Omani Arabs besieged Fort Jesus for nearly two years before taking it in December 1698. Oman became the nominal power on the coast, though the towns grew more and more independent, flourishing as city states until the accession to Oman's sultanate of the powerful Seyyid Said in 1806. Beginning in the 1820s Seyyid campaigned to bring the coast under his sway, shifting his headquarters to Zanzibar and succeeding by 1840 in ruling the coast.

Seyyid's campaigns coincided with growing European interest in Africa. The missionaries Johann Ludwig Krapf and Johannes Rebmann established a mission at Rabai, outside Mombasa, in 1844–46, and in 1847 Rebmann became the first European to venture into Kenya's interior. Rebmann saw Kilimanjaro in 1848; Krapf saw Mount Kenya in 1849. Richard Burton and John Speke, and later Speke and James Grant, explored Tanzania in the late 1850s and early 1860s, but the first to explore very far into Kenya was the Scot Joseph Thomson, who crossed Masailand in 1883.

With its mighty sea power and campaign to end the slave trade, Britain became the European nation with the most influence on the coast, rivaled by Germany; the Berlin Conference of 1884–85 and a series of treaties led to Kenya's being included in the British "sphere of influence," Tanzania within Germany's. Sir William Mackinnon's Imperial British East Africa Company (IBEA) won a concession in 1888 to develop trade in the interior. IBEA's activities were focused on Uganda, but even though the way to get there was through Kenya, that area seemed unimportant at the time, since it didn't even have a name. Uganda became a British protectorate in 1894, and when IBEA passed out of existence because of excessive unprofitability, the rest of its concession became Britain's East Africa Protectorate on June 15, 1895. Shortly, Parliament decided to build a railway to Uganda, since it was thought it had the greatest potential and was, additionally, at the source of the Nile. So the railway became Kenya's raison d'être.

The railway, built from Mombasa to Kisumu on Lake Victoria from 1896 to 1901, is an epic story. It was a mammoth building project that Elspeth Huxley dubbed "the most courageous railway in the world." Malaria and dysentery disabled and killed hundreds of workers imported from India, and the animal toll was higher. Kamba and Kikuyu raiders åttacked the railhead party, and Nandi warriors waged a long guerrilla war against the railway. Ants and guinea fowl undermined embankments. Sudden rains in the middle of a dry season melted 75 miles of earthworks. Man-eating lions held up the building of the Tsavo River Bridge, gobbling up 28 workers before being tracked down and shot. The railway builders were struck down by heat in the Taru Desert, suffered from ice and sleet at Mau Summit. "It seemed," wrote the railway's official historian, "as if the very spirit of Africa resented the intrusion of the white man's railway." But finally, on December 20, 1901, the tracks reached Port Florence (Kisumu) on Lake Victoria.

The railway had passed Nairobi in 1899, and in a few years the frontier town was capital of the protectorate. Big-game hunters arrived as Kenya's first tourists, setting off like Teddy Roosevelt from the Norfolk Hotel with great lines of porters. An early governor encouraged British settlers, and soon an enormous chunk of the fertile Highlands was the preserve of "Europeans" (as whites in Africa are called). Reality was recognized in 1920 when the protectorate became Kenya Colony, governed by a Legislative Council dominated by white settlers. Under the pioneer agriculturalist Lord Delamere, the Europeans resisted the attempts of even the former railway-worker Asians (now become retail traders) to gain a voice in government, and the middle years of colonial Kenya are remarkable only for their dullness. The Europeans had it good—big farms on rich land, plenty of cheap African labor to help re-create the British way of life: fox hunts, high tea, estates with high hedges, polo tournaments, clubs, black-robed judges with powdered wigs, the lot. The Africans progressed in certain ways, carried along by colonial momentum, encouraged by few Europeans. Those who demanded anything resembling white settler rights were, however, quickly put down; Harry Thuku, a 1922 rebel, was locked up, then shipped off to remote Kismayu on the Somali coast.

But you can't lock up everybody. The colony's largest tribe, the Kikuyu, provided the mass of the movement against colonial rule in the early 1950s—the Mau Mau, at first merely a terrorist society, then a nationalist movement, now regarded as Kenya's freedom fighters, with a prominent display of their homemade guns in the National Museum in Nairobi. It was after a spate of killings that the colonial government declared the Emergency on October 20, 1952, with the immediate roundup of a hundred political leaders. The most prominent, including Jomo Kenyatta, were tried, convicted, and sent to exile in the Northern Frontier District. The Land and Freedom Armies, the "forest fighters," went into the Mount Kenya and Aberdare forests to wage war against the whites, who fought back with regiments, bombers, special tracker teams, brainwashing. The casualties were many, including 11,503 Mau Mau, 167 members of the security forces, and 1,819 African civilians killed. Thousands of Kikuyu, Embu, and Meru —two-thirds of whom took the Mau Mau oath—were detained; village life was broken up, almost all political activity proscribed. The Mau Mau lasted until 1957, although the Emergency wasn't over until 1960.

The handwriting on the wall was now in shouting letters; colonial Kenya was doomed. Africans gained representation in the Legislative Council in 1956; the White Highlands were opened to black ownership in 1960. The same year, British Prime Minister Harold Macmillan gave his famous "winds of change" speech, and by then half of Africa had won *uhuru,* freedom; and, in exile, Kenyatta was elected president of the Kenya African National Union (KANU). Tanganyika won independence in December 1961, Uganda in 1962. Inexorably, the white settlers gave way as Britain granted more and more power to the black majority. On June 1, 1963, the country won internal self-government, with the recently released Kenyatta as prime minister. On December 12, 1963, the Union Jack was lowered for the last time, and the black, red, and green flag of Kenya raised. A year later Kenya became a republic.

Still led by Kenyatta—the Mzee or "honored old man" (he is in his eighties)—Kenya is a de facto one-party (KANU) state with a one-house parliament; elections for both president and National Assembly are held every five years. Unifying the major and minor tribes, the large Asian population, and the 40,000 resident Europeans of Kenya is Kenyatta's spirit of *harambee,* roughly translated as "let's all pull together." Despite *harambee* the government's aim is the Africanization of the economy, a continuing process of revoking noncitizen trading licenses and work permits to enable blacks to assume control of their own country in fact as well as name. This Kenyanizing of Kenya is being accomplished without the violence seen in Uganda in 1972–73.

Unlike neighboring Tanzania, Kenya is quite capitalist, with the government encouraging foreign investment in several ways, not the least by fostering Kenya's image as a progressive, stable nation. Coffee, tea, pyrethrum (a natural insecticide), and other exports bring in a large income, though the No. 1 money-earner is now tourism—$100 million a year.

Some Vital Statistics. Area: 224,960 sq. mi. (582,647 sq. km.), about the size of Texas.

Population: 12,067,000 (est. 1972), about the population of Pennsylvania. Population density: 50 per sq. mi. The last census counted 40,000 Europeans, 139,000 Asians, and 28,000 Arabs in Kenya (of all these groups, a total of 89,000 were citizens of Kenya).

Cities: Nairobi (1972 est. pop. 597,000) is the capital and largest city. Mombasa (est. pop. 286,000) is the second city and major port. Other towns (1969 figures): Nakuru (47,151), Kisumu (32,431), Thika (18,400), Eldoret (18,196), Nanyuki (11,624), Kitale (11,-573), Malindi (10,757).

Gross national product (1971): $1.725 billion ($140 per capita).

Currency

The basic unit of currency is the shilling, divided into 100 cents. Figures are written in the old British style: e.g., 10 shillings as 10/–; 5 shillings and 75 cents as 5/75; 50 cents as –/50. Shilling is also abbreviated as *sh.* and *shs.* There are shilling currency notes in 5/–, 10/–, 20/–, 50/– (uncommon), and 100/– denominations; coins of –/05, –/10, –/25 (uncommon), –/50, 1/–, and 2/– (uncommon). An unofficial unit, the pound, consisting of 20/–, is often used in government finance and newspaper headlines. To convert pounds to shillings, simply double pounds and add a zero.

As of mid-1974 one shilling has an official value of 14 American cents, with $1 equal to 7/14. The shilling is pegged to the dollar. The quick method of converting shillings to dollars is simply to divide shillings by 7. Here is a quick conversion table, based on 7/14 = $1:

$$1,000/- = \$140$$
$$500/- = \$70$$
$$100/- = \$14$$
$$75/- = \$10.50$$
$$50/- = \$7$$
$$25/- = \$3.50$$
$$10/- = \$1.40$$
$$5/- = \$.70$$
$$1/- = \$.14$$
$$-/50 = \$.07$$
$$-/10 = \$.014$$

You should know that the Kenya shilling, while a relatively stable African currency, is inflated, having a Zurich (free market) value of about 10/– to $1, and that an active black market exists in Nairobi and, to a lesser extent, Mombasa. Dealing on the black market is illegal.

Planning a Trip

What to See and Do

You cannot go to Kenya and *not* visit a game park any more than you can go to Greece and not see ancient ruins. The question is which parks to go to. If you are not on an organized tour, we would suggest a series of individual safaris from Nairobi to destinations individually determined. If you want a broad selection of the best beasts, birds, and scenery, you should go to *Nairobi National Park, Tsavo West, Amboseli,* and *Lake Nakuru* and then spend a night at a game-viewing lodge. The choices are now more than just *Treetops.* Also in the Aberdare forest is *The Ark,* our personal favorite; on the slopes of Mount Kenya are *Secret Valley* (leopards are the attraction) and *Mountain Lodge,* both of which leave something to be desired; and, near Tsavo West, the Hilton *Salt Lick Lodge,* new in 1973. See our more extensive comments on each of these "tree hotels."

After a game-viewing lodge, the best parks to visit if you have the time are *Masai Mara* and *Samburu,* which is good for not so common animals such as the thin-striped Grevy's zebra and reticulated giraffe. The other game parks and wildlife areas are definitely off the beaten track and should be considered by those who have the time, or those who like out-of-the-way places. In this category we include *Marsabit,* home of elephants with mammoth tusks, and *Lake Rudolf,* the "jade sea," named for the crown prince of the Mayerling romance. Both are in the rugged Northern Frontier District (NFD—not its official name but in common use); if you don't have the time to drive, fly to both places. *Meru,* associated with Joy Adamson's Elsa, has a new lodge but takes a chunk out of your schedule unless you fly. Travelers with a month or more can consider the various attractions of western Kenya —*Mount Elgon, Cherangani Hills* and *Kerio Valley, Saiwa Swamp sitatunga sanctuary*—and *Lake Baringo.*

Places which can be seen along the way include *Lake Naivasha* (especially if you're a birdwatcher), *Thomson's Falls* (Nyahururu), and three of Kenya's prehistoric and historic sites—the ruined Arab city of *Gedi* near Malindi, and the *Hyrax Hill* and *Kariandusi* excavations, both near Nakuru. *Kericho* and the tea estates make a very worthwhile stopover on the way to Masai Mara.

It is not worthwhile for Americans to make the *coast* a main destination, not unless you're a beach nut looking for a new sunspot; but if you're in Kenya a month, the coast is an attractive detour, not for the beaches alone but for *Mombasa* (with *Fort Jesus,* the mammoth 16th-century Portuguese fort), the two *Marine National Parks,* Gedi, and *Shimba Hills,* the sable antelope preserve. For sunning, we'd pick the *South Coast,* particularly *Diani Beach;* north of Mombasa, the best place is *Watamu.*

What about *Lamu,* the island town of narrow streets and Arab culture? We'd say yes, even if you're not seeing the rest of the coast. But you have to fly, since the road up is primitive.

Finally, if you're reasonably fit and under 50 (or very fit at any age), you should consider a walking trip on *Mount Kenya,* second-highest mountain in Africa. The giant vegetation, the fabulous views, and the whole mountain experience are thrilling.

The energy crisis in early 1974 seemed to make a substantial impact in Kenya—as in other African countries—mainly in higher prices for gasoline (in February a liter of petrol in Nairobi cost between 1/28 and 1/60—that is, between U.S.$.71 and .91 per gallon), with availability unaffected. The price increase will, in turn, increase the cost of package-tour land arrangements.

How Long to Stay Where

Any place improves with time, and game parks are no exception. First-timers in Africa tend to prefer ten game parks in ten days; repeaters would rather spend ten days in one park. Minimum stays:

Nairobi: At least one day for sightseeing (including the National Museum, two hours; National Park, three hours to half a day), one more full day for thorough shopping.

Lake Nakuru: Half a day if you're not a keen birder. Not necessary to stay overnight in the vicinity unless you camp, which is a pleasant experience here.

Tsavo West: Full day and half a day (two overnights).

Tsavo East: Full day, one overnight at Voi Lodge.

Amboseli: At least one night, two half-days.

Masai Mara: Two nights with a full day in between.

Samburu: At least one overnight, two half-days, easily stretched to longer.

Marsabit: One and a half days, two nights—since it takes a long time to get there by road.

Treetops, etc.: Strictly one-night stands.

Mount Kenya: To walk up "Tourist Peak" (Point Lenana), two days (one night on the mountain) is the minimum, but we'd say stretch it to three days, two nights. Four days takes you around the peaks, and you'll need about that long to do the top peaks, Batian and Nelion.

Lake Rudolf: If you're driving, don't plan for less than a week total. If you're flying, two nights.

Mombasa: Full day of sightseeing and shopping. Overnight in the city is not necessary—the beach hotels are close, better.

Malindi and *Watamu:* Malindi town needs little attention. Give Gedi two hours in the morning or late afternoon. One half-day for a glassbottom-boat trip with goggling out to marine park reefs. In short: two days, two nights.

Lamu: One day if you're flying.

Where to Stay

Of the five countries in this guide, Kenya has the most accommodations in the widest range for the most budgets. In short, do not worry where you can stay, since there are not only lots of regular hotels, game lodges, resorts, and game-viewing lodges but also self-service *bandas* where you prepare your own food, forest department and government rest houses, mountain huts, fishing camps, luxury tented camps, ordinary campgrounds and campsites, YMCAs and YWCAs, youth hostels, and, if you choose carefully, lots of African *hotelis,* though hardly any can be recommended.

The Ministry of Tourism and Wildlife began classifying hotels in 1971, and a new edition was published in 1974. All 164 classified hotels fit one of three categories—town hotels, vacation hotels, and country hotels—and within that category are rated on an A*, A, B*, B, C, and D system, except in the country hotels class, with only A, B, and C ratings. As a rule, most D hotels are barely adequate for American tourists, but they rarely have bedbugs. C hotels are usually good value. Both C and D are older, colonial-era hotels. Hotels above C are of the American standard, though they may not be modern. We haven't always agreed with the government ratings, but we have included them.

Service charge is variably 5 or 10 percent. There is also a 10 percent government tax on accommodations only (7½ percent on room and full board), and a 2 percent training levy on accommodations, food, and beverage (to be used to fund and support the future Hotel Training Centre, Nairobi).

Except for the few top international-class hotels in Nairobi, most hotels in Kenya serve a big English breakfast included in the charges. Game lodges typically charge for three meals.

During the off-season on the coast, May–June, many beach hotels shut their doors, and those that stay open offer a lower rate. Some inland hotels also have an off-season rate, and many give Kenya residents lower rates all year.

As usual, we note the room charges for singles and doubles *with* private bath or shower.

Booking Accommodations

For the top Nairobi hotels almost anytime, and the game lodges December–February and July–August, reservations have to be made as far in advance as possible.

Booking for several hotels and lodges and self-service lodges is consolidated at various Nairobi offices. Addresses:

A. A. & Bunson Travel Ltd., at Automobile Association HQ, Westlands, Box 45456, Nairobi; tel. 46826; cable EASIGO. Bookings for Kitani Lodge, Ngulia Safari Camp, Aruba Lodge, Leopard Rock

Lodge, Buffalo Springs Camp, Lake Baringo Self-Service Lodge, Turtle Bay Hotel, Kenya Beach Hotel, Ngobit Fishing Lodge, Marsabit Tented Lodge, Naivasha Marina Club, Tea Hotel, Lake Rudolf Angling Lodge.

African Safari Lodges Ltd., Lugard House, Government Road, Box 46020, tel. 28760; cable CENTBOOKING. Bookings for the African Safari Club hotels: Dolphin, Watamu Beach Club, Coral Beach, Bahari Beach, Silver Beach, Tsavo Inn, Sigala Lodge.

African Tours & Hotels Ltd., Consolidated House, Standard St., Box 30471, tel. 29251; cable AFTOURS. Bookings for Eliye Springs, Hunter's Lodge, Kilaguni Lodge, Mountain Lodge, Namanga Hotel, Safariland Lodge, Mnarani Club, Trade Winds, College Inn.

Forest & Frontier Lodges Ltd., Norwich Union House, Mama Ngina St., Box 48559, tel. 34411, 34414; cable HYRAX. Bookings for Cottars Camp (Tsavo Tsafaris), Masai Lodge, Isaak Walton Inn.

Game Department, behind National Museum, Museum Hill, Box 40241, tel. 20671. Bookings for Ol Tukai Lodge, Buffalo Springs bandas, also camping in Amboseli, Masai Mara, and Samburu.

Hilton Hotels, Nairobi Hilton, Mama Ngina St., Box 30624, tel. 34000; cable HILTELS. Bookings for Nairobi Hilton, Taita Hills Lodge, Salt Lick Lodge. (Hilton hotels anywhere take bookings.)

Kenya Safari Lodges & Hotels Ltd., Panafric Hotel, Kenyatta Ave., Box 49972, tel. 25655; cable KSLHOTEL. Bookings for Ngulia Lodge, Voi Lodge, Mombasa Beach Hotel.

KTDC Hotel Management Company, 4th floor, Standard Bldg., Kenyatta Ave., Box 42013, tel. 29751, 23488; cable TOURIST. Bookings for the new Kenya Tourist Development Corp. properties: Marsabit Lodge, Njiru Country Club, Meru Mulika Lodge, Casuarina Hotel (taken over), Mount Elgon Lodge, Kisumu Hotel (last two expected to be open in 1975).

Percival Tours, IPS Bldg., Kimathi St., Box 43987, tel. 33275; cable TOURPERCY. Bookings for The Ark and Aberdare Country Club.

Serena Lodges and Hotels, IPS Bldg., Kimathi St., Box 48690, tel. 26701/2; cable SERENA. Amboseli and Mara Serena lodges, Serena Beach Hotel, future Nairobi Serena Hotel.

Wildlife Lodges Ltd./Kenya Hotels Ltd., New Stanley House, Standard St., Box 47557, tel. 22860; cable WILDLODGES. Bookings for Samburu Lodge, Keekorok, Treetops, Outspan, Secret Valley, Lake Naivasha Hotel.

When to Go

The American and European winter is when the hotels are most crowded with package tourists. The tourist high season of December–March is roughly comparable with the U.S. summer, and that means mostly hot: hot and humid along the coast and Lake Victoria, hot and dry almost everywhere else. The other nice season inland is August–October, overlapping the busy July–September second tourist season. The three most popular months are July, February, and October.

The long rains are supposed to come between late March and June, the short rains in November–December. The rains are most unpredictable, however, and no resident of Kenya would ever bet on when they'll come. When they do, you can still be a tourist, taking advantage of low-season rates at many hotels and lodges. The main difficulty is in driving, especially in the legendary bottomless black-cotton soil of Masai Mara and a few other places. Even during the rainy season, however, it doesn't rain that much, it doesn't rain all day, and it doesn't even rain every day. During the long rains the average rainfall is 18 inches around Nairobi, while the short rains total 5 to 10 inches.

Temperatures can vary remarkably. Nairobi, at 5,500 feet, has cold Julys, but never below 33°F. Except in the NFD (Lake Rudolf, Marsabit), the heat of the day in most game parks is no higher than a California summer, 85–95° in midday; but nights can be chilly by comparison. Mombasa and the coast have only ordinary summer daytime heat (mean maximum is 86°), but the humidity (mean is 75 percent) can make it unbearable unless you have a cool drink in your hand.

June and July, and perhaps part of August as well, are generally cloudy, cool—and a bit dismal.

School holidays, which affect the availability of self-service lodging and camping space, are during Easter and, roughly, July 20–September 11, December 7–January 7.

Tourism Authority

The Ministry of Tourism and Wildlife, New Jogoo House, Harambee Ave., Box 30027, Nairobi; tel. 28411 (address letters to Permanent Secretary). Tourism offices are located at 15 East 51st St. (across from St. Patrick's), New York 10022; tel. (212) 486-1300; at 318 Grand Bldgs., Trafalgar Square, London WC2; also in Paris, Frankfurt, and Stockholm. Government's Kenya National Travel Bureau (Box 42013, Nairobi) runs the downtown Nairobi Tourist Information Bureau (tel. 23285, 21855) and the airport information desk (tel. 82111), and may be more helpful than the ministry.

There is an official tourist office in Mombasa in the Jubilee Insurance Bldg., Kilindini Road (above the Tusks), Box 80091, tel. 23465.

Maps

Good maps of Kenya, Nairobi, and the national parks (but not the game reserves) are available. The casual tourist should start with the Shell road map (see below). Survey of Kenya maps (marked SK in the list below) are available from the Public Map Office, Harambee Ave. (next to the President's Office), Box 30089, Nairobi; catalog costs 1/−. Some SK maps and the oil company maps are available from the Tourist Information Bureau (see p. 169) and from the Automobile Association (p. 107). Include approximate postage.

Kenya, general: A colorful, barely functional tourist map (1:2 million) is published by the Survey (SK-72, price 5/−, available free outside Kenya at tourist offices). It has climate charts and sketch maps of Nairobi and Mombasa. More useful are the two sheets of SK-57 (price 12/50 for both) at 1:1 million. *Kenya, roads:* The best map is by Kenya Shell (price 6/−). It's a pretty map, though the information shown is not always accurate and the roads not always in existence; in fact, the 1973 edition shows little change from the 1968 edition. SK-81 (price 7/−) also has its faults, but the two together will get you around the marked roads. The Esso, Caltex (AA), and Total maps of East Africa are miserable productions.

Nairobi: SK-46 (7/50) is very handsome and useful. Small maps are in *Nairobi Handbook, What's On,* and publicity handouts. *Mombasa:* SK-54 (5/−) is the best available. *Coast:* Most detailed is SK-79 (7/−). *Game parks:* Caltex has a series of maps (5/− each) which are inadequate to dreadful, with an oblique projection, covering Samburu, Meru, Amboseli, Nakuru/Naivasha, Tsavo. Superior and useful are the Survey parks maps (5/− each) of Nairobi Park (SK-71), Tsavo West (SK-78), Tsavo East (SK-82), Keekorok area of Masai Mara (SK-69), Meru (SK-65). Amboseli is best covered in the 1:250,000 "Amboseli" sheet, Mount Kenya and the Aberdares on "Nyeri" sheet, Masai Mara (entire) on "Narok" sheet. The National Parks' Lake Nakuru guide (10/−) has the best map of that park. Nothing is available on Marsabit except two 1:100,000 sheets dividing the area in two. *Mount Kenya:* SK-75 (DOS-302) shows peaks, valleys, and the top part of the access trails in relief. The 1:50,000 sheets are antique. Schriebl & Schneider has a fine 1:5,000 map of the central peaks; price about $4.25 from Alpina Technica Productions (West Col Productions), address p. 250.

Books to Read

The following list contains books on both Kenya and East Africa.

Adamson, Joy. *The Peoples of Kenya.* New York: Harcourt Brace, 1967; London: Collins, 1967.

Blixen, Karen von (Isak Dinesen). *Out of Africa.* New York: Random House, 1970 (also Vintage paperback).

Brown, Leslie. *East African Mountains and Lakes.* Nairobi: East African Publishing House, 1971 (paperback).

Cole, Sonia. *The Prehistory of East Africa.* New York: Macmillan, 1963, and New American Library paperback, 1965.

Coupland, (Sir) Reginald. *East Africa and Its Invaders.* Oxford: Oxford University Press, 1938; New York: Russel & Russel, 1965.

Harlow, Vincent, et al., eds. *History of East Africa, Vol. II.* Oxford: Clarendon Press, 1965. (See also Oliver, below.)

Huxley, Elspeth. *The Flame Trees of Thika.* New York: Morrow, 1959, and Pyramid paperback and Apollo paperback. London: Chatto & Windus, 1959, and Penguin paperback, 1962. *White Man's Country: Lord Delamere and the Making of Kenya.* 2 vols. London: Chatto & Windus, 1935; New York: Praeger, 1968.

Kenyatta, Jomo. *Facing Mount Kenya: The Tribal Life of the Gikuyu.* London: Secker & Warburg, 1938; New York: Vintage paperback, 1962. *Suffering Without Bitterness: The Founding of the Kenya Nation.* Nairobi: East African Publishing House, 1968; New York: International Publications Service, 1969.

Kirkman, James. *Men and Monuments of the East African Coast.* London: Lutterworth Press, 1964.

MacPhee, A. Marshall. *Kenya.* New York: Praeger, 1968; London: Ernest Benn, 1968.

Marsh, Zoe A., and Kingsnorth, George W. *An Introduction to the History of East Africa.* 4th ed. New York and Cambridge: Cambridge University Press, 1972. (Also paperback.)

Miller, Charles. *The Lunatic Express: An Entertainment in Imperial-*

ism. New York: Macmillan, 1971; London: Macdonald, 1972; now
in paperback.

Mitchell, John, ed. *Guide Book to Mount Kenya and Kilimanjaro*.
Nairobi: Mountain Club of Kenya, 1971. (Availability, see p. 250.)

Mollison, Simon. *Kenya's Coast: An Illustrated Guide*. Nairobi: East
African Publishing House, 1971 (paperback).

Morgan, W. T. W., ed. *Nairobi: City and Region*. Nairobi: Oxford
University Press, 1967 (paperback).

Ogot, B. A., and Kieran, J. A., eds. *Zamani: A Survey of East African
History*. Nairobi: East African Publishing House/Longman Kenya,
1968 (paperback).

Oliver, Roland, and Mathew, Gervase, eds. *History of East Africa,
Vol. I*. Oxford: Cladendon Press, 1963. (See also Harlow, above.)

Robson, Peter, *Mountains of Kenya*. Nairobi: East African Publishing
House, 1969 (paperback).

Rosberg, Carl, and Nottingham, John. *The Myth of 'Mau Mau': Nationalism in Kenya*. New York: Praeger, 1966; Nairobi: East African
Publishing House, 1966 (paperback).

Ross, W. McGregor. *Kenya from Within*. London: Frank Cass, 1968.

Newspapers

The two Nairobi dailies in English, the *East African Standard* (Box
30080) and the *Daily Nation* (Box 49010), and the two Sunday
papers, the *Sunday Nation* and the *Sunday Post* (Box 30127), make
interesting reading before a trip to Kenya.

Other Sources of Information

Kenya National Chamber of Commerce & Industry, Box 47024,
Nairobi; tel. 20866. *Department of Information,* Information House,
Hakati Road (off Tom Mboya St.), Box 30025, Nairobi; tel. 23201.
Industrial & Commercial Development Corp., Box 45519, Nairobi; tel.
22031. *Kenya Tourist Development Corp.,* Standard Bldg., Kenyatta
Ave., Box 42013, Nairobi; tel. 29751, 23488.

Inside Kenya Today is published quarterly by the Ministry of Information; subscriptions 33/– a year postpaid to the U.S. or Europe, 2/–
at Nairobi newsstands. *Safari: The Tourist Magazine for East Africa*
is a monthly costing 2/50 on the street, 44/– ($7) a year postpaid
outside Africa, from News Publishers Ltd., Box 30339, Nairobi. *Kenya
Past and Present,* published by the Kenya Museum Society, Box 40658,

Nairobi, is free with membership of 70/– (overseas rate) per year.
Africana, published by the Wild Life Society, see p. 136. East Africa
Natural History Society *Bulletin* and *Journal,* see p. 138. The Ministry
of Tourism and Wildlife has recently started producing two quarterly
magazines (free on request to the Permanent Secretary): *Hotline,* for
the general reader, and *Newsletter,* for the Kenya tourist industry.
Finally, there's the Block and Hallways hotels-sponsored *Maridadi,* a
quarterly magazine costing 40/– per year (air) from Box 48350,
Nairobi.

Entry Requirements

Immigration

American citizens entering Kenya on tourist, business or transit visas
are required to have their passport; a visa; a ticket to leave; a vaccination certificate for smallpox, cholera, and yellow fever; and, in the case
of businessmen, a letter of recommendation for business travel. Persons
coming overland or intending to leave overland are admitted without
the ticket to leave, but some proof of intention and ability to leave has
to be shown, or else a 5,000/– bond may have to be posted.

On arrival you will be issued a visitor's pass, which is usually for a
three-month visit. The visitor's pass remains valid as long as you don't
travel outside East Africa proper. Separate *visas* are necessary for Tanzania and Uganda.

Commonwealth citizens, along with Germans, Danes, Italians, Nor-
wegians, and a few others, do not need visas.

To obtain a visa, go to the nearest Kenya diplomatic mission (four
weeks ahead of time is advised), submit your passport and one copy
of the form, a round-trip ticket (or onward ticket or airline or travel
agency letter), and $3.15 (22/–) visa fee. No photos are necessary.
Visas are usually valid for multiple entries during a 12-month period,
with duration of visit normally three months. You can get a visa by
mail by sending a stamped, self-addressed envelope for return by certi-
fied or registered mail. Note: If you intend to stay for six months or
more you must apply for a visitor's pass *before* applying for a visa.

Inquiries and renewals of visas and visitor's passes: Chief Immigration Officer, New Jogoo House (ground floor), Harambee Ave. (at
Taifa Road), Box 30191, Nairobi; tel. 28411. Note: The immigration
offices in Nairobi and Mombasa can issue visas for Tanzania and
Uganda.

Diplomatic Missions of Kenya

Ethiopia: Embassy, Fikre Mariam Aba Techan Road, Box 3301, Addis Ababa; tel. 120033. *Great Britain:* High Commission, 45 Portland Place, London W1; tel. 01-636 2371. *USA:* Embassy, 2249 R St., N.W., Washington, D.C. 20008; tel. (202) 387-6101. Tourist and visa office, 15 East 51st St., New York 10022; tel. (212) 486-1300; visa applications accepted 11 A.M.–5 P.M. Mon.–Fri., processing takes 24 hours; bring $3.15 visa fee with correct change. *West Germany:* Embassy, Hohenzollernstrasse 12, 53 Bonn-Bad Godesberg 1. *Zambia:* High Commission, Kafue House, Cairo Road, Box 3651, Lusaka; tel. 75897.

Kenya also has missions in China (People's Republic), Egypt, France, India, Nigeria, Somalia, Sweden, U.S.S.R., and Zaire.

The immigration departments of Tanzania (Ohio St., off City Drive, Box 512, Dar es Salaam; tel. 27291) and Uganda (35 Jinja Road, Box 7165, Kampala; tel. 31031) issue visas for Kenya.

Customs

Persons 16 years or older may import, duty-free, their own clothing and toilet articles, 200 cigarettes (or 50 cigars or 8 ounces of tobacco), one pint of perfume or toilet water, one pint of spirits or wine. Tourists intending to stay less than six months need not worry about quantity of camera equipment or, usually, amount of film, though you may have to declare quantities to the customs officer on arrival. You are not usually required to fill out any customs declaration, but be ready to make a verbal declaration of luxury items.

Export of game trophies or skin articles requires an export permit.

Inquiries: East African Customs & Excise Department, Custom House, Box 90601, Mombasa, Kenya; tel. 21244. Nairobi Customs Office, E.A. Community Bldg., Ngong Road, Box 40160, Nairobi; tel. 26411.

Currency Control

You may import as much foreign currency—cash or traveler's checks—as you want, as long as you want, as long as you declare it. You can take out as much as you brought in.

Entering or leaving East Africa, you cannot import or export Kenya shillings in any amount, small coins being an exception. (Previously you were allowed 250/–.) Within East Africa, as far as Kenya is concerned, you can carry 100/– only, but this may be liable to seizure in the other two countries. Traffic in Uganda and Tanzania shillings is not allowed; the three currencies lost their interchangeability in 1971. East African traveler's checks are the best way to carry local money.

Once you have changed dollars or whatever to Kenya shillings, they are acceptable as payment for all bills in Kenya except for air tickets to points outside Kenya (unless you have the pink bank-exchange slips) or in payment for any goods you may import into Kenya.

Under no circumstances rip up or destroy any Kenya currency.

While there is an active black market in Kenya, foreign currencies may legally be changed only in places displaying a license to accept foreign currency—that is, all banks, most hotels, and a few other places. The Central Bank of Kenya warns that jail sentences may be imposed on those who change money illegally at Asian shops or wherever. A few tourists have been nabbed for dealing with moneychangers who approached them on the street.

Vehicle Documents

If you are driving a car registered outside East Africa, you will need a Carnet de Passages en Douanes (triptyque) issued by a recognized auto club. The carnet will be stamped at the first frontier post in East Africa and the exit *souche* at the last border point. You don't need a carnet if driving an East Africa-registered car between the countries.

A non-East African vehicle needs, within seven days of arrival, an International Circulation Permit, issued free by the Licensing Officer, Road Transport Branch, Gill House, Government Road, Box 30440, Nairobi; tel. 26624. You have to present ownership papers, carnet or customs duty receipt, and insurance certificate.

All vehicles have to be covered by third-party liability insurance. Short-term insurance never seems to be purchasable at the border, but it can be easily, though not inexpensively, bought in Nairobi. While there are many insurance companies in Nairobi, the Automobile Association's agent is J. H. Minet & Co. (K) Ltd., 5th floor, New Stanley House, Kaunda St., Box 20102, Nairobi; tel. 28861.

You can drive in Kenya on an International Driving Permit, or your own state or national license for 90 days if it is endorsed by the Road Transport Branch.

Finally, all vehicles not registered in Kenya should carry an approved nationality plate ("USA," "D," or whatever).

Firearms

Rifles, guns, and a limited amount of ammunition are allowed into Kenya duty-free, but police permits are necessary before they are released by customs. Fully automatic or semiautomatic rifles or shotguns are prohibited. Hunting safari firms will arrange all the necessary import papers. Inquiries: Central Firearms Bureau, Box 30263, Nairobi.

Getting to Kenya

By Air

Nairobi's Embakasi Airport is served by East African Airways (EAA), Aeroflot, Air France, Air India, Air Madagascar, Air Malawi, Air Zaire, Alitalia, Austrian Airlines, British Airways (BOAC), British Caledonian, Egyptair, El-Al, Ethiopian Airlines, KLM, Lufthansa, Olympic, Pan American, PIA, Sabena, SAS, Somali Airlines, Sudan Airways, Swissair, and Zambia Airways.

From Europe: From London: British Airways 11Xwk (incl 3X nonstop), Zambia Airways 1Xwk, British Caledonian 4Xwk, Sudan Airways 1Xwk, EAA 10Xwk (incl 1X nonstop). From Frankfurt: Lufthansa 2Xwk (nonstop), EAA 1Xwk. From Rome: Alitalia 3Xwk (nonstop). From Paris: Air France 2Xwk. There are also flights 1X or 2Xwk from Zurich, Geneva, Athens, Amsterdam, Munich, Copenhagen, Vienna, Brussels, Moscow, and Nicosia.

From the U.S.: From New York: Pan Am 2Xwk.

From other African countries: From Dar es Salaam: EAA 28Xwk. From Entebbe: EAA 13Xwk (11X nonstop). From Johannesburg: British Airways 7Xwk, Alitalia 1Xwk, Lufthansa 2Xwk, SAS 1Xwk, Olympic 2Xwk, El-Al 1Xwk, Swissair 1Xwk (all but Swissair nonstop). From Lusaka: Zambia Airways 6Xwk (4X nonstop), EAA 3Xwk (1X nonstop), Alitalia 1Xwk (nonstop). From Addis Ababa: Ethiopian Airlines 3Xwk, EAA 3Xwk (all nonstop). From Blantyre: Air Malawi 3Xwk, EAA 1Xwk (all nonstop). From Cairo: Egyptair 2Xwk (1X nonstop). From the Seychelles: British Airways 3Xwk, British Caledonian 1Xwk (all nonstop). From Tananarive: Air Madagascar 1Xwk, Air France 1Xwk (nonstop). There are also flights to Nairobi from Tanga, Arusha, Zanzibar, Mauritius, Kinshasa, Bujumbura, Kigali, Mogadishu, Majunga, Accra, Douala, Dakar, Monrovia, and Lagos.

From elsewhere: There are flights from Bombay, Aden, Karachi, Jeddah, and Tel Aviv.

Mombasa (Port Reitz International Airport) is served directly by German charters, will soon be served directly from other points outside East Africa.

There are weekly charter flights from London to Nairobi; see p. 52.

Sample fares, one-way, economy/tourist class, valid for a year, to or from Nairobi, are listed below only as an indication of current fares (Feb. 1974), which are structured by, and change fairly often at the whim of, IATA, partially in response to international monetary and fuel crises. (Add 20% to figures below to get approximate early 1975 fares.)

from/to Nairobi	U.S. dollars	Kenya shs.	other currency
Addis Ababa	120	855	E$248
Arusha	22	160	T.shs. 160
Blantyre	146	1,113	MK125
Cairo	315	2,249	Eg. £137
Chicago	685–735	5,143–5,516	
Dar es Salaam	64	455	T.shs. 455
Entebbe	46	330	U.shs. 330
Frankfurt	503	3,592	DM1251
Johannesburg	209	1,494	R144
Kinshasa	274	1,958	Zaires 137
London	503	3,592	£201
Lusaka	156	1,113	ZK100
Montreal	666–712	4,754–5,088	Can.$635–680
New York	643–693	4,810–5,183	
—14/45-day excursion fare (round-trip)	927–1,000	6,396–6,900	
Paris	499	3,565	FF2,299
Rome	464	3,311	Lire 257,200
San Francisco/Los Angeles	819–869	5,651–5,996	
Seychelles	166	1,188	S.Rs. 889
Zanzibar	58	415	T.shs. 415
Zurich	499	3,565	SF1,559

Excursion fares (which allow two stopovers between New York and Nairobi) are generally available on most routes. Always check with a travel agent about the current applicable fares.

Airports

Embakasi Airport, 13 km south of Nairobi, is the main airport, completed in its present form in 1957. In 1973 the government let the first contract for a $45.7 million expansion which will essentially create a new airport perhaps as early as 1976, solidifying Nairobi as East Africa's gateway. The present terminal has the Simba Restaurant and Bar (credit: DC), outdoor flight observation deck (admission –/50), snack bar, bookshop, curio shop, Barclays Bank (8:30 A.M.–midnight all week), duty-free shop, hotel reservations desk, information counter (tel. 82111, ext. 801, 802), airline information desk (tel. ext. 570, 574), Kenatco taxi service, and an Avis car-hire counter.

East African Airways has a 5/– bus service to the downtown terminal on Koinange St., several blocks from the major hotels. Terminal tel. 29291. You should pay no more than 25/– for a taxi to a downtown hotel from the airport.

Nairobi's Wilson Airport, Langata Road, is used by light aircraft, including flying safaris.

Mombasa's international airport is Port Reitz Airport, 13 km northwest of downtown on the mainland. It, too, is undergoing an expansion program, costing $31 million, to result in an airport capable of taking jumbo jets by 1976.

There is an EAA bus to the downtown terminal on Kilindini Road, tel. 21251. A taxi should cost 25/– into town.

Kenya has a few airfields with paved landing strips, but safari lodges, isolated hotels, and such have dirt or grass landing strips.

Departure tax: Kenya levies a 20/– departure tax on those leaving the country. Have this fee with you in shillings when you check in.

By Boat

Mombasa is the main Eastern African port served by freighters and one passenger line (Lloyd Triestino). Details, p. 53. You can get to Kenya from neighboring countries by irregular coastal boats, and from Uganda or Tanzania across Lake Victoria on the M.V. *Victoria,* an East African Railway steamer; see p. 324. Last, but scarcely least, you can sail between Mombasa and the Persian Gulf in an Arab dhow, schedule depending on the season. Trip takes 10–14 days, costs about 250/–. You take your own food, sleep on deck. Good luck.

By Train

You can take the train from Uganda and Tanzania into Kenya, with through service on East African Railways from several points. There's twice-a-week through service from Dar es Salaam and Tanga to Nairobi or Mombasa, but Dar–Nairobi takes just half an hour less than two whole days. EAR has daily service Kampala–Nairobi taking 24 hours (overnight, arrival in the afternoon). There is first-, second- and third-class service; first-class cars have two passengers in a compartment, and second-class six passengers, while third-class has no compartments, just benches. Bedding can be hired for 7/– on unbroken journeys. Some trains have dining cars with breakfast 7/–; lunch 10/–; dinner 11/–.

Sample fares (first-, second- and third-class fares in that order): Dar–Nairobi—169/–; 88/10; 30/60. Dar–Mombasa—138/80; 72/20; 25/40. Kampala–Nairobi—106/50; 55/40; 19/90.

Inquiries address, p. 103.

By Bus

There is fast bus service by East African Road Services from Tanzania (Dar es Salaam, Arusha, Moshi) and Uganda (Kampala) to Nairobi and Mombasa. Service and fares are as follows: *Dar–Nairobi* 3Xday; 18½-hr trip; fare—57/50. *Moshi–Arusha–Nairobi* 2Xday; 6½–8½-hr trip; fare—12/50 from Arusha; 17/– from Moshi. *Arusha–Moshi–Mombasa* 2Xday; 7½–10-hr trip; fare—17/– from Arusha; 14/– from Moshi. *Kampala–Nairobi Express* 2Xday; 13–15-hr trip; fare—41/– night; 38/– day. *Kampala–Kisumu–Nairobi* daily; 20½-hr trip; fare—18/50 to Kisumu; 32/50 to Nairobi. Inquiries address, p. 103.

There is also frequent service on small bus lines from Dar to Tanga and Mombasa, fare about 30/–; inquire in Dar.

Merali Bus Services (Box 366, Arusha; tel. 2137) has a daily service Moshi–Arusha–Nairobi. Fare is 12/50 second class, 20/– first class from Arusha; 16/– and 25/– from Moshi.

By Car

There are two main paved roads into Kenya, one each from Uganda and Tanzania on the following routes: Kampala–Jinja–Tororo–Eldoret–Nakuru–Nairobi (our Route K-10), and Arusha–Namanga–Nairobi (Routes T-2 and K-5). Other routes are mostly dirt even if well traveled.

Secondary routes from Tanzania are Moshi–Taveta–Voi–Nairobi (Routes T-4, K-4, K-1), which has a dirt section in the middle between Taveta and Voi; Tanga–Horohoro–Mombasa (Routes T-5 and K-3), of which the Tanzania section is poorly maintained dirt while the section in Kenya is tarred; and Seronera (Serengeti)–Keekorok (Masai

Mara)–Narok–Nairobi (Routes T-1 and K-6), which is good dirt. All can be traveled in ordinary sedans.

The roads from Ethiopia and Somalia are scarcely tourist routes. We've seen VW Bugs and Citroëns on the Addis Ababa road, so you need not have a four-wheel-drive. We know nothing about the Somalia road except that few travelers bother with that country. There is little land commerce besides nomadic herdsmen between Sudan and Kenya.

Trip times: Arusha–Nairobi, 4–5 hrs. Tanga–Mombasa, 3–4 hrs. Kampala–Nairobi, 1½ days. Dar–Nairobi, 2 days. Addis–Nairobi, 4–6 days.

Gasoline: Plenty available on the primary and secondary routes from Uganda and Tanzania. You'd better carry a couple of jerrycans Addis–Nairobi.

Border posts on the main routes: from/to Uganda—Malaba and Busia. From/to Tanzania—Isabania, Keekorok (Masai Mara–Serengeti), Namanga, Loitokitok, Taveta (Tsavo), Lunga Lunga–Horohoro (coast). From/to Ethiopia—Moyale–Moiale. From/to Somalia—Libol (on Garissa-Kismayu road).

Getting around Kenya

Travel Agents

Some of the main travel agencies in Kenya that make hotel, transport and car-hire, and tour bookings are as follows:

In Nairobi: A. A. & Bunson Travel Service Ltd., Westlands (near Agip Motel), Box 45456, tel. 46826; cable EASIGO. *ETCO Ltd.* (Express Transport), Express House, Kimathi St., Box 40433, tel. 34722; cable EXPRESTRAVL. American Express representative. Also storage, shipping, customs clearance, transport. *Kearlines Ltd.* (J. W. Kearsley Ltd.), Town House, Wabera St. (at Kaunda St.), Box 41564, tel. 32299; cable KEARLINES. Also moving, storage, packing, transport, shipping. *Mackenzie Dalgety Travel Services Ltd.*, Hamilton House, Wabera St., Box 30345, tel. 23131. *Mitchell Cotts & Co. (EA) Ltd.*, Cotts House, Wabera St., Box 30182, tel. 32320.

In Mombasa: Bunson Travel Service (Msa) Ltd., Southern House, Kilindini Road, Box 84965, tel. 20501; cable EASIGO. *ETCO Ltd.*, Nkrumah Road, Box 90631, tel. 24094; cable ETCO. American Express representative. *Kearlines Ltd.*, Kilindini Road (opposite EAA terminal), Box 84675, tel. 20304; cable KEARLINES.

Student and low-budget travel companies in Nairobi: Odd Jobs

(Rent-a-Car Tours & Safaris), Koinange St. at Monrovia St., Box 46590, tel. 25498. Odd Jobs helps low-budgeters share cars, find cheap hotels, etc. *Sun Sea & Safari Ltd.*, Kimathi St. (near Caltex), Box 20393, tel. 29488. SS&S handles charter flights, other low-budget travel. *Sunshine Holidays Ltd.*, Cabral St., Box 44099, tel. 25427. Charter flights. *Acharya Travel Agency*, Government Road, Box 42590, tel. 20960. Charter flights.

Credit card acceptance: Bunson—DC. ETCO—AE. Kearlines—BA.

By Air

East African Airways serves only four towns: Nairobi, Mombasa, Malindi, and Kisumu. Services and fares (tourist-class) are as follows: *Nairobi–Mombasa*—39Xwk incl 11X nonstop on DC-9, 8X on a Friendship 27; regular fare—240/– one-way; 432/– return; 258/– 6-day excursion, return. *Nairobi–Malindi*—daily; fares same as to Mombasa. *Mombasa–Malindi*—daily; regular fare—80/– one-way; 144/– return; 85/– 6-day excursion, return. *Nairobi–Kisumu*—4Xwk; regular fare—180/– one-way; 324/– return; 200/– 6-day excursion, return.

Caspair and its associate Tic-Air offer scheduled charter service between Nairobi and Kisumu (5Xwk), Nakuru (2Xwk), Eldoret (5Xwk), Kitale (5Xwk), Ferguson's Gulf (3Xwk), Juba, Sudan (1Xwk) and Garissa (2Xwk), and between Malindi and Lamu, Hola and Garissa (2Xwk). Return fares from Nairobi: to Eldoret—324/–; Ferguson's Gulf—720/–; Juba—1,530/–; Kitale—360/–; Kisumu— 324/–; Nakuru—238/–; Garissa—315/–; Malindi—690/–; Lamu— 530/–. Tic-Air operates daily Malindi–Lamu; day return—150/– per seat; monthly return—250/–; one-way, depending on demand—80/–.

Air Kenya has regular once-daily service to the remote locations in northern Kenya. One-way fares (approx.) from Nairobi to: Meru Mulika—189/–; Nanyuki—133/–; Samburu—196/–; Marsabit— 308/–; Loyengalani (3Xweek only)—343–; Ferguson's Gulf (4Xwk only)—371/–; Eliye Springs—364/–.

Airstrip-hotel transfers are easily arranged with the air charter company.

Caspair and Air Kenya inquiries, see under "By Air Charter."

Airline Offices

East African Airways (operated by the three countries) has the following offices in Kenya: Sadler House, Koinange St., Box 41010, Nairobi; tel. 29291 (also city offices in Hilton, Mama Ngina St.; Inter-Continental Hotel, City Hall Way; Mackinnon Bldg., Kimathi St., all same tel. 29291. Embakasi Airport, tel. 82111. Jubilee Insurance Bldg., Kilindini Road, Mombasa; tel. 21251/9. Mombasa Port Reitz Airport, tel. 73501. Also Eldoret, Kitale, Kisumu. Overseas offices: 600 Fifth Ave., New York 10036; tel. (212) 757-2327; 46 Albemarle St., London W1; tel. 01-493 8973; also Addis Ababa, Athens, Bombay, Copenhagen, Frankfurt, Lusaka, Paris, Rome, Stockholm, Zurich, and many Tanzania and Uganda locations.

Other airlines with offices in Nairobi are: *Air Madagascar*, Hilton Hotel, Mama Ngina St., tel. 25286. *Air Malawi*, Hilton Arcade, tel. 22221. *Air Zaire*, Shretta House, Kimathi St., tel. 24786. *British Airways (BOAC)*, Prudential Assurance Bldg., Wabera St., tel. 34362. *British Caledonian*, Mutual Bldg., Kimathi St., tel. 23071. *Egyptair*, balcony floor, Shankardass House, Government Road, tel. 26821/2/3. *Ethiopian Airlines*, Mansion House, Wabera St., tel. 26631. *Pan American*, Commerce House, Government Road, tel. 23581. *Sudan Airways*, Mondlane St., tel. 25129. *TWA*, IPS Bldg., Kimathi St., tel. 32334/5. *Zambia Airways*, Hilton Arcade, Mama ‧Ngina St., tel. 24722. Others with Nairobi offices are Aeroflot, Air Canada, Air France, Air India, Alitalia, El-Al, Japan Air Lines, KLM, Lufthansa, Olympic, PIA, Qantas, Sabena, SAS, and Swissair. Most airlines with offices at Embakasi Airport are on extensions of tel. 82111.

By Air Charter

Firms having small planes for hire (23 models in all) include: *Air Kenya Ltd.* (formerly Wilkenair), Wilson Airport, Box 30357, Nairobi; tel. 21063; cable WILKENAIR; also in Mombasa (Box 84700, tel. 73320), Malindi, and Nanyuki. *Amphibians Air Charters*, Ukunda, Box 80607, Mombasa; tel. Diani 5. *Caspair Ltd.*, Commercial Bank House, Standard St., Box 42890, Nairobi; tel. 29161/2; cable INTECCO. *Kenya Air Charters Ltd.*, Wilson Airport, Box 30603, Nairobi; tel. 23863; cable AIRBORNE. *Safari Air Services Ltd.*, Wilson Airport, Box 41951, Nairobi; tel. 27225; cable ATOMIC. *Tic-Air Charters Ltd.*, Box 146, Malindi; tel. 153; Nairobi office with Caspair. *Z. Boskovic Air Charters Ltd.*, Wilson Airport, Box 45646, Nairobi; tel. 27008; cable BOSKY.

Most single- and twin-engine models, seating up to 9 passengers, are available. Prices are standard. Examples: Piper Cherokee 180D single-engine (3 passengers)—2/60 per mile. Piper Comanche twin

(3 pax) and Cherokee 6 single and Cessna 206 single (both 5 pax)—4/– per mile. Piper Aztec and Seneca twins, Beechcraft Baron twin and Cessna 310 twin (all 5 pax)—5/– per mile. Piper Navajo twin and Cessna 401 twin (both 7 pax)—6/– per mile.

Demurrage or waiting time, roughly equivalent to a rent-a-car's minimum daily mileage, is also standard, with single-engine planes charged at 1/– per mile for less than 300 miles per day averaged over the charter period, and twins 2/– per mile for less than 400 per day.

Since planes fly a beeline, you can figure out mileages from place to place by using a ruler on a map, or you can write and ask for the estimated cost of an itinerary.

Air charter firms can set up ground transportation in game parks and elsewhere.

By Train

The main line of East African Railways in Kenya goes from Mombasa through Voi to Konza, Nairobi, Gilgil, Nakuru, Eldoret, Tororo, and on to Kampala. A main branch goes from Nakuru to Kisumu, and there are branch lines and connections from Voi to Moshi, Konza–Magadi, Nairobi–Nanyuki, Gilgil–Thomson's Falls (Nyahururu), and Eldoret–Kitale. A line is proposed from Konza (south of Nairobi) to Kikuletwa (east of Arusha), which will pass through Amboseli and go past Kilimanjaro.

Undoubtedly the best, most traveled (by tourists), and most famous run is Nairobi–Mombasa, a 14-hr (overnight) service with trains leaving either city at 6:30 P.M. and arriving at the other at 8 or 8:30 the next morning. Accommodations in first class are comfortable and the multiple-course meals quite good.

To get to Lake Victoria to catch the round-the-lake cruise, there is a daily overnight service Nairobi–Kisumu. For lake service, see p. 324.

Rail buffs like the numerous steam engines used by EAR on many services. A very scenic trip is Nairobi–Nakuru, going down the Escarpment and across the Rift Valley; this service is twice daily and takes about 6 hours.

Specimen fares (first-, second-, and third-class fares, respectively): Nairobi–Mombasa—82/50; 42/90; 15/80. Nairobi–Nakuru—28/–; 14/60; 6/60. Nairobi–Kisumu—61/80; 32/20; 12/30.

You can take a car with you on the train, with single charge Nairobi–Mombasa being 243/60, return 456/80.

For bedding and meal charges, see p. 98.

The railway terminal in Nairobi (tel. 21211) is at the end of Government Road, south of Haile Selassie Ave., about 1 km from the Hilton. In Mombasa, the train station (tel. 21211) is at the north end of Haile Selassie Road, 1½ km from the downtown hotels.

Inquiries: Chief Traffic Manager, Box 30006, Nairobi; tel. 21211. Reservations in Nairobi and Mombasa at same tel. 21211.

By Bus

Bus transport in Kenya is the people's transport, and buses go simply everywhere, even to remote places like Marsabit, because people live there. The basic networks are operated by East African Road Services and Kenya Bus Services.

EARS runs daily buses on the following routes: Nairobi–Mombasa (3Xday), 8–10½ hrs. Nairobi–Nyeri, 4 hrs. Nairobi–Nyeri–Naro Moru–Nanyuki–Meru, 8 hrs. Nairobi–Naivasha–Nakuru–Kericho–Kisumu, 8½ hrs. Nairobi–Kisumu Express, 6½ hrs. Nairobi–Nakuru–Molo–Eldoret–Soy–Kitale, 9 hrs. Nairobi–Thomson's Falls (Nyahururu), 4 hrs.

Specimen fares: Nairobi–Mombasa—25/50 day; 27/50 night. Nairobi–Nakuru—11/50. Nairobi–Kisumu—20/–. Nairobi–Kitale—24/–. Nairobi–Nanyuki—14/– or 15/80. Mombasa–Malindi—11/25 (maximum). Mombasa–Lamu—22/50 (maximum).

Most long-distance buses leave Nairobi from the Country Bus Terminal, Pumwani Road. You can get there by walking west on Haile Selassie Ave. or south on River Road to a big traffic circle, then taking Pumwani Road between the market and the mosque. The Kenya Bus terminal in Mombasa is on Jomo Kenyatta Ave.

Inquiries and booking: *EARS,* Racecourse Road, Box 30475, Nairobi; tel. 26155, 23476/8. *Kenya Bus Services,* Box 40238, Nairobi; tel. 23286, 50304. *EARS,* Mombasa, tel. 23643. *Coast Bus Service,* Box 82414, Mombasa; tel. 20916; Nairobi, tel. 29494. *Goldline Ltd.,* Box 10098, Nairobi; tel. 25279; Box 83542, Mombasa; tel. 20027.

EARS timetable and fares booklet costs 2/–.

By Tour Bus

Ordinary transport, generally in minibuses, is easily arranged to Treetops, The Ark, Mountain Lodge, and Salt Lick Lodge. When you make your booking at the Nairobi reservation office concerned, you can reserve a minibus seat (sample—100/– round-trip to Mountain Lodge) if you don't have your own transport.

United Touring Co. (p. 114) virtually has scheduled coach service Nairobi-Mombasa to Voi town, Taita Hills Lodge, Maneaters Motel, Mtito Andei, and Hunter's Lodge, with connecting links to Kilaguni, Ngulia, Voi, and Salt Lick Lodges. Nairobi to Mtito Andei—105/–, to Voi 145/–, to Taita Hills Lodge—160/–. Mombasa to Voi—70/–. Mtito Andei to Kilaguni—45/–, to Ngulia—70/–.

By Long-Distance Taxi

One of the cheapest transport services is Peugeot long-distance taxi: from Nairobi to Mombasa (four times daily) is only 50/– per person, 55/– for the front seat (or 250/– for the whole car). *Mombasa Peugeot Service,* Duruma Road at Latema Road, Box 45274, Nairobi; tel. 27858, 24977 (Mombasa tel. 25551), also operates Nairobi–Malindi and Mombasa–Malindi. *Rift Valley Peugeot Service* (RVP), Box 354, Nakuru; tel. 2513 (Nairobi tel. 26374), has similarly inexpensive service between Nairobi, Nakuru, Kisumu, Eldoret, Kitale, and Kericho. Lamu's New Mahrus Hotel operates a Mombasa–Lamu taxi service; details from Box 25, Lamu, or Box 81564, Mombasa, tel. 20816.

By Rent-a-Car

We devote much space below to a cost analysis of rent-a-cars and car-hire firms, both in Nairobi and in Mombasa, because we believe renting a car offers the best opportunity for a traveler to see more of East Africa at lower cost than taking a package tour, especially if he is willing to camp and/or stay at inexpensive (but still tourist-class) hotels. (See pp. 38–43.)

As is the case in the U.S., car-hire firms charge such a variety of rates that it is difficult to compare them. Only a couple companies pay for gasoline. Some companies offer a better deal for long safaris, by charging no daily rate or offering a percentage off the total cost.

We can't really recommend any particular firms. Americans will immediately recognize the names of Hertz and Avis—but it so happens these two charge more than just about any other company, which is surely the worst exploitation of Americans we've heard of. Some might say that the car-hire firm with the cheapest rates might have cheap to worthless vehicles. Well, perhaps so.

In the two lists below, 14 of the most common vehicles available in Nairobi and 8 of the most available in Mombasa are listed in order of their relative cost. Following the vehicle model is the *average price for one day, 100 km (62 miles)*—say, around Nairobi and into the game park. Following that are the names of the *firms with the cheapest rates* for that car, then the *lowest rate available* for one day, 100 km.

For more on car hire in Africa, see pp. 30–33.

NAIROBI CAR HIRE

VW Beetle: Average for one day, 100 km—85/45. Cheapest rates—Aladin's, Jambo, Odd Jobs, Kenya Mystery, Habib's. Lowest rate available—53/70. *Toyota Corolla:* Average—86/50. Cheapest—Kenya Mystery, Bestway. Lowest—65/–. *Ford Escort:* Average—92/85. Cheapest—Jambo, Park, Habib's, Bestway, Ivory. Lowest—62/–. *Datsun 1200:* Average—94/75. Cheapest—Kenya Mystery, Across Africa, Warthog, Archer's. Lowest—65/–. *Fiat 124:* Average—98/95. Cheapest—Bestway, Lighttours, Nyati. Lowest—82/50. *Toyota Corona:* Average—112/50. Cheapest—Thorn Tree, Rhino. Lowest—100/–. *Datsun 1600:* Average—113/20. Cheapest—Kenya Mystery, Warthog, Across Africa. Lowest—85/–. *Peugeot 404:* Average—115/40. Cheapest—Bestway, Odd Jobs, Habib's. Lowest—92/50. *Ford Capri:* Average—131/65. Cheapest—A. A. & Bunson, Car Hire Services. Lowest—125/–. *Mercedes 200:* Average—165/55. Cheapest—Warthog, Odd Jobs, Jambo, Car Hire Services. Lowest—121/50. *VW Bus:* Average—169/65. Cheapest—Jambo, Odd Jobs, Kenya Mystery, Warthog. Lowest—124/–. *Land-Rover 109:* Average—180/50. Cheapest—Jambo, Warthog, Archer's, Habib's, Odd Jobs. Lowest—124/–. *Toyota Land Cruiser wagon:* Average—190/–. Cheapest—Car Hire Services, Donald Vincent. Lowest—180/–. *VW Camper:* Average—191/10. Cheapest—Aladin's, Jambo, Warthog. Lowest—108/50. Other popular cars are Renault 12, Peugeot 204, 304, and 504, Datsun 1000 and 1800, Ford Cortina and Toyota Crown.

Car-hire firms in Nairobi are listed below in categories according to the relative costliness of the vehicles they rent. Addresses not given here can be found on pp. 113–114.

Low rates: Aladin's Car Hire Ltd., Industrial Area, Box 44670, tel. 26070, 34315. *Bestway Tours & Safaris Ltd.* Prices up to medium-low. *Jambo Safaris Ltd. Kenya Mystery Tours (Car Hire) Ltd.*, Phoenix House Arcade, Kenyatta Ave., Box 30442, tel. 21366. *Rent-A-Car Tours & Safaris (Odd Jobs)*, Koinange St. at Malik St., Box 46590, tel. 25498. *Park Tours & Safaris Ltd.*

Medium-low rates: Across Africa Safaris Ltd. East African Sun Sea & Safari Ltd. (same as Low Budget Car Hire & Tours Ltd.). *Habib's*

Cars, University Way, Box 48095, tel. 23816/7; also at Agip House, Haile Selassie Ave., tel. 20463. *Ivory Safaris (Car Hire) Ltd.,* Bruce House, Standard St., Box 45209, tel. 23013. *Light Transport Co. Ltd. (Lighttours). Sunny Safaris Ltd. Tayler's Travel Center Nairobi Ltd.,* Ambassadeur Hotel, Government Road, Box 42578, tel. 22838. *Thorn Tree Safaris Ltd.* Prices to medium-high. *Travel Experts (K) Ltd.,* Caltex House, Koinange St., Box 43912, tel. 26581/2; cable TRAVELEX-PRESS. *Warthog Safaris Ltd.,* 1st floor, National House, Koinange St., Box 43010, tel. 32483. Many rates low.

Medium-high rates: A. A. & Bunson Travel Ltd., Westlands (near Agip Motel), Box 45456, tel. 46826. Gasoline included. *Avis (Kenya Rent A Car Ltd.),* Kenyatta Ave. (opp. 680 Hotel), Box 49795, tel. 21324/5/6/7; cable AVISCARS; also stations at Nairobi Hilton and Embakasi Airport. *Car Hire Services Ltd.,* Vic Preston's Shell Station, University Way, Box 42304, tel. 22813/4. Gasoline included. *Donald Vincent Tourism Ltd.,* Standard St., Box 41746, tel. 28705/6/7; cable VINSURE. Some high rates. *Larsen's Car Hire & Transport Ltd.,* corner Bunyala and Baricho roads, Industrial Area, Box 46164, tel. 58864. Some high rates. *Mini-Cabs & Tours Co. Ltd. Nyati Tours Ltd. Pollmans Tours & Safaris Ltd.,* International House, Mama Ngina St., Box 45895, tel. 27250; cable ORYX.

High rates: Eboo's Tours & Safaris Ltd. Hertz (United Touring Co. Ltd.). Gasoline included.

Widely varying rates: Archer's Cabs Ltd., Simonian Caltex Station, Koinange St., Box 40097, tel. 20289; also in Mombasa (Agip station, Kilindini Road, tel. 25362). *Rhino Safaris Ltd. Tembo Tours & Safaris Kenya Ltd.*

MOMBASA CAR HIRE

Mini-Moke (resembles a beach buggy): Average for one day, 100 km—90/10. Cheapest rates—Palm, Jubilee, Bellerive, Avenue, Highways. Lowest rate available—75/–. *Ford Escort:* Average—91/75. Cheapest—Bellerive, Palm, Highways, Avenue. Lowest—75/–. *VW Beetle:* Average—92/45. Cheapest—Palm, Jubilee, Bellerive, Avenue, Jumbo, Highways. Lowest—75/–. *Toyota Corolla:* Average—93/90. Cheapest—Jumbo, Palm, Bellerive. Lowest—77/50. *Fiat 124 or 125:* Average—115/45. Cheapest—Avenue, Kuldip's. Lowest—96/40. *Peugeot 404:* Average—119/70. Cheapest—Jubilee, Palm, Highways, Avenue. *Mercedes 200 or 220:* Average—159/55. Cheapest—Jumbo, Avenue. Lowest—110/–. *VW Bus:* Average—176/10. Cheapest—Avenue,

Pollmans. Lowest—152/80. Other popular cars are Morris 1000, Renault 12, Ford Cortina and Taunus 17M, Peugeot 204 and family saloon, Toyota Crown.

Car-hire firms in Mombasa are listed below in categories according to the relative costliness of the vehicles they rent. Addresses not given here can be found on p. 114.

Low rates: Avenue Motors. Bellerive Tours, Kilindini Road, Box 83003, tel. 20651. *Highways Ltd. Jubilee Tours & Safaris Ltd. Jumbo Tours Ltd. Palm Tours Ltd.* •

Medium rates: Pollmans Tours & Safaris, Rex Hotel, Kilindini Road, Box 84198, tel. 23825. *Savannah Travel & Tours Ltd.*

Medium-high rates: Kuldip's Touring Co., Kilindini Road (next to Rex Hotel), Box 82662, tel. 25928.

Medium-high to high rates: Bigways Tours & Safaris Ltd. Gasoline included. *Lemax Tours & Travel Ltd.,* off Kilindini Road (opp. Anglo Swiss Bakery), Box 83611, tel. 23674. Gasoline included. *Nyati Tours Ltd.,* Kilindini Road (opp. Kenya Commercial Bank), Box 81763, tel. 23943. *Palmtree Tours & Safaris Ltd.*

High rates: Avis (Kenya Rent a Car Ltd.), Kilindini Road, Box 84868, tel. 23048, 20465; also at Port Reitz Airport, same tel. *Hertz (United Touring Co. Ltd.).* Gasoline included.

Driving in Kenya

Drive on the left, overtake on the right. Give way to traffic coming from the right, except when you're in a traffic circle, in which case keep going.

Gasoline price, availability: see p. 84.

Auto club: The Automobile Association of East Africa (AAEA), founded in 1919, has about 15,000 members and offers the usual range of services, including 50/– towing vouchers, road emergency service (in Nairobi, Mombasa, Mtito Andei, and Lanet, near Nakuru), road information, and route planning. There is supposedly some kind of reciprocation with other motor clubs, but this doesn't get you very much. Membership: 75/– per year plus 25/– entrance fee. The AA has a brand-new headquarters at Westlands shopping center, Box 40087, Nairobi; tel. 46826. The club sells many road maps and miscellaneous publications. The AA's *Official Touring Guide to East Africa* (price 22/–), issued yearly, is about 270 pages of badly organized information, some outdated, some useless, some useful. AA accepts DC credit card.

Vehicle servicing, repairs, spare parts: Nairobi's mechanics are probably the best in Eastern Africa. Service is also fairly cheap compared with stateside prices, though parts can be awfully expensive. Nairobi, Mombasa, and quite a few of the smaller towns like Kisumu, Nakuru, Nyeri, and Nanyuki have many car dealers, servicing agents, and garages that can work on most makes, including the following: *Land-Rover* and *Volkswagen* (Cooper Motor Corp., Haile Selassie Ave., Box 30135, Nairobi; tel. 35043; also Mombasa, Nakuru, Kisumu), *Toyota* (Westlands Motors Ltd., Koinange St., Box 30515, Nairobi; tel. 35833; Toyota agents elsewhere), *English Fords* (Hughes Ltd., Kenyatta Ave., Box 30060, Nairobi; tel. 27091; also Mombasa, Kisumu, Nakuru, Eldoret, Nanyuki, Meru, Nyeri, Thika, Thomson's Falls, Kericho), *Datsun* and *Mercedes* (D. T. Dobie & Co. Ltd., College House, Koinange St., Box 30160, Nairobi; tel. 31505; also Mombasa, Nakuru, Nanyuki, Malindi, and elsewhere), *Peugeot* (Marshalls Ltd.), as well as Fiat, Volvo, Isuzu, Jeep, BMC, Jaguar, Rolls, Mazda, BMW, Alfa, Subaru, and nearly every other kind of car—but no GM cars and few American models.

Used vehicles: Most private sellers advertise in the *East African Standard;* used-car dealers advertise in the *Sunday Nation.* Among the dealers in Nairobi are: Twiga Motors Ltd., Box 41793; Car Dealers (1969) Ltd., Box 45450; Nairobi Car Sales, Box 46908; Sembi Car Sales Ltd., Box 43283; and Joginder Motors Ltd., Box 43177. The new-car dealers listed above also have used models. The big tour companies, especially UTC (p. 114), automatically sell off VW buses and other tour vehicles after a certain number of miles, and advertise periodically. On the subject of buying a car in East Africa, see p. 45.

Spare parts: Hughes Ford Motorist's Supermarket, Kenyatta Ave., Nairobi, has a good range of automobile accessories and equipment.

Camping in Kenya

Of the five countries in this book, Kenya is the most developed for tent camping, which is by far the most economical kind of accommodation. Camp fees are rarely more than 5/– per person, compared with 40 times that amount for a game lodge. Among the game parks, camping is allowed at all but Nairobi National Park and Shimba Hills, and at Lake Nakuru, tenting is the only way to stay inside the park (a delight it is, too). In some parks—Tsavo West and East, Samburu, Amboseli, Meru—an alternative is to stay in a self-service *banda,* which is a simply furnished cottage equipped with all the crockery and utensils you'll need, with bedding, lantern, and stove available, if you need them, for a small fee. The charge is generally 35/– per person. Hardly a soul has a trailer or camper in East Africa.

Camping equipment is manufactured or imported by the following Nairobi firms: *Low & Bonar (E.A.) Ltd.,* Dundee House, St. John's Gate (near Donovan Maule Theatre), Box 42759, tel. 26791. *Ahamed Bros. Ltd.,* Kenyatta Ave. (at Muindi Mbingu), Box 40254, tel. 29467/8. *Alibhai & Co. Ltd.* (tents, tarps only), Aliken House, Kimathi St., Box 40201, tel. 20571. Catalogs available from all three. Camping equipment purchased new is not cheap, but if you're planning a longish safari, it may be more worthwhile than renting. Some sample Low & Bonar prices, early 1974:   8-by-6-foot "Karen" single-roof ridge tent, 760/– or 985/–. 9-by-14-foot "Namanga" double-roof ridge tent with fly and veranda, 2,610/– or 3,525/–. 9-by-13-foot "Malindi" metal-frame tent, 1,785/–. 7-by-5½-foot "Kwikpich Major" mountain tent, 530/–. Camp beds, 175/– to 345/–. 2-in-thick foam mattress, 38/– to 66/–. Camp tables, 67/– to 245/–. Camp chairs, 80/– to 345/–.

You can rent camping equipment in Nairobi but the cost is high for a long safari. Firms renting equipment: *Low & Bonar* (tents, beds, tables, chairs). *Ahamed Bros.* (all items). *Thorn Tree Safaris* (same gear as Ahamed at higher rates). *Nairobi Afri-Gas Distributors,* Kimathi St., Box 44922, tel. 27641 (propane lanterns, stoves only). Sample Ahamed rates, early 1974: 12-by-8-foot "Kongoni" tent with veranda, 50/– for first day, 12/50 each following day. 2 camp beds, 2 chairs, 1 table—15/– first day, 10/– each following day. Bedding for 2 persons—50/–, then 20/–. Double-burner stove—16/–, then 4/–. Camp lantern—same. Kitchen box (including stove, lantern, cooler box, utensils, etc.)—65/–, then 20/–.

Camping gas (propane): BP, Caltex, Esso, Agip, and Shell have propane camping gas in large rental tanks; Camping Gaz (Bleuet) propane cylinders are available everywhere (Low & Bonar, for instance), Primus cylinders infrequently (Agipgas on Cabral St. has Primus Grasshopper butane cylinders). White gas is *not* available, but kerosene is. Propane cylinders with American fittings can be refilled (5/– per kilo) at Essogas, Tom Mboya St.

Camping safari packages: You don't have to do the whole thing from scratch. Ahamed Bros. has camping safari package tours of 4, 8, 12, and 16 days, chauffeur-driven, with a camp attendant for an extra charge, for $25 to $40 per person per day (see package KP-37). UTC-

Hertz (address p. 114) in early 1974 started a do-it-yourself program in which 2 persons get unlimited mileage (you pay gas) on a Datsun 160B or similar, with camping equipment, for a shade under $25 per person per day, minimum 3 days, restricted to Kenya and Northern Tanzania (on going into Tanzania with camping equipment, see important note on p. 320). Thorn Tree Safaris (p. 114) also has a camp-and-drive plan.

Kimbla Safaris (Bruce Travel in Nairobi) has low-budget camping safaris—950/ – one week, 1,900/– two weeks, 2,550/– three weeks.

Safaris and Safari Operators

The personally tailored, professionally guided luxury safari is the most comfortable and most expensive—and perhaps most satisfying—way to see East Africa. As the center of the tourist industry, Nairobi has a multitude of safari operators who can arrange just about any kind of safari, trip, tour, adventure, or expedition. If you have no special interest, you can perhaps combine a package tour to accessible places (accommodations in hotels and lodges) with a private safari to remote places (accommodations in a luxury tented camp); a safari firm will arrange both tour and safari.

If you're not sure what you want, write to a safari firm with a brief list of your needs and requirements, and most will advise you. Mike Higginson's Contact (E.A.), "consultant and agent for safaris and all matters relating to travel in East Africa," has wide connections and will give advice and information on types and costs of various safaris, without charge, and also handles bookings.

Most safaris run their own movable luxury tented camp with a minimum camp staff of six; clients are usually transported by Land-Rover or Land Cruiser (air charters are often used for long hauls), and the camp is moved by a huge truck. Everything is done in style, like a hunting safari, with deep-frozen meat, iced champagne, and hot baths—and you pay for it. The usual three- or four-week safari on your own itinerary costs an average of $230 a day for a party of two; we took six safari operators at random, and their daily charge ranged from $185 to $285. Less expensive safaris are possible, but the clients may be more crowded in a Land-Rover, tents may be smaller, camp staff fewer. Len Bonnett, for instance, runs low-budget safaris at 400/– per day (100 miles) plus 140/– per person. Even with the higher-priced firms, the more people, the cheaper the head. You can get a modest camping safari on your own itinerary, with a professional guide, at $60 to $90 per person per day for a group of 10 to 20—not too different in price from the common or garden package tour. Make your demands and budget known to a safari firm, and it will tell you if it can be done.

Most hunters will take out photo safaris for about $250 for one client per day (another $30 for a second person). Remember that not every safari is led by a professional hunter (white or otherwise).

Safaris *must* be booked about a year in advance.

Highly rated by other tour and safari firms are Ker, Downey & Selby; Abercrombie & Kent; and Root & Leakey's Photo Safaris.

Following is a list of safari operators, all in Nairobi unless indicated otherwise: *Abercrombie & Kent Ltd.*, 4th floor, Vedic House, Mama Ngina St., Box 20224, tel. 34955/6/7; cable KENTOURS. *African & Alpine Safaris Ltd.* (David Lockwood), with Abercrombie & Kent. *African Travel Advisors Ltd.* (Eddie Hoarau), International House, Mama Ngina St., Box 47775, tel. 35406; cable AFTRAV; group charter and tours. *John Alexander Safaris*, Box 125, Nanyuki; tel. 2175. *Bateleur Safaris Ltd.*, Nairobi Hilton mezzanine floor, Box 42562, tel. 27048; cable BATELEUR. *Len Bonnett*, Box 15516, tel. Langata (89) 558. *Bruce Safaris (E.A.) Ltd.*, Box 40662, tel. Karen (88) 2617; cable BRUSAFARI. *Contact (E.A.)* (Mike Higginson), Box 40603, tel. 65060; cable HABARI. *Ellerman Lines Safaris Ltd.*, City House, Wabera St., Box 49952, tel. 29566; cable ELLERSAF. *Karl Pollman & Gordon Harvey Wildlife Safaris*, Mutual Bldg., Kimathi St., Box 44239, tel. 21768; photographic. *Ker, Downey & Selby Safaris Ltd.*, New Stanley House, Standard St., Box 41822, tel. 20667. *Kimsafaris Ltd.*, Box 277, Nanyuki; tel. Nairobi 66783; cable KIMPEN Nanyuki; personal safaris. *Kingfisher Safaris*, Box 29, Malindi; tel. 123; deep-sea fishing, Tana River safaris. *Kudu (Africa) Ltd.*, Express House, Kimathi St., Box 72450, tel. 31063; cable KUDU; photographic. *Mountain Safaris* (Clive Oak-Rhind), Box 49706, tel. 26608. *Root & Leakey's Photographic Safaris Ltd.*, Ottoman Bldg., Kenyatta Ave., Box 43747, tel. 27217; cable ROOTLEAKEY. *Safari-Camp Services* (Dick and Diana Hedges), Box 44801, tel. Langata (89) 483; group and student camping safaris. *Safari Desk Ltd.* (J. N. Hopcraft), IPS Bldg., Kimathi St., Box 47272, tel. 25525; cable SAFARIDESK; scientific safaris. *Safaris Unlimited* (Rift Valley Horse Safaris; Tony Church), with Abercrombie & Kent, tel. 32132; cable ANTHILL; horse and pony treks. *Sirikwa Safaris* (Tim and Jane Barnley), Box 332, Kitale; tel. 408; Western Kenya, NFD specialists. *Snowline Safaris* (Mrs. Amber May), Box 2, Nanyuki; tel. 2193; horse and zebroid safaris on Mount Kenya, in NFD. *Trans-Africa Guides* (Robert A. Lowis), Box 49538; cable RALOWIS; personal safaris. *Wilderness Trails* (Peter Hankin), with African & Alpine Safaris; walking safaris in NFD. *Zanji Safaris,* Standard Bldg., Wabera St., Box 20033, tel. 29662; cable ZANJI.

(Note: Because of on-going "Kenyanization" of the tourist industry, some European-owned and operated firms may cease operations or change hands.)

Package Tours and Tour Operators

The number of all-inclusive package tours around Kenya and East Africa, starting from Nairobi and Mombasa, is almost beyond count. Some 40 tour operators operate more than 600 tours—on more than 120 different itineraries—within Kenya from Nairobi alone. Not all the tours are good, but not all of them are the usual rush-rush group trips from this blurred sight to that bland hotel, although such tours tend to be the most numerous and the cheapest. What is certain is *there is a more varied offering among Nairobi tour operators than you will ever find in the U.S.* For this reason, we list many reliable tour operators and a good selection of what they have to offer. As suggested in the Introduction, there is no reason why you and a U.S. travel agent (or, better, one in Nairobi), armed with the listing below and what you have sent away for, cannot put together an economy safari almost on your own itinerary—combining short package tours with trips by rent-a-car (chauffeured if you like) to less common destinations, or even with a short professionally guided luxury safari to some special place or to do something different. An organization like Contact (address p. 111), or big safari firms, will help you do this.

Operators highly rated by other tour and safari firms are Thorn Tree (which has staff members who speak French, German, Spanish, and Scandinavian languages) and United Touring Company (UTC, connected with Thos. Cook), the biggest tour operator, with a fleet of 500 vehicles in Eastern Africa. Operating basically inexpensive tours are East African Sun Sea & Safari, Jambo, and Odd Jobs. Generally expensive tours are run by Archer's, Eboo's, Flamingo, Kearline, Silver Spear (American Express), and UTC. Prices of other operators vary. Specialized companies worth mentioning are Kenya Mystery and Yellow Bird, which have several "meet the people" tours.

In 1973 Kenya had no fewer than 192 tour operators, along with

111 car-hire companies and 41 safari outfitters. Only a fraction of the number of tour operators—mainly long-established firms—are listed here.

Nairobi tour companies: *Across Africa Safaris Ltd.,* Bruce House, Standard St., Box 49420, tel. 21593; cable ACROSAFARI. *Ahamed Bros. Ltd.,* Kenyatta Ave. at Muindi Mbingu St., Box 40254, tel. 29467/8; cable OUTFITTING. *Archer's Tours,* New Stanley Hotel, Kenyatta Ave., Box 40097, tel. 20289 (also at Inter-Continental Hotel). *Bestway Tours & Safaris Ltd.,* Woolworths Bldg., Kenyatta Ave. (at Kimathi St.), Box 44325, tel. 22297; cable BESTWAY. *Big Five Tours & Safaris Ltd.,* 2d floor, Gilfillan House, Kenyatta Ave. (opp. 680), Box 10367, tel. 29803. *Dik Dik Safaris Ltd.,* Hilton Hotel, Box 43004, tel. 23268; cable DIKDIK. *East African Sun Sea & Safari* (Low Budget Car Hire & Tours Ltd.), Tubman Road (top of Kimathi St.), Box 20393, tel. 29488, 35365/6. *Eboo's Tours & Safaris Ltd.,* Corner House, Kimathi St., Box 30098, tel. 21666; cable EBOOS. *Equatorial Travels Ltd.,* Ambassadeur Hotel, Government Road, Box 49021, tel. 28185; cable ESCORTS. *Flamingo Tours Ltd.,* Livingstone House, Kimathi St., Box 44899, tel. 28961; cable FLANTOURS. *Hansmax Tours & Travel Ltd.,* 1st floor, National House, Koinange St., Box 28703, tel. 27432. *Ivory Safaris Ltd.,* Mama Ngina St., Box 45209, tel. 26623; cable IVORARI. *Jambo Safaris Ltd.,* Silopark House, City Hall Way, Box 30495, tel. 22096; cable JAMBO.

Kearline Tours, Wabera St., Box 41564, tel. 32299; cable KEARLINES. *Kenya Mystery Tours Ltd.,* Koinange St., Box 30442, tel. 21366/7. *Kibo Safaris Ltd.,* Malika House, Muindi Mbingu St., Box 42518, tel. 20850; cable KIBOSAFARI. *Lighttours,* Esso House, Mama Ngina St., Box 18133, tel. 29110; cable LITRACO. *Malaika Safaris Ltd.,* Kenyatta Ave. at Kimathi St., Box 45351, tel. 23916; cable MALAIKA. *Mini-Cabs & Tours Ltd.* (Micato Safaris), Government Road (opp. Kenya Cinema), Box 43374, tel. 29058/9. *Nilestar Tours* (*International*) *Ltd.,* Kenyatta Ave., Box 42291, tel. 29501. *Nyati Tours Ltd.,* Hilton Hotel Arcade, Box 46841, tel. 26896. *Park Tours & Safaris,* Kenyatta Ave. at Government Road, Box 43671, tel. 24421. *Paw-Line Tours & Travel Ltd.,* Silopark House, City Hall Way, Box 40109, tel. 23495.

Rhino Safaris Ltd., Hilton Hotel Bldg., City Hall Way, Box 48023, tel. 28102; cable RHINOKAMP. *Silver Spear Tours Ltd.,* Express House, Kimathi St., Box 40500, tel. 20333; cable SILVERTOUR. *Sunny Safaris Ltd.,* Banda St., Box 74495, tel. 27659; cable SUNNY. *Tembo Tours & Safaris* (*K*) *Ltd.,* Hilton Hotel Arcade, Box 46595, tel. 29573; cable

SIMBA. *Thorn Tree Safaris Ltd.*, Esso House, Kaunda St., Box 42475, tel. 25641; cable ACACIA. *Travel Bureau Ltd.*, Cariboo House, University Way, Box 43230, tel. 21716/7. *United Touring Co. Ltd.* (UTC), Travel House, Muindi Mbingu St., Box 42196; cable OVERTOURCO. *Yellow Bird Safaris (K) Ltd.*, Vedic House, Mama Ngina St., Box 49975, tel. 22753; cable YELLOWBIRD.

Mombasa tour companies: *Avenue Motors Tours & Safaris,* Kilindini Road, Box 83697, tel. 25126. *Bigways Tours & Safaris Ltd.*, Kilindini Road, Box 80184, tel. 20283. *Highways Ltd.*, Kilindini Road (by the Tusks), Box 84787, tel. 26886. *Jubilee Tours & Safaris,* Kilindini Road (opp. EAA terminal), Box 80645, tel. 24189. *Jumbo Tours Ltd.*, Kilindini Road, Box 80717, tel. 20418. *Palm Tours Ltd.*, Kilindini Road (opp. Uhuru Garden), Box 81045, tel. 21152. *Palmtree Tours & Safaris Ltd.*, Bishop Mwangombe Road (off Kilindini Road), Box 85215, tel. 21041. *Savannah Travel & Tours Ltd.*, Kilindini Road (opp. Jubilee Insurance), Box 83644, tel. 23456; cable STAT. *United Touring Co. Ltd.* (UTC), Castle Hotel, Kilindini Road, Box 84782, tel. 20741.

Air safari operators, all in Nairobi: *Kenya Flying Safaris Ltd.*, Silopark House, Mama Ngina St., Box 40696, tel. 20545; cable FLYSAFE (associated with Z. Boskovic Air Charters). *Lindblad Travel & Tony Irwin (E.A.) Ltd.*, Norwich Union House, Mama Ngina St., Box 48559, tel. 34411; cable HYRAX. *Safari Air Services Tours Ltd.*, Wilson Airport, Box 41951, tel. 27225; cable ATOMIC.

Note: "Kenyanization" may cause changes in ownership and management of European safari and tour operators.

We cannot list all the packages and all the prices; if we did, it would be a forbidding catalog. What we do below is list some of the basic itineraries, most of the single-destination tours, and some special (and possibly expensive) tour-safaris.

Many tours are "seat in car" tours—packages with a set itinerary that have frequent departures and operate on a basis of seven people in a minibus. These are more likely to be bargains than private-car tours—packages with no schedule of departures, in which the price depends on how many are taking the tour. Anyone can set up a private car tour on his own itinerary, but we list some tours below so you can see how much, approximately, one would cost to certain destinations. Seat in car is abbreviated SIC, private car is PC. If tour operators are not mentioned, the tour is offered by several firms. Some packages below are run by safari firms (listing pp. 111–112).

Prices are changeable; see pp. 84–85.

The list is divided into two sections: packages around Kenya and those around East Africa. Tours begin in Nairobi, Mombasa, and Malindi, but we list none from Malindi.

PACKAGE TOURS AROUND KENYA

From Nairobi:

KP-1: *Nairobi City Tour*. National Museum, Snake Park, shopping areas, Parliament, sometimes Arboretum. 2–3 hrs. 21/– to 30/– SIC, 45/– each of 2 in PC. *Bomas of Kenya* is sometimes included; alone, cost is 45/– to 65/–.

KP-2: *Nairobi National Park*. Usually incl Animal Orphanage; run midmorning and midafternoon (Yellow Bird has a 6–10 A.M. tour, 70/– each of 3). 3-hr tours: 40/– to 45/– SIC; 60/– to 100/– each of 2 in PC. 4 hrs: 42/– to 60/– SIC. 5 hrs: 60/– to 65/– SIC. Thorn Tree and Jambo 5-hr tours incl coffee at the Hippo Pool. (Incidentally, 3 hrs is too short; make it 4 or 5, and go in the morning.) The park tour is often combined with Masai Lodge lunch and Masai *manyatta* dancing/Bomas of Kenya.

KP-3: *Nairobi by Night*. Paw-Line's 200/– tour incl African dancing, barbecue, International Casino floor show and gambling, and a nightclub. Odd Jobs' 105/– tour incl drink at Panafric's Simba Grill, Starlight Club, Casino dinner, show, and gambling; 75/– tour incl Swiss Grill dinner and dancing instead of Casino. Travel Bureau's 100/– SIC tour incl Casino dinner and show, Hallian's nightclub, Swiss Grill. Kenya Mystery—140/–.

KP-4: *Nairobi City and Racecourse Sunday Tour*. Sunny Safaris runs this 89/– tour 10:30 A.M.–6:30 P.M. on race-meeting Sundays, incl Museum, Snake Park, Racecourse lunch and tea.

KP-5: *Ngong Hills*. Archer's has a half-day circuit for 154/– per car. Malaika's 4-hr tour is 70/– each of 2 in PC. Sun Sea has 5-hr city and Ngong Hills tour for 60/– SIC.

KP-6: *Ngong Hills–Rift Valley–Kitengela Game Conservation Area Horse Safaris*. Safaris Unlimited has bush-trained, crossbred Arab and Somali horses for safaris and treks. 1 day of horsing around in the Ngongs is 161/– each of 2; 119/– each of 4. A 2-day trip (overnight in tented camp) to Ngongs and Kitengela game area (borders Nairobi

Park) costs 637/– each of 2; 322/– each of 4. Pony treks are 91/– each of 2 for half-day to Ngongs. 3-hr Kitengela ride is 65/– each of 2.

KP-7: *Limuru High Country–Rift Valley Viewpoint.* 3 hrs: 50/– to 110/– SIC; 65/– to 105/– each of 2 in PC (Lighttours, Eboo's, Malaika). Archer's charges 154/– per car.

KP-8: *Lake Nakuru.* Day trip incl Escarpment, sometimes Lake Naivasha tea, Menengai Crater. 140/– to 175/– SIC; 320/– to 375/– each of 2 in PC.

KP-9: *Lake Naivasha.* Day trip for 100/– to 175/– SIC (Lighttours, Jambo, Across Africa, Tayler's, Ivory).

KP-10: *Masai Tour.* 4–5-hr tour incl visit to *manyatta* for Masai dancing, refreshments at ranch. 85/– to 105/– SIC. Daily departures. Very popular tour. Nyati, Kenya Mystery, Bestway, Malaika incl Lake Nakuru in day tour, 230/– to 350/– each of 2. Malaika doubles up Masai and Kamba (below) for 85/–; Kenya Mystery puts together Masai and Kikuyu (below) for 140/–, also has a new Masai tour to Lukenya Hill Caves and dancing at Small World Country Club.

KP-11: *Kikuyu Tour.* Specialty of Kenya Mystery. (1) Kikuyu–Ngure Safari—dancing (4 teams), visit to market, Harambee School, handicraft center, fields and intensive farm, tea with Kikuyu, local food; 2d and 4th Sundays; 85/– SIC. (2) Limuru Safari incl tea and coffee estates, market, farming college, dancing; Wednesdays; 85/– SIC. (3) Rioki coffee estate, dancing, market, *shamba* (farm); 85/– SIC. (4) "An African Evening" to Kikuyu farm, Ndumo and Kibata dancing, barbecue dinner, and local foods; 85/– each of 15–19 people. Yellow Bird has a different Kikuyu tour to Githunguri and Kabaa, with dancing; Sundays, Mondays; 77/– each of 3.

KP-12: *Kamba Tour.* Kenya Mystery tour incl sisal plantation, Kamba dancing, handicraft shop, school choir, local food, mixed farm; 1st and 3d Sundays; 85/– SIC. Yellow Bird offers a "Kamba Evening" at the Small World Country Club, with dancing, barbecue; Tuesdays, Thursdays; 70/– each of 3.

KP-13: *Treetops or The Ark.* Go up to Outspan or Aberdare Country Club for lunch, overnight at Treetops or The Ark, return to Nairobi in morning. 322/– to 392/– SIC; 588/– to 714/– each of 2 in PC. Treetops etc., plus Mount Kenya Safari Club lunch: 540/– to 650/– each of 2–3 (Lighttours, Thorn Tree, Ivory, Rhino). Some tour operators may offer a stop at the new Village Dancers Hotel for lunch, dancing show, for 60/– extra.

KP-14: *Secret Valley Lodge.* Up to Sportsman's Arms, overnight at

Secret Valley, back to Nairobi in morning. No lunch, no shower. 322/– to 450/– SIC; 650/– to 689/– each of 2 in PC.

KP-15: *Mountain Lodge.* No lunch. Proceed directly to lodge, return Nairobi in morning. 322/– to 380/– SIC.

KP-15A: *Salt Lick Lodge.* 2-day tours to new game-viewing lodge near Tsavo costs about 580/– SIC.

KP-16: *Mount Kenya Safari Club.* Overnight in luxury. 525/– to 588/– each of 2–3. Lighttours has day trip for 350/– each of 2 in PC.

KP-17: *Masai Mara.* 2 days: 500/– to 560/– SIC; 742/– to 895/– each of 2 in PC. 3 days: 707/– to 1,089/– each of 2–3.

KP-18: *Amboseli.* 1-day express: 300/– to 440/– SIC. 2 days (overnight plus 1 game run, sometimes 2): 420/– to 460/– SIC; 826/– to 1,065/– each of 2 in PC. Extra days 175/– to 245/– each of 2–3. Economy tours (overnight in Namanga or Ol Tukai Lodge) also available.

KP-19: *Tsavo West.* 1-day express: 300/– to 350/– SIC. 2 days (overnight Kilaguni or Ngulia plus 1 game run, maybe 2): 420/– to 460/– SIC; 620/– to 895/– each of 2 in PC. Extra days: 175/– to 245/– each of 2–3. Economy tours (overnight Tsavo Inn): 462/– each of 3 (Thorn Tree Safaris). UTC has 4-day PC tour, nights at Ngulia, for 1,610/– each of 2. 1-day air express to Kilaguni plus game run: 425/– each of 4 (Caspair).

KP-20: *Tsavo Tsafaris.* Overnight(s) at Cottars Camp in luxury, game viewing in Tsavo East concession area. 2 days: 658/– each of 3; extra days 245/– (Thorn Tree). 3 days: 875/– each of 2 (Jambo).

KP-21: *Samburu.* 3 days: 920/– to 930/– (Tembo, Big Five). 1-day air express: 450/– to 595/– each of 4 (Safari Air, Caspair).

KP-22: *Meru.* 3 days: 735/– each of 2 (Jambo).

KP-23: *Marsabit Air Safari.* 2 days: 1,330/– to 1,400/– each of 2–4 (Lighttours, Safari Air).

KP-24: *Lake Rudolf Air Safari.* To Eliye Springs. 2 days: 750/– each of 4–5 (Caspair), 1,285/– or 1,505/– each of 2 (Lighttours, Safari Air). 3 days: 1,655/– each of 2 (Lighttours).

KP-25: *Lake Baringo Air Safari.* 1-day express: 460/– to 630/– each of 2–4 (Lighttours, Safari Air).

KP-26: *Mount Kenya.* 1–4-day walks (Naro Moru River Lodge) and 1–4-day horse and zebroid safaris (Snowline Safaris). See p. 249 for details.

KP-27: *Lamu Air Safari.* 1-day express: 680/– each of 4 (Caspair). 2 days: 900/– to 1,100/– (Kenya Mystery, Caspair, Ahamed Bros.).

4 days: 1,400/– to 1,500/– (Travel Bureau, Ahamed Bros.), 5,705/– each of 2 (Abercrombie & Kent).

KP-28: *Treetops or Ark or Secret Valley or Mountain Lodge, and Mount Kenya Safari Club.* Overnight at each. 760/– to 924/– SIC.

KP-29: *Treetops or Other and Lake Nakuru.* 2 days (1 night): 490/– to 665/–. 3 days (2 nights): 678/– to 910/–.

KP-30: *Treetops or Other and Samburu.* 3 days: 930/– to 1,170/–. 4 days: 1,218/– each of 3 (Thorn Tree).

KP-30A: *Treetops* or *Ark, Samburu, and Meru.* 6 days: 2,212/– SIC; 3,157/– each of 2 in PC (UTC).

KP-31: *Treetops or Other, Mount Kenya Safari Club, and Samburu.* 4 days: 1,330/– to 1,640/– each of 2. 5 days: 1,050/– SIC (Archer's), 1,785/– to 1,970/– each of 2 in PC, 1,520/– each of 3 (Thorn Tree).

KP-32: *Treetops or Ark, Mount Kenya Safari Club, Samburu and Nakuru.* 4 days: 1,687/– each of 2 in PC (African Roadways). 5 days: 1,876/– each of 2 in PC (Kearlines).

KP-33: *Treetops, Nakuru, and Masai Mara.* 4 days: 1,290/– to 1,835/– (Eboo's, Travel Bureau, Nyati).

KP-34: *Treetops or Ark, Nakuru, Kericho, and Masai Mara.* 5 days: 1,610/– each of 2 (Across Africa).

KP-35: *Treetops or Other, Mount Kenya Safari Club, Samburu, Nakuru, Kericho, and Masai Mara.* 7 days: 2,340/– each of 2 (Lighttours).

KP-36: *Treetops, Mount Kenya Safari Club, Samburu, Lake Rudolf, Masai Mara, and Tsavo East Air Safari.* 15 days: 8,345/– each of 2 (Safari Air).

KP-37: *Ahamed's Camping Safaris.* Naivasha, Masai Mara, Nakuru, Aberdares, and Outspan lunch; 4 days; 1,820/– each of 2. Same plus Naro Moru, Meru, Mount Kenya Safari Club, and Samburu; 8 days; 3,640/– each of 2. All above plus Nairobi, Nairobi Park, Nairobi by Night, Tsavo West, Malindi, Gedi, and Tsavo East; 12 days; 5,460/– each of 2. Foregoing plus Lamu by air; 16 days; 7,280/– each of 2. Chauffeur-driven. (See also pp. 109–110.)

KP-38: *Tsavo East and West.* 3 days: 700/– each of 4 (Safari Air), 1,190/– or 1,246/– (Silver Spear). 6 days: 854/– each of 2 in PC (UTC).

KP-38A: *Tsavo and Taita Hills.* UTC has several half-day tours, each 135/– (min. 2 persons) from Taita Hills Lodge, visiting Tsavo West or East, WWI battlegrounds, Ponderosa Game Sanctuary, or the

Taita Hills. Full-day tour visits Tsavo West, Lakes Jipe and Chala, and the battlegrounds—245/– each of 2.

KP-39: *Amboseli and Tsavo West.* 2 days (overnight Tsavo): 441/– to 749/– SIC. 3 days (overnight each park): 700/– to 910/– SIC; 812/– to 1,575/– each of 2 in PC.

KP-40: *Amboseli, Tsavo West, Salt Lick Lodge, and Tsavo East.* 4 days: 1,771/– each of 2 in PC (African Roadways).

KP-41: *Tsavo and Beach.* 4 days: 1,113/– each of 4 (Jambo).

KP-42: *Diani Beach and Lamu Air Safari.* 2 days: 980/– each of 4–5 (Caspair).

KP-43: *Marsabit and Samburu by Road.* 5 days: 2,940/– each of 2 (Travel Bureau).

KP-44: *Lake Rudolf and Marsabit Air Safari.* 3 days: 2,000/– each of 2 (Lighttours).

KP-45: *Wajir and Lamu Air Safari.* 2 days: 1,400/– (Kenya Mystery).

KP-46: *Sankuri Tented Camp–Tana River Canoe Safari.* 3 days: 3,376/– for 2 by road to Garissa; 3,776/– for 2 by air (African & Alpine Safaris).

KP-47: *Tana River Tented Camp Safari.* 3 days: 1,106/– each of 2 (Silver Spear).

KP-48: *Malindi, Lamu Archipelago and Manda Island Tented Camp Safari.* 9 days: 11,410/– each of 2; 16 days: 17,710/– each of 2 (Abercrombie & Kent).

KP-49: *Wilderness Trails Walking Safari.* In area 10 miles west of Isiolo. Movable camp. Designed after successful Zambia foot safaris. 5 days: 5,600/– for 1–2; 7,200/– for 3; 8,000/– for 4 (Wilderness Trails). Also 2, 3, 4 days.

KP-50: *Northern Frontier Trek Safari.* Luxury tented camps, hunterguide, two vehicles. 10 days: 15,645/– for 1; 8,351/– each of 2; 5,922/– each of 3 (African & Alpine Safaris).

KP-51: *Northern Frontier Camping Safari.* 15 days to Meru, Marsabit, Lake Rudolf, and Maralal: 6,202/– each of 5 in vehicle, min. group of 10 (UTC).

KP-52: *Northern Frontier Camel and Zebroid Safari.* 4 days: 1,400/– each of 2 (Snowline Safaris).

KP-53: *Northern Frontier Camel Trek Safari.* 8 days from near Barsaloi to near Serolevi: 6,496/– each of 4; 4,879/– each of 8 (African & Alpine Safaris).

From Mombasa:

KP-54: *Mombasa City Tour.* Wailing Mosque, Ivory Room, Fort Jesus, Old Town, Bazaar, Kamba carvers. 3 hrs: 30/– to 55/– each of 2–3. Bigways' 6-hr tour incl drive up North Coast, 98/– each of 2.

KP-55: *Malindi, Gedi, Watamu Marine National Park, Giriama Dancing.* 1 day: 180/– to 245/– each of 2.

KP-56: *Shimba Hills and South Coast.* 1 day: 150/– to 170/– each of 2.

KP-57: *Lamu Air Safari.* 1 day: 370/– (UTC–Air Kenya).

KP-58: *Tsavo East.* 1 day: 275/– to 350/– each of 2; 336/– to 431/– each of 2 in PC.

KP-59: *Malindi and Tsavo East.* 2 days: 700/– each of 2 (Avenue Motors).

KP-60: *Tsavo East and West.* 2 days: 455/– to 700/– each of 2; 784/– to 1,010/– each of 2 in PC. 3 days: 850/– each of 2 (Highways). 6 days: 903/– each of 2 in PC (UTC).

KP-61: *Amboseli, Tsavo East and West.* 3 days: 1,225/– each of 2 (Avenue Motors); 1,351/– each of 2 in PC (African Roadways).

KP-62: *Tsavo West, Taita Hills, and Salt Lick Lodge.* 2 days: 678/– each of 2 (Highways). 3 days (overnights at each lodge): 917/– each of 2 (Highways).

PACKAGE TOURS AROUND EAST AFRICA

From Nairobi:

KP-63: *Ngorongoro Air Safari.* 1 day: 805/– each of 4 (Safari Air).

KP-64: *Serengeti Air Safari.* 1 day: 325/– (Travel Experts); 763/– each of 4 (Safari Air).

KP-65: *Ngorongoro and Lake Manyara.* 4 days: 1,130/– (Nyati, Big Five); 1,490/– each of 2 in PC (Lighttours).

KP-66: *Serengeti and Masai Mara.* 3 days: 920/– (Ivory).

KP-67: *Masai Mara, Serengeti, and Mount Kenya Safari Club Air Safari.* 7 days: 5,271/– each of 2 (Flamingo).

KP-68: *Treetops, Masai Mara, Serengeti, Lake Manyara, and Tarangire Air Safari.* 5 days: 5,177/– each of 2 (Kenya Flying Safaris).

KP-69: *Amboseli, Lake Manyara, and Ngorongoro.* 4 days: 1,260/– to 1,400/– SIC; 1,610/– to 2,044/– each of 2 in PC. 5 days: 1,450/– to 1,600/– SIC; 1,910/– to 2,365/– each of 2 in PC.

KP-70: *Amboseli, Kilimanjaro (Marangu), and Tsavo West.* 4 days: 945/– to 1,050/– SIC; 1,260/– to 1,770/– each of 2 in PC.

KP-71: *Arusha, Lake Manyara, Ngorongoro, and Amboseli.* 5 days: 990/– to 1,600/– SIC; 2,345/– each of 2 in PC (Travel Bureau).

KP-72: *Amboseli, Kilimanjaro (Marangu), Tsavo West, and Mombasa Beach.* 6 days: 1,277/– to 1,540/– SIC each of 4 (Jambo, Big Five, Dik Dik, Tembo).

KP-73: *Amboseli, Shira Plateau, Osirwa Cottages, Kilimanjaro (Marangu), Tsavo West, and Tsavo Tsafaris Camp.* 6 days: 1,960/– each of 2 in PC (Across Africa).

KP-74: *Amboseli, Lake Manyara, Ngorongoro, Kilimanjaro (Marangu), and Tsavo West.* 6 days: 1,277/– each of 4 SIC (Jambo); 2,681/– to 2,856/– each of 2 in PC (Travel Bureau, African Roadways).

KP-75: *Amboseli, Arusha National Park, Kilimanjaro (Marangu), and Tsavo West.* 5 days: 1,022/– each of 4 (Jambo).

KP-76: *Masai Mara, Serengeti, Olduvai Gorge, Ngorongoro, and Lake Manyara.* 6 days: 1,680/– to 1,950/–; 7 days: 1,950/– (Hansmax, Kibo).

KP-77: *Camping Safari to Masai Mara, Serengeti, Ngorongoro, Lake Manyara, and Mombasa Beach.* Small crowd in Land-Rover, rough camping. Mostly under ages 30–35. Bargain safari is part of Siafu London–Nairobi expedition. 14 days: 1,176/– (Bruce Travel, Koinange St., Box 40809, Nairobi; tel. 26794).

KP-78: *Masai Mara, Lake Manyara, Tarangire, Treetops, Mount Kenya Safari Club, Samburu, Naivasha, Nairobi, and Malindi Air Safari.* 15 days: 9,467/– each of 2 (Kenya Flying Safaris).

KP-79: *Masai Mara, Serengeti, Fort Ikoma, Lake Lagarja, Ngorongoro, Tarangire, Amboseli, Tsavo West, Nakuru, Naivasha, Treetops or Ark, and Samburu by Road.* 20 days: 7,845/– each of 2 (Safari Air).

KP-80: *MILK RUN (Masai Mara, Serengeti, Olduvai Gorge, Ngorongoro Crater, Lake Manyara, and Amboseli).* 7 days: 1,960/– to 2,434/– SIC; 2,580/– to 2,980/– each of 2 in PC (African Roadways, Lighttours). 8 days: 2,800/– to 3,925/– each of 2 in PC (Bestway, Ivory, Travel Bureau).

KP-81: *Milk Run plus Tsavo West.* 8 days: 2,790/– each of 3 (Thorn Tree). 9 days: 3,575/– each of 2 in PC (Eboo's).

KP-82: *Milk Run plus Kilimanjaro (Marangu) and Tsavo West.* 9 days: 2,044/– to 2,780/– (Jambo, Big Five, Nilestar, Nyati, Ivory).

KP-83: *Milk Run plus Arusha National Park, Mount Meru Game Sanctuary, and Tsavo West.* 11 days: 3,950/– each of 3 (Thorn Tree).

KP-84: *Milk Run plus Arusha, Kilimanjaro (Marangu), Tsavo West, and Mombasa Beach.* 11 days: 2,800/– (Dik Dik).

KP-85: *Milk Run plus Lake Nakuru and Treetops.* 8 days: 3,455/– each of 2 in PC (Eboo's). Plus Mount Kenya Safari Club, 9 days: 3,800/–. Plus Safari Club and Kericho, 12 days: 4,490/–.

KP-86: *Milk Run plus Kericho, Lake Nakuru, Mount Kenya Safari Club, Treetops or Ark, Tsavo West and East.* 13 days: 4,326/– each of 2 in PC (Silver Spear).

KP-87: *Milk Run plus Kericho, Treetops or Secret Valley, Mount Kenya Safari Club, Samburu, Kilimanjaro (Marangu), and Tsavo West.* 18 days: 7,182/– each of 2 in PC (Archer's).

KP-88: *Ker, Downey & Selby Deluxe Camping Safari Packages.* These ritzy tours, guided by a professional hunter, take in game parks, with accommodations in luxury tented camps, at a price 10 percent less than a special itinerary. 9 days to Masai Mara, Serengeti, Lake Manyara: 20,755/– for 2. 11 days to same plus Amboseli: 25,225/– for 2. 14 days to Masai Mara, Serengeti, Ngorongoro, Lake Manyara, Amboseli: 32,340/– for 2. 20 days to same plus Tsavo West: 46,200/– for 2. 23 days to all above plus Mombasa and Shimba Hills: 48,920/– for 2.

From Mombasa:

KP-89: *Zanzibar Air Safari.* 1 day: 450/– each of 2 (UTC–Air Kenya).

KP-90: *Lake Manyara and Ngorongoro Air Safari.* 2 days: 1,175/– each of 2 (Air Kenya).

KP-91: *Tsavo West and Kilimanjaro (Marangu).* 2 days: 700/– each of 2 in PC (Savannah, Avenue Motors). 3 days: 1,100/– each of 2 in PC (Savannah).

KP-92: *Tsavo East, Lake Manyara, and Ngorongoro.* 4 days: 1,547/– to 1,700/– each of 2 in PC (Highways, Bigways).

KP-93: *Tsavo East, Kilimanjaro (Marangu), Lake Manyara, and Ngorongoro.* 4 days: 1,876/– to 2,065/– each of 2 in PC (Avenue Motors, African Roadways).

Travel by Credit Card

The following Nairobi, Mombasa, and Malindi tour operators, safari firms, car hire companies, air safari operators, and travel agencies accept American Express, BankAmericard/Barclaycard, and/or Diners Club cards as indicated. We list these companies all together because the services offered by many overlap. *A. A. & Bunson*—DC. *Abercrombie & Kent*—AE, BA, DC. *Across Africa*—AE, DC. *African Roadways*—AE. *African Tours & Hotels*—AE, BA, DC. *Air Kenya*—DC. *Avis*—AE, BA, DC, Avis. *Bunson Travel*—DC. *Car Hire Services*—BA, DC. *Donald Vincent Tourism*—DC. *Eboo's*—AE. ETCO—AE. *Flamingo Tours*—DC. *Habib's*—AE. *Hertz*—AE, BA, DC, Hertz. *Highways*—BA, DC. *Jambo*—BA, DC. *Kearlines*—BA. *Kingfisher Safaris*—DC. *Lindblad Travel & Tony Irwin*—BA, DC. *MiniCabs & Tours*—AE, DC. *Nyati*—AE, DC. *Pollmans*—BA, DC. *Rapid Road Services*—AE, BA. *Rhino*—AE, BA, DC. *Root & Leakey's Photo Safaris*—DC. *Safari Air Services*—AE, DC. *Savannah*—BA. *Silver Spear*—AE. *Tembo*—BA, DC. UTC—AE, BA, DC. *Yellow Bird*—DC.

General Information

Language

The official language of Kenya, it was announced in 1973, will be Swahili, but English is likely to remain the most important language for some time to come. The tourist will find English spoken nearly everywhere by someone, while Swahili is understood by all but remote tribes. There is a "pure" Swahili spoken on the coast and in classrooms, a simpler "upcountry" Swahili spoken everywhere else.

Swahili is fairly easy to pronounce. *Every letter should be sounded.* Most of the consonants are the same as in American English, with these exceptions: *g* is always hard, as the *g* in "got"; *dh* is pronounced as *th* in English, as in "this" and "that"; *m* and *n,* when followed by a consonant, as in *mtoto* child), or Ngong, are hummed rather than pronounced. The vowels are pronounced as follows:

a as the *a* in mama
e as the *e* in get, or the *ai* in pail
i as the *ee* in reel
o as the *o* in cold
u as the *u* in crude, or the *oo* in cool

The standard greeting is *jambo* ("hello"). A reply is *jambo sana* (literally "hello very much"; roughly "hi to you, too"). One may then ask *habari?* ("how are you?" or "what's your news?"). The answer, no matter how rotten you feel, should first be *mzuri* ("good"; pronounced like Missouri); you can follow this with *lakini* and relate your problems. Or you can ask in return *habari yako?* ("how are you?"). After the response, business or whatever can proceed.

Here are a few words which may be useful in East Africa:

hello	jambo (JAH-mboh)
how are you?	habari? (hah-BAH-ree)
well	mzuri (mih-ZOO-ree)
thank you	asante (ah-SAH-nteh)
thank you very much	asante sana (ah-SAH-nteh SAH-nah)
good-bye	kwaheri (kwah-HEH-ree)
please	tafadhali (tah-fah-THAH-lee)
bring me	lete (LEH-teh)
I want	nataka (nah-TAH-kah)
food	chakula (cah-KOO-lah)
coffee	kahawa (kah-HAH-wah)
tea	chai (chy)
water	maji (MAH-jee)
beer	beer *or* tembo (TEH-mboh)
milk	maziwa (mah-ZEE-wah)
bread	mkate (MKAH-teh)
meat	nyama (NYAH-mah)
fish	samaki (sah-MAH-kee)
salt	chumvi (CHOO-mvee)
sugar	sukari (SOO-KAH-ree)
hot	moto (MOH-toh)
cold	baridi (bah-REE-dee)
I want a cold beer	nataka tembo baridi (nah-TAH-kah TEH-mboh bah-REE-dee)
yes	ndio (NDEE-yoh)
no	la (lah)
slowly	polepole (POH-leh-POH-leh)
quickly	upesi (OO-PEH-see)
where is . . .	wapi (WAH-pee) . . .
a good hotel?	hoteli mzuri? (hoh-TEH-lee mih-ZOO-ree)
a telephone?	simu? (SEE-moo)
a garage?	garagi? (gah-RAH-gee)
a drugstore?	duka la dawa (DOO-kah lah DAH-wah)
the American consulate?	balozi ya Marekani? (bah-LOH-zee yah mah-ree-KAH-nee)
a police station?	steshini polisi? (stah-SHEH-nee poh-LEE-see)

the main road?	barabara? (BAH-rah-BAH-rah)
the market?	soko? (SOH-koh)
the bus station?	kituo cha basi? (kee-TOO-oh chah BAH-see)
the railway station?	steshini la gari? (stah-SHEH-nee lah GAH-ree)
how much?	ngapi? (NGAH-pee)
I don't understand	sielewi (see-eh-LEH-wee)
left	kushoto (koo-SHOH-toh)
right	kulia (koo-LEE-ah)
one	moja (MOH-jah)
two	mbili (MBEE-lee)
three	tatu (TAH-too)
four	nne (N-neh)
five	tano (TAH-noh)
six	sita (SEE-tah)
seven	saba (SAH-bah)
eight	nane (NAH-neh)
nine	tisa (TEE-sah)
ten	kumi (KOO-mee)
eleven	kumi na moja (KOO-mee nah MOH-jah)
twelve, etc.	kumi na mbili (KOO-mee nah MBEE-lee)
fifty	hamsini (hah-MSEE-nee)
hundred	mia moja (MEE-ah MOH-jah)
toilet	choo (CHOO)
men	wanaume (wah-nah-oo-meh)
women	wanawake (wah-nah-WAH-keh)
my name is . . .	jina langu (jee-nah LAH-ngoo) . . .
what is your name?	jina lako nani? (jee-nah LAH-koh NAH-nee)
I need a guide	nataka mwongozi (nah-TAH-kah mwoh-NGOH-zee)
I want a ticket to Nairobi	nataka tikiti ya Nairobi (nah-TAH-kah tee-KEE-tee yah Nairobi)
what time does the bus leave?	basi yatoka saa ngapi? (bah-see yah-TOH-kah sah NGAH-pee)
what is the fare?	ni bei gani? (nee BEH-ee GAH-nee)
I need a mechanic	nataka mekanika (nah-TAH-kah meh-kah-NEE-kah)

I need a doctor	nataka daktari (nah-TAH-kah dahk-TAH-ree)
may I take photos?	naweza kupiga mapicha? (nah-WEH-zah koo-pee-gah mah-PEE-cha)
today	leo (LEH-oh)
yesterday	jana (JAH-nah)
tomorrow	kesho (KEH-shoh)

A basic book for more phrases and some grammar is *Swahili Phrase Book for Students and Travelers* by T. L. Gilmore and S. O. Kwasa (New York: Ungar, 1963; $4.75). For the more ambitious and studious: *Swahili* ("A Teach Yourself Book") by D. V. Perrott (New York: McKay, 1956; $3.50).

Note: Do *not* use "boy" to call a waiter, or to refer to any African. In Kenya, "steward," "waiter," or even *bwana* ("sir," "mister") is used; in Tanzania *rafiki* ("friend," "comrade") seems *de rigueur*. "Native" is taboo; "Africans," "Kenyans," "blacks," are approved.

Time

East Africa time is three hours ahead of Greenwich Mean Time (GMT plus 3), two hours ahead of British Standard Time and Mid-European Time, eight hours ahead of U.S. Eastern Standard Time, eleven hours ahead of Pacific Standard Time. When it is noon in Nairobi, it is 9 A.M. in London, 4 A.M. in New York, and 1 A.M. in San Francisco.

Weights and Measures

Mainly metric at the market and gas stations and on road signs, though people still talk of miles and feet and pounds.

Electricity

220–240 volts AC, 50 cycles.

Holidays

Jan. 1—New Year's Day. Good Friday. Easter Monday. May 1—Labor Day. June 1—Madaraka Day (anniversary of self-government, 1963). 1st Monday in August—Bank Holiday. Oct. 20—Kenyatta Day (anniversary of the Mzee's arrest Oct. 20, 1952, same day the Emergency was declared). Dec. 12—Jamhuri Day (anniversary of Independence, 1963). Dec. 25—Christmas. Dec. 26—Boxing Day. In addition, Id-ul-Fitr (breaking the fast of Ramadan), a movable holiday, is a public holiday. Id-ul-Azha and Maulidi are observed by Moslems, and Hindus have several holidays also.

Hours of Business

Office and shop hours are generally 8 or 8:30 A.M. to 4:30 or 5 P.M., with Nairobi lunch closing 1–2 P.M., Mombasa 12–2 P.M. Things are generally shut Saturday after 1 P.M. and all day Sunday. However, many shops of all types are open daily until 6 or 7 P.M., and Saturday afternoon and Sunday, either all day or in the morning.

Banks in Nairobi are open 9 A.M.–1 P.M. Monday–Friday; 9–11 A.M. Saturday. Banks in Mombasa are open 8:30 A.M.–12:30 P.M. weekdays; to 11 A.M. Saturday.

Bars generally serve 11–2 and 5–11.

Banks

Barclays Bank International Ltd., main branch, Queensway House, Mama Ngina St., Box 30011; tel. 23161; cable BARCLADOM. Plus Government Road (two), Muindi Mbingu St., Kenyatta Ave., Enterprise Road, Westlands and Embakasi Airport branches; 4 branches in Mombasa, and 36 elsewhere in Kenya. *Kenya Commercial Bank Ltd.,* main branch, Government Road, Box 30081, tel. 20681; cable KENCOM. Plus 5 other branches in Nairobi, 3 in Mombasa, 29 elsewhere. *Standard Bank Ltd.,* main branch, Kenyatta Ave., Box 30001, tel. 35304; cable DERBY. Plus 5 other branches in Nairobi, 3 in Mombasa, 23 elsewhere. *Commercial Bank of Africa,* main branch, Wabera St., Box 30437, tel. 28881; cable COMAFBANK. Also Mama Ngina St. and two other Nairobi branches, one in Mombasa. Associated with the Bank of America. The Bank of Baroda, Bank of India, National Bank of Kenya, and Algemene Bank Nederland also have offices.

Diplomatic Representatives in Kenya

All the following have offices in Nairobi, with Mombasa offices as indicated: *Canada*—High Commission, IPS Bldg., Kimathi St., Box 30481, tel. 34033. *Egypt*—Embassy, Total House, Koinange St., tel. 25991. *Ethiopia*—Embassy, State House Ave., tel. 23941. *Germany (West)*—Embassy, Embassy House, Harambee Ave., Box 30180, tel. 26661/2. Consul, Mombasa, tel. 24938. *Great Britain*—High Commission, Bruce House, Standard St., Box 30465, tel. 35944. Ralli House,

Nyerere Ave., Mombasa; tel. 25453. *Malawi*—High Commission, Gateway House, off Government Road, tel. 21174. *Somalia*—Embassy, International House, Mama Ngina St., tel. 24301. *Sudan*—Embassy, Shankardass House, Government Road, tel. 20770. *Tanzania*—Visa Office, Kenya Immigration Department, New Jogoo House, Harambee Ave., Box 30191, tel. 28411. (Tanzania Tourist Centre, IPS Bldg., Kimathi St., Box 48610, tel. 26888, 32421.) *USA*—Embassy, Cotts House, Wabera St., Box 30137, tel. 34141. *Zambia*—High Commission, International House, Mama Ngina St., tel. 35972.

Other countries with representatives in Nairobi include Australia, Austria, Belgium, Brazil, Bulgaria, China (People's Republic), Colombia, Cyprus, Czechoslovakia, Denmark, Finland, France, Ghana, Greece, Hungary, India, Iraq, Iran, Ireland, Israel, Italy, Japan, Korea (South), Kuwait, Lesotho, Liberia, Malagasy Republic, Malaysia, Netherlands, Nigeria, Norway, Pakistan, Poland, Rumania, Rwanda, Spain, Sri Lanka (Ceylon), Swaziland, Sweden, Switzerland, Thailand, Turkey, USSR, Vatican, Yugoslavia, and Zaire.

Health

Health hazards need not worry you in Kenya, though see our section on health in the Introduction. Tap water is safe in Nairobi, Mombasa, and major towns; tourist hotels in game parks have piped, filtered water but will warn you if you cannot drink from the tap. Campers will have no great problem obtaining potable water; it can always be boiled.

There are good doctors, hospitals, dentists, and medical specialists in the cities and major towns.

Many tourists join the Flying Doctors' Society; see Introduction.

Most visitors use the private Nairobi Hospital, on Argwings-Kodhek Road, tel. 21401. The Aga Khan Platinum Jubilee Hospital, on 3d Parklands Ave. near the City Park (tel. 55301), is also good. The U.S. Embassy (tel. 34141) has the names of doctors and dentists. In Mombasa, the main hospital used by visitors is the Katharine Bibby Hospital, near Fort Jesus, tel. 24191.

Nairobi ambulance, tel. 22396, 24066.

Mail, Telegrams

From East Africa, it costs –/70 to send an aerogramme to the U.S. or any other country outside Kenya, Tanzania, and Uganda. Airmail letters to the U.S. cost 2/50 for the first and second 10 grams, then 2/– per 10 grams; to Britain and the Continent, 1/50 for the first and second 10 grams, then 1/– per 10 grams. An airmail postcard to the U.S. is 1/30; to Britain and Europe –/70.

Ordinary surface mail to the U.S. costs –/70 up to 20 grams, 1/30 up to 50 grams, 2/– up to 100 grams, 4/– up to 250 grams. A parcel sent sea mail costs about 60/– for 10 kilos (22 pounds), the maximum weight acceptable. Sea mail at its fastest is four weeks; at its slowest, forever or never.

Aerogrammes within East Africa cost –/40, a 10-gram airmail letter –/50, an ordinary letter –/40.

The General Post Office in Nairobi is on Kenyatta Ave. opposite the New Avenue Hotel; tel. 20617. Post office hours in Kenya generally are 8 A.M.–12:30 P.M., 2–4:30 P.M. Monday–Friday, 8 A.M.–1 P.M. Saturday. The Nairobi GPO is open 8 A.M.–6 P.M. Monday–Friday, 8 A.M.–5 P.M. (stamps to 6 P.M.) on Saturday; stamps are sold 9–10 A.M. Sunday.

The main post office in Mombasa is on Digo Road, two blocks west of Kilindini–Nkrumah Road.

In Nairobi, international cables can be sent from Extelcoms House, Haile Selassie Ave., open 24 hours; or from any other post office during regular hours. Cable rates to the U.S. from anywhere in East Africa are 2/20 per word, minimum 7 words (night letter of 22 words costs 24/20), to Britain 1/85 per word regular (22-word night letter 20/90).

Telephone Calls

Pay telephones in Kenya (as well as Tanzania, Uganda, Zambia, and Malawi) are a bit complicated for Americans; but Britons will know what to do. First, put the necessary coin (–/50 in East Africa, 5n in Zambia, 5t in Malawi) in the slot but *don't* push it in; next, pick up the receiver and dial your number when you hear the dialing tone (a continuous low-pitched burr); listen for the ringing tone (double burr, reminiscent of a busy signal), and when you hear someone answer, *push the coin down into the slot before you talk,* otherwise your party can't hear you.

Ordinary phones work the same as in the U.S., but you must dial more slowly and be more patient.

From nonpublic phones in East Africa, you can make direct calls to the U.S., Britain, and most European countries. Calls are charged for the first three minutes, then each extra minute. The charge for a three-minute call to the U.S. is 57/– station-to-station (19/– for each additional minute), with person-to-person costing 38/– more. Three minutes to Britain is 45/–. With trunk dialing (STD) phones, dial 0196 for a call to the U.S.; connection may be on demand. To book a call, dial 0195. Dial 0191 for international directory inquiries.

Public phones in Nairobi are at the main downtown hotels, post offices, National Theatre, Kenya Commercial Bank (Government Road), and the Nairobi train station.

In Nairobi and Mombasa, dial 00 to get the operator, 991 for a directory inquiry, 993 for the correct time, 999 for fire, ambulance, and police emergencies.

Shopping

Nairobi is the department store of East Africa, with more shops selling more of nearly everything—including many locally made things—than Dar es Salaam, Arusha, Addis Ababa, Lusaka, Blantyre. This is not to say that everything is a bargain. Ethiopian crosses are cheaper (and cheap) in Addis, and you have more choice; Makonde sculpture is best bought in Dar, shells anywhere on the coast. Among the good buys in Nairobi (and Mombasa): fabrics, animal-skin articles (even though the trade is reprehensible), safari clothes and boots, crafts, prints, reproductions and photos, sisal items, soapstone, meerschaum pipes, flamingo feather corsages, coffee and tea, traditional items, basketwork, beadwork, modern jewelry and gemstones, spices, sheepskins, shells.

If you have a limited amount of time in Nairobi, we suggest you try these shops: *Zebra Crafts,* Koinange St. at Kenyatta Ave.; *Maendeleo ya Wanawake* ("Progress for Women"), Muindu Mbingu St. opposite 680 Hotel; *African Heritage/Pan African Gallery,* Kenyatta Ave. opposite 680; *Studio Arts 68,* Standard St. near New Stanley; *East African Wild Life Society* (*EAWLS*) *shop,* Hilton Arcade mezzanine; *Hirji Devraj,* Biashara St. near Muindi Mbingu; and *Y-Crafts* (YMCA), Uchumi House, Aga Khan Walk.

Shops mentioned below are mostly in Nairobi; Mombasa shops are so identified. Most accept major credit cards.

Fabrics are among the outstanding buys. They are available at Lucky Wear, Abdulla bin Abdulla, African Drapering, and Kitenge Palace; in Mombasa at Wawira Traders, Biashara St. There are several designs: *kikoi,* a style that originated with the Arabs, is a simple, straight, wraparound piece of brightly printed cloth which you tuck in at the waist; it reaches to the ankles; also *khanga* and *kitenge* (see

p. 337). Ready-made *kitenge,* long casual muumuus in *khanga* designs, and dresses from the imaginative Maridadi designs are available for 40/– up to 240/– at Shangri-La Boutique, Jax Bazaar, Studio 68, Cultural Heritage, Kitenge Palace, Paa-ya-Paa Gallery, and elsewhere; in Mombasa at Mirpuri's, Glamour I.T., Kabani Kitenge Shop.

Safari clothes in bush tan color are or are not good buys. Hardly anyone wears them except tourists on safari; on the other hand, a long-sleeved safari jacket is a nice addition to a stateside wardrobe. Sample prices (at Colpro): jacket—75/– cotton; 125/– wash 'n' wear; stiff-brim hat—45/–; ladies' outfit with pants or skirt—190/–; sleeveless hunting jacket (which white hunters sport)—75/– or 125/–; safari shirt—35/–. Ahamed Bros., the famous outfitters, will tailor-make an outfit before you arrive; send for measurement sheets to Box 40254, Nairobi; their work is of the highest quality. Safari clothes are also available at a rather wide range of price and quality at Colpro, Clayton's, Esquire, Kant's, Jax (ladies), Pop-In. Locally made Bata *safari boots,* which everybody wears and which resemble desert boots, are a bargain at 35/– (ladies'), 50/– (men's). *All silk scarves* of quality, with African birds by Rena Fennessy, zebras, lions, etc., at Rowland Ward's, 70/– to 75/–, also at Madame Louise. Warmer would be *sheepskin coats* made in Nakuru from sheep raised in the Highlands of Kenya. Nakuru Tanners (Box 225, Nakuru) has the best, well-tanned sheepskins (do not buy the poorly tanned ones offered by Escarpment roadside vendors) and sheepskin coats: full-length—350/–; duffle—300/–. Mrs. Peggy Nash (Box 30, Molo), Mrs. G. Southey (P.O. Turi), and other Highland sheep-country British ladies produce *handspun yarn,* available in natural off-white or gray-brown black or in autumnal colors (from herbs, roots, natural dyes) at 3/25 to 4/– per ounce-skein.

Jewelry for ears, neck, wrists, and fingers—and, if you're of a mind to, nose, ankles, upper arms, and thighs—is widely available. Traditional jewelry, such as beadwork, ostrich eggshell necklaces, copper or iron bracelets, and aluminum bangles, is hard to price; look for it in Studio 68, Manyatta Gallery, Zebra Crafts. Alan Donovan of African Heritage has collected old and odd bits and pieces from all over Africa and created expensive composite jewelry, mainly necklaces. Modern jewelry can be low-priced: well-designed copper necklaces and bracelets at Waa, Hirji Devraj, Rowland Ward's, John W. Hyland Ltd., and EAWLS shop; modern Masai beadwork at Zebra Crafts and Maendeleo; heavy silver jewelry at Cultural Heritage; select gold, silver, copper, and gemstone items at EAWLS shop. *Gemstones* and *gemstone jewelry* include tanzanite (a recently discovered precious stone), rubies, rhodolite, garnets, bloodstone, sapphire, and malachite, available at Apollo Watch Co., Elton's, African Jewels, and Beth (which is also in the duty-free departure lounge, Embakasi). Copper and silver versions of *usinga*—good-luck elephant-hair bracelets—are available for 15/– at EAWLS shop. Elephant-hair *usinga* made only from drought victims are sold at EAWLS; anything available on the street, 10/– and up or down, is either plastic or from poached elephants.

Among drinkable souvenirs are *liquor and spirits, coffee,* and *tea,* all produced in Kenya. Mount Kenya Liqueur, distilled from coffee, is perhaps not as good as Kahlúa; cost is 57/–, but check duty-free shops as you travel. Kenya Cane, a new ginlike liquor made from molasses, is 23/50 a small bottle, 45/– a fifth. Arabica coffee, either ground or unground, is sold at the Kenya Coffee Houses in Nairobi and Mombasa for 3/60 per quarter-kilo in the special Coffee House Blend (try a cup for –/80). Tea, loose or in tea bags, is sold under the green and yellow Brooke Bond label; 250 grams of "Green Label" is 3/20; 500 grams of "Gold Label" is 7/–. Kaitet-label tea bags cost 1/45 for 25. Rowland Ward's has distinctive and expensive Bavarian-made *glassware*— a series of glasses, tumblers, tankards, goblets, jugs, and decanters etched with lions, elephants, rhinos, etc., also English-made *china* with Rena Fennessy birds.

Spices at incredibly low prices in bulk (large or small quantities) can be found at several Biashara St. *dukas.*

Like old jewelry, such traditional items as camel-stomach oil holders, honey containers, gourds, wrist knives, and cowbells are difficult to price. Look in Maendeleo, Zebra Crafts, and African Heritage. Spears and shields are costly or not, depending on how new they are. An 8-foot Samburu spear that is genuine will have a hand-beaten head, with well-worn wooden shaft joined to a somewhat pointed metal bottom shaft, and all three pieces will fit snugly together (but you can take them apart); cost is 50/– to 120/– in shops, 30/– or so on the Isiolo road. Try Zanzibar Curio Shop, Zebra Crafts, Studio 68, Kenya Souvenirs & Crafts, City Furriers, Ashiki, African Heritage, Rowland Ward's, and, in Mombasa, Wason's Tourist Centre.

Dolls, toys, and games: Chess sets carved in black and pink soapstone cost 140/– at Y-Crafts; black ebony and white something-wood sets are 100/– to 200/– around town. Authentic *bao* games, a game played with stones in a series of indentations in a board (known to

Stone Age man in East Africa, to the Axumites in Ethiopia), are 80/– to 100/– at Zebra Crafts, pricier at African Heritage. For children, rope dolls (10/– to 15/–), cute stuffed rhinos and elephants (16/50 to 45/–), and ochered wooden Turkana dolls, suitably dressed in leather apron and beads (70/– at Zebra Crafts), are available; East African Mattings has clever sisal-rope lions for 25/– and 35/–. Simple wooden jigsaw puzzles (a three-part elephant, a multipart Africa map) for small children can be bought at Hirji Devraj. The National Museum has wildlife coloring books for 7/–.

Teak, ebony, mango, sesame, and jackfruit wood *Arab (or Zanzibar) chests,* brass-studded and plated, with up to four drawers and maybe a secret compartment, are available from jewelry box to footlocker size. Poorly made but expensive new ones are available, but the old good ones are hard to find and very dear. For new ones, try the Zanzibar Curio Shop in Nairobi, Coast Zanzibar Curio Shop in Mombasa. A chest 4 by 1½ by 2 feet is about 1,500/–. If you go to Mombasa during the dhow season (December–April), you can buy a chest, perhaps an old one, directly off the dhow or at the customs sheds; check also Shariff M. A. Shatry (Mbarak Hinawy Road, Old Town), Lamu Craft (opp. Fort Jesus), and M. A. Timami (Ndia Kuu St., Old Town); made-to-order chests at Wananchi Curios Centre (Ndia Kuu St.). An import that makes a conversation piece is a conical brass *Arab coffee vendor's pot,* with handle for carrying, tray for hot coals, detachable cup; 125/– in Mombasa, up to 250/– in Nairobi. Try Wason's Tourist Centre and Coast Zanzibar Curio Shop in Mombasa.

Our opinion of the traffic in *game skins, horns, trophies, ivory,* etc. is pretty low. Do you really want to go to East Africa to admire the wildlife that the rest of the world lacks—and then take home a gazelle-hide drum or elephant-foot stool with zebra-skin top? There's a worthy government ban on spotted cat furs—and, recently, on new ivory—and if you buy anything that was once running around free and alive on the savanna, get a Game Department export license from the seller. Prices are high and change often. *Shells* are perhaps in the same category as skins, but at least there's more sea than savanna to pick from. Try Mombasa shops, vendors at coast hotels, and the H. B. Fishing Service in Malindi. Very objectionable are pictures made from butterfly wings. However, *flamingo feather corsages* (about 35/–) are all right to buy because the feathers were discarded by the birds and picked up by a Nakuru mission that has the concession.

Crafts, a catchall category, make better presents than game skins.

Maendeleo, Y-Crafts, Prison Industries shops (Langata Road in Nairobi; near Mtwapa Bridge on North Coast road) and the Home Industries Center in Mombasa offer a wide selection of handy, well-made items: beadwork, pottery, sisal and basketware, leatherwork, clothes. East African Mattings has 18-piece, 6-place sets of *sisal placemats* in a variety of pleasing colors for 33/– a set. The stalls in and around the Municipal Market, and Dafina and Hirji Devraj, are also worth checking, but almost every curio shop has some good contemporary crafts. Pink (best) and black (shoe polish) *soapstone carvings,* including handsome vases, eggs, candlesticks, lions, and crocodiles, are generally available at fair prices. Lowest prices at the sidewalk vendor in front of the New Avenue Hotel.

There is, at last, that indefinable category of *curios,* another catchall, this one including gewgaws, knickknacks and most slick, highly polished, mass-produced *Kamba carvings*—elephants, masks, salad servers. Available anywhere at negotiable prices.

The best art by Africans is probably *Makonde sculpture,* done by Tanzanian tribesmen, and best bought more cheaply and from a wider range in Tanzania (see p. 336). Nairobi sellers include Panorama, Sifa, Kumbu Kumbu, Arts 680 (flabbergasting prices), Shanta Craft, Manyatta Gallery, and Zawadi; in Mombasa at Zawadi also, Wason's and Mombasa Art Centre. *Paintings* by African and Western artists, including some extremely good wildlife paintings, can be found at Gallery Watatu, Paa-ya-Paa, Tryon Gallery, and East African Wild Life Society Gallery. *Reproductions* of Joy Adamson's famous portraits of Turkana, Masai, and other peoples of Kenya—20/– to 30/– for small or large reproductions—are sold at the National Museum shop, EAWLS shop, and Firmin Studio; some of the pictures also appear in her *Peoples of Kenya* (p. 90). Rena Fennessy *bird prints* are found at EAWLS and Rowland Ward's, also bookshops. Striking *lithographs* of African women and their dress, by Thelma Sanders, are high-priced but very much worth wall space; at Gallery Watatu and African Heritage. *Photographs* are an attractive and less expensive alternative. Superb black and white wildlife photos, up to mural size, by Mohamed Amin and Masud Quraishy are available from Wildlife Photographers (Box 45048, Nairobi); prices from 30/– for 12 by 15 inches up to 210/– for 3 by 2 feet to 525/– for a 5-by-3-foot photo that can rival anything in your living room in eye appeal. Amin/Quraishy also do photomurals of your own pix (write Photomural/Photofinishers, Box 45259). The 12-by-15-inch prints cost 30/– at EAWLS, Watatu, and elsewhere. Large (25 by 34 inches) color prints from Mirella Ricciardi's splendid *Vanishing Africa,* signed and numbered, cost 400/– from Tryon Gallery. (Picture books, incidentally, are not bargains; shop at home.)

The *sounds* of twittering birds, hungry lions, and singing Luos have been recorded on several records (40/– or 45/–), many cassettes, and several 45s, so you can sit back and hear grunting hippos in stereo as you think about your second safari to Africa.

Wildlife and Game Parks

Like every other country, Kenya came late to conservation, with little but hunting regulation (by itself, not enough) until after World War II. But in Kenya's case, it wasn't *too* late, and the country has leaped far ahead since President Kenyatta's 1963 manifesto pledging the government to conservation "with all means at its disposal." Nairobi National Park—the first—was established in 1945, followed three years later by the gigantic Tsavo West and Tsavo East, Mount Kenya in 1949, the Aberdares in 1950. Then there was a pause until Lake Nakuru was officially made a bird sanctuary in 1961. In an 18-month spurt in 1966–68, Meru, Mount Elgon, and two lagoon-and-coral reef areas off Malindi and Watamu were declared national parks, and the Aberdares, Mount Kenya, and Lake Nakuru were expanded. East Lake Rudolf, part of Amboseli, and the coast at Kisiti were to be dedicated in early 1975. Next on the national parks list are Saiwa Swamp near Kitale and perhaps Lake Hannington.

There are also the famous game reserves: Amboseli (until early 1975), Mara (run by the Masai county council), Samburu, and the small, unpublicized Lambwe Valley Game Reserve, which is a roan antelope sanctuary. There are national reserves (Marsabit, Shimba Hills, and the area surrounding the two marine national parks), game conservation areas (West Chyulu near Tsavo West, Kitengela bordering Nairobi Park, and five others), photography blocks (one bordering Meru, another next to Samburu, and four others), and one nature reserve (Southwest Mau). The Forest Department tolerates all but destructive game in the government forests.

But even with all this protection, including rigidly controlled hunting and constant warfare against poachers, and, in September 1973, a six-month-long ban on elephant hunting, wildlife is still somewhat on the defensive in Kenya, and the government, like any other, cannot single-mindedly pursue conservation at all costs. With an expanding population, all land must pay, and so must wildlife areas. Tourism would seem to be the answer, but as Dr. D. R. M. Stewart of the Game Department, for one, notes, "A large part of the financial benefits of tourism tends to accrue elsewhere . . . and an individual national park seldom shows much profit." There are other problems with Kenya's conservation policy, such as the drawing of park boundaries without regard to animals' migration habits, and the absence of such species as Grevy's zebra and reticulated giraffe from the national parks (they are in Samburu Game Reserve, however). Dr. Stewart notes that a landowner may legally get rid of wildlife that threatens his interests, but the laws don't give him any incentive to conserve the animals. One basic problem, as farmers and ranchers know, is that wildlife can be a bloody nuisance. The national parks system has a wildlife education program designed to combat people's ignorance of conservation, and more ways are being found to see that the people who have to put up with wildlife get some benefit from foreigners traveling thousands of miles to see it.

The 1974–78 Development Plan calls for both a wildlife training institute and a Wildlife Conservation and Management Service (with a research division) along with increased antipoaching field forces.

Conservation society: The East African Wild Life Society (EAWLS), founded in 1961, has been growing at the same speed as Kenya's park system. Every year, using the proceeds from membership fees, sales, and so forth, the society makes grants to support research, run surveys, and aid antipoaching patrols, and for wildlife education and the rescue and relocation of endangered animals. For its members and the general public, EAWLS publishes the big, glossy *Africana* quarterly, and for a scientific audience the quarterly *East African Wildlife Journal*. Ordinary overseas membership in the society is 70/– ($10), and East African membership 40/–; members receive *Africana*. Membership and inquiries: EAWLS, mezzanine of Hilton Hotel Arcade, Mama Ngina St., Box 20110, Nairobi; tel. 27047/8. *Africana* subscriptions only: Box 49010, Nairobi; 76/– ($11) airmail to U.S., 24/50 ($3.50) surface mail.

Game Park Entry Fees

Game reserves charge varying amounts; see descriptions in route notes. All national parks, except Tsavo East and the marine parks, charge the same fees: resident of Kenya—5/– per day; nonresident—

20/–; children up to 16 years—1/–; vehicle—10/–. Tsavo East and Shimba Hills National Reserve fees: resident—2/50; nonresident—10/–; children up to 16 years— –/50; vehicle—10/–. Marine parks, see p. 209. Only camping fees are charged at Marsabit. If you are a bona-fide resident of Kenya, you can get a bargain private-car pass for two or five residents for one or all parks for a calendar six months or a calendar year. For instance, a six-month pass for two persons in a car to enter all the parks costs 180/–. Passes from Kenya National Parks Headquarters, Langata Road (at Nairobi National Park main gate), Box 42076, Nairobi; tel. Langata (89) 493.

Exclusive occupancy of one of the six photography blocks (adjacent to Masai Mara, Meru, Samburu, and between Nairobi and Amboseli) costs 1,000/– per week for one to five persons, 4,000/– per week for six to twenty persons. It can be cheaper than a national park or game reserve, and less populated. Booking to Game Department (address, p. 87). Entry is free to the seven game conservation areas, but you have to book at the Game Department first, in theory.

Birdwatching

Please don't skip this section, even if you think there are only three kinds of birds (sparrows, pigeons, and chickens) and, anyway, only peculiar, silent people with binoculars watch birds. Quite frankly, before we went to East Africa, we weren't really aware of birds, either, but we were captivated the very first day with the profusion of birds around our hotel—bright yellow weavers, clever "little brown birds," birds that went "tink tink" or "tootle" somewhere off in the bushes, birds that wagged their tails, and more. There are birds of all feathers all over Kenya. Lake Nakuru's million flamingos are one of the world's great natural spectacles—and tourist sights. At Kilaguni Lodge in Tsavo West, incredibly colorful superb starlings (blue coat and red pants) run among the people, keeping beady white eyes sharp for bread crumbs. There are some big birds that stand out in the crowd—ostriches, the peculiar-looking secretary bird, the stunning crowned crane. Birds are everywhere, and you need not sprain your neck or strain your eyes to find them. You need no elaborate equipment, just a pair of ordinary binoculars (we used a 7x35 pair that cost only $15) and John G. Williams's bird field guide (see p. 10), which describes and illustrates 428 species and enumerates the characteristics of another 324—out of a grand total, in Kenya alone, of 1,030 or 1,032 species—a record exceeded, possibly, by Ecuador and Colombia. By comparison, Britain has about 440 species, North America 800 (no one state has more than 450).

The East African Natural History Society (EANHS), connected with the National Museum, where it has its offices and library, is the de-facto ornithological society in East Africa. It has weekend field trips and, Wednesdays at 8:45 A.M., a bird walk in or around Nairobi (meet in front of the museum). EANHS membership is 50/– a year. Inquiries: Hon. Secretary, EANHS, Box 44486, Nairobi; tel. 20141.

The museum has a very comprehensive display of East African birds, largely put together by Williams. That ornithologist has written that the mildly knowledgeable birdwatcher can count on seeing 600 to 800 species in a month or five weeks, depending on the season, weather, and places visited. Keen birders should see Williams's national parks guide (p. 10) for checklists of birds in the game parks.

Historic and Prehistoric Sites

‚ Kenya has—alas—no concerted program for the discovery, preservation, and opening to the public of historic and prehistoric sites. There are two prehistoric sites on the Nakuru road—Kariandusi and Hyrax Hill—and a famous one southwest of Nairobi—Olorgesailie, which is a national park. All three are under the administration of the National Museum. Three historic places are preserved and open: Fort Jesus, the old Portuguese fort that was oft besieged; Gedi, the "mysterious" Arab ruins; and Jumba la-Mtwana, another set of ruins, both north of Mombasa.

There are other historic places which we detail in the route descriptions.

Sports

As a former British colony, with many ex-colonials still in residence, Kenya has a multitude of sports, some very British, some more universal. There is, for example, the Limuru Hunt, a hounds-and-horses affair every Sunday from April to mid-December; and there are polo, rugby, and cricket. There are also clubs and facilities for golf, horseback riding, show jumping, swimming, sailing, motor racing, pistol and rifle shooting, judo, skin diving, cave exploration, fencing, squash, hiking and climbing, flying, soccer, fishing, water skiing, basketball, bowling, boxing, tennis, hockey, and go-carting. The Tourist Information Bureau (p. 169) has details.

Kenya is beginning to push the idea of a golfing safari for the golfer who has tried Ireland, Scotland, and Portugal. Kenya has ten 18-hole courses in attractive country. Green fees are low (10/– on a weekday, average), so are caddies' fees (16/–). Special rules apply when you find a snake wrapped around your ball. Top courses: Muthaiga, Limuru, Highlands, Royal Nairobi, Karen, also the Golf Range.

Water Sports

The Kenya coast is deservedly popular during the European winter for its sun, sea, and sand, and water-sports facilities are available from Malindi south to the Pemba Channel, and at Lamu. The white sand beach extends along half the coast, and except for unpredictable and seasonal amounts of seaweed, swimming in the warm water is fine, with no danger of sharks within the reefs. Off most beaches at low tide, however, swimming is not good or is impossible—but then you can go reef walking (wear tennis shoes to protect your feet). All the beaches are public, and accesses are supposed to be provided, but the best way to sample the sea is to enter through a hotel, which won't have any facilities for changing unless you're a guest. Nonguests are charged 5/– to use the pool. Surfing is possible in Malindi Bay, but the waves aren't very exciting. Water skiing is possible in the creeks (Kilifi, Mtwapa, Tudor at Mombasa). Kenya Marinas, Bahari Club, "K" Boats, and MacConnel (addresses under "Fishing" below) and Seafarers and Ocean Sports (see hotel listings, Route K-2) have water skiing at 1/25 to 2/– per minute to 80/– per hour, or 5/– per circuit at the hotels. Mini-sailboats are available at most hotels and marinas for 15/– or 25/– per hour. The marinas have motorboats costing 40/– per hour and up.

A very popular water activity up and down the coast, but especially at the Malindi and Watamu Marine National Parks, is goggling (snorkeling, skin diving), best done from a boat at low tide over a coral garden or other part of a reef (ask locally, or see Simon Mollison's *Kenya's Coast*). Goggling is often combined with a glassbottom-boat trip in which mask, flippers, and snorkel are usually included in the 10/– to 20/– per person charge for a two-hour-plus trip. Goggling and glassbottom boating can be arranged at the marinas and most hotels, with the Malindi and Watamu hotels having the best goggling areas close at hand. Seafarers arranges general reef goggling, underwater photo safaris, and Mida Creek goggling for 10/– per person per hour, minimum four persons. Driftwood Club's Afro-Sub Diving School and

Kenya Marinas both have scuba-diving equipment. Driftwood Club will give five lessons (to third-class standard) for 380/–, and will take experienced divers on a two-hour diving expedition or take beginners goggling with an aqualung for two hours for 80/– per person. Kenya Marinas charges 120/– per dive for two or three persons, with free instruction. Ocean Sports and MacConnel have aquanauts (two-man floating air compressors with long hoses) for 40/– per hour plus cost of boat. Nikonos underwater cameras are available for 20/– per hour or 40/– per goggling trip at Kenya Marinas, Driftwood Club, and elsewhere.

Between Mombasa and Kikambala on the North Coast, you can get from one hotel to another or to a marina for 20/– to 25/– by taxi or hotel transport.

Fishing

Kenya has superb big-game fishing in the Indian Ocean but tourists are also lured to inland waters—Mount Kenya and Aberdare trout streams and Lakes Rudolf and Naivasha.

Deep-sea fishing: Kenya offers as exciting big-game fishing as can be found anywhere. Fish to be caught in these waters include tuna, marlin (black, blue, and striped), sailfish, broadbill swordfish (rare), wahoo, kingfish (the most sought-after eating fish), barracuda, black runner, rainbow runner, shark (including fighting mako), bonito, kolikoli, karambesi, and dolphin (dorado or felusi). The largest fish caught so far on the coast was landed in March 1973 when a West German champion angler brought in a 748-pound tiger shark on a 130-pound line after battling it for two and a half hours. The biggest marlin was a 510-pound black marlin, the heaviest sailfish 145 pounds. In the Pemba Channel in the 1972–73 season, all-Africa and Kenya records were claimed for striped, blue and black marlin, and tiger, mako, hammerhead, and sand shark. The world-record cobia was caught off Mombasa in 1964.

Height of the season is October–December. Billfishing is best October–March; smaller fish can be taken well all year. There are several fishing tournaments.

Deep-sea fishing outfits are found where there is a break in the reef —Mombasa, Kilifi, Mtwapa, Malindi, and Pemba Channel. Boats, ranging from 14-foot outboards to 30-foot-plus inboards of the "Coronet" class, are hired on a fully inclusive basis with experienced crew, rods, reels, wet bait, lures, harnesses, fighting chairs, safety equipment, marine toilet.

Book the fishing trip at least two days in advance, or as far ahead as you can. Plan on the best fishing being done dawn to midday.

Some fishing charter firms are as follows: *"K" Boat Services Ltd.*, Box 82345, Mombasa; tel. 20822; takes DC card. *Bahari Club Ltd.*, Box 90413, Mombasa; tel. 71316. *Pemba Channel Fishing Club*, Shimoni (p. 223). *Mnarani Club*, Kilifi (p. 206). *Seafarers* and *Ocean Sports*, Watamu (p. 211). *H. B. Fishing Service*, Box 70, Malindi; tel. 28. *Kingfisher Safaris*, Malindi (p. 111). *F. G. MacConnel & Co. Ltd.* (Mtwapa Creek), Box 82849, Mombasa; tel. Kikambala 2Y9. *Kenya Marinas Ltd.* (Mtwapa Creek), Box 15070, Kikambala via Mombasa; tel. Kikambala 2Y7.

Sample prices: "K" Boats—four-fisherman boats of various sizes, 300/– to 500/– per six hours. Bahari Club—four-man boat, 60/– per hour (three-hour minimum); eight-man boats for 300/– per morning or afternoon. Kenya Marinas—four-man boat for 320/– per four hours (minimum); six-man boat for 480/– per four hours. Pemba Channel Fishing Club—four-man boat for 75/– to 85/– per hour (four to six hours minimum). With a couple of exceptions (H. B. Fishing Service, for one), fish belong to the person catching them, and can easily be sold for –/50 or more per pound. Fishing license costs 40/– at hotels, clubs, marinas.

Inshore fishing for snappers, bream, grunters, jacks, rockcod, and catfish costs 25/– to 40/– per hour inclusive. Also popular on the coast is fishing from rocky headlands, surf casting or hand lining inside the reef, and underwater spear fishing for rockcod, peacock, and parrot fish. Charter boat outfits and most hotels can make arrangements.

Inland, the most serious fishermen head for Lake Rudolf, where the prize is Nile perch (present record is 238 pounds) and the smaller but ferocious fighting tigerfish. Eliye Springs and Lake Rudolf Angling Club are both fishing centers.

Fishing in the Mount Kenya, Aberdares, Mau Escarpment, Cherangani Hills, and Mount Elgon streams for rainbow and brown trout appeals mostly to locals, but visitors with or without transport or equipment can easily make a trout-fishing weekend trip to Ngobit Fishing Lodge or Naro Moru River Lodge or the Isaak Walton Inn. Because of poaching, average weight of trout caught is about 1½ pounds, though record brown trout is 10 pounds 8 ounces, rainbow 12 pounds

11 ounces. There is no closed fishing season. Rainbow trout bag limit is six, brown trout four. One-hook flies only. License is mandatory even on private land; cost is 5/– for 48 hours, 10/– for two weeks, obtainable locally. Further information from the Fisheries Department, behind National Museum, Museum Hill, Box 40241, Nairobi; tel. 24865, 23592.

Go to Lake Naivasha for black bass (up to 9 pounds), numerous species of tasty tilapia (up to a pound), and other coarse fishing. The lake hotels and Carnelley's Fisherman's Camp have boats for rent. Lake Baringo is also good for coarse fishing.

Hunting

Long before Kenya was known for its game parks it was known for its hunting of game. Philosophically and morally, the authors feel that hunting for trophies is an atavistic blood sport, and that the lucrative hunting safari business caters to the whims of a privileged few at the expense of the finest individual members of such beautiful or rare species as the bongo (you can shoot a female for 1,500/–), gerenuk, reticulated giraffe, kudu, leopard, black and white colobus monkey, oryx, rhino, Grevy's zebra. We're against hunting, as we're against elephant-foot stools and zebra-skin cigarette boxes. Our opinion is not ours alone. Heeding the cries of conservationists, and noting its dwindling population of elephants, Kenya banned the hunting of elephants for several months in 1973–74, and Tanzania followed with a permanent ban on *all* hunting.

The East African Professional Hunters' Association (Box 40528, Nairobi) can provide details on safari firms, hunting regulations, and so forth.

For photo safaris, which are usually led by a professional hunter, see pp. 111–112.

Nairobi

Nairobi, Kenya's capital with a population (est. 1972) of 597,000, is the certain destination of practically every traveler to East Africa. Not only the region's most cosmopolitan city, but also its main commercial and transport center, Nairobi has roaring lions not 5 miles from the Hilton, and so is a natural safari center. A mile above sea level, it has a temperate climate and sports two slogans: "City of Flowers," which it is, and "City in the Sun," which it is except in July and August.

Like most African cities Nairobi is new, and like Lusaka it was founded because of a railway. The Masai called the area Nakusontelon, "the beginning of all beauty," and the stream that bisected it the Uaso or Enkare Nairobi, "cold water." In 1896 Sergeant Ellis of the Royal Engineers established a staging depot there for oxen and mules used by the Protectorate government, and in June 1899 the railhead of the Uganda Railway reached Nairobi. The European in charge of plate laying said it was "a bleak, swampy stretch of soppy landscape, devoid of human habitation of any sort, the resort of thousands of wild animals of every species." Its big advantage was that it was the last flat place before the uplands leading to the Escarpment, which the railroad builders knew would be a devil to build tracks down, and so the railway shifted its headquarters to Nairobi in July 1899. The next month Ukamba Province administrator John Ainsworth moved his office to the new town, setting it up across the Nairobi River on Museum Hill. Relations between government and railway were bad to begin with. One man who had friends in both camps found it impracticable to visit both on the same day. In 1900 Ainsworth moved his headquarters to the north end of Government Road, and on April 16, 1900, he promulgated the Nairobi Municipal Regulations, the official start of today's city.

It wasn't a pretty town—lines of tents and corrugated iron barracks, a massed group of Indian *dukas* (shops) here, the railway yards there, a soda water factory, and a rickety hotel called Wood's. Initial commercial development was on Victoria (now Tom Mboya) Street. Plague broke out in the bazaar in 1902, and on the advice of a doctor the place was burned to the ground. After a 1904 plague the local authorities began campaigning to move the town to a more healthful site. The railway was opposed, and the matter was debated until it was too late to move. Then, finding it inconvenient to govern from humid Mombasa, the Protectorate administration moved to cool, central Nairobi in 1907. By then the old Norfolk Hotel was the scene of safaris: Teddy Roosevelt's set off from there with each of 500 blue-coated porters carrying a 60-pound load; that "conservation president" personally shot 296 animals in ten months.

By 1910 the town had a population of 14,000, including 600 Europeans. There were stone government buildings, a hospital, three hotels, churches, temples and a synagogue, an almost-finished railway

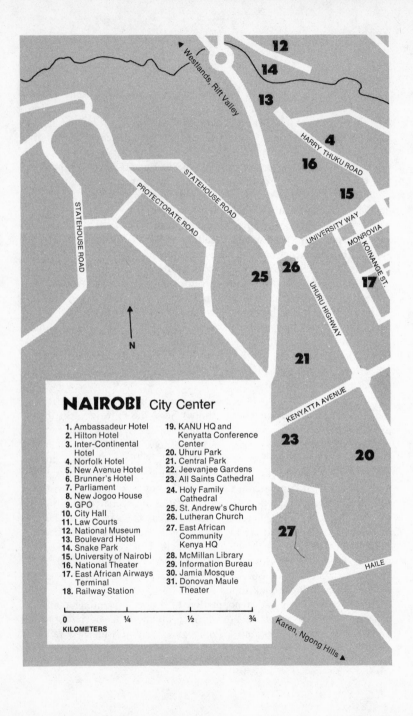

NAIROBI City Center

1. Ambassadeur Hotel
2. Hilton Hotel
3. Inter-Continental Hotel
4. Norfolk Hotel
5. New Avenue Hotel
6. Brunner's Hotel
7. Parliament
8. New Jogoo House
9. GPO
10. City Hall
11. Law Courts
12. National Museum
13. Boulevard Hotel
14. Snake Park
15. University of Nairobi
16. National Theater
17. East African Airways Terminal
18. Railway Station
19. KANU HQ and Kenyatta Conference Center
20. Uhuru Park
21. Central Park
22. Jeevanjee Gardens
23. All Saints Cathedral
24. Holy Family Cathedral
25. St. Andrew's Church
26. Lutheran Church
27. East African Community Kenya HQ
28. McMillan Library
29. Information Bureau
30. Jamia Mosque
31. Donovan Maule Theater

0   ¼   ½   ¾
KILOMETERS

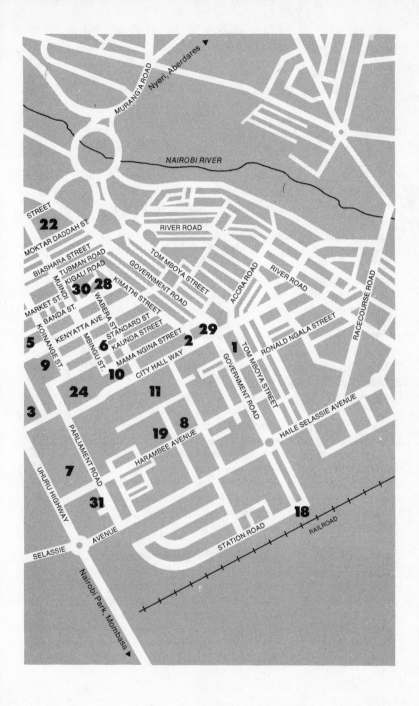

station, three main streets planted with eucalyptus trees, gardens everywhere, and electric lights. The boundary was enlarged in 1920 and 1927, a Municipal Council was formed in 1928, and in the 1930s the town lost its Wild West appearance when more urban-looking buildings went up. On March 30, 1950, Nairobi became the first colonial municipality in Africa to gain city status.

With boundaries last enlarged in 1963, to 266 square miles, Nairobi includes 44-square-mile Nairobi National Park and all of Embakasi Airport. But the downtown area will inevitably expand skyward rather than outward, since, like Chicago's Loop, the central area is restricted: by the Nairobi River (a sluggish stream) on the north, the railroad on the south, and a bluff (Nairobi Hill, "the Hill") and Uhuru Highway, a six-lane expressway, on the west. Besides the 743-acre central area, there are five urban-suburban sections: Upper Nairobi (the largest part) to the north and west, where most of the European population and the well-off Africans and Asians live; Parklands-Eastleigh, where the vast majority of the Asians live; Nairobi South (Asian); and Eastlands (almost exclusively African); and the Industrial Area to the south.

The commercial section, boasting several skyscrapers (one with a revolving restaurant), is largely within the University Way–Koinange Street–City Hall Way–Tom Mboya Street quadrilateral. The national government was until the 1948 master plan largely on the Hill; the plan recommended relocation to the underdeveloped area, now called City Square, between City Hall Way and Haile Selassie Avenue, in which principal government buildings now are located.

Nairobi certainly disappoints those looking for an African city, though the first-time visitor will generally find it an exciting place to be. But after a couple of days, you want to go off and see *Africa,* with flat-topped acacias, elephant and giraffe, villages with grass huts, equatorial snow-capped mountains. However, there's no better place to start than Nairobi, which deserves at least two full days of a traveler's itinerary.

Nairobi Walking Tour

Following is a 4-km walking tour that goes through the main business area to the National Museum, then heads back by a different route. It can easily be shortened; trace it out on a map beforehand.

Begin at the *Information Bureau,* cross to the *Hilton Hotel* (1969), a handsome round gray tower on top of a rectangular street block. The interesting murals in the lobby were painted by American Jony Waite. Cross *Mama Ngina Street,* named for the president's wife (it was formerly Queensway), and walk up the right side to *Kimathi Street* under the white-columned shopping arcade. The street was named, at Independence, for Dedan Kimathi, Mau Mau leader of the Aberdare forest fighters, executed in 1957. At the major intersection, marked by a large traffic circle (Lord Delamere's statue once stood here), is *Kenyatta Avenue,* planned very wide in Nairobi's pioneer days so that 12-span oxcarts could turn around easily. On the left is the famous *New Stanley Hotel,* dating to 1913 on its present site. On the Kimathi Street side is the equally well-known *Thorn Tree,* a sidewalk café so named from the three-story-high yellow-barked acacia growing among the tables and tourists.

Cross Kenyatta and continue up Kimathi. At the end of the street, go through Mugutha Alley (next to Lexikon College) from Tubman Road (formerly Hussein Suleman) to *Biashara Street* (formerly Bazaar Street), where you turn left and walk past many open-fronted Indian *dukas* selling fabrics, spices and fireworks (that combination), clothes, and curios. At Muindi Mbingu Street, turn right and walk up past *Jeevanjee Gardens,* with a statue of an unknown lady, to University Way. Go straight across and up *Harry Thuku Road* (formerly College Road). Thuku (1895–1970), one of the founders of the Kikuyu Central Association, was arrested March 14, 1922, for protesting against the use of African forced labor, and was held at the *Central Police Station,* at the corner here. A crowd gathered outside, became unruly, and was fired on; several died. Thuku was exiled to Kismayu (Somalia) until 1930. Walk up the street, with the University of Nairobi and bougainvillaea gardens on your left and right, to the *Norfolk Hotel,* a famous old colonial hostelry, founded in 1904. In the "old hairy rough days of Kenya," wrote Robert Ruark, "if a bit of a fight brewed in the bar the boys were apt to settle it straight off with knives or pistols, bang on the verandah or in the court." In the courtyard now are two *aviaries* worth seeing, also a *semicovered wagon* from the pioneer days. Opposite the Norfolk is a cultural complex including the *Kenya National Theatre* on the right and the *Kenya Cultural Centre,* which follows the curve of the driveway to the left; between them is a huge pink-flowered bombax tree. The theater, opened in 1952 as the first British colonial national theater, is self-supporting and hosts films and plays put on by local groups; it is also responsible for keeping the 1960 Cultural Centre, housing the British Council and areas for ballet, music, drama, alive and functioning.

Continuing up Harry Thuku Road you pass the *Voice of Kenya* studios. VOK operates all the country's radio and TV, broadcasting radio programs mainly in English and Swahili but also in 16 tribal languages.

Pass between VOK and the Boulevard Hotel, emerging on *Uhuru Highway,* formerly the railway corridor, opened as a six-lane express-way in 1952. The well-landscaped traffic circles and center strip on the highway (and elsewhere) are the work of Peter Greensmith, for-mer city landscaper (his nursery on Kiambu Road is a delight of flowers). Continue on the sidewalk to the traffic circle, then bear right up Museum Hill, passing by or through the small, pretty *Ainsworth Garden* and *War Memorial Garden.* The hilltop building with the zig-zag roof is the posh *International Casino.* Turn right on Museum Road to the *National Museum,* founded as the East Africa and Uganda Natural History Society museum in 1910. The basis of the present complex was built in 1928–29. The first habitat—the bongo group— was prepared in 1929 and is still on view. The wing to the right of the entrance was opened in 1953, and the Conservation Gallery to the left was built 1972–73. The museum's exhibits include a very large collec-tion of East African birds, insects (there are 100,000 to 200,000 species in the region, including 700 to 800 species of butterflies and 7,000 to 8,000 species of moths), mammals (Ahmed the late famous elephant will be displayed in time), fish, prehistory, ethnology (a fascinating collection of tribal weapons, musical instruments, orna-ments, and decoration): also on display are some of Joy Adamson's 800 priceless tribal portraits and many of her flower watercolors, and in the lobby are homemade guns used by the Mau Mau. The museum, which is directed by Richard Leakey, son of the late Dr. L. S. B. Leakey, is a research museum, housing the Centre for Prehistory and Palaeon-tology (to become the Institute for African Prehistory) and the Institute of African Studies, and it sponsors expeditions (see East Rudolf, p. 267). Opposite the museum is the famous *Snake Park* and, adjacent, the *Aviary.* The Snake Park has a snake population of about 500 (there are 169 species of snakes and reptiles in East Africa). Most are fed every two weeks, grass and sand snakes once a week, croco-diles and alligators three times a week. Snakes are usually milked for their venom Wednesdays at 5:30 P.M. (check by ringing 24638). The

Museum and Snake Park are open daily 9:30 A.M.–6 P.M. (Snake Park to 9 P.M. Wednesday). Separate entry fees to both: nonresident adult— 5/–; resident—2/–; children—2/– and 1/–. Museum tours are available periodically during the day. Inquiries, tel. 20141.

Half the walking tour ends here. If you're not footsore, head back the way you came to the Norfolk, then bear right past the Cultural Centre into the *University of Nairobi* quadrangle. Founded in 1952 as the Royal Technical College, with the first building opened in 1955 and the first students accepted the next year, the college later merged with Gandhi Memorial Academy and became a full-fledged university in 1970. It has ten faculties with a 350-man academic staff and an enrollment of about 4,200. The 18-acre central campus is attractively landscaped, with modern buildings (*Gandhi Library, Taifa Hall, Education Building,* and *Science Faculty* around the courtyard) and some sculpture, the biggest being the sinuous *Jajnik Memorial Fountain,* by F. V. Foit, installed in 1962. Exit on University Way, crossing that street and going down Koinange Street (auto row), detouring by the East African Airways terminal to the *Paa-ya-Paa Gallery,* an African-founded gallery with frequent displays and exhibitions of African and Western contemporary art. Past Tubman Road you come to the *Municipal Market,* a pastel building with a soaring roof. Walk through the market (good pictures from the balcony inside) past flower, fruit, vegetable, and curio stalls, and exit on Muindi Mbingu Street, turning right. Walk down to Banda Street and turn left, coming quickly to the *Jamia Mosque* of the Sunni sect of Islam, built in 1925–33 in an Arabian style. After removing your shoes you may go inside. Next door is the *McMillan Memorial Library,* which appropriately has a pair of stone lions guarding the portico entrance. The library, built 1929–31 and named for Sir William Northrup McMillan (see p. 236), has a good Africana collection. At the library steps, turn down Library Street toward Kenyatta Avenue. On the corner is the *Bank of India,* a building which as Memorial Hall was where Kenya's Legislative Council met from 1924 until the new Parliament was constructed in 1954. On either side of Kenyatta are world war memorials, one with two life-size *askaris* (native soldiers) and a carrier (porter). Go right along Kenyatta, crossing at Koinange. At the intersection next to the *General Post Office* (1961–62 reconstruction), is the *Nairobi Milliary Stone,* erected in 1939 as a memorial to L. D. Galton-Fenzi (died 1937), founder of the Automobile Association of East Africa in 1919 and pioneer of several driving routes. The stone's quaint calligraphy indicates it stands 5,474.37 feet above sea level and is exactly 3,256 miles from Alexandria. Go down Koinange past the Milliary Stone, coming to the Roman Catholic *Cathedral of the Holy Family,* founded in 1960 on the site of the earlier cathedral. The 198-foot campanile has three bells from the old church; the interior, designed with simple lines, has stained glass windows towering on three sides of the marble altar. Nairobi's archbishop was made a cardinal in 1973.

Go left to Muindi Mbingu Street, then turn right, then left at Mama Ngina Street. The big building is *City Hall,* dedicated "as an act of faith" during the Emergency; to tour, ring 24281. Continue straight along Mama Ngina. At Wabera Street is a good vista to the right, taking in the old, imposing *Law Courts,* the round teepee-roofed *Kenyatta Conference Centre* (1973) and the handsome round 34-story *KANU Tower Building,* housing the offices of the ruling Kenya African National Union. The $11.4-million complex, under construction for six years, was inaugurated by the 1973 World Bank–IMF Conference and is now temporary headquarters of the *Environment Program Secretariat,* the first U.N. agency headquartered outside the U.S. or Europe. The 28th floor of the tower is a revolving restaurant. Continue along Mama Ngina past one of the handsomest buildings in Nairobi, the white and rust-red *International House,* a $4.1-million structure opened in 1972. Across the streeet is the Hilton, and the tour ends.

Other Places of Interest

On Harambee ("let's all pull together") Avenue are the *Parliament* buildings, a two-story yellow-stone structure with a twelve-story clock tower, opened as the Legislative Council building in 1954 and now the seat of the unicameral National Assembly. Some interesting things can be seen on a tour (call the Sergeant-at-Arms, tel. 21291, ext. 256): nicely carved doors on the Parliament Road side; twelve African figures sculpted in relief above the public entrance; a display of shields of the ten most important tribes; the Seal of Independence; the 50 Kenya Tapestries illustrating the pioneer history of the country, woven by the East African Women's Guild, hanging in the Long Gallery; a conference table made from 33 different kinds of Kenya wood; a set of mosaics, by Margaret Cullen and Ruth Yudelowitz, on "Peoples and Produce of Kenya"; the basement Chamber of Meditation, decorated with murals. The old Council Chamber dates from the original building, but the National Assembly meets in the 1965 version, reached by a spiral staircase. In the attractive garden is a statue of President Kenyatta, shown with his celebrated fly whisk raised. To hear legislative debates, apply at the Harambee Avenue entrance.

Across from Parliament is *Uhuru Park,* completed in 1970, with a lakeside restaurant. Almost in the park, on Kenyatta Avenue, *All Saints' Cathedral* (Anglican), or the Cathedral of the Highlands, begun in 1917, finished in 1922, and extended in 1949, is a most English-looking church with a square tower and Gothic arches.

On Haile Selassie Avenue are a number of new, large commercial and government buildings, including the very imposing *Central Bank of Kenya* (1972), a gray concrete fortresslike building with a parking-lot access ramp sweeping into the second story on the right side. Farther along is *Kahawa* ("coffee") *House,* headquarters of the Kenya Planters Cooperative Union (whose initials are obscured in the decorative logo in front), where you can see the coffee auction Tuesday morning at 10 during the season (call 28761).

Two parks worth visiting are the Arboretum and City Park, both short taxi rides from downtown. The 100-acre *Arboretum,* established in 1907 as a place where imported plants could be tried out, is a delightfully peaceful place for walking among the labeled trees. The 1958 guidebook costs –/50. Next to the Arboretum entrance is the *Kenya Arts Society,* founded in 1922; the gallery has works for sale. At the 300-acre *City Park* are Boscawen House, with Central American philodendrons and other exotics; the City Nurseries, with more than 100 species of bougainvillaea (call 65551 before visiting); and a maze with hedges about 2 feet high. Women should have male escorts at the park, which is open dawn to dusk.

Tuesday and Thursday mornings you can visit the *St. John's Community Centre* in Pumwani. This is the workshop and shop (seconds are a bargain) of the Maridadi designs.

For *Nairobi National Park,* which is only a few miles from downtown, see Route K-14, Km 8. For other places of interest in Nairobi's vicinity, see the beginnings of Routes K-1, 7, 10, 12, 13, and 14.

Accommodations

Nairobi has the most, and best range of, accommodations in Eastern Africa, lacking only a super-deluxe Ritz for kings and the very rich. Lodging in the city can be cheap but you have to pay about $10 to get a reasonably adequate double. Low-budgeters have a lot to choose from, but only a few places are not basically depressing. Better than staying in a cheap hotel, we'd say camp at Rowallan Camp or Westwood Park Country Club.

In the listing below, hotels are divided into these categories: Expensive—In Town; Expensive—Out of Town; Moderate; Budget. Within each category we've ranked the hotels roughly according to overall quality, style, and price. Because of the sheer number of hotels, we have cut out many which, on investigation, offered poor accommodations for too much money.

Many hotel dining rooms are not mentioned below, since they are described under "Where to Eat."

Under construction or planned are an 8-floor, 176-room *Holiday Inn,* at Kirk and Protectorate roads; a sizable *Hyatt Hotel,* at Kenyatta Avenue and Uhuru Highway; a Kenya Tourist Development Corp. hotel; and the 200-room *Nairobi Serena,* opening mid-1975.

EXPENSIVE—IN TOWN

Nairobi Hilton, Box 30624, tel. 34000; cable HILTELS. Takes up a whole block between Mama Ngina St. and City Hall Way. 335 dbls, 4 sgls, incl 4 suites, all rms w/bath, a-c. Rates: bed only: sgl—155/– to 190/–; dbl—230/– to 270/–; also low season rates. Credit: AE, BA, DC. 1969 Hilton's 19-floor round tower is a skyline landmark. Lower floor rooms a bit squeezy, but all are uniform and uniformly comfortable, with an African motif here and there. Housekeeping not too thorough. Public areas very busy. Several restaurants. Pool. Underground parking. Rating: 1st-class international; you get what you pay for, and get a good view besides. ★★ in our book. Govt. class A*.

Norfolk Hotel, Box 40064, tel. 35422; cable NORFOLK. On Harry Thuku Road opposite National Theatre, 15-min. walk from downtown. 67 sgls, 93 dbls, and 10 cottages (total 280 beds), all but 30 rms w/bath. Rates: bed only: sgl—140/–; dbl—270/–; cottage—400/– to 800/–; older sgl w/o bath—80/–, dbl—150/–; prices incl tax, levy, service. Credit: AE, BA, DC. Built in 1904, Norfolk exudes character and colonialism. It grew with the city, adding rooms, wings, cottages; the whole of it·is well managed by the Block chain. Best rooms are new doubles, 1937-wing doubles, and the cottages. Central courtyard has aviaries, manicured lawn, semicovered pioneer wagon. Pool, sauna in another yard. Veddy British dining room, popular Lord Delamere snack terrace, steak room. Rating: 1st-class international, preferred by safari clients and The Rich. ★★★ for atmosphere, character, excellent staff, comfort, congeniality. Govt. class B (strange!).

Hotel Inter-Continental Nairobi, Box 30667, tel. 35550; cable IN-HOTELCOR. City Hall Way at Uhuru Highway. 430 dbls w/bath, balcony. Rates: bed only: sgl—155/– to 190/–; dbl—230/– to 270/–. Credit: AE, BA, DC. Pan Am- and government-owned hotel is huge (apparently the largest hotel complex in Eastern Africa—860 beds), modern, bland, and chock-full of package tourists. Lobby tends toward the gauche, has shops, offices. Rooms are standard Inter-Continental—straw furniture and colorful fabrics, relaxing but undistinguished. Worn spots on walls tell of hotel's constant use since 1969 opening. 3 bars, 3 restaurants. Parking. Pool. Rating: 1st-class international, less inviting than the Hilton in this class. ★. Govt. class A*.

New Stanley Hotel, Box 30680, tel. 33233; cable SNUGGEST. Kenyatta Ave. at Kimathi St. 70 sgls, 152 dbls, 7 suites, all w/bath. Rates: bed only: sgl—147/– or 171/50; dbl—245/– or 269/50, incl tax, levy, service. Credit: AE, BA, DC. Eight-story hotel dating to 1913 and 1929, New Stanley has been renovated, extended since. All rooms choice, comfortable, every floor with a different color scheme, its own nice lobby area. Table d'hôte restaurant plus deluxe Grill Room, busy Thorn Tree café, modern Safari Bar, famous Long Bar, arcade shops. Rating: 1st-class international, one of the best hotels in town. ★★. Govt. class A.

Panafric Hotel, Box 30486, tel. 21245; cable PANAFOTEL. Kenyatta Ave. 1 km from GPO. 76 sgls, 84 dbls, all w/bath, balcony. Rates: B&B: sgl—126/50; dbl—232/–. Credit: AE, BA, DC. Big (8 floors), bland, stucco-and-concrete building, inexpensively designed, put up in 1965 by BOAC, the government, and others. Up from the functional lobby (Muzak-filled) are modern rooms with unfancy furniture, thin carpeting; rooms are bruised here and there, some chairs threadbare, carpets with scattered spots, white walls need repainting. This is a Govt. class A hotel? Nice pool, lawn. Simba Grill dining room, Flamingo Garden café. Parking. Rating: 2d-class international. Late note: Hotel underwent a half-million-dollar modernization and decoration program in 1974.

Hotel Ambassadeur, Box 30399, tel. 26803; cable AMBASSOTEL. Government Road opposite Hilton. 20 sgls, 60 dbls, 10 trpls, all w/bath. Rates: B&B: sgl—80/–; dbl—140/–; trpl—190/–. Credit: BA, DC. Seven-story hotel built 1961–62 as 1st-class establishment, now slipping. Plain doubles have corkblock floor, red or blue pattern drapes, bedspreads. Dining room plus La Taverna (à la carte) and snack bar. Rating: 2d-class international, getting raggedy around the edges, but basically a better hotel than, say, the 680. Govt. class B.

Six-eighty Hotel, Box 43436, tel. 32680; cable SENTRIGUEST. Kenyatta Ave. at Muindi Mbingu. 340 dbls (incl 4 suites) w/bath or shower. Rates: bed only: sgl—136/– to 189/–; dbl—208/–, incl tax, levy, service. Credit: BA, DC. New in 1972, the 680 (number of beds) caters to big tours fitting into posh-dorm-like rooms. Best are expensive higher-floor doubles with balcony over Kenyatta Ave. The Minute Chef dining room and the Pub snack bar leave no impression. Rating: 2d-class international, sterile but conveniently located; may mellow with age.

Hotel Milimani, Box 30715, tel. 21004, 25821. 1.6 km from GPO on Milimani Road. 75 dbls w/bath, balcony. Rates: B&B: sgl—122/–; dbl—196–/; incl tax, levy, service. Credit: BA, DC. 1972 hotel for middle-budget travelers, on par with the 680 in its inexpensive construction, mediocre style (new Swiss management may make changes), great capacity to accept packages. Five floors high, Casblah-white exterior, highly polished floors, pleasing rooms. Malaika dining room and nightclub. Pool. Rating: 2d-class international, a bit expensive for what you get.

Hotel Boulevard, Box 48945, tel. 27567; cable ARCHOTEL. Located at end of Harry Thuku Road, 1.6 km from downtown. 72 dbls (incl 2 suites), all w/bath. Rates: B&B (Continental): sgl—116/–; dbl—183/–, incl. Credit: DC. 1970 modern, with grounds, Boulevard has uninspired European rooms with balconies over nice gardens. Dining room has black vinyl furniture, beige and orange color scheme, à la carte menu, slow service, and view toward Museum and Snake Park. Best part is garden, pool, terrace. Rating: 2d-class international, favored by British, German packages.

New Avenue Hotel, Box 42382, tel. 28711; cable AVENUE. Kenyatta Ave. at Koinange St. 52 dbls, 16 sgls, all w/bath or shower. Rates: B&B: sgl—94/–; dbl—184/–, incl. Credit: AE, BA, DC. 1929 hotel remodeled 1952. Pleasant, older, urban (no grounds); favorite of German, French tours. Rooms clean, cheerful, have balconies over Kenyatta Ave. Dining room plus Topaz Grill. Rating: 1st-class local, good bet. Govt. class B.

College Inn, Box 30471, tel. 20268; cable AFTOURS. University Way near Muindi Mbingu, short walk from downtown. 10 sgls, 24 dbls, 8 trpls, all w/bath or shower. Rates: B&B: sgl—72/– or 84/–; dbl—144/–; trpl—180/–, incl tax, levy, service. Credit: AE, BA, DC. Modest urban hotel, businesslike, unprepossessing. Singles are cubbyholes that get kitchen noise, doubles larger but get University Way noise. Not much on atmosphere. African Tours & Hotels plans a new flagship hotel. Rating: 1st-class local, was overpriced, still is a bit. Govt. class B (!?).

EXPENSIVE—OUT OF TOWN

Masai Lodge, Box 20130, Nairobi; bookings to Forest & Frontier Lodges (p. 87). Just outside Nairobi National Park near Masai Gate, 17 km from downtown via Park (pay fee), 23 km if going via Magadi Road. 15 dbls, going to 35 dbls; all rms w/bath. Rates: B&B: sgl—155/–; dbl—255/–, incl tax, levy, service. Daily membership—5/– per adult. Credit: DC. 1972 Masai Lodge is the closest game lodge to the city, makes a good base if you have a car (transport otherwise difficult). Like new lodges in Meru, Amboseli, Mara, this one is styled after a Masai *enkang,* with each comfortable room in its separate mud-gray-colored, four-humped square igloo, whole complex with humped main building surrounded by thorn hedge. Decor is African Modern: cowhide chairs, flagstone floors, Masai motifs. Airy dining room (à la carte and table d'hôte) has good view over Kingfisher Gorge into the park. Animals on view, birdwatching good, too. Rating: 1st-class international, gets our ★★ for desirable location, comfort.

Safari Park Hotel, Box 45038, Nairobi; tel. Ruaraka (80) 2311; cable EAGLEHOTEL. On Thika Road 11½ km from Uhuru Highway. 3 sgls, 67 dbls (3 trpls), all w/bath or shower. Rates: B&B: sgl—106/–; dbl—156/–, incl. Credit: BA, DC. Country hotel (formerly the Spread Eagle) set in 33 acres of grounds, convenient if you have a car (bus service every 2 hours). Rooms uniformly pleasant, simple, cool. Old-fashioned, woody dining room (table d'hôte), handsome billiard room, big warm lounge with white piano, stone fireplace; 4 bars, sunny terrace with big sculpture-fountain by Gregory Maloba. Nairobi HQ of several European package tours. Rating: 2d-class international, a fine place which we'll give a ★. Govt. class B*.

Westwood Park Country Club, Box 41737, Nairobi; tel. Karen (88) 2233, 2347. Ngong Road, 17 km from the city. 73 dbls plus 4 cottage dbls, all w/bath or shower. Rates: FB: sgl—130/–; dbl—184/–, incl tax, levy, service, membership. Credit: BA, DC. Not so much a country club as a country resort hotel: big grounds (80 acres), 2 pools, tennis, mini-golf (real golf nearby), riding. Main building is big stone manse (part was first farmhouse Karen Blixen lived in) with long terrace, friendly bar, largish dining room. Doubles in old wing solid, comfortable; doubles in new Spanish-style wing more softly styled. Transport into town once daily. Many German packagers lodge here. Rating: 2d-class international, country fresh. Govt. class C.

Kentmere Club, Box 49666, Nairobi; tel. Kentmere (735) 253. Limuru Road, 22½ km from downtown (see Route K-12). 4 sgls, 8 dbls, all w/bath. Rates: B&B: sgl—146/–; dbl—177/–, incl tax, levy, service, 10/– daily membership. Credit: DC. Known mainly for its delicious food, Kentmere also has a few country-inn rooms, each with antique furniture, Dutch door opening onto lush gardens. Walkways among the fuchsias and bougainvillaea bring you to patio, Tudoresque bar, members' lounge, very proper dining room. Rating: 1st-class local, very quiet, idyllic safari base (Ellerman Lines Safaris owns it). ★★.

Njiru Country Club, Box 47166, Nairobi; tel. Ruaraka (80) 2597/8; cable NJICLUB. Dandora Road off Thika Road (turn right past Fox drive-in), follow signs. 1973 country club has accommodations, restaurant. Rates: bed only: sgl—70/–; dbl—130/–. Credit: DC.

MODERATE

Fairview Hotel, Box 40842, tel. 31277; cable FAIRVIEW. Bishop Road off Valley Road, 1.8 km from GPO. 27 sgls, 46 dbls; 40 rms w/bath or shower. Rates: B&B: sgl—52/65 to 76/05; dbl—99/45 to 117/–; incl tax, levy, service. Sloganed "the country hotel in town," Fairview has 5 acres landscaped by Peter Greensmith, 1933 central building, 1959 annex, pleasant, light rooms (some with Persian rugs). Cream-colored lobby is busy with lounge, bar; dining room is adjacent. Rating: Very good 1st-class local, best hotel for the price, our choice for middle-budgeters. Gets a ★. Govt. class C.

Mayfair Hotel, Box 42680, tel. 56931; cable MAYFAIR. Waiyaki Way 2½ km from GPO. 16 sgls, 122 dbls, 5 suites, almost all w/bath. Rates: B&B: sgl—72/50 to 102/50; dbl—112/50 to 132/50; cheap annex sgl w/o bath—32/50; dbl w/o bath—57/50. Credit: AE, DC. Built 1948, renovated 1967, new wing added 1971–72. Rooms clean, simply furnished; new rooms stark, more modern; suites waste of money. Gardens need attention; pool and Oasis Club are nice. Rating: 1st-class local, good for middle- to low-budget travelers. Govt. class B.

Grosvenor Hotel, Box 41038, tel. 21034. Girouard Road, 2.2 km from GPO. 43 dbls, 31 sgls, most w/bath or shower. Rates: B&B:

sgl—80/–; dbl—120/–, incl tax, levy, service. Credit: DC. Respectable, middle-class, middle-aged hotel with old, styleless rooms (best ones in former BOAC wing). Big bare dining room. Hotel needs painting. Grounds pleasant, includes pool, Beer Garden for outdoor lunch. Rating: 1st-class local, slipping. Govt. class C.

Safariland Hotel, Box 48119, tel. 55000, 55795. Chiromo Lane off Chiromo Road, 2.4 km from GPO. 73 dbls, 2 sgls, all w/shower. Rates: B&B: sgl—50/–; dbl—85/–. 1930s Safariland rambles around its grounds, even jumping across a street. Rooms unassuming, open onto center garden. Woody bar, indoor-outdoor lounges, pseudo-Tudor dining room (two menus) with immense antique mirror-lined buffet. Mammoth pool, too. Rating: 1st-class local, good for the money. Govt. class D.

Devon Hotel, Box 41123, tel. 56213; cable DEVONHOTEL. Chiromo Road, 2 km from GPO. 31 sgls, 37 dbls, almost all w/o bath. Rates: B&B: sgl w/o bath—62/–; dbl w/shower—132/50, incl tax, levy, service. Built 1930s, Devon is old but very well kept, with immaculate but plain, small rooms. Homey lounge has local-people-paintings; gold and white dining room serves mainly table d'hôte. Devon gets few tourists. Rating: Old and pleasant 1st-class local, definitely overpriced. Govt. class C.

Motel Agip, Box 14287, tel. 45272. Waiyaki Way near Westlands traffic circle, 3.6 km from GPO. 9 sgls, 123 dbls, all w/bath. Rates: B&B: sgl—74/–; dbl—123/–, incl tax, levy. Nairobi's only motel lacks U.S. motel amenities, comfort. Half the rooms date to 1964, rest from 1973; they feature parquet floors, otherwise do not shine. Clean—but we've heard alarming reports of shoddy housekeeping, room service. Free hourly transport into town. Rating: Very plain 2d-class international. Govt. class B.

Hurlingham Hotel, Box 43158, tel. 27795. Argwings-Kodhek Road, 3 km from GPO. 11 sgls, 6 dbls, all w/o bath. Rates: B&B: sgl—45/–; dbl—90/–. Small, cozy, friendly—feels like somebody's home, but maybe a bit funky. Lounge has owner's collection of prints, posters, gourds, shields, books, Maridadi pillows, TV (unusual). Cute, tiny bar, appealing little dining room. Garden terrace. Rooms not so great, could use work. Rating: Quiet, enticing 1st-class local, good bet if you don't mind sharing a bathroom. A ★ is warranted. Govt. class D.

Equator Inn, Box 49279, tel. 23331; cable EQUATORINN. Crauford Road, 2 km from GPO. 13 sgls, 17 dbls, only 6 w/bath. Rates: B&B:

sgl—50/–; dbl—90/–. Well-kept, quiet hotel dating from 1940s. Rooms are clean, not plush. Rating: 1st-class local, one of the few better places in this price range. Govt. class D (?).

New Ainsworth Hotel, Box 40469, tel. 55574; cable AINSWORTH. Westlands Road very near Museum. 14 sgls, 24 dbls, incl 28 w/bath. Rates: B&B: sgl—50/–; dbl—90/–. Built 1909–10, hotel has been "New" since its new owners. A secluded place, with shady courtyard, cactus garden, New Ainsworth is favored by Americans doing Museum research nearby. Rooms are as personable as rest of hotel. Rating: 1st-class local, good for families. Govt. class C.

Hotel Omar Khayyam, Box 43912, tel. 26555. Argwings-Kodhek Road, 3 km from GPO. 12 dbls w/bath. Rates: B&B: sgl—55/–; dbl—90/–. Motelish, blahish, 1971 suburban hotel has one or two Persian motifs, new and clean rooms. Rating: 1st-class local, but for character, go next door to Hurlingham.

Brunners Hotel, Box 40949, tel. 29961; cable BRUNNERS. Entrance on Muindi Mbingu St. 33 sgls, 55 dbls; 49 rms w/bath. Rates: B&B: sgl—45/– to 60/–; dbl—80/– to 100/–, depending on season. Built in 1948, Brunners is known by more people for its big off-the-street lounge with lingering colonial atmosphere, nice place for coffee and a look at the paper. Upstairs rooms functional, somewhat shabby. Draws low-budget packagers who like to be downtown. Rating: Less than 1st-class local, but respectable and conveniently located. Govt. class C.

Hotel Chiromo–Swiss Grill, Box 44677, tel. 46821; cable SWISSGRILL. Chiromo Road, 2.2 km from GPO. 6 sgls, 32 dbls, most w/bath or shower. Rates: B&B: sgl—50/–; dbl—90/–. Credit: BA. Chiromo, opposite the same-named forest, was established at the Swiss Grill in 1965. Rambling structure has rooms in wings around lawn; buildings, rooms, lawn all a bit unkempt. Rooms dull but clean. Small pool, sauna to come. Rating: 2d-class local, okay for low-budget packages, but it needs painting, renovation. Govt. class C.

New Continental Hotel, Box 14301, tel. 60321. On Rapta Road, Westlands, 4 km from GPO. 18 sgls, 21 dbls, all w/bath or shower. Rates: B&B: sgl—50/–; dbl—90/–. Started 1953, now run by Naivasha Safariland's owners, this homey hotel has a pleasant little lounge, inner courtyard with thorn tree and vines, not so great rooms (well-used furniture, spotted carpets). Hourly transport to town. Rating: Would be good 1st-class local if rooms were better, but okay for price. Govt. class C.

United Kenya Club, Box 42220, tel. 28621. State House Road near

Uhuru Highway. 10 luxury dbl bed sitting rooms, 36 other rms. Rates: FB: sgl—50/– or 55/–; dbl—95/–, plus monthly membership—10/–. Club founded late 1940s to bring all races together. New yellow-and-green buildings, pleasant grounds overlooking university athletic fields.

Plums Hotel, Box 40747, tel. 55646. Plums Lane near Ojijo Road, 2.6 km from GPO. 39 sgls, 9 dbls, most sharing bath. Rates: B&B: sgl—55/–; dbl—90/–. Asian-run hotel in suburbs (no grounds) has reasonably large, comfortable, quiet rooms. Rating: Less than 1st-class local, attractive to low-budget German travelers. Govt. class D.

Hotels in the moderate price range that are absolutely not worth paying to stay in, and aren't worth the space to describe, are the Esperia, Gaylord Inn, Impala, Normandie, Roma, Treeshade, Westview, and Windsor.

BUDGET

YWCA International House, Box 40710, tel. 20707. Protectorate Road, 1.2 km from GPO. 38 sgls, 30 dbls (7 for married couples), none w/bath. Rates: B&B: sgl—30/– or 35/–; dbl—50/– or 60/–; 4-bedded room or dorm—20/– per person. For single females, married couples. Y rambles over gardened hill, has college-dorm-like rooms, clean with bare essentials. Not safe to cross Uhuru Park below hostel after dark (take a taxi). Rating: Good inexpensive place for budgeting couples and women.

YMCA, Box 30330, tel. 22217. Next to United Kenya Club, State House Road. 12 rms w/bath plus 120 beds in dorms. Rates: FB: dorm bed—30/–; sgl—45/–. Pool, luggage deposit. Good reports on this from pennywise travelers.

The following hotels, downtown, vary a lot in quality. Look before you book, or take your chances: *Hotel Pigalle,* Box 14294, tel. 28203. Moktar Daddah St. Rates: B&B: sgl—50/–; dbl—87/–, incl tax, levy, service. Sloppily run, sloppy-looking. Rating: 3d-class local. Govt. class D. . . . *Hotel Fransae,* Box 47247, tel. 28817. Moktar Daddah St. Rates: B&B: sgl—45/– or 50/–; dbl—70/–. Govt. class D. . . . *Hotel Emsley,* Box 49860, tel. 23437. Tsavo Road (next to Embassy Cinema). Rates: B&B: dbl—50/– or 55/–. Govt. class D. . . . *Hotel Embassy,* Box 47247, tel. 24087. Tubman Road. Rates: B&B: sgl—45/– or 50/–; dbl—70/–. Govt. class D. . . . *Jumbo International Hotel,* Box 30569, tel. 29644. Murang'a Road, across traffic circle from Globe Cinema. Rates: B&B: sgl—35/–; dbl—55/–. . . . *Abbey Hotel,* Box 28265, tel. 31487. Gaborone Street (behind Ambassadeur

Hotel). Rates: bed & tea: sgl—20/–; dbl—35/–. . . . *Hotel Gloria,* Box 10345, tel. 28916. Ronald Ngala St. Rates: B&B: sgl—44/–; dbl—55/–. . . . *Hillcrest Hotel,* Box 14284, tel. 60060. Waiyaki Way near Westlands shopping center. Rates: bed & tea: sgl—30/–; dbl—50/–. . . . *City Lodge,* Box 41604, tel. 28663. Tom Mboya St. (behind Ambassadeur). Favored by Peace Corps Volunteers. . . . *Iqbal Hotel,* Latema Road (near Odeon Cinema). Rates: bed in quadruple: 10/–. Reasonably clean, safe for single women, says one. . . . Low-budgeters in dire need (no freeloaders) can stay for free at the *Ramgharia Sikh Temple,* off Racecourse Road. . . . *Nairobi Youth Hostel,* in Salvation Army Bldg., Racecourse Road (opp. Kariokor Market) has two dormitories, is cheap.

Camping

There are three places to camp. Cheapest is the *City Park Campground,* haunt of low-budget travelers, mostly overland expeditions and some hitchhikers. City Park is off Limuru Road, opposite the Aga Khan Hospital, 3.8 km from downtown. Booking is allegedly necessary (City Park Superintendent, Box 30075, Nairobi; tel. 55371). Fee: 2/50 per tent or vehicle per night. Facilities: Running water, toilets; campers have found discreet showers possible at the Inter-Continental's pool, among other places. Some shade, not much privacy, but lots of social life. Watch your property. *Westwood Park Country Club,* in Karen 20 km from the city (go out Ngong Road), permits camping for 10/– per person per night, with use of facilities for additional charge. Bookings to Box 41737, Nairobi; tel. Karen (88) 2233. *Rowallan Camp,* the campground of the Boy Scouts, is in 30 acres of the Ngong Forest, next to Jamhuri Park off Ngong Road, 10 km from town. Visitors are encouraged. Charges: 2/50 per person plus 2/50 per vehicle for camping, 2/– to use the pool. Bookings or info: Camp Warden, tel. 66911.

Where to Eat

Nairobi has a multitude of restaurants and coffeehouses, a selection of which is below. Food critic Craig Claiborne in 1971 found half a dozen restaurants to please his palate, and more have proliferated since, with not one, but two Japanese restaurants. Food is reasonably inexpensive in Kenya, but, as ever, the method of preparation jacks up the price, as does the style with which the bill is presented.

Every hotel has a dining room, and some have several.

African cuisine is the specialty of no particular restaurant; indeed, local food is served mostly at jerrybuilt "kiosks" in the Industrial Area, African markets, and elsewhere. The Kenya Tourist Development Corporation (KTDC), when it builds its headquarters, plans to have a good African restaurant on the ground floor. Until then, try the Simba Grill (Panafric Hotel) and the Norfolk special Wednesday lunches; the Simba's regular à la carte menu also has several African dishes.

Restaurants are listed below roughly in order of quality, price, style. Reservations are advisable at the ones with listed telephones. Top restaurants are usually open only for lunch (12:30 to 2) and dinner (7 to 10, later on Saturday), and most are closed Sunday. Jacket and tie are necessary at the classier places at night.

CONTINENTAL

New Stanley Grill Room, tel. 33233, and *dining room,* tel. 27456. Grill Room closed Saturday lunch, all day Sunday. Grill Room is the most expensive, nicest eatery in town. Old, plush, red, dark, it looks like an old New York hotel dining room. Minimum charge—17/–. On the menu: Burgundy snails in shell, avocado soup and chili, Nile perch Grenobloise, lobster New Stanley, escalope Holstein, carpetbag steak with oysters, tournedos Rossini, châteaubriand for two, lamb chops New Stanley special. Entrées—14/– to 43/–. Hotel's dining room has 19/– lunch, 25/– dinner. Friday smorgasbord—28/–; Sunday Italian dinner—25/–. Credit: AE, BA, DC.

Le Chateau, at the Inter-Continental, tel. 29661. Rooftop restaurant, cocktail lounge, exceedingly French in the American style: stone here and there, big chandeliers, French motifs. Band nightly except Sunday. Very pricey. Weekday buffet lunch—25/–. Long à la carte menu (English, French, German): smoked ham and upcountry melon, lobster cocktail, pan-fried mountain trout with cream sauce, broiled lobster, chicken Kiev, roast farm duckling with cherries Montmorency, chicken Surabaya in curry sauce, châteaubriand for two. Entrées— 21/– to 46/–. Credit: AE, BA, DC.

Amboseli Grill, at the Hilton, tel. 29751, ext. 258. One of the posher eating places, with a semi-African though modern decor, with charcoal and copper colors dominating, big copper grill, lionskins on the backs of chairs (in a place named for a game park!). Prices fairly high (entrées—21/– to 34/50). Samples: real turtle soup laced with aged sherry, fresh Mount Kenya river trout, rock lobster thermidor, sirloin, spit-roasted Naivasha duckling (chef's specialty). Credit: AE, BA, DC.

Kentmere Club, in Limuru (see Route K-12), tel. Kentmere (735) 253. One of Nairobi's finest restaurants. Dining room is timbered but —this is Africa—has a reed roof. Red placemats, English china, bird prints on the wall, fireplace, fresh flowers everywhere. Popular for country lunch. Menu is select, rich, and mostly French: Mombasa oysters, king crab, mushrooms à la Gregoire, plump English pigeons, roast duckling, lamb cutlets, rainbow trout, marmalade duck. Entrées— 14/50 to 29/50. Temporary membership—10/– for four people. Credit: DC.

Farm Hotel, in Limuru (see Route K-12), tel. Tigoni (76) 323. Immaculate old stone farmhouse disguises what some call the best French restaurant in Nairobi. Dishes on à la carte menu range from 19/– up to 29/–, include Aylesbury duckling, pork fillet à la crème, turtle soup, trout aux amandes, tournedos Rossini. Note: As a hotel (★) it has a mere two doubles, either of which will do for an extremely quiet country weekend. Rates: B&B: double—90/–. Credit: DC.

Alan Bobbe's Bistro, Caltex House Arcade, Koinange St., tel. 21152. Closed Sunday. Calling itself "a corner of France in the heart of Africa," the Bistro has split-level black, blue, red, and white dining rooms, the upstairs section being most intimate. Winston Churchill was first to sign the guestbook. High-priced (entrées—25/– and up) menu is handwritten: smoked Dutch eel, half-dozen escargots, onion soup, chicken Creole, young duckling Bistro style, steak Diane, banana flambé Bobbe. Good wine list. Credit: AE, DC.,

The Tsavo Restaurant, in the Hilton, tel. 34000. Olive and green in decor, has better view than fancier Amboseli Grill. Big place serves hot and cold buffet for lunch (safari lunch—19/60 inclusive) and dinner, plus some à la carte: spaghetti alla carbonara, chef's salad bowl, grilled spring chicken, filet mignon. Entrées—13/80 to 21/80 inclusive. Credit: AE, BA, DC.

Simba Grill, at the Panafric, tel. 35166. Decor is pleasant—red, white, and wood—and the bar is highly polished stone. Dancing nightly until midnight, 1 or 2 A.M. Table d'hôte lunch (15/–) and dinner (20/–), also à la carte menu in French and Swahili: grilled sole, fondue Bourguignonne, half lobster, T-bone, tournedos à Niçoise and many Kenya dishes. Entrées—16/– to 35/50. Wednesday is the special Kenya lunch: *muteta* soup (Kikuyu), *matoke* (Uganda banana dish), *githeri* (maize and beans), *sukuma wiki* ("sees you through" vegetable dish), *mseto, ugali,* grilled leg of impala and other meats. Credit: AE, BA, DC.

Marino's, mezzanine of International House, Mama Ngina St., tel. 27150. Closed Sunday. Has an uncozy, cavernous dining room, outdoor terrace, long bar. The chef is Marino Lavarini, formerly of Lavarini's. Selections: escargots Bourguignonne, lasagne al forno, veal escalopes with mushroom sauce, châteaubriand for two, zabaglione with Marsala. Wines. Entrées—12/50 to 40/–. Credit: BA, DC.

Lavarini's, Government Road, tel. 20359, 28613. Closed Sunday lunch. Very popular, noisy, friendly, wood, stucco, and stone restaurant with fountain in the middle of room. Less formal than Marino's. Minimum—10/–. Good for pizzas—10/50. Items: minestrone, ravioli in brodo, lobster thermidor, grilled steak pizzaiolla, tournedos Rossini, Irish coffee. Entrées—6/– to 28/–. Credit: AE, BA, DC.

Swiss Grill (Club Le Chalet), at Hotel Chiromo–Swiss Grill, tel. 56821/2/3. Closed Sunday. Guests enter free, others pay 5/–. Dinner is 8–10, band goes on to 1:30 or 2. Very woody place with stucco walls, heavy furniture. Entrées—14/50 to 33/–. Items: Rainbow trout, lobster thermidor, fondue for two, prime fillet steak, piccasa Milanese, tournedos Rossini. Guests can have table d'hôte lunch—12/50; dinner —15/–. Credit: BA, DC.

La Taverna Grill, at the Hotel Ambassadeur, tel. 26803. Quite nice second-floor restaurant. Bargain salad buffet at lunch—6/75. Entrées —8/– to 17/50 and up. Menu items: Malindi melon and ginger, real turtle soup, rainbow trout meunière, poached kingfish, ravioli Niçoise, escalope Viennoise, roast Longonot capon Côte d'Azur, tournedos Bordelaise, American porterhouse. Credit: DC.

Hotel Milimani dining room (Malaika Club), tel. 29461. Three hexagons connected together, with colorful murals, solid wood floor. Entrées (10/50 to 25/–) include lobster thermidor, Kenya rainbow trout, shrimp omelet, roast capon and mushrooms. Malaika Club, open 10 P.M.–3 A.M., serves dinner also. Credit: BA, DC.

International Casino. See "Nightlife" below.

Masai Lodge dining room. The only place you can dine in Nairobi and have any chance of seeing wildlife: the split-level dining room faces Nairobi National Park across Kingfisher Gorge, and the lodge itself is in Kitengela Game Conservation area; one end of the lodge overlooks a salt lick. Giraffe, zebra, waterbuck, lion, and leopard (baited for) have been seen. Nonguests pay 5/– to get in. Table d'hôte dinner is 22/50. Entrées run 15/– and up. À la carte selections:

soup made from seafish, shrimp, and port, gnocchi à la Romana, deep-fried oysters, chicken Bijou, crêpes au porc, *ugali,* veal piccata New York. Credit: DC.

Topaz Grill Room, at the New Avenue Hotel, tel. 28711. Decor is green and white, bamboo and rock, abstract paintings and Arab coffee pots. Dancing nightly except Sunday. Salad buffet lunch—6/– including coffee, cheese, biscuits. À la carte plates start at 10/–. Items: oysters, Nile perch, prawns Lisette, *ugali,* Limuru duckling, capon dressed. Credit: AE, BA, DC.

Agip Restaurant, on Waiyaki Way, Westlands, tel. 45272. Unassuming decor but varied lunch and dinner menus, entrée price 12/50 to 32/–. Selections: grilled chicken, lobster thermidor, escalope paprika, châteaubriand, chicken California, crêpes flambées. Wines.

Lobster Pot, Cabral St. at Tom Mboya St., tel. 20491. Closed Sunday. Bar-lounge plus small dining room adjacent. Seafood, obviously, entrées 8/50 low but typically 17/– to 29/–. Avocado shrimp cocktail, real turtle soup, Dover sole Colbert, broiled lobster with butter, prawn curry, rum omelet flambé. Credit: AE, DC.

P.A.'s, Silopark House, Mama Ngina St., tel. 28683. International menu.

Angus, 1st floor, Uchumi House, tel. 24306. New place with bar decorated with murals, somewhat friendly dining room with plaid tablecloths. Mostly steaks (10/– to 14/– for a fillet) but also some Greek dishes—stifatho, moussaka, Greek savoy (9/– to 11/–).

Arturo, 1st floor, Lugard House, Government Road (next to Kenya Cinema), tel. 26940. Unstylish but pleasant Italian-Continental restaurant. Entrées (8/50 to 12/50 mainly) include spaghetti Bolognaise, lasagna Arturo, seafish fillet Livornese, fillet steak Parmigiana, liver Veneziana. Credit: AE, DC.

Steak House, Corner House, Kaunda St. near Kimathi St., tel. 23093. Closed Sunday lunch. Bargain place for steaks (9/– to 17/–), though the restaurant itself isn't much on style. Credit: AE, BA, DC.

CASUAL MEALS

Kenyan Coffee Shop, in the Hilton. Serves the guests breakfast (American—15/30; Continental—10/25!), informal meals and snacks. Atmosphere and style very American. Hamburger, club sandwich, minute sirloin, fresh tilapia, *ugali* runs 8/45 to 10/95—not cheap. Credit: AE, BA, DC.

Coffee Banda, at the Inter-Continental. Bamboo booths, counter service. Pix of wildlife. But very American. Casual eating: hot dogs, steak sandwich, hamburger, fried chicken, beef kebab Masai, tilapia in coconut milk, *irio,* banana boat, apple pie à la mode. Prices start at 6/50 for two dogs or a burger. Open 6 A.M.–2 A.M. Credit: AE, BA, DC.

The Thorn Tree, Kimathi St. The New Stanley's sidewalk café, a Nairobi meeting place. A tall thorn tree shoots up from the middle of the floor; it's a replacement for one that died of floor cleaning liquid, but this one may die of traffic noise and auto pollution. The service is lousy, but the people-watching is good. Hamburgers sell for 5/10; menu also has Longonot club sandwich, BLT, chef's salad, Bombay curry, "Hunter's Delight" omelet, spaghetti, fountain items. Open 7 A.M.–midnight. Credit: AE, BA, DC.

The Lord Delamere, at the Norfolk. The Delamere is the hotel's à la carte and casual meal-and-drinking complex, with a terrace and a couple of adjacent rooms, one with shining copper-covered tables. Snacks served 11–3, 6–10. Delamere offers Lamu prawn cocktail, Hungarian goulash soup, cheeseburger, cold meat buffet with potato salad, lake fish fillets, charcoal-grilled sirloin, filet de boeuf au poivre, Molo lamb chops, at prices 5/– to 12/50. Off the lobby is the hotel's table d'hôte dining room (tel. 35422) with starched white tablecloths: 20/– lunch; 25/– dinner. Special 25/– "Kenya Lunch" Wednesday— a dozen of the tastiest African (Luo, Kamba, Kikuyu) dishes of fish, chicken, game meat, beef, and vegetables, not the most traditional but good. Sunday curry lunch is also 25/–. Credit: AE, BA, DC.

Terrace Restaurant, at the Inter-Continental. By the oval pool. Lunchtime and dinner barbecue (19/– to 30/–): chicken with herbs, double lamb chops, T-bone, grilled lobster (in season). Sunday buffet —21/50; Orient buffet—21/–.

Oasis Club, at the Mayfair Hotel. Nonguests can use pool for 5/– weekdays, 7/50 weekends. Club menu has good plank steak with salad and chips: large—12/50; small—8/50; plus grilled steak marinated in spices—17/50. Credit: AE, DC.

Sunflower/Moonflower and *Lamu Coffee House,* Bruce House, between Standard and Kaunda, tel. 35097. Mini eating complex: Lamu (open to 7 P.M.) is indoors and on shady terrace, has copper-covered tables, copper stools, and padded benches in stuccoed rabbit warren of alcoves and niches; coffee, tea (1/– each), and tasties on a self-service basis. Attached is Sunflower, lunch-daytime restaurant with sand-wiches, mixed salad; and Moonflower, dinner-nighttime version of the same place (last orders at 10) with casserole (15/–) the specialty. Credit: DC.

Supermarket Roof-Top Cafeteria, Aga Khan Walk. Has three-course lunch with coffee/tea for 6/50.

Kentucky Fried Chicken, in 680 Hotel, Kenyatta Ave., also at Westlands. If you must.

ORIENTAL AND INDIAN

Pagoda, 1st floor, Shankardass House, Government Road (by Kenya Cinema), tel. 27036. Closed Sunday. Outdoor terrace is nice on warm evenings. Half-portions of Chinese are 8/50 basic. Credit: AE, DC.

Hong Kong, Koinange St. near University Way, tel. 28612. Closed Sunday. Peaceful place with white, red, and black decor, a nice man-agement. Reasonably inexpensive menu of quite tasty plates, with half-portions running 6/50 to 9/50. Roast duck, chicken bird's nest soup, stuffed Chinese mushrooms can be specially ordered. Credit: DC.

Mandarin, Tom Mboya St. (opposite Standard Bank), tel. 20600. Small, noisy, fairly expensive. Minimum—12/50. Half-portion prices: sweet and sour—8/– to 12/–; deep-fried—7/– to 12/–; bamboo shoot, bean sprout, and mushroom dishes—6/– to 12/–; foo yong—8/– to 12/–; soy sauce, oyster sauce, and gravy dishes—7/– to 14/–; rice and noodle—7/– to 12/–. Credit: AE, DC.

Bamboo Shoot, Tom Mboya St. (opposite Odeon Cinema), tel. 28009. Long, long menu is mainly Chinese with many Indian and Indonesian dishes. Modern decor with national motifs. Indian plates about 16/50; Indonesian dishes 19/– to 22/50; Chinese portions 10/– to 13/–. Credit: DC.

Samurai, 1st floor, Elite Arcade, Kimathi St., tel. 31626. You can sit around a counter at the cooking area and watch the Japanese chefs prepare, or you can sit in small adjacent rooms. Business lunch in-cludes soup, rice, coffee, and entrée—15/–. Dinner plates (19/50 to 30/–) include prawn tempura, sukiyaki, trout with pon-zu (soy and lemon), kushi katsu (deep-fried pork on skewers with vegetables). Credit: DC.

Akasaka, in the 680 Hotel, Standard St. side, tel. 20299. Sleek Japa-nese restaurant with moderately high-priced dishes (20/– to 25/–) such as beef sukiyaki, shrimp and vegetable tempura, sjitate or chicken soup, vinegared dish of cuttlefish. Main part of restaurant has tables; you sit on floor in private room.

Three Bells, Tom Mboya St. (behind the Ambassadeur), tel. 20628. Specialists in Indian food, offering mild, medium, and hot dishes. Not much atmosphere. Chicken, lobster, and other curries—8/50 to 16/50; tandoori chicken or prawns—14/50; fish dishes—7/50 to 15/–. Credit: AE, DC.

Moti Mahal, Muindi Mbingu St. near Monrovia St. Well-rated Indian restaurant. All curry, masala plates—7/– to 10/–; soups—2/–; green masala steak—7/50; also kebabs, samosas, bhajia, katlas, chops.

Curry Pot, Government Road near Moktar Daddah St. Clean place serving Indian food—6/50 to 12/50, masala chicken and chicken paprika tandoor—9/–.

Tropicana Curry Center, Kimathi St. We have a good report on this one.

Omar Khayyam, Argwings-Kodhek Road, tel. 26555. Persian cuisine.

Sunset Strip, Latema Road (off Tom Mboya). Freak haven: you can fill up for about 3/50 or 4/– on mostly Asian food. Special is chapati (like a tortilla) topped with minced meat and an egg, only 2/–.

COFFEE HOUSES AND SNACK PLACES

The Coffee House, Mama Ngina St., and *Uchumi Coffee House,* in Uchumi House arcade, both operated by the Coffee Board of Kenya, serving the best (Coffee House Blend) and cheapest (–/80) cup of coffee in town. Good in hot weather: ice cream coffee float—1/80. Closed evenings, Sundays.

The Coffee Bean, in the Hilton. Daytime coffee nook with bottomless cup—1/60. Open to 6 P.M.

Lamu Coffee House. See Sunflower/Moonflower above.

Ciroco, Kimathi St. Half off sidewalk, half inside. Stylish decor but unkempt. Belgian waffles are the specialty—3/– to 5/–. Open to 10 P.M.

Cona Coffee Bar, Mama Ngina St. Coffee—1/–. Opens at 7 A.M.— earlier than the Coffee House opposite.

Mocha, corner of Koinange and Moktar Daddah. Little place open to midnight, has the best hamburgers in town, with onion—2/25 (have two).

Coffee Bar, corner Mama Ngina St. at Muindi Mbingu. Funky place with theatrical decor. Good for hot chocolate after a late movie.

Batchelor's Bakery, Wabera St. Not a sit-down place. Walk in and buy a scrumptious hot meat or chicken pie to munch on the street—1/– and up.

Getting Around

Nairobi's downtown area is compact, so walking is the best way to get around.

Taxis: City Council-licensed taxis, in ranks here and there, are easily spotted by the broad yellow stripe painted on them. You can get charged by the meter (first mile or part thereof at 2/–, additional quarter-miles at –/50, plus 2/– for every 15 minutes of waiting) or by negotiating with the driver (complaints about overcharging, tel. 26561). Call cabs from *Archer's Cabs,* tel. 20289, 21935; *Mini-Cabs,* tel. 29058; and *Kenatco Transport,* tel. 25123, 21561. Do not pay more than 25/– to get from the airport to town in a regular cab, no more than 32/– (small) or 48/– (large) for a call cab. *Nairobi Handbook* has a long list of recommended call-cab fares to various points.

Buses: Local bus transport is very cheap. Kenya Bus Services (tel. 50304) runs the basic network, but there are single-bus lines and private buses. KBS route map is at the bus stop behind the Hilton on City Hall Way; the Information Bureau next to the Hilton can also help you get the right bus.

Street names: To celebrate the tenth anniversary of self-government in 1973, the government ordered all colonial street names to be replaced with African ones. This meant that a nasty old colonial governor (Northey) and the man who founded Nairobi (Sergeant Ellis) both got tossed out, bathwater and baby. In this chapter we have substituted the new names, since the street signs were changed quickly. Since the maps may not change so quickly, here is a brief list of some of the old and new names:

Queensway to Mama Ngina St.
Sgt. Ellis Ave. to City Hall Way
York St. to Kaunda St.
Portal St. to Banda St.
Hussein Suleman Road to Tubman Road
Bazaar St. to Biashara St.
Gulzaar St. to Moktar Daddah St.
Malik St. to Monrovia St.
Northey St. to Cabral St.

Coryndon St. to Mondlane St.
Lugard Lane to Nkrumah Lane
Duke St. to Ronald Ngala St.
Sclaters Road to Waiyaki Way
Salisbury Road to Chiromo Road
Fort Hall Road to Murang'a Road
Ainsworth Hill to Museum Hill
Marlborough Road to Nyerere Road
Buckleys Road to Bunyala Road
London Road to Lusaka Road

The renaming was to affect 246 street names.

Information Bureau

The Kenya Tourist Development Corporation (KTDC) operates the Tourist Information Bureau in the landscaped oval in front of the Hilton. Address: Box 42278; tel. 23285. Open 8:30 A.M.–12:45 P.M., 2–4:30 P.M., Monday–Friday; to 12:30 Saturday. They can answer some questions, also sell you maps, give you brochures, and will take hotel and tour bookings for all over Kenya.

"What's On . . ."

The *Daily Nation* publishes a 32-page weekly guide called *What's On,* distributed free at hotels, tour operators, shops. It has plenty of advertisements, a good amount of inaccurate, incomplete, and outdated editorial information, and not much about what's on. See the entertainment pages in the *Nation* and the *Standard,* and ask.

Nightlife

Compared with other cities in Eastern Africa, Nairobi swings after dark, though the casual visitor will think the evening streets look somewhat deserted. But step outside the Hilton and hear Hallian's noise clear from Tom Mboya Street, or look in the lobby-bar of the Donovan Maule Theatre.

Top of the nightspot list for sheer class is the *International Casino,* near the National Museum; tel. 46000, 46627. Opened in December 1969, the Casino seats 400 in the nightclub section, also has room where roulette, chemin de fer, and baccarat get more attention than the Bluebell Girls. Five-course table d'hôte dinner (chosen from a menu) plus show, dancing, and admission to game room costs 60/–;

otherwise 20/– for the show, 10/– Casino entrance. Tab is not bad. Credit: AE, DC.

Very plush is the *New Stanley Grill Room,* tel. 33233. À la carte meals (see above, "Where to Eat") are served to 11, band goes on to 2. Cabaret or entertainment cost extra. *Le Chateau,* at the Inter-Continental, tel. 35550, has a show. The other big hotels also have music, dancing, but no show: *Tsavo Restaurant,* at the Hilton, tel. 34000; and the *Simba Grill,* at the Panafric, tel. 35166. Credit (at four above): AE, BA, DC. New on the scene is the *Malaika Club,* at the Hotel Milimani, tel. 21004. Dancing plus floor show (imported or local talent) costs 20/– without dinner, 40/– with. Credit: BA, DC.

Most of the popular action is at the regular nightclubs. Possibly the most crowded place in town is the *Starlight,* Crauford Road near the Panafric; tel. 22716. Good band, occasional entertainment, outdoor beer garden. The loudest place, on the other hand, must be *Hallian's,* Tom Mboya St., tel. 23628, featuring hilarious drinking, loud band, disco, dancing to dawn; costs a couple shillings to get in. The *Sombrero,* Moktar Daddah St., tel. 27949, has cabaret with imported strippers, continuous after 11:30, and a smoky atmosphere. On the same street is the *Rainbow,* tel. 33480, with Congolese (Zairean) music, African strippers, cabaret after 11:30, dancing from 9, also traditional dancing; costs 7/50 to enter.

Somewhere in the middle is the *Club Le Chalet* at the Hotel Chiromo–Swiss Grill, tel. 46821. The club is often featured on Nairobi by Night tours as an alternative to the Casino for dinner, dancing. Nearby: *Club 1900,* next to the Safariland; tel. 46461. Supper, disco dancing nightly (7–12); 10 bob to get in. The local populace likes discos, and there are several Fridays and Saturdays, including at the *Golf Range,* Langata Road; *Westwood Park Country Club,* Ngong Road, Karen; *The Tavern,* at the Inter-Continental; *Dambusters Club,* Wilson Airport, tel. 20001 (Dambusters has an English pub atmosphere, welcomes overseas visitors). Those under 20 can head for the *Impala Club,* Ngong Road; it's a football (i.e., soccer) club with a 200-decibel rock band Fridays. Mayfair Hotel's *Oasis Club* has a Wednesday disco. It costs 5/– to get into most discos.

Culture and Entertainment

Nairobi has enough of each to keep a large resident and tourist population reasonably busy. It has, for one, East Africa's only professional theater, the *Donovan Maule Theatre Club,* located opposite

Giraffes have to do the splits to get a drink of water, but they can recover from this position quickly in case of danger. In Nairobi National Park, Kenya.

Three young lions (males on either side of the female) in Nairobi National Park. You've never felt ignored until you've been ignored by a lion.

Cape buffalo in bushes at Amboseli Game Park, Kenya. He looks ill-tempered and mean and he *is*.

Mirror reflections in the Zambezi River of the riverine gallery forest, above Victoria Falls.

Shore of Lake Malawi.

Priest in a rock-carved church in Lalibela, Ethiopia. He is carrying *(left)* a Lalibela cross and *(right)* a prayer stick, used for leaning on during services.

Woman selling potatoes at the Saturday market, Gondar, Ethiopia.

Children. Kolo, Tanzania.

Zebras in Serengeti National Park, Tanzania. This shows how optically confusing zebras can be, proving that the black-and-white stripes are a form of protection.

Eland, among the largest of antelope, at Mount Kenya Safari Club. Scientists are attempting to domesticate eland for meat and milk.

Elephants in Tsavo West National Park, Kenya, seen from the terrace of Kilaguni Lodge.

St. George killing the dragon, a mural in the church of Debre Berhan Selassie, Gondar, Ethiopia. St. George is the national saint of Ethiopia.

Parliament between Harambee and Haile Selassie avenues. The company has a continuous series of comedies, thrillers, and revivals, so that there is always something on. Performances are usually on the following schedule: Tuesday at 6, Wednesday and Thursday at 9, Friday at 5:15 and 9, Saturday at 6 and 9:30. Day membership is 10/–, monthly membership 30/–; seats are 15/–. Reservations, tel. 22300. *What's On* and the newspapers have details on the current play.

The other theater is the *Kenya National Theatre,* opposite the Norfolk Hotel, rented out at any one time for a play by the Theatre Group, the National Theatre Company, the City Players, or other groups, or for a concert by visiting soloists, or to the Kenya Film Society for biweekly films (see below), or Bevia Lambe's Puppet Theatre. Concert tickets are usually 20/–. See the daily papers or phone 20536.

New in 1973 is the *Bomas of Kenya* complex on Forest Edge Road near Nairobi National Park. It is an 80-acre government-developed cultural facility in two parts: a huge, round, thatched-roof, 2,000-seat auditorium where the two 36-member dance troupes present traditional dancing, singing, and drumming; and an African village composed of 16 compounds, each containing the huts, grain bins, and so forth of a Kenya tribe. Eventually, craftsmen will live in each compound and sell their carvings, baskets, and other crafts. Afternoon performances are Monday to Friday at 2:30 P.M., weekends at 3:30; evenings at 9 P.M. Admission: 22/50 for adult nonresidents (10/– per child), 5/– for residents. Tours, with lunch, cost about 45/–. Inquiries, tel. Langata (89) 642 or 672. Bomas is located on Route K-14, Km 10.

Other traditional dancing can be seen at the Small World Country Club, on the Mombasa Road (p. 190), and elsewhere outside town; see package listings KP-10, 11, and 12.

Cinemas

First-run downtown cinemas are the brand-new *Nairobi Cinema,* Uchumi House, Government Road (opposite the Hilton across City Hall Way), tel. 26603; the *20th Century,* Mama Ngina St., tel. 27957; and the *Kenya,* Government Road, tel. 27822, 24677. All are air-conditioned. Second-run theaters include the *Odeon,* Tom Mboya St. (at Latema Road), tel. 22030; the *Metropole,* Adams Arcade, Ngong Road, tel. 66967, 67158; and the *Casino,* River Road (at Maganbhai Road), tel. 24472. There are two drive-ins: the *Fox,* Thika Road, and the *Belle Vue,* Mombasa Road. The *Embassy, Globe, Shan,* and *Lib-*

erty play Indian movies exclusively (but no Satyajit Ray!). The *Cameo*, Kenyatta Ave., plays skin flicks.

Movies are usually shown at 5 and 9 P.M., with at least half an hour of ads and newsreels. Admission prices at the first-run theaters start at 6/−.

The *Kenya Film Society* (Box 72148) has a 50- or 60-film schedule of good films, mainly European. The society advertises in the Thursday *Standard,* the *Sunday Nation,* and the *Sunday Post.* Bona-fide tourists and visitors are admitted at the door for 10/−.

Art Galleries

All that are so dubbed are not galleries. Some Nairobi "galleries" are merely sculpture and curio shops; the real ones, listed here, are U.S.-type selling galleries, with occasional shows. *Gallery Watatu,* 1st floor, Standard St. (above Studio Arts 68), tel. 28737. Watatu runs the *New Stanley Art Gallery* off the hotel lobby. *Paa-ya-Paa Gallery,* Sadler House, Sadler Lane (off Koinange St. behind EAA terminal), tel. 26755. *Tryon Gallery,* lobby of International House, Mama Ngina St., tel. 27886. Wildlife and sporting paintings and prints. *East African Wild Life Society Gallery,* mezzanine floor, Hilton Hotel Arcade, Mama Ngina St., tel. 27047. *Kenya Arts Society,* on Arboretum Road, tel. 25891.

Through the Watatu and the Tryon you can contact such excellent resident artists as Rena Fennessy, Jony Waite, and Thelma Sanders.

Libraries

McMillan Memorial Library, Banda St., has a good Africana collection. *American Library* (USIS), Shankardass House, Government Road. *British Council Library,* opposite Norfolk Hotel. *Goethe-Institut,* Harambee Ave. *Alliance Française,* Tom Mboya St. *East Africa Natural History Society–National Museum Library,* at the Museum; EANHS, Museum Society members or serious researchers only. *University of Nairobi—Gandhi Library;* inquire about reader's cards.

Churches

Anglican: All Saints' Cathedral, Kenyatta Ave., tel. 20715. *Lutheran:* Lutheran Church, Uhuru Highway at University Way, tel. 66169. *Nondenominational:* Nairobi Chapel, Protectorate Road. *Presbyterian:* St. Andrew's Church, top of University Way, tel. 48353.

Roman Catholic: Holy Family Cathedral, Parliament Road, tel. 20971. *Methodist:* Lavington Church (associated with Anglican and Presbyterian churches), tel. 48352. Also Baptist, Christian Scientist, Pentecostal, Quaker, Mennonite, Seventh-Day Adventist, Salvation Army, Greek Orthodox, Jewish, Baha'i, Hindu, Moslem, Sikh, and Ismaili services. Saturday newspapers have times of services.

Shops and Services

You can get just about anything in Nairobi; it may not be cheap, but it's probably available. Nairobi is a travel headquarters, and it is easy to outfit an expensive or a cheap safari.

Army surplus equipment (tents, clothes, etc.): Young Traders Ltd., Moktar Daddah St.

Bakeries: Ovendoor, Westlands. Batchelor's, Wabera St.

Barbers: Boston's, Baring Arcade, Kenyatta Ave. Queensway Hairdresser, Vedic House Arcade, Mama Ngina St.

Body builder (for roof racks, sleeping platforms, or whatever): Kehar Singh, Baricho Road (Industrial Area).

Books: Prestige Booksellers, Mama Ngina St., Box 45425. The Bookshop, Kaunda St., Box 30247. S. J. Moore, Government Road, Box 30162. Toddler Bazaar, Market St., has thousands of secondhand paperbacks for taking on safari. East African Wild Life Society (p. 136) has wildlife books.

Cameras, optics: Elite Camera House, Kimathi St. and elsewhere. Ebrahim Camera House, IPS Bldg., Kimathi St. Sapra Studio, Kaunda St. *Rental:* Nilestar Photo-Cine, Kenyatta Ave. Also Ebrahim. (Telephoto lenses and cameras rent for 20/– or 25/– per day.)

Camping equipment, new and rental: See p. 109.

Camping gas: See p. 109.

Five-and-ten items: Woolworths, Kimathi St. at Kenyatta Ave., also at 680 Hotel, Kenyatta Ave.

Freight forwarders: Schenker & Co., International House, Box 46757. See travel agents, p. 99.

Hairdressers: Elegance, Hilton, tel. 21923. Carina, City Hall Way, tel. 27626. Elton's, Standard St., tel. 32534.

Hardware: Alibhai Shariff, Kimathi St., also Government Road. Hardware Stores Ltd., Government Road.

Inoculations: Inoculation Centre, City Hall, Room 44, tel. 24281.

Jewelers: Bradley, Mama Ngina St. Apollo Watch Co., Hilton.

Laundry, cleaning: Pearl, Koinange St., also Vedic House Arcade. White Rose, Kenyatta Ave. Laundromat, Mpaka Road (near post office), Westlands (washing load—6/−; drying cycle—1/−).

Liquor: Nairobi Wines & Spirits, Wabera St.

Lumber: Timsales, Enterprise Road (Industrial Area).

Office space: Office Hotels Ltd., International House, Mama Ngina St. Box 48747 (office—60/− per day, 250/− per week; also typing, telex, duplicating, etc.).

Opticians: V. M. Browse, New Stanley House, Standard St. Lens Ltd., Kimathi St.

Packing, wrapping: Mr. Wilson, tel. 24682. Packing, crating done by freight forwarders for 10/− per cubic foot. Bully the curio shop into packing and sending it for you, and get it in writing.

Pharmacies (*chemists*): Robson Chemist and Mansion Pharmacy, both Wabera St. Cosmopolitan Chemist, Kimathi St.

Photocopying: Xerox copyroom, International House lobby, Mama Ngina St. (1/− per copy).

Photo shops: Colorama Studios, Government Road (color film processed in a day). Studio One, Lugard House, Government Road. See "Cameras, optics" above.

Real estate agents: Tyson's, Box 48228. Velco Properties, Box 30282. Colburn's, Box 41922. Estelle Glass, Box 74706. Thursday newspapers carry the week's rental, sale listings.

Secretarial bureaus: Dorothy Wood, Mansion House, Wabera St., tel. 28178. Alison Keane, Queensway House, Kaunda St., tel. 25416.

Shoe repair: Shoecraft Ltd., Government Road.

Sports equipment: Nairobi Sports House, Government Road.

Supermarkets: Finefare, Kijabe St. (good prices). Supermarket Ltd., next to Uchumi House. K&A, Kenyatta Ave. Westlands Self-Service Store and Future Stores, both Westlands.

Mombasa

Kenya's second-largest city (1972 est. pop. 286,000) and East Africa's main port, Mombasa, like Beirut, Istanbul, or Singapore, conjures up images of inscrutable mystery and romance—one of those places that even after you've been there retains that aura. Perhaps it's because Mombasa is, like the other cities, a world port, with attendant legends and stories; perhaps it's because of Old Town, and the dhows in the old harbor, and Fort Jesus, and the mingling of many races—Africans, Swahili, Arabs, Asians, Europeans, even Chinese.

Though the 5½-square-mile island city has few buildings older than the last century, Mombasa is one of the oldest settlements on the coast. But like other places, very little is known about it before the Portuguese came. It may have been visited by Phoenician sailors about 500 B.C. It may be the Tonika of that 1st-century travel guidebook, *Periplus of the Erythraean Sea*. But there is little believable documentary evidence.

Mombasa's written history really begins with Vasco da Gama, who sailed into the harbor April 7, 1498; he quickly left after an unenthusiastic reception and sailed on to Malindi, where he was welcomed. But Mombasa became a port of call for Portuguese vessels on the way to Goa, and was periodic victim of the usual Portuguese method of diplomacy, which was to conquer by threat, cannon fire, and demand for tribute. The Portuguese ruled from Goa on the coast of India, with local headquarters in Mozambique and an outpost in Malindi. Given the nature of the Europeans' business methods, coastal towns periodically rebelled, and Mombasa—then a big trading center with a population of 10,000—seemed to be more rebellious than others. So it was attacked, sacked, and burned four times (1505, 1528, 1587, and 1589 —naturally, there is nothing left of medieval Mombasa). The last attack was carried out with a rather ferocious ally, the cannibalistic Zimba, who had been eating their way up the coast for years. The Portuguese decided in 1593 to build a fort to keep Mombasa tame. The Sheikh of Malindi was brought in as sultan, and the Portuguese settled inside Fort Jesus' thick walls as masters of the coast for the next 100 years. The local Arabs revolted in 1631 and massacred all the Portuguese on the island; but others came the next year and reconquered town and fort. But Portugal soon had a rival on the Indian Ocean: the Sultan of Muscat and Oman, who in the mid-17th century began attacking the Portuguese (already threatened by other European powers) up and down the coast, finally driving them into two strongholds, Mombasa and Mozambique. After a 33-month siege, Fort Jesus was taken by the Omani Arabs in 1698, and the coast became a province of Oman, a Persian Gulf state. The Portuguese recaptured Mombasa briefly in 1728, for the last time. The sultan went back to Oman, leaving in control the Mazrui family, which not surprisingly became rather independent. Mombasa prospered and became fat, attracting the attention of a later Omani sultan, the famous Seyyid Said. Seyyid

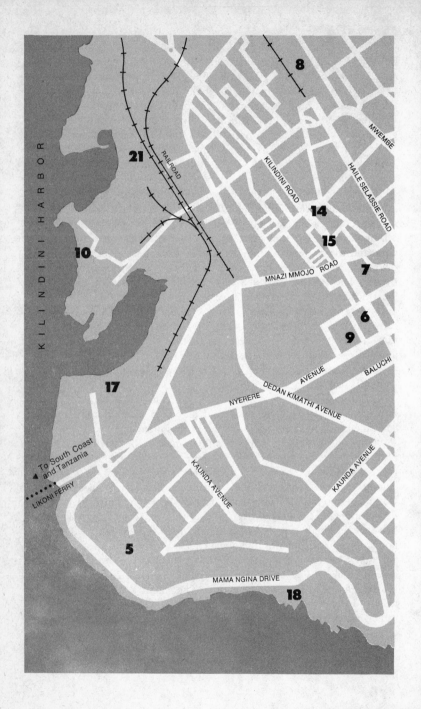

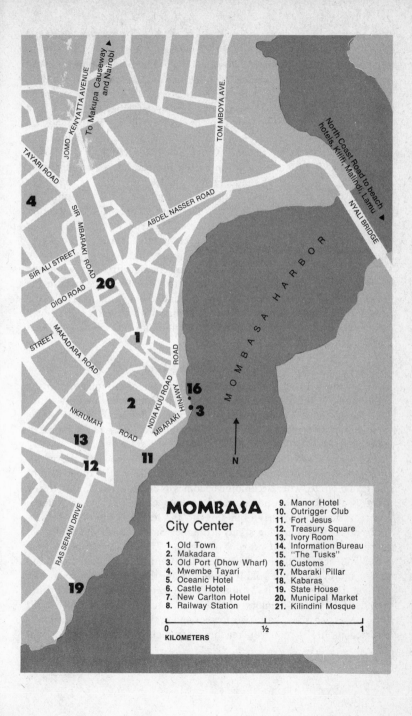

MOMBASA
City Center

1. Old Town
2. Makadara
3. Old Port (Dhow Wharf)
4. Mwembe Tayari
5. Oceanic Hotel
6. Castle Hotel
7. New Carlton Hotel
8. Railway Station
9. Manor Hotel
10. Outrigger Club
11. Fort Jesus
12. Treasury Square
13. Ivory Room
14. Information Bureau
15. "The Tusks"
16. Customs
17. Mbaraki Pillar
18. Kabaras
19. State House
20. Municipal Market
21. Kilindini Mosque

0   ½   1
KILOMETERS

MOMBASA HARBOR

NYALI BRIDGE

North Coast Road to beach
hotels, Kilifi, Malindi, Lamu ▶

To Makupa Causeway
and Nairobi ▲

JOMO KENYATTA AVENUE

TAYARI ROAD

SIR MBARAKI ROAD

SIR ALI STREET

DIGO ROAD

MAKADARA ROAD

STREET

NKRUMAH ROAD

RAS SERANI DRIVE

ABDEL NASSER ROAD

TOM MBOYA AVE.

NDIA KUU ROAD

MBARAKI HINAWY ROAD

N

seized the island of Pemba, alarming the Mazrui in Mombasa, who then coaxed the commander of a British coast-charting expedition, Captain Owen, to set up a British protectorate. "Owen's Protectorate" was short-lived—1824–25—and the British left the Arabs to fight among themselves. After four expeditions Seyyid finally took possession of Fort Jesus in 1837. He had by that time moved his headquarters from Muscat to Zanzibar, and it was Zanzibar's red flag which officially flew over Mombasa and the Kenya Protectorate (a 10-mile-wide coastal strip) until Kenya's independence in 1963.

The traveler to Mombasa should have an interesting time in this hot, humid city, and will enjoy it if he takes care to dress for the weather (light and casual clothes, sunglasses, and maybe even a hat), seek shelter from the midday heat, and never be too far away from something cold and refreshing, like a shower, a swimming pool, the ocean, or a drink. Most tourists, unless staying on the outskirts of town at the Oceanic, will probably prefer to stay across Nyali Bridge, where the hotels have their own beaches just beyond the swimming pool, and make short trips into the city. If combined with drives on the north and south coasts, Mombasa is worth a minimum stay of two or three days.

Mombasa Walking Tour

Following is a reasonably short walking tour of Mombasa, starting and ending at the Castle Hotel terrace. The tour takes in Fort Jesus, Old Town, the dhow port, and lesser points of interest. Other sights can be seen by renting a taxi for an hour or two (20/– per hour maximum charge).

From the Castle Hotel, walk east on Kilindini Road to the major intersection with Nyerere/Digo Road, continuing on the other side of the traffic circle, where Kilindini becomes Nkrumah Road. Just to the right is the Roman Catholic *Holy Ghost Cathedral*. After Baluchi Street, the area behind the buildings to the left is Jamhuri Park, with indigenous trees and plants and a number of structures including two mosques and the *Lord Shiva Temple,* a 1952 Hindu temple with a silver door leading to the shrine, sacrificial altars and sacred trees, and on top a crock of solid gold. Continuing on, the street becomes a little quieter. On the right is *Mombasa Memorial Cathedral* (Anglican), founded in 1903 in memory of Bishop Hannington (see p. 280), built in the Moorish style, with two towers and a silver-colored roof; it was restored in 1955. Soon you reach a very picturesque part of colonial

Mombasa, *Treasury Square,* off to the right, with several public build-ings including un-bank-looking banks, the *municipal building,* and the *old post office,* near which the railway station was until 1932. On Mvita Road next to Brooke Bond, and near the old PO, is the *Game Department Ivory Room,* established in 1912 as a storage and display room for elephant tusks (ivory), rhino horns (in demand as an aphrodisiac), hippo teeth (used for carvings), and other trophies recovered from poachers or collected from animals that died or were shot on control. There are twice-yearly auctions. At the December 1972 auction, more than $710,000 worth of ivory and trophies was sold, including 2,600 pieces of ivory, 359 rhino horns, and 553 hippo teeth (this gives some idea of how much poachers don't get away with). Private dealing in ivory was prohibited indefinitely September 1, 1973. You can visit the Ivory Room 7:45 A.M.–noon, 2–4 P.M. Monday–Friday, until noon Saturday.

Just past Treasury Square on the right are the *Law Courts,* opened in 1902. You are now outside *Fort Jesus,* the 1593 Portuguese fort (with a museum) that is one of the only remaining Portuguese build-ings on the East African coast and is Mombasa's main historical at-traction. From the bottom of the ditch (now a parking lot) near the entrance, the coral-block walls tower 52 feet, although they were originally constructed a bit shorter. Designed by an Italian military architect, and taking two years to build, Fort Jesus is a two-acre struc-ture that is roughly rectangular, with four corner bastions and a rec-tangular projection pointing out to sea. Its original ramparts were quite wide, with firing steps and gunports, and around the fort was dug a ditch from 10 to 40 feet wide and deep. The fort was virtually im-pregnable and was taken by attack only once in its history (it fell by treachery far more often). The central court contains (or contained) barracks, a chapel or church, cistern and well, guardrooms, powder magazine, priest's house, and governor's house. Mateu Mendes de Vasconcelos, the last captain of Malindi and the first captain of Mom-basa, was in charge of construction, carried out by Goan masons and Malindi laborers. The fort was dedicated April 11, 1593. The elliptical bastion and outer gate were built after the Arab revolt of 1631, while the battlements and parapets were rebuilt a number of times. The in-scription over the entry dates to 1648. James Kirkman's 24-page guide-book (price 1/50) gives full details.

In its turbulent history, the fort changed hands several times, and for at least 250 years the history of the fort is the history of Mombasa.

The major event in its history was the Great Siege by Omani Arabs from March 13, 1696, to December 13, 1698. The original garrison, 50 Portuguese and 1,500 loyal Swahili, held out through 1696 and was reinforced from Goa at Christmas. But these saviors brought the plague with them, and by the end of August 1697 the only Portuguese survivor was a teenager, while the commander was a Swahili named Bwana Daud. The ship that had brought the first reinforcements unluckily was wrecked on a shoal when it came back in September, and the crew became the new Fort Jesus garrison. In December 1697 a hundred soldiers landed and replaced Bwana Daud and the ship's crew, but that garrison too was decimated by plague, a more effective weapon than Arab guns. At the end of the year only eight Portuguese, three Indians, two African women, and one African boy were alive. The Arabs came over the wall near the S. Mateus gate on the night of December 12, 1698, but the defenders, holed up in one of the cavalier bastions, held them off until the next morning, when the captain was killed and the remnants surrendered. Two of the defenders told the Arabs there was gold in the powder magazine, led them to it, and blew it up, killing themselves and several Arabs. Portuguese reinforcements came into the harbor a few days later but sailed away when they saw the red flag of Oman over the fort.

The Portuguese tried and failed twice to take the fort, and finally reoccupied it bloodlessly in 1728, only to be driven out the next year, after which Mazrui-led Arabs and Omani Arabs alternated in holding the fort. The Sultan of Zanzibar used the fort from 1837 on as a barracks, and Fort Jesus became dilapidated. The last shots fired in anger were in 1875 when British men-of-war bombarded the fort to help put down a mutiny. Fort Jesus was used as a prison from 1895 until 1958 when it became a public monument; work was undertaken by James Kirkman to restore and excavate the fort, with funds from the Gulbenkian Foundation. The museum houses artifacts, including much porcelain, from the fort and from Gedi, Ngwana, Manda, and elsewhere on the coast. Fort Jesus is open daily 9 A.M.–6 P.M. Admission: nonresident adult—5/–, child—2/–; resident adult—2/–, child —1/– (half-price on weekends).

Exiting Fort Jesus, you may wish to hire a guide (dicker down to 5/–) for a tour through *Old Town,* the warren of narrow winding streets and tall shuttered houses across Nkrumah Road from the fort. Access is on either Ndia Kuu Road or Mbarak Hinawy Road (formerly Vasco da Gama Street). Besides the goldsmiths, ivory carvers, silk dealers, perfumemakers, spice merchants, and numerous other open-fronted shops, points of interest include the *Manadhara/Mandhry Mosque,* established about 1570, possibly the oldest mosque (out of 49) in Mombasa; the *Mombasa Club,* founded 1893, just on the outskirts near the fort; the *bazaar,* the area on Langoni Road (off Digo Road to the right of the municipal market); and the *Old Port,* which is entered at the Customs House in Government Square. A word with the customs officer on duty will get you by the "no admittance except on business" sign. The Old Port was the principal harbor for hundreds of years until the railway builders started Kilindini port on the other side of the island, but today it is Mombasa's *dhow port,* also sheltering other local and coastal craft.

Dhows, which you may see here anytime from December to April, are blown to the East African coast from the Persian Gulf, Arabia, and India by the *kashazi* monsoon wind, and are sent back on the south wind. They come in carrying brass-decorated chests, Arab silverware, Persian carpets, spices, dried dates, tiles, and Arab furniture, and they take away with them ivory and horn, skins, sugar, coffee, dried fish, coconut oil, sim sim oil, ghee, charcoal, timber (*boriti* or mangrove poles), steel bedframes, bottles. It is a dying trade: from the beginning of the century until the late 1940s, up to 350 dhows came in during the season, but Old Port now sees only 40 dhows a year. But many dhows (a broad category covering many crafts; see p. 347), though equipped with diesel engine and propane stove in the galley, still make a ceremony of entering Mombasa harbor with lateen sail catching the wind, flags flying, the crew beating drums. If any dhows are in Old Port, a visit to one is easily arranged, and you may inspect (and perhaps buy) some of the more interesting cargo such as chests and carpets, on board or in the customs shed. (And if you're interested you can arrange passage for about 250/– to the Persian Gulf.) After the dhows clear customs and discharge their cargo, they lie in Old Port awaiting their turn to go to the *careening area* north of the harbor. Careening is like drydocking: the dhow is beached and the crew works at repairs and caulking the hull, which is held upright by gins and shear legs. When the tide is out, you can walk up to the careened dhows and watch the process. Below Fort Jesus you may see the sails laid out for repairs. John H. A. Jewell's *Dhows at Mombasa* (Nairobi: East African Publishing House, 1969) has a wealth of information (and pictures).

Just past Samji Kala & Company on Ndia Kuu is a narrow lane

leading to *Leven Steps* (or the *Old Slave Steps*), which go down to the original wharf. They were built by Lieutenant Emery of the H.M.S. *Leven,* one of the British ships in the area 1824–26. Also near Customs, as your nose will tell you, is the *Fish Market.*

Most of Old Town is not that old, nor is it very Arab; few buildings are older than the 19th century, and the area is mostly Asian in character. The Old Port area is on the site of the Portuguese and Omani Mombasa, and the medieval Mombasa is the northern part of Old Town. Walk toward Digo Road (you may have to ask locals to point the way) and come out near the *Municipal Market,* worth a look into, then go up *Sir Mbaraki Road,* named for one of the Arab *liwalis* (governors) of the coast. Opposite the *War Memorial* (four *askaris*) is *Mwembe Tayari Market,* a definitely African market where *kikois,* beaded caps, maize cobs and meal, dried fish, herbs, and (one guidebook notes) voodoo ingredients are sold. Taking a little circle in Mwembe Tayari ("the place of the ripe mango"), come out on *Sir Ali Street,* named for another *liwali,* and go right, cross Haile Selassie Road, pass the *Sheikh Jundani Mosque,* which cost $210,000 to build in 1870, and come out on Kilindini Road opposite the Castle Hotel terrace, where you can order up a cold beer.

Other Places of Interest

There are a few points of interest that can be included in a general driving tour of the island. *Kilindini Harbor,* named for the people who once comprised a large part of old Mombasa's population, is the main port north of Durban, handling 2,000 oceangoing ships, 40,000 passengers, 5 million tons of cargo a year. The port has 13 deep-water berths (2 more are to be finished in 1974, 2 more are planned) and processes 55 percent of East Africa's imports, 63 percent of exports. "K" Boat Services (tel. 20822/3) has harbor cruises in the tourist season. *Mbaraki Pillar* off Nyerere Road (take a right just before the traffic circle and Likoni Ferry) is a 25-foot-high pillar tomb, dating from the 17th or early 18th century. *Kilindini Mosque,* or the Wailing Mosque or the Mosque of the Three Tribes, located off Makarios Drive, is a ruin excavated in 1950; it was built in the 18th century, rebuilt in the early 19th. In the golf course on Mama Ngina Drive are the ruins of *Fort St. Joseph,* or the *Kaberas Redoubt,* an oval-shaped structure erected by the Portuguese and now in ruins. Legend states that an underground passage goes to Fort Jesus, but this has not been proved. Finally, there are *the Tusks,* four gigantic sheet-metal elephant tusks arching over the main street, Kilindini Road, not far from the Information Bureau.

For places of interest on the immediate north and south coasts, see the beginnings of Routes K-2 and K-3.

Accommodations

Note: "Mombasa" hotels listed in tour brochures are often on the North Coast (our Route K-2); see also South Coast (K-3). Following are on Mombasa Island (the city).

Oceanic Hotel, Box 90371, tel. 26191; cable COASTOTEL. Off Oceanic Road, about a mile from town center. 18 sgls, 67 dbls, all w/bath. Rates: B&B: sgl—120/–; dbl—186/–. Credit: AE, BA, DC. Best on Mombasa Island, 1958 hotel has 5 floors of rooms, 4 floors with balconies, air-conditioning, nice furnishings, bath with bidet. Spacious grounds, pool; free transport to hotel's private North Coast beach. Rating: 1st-class international, perfect for those who want to be in town and enjoy coastal resort amenities. A ★ from us. Govt. class A.

Outrigger Club, Box 82345, tel. 20822. On Kilindini Harbor next to "K" Boat Services, about 2 km from town center. 44 dbls w/bath, a-c, balconies. Rates: B&B: sgl—125/–; dbl—200/–. 1973 Outrigger's attraction is its harbor site; the rooms are only standard modern. Blue and chartreuse dining room has table d'hôte, à la carte menus. Pool. Rating: 2d-class international, but no bargain.

Manor Hotel, Box 84851, tel. 21822; cable MANORIAL. Nyerere Avenue, 1 block from Kilindini Road. 4 sgls, 37 dbls w/bath; 10 sgls, 5 dbls w/o bath; some rms w/a-c. Rates: B&B: sgl w/a-c, bath—81/90; dbl w/a-c, bath—117/–; incl tax, levy, service. 50-year-old Manor is a colonial town hotel catering to tourists, businessmen. Best rooms have old, nice furnishings, well maintained. Outdoor verandas, airy colorful dining room. Rating: 1st-class local, superior to Castle. ★. Govt. class B.

Castle Hotel, Box 84231, tel. 23403. Kilindini Road near main traffic circle. 15 sgls, 47 dbls, some w/bath, most w/shower. Rates: B&B: sgl—45/–; dbl—70/– or 80/–. Castle's sidewalk veranda café is Mombasa's tourist mecca. The 3 floors of rooms are old, funky, clean. Rating: Between 1st- and 2d-class local. Govt. class C.

New Carlton Hotel, Box 84804, tel. 23776. Kilindini Road, 2 blocks from Nyerere Ave. 4 sgls, 21 dbls, all w/bath, a-c. Rates: B&B: sgl—95/–; dbl—137/–, incl tax, levy, service. Credit: DC. Central, downtown New Carlton is fine, functional with adequate, nothing-special rooms. Rating: Less than 1st-class local; Steak House Bar & Seafood Room has more of interest than the rooms. Govt. class B (?).

Hotel Splendid, Box 90482, tel. 20967/8; cable HOSPLENDID. Sir Ali St. at Sheikh Jundani Road. 8 sgls, 36 dbls, 6 family rms; 40 rms w/bath. Rates: B&B: sgl—27/50 to 40/–; dbl—50/– to 65/–. Main building and adjacent annex have some large, airy rooms with stone floors, balcony, no decor to speak of. All quite adequate, quite clean. Management here cares. Rating: 1st-class local, best place in city for middle budgets. Govt. class C.

Lotus Hotel, Box 90193, tel. 23637. Cathedral Road behind the Anglican Cathedral. 24 dbls w/bath or shower. Rates: B&B: sgl—40/– to 60/–; dbl—75/– to 100/–; a-c 10/– extra per day. Older hotel, refurbished 1972, Lotus is quiet, clean, convenient. Plain, functional rooms are around a Spanish-style central courtyard; bar, lounge, dining room continue the Spanish decor. Rating: 2d-class local, good for budgeters. Govt. class C.

Tudor House Hotel, Box 80291, tel. 21470. On Tom Mboya Ave., 2 km from Makupa Causeway. 4 sgls, 21 dbls, all w/bath or shower. Rates: B&B: sgl—30/–; dbl—50/–. Far-from-madding-crowd Tudor is good for budget travelers with cars. Most rooms overlook Port Tudor, are simply furnished, clean. Rating: 2d-class local, quiet and pleasant bargain.

Rex Hotel, Box 84800, tel. 23919. Kilindini Road. 16 dbls, 11 sgls, 6 family rms. Rates: B&B: sgl—32/– or 43/–; dbl—50/– or 75/–. Big white building disguises functional, well-used lounge and bar, small, quiet dining room, antique elevator, rambling corridors, neat but scarcely fashionable rooms. Rating: 2d-class local, okay for shilling savers. Govt. class D.

Hotel Excellent, Box 82192, tel. 25124. Haile Selassie Ave. 16 dbls, trpls. Rates: B&B: 55/– per person. 3-story city hotel, brand-new in late 1972. Rooftop garden.

Palm Court Hotel, Box 80506, tel. 23834. Nkrumah Road. 5 sgls, 18 dbls, 4 family rms, all sharing bath. Rates B&B: sgl—24/–; dbl—48/–. Saw better days several decades ago, if then. Elderly rooms open on tiled roof, are fairly clean. Rating: 2d-class local or lower.

Look before you book: *Hotel Skyway,* Box 83033, tel. 24945. Kilindini Road near Standard Bank. 23 rms. Rates: bed only: sgl—22/50 or 27/50; dbl—32/50 to 42/50. Clean enough but awful-looking. Rating: 3d-class local. . . . *YMCA,* tel. 25426. Rates: 30/– full board in dorm. Bad reports on this Y. . . . *Hotel Astra,* Box 98419,

tel. 23004. Haile Selassie Road near Sir Ali St. Rates: B&B: sgl—
40/–; dbl—50/–. . . . *New Bristol Hotel,* Box 81649, tel. 20005.
Baluchi St. off Nkrumah Road. 4 sgls, 8 dbls, 2 family rms, all sharing
bath. Rates: B&B: 20/– per person. Rooms okay-clean, open off
rooftop. Rating: 3d-class local, pretty funky but, then, pretty cheap
too. . . . *Tusk Lodge,* Box 81637, tel. 20077. Kilindini Road near
the Tusks. Rates: bed & tea: sgl—12/50; dbl—25/–. . . . *Cosy
Guest House,* Box 81274, tel. 21917. Haile Selassie Road. Rates: bed
only: sgl—15/–; dbl—30/–. . . . *Chui Lodge,* Box 98823, tel.
26268. Kitumbo Road. Rates: B&B: sgl—15/–; dbl—20/–. . . .
Savoy Hotel. Digo Road between GPO and market. Rates: 6/50 for
bed in trpl.

Camping

Closest is Timbwani Camping Site (other side of Likoni Ferry),
but better is Twiga Lodge (Route K-3, Km 20). Just across Nyali
Bridge (first right, then go past cement silos) is Mombasa Marina,
Box 80736, offering camping for 12/50 per site.

Where to Eat

Tamarind, just across Nyali Bridge, tel. 71747. Closed Monday.
Pleasure to eat here: posh new (1972) Arab-white waterside establishment (good views from patio over water to Mombasa). Dinner minimum—20/–, but you can fill up on near that amount. Entrées (18/50
to 33/–) include whole crab, prawns in whiskey sauce, 600-gram
lobster Tamarind sautéed in butter, T-bone, lamb kebabs; also Mombasa oysters, *supu ya samaki* (Kenya version of bouillabaisse), pâté of
duck. Businessman's lunch—4/50 to 8/–.

Le Gourmet Grill, at the Nyali Beach Hotel, tel. 71551. Intimate
place but too small and, as evening gets older, too warm despite the
air-conditioning. High prices for take-a-chance mediocre or tasty dishes.
Menu selections: burgundy escargots, Mombasa oysters, chilled gaz-
pacho Castellana, charcoal-grilled half-lobster, broiled kingfish steak
Clara Ward, tournedos Reine Cleopatra. Entrées—17/50 to 27/50.
Credit: AE, DC.

Mombasa Beach Hotel dining room, tel. 71861. Decor is blue and
white, plants and baskets; there's a sea view, too. Air-conditioned to
the point of chilliness. Table d'hôte lunch—15/–; dinner—20/–. À la
carte plates run 13/50 to 28/–, include crab cocktail, clear turtle soup,
pan-fried fillet of red snapper, coastal prawns Provençale, fillet steak

with sauce Béarnaise, entrecôte Bordelaise, fresh lobster salad. Credit: BA, DC.

Oceanic Hotel dining room, tel. 26191. Dining room (adjacent to Mombasa International Casino) has table d'hôte lunch—15/–, dinner —17/50 or 20/–, also à la carte (entrées—16/50 to 33/50). Items: Mombasa oysters, lobster thermidor, prawns, fondue Bourguignonne, veal escalope cordon bleu, châteaubriand for 2. Credit: AE, BA, DC.

Bellerive, Kilindini Road next to Hotel Skyway. High-ceilinged and half open to street; clean. Entrées (7/50 to 18/50) include curried lobster, crab mayonnaise, prime cut of grilled kingfish, kofta curry, spaghetti. Credit: BA, DC.

Bella Vista, Kilindini Road over Agip station, tel. 24132. Air-conditioned and pleasant for lunch, dinner. Dishes 7/– to 22/–, include lobster Americaine, prawns Cardinal, spaghetti, steak pili-pili, pork escalope. The Italian dishes aren't terrible.

Manor Hotel dining room, tel. 21821. If it's hot inside, eat on the veranda. Table d'hôte lunch—11/– (Sunday—12/50); dinner—12/50 (weekends—15/–), which is good value. À la carte menu is routine.

Castle Hotel dining room, tel. 39591. Cool, breezy, long, high-ceilinged. Table d'hôte lunch—11/50; dinner—12/50. Some à la carte.

New Carlton Steak House & Seafood Room, at the New Carlton Hotel, tel. 23776. Three-part restaurant with stuffed fish on the wall in one room. Entrées—8/– (for seafish fillet) and up.

Hong Kong, Kilindini Road (way west of Tusks), tel. 26707. Same management as Nairobi's Hong Kong. Bamboo and lanterns and red. Half-portions: prawns—8/50 to 10/50; foo yong—6/50 to 7/50; chop suey—8/50 to 9/50. Credit: AE, DC.

Golden Dragon, at the New Florida nightclub, Mama Ngina Drive. Chinese dinner from 6:30 P.M. to 2:30 A.M. Soups—3/50 to 9/50; half-portions—7/50 to 15/50.

Chinese Overseas Restaurant, Kilindini Road opposite Jubilee Insurance, tel. 21585. Plain, air-conditioned, more expensive than the Hong Kong.

Hotel Splendid Roof Garden Restaurant, tel. 20967. Plain, very clean, with menu heavy on Asian dishes—chicken, prawns, mutton or fish curry or masala, with rice or chapati, also barbecued chicken tikka, shish kebab, mishkaki.

Curry Bowl, Kilindini Road near Mnazi Mmoja Road. Nice-looking place with Indian menu (dishes 4/– to 8/–), also British-Continental and seafood menus.

Singh Restaurant, Mwembe Tayari Road at Station Road. Sikh Indian cooking, hottest curries in Mombasa.

Kenya Coffee House, Kilindini Road opposite Caltex station. Run by Coffee Board of Kenya. Coffee—1/–.

Castle Hotel terrace. Best snack place in town. Coffee—1/–; Allsopps Pilsner—3/15; small Coke—1/30. Ignore the curio sellers on the sidewalk and watch Mombasa stroll by in the heat.

Wimpy and *Kentucky Fried Chicken,* Kilindini Road.

Getting Around

City-licensed taxis have a broad yellow band on them, charge rates by the meter, about the same as Nairobi's. Sightseeing is 20/– per hour, maximum. Buses go all over but are hot riding. Kenya Bus Services, tel. 24851; terminal is on Jomo Kenyatta Road.

Information Bureau

Located just above the Tusks on Kilindini Road, the Information Bureau is run by the Mombasa & Coast Tourist Association, Box 95072, Mombasa; tel. 25428. Open 8–12, 2–4:30 weekdays, 8–12 Saturday. Bureau publishes *Your Guide to Mombasa, Malindi and the Kenya Coast* (3/–), reasonably useful booklet with a poor city map.

"What's On . . ."

The free weekly *Mombasa Advertiser* has advertisements, some articles, and a calendar.

Nightlife, Entertainment

Mombasa at night is duller than Nairobi. About the only nightspot for tourists has been the *New Florida Nightclub* on Mama Ngina Drive (views over the harbor), tel. 25970. It is very dark, very big, and cooled by sea breeze, and has live music and a floor show at 11:30 P.M. Ten bob to get in. Credit: DC. New in 1973, however, is the *Mombasa International Casino,* tel. 25201. The games are roulette, punta y banco, craps, blackjack. The Casino is located at the *Oceanic Hotel,* which has dinner dancing. Sailors may wish to dive into the *Sunshine Night & Day Club* or the *Casablanca,* both on Kilindini Road, or the *Star,* Nkrumah Road.

There is no professional theater, but the *Little Theatre Club* has periodic amateur productions. Among the cinemas, the *Kenya, Regal, Moons, Drive-In,* and *Naaz* show both Western and Indian movies;

check the *Daily Nation* and the *East African Standard,* which have Mombasa editions. The Kenya and the Naaz are air-conditioned.

The hotels have most of the nightlife, and if you're staying in the city, it's not impossible to taxi up the North Coast to the discos or other entertainment at the Nyali Beach Hotel, Mombasa Beach Hotel, or those farther up; the newspapers have details on activities.

Churches

Mombasa has Anglican and Roman Catholic cathedrals plus Presbyterian, Methodist, Baptist, Lutheran, Seventh-Day Adventist, and other churches. The Information Bureau and the Saturday newspapers have details on times of services.

Shops and Services

In listing below, places mentioned are on Kilindini Road unless specified otherwise.

Books: Huseini Stationery Mart, Digo Road.

Barber: Stylish (opposite Agip station).

Camping gas: Essogas (opposite Agip station).

Clothes: Deacon's (next to Central Pharmacy at main intersection).

Groceries: Omees.

Hairdresser: Noorjan's, tel. 23445. Carita, tel. 23661.

Jeweler: Chandaria, Digo Road at Haile Selassie Road.

Optician: Oskar Walch, near Digo Road.

Pharmacies: London Pharmacy (opposite Rex Hotel). Modern Pharmacy, Digo Road. Night pharmacist, tel. 24038.

Photo shops: Elite Photographic (near bend in Kilindini Road). Photokin (at Castle Hotel).

Photocopying: Pioneer Electronics.

Water sports and outdoor gear: Wason Stores (Wason's Tourist Centre).

Route K-1: Nairobi–Mombasa

This route is economically important as half of Kenya's main trunk road (the other half is Route K-10), but it is not totally interesting as a tourist route despite the fact that it goes between Tsavo West and Tsavo East game parks and is historically important as the 19th-century caravan route and railway corridor from Mombasa to Lake

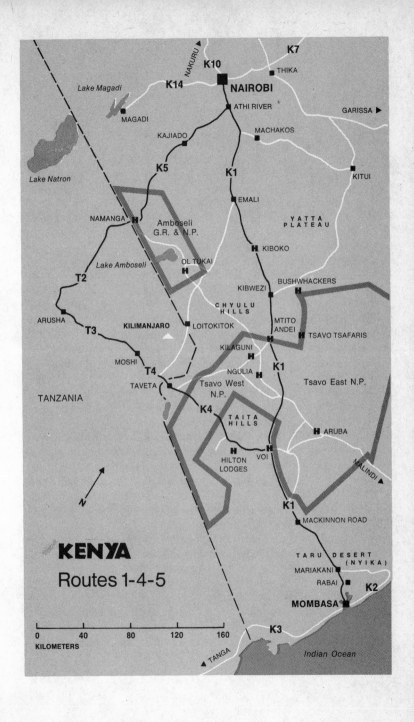

KENYA
Routes 1-4-5

Victoria and Uganda. Tourists going all the way to Mombasa should fly or, for an interesting, comfortable trip, take the night train. Drivers should be alert on this busy road.

Beginning at Kenyatta Avenue, go south on Uhuru Highway. Km 2: Turnoff (R) on C58 (Aerodrome/Langata Road—our Route K-14) to Nairobi National Park main gate, and on. Km 6: East Gate (Mombasa Road Gate) of Nairobi Park (R). Km 10: Turnoff (L) on B10 to *Embakasi Airport* 3 km, completed in 1957 with the help of 5,000 Mau Mau detainee laborers, now undergoing a $45.7 million expansion program. Embakasi handles a million passengers per year.

You are now on the *Athi Plains,* blending into the *Kapiti Plains,* a total of 800 square miles of grassland whose gregarious zebra and antelope move into Nairobi Park during the dry season. The scenery is big, the sky is big.

Km 26: Turnoff (R) on A104 (our Route K-5) to Cheetah Gate of Nairobi Park and on to Amboseli and Tanzania.

Km 34: *Small World Country Club* (R), Box 78, Athi River; tel. (81) 239. Rates: B&B: sgl—45/–; dbl—72/–, incl 5/– temporary membership, tax, levy. New in 1972–73, Small World is less a place to stay (it has new rondavel doubles) than a place for a day or evening visit to see the three resident teams of dancers—two Kamba, one Embu—performing from 4 P.M. weekends, from 9 P.M. Tuesday–Friday. Groups can make special booking, get barbecue lunch or dinner, dancing, *muratina* (African beer), and African food for 15/– per person (minimum 6). See package listing KP-12.

Km 45: Turnoff (L) on C97 to Machakos 19 km and Kitui 119 km, the two centers of the *Kamba,* the fourth-largest tribe with a population of 1.1 million in the 1969 census. Until a hundred years ago the Kamba were primarily pastoral, but the situation has reversed itself, and farming (maize, coffee, vegetables, fruit) is more important than herding. The Kamba are regarded as famous hunters, soldiers and policemen, and woodcarvers.

Km 109: Turnoff (R) on C102 to Sultan Hamud 1 km, Lemi Boti Gate of Amboseli game park 70 km, Loitokitok 110 km. At *Loitokitok,* at the base of Kilimanjaro, is the *Outward Bound Mountain School,* dedicated to building the self-reliance of young people and future leaders of the East African countries.

Km 122: Emali (R), and 1 km later a turnoff (R) on E401 alternate to Amboseli. Km 154: *Kiboko* (Swahili, "hippopotamus"), a little oasis made even pleasanter by *Hunter's Lodge.* Bookings to African

Tours & Hotels (p. 87). 54 rms, incl 12 trpls, most w/bath. Rates:
FB: sgl—96/–; dbl—176/–; trpl—255/–; sgl in dbl—109/–; incl
tax, levy, service. Credit: AE, BA, DC. White stucco, tile-roofed lodge,
originally built by a hunter named J. A. Hunter in 1955, remodeled
since, is next to dammed-up Kiboko Springs, where animals come to
drink. There are birds galore and, in addition, 40 miles of game-
viewing roads (van goes out morning and evening) and a lookout
tower over a floodlit salt lick 800 yards away. Rooms are pleasant;
new pentagonal triples have balconies overlooking the springs. Snack
bar caters to highway travelers. Rating: 2d-class international. We
give it a ★ as an all-around pleasant way station. Govt. class B.

Km 168: *Makindu* ("palm trees"). Km 190: *Kibwezi,* where the
first Kenya coffee was planted, in the 1890s, first by French, then by
Scottish missionaries. Here you turn left on B7 to get to Masalani,
Bushwhackers Camp 27 km, Kitui 139 km. *Bushwhackers Safari Camp,*
P.O. Kibwezi. After turning, go straight for about 10 km, turn sharp
right at signpost, go another 1½ km, bear left, and then go straight
to the camp, 14½ km from the Kitui Road. Self-service lodge has
32 beds in 12 fully furnished, equipped rooms in one- to three-roomed
bandas. Camp has small store, but bring your own food. Rates: 20/–
or 25/– per person; 7/50 to 15/– in shelter. **Camping** at 7 sites on
edge of Bushwhackers. Charge: 5/– per person. Bushwhackers is a
good place for a weekend of birdwatching, with birds in and around
the Athi River and on the camp's bird tables. Fishing in the river.

South of Kibwezi and all the way to Voi, you pass through a zone
of grotesque, fat-trunked, photogenic *baobab trees* (*Adansonia digi-
tata*), whose rootlike branches appear to be reaching into the sky in
agonized despair. The baobab seems to be growing upside down,
which African storytellers say is by God's order, since the baobab
refused to grow where it was first placed. The dry fruit pulp of the
tree yields cream of tartar, pectin, and the highest known concentra-
tion of vitamin C. Dissolved in water, the pulp produces a somewhat
refreshing drink. The inner bark can be plaited into a strong fiber or
manufactured into coarse wrapping and packing paper. The fruit, seeds,
leaves, and bark are all used in the preparation of traditional medicines.
The large trunks have been hollowed out on occasion and used
variously as water storage tanks, bus stop shelters, toilets, and refuges
from marauders. Many tribes worship the baobab as a fertility symbol.
Sometimes logs are hung like Christmas tree decorations in the baobab's
branches; the logs are hollow and are to attract bees for honey.

Tsavo National Park

Km 220: *Mtito Andei* ("forest of vultures"), a road town that is a main rest stop for highway traffic. To the right is Mtito Andei Gate into *Tsavo West,* to the left a gate into *Tsavo East* to Tsavo Tsafaris (Cottars Camp) 26 km. Though the two parks are run separately, they are officially one *Tsavo National Park.* At 8,034 square miles, Tsavo is the largest national park in East Africa—and it's larger than New Jersey or Wales. A vast arid and semiarid expanse of savanna, acacia woodlands, rocky outcrops and ridges, open plains, riverine forest belts, and palm thickets, Tsavo is so big that two large areas are basically undeveloped for tourists. Established in 1948, Tsavo has more than 2,000 km of good roads, all well signposted.

There is an extraordinary amount of wildlife, surprising in a park so poorly watered. The Tsavo River in Tsavo West and the Athi in Tsavo East flow all year; others are rivers when it rains. How little permanent water there is became dreadfully apparent during 1960–61 when thousands of the larger mammals, including elephants and rhinos, died; a decade later another drought killed off another 1,200 to 1,500 elephants out of a population (aerial census) of 13,000 in Tsavo East and 7,000 in Tsavo West. Ever since the big drought a controversy has raged in the press and in conservation circles about Tsavo's elephants, centering on the question of the effect of elephants on the park. Enormously destructive in their feeding habits, elephants can eat 400 to 600 pounds of grass, branches, bark, fruit, and seed pods a day (and drink up to 200 quarts of water), and will knock over a tree just to get a few choice leaves from the top. Some conservationists want to see the herds cropped so that (a) they will not damage the land as much, and (b) droughts will have a lesser effect, since there will be more water and forage. Other conservationists maintain that Tsavo, like other parks, has a natural cycle (visible in Amboseli today), and that elephants play an important ecological role in the transition of woodland to grassland and back again. In any case, a "Water for Wildlife" program was launched to head off a repetition of the 1960–61 drought's wholesale killing, and three bore holes have been drilled and three waterholes created in both parts of the park to relieve feeding pressure on the areas adjacent to the permanent rivers. Unfortunately the program was not as successful as had been hoped, for the 1973–74 drought once again saw elephants and thousands of other animals dying of thirst and hunger, often in front of helpless tourists.

Drought is not the only killer of wildlife. Poachers—increasingly mechanized, well-financed and professional—have been killing an estimated 15,000 elephants a year (out of country-wide population of 150,000).

Besides elephants and black rhinos (which number 6,000 to 8,000), Tsavo is famous for lions (historically for the man-eating variety; see Km 276 below), lesser kudu (look in the dry brush along the

Dik-dik

Galana River), oryx, gerenuk, *dik-dik* (tiny gazelle often seen hiding in the brush), and klipspringer (look in rocky outcrops). In Tsavo West, at least, it is hard to travel a mile without wanting to stop to look over a red-dusty elephant or zebra, a galloping oryx, or a hiding dik-dik. As a big park with many types of terrain and vegetation, Tsavo has, also, incredible birdlife; John G. Williams counted 523 species. Two books have been written about Tsavo by the warden's wife, Daphne Sheldrick, *Orphans of Tsavo* and *The Tsavo Story*.

Drive around Tsavo West

A 170-km route starting at Mtito Andei Gate and ending at Tsavo Gate will take you to all the places of interest and, generally, the best game-viewing areas. Numbers mentioned below are numbered signposts; the park map, showing these, is a good one.

Head first for the *Park Headquarters* at Kamboyo, where you can check the location of wildlife, then continue to *Kilaguni Lodge,* worth a stop because the lodge waterholes attract game and for the superb views of the Chyulu Hills and down across a valley and up to Kilimanjaro. A detour from the Kilaguni area will take you to *Shaitani,* ("devil"), a volcano recently extinct and still covered with black lava. A legend says that a Kamba village was buried by the lava, and that you can hear people talking, dogs barking, goats bleating, cattle lowing. It is said that (a) you may feel a powerful urge to climb the hill, but if you do, you won't return, and (b) the only way to survive a night spent near the hill is to leave food to feed the spirits. The volcano is climbable, and the warden has created a nature trail that goes into one of the animal-bone-filled caves. The road continues through the 145-square-mile *West Chyulu Game Conservation Area* (Chyulu Hills) to Lemi Boti Gate, Amboseli. From Kilaguni you pass the *Five Sisters,* young volcanic cones, and arrive at *Mzima Springs,* the single most famous destination in Tsavo. The *Chyulus,* which are ash or cinder cones rising to 7,120 feet, attract much rain and act something like a sponge. For reasons geological, the water goes underground and suddenly emerges from beneath black rocks at Mzima Springs. It is a spectacle—crystal water gushing forth at the rate of half a million gallons a day, flowing through Top Pool, then Long Pool, disappearing beneath the lava again, then reemerging as the Mzima River and flowing into the Athi. Above the springs, and carefully designed to preserve the beauty of the area, is a pumping station that sends sweet pure water all the way to Mombasa through what is said to be the longest concrete water pipeline in the world. (Notwithstanding, the pipeline is problem-plagued.) The Mzima area is an oasis: while vervets scamper in the brush and in the trees, hippos and crocodiles and fish live what looks like an idyllic life in the clear water. You can see all this from an underwater viewing tank (first built in 1955 at the suggestion of two Disney photographers).

Vervets are the commonest monkeys you will see: a small, light-gray or yellowish olive monkey with a completely black face fringed with white whiskers, and with black feet and black tail-tip. They look cute and do hang around, but don't feed or tease them. No need to describe the *hippopotamus.* Hippos swim well (though young must be taught) and can, because of their high specific gravity, walk on the bottom; they can stay under for as long as six minutes but usually only two. They loaf and sleep during the day, leave the water and forage as far as several miles during the night, eating 130 pounds of grass and aquatic plants. Hippos will fight among themselves, sometimes using well-toothed mouths. The hippo's most common noise is a series of booming grunts. Never stand between a hippo and water. If you are lucky you will be in the viewing tank when a *crocodile,* silently, frighteningly, glides by. Believe whatever warnings you hear about crocodiles, and as a rule in Africa, don't swim in anything but a swimming pool or the ocean, and don't walk too close to the bank of a croc-infested river, for one sweep of the reptile's powerful tail will get you where he wants you. More people in Africa are killed by crocs and hippos than all the other species combined, according to Joan and Alan Root, makers of the films *Mzima* and *Baobab.* Crocodiles differ from alligators (none in Africa, by the way) in having a longer, tapered head and two big teeth which are outside the mouth when closed.

From Mzima Springs, head toward signposts 11A and 30 and *Poacher's Lookout,* where you can alight from your vehicle for a high look around. Drive south toward 53, then up to 53A, past Mzima and Kilaguni to get to another set of roads, going south at 9 to jet-black, volcanic *Chiemu Crater* and on to 55, then straight through rocky *Rhino Valley* (not always) to *Roaring Rocks.* There you can get out and walk 50 feet up the rocks and look 300 feet down the other side, and hear the roaring sound of the wind on the rocks. Backtrack a bit to 16 and 17 and southeast past Ngulia Hill (5,983 feet), which has original forest of the type that once covered Tsavo, to the *Ndawe Escarpment* (4,127 feet), on which is *Ngulia Lodge,* good place for a cold drink and a peek at the waterhole action, if any. Go back to 18, over to 19, 20, and 21, then down to 23, where you can drive along a stretch of the *Tsavo River* before exiting at *Tsavo Gate.* Direct return to Mtito Andei on the highway is 47 km, on park roads 70 km.

Drive around Tsavo East

Tsavo East is less interesting than West—it seems to have more flat expanses of rather boring bush, and more bush. (A mapmaker who had been in Africa too long once penciled in the place name "Mamoba" across a big section of bush country. Co-workers puzzled over this before the cartographer confessed it was an acronym—"miles and miles of bloody Africa.") Like the Sahara or the NFD, however, bush can have its attractions, in this case large herds of the famous red (from the dust) Tsavo elephant, and a couple of interesting sights. On a 150-km route, begin at Voi Gate and head toward *Voi Safari Lodge,* passing the turnoff to *Park Headquarters,* where you can inquire about wildlife locations, and *Tsavo Research Centre.* At the lodge is a telescope on a balcony above the waterhole, and below is an Ark-like "dungeon" so you can get on top of the animals without their getting on top of you. Lizards are very active around the lodge, and in front are a couple acacias with noisy *weaverbird colonies.*

Drive north to *Mudanda* ("strips of drying meat") *Rock,* a huge, whale-back rock outcrop with a sheer drop from a ledge on the east side to a pool below; you can sit on the ledge and watch the animals, including many elephants, come to drink in dry weather (best time—February–March). Pass Manyani Gate and arrive at the *Tsavo River,* which near *Observation Hill* joins the Athi to form the *Galana River.* Across the river is one end of the *Yatta Plateau.* An extraordinary geographic feature that begins 270 km away near Thika, it is one of the longest lava flows in the world, but the lava is on top of other rock, forming a ridge. The long sinuous ridge (only 2 km across) is puzzling, for it could represent a lava flow along a river valley that has now eroded away, or it could be that lava filled a fissure in rock that has now eroded away.

Drive west along the Galana, generally a good viewing area. All the area north is an undeveloped *Wilderness Area,* uninhabited, hot, waterless, crossed by only a few tracks. Only one party at one time is allowed in the area, and because it is remote, a ranger-guide must accompany the group. Inquiries to the Tsavo East Warden. Down past some rapids you will come to *Lugard's Falls,* best seen in dry weather when the river is down, revealing the fascinating shapes and colors of the rocks, and the falls, which rapidly twist this way and that in a mad rush down. The guidebooks say the falls are narrow enough to stand astride, but after we saw them, we would warn against anything that foolish (a German tourist was killed doing it a couple years ago). The falls were "discovered" by Frederick D. Lugard (later Lord Lugard) in 1890 when the young army captain was hired by the Imperial British East Africa Company to open up a route along the Sabaki-Athi between Mombasa and Machakos. Just downstream from the falls is *Crocodile Point,* from which you may see the lazy log-shapes of basking crocs. Continue to signpost 163 and turn south along Rhino Ridge to 107 and then *Aruba Dam,* a 211-acre artificial lake situated on the seasonal Voi River, which flows from the Taita Hills. Aruba is one of the only watering spots in miles and so attracts game. (Alternatively, from Crocodile Point you can continue straight along the Galana to Sala Gate, then go southwest to Aruba; this adds 80 km to the drive.) From Aruba, drive west along the Voi River to Voi Gate.

When to Visit

Tsavo can be visited anytime, but the game is more concentrated in the dry seasons, with January–March being particularly good.

Getting There, Getting Around

Tsavo West can be visited on a package tour from Nairobi as short as one day (if you're really in that much of a hurry); Tsavo East is more commonly visited from Mombasa and Malindi. For Tsavo West, see packages KP-19, 37–41, 60–62, 70, 72–75, 79, 81–84, 86–88, 91; and TP-28; for Tsavo East, KP-20, 36–38, 40, 58–61, 86, 92–93. There are airstrips near Kilaguni, Ngulia, and Voi lodges, and transport is available at the lodges for game viewing. There are five gates into Tsavo East, four into West. The park roads are excellent dirt.

Accommodations

A wide range of accommodations is available inside West and East and outside the park. All are described below. A bit farther away are Bushwhackers Camp (Km 190 above), Hunter's Lodge (Km 154 above), and Hilton's Taita Hills Lodge and Salt Lick Lodge (see Route K-4).

Tsavo West accommodations: *Kilaguni Lodge,* bookings to African Tours & Hotels (p. 87). 33 km from Mtito Andei. 37 trpls plus 4 qdrpl cottages, all w/bath. Rates: FB: sgl—220/–; dbl—330/–; trpl—438/–, incl tax, levy, service. Credit: AE, BA, DC. Best feature of Kilaguni is superb location on edge of shallow, Eden-like valley (Kilimanjaro rises majestically in the background), with a couple of elephants here, a line of zebras moving behind some trees there, everywhere impalas and gazelles. Though not billed as such, this is a game-viewing lodge—the long, stone terrace-dining room-bar is the place; bring binoculars and be quiet. The pentagonal rooms of the 1962–63 lodge are comfortably furnished. Meeting space for 300 was added in mid-1974. Menus are adequate table d'hôte (breakfast—11/–; lunch —22/50; dinner—26/–). Pool. Rating: 2d-class international and overpriced, but worthy of ★★. Govt. class B. . . .

Ngulia Safari Lodge, bookings to Kenya Safari Lodges (p. 87). 39 km from Tsavo Gate. 52 dbls w/bath. Rates: FB: sgl—198/–; dbl— 300/–. Credit: DC. Built 1969, Ngulia has a long view of a broad sweep of Tsavo River valley, with modern rooms facing either the valley or waterholes. Lobby and bar-lounge are huge, too airy. Pool. Rating: 1st-class international but uninspired and overpriced. Kilaguni is more intimate and has far better game watching. But Ngulia gets a ★. Govt. class A. . . . *Kitani Lodge and Shelter Camp,* bookings to A. A. & Bunson (p. 86). 58 km from Mtito Andei. Self-service lodge has 6 fully equipped double bandas. Rates: 30/– per adult, 15/– per child, plus 2/– per lamp, refrigerator, or stove, 5/– per bedding roll, if required. Not far from the lodge is an equipped, makuti-roofed shelter with two rooms (triples) and veranda, outside fireplace, for a maximum of 6 persons. Rate: 75/– for the whole shelter; 5/– per bedroll. . . . *Ngulia Safari Camp,* bookings to A. A. & Bunson (p. 86). 6 self-service bandas, each with 2 beds; no bed linen or blankets available. Rates: 30/– per adult, 15/– per child, plus 2/– per stove, fridge, lamp, if required. Very adequate accommodations. Good view. . . . **Camping:** Best campground is 1 km inside Mtito Andei Gate. Running water (potable), toilets, showers. Some shade from acacias, baobab. Lots of twittering weavers in the trees, redbilled hornbills and superb starlings sharing your tentsite. Map shows campsites near Tsavo Gate and signpost 44; inquire about these. Fee: 5/– per person.

Tsavo East accommodations: *Voi Safari Lodge,* bookings to Kenya Safari Lodges (p. 87). Near Voi Gate. 50 dbls w/bath. Rates: FB: sgl—198/–; dbl—300/–. Credit: DC. 1967 lodge is nestled nicely on a rocky hillside overlooking the southern Tsavo East plains, blending in well with its environs. Rooms, in 2- and 3-story blocks, are typically smallish but comfortable. Dining room (table d'hôte) has good-quality food. Pool. Telescope, underground chamber for viewing waterholes. Rating: 1st-class international. ★. Govt. class A. . . .

Tsavo Tsafaris (Cottars Camp), bookings to Forest & Frontier Lodges (p. 87). 26 km east of Mombasa Road, turnoff in Mtito Andei opposite Tsavo West Gate. Luxury tented camp is in a private concession area; access is by booking-office voucher only; private cars are left on one side of Athi River and guests are ferried across. Rates: FB: sgl—172/–; dbl—287/–, incl tax, levy, service. Credit: AE. Transport around area in Land Cruisers is extra. Dining room, though breakfast and lunch are served outside; also al fresco bar. Fishing in Athi River (tilapia over 3 pounds). Birdwatching: 258 species. . . . *Aruba Lodge,* bookings to A. A. & Bunson (p. 86). 35 km from Voi Gate. 6 equipped self-service bandas, each a double with bath and kitchen. Rates: 30/– per adult, 15/– per child, plus 2/– per stove or lamp, 5/– per bedroll, if required. . . . **Camping** is good at two places: Aruba

Lodge and near Voi Gate. Toilets, showers, drinking water at both. Fee: 5/– per person.

Accommodations outside the park: *Maneaters Motel,* Box 74308, Nairobi. On Mombasa Road at Km 276. Has 28 dbls (to be increased to 40) w/shower. Design of this 1974 motel is based on the interruption of the building of the Uganda Railway in 1898–99 by a couple of man-eating lions (see below, Km 276). Tourists need not fear for their lives, though some of this happened at Tsavo Station, across the road. The motel consists of a main building with open-air dining room, overlooking a loop of rail on which sit 14 (to be increased to 20) genuine boxcars (in local railway parlance, CGBs—for "covered good bogies"), each boxcar remodeled into two bedrooms, each with private shower. At one end of the line of CGBs will be an 11-Class steam locomotive. Within the space created by the boxcars is a garden and pool. To discourage would-be man-eaters, there is a 5-foot trench around the motel. Each boxcar, incidentally, faces Tsavo West, with views of the Chyulu Hills and Taita Hills. . . . *Tsavo Inn,* P.O. Mtito Andei; tel. 1Y1; or bookings to African Safari Lodges (p. 87). Near Mtito Andei Gate. 4 sgls, 23 dbls, 5 trpls, all w/bath. Rates: FB: sgl—164/–; dbl—222/50, incl tax, levy, service charge. Credit: AE, DC. Mainly used by African Safari Club's German and Swiss packages, the Tsavo Inn makes a pleasant rest stop. Rooms are oldish, cool, comfortable. Snack and sandwich bar, table d'hôte dining room (breakfast—10/–; lunch—12/50; dinner—15/–), upstairs bar, green lawns, pool. Rating: 1st-class local. Govt. class B. . . . *Sigala Lodge,* Box 28, Voi; tel. 4; or bookings to African Safari Lodges (p. 87). 3 km off highway at Voi. 18 dbls, 2 qdrpls, all w/bath. Rates: B&B: sgl—85/–; dbl—110/–. Credit: AE, DC. 1949 hotel is just like an aged Midwest motel, with two-in-a-cottage, musty, old-fashioned rooms. Agreeable dining veranda with fishing-net globes hanging from the ceiling; but beware bugs in the Rice Krispies. Pool. Rating: 2d-class local, not recommended. Govt. class C.

Picking up the route at Mtito Andei, you drive south through Tsavo West until Km 276, *Tsavo Station* and the bridge across the Tsavo River, famous from Colonel J. H. Patterson's best-selling *The Man-Eaters of Tsavo* (1907, reprinted 1947). Here at Mile 131 during the building of the Uganda Railway, the completion of the bridge was delayed by the frightening eating habits of two Tsavo lions. A four-month building job stretched into almost a year, from March 1898 to

February 1899. When the railhead reached here, the lions carried off two plate layers while a temporary bridge was being built, then the tracks pushed on. Patterson was put in charge of constructing a permanent span some 300 feet long, no small task. There were several construction camps in a four-mile radius, and the man-eaters began to carry off Indian workers in eat-and-run attacks. Patterson, an experienced hunter of tigers in India, found himself building the bridge during the day and lying in wait for the lions at night. Finally, after months, more killings, frustration, near-misses, and many sleepless nights, Patterson killed one lion on December 9, then set out after the other one, which he had already wounded. It took six shots to bring down that one. The stuffed, very bullet-scarred lions are in Chicago's Field Museum. The lions had killed 28 Indians plus about 100 Africans in surrounding villages. As for Patterson's bridge, it finally opened February 7, 1899, and immediately withstood a raging flood. The Germans blew it up during World War I.

Km 323: Turnoff (R) on A23 (our Route K-4) to Taita Hills, Salt Lick Lodge and Taita Hills Lodge, Mbuyuni Gate of Tsavo West, Taveta, and Tanzania. After this turnoff is one (L) into *Voi* (pop. 5,313), an ugly town with no appeal, but it's the gateway to Tsavo East and in the midst of a sisal-growing area.

Km 402: *Mackinnon Road,* a small town and train station so called from the rough highway built in the late 1880s and early 1890s from Mombasa to Kibwezi, the first attempt at road building in Kenya. After Mackinnon Road you cross a barren, desolate country known to explorers as the *Taru Desert,* now more generally known as the *Nyika,* or thorn country. This semiarid land ends about Km 455, *Mariakani,* with a turnoff (L) on C107, shortcut to Kilifi and the North Coast road, 50 km. About 11 km northeast of Mariakani on this road, at a place called *Giryama* on the maps, is the *kaya* or large, walled enclosure with the central tribal council house of the *Giriama;* it is the most accessible of the dozen *kaya* that are preserved.

Km 470: *Mazeras,* location of *Mombasa's Municipal Nurseries.* Entry free to see lots of flowers. Just north of the Botanical Garden is a turnoff (R) to the missionary center of *Rabai,* located on top of an escarpment 13 km from the coast, with good views. Johann Ludwig Krapf, a missionary-explorer, arrived in Mombasa in 1844 after service in Ethiopia, and was joined by Johannes Rebmann in 1846, when they established the Rabai mission of the Church Missionary Society (CMS), an English group though both men were German. This was the first mission in East Africa since the Portuguese. Both made the first recorded journeys into the interior, with Rebmann seeing Kilimanjaro in 1848 and Krapf Mount Kenya in 1849. Rebmann later moved to the Kilimanjaro area and Krapf continued at Rabai, starting East Africa's first school and compiling the first Swahili dictionary (he translated the Old Testament as well). Krapf's house is in ruins, but Rebmann's cottage to the right of the 1879 church is still used; the school opposite was the first church. Slaves found sanctuary at the mission and were given "charters of freedom" under the large mango tree outside.

Km 473: About here you enter the *Ten-Mile Strip,* theoretically part of the Sultan of Zanzibar's dominions until Kenya's Independence. The people you see in roadside villages surrounded by palm trees are not necessarily all one tribe, but they are probably of the Nyika or Mijikenda ("Nine Tribes") group, consisting of the Digo and Giriama (the two most populous tribes) and seven smaller tribes, with a 1969 population total of 520,520.

Km 481: Turnoff (L—at BP station) to *Port Reitz (Mombasa) Airport.* Km 489: *Makupa Causeway,* a permanent connection of Mombasa Island to the mainland. It was built as a railway bridge in 1896, later turned into a causeway. In 3 or 4 km you will be in downtown *Mombasa* (see separate section above).

Route K-2: Mombasa–North Coast–Malindi–Lamu

Because of the many resort hotels between Mombasa and Malindi, this is one of the best-traveled tourist routes. Historically, it is also the most interesting, and all the water sports, including fishing, make the route one long playground, mainly for Germans (who spend 80 percent of their Kenya time at the beach), Swiss, and other Europeans. There are many beach hotels, and more are planned. For some of the new, adequate, but characterless beach hotels, we have pared the description to a few words.

Nyali

Begin in downtown Mombasa at Kilindini Road, going north out of the city on Digo Road (B8). It's paved all the way to Malindi. In 2 km you cross the 1931 *Nyali Pontoon Bridge* (toll) to Nyali. To the right are the Tamarind Restaurant, English Point, and Princes Park (Mombasa Showground); straight is Nyali Beach and Hotel 4 km.

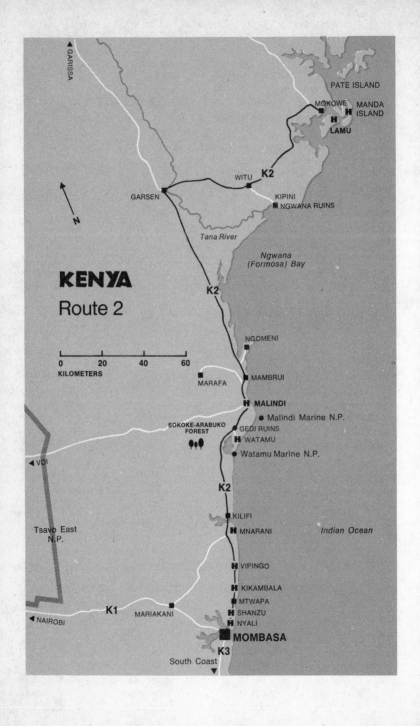

Nyali (Swahili, "clearing") was first a sisal estate, then developed as an exclusive residential estate in the late 1930s. *English Point* (on Cement Road near Mombasa Marina, where there's **camping**) is a little hill with a gleaming white *monument to Dr. Krapf* (see Route K-1, p. 200) and nearby an enclosure with the graves of his wife and child, who died of fever shortly after arriving in Mombasa.

Km 3: Turnoff (L) to *Bahari Club,* water sports center and marina. Near here is the *Emmanual Church,* solid old church built in 1875 as the base of the *Freretown Mission.* Freretown, named for Sir Bartle Frere, an antislavery leader, was established by the Church Missionary Society in 1874 for about 600 slaves liberated from Arab dhows by the Royal navy. Freretown was twice (1880, 1895) attacked by Swahili slavers from Mombasa. Nyali **accommodations:** *Nyali Beach Hotel,* Box 90581, Mombasa; tel. 71551/2; cable NYALOTEL. 15 sgls, 172 dbls, all w/bath, 21 garden cottage rms w/shared baths. All w/a-c. Rates: FB: sgl—140/– to 160/–; dbl—220/– to 240/–. Credit: AE, DC. The Norfolk of beach hotels, a rambling place opened 1952, expanded 1962, new wings, cottages, renovations since. Main building doubles plain but pleasant; cottage rooms fancier, cheaper. Colonnaded terrace, open-air dance floor, 2-story pool deck and lounge, intimate bar, downstairs Grill Room as well as cool dining room. Whole hotel is exceedingly well kept, and though drawing packages, has the atmosphere of a hotel catering to individuals. Rating: Superior 1st-class international and worthy of ★★. Govt. class A. . . . *Mombasa Beach Hotel,* Box 90414, Mombasa; tel. 71861; bookings to Kenya Safari Lodges (p. 87). Turnoff at Km 8. 100 dbls w/bath, a-c, balcony w/sea view. Rates: FB: sgl—210/–; dbl—312/–. Credit: BA, DC. Long, stark, 4-story blocks look out on beach; rooms have sleek, modern metal furniture, are bright, airy. Nautically decorated bar, cool blue dining room, large pool, fish pond, busy terrace. Hidden sandy coral-cove shelters private parties, barbecues, dances. Rating: 1st-class international, well liked by American Express packagers. ★★. Govt. class A. . . . *Reef Hotel,* Box 82234, Mombasa; tel. 71771; cable REEF. 1st-class international but not distinctive. . . . *Bahari Beach Hotel* and *Silver Beach Hotel,* bookings to African Safari Lodges (p. 87). New in 1974.

Bamburi

Km 10: *Bamburi* beach resort area. Kenyatta Beach is a fully public beach (actually, the others are, too) owned by Mombasa Municipal

Council; it is signposted. President Kenyatta's Thiririka beach house is along here. **Accommodations** (turnoffs Km 10-12): *Severin Sea Lodge,* Box 82169, Mombasa; tel. Bamburi (85) 215, 239. 50 dbls incl 2 suites, all w/bath, balcony, a-c. Rates: FB: sgl—160/–; dbl—220/–; also low season rates. Credit: DC. 1972 Sea Lodge hosts mostly Germans, plans to lure Americans. Couple dozen 2-story rondavels, each with 4 colorful, modern doubles; main building complex of round lobby, round dining room, round bar-lounge . . . and on; the pool is figure-8-shaped, while Kenyatta Beach is long and sandy. Rating: 1st-class international, quite classy. ★. . . . *Kenya Beach Hotel,* Box 81703, Mombasa; tel. Bamburi (85) 250; cable KENBEACH; bookings to A. A. & Bunson (p. 86). 60 dbls incl 2 suites, all w/bath or shower, a-c. Rates: FB: sgl—180/–; dbl—220/–; also low season rates. Credit: DC. New in 1972, constructed in series of 2-story octagons with makuti roofs; rooms colorful, cool. Octagonal main building has zesty dining room with table d'hôte, small à la carte. Mostly Scandinavian clientele, some British. Rating: 1st-class international, handsome but pricier than others. ★. . . . *Whitesands Hotel & Lido,* Box 91073, Mombasa; tel. Bamburi (85) 253. 2d-class international, unmemorable. . . . *Ocean View Beach Hotel,* Box 81127, Mombasa; tel. Bamburi (85) 230. 2d-class international, nothing special. . . . *Bamburi Beach Hotel,* Box 83966, Mombasa; tel. Bamburi (85) 261, 232. 2d-class international, quite modest. . . . *Coraldene Beach Hotel,* Box 80940, Mombasa; tel. Bamburi (85) 216. 1st-class local, casual, easygoing, good for budgeters. . . . *Sandpiper Cottages,* Box 82686, Mombasa; tel. 21854; cable ZONIKRI. . . . **Camping** on bumpy, coral-rock grass lot by the Coraldene driveway; hot shower, bath in room block. Fee: 5/– per person. No camping at Whitesands.

Shanzu

After Bamburi comes *Shanzu.* Some say *Shanzu Beach,* by the Dolphin Hotel, is the best on the North Coast because you can swim at low tide. **Accommodations** (turnoffs Km 13-15): *Dolphin Hotel,* Box 81443, Mombasa; tel. Shanzu (84) 232; bookings also to African Safari Lodges (p. 87). 110 dbls w/bath and shower, half w/a-c. Rates: FB: sgl—140/–; dbl—190/– (220/– w/a-c). Credit: AE, DC. Dolphin, heavily populated with African Safari Clubbers from Europe, is modern, busy-active hotel with 2-story block rooms colorful, breezy. Long dining room is table d'hôte. Rating: 2d-class international, peppy place. . . . *Coral Beach Hotel,* same address as Dolphin. 2d-class international, standard (Dolphin is better). . . . *Don's Inn,* Box 82879, Mombasa; tel. Shanzu (84) 221. 3 dbls w/a-c. Rates: bed only: 40/— per person in rm w/o bath; 60/— in rm w/bath. Don's Inn (ex-Shanzu Frigate) is seafood restaurant and country inn on the beach. Three rooms extremely nice; one, plushy and royal, is best individual room on the coast. Informal dining rooms decorated with antique menus. Entrées—11/— to 20/—. Rating: Local but distinctive, good for quiet beach holiday. ★. . . . *Casuarina Hotel,* bookings to KTDC (p. 87). Motley, nondescript international class; go elsewhere. . . . *Boulevard Beach Hotel,* Box 84907, Mombasa; tel. Shanzu (84) 273. New in 1973. . . . *Serena Beach Hotel,* bookings to Serena Lodges & Hotels (p. 87). 120 rooms, (a-c). Rates: FB: sgl—150/—; dbl—220/—. New in 1974, Serena Beach resembles an 18th-century Swahili village such as Lamu. Rating: 1st-class international.

Mtwapa

Km 16: *Prisons Industries Showroom* (L) welcomes visitors. Immediately after, *Mtwapa Creek Bridge* (toll)—no more "singing ferry" here. Across the bridge, turnoff (R) to *Kenya Marinas, F. G. MacConnel Marina, Mtwapa Marina.* Kenya Marinas in 1974 was to open East Africa's first *shark aquarium.* About 1½ km past this turnoff is another to *Jumba la-Mtwana* ("slave master's house"), a set of ruins including a picturesque mosque almost on the beach, a pillar tomb, an amphitheaterlike walled building, houses, including one built with more than one story, a city wall, and wells. The mosque dates from the late 14th or early 15th century. James Kirkman completed excavations here in 1972, and the site is open to the public. **Camping** for 6/— per person at Kenya Marinas; grassy field, toilet, clubhouse.

Kikambala

Km 20: *Kikambala,* a less developed beach resort area. The beach is 4 miles long but has a lot of seaweed, and you can swim at high tide only. But the reef is easily accessible when the water is out. **Accommodations** (turnoffs Km 23-24): *Whispering Palms Hotel,* P.O. Kikambala via Mombasa; tel. 6. 6 sgls, 154 dbls, all w/bath or shower, 40 w/a-c. Rates: FB: sgl—110/—; dbl—160/— to 200/—; also low season rates. Credit: BA, DC. Built 1961, added to in 1972. Grounds are ill-kept, rooms adequate. Renovations in progress late 1973. 3 pools. Rating: Local-international, quite ordinary. Govt. class B. . . . *Sun 'n Sand Hotel,* Box 98501, Mombasa; tel. Kikambala 8, Mombasa 26265.

1st-class local, lusterless. Govt. class D. . . . *Kanamai Conference &
Holiday Centre* (*Kanamai Youth Hostel*), P.O. Kikambala via Mombasa; tel. 12Y4. Rates: bed only: dorm—6/– per person; 4-bed rm—
8/– per person; 2-bed rm—10/– per person; self-service cottage—15/–
per person (minimum 70/– per day, high season). Methodist-run
Kanamai is mainly for low-budget travelers, whether youth or
missionaries or Africans. Rooms clean, spartan. Matter-of-fact dining
room has 3 different menus, basic-to-dreadful food. Saline water
showers. . . . *Hoare Alzo Estate cottages,* P.O. Kikambala via Mombasa; tel. 15. . . . *Beachcomber Cottages,* Box 95060, Mombasa; tel.
25171. . . . **Camping** at Hoare Alzo for 5/– per person in pleasant
pasture. Toilet, shower. Also hostellike bunkhouse sleeping 6, with
kitchen, shower, for 15/– per person or 60/– for whole place. If you
have food, this is far better than Kanamai, where camping is 3/–
but campers have no privacy.

Kilifi

After Kikambala, you pass through a sisal estate, with baobab trees
scattered here and there. The area here (Km 30) is called *Vipingo;*
on the beach may be developed a 400-bed Tropicana Beach Club and
a 280-bed Hotel Tropicana. Km 49: Turnoff (L) on C107 to Mariakani 50 km (shortcut to Mombasa–Nairobi road). Km 52: Turnoff
(R) to *Takaungu,* with some minor ruins dating to the 17th century.
You are now in the *Kilifi* area, developing as a resort around the
mouth of the wide *Kilifi Creek.* Just south of the free ferry is a turnoff (R) to Mnarani Club 1 km, Seasafaris/Kenya Diving School, and
Mnarani ruins. *Mnarani* ("lighthouse") is the old Kilifi; it has 14th-
to 17th-century ruins including a group of tombs (and a pillar tomb)
and a mosque which Kirkman calls "one of the most elaborate in
East Africa" with inscriptions in 18-inch-high letters. A local guide is
advisable. On the road just before the ferry is the *Kilifi Serpentarium*
(L), a snake house with Kakamega Forest and many local snakes.
Admission: 2/– for adults; –/50 for children. On the other side of
the creek, *Kilifi town* (pop. 2,662), is a district HQ. Kilifi Creek is
good for birdwatching, with 127 species recorded. The area between
the town and the sea is good during the spring migration, mid-March–
April. **Accommodations:** *Mnarani Club,* Box 14, Kilifi; tel. 18; cable
MNARANI; bookings to African Tours & Hotels (p. 87). Turnoff at
Km 55. 4 sgls sharing bath, 43 dbls w/bath. Rates: FB: sgl—93/– to

180/–; dbl—196/– to 270/–, incl tax, levy, service; plus 20/– daily
membership; also low season rates. Credit: BA, DC. Club dates from
1940s but was recently modernized with BOAC money. Site on a bluff
gives a sheltered harbor for club boats; upstream grow tiny, yummy
oysters which find their way to the club kitchen; lunch—16/–, dinner—
21/50. Rooms passably modern, airy, woody. Open-air dining room,
terrace. Pool. Rating: 2d-class international. ★. Govt. class B*.

Between Kilifi and Watamu the road passes the *Sokoke-Arabuko
Forest,* mostly on the left. The forest has natural ebony, some rare
animals (Zanzibar duiker, yellow-rumped elephant shrew) and much
birdlife, including some rare species, though neither animals nor birds
are easy to see.

Gedi

Km 100: Turnoff (R) on E899 (paved) to Gedi ruins 1½ km,
Watamu Marine National Park 7 km, Blue Lagoon, Turtle Bay, Mida
Creek 11 km, Watamu village, Watamu beach hotels 7–7½ km. *Gedi*
is a ruined Arab city of the 15th century. It is not of great historical
importance; indeed, there are no documentary references other than one
map to Gedi, or Quelman, as it may have been called. Its importance
is that it is typical of historical Arab coastal towns; Gedi is also the
only big set of ruins which the public is encouraged to visit.

Gedi (Galla *gede,* "precious") consists of the ruins of a city wall
enclosing about 45 acres, a palace, a great mosque and smaller mosques,
14 large houses, 3 pillar tombs, a market, and wells. It was declared a
national park in 1948, when James Kirkman was appointed to excavate
and restore. During 1948–58 an immense amount of bush was cleared,
walls were shored up or rebuilt, wells emptied. Besides the concentrated urban area near the entrance and museum building, several
isolated buildings were also excavated. The digging, Kirkman reported,
"produced no great thrills," but there are some mysteries still. The
location—4 miles from the sea, 2 miles from navigable Mida Creek—
is a mystery. So is the fact that the Portuguese nowhere mentioned
Gedi, even though they were 15 km away in Malindi for nearly a
century. And there is no confirmation of the destruction of Gedi in
the early 1500s, which may be, says Kirkman, the only dramatic event
in its history.

The city was apparently founded sometime in the 1200s, though the
only dated monument, a tomb, is inscribed 802 in the Moslem calendar,

or A.D. 1399. Gedi wasn't much until the mid-1400s when the Great Mosque and town wall were built. It was abandoned and partially destroyed in the early 1500s, perhaps in connection with a Mombasa punitive expedition against Malindi in 1529. It was reoccupied, perhaps by Somalis, at the end of the century and partially reconstructed, then abruptly abandoned again between 1625 and 1650, possibly because the inhabitants heard the nomadic Galla, whose policy was extermination, were coming. Gedi then became a lost city, not really rediscovered until the 1920s.

Gedi is worth a couple hours of strolling in either the cool early morning or late afternoon—the latter is when the ruins are the most romantic, and the most eerie. Kirkman's 1/− guide is good. After the *Dated Tomb,* follow the path over the town wall near the *Tomb of the Fluted Pillar,* a perhaps phallic pillar tomb. In front of you is the *Great Mosque,* put up in the mid-15th century, reconstructed 100 years later. A typical *jumaa* or congregational mosque, it has three doors in each wall; the *qibla,* as is usual, shows the direction of Mecca. Go through the mosque to the *Palace,* which with annex covers a quarter-acre. It has a sunken court, reception court, audience court, washing court, and several other courts, and more than 50 rooms of various sizes and uses. In a strong room were kept valuables such as cowrie shells (40,000 cowries equaled one gold dinar). In the main block is an interesting room entered by stepping over a *fingo,* a pot containing a piece of paper inscribed with a spell. When it was buried with appropriate ceremony, a jinn would come to live in the pot. If anybody came into the house who was up to no good, the jinn would get him first. The rest of the buildings in this area are ten houses built cheek by jowl and named for something found in them during the excavations. The oldest house still in its original condition is the late-14th-century *House of the Cowries.* Others were modified in the 15th and 16th centuries. The houses and other buildings were constructed of coral rag (cut from the coral ridge under Gedi), red earth, and coral lime. The one-story houses had flat lime-concrete roofs supported by squared mangrove poles no more than 8 feet long, which results in long narrow rooms; the floors were lime-concrete with coral chips. The *House of the Sunken Court* is one of the most elaborate. Return to the Fluted Pillar, take the path to the left past the *House of the Dhow,* named from the drawing scratched into the plaster, and go around to the South Gate on the *Inner Wall,* constructed in the late

1500s to enclose a smaller area than the original 9-foot-high *Outer Wall*. The path crosses to the Outer Wall, then back to the Inner Wall, thence back to the gate and museum.

Gedi is open daily 7 A.M.–6 P.M. Admission: 5/– per nonresident adult, 2/– per child; residents are charged 2/– per adult Monday–Friday, 1/– on weekends and holidays. Do not climb or stand on the walls or stamp or tap on the plaster floors. For package tours visiting Gedi, see listings KP-37, 55.

Watamu Marine National Park

The highway turnoff to Gedi also goes to the *Watamu* beach hotels. This part of the coast includes the *Watamu Marine National Park,* 3 square miles of white coral sand beaches, blue water, and coral reefs full of colorful marine life—gaudy tropical fish, crimson starfish, tiger-striped eels, shells of many sizes and shapes, blue, brown, purple, and gold coral. This and 1½-square-mile *Malindi Marine National Park* off Casuarina Point, Malindi, were established in 1968 as the first marine parks in Africa. Inside the parks you cannot kill, injure, capture, or disturb any life or remove any live or dead fish, animal, shell, or plant. You can get a free permit for passage and anchorage of boats, and there is free swimming, water skiing, walking, and picnicking without permit. The only park fee you pay is for goggling (skin diving, snorkeling)—10/– per day for nonresidents, 2/50 for residents, 1/– per child; tickets from the main office at Malindi, or at Casuarina Point and near Ocean Sports, Watamu. Both parks are enclosed in the 82-square-mile *Marine National Reserve,* where all activities including goggling are allowed without fee or permit, but spearing fish and collecting shells or coral are prohibited. The reserve extends from about 100 feet inland out to the 3-mile territorial limit. Malindi Marine Park includes Casuarina Point (and, on either side of it, Leopard Point and Chanoni Point), the coastal reef, Barracuda Channel (too deep for goggling), and the two main reefs, North Reef (whose Coral Gardens are in shallow, clear water) and Barracuda Reef. Watamu Park includes all of Mida Creek mouth and Big Three Cave, Turtle Bay and its peculiarly shaped island, the shallow-water Coral Gardens, and Whale Island; Blue Lagoon is outside the park. Big Three Cave is so called because it is the home of three (sometimes more) large (up to 800 pounds) groupers, or rockcods, best seen at high neap tide. Inquire at Ocean Sports or Seafarers. To identify coral, shells, and fish, see the 10/– parks guidebook. *Mida Creek* is partly in the park; watching shore birds is good late March–April; the bird count is 388 in 18 days.

When to Visit

Best months for the coast are October–March. Goggling and glass-bottom boating are best at low tide, when there is better visibility; a spring low tide half-exposes much shallow coral reef.

Getting There, Getting Around

The most efficient way to get there is to take a German or Swiss package tour, or you can fly to Malindi from Nairobi or Mombasa and get a hotel minibus to collect you. See package listings KP-37, 48, 55, 59, 78. Arrangements are easily made to take a glassbottom-boat trip to the Coral Gardens (price 10/– to 25/–), with goggling gear (mask, snorkel, flippers) usually included, or to explore elsewhere in the reefs or Big Three Cave. For general water-sports costs, see p. 139–40.

Accommodations

All the following are 7–7½ km from the highway at Km 100, and all but Watamu Beach Hotel are on the edge of Watamu Marine Park. For accommodations near Malindi Park, see Malindi below. *Turtle Bay Hotel,* Box 457, Malindi; tel. 23; cable TURTLEBAY; bookings also to A. A. & Bunson (p. 86). 90 dbls, all w/bath, 70 w/sea view, 3 w/a-c. Rates: FB: sgl—120/–; dbl—240/–; also low season rates. Credit: DC. Classiest hotel of the 9 in Malindi-Watamu, the Turtle Bay draws a very European crowd but can be recommended to Americans: the hotel is outstanding, and the location on a white sandy cove is magnificent. Hotel is arranged on several levels, main building plus 2 blocks of rooms, which have cool stone floors, bright bedspreads, drapes, wall hangings—rooms are clean, well kept, appealing. Lobby and lounge are big and bright, dining room the most spectacularly friendly riot of color in Kenya. Pool is largest in Malindi area. Rating: 1st-class international, deserving ★★. . . . *Watamu Beach Club Center,* Box 300, Malindi; tel. 101; bookings also to African Safari Lodges (p. 87). 123 dbls w/bath. Rates: FB: sgl—60/– to 110/–; dbl—120/– to 220/–. Credit: DC. Best of the Safari Club hotels catering to European packages. Rooms are arranged on a hillside (most popular location) and along the beach. Pool, lots of water sports, camel to ride on in the surf, games, dances, wine voyage on an old sailing ship (25/– per person). Table d'hôte menus heavy on seafood; bar has an aquarium (unusual). Rating: 2d-class international, great place to have fun. ★. Govt. class C (eh?). . . . *Seafarers,* Box 274, Malindi; tel. 198. 61 dbls, most w/shower. Rates: FB: sgl—50/– to 100/–; dbl—110/– to 150/–, plus 2/50 per person daily membership. Primarily a water-sports club, Seafarers added new rooms to its family cottages and old rooms in order to attract packages. New rooms have airy, modern interiors, face the sea. Old rooms are serviceable cottages. Central building is most attractive; standard menu plus à la carte (entrées—17/50 to 20/–). Rating: Local-international, pleasing place. . . . *Ocean Sports,* Box 340, Malindi. 12 dbls, 2 sgls, all w/bath or shower. Rates: FB: sgl—65/– to 100/–; dbl—130/–. Credit: DC. Closed May–June. Hotel is one of a very few on the coast in catering to individual travelers. Congenial atmosphere in simple, clean rooms, open-air dining room-lounge-bar. Emphasis here on water sports. Rating: 1st-class local, our choice for middle budgets. Govt. class D (?). . . . **Camping** in grounds of private house near Ocean Sports (inquire there). Shower, toilet, no shade. Fee high: 15/– per person.

Km 113: Turnoff (L) to Malindi Airport. Km 115: Malindi traffic circle. Go right to get to Casuarina Point and Malindi Marine Park, Driftwood Club, Silversands campground; go straight to town and other hotels, passing a turnoff (L) on C103 to Tsavo East (Sala Gate 105 km, Voi 193 km).

Malindi

Malindi (pop. 10,757) has been a beach resort and deep-sea fishing (mainly billfish) center since before World War II, but it is only since 1965, when the first package tour came, that it has really grown. Forty percent of the jobs in town are now in tourist industry. Malindi is historic, but no one knows when its history began, with the only certainty being that the Portuguese navigator Vasco da Gama called here in 1498. Before that, there were places called Ma-Lin or Melinde or Malindi somewhere on the East African coast, with the name occurring first in a Chinese geography written in the 9th century. Vasco da Gama sailed into Malindi roads April 13, 1498. The town was apparently quite prosperous then and, says James Kirkman, probably looked as Lamu does today. The friendly ruler supplied da Gama with food and water and a pilot to guide his way to Calicut on the Indian coast, and the Portuguese ships sailed away April 28, leaving behind a *padrão* or cross (see below).

Then began Malindi's time in the limelight: it continued its profitable trade in rhino horn, tortoise shell, ivory, cowries, and ambergris while becoming the center of Portuguese activity north of Mozambique. All the Portuguese on the coast took refuge here in 1589 when the Turk Mirale Bey came rampaging along, but he was driven away by cannon fire. The next year the town was attacked by the cannibalistic Zimba, who had killed 3,000 people at Kilwa in 1586 and ate quite a few in Mombasa in 1589. The Zimba were themselves attacked in the rear by the Segeju, Malindi's allies, and almost annihilated; the toothless remnants fled back to the Zambezi. Then, in 1593, the Portuguese decided to set up their headquarters in Mombasa, building Fort Jesus and naming Malindi's sheikh as Sultan of Mombasa. Malindi swiftly declined; in 40 years it was one-third the size, and travelers' accounts for the next 200 years speak of it as ruined or dilapidated until, as Dr. Johann Ludwig Krapf found in 1845, it was apparently deserted completely. Malindi was refounded in 1861 to grow grain for the Sultan of Zanzibar, and it had a brief period of prosperity as a slave market. When the British came, slave trading was halted, and Malindi again became a nothing town until its development as a resort (the Blue Marlin Hotel dates to 1931, Lawford's to 1934).

There remains little that is historic in the town, with few buildings predating 1880. Of great importance is the *padrão* or *cross of Vasco da Gama,* a pillar of local stone surmounted by a small squarish cross of Lisbon stone engraved with Portugal's coat of arms. Da Gama had it erected in 1498 in front of the sheikh's house, but it was taken down, then reerected in 1512. It apparently fell down and was put on its squat tower before 1593. To get there, go south along Sea Front Road, continue on Mnarani Road, pass the "footpass" sign, and go left along the cliffs out onto the promontory at the southern end of the harbor. The cross is one of the only Portuguese relics on the coast. On the road to Silversands is the *Portuguese Chapel,* a small building incorporating in its southeast corner some Portuguese ruins. Other sites of interest: Two *pillar tombs,* one dating to the late 1400s, are in front of the modern mosque. According to James Kirkman, "pillar tombs are the one architectural invention of the coast of East Africa"; he says they are supposed to be phallic, but Arabs disagree. Other than a *ruined mosque,* there are no Arab relics in Malindi. The *old town,* which is not much more than a century old, is at the southern end of the harbor. Not far from the village green is the *Vasco da Gama Monument,* a white stone billowing sail emblazoned with the Cross of the Order of Christ, on top of a 20-foot pillar in a mosaic pool. It was unveiled by a Portuguese official in 1960; two brass plaques were subsequently stolen. The *District Officer's house,* completed 1890, is typical of 19th-century English colonial architecture.

Down at the *harbor* you can see Bajun fishermen repairing fishnets, also some of their boats. Next to the African market are some *Kamba carvers.* Other than seeing the sights, swimming, goggling, and loafing, there is golfing at the nine-hole course of the Malindi Golf and Country Club (temporary membership 2/–) and horseback riding (Alfred Ruesch, Ngowe Road, tel. 174). You can also visit *Birdland* on Silversands Road. It is a private bird sanctuary with 1,000 mostly local birds but some South American and Australian imports; there's a walk-in aviary with 60 species. Admission: 5/–. For details on *Malindi Marine National Park,* see Km 100 above.

As a resort, Malindi has something wrong with it: the Sabaki River, which flows into the sea 4 miles north, bleeds great amounts of brown mud into Malindi harbor. The water off the four big hotels is, for several months a year, the same color as the East River, though perhaps cleaner. (The mud doesn't go as far as the marine park, however.) Additionally, Malindi is just not that attractive a town. We found Watamu far nicer, and suggest you lodge (and swim) there instead.

Accommodations

Hotel Sindbad, Box 30, Malindi; tel. 7; cable SINDBAD. 4 sgls, 67 dbls, all w/bath, a-c. Rates: FB: sgl—100/– to 150/–; dbl—130/– to 200–. Credit: BA, DC. 1946 hotel augmented, refurbished 1969–70. Arabesque design and decor. Rooms smartly furnished, those fanciest which are priciest. Peppy, Persian rug-lined lounge, bar, dining room. Pool. Mostly British clientele. Rating: 1st- to 2d-class international, depending on your room. Best hotel in Malindi, we'll give it a ★. . . . *Eden Roc Hotel,* Box 350, tel. 8; cable EDENROC. 2d-class international, big and bland. . . . *Lawford's Hotel,* Box 20, tel. 57, 6; cable LAWFORDS. 2d-class international, commendable. . . . *Blue Marlin Hotel,* Box 54, tel. 4; cable MARLIN. 1st-class local, standard, characterless. . . . *Driftwood Club,* Box 63, tel. 155. 3 km south of town on Silversands Bay. 54 beds in 25 thatch-roofed bandas. Rates: B&B: best cottage—50/– to 60/– per person; cheap cottage—27/50 per person; also low-season rates. Daily membership 2/– per day, 10/– per week. Closed May–

June. 1965 banda colony caters to individuals (mainly locals), has no plans to change face or mind. Cottages homely, basic; grounds passable, pool round. Choice of fish or meat at meals. Rating: 2d-class local but a beachy low-budget buy. . . . *Indian Ocean Hotels* project may be revived, and *Fisherman's Hotel,* 220 beds, is planned. Now under construction on Silver Beach is Malindi's newest international-class hotel, the *Malindi Bustani,* 154 doubles, to be completed in late 1975. . . . Houses and bungalows rented by Allen & Charlton, Box 301, tel. 70. . . . *Silversands Tourist Paradise,* Box 27, tel. 78. And Malindi Town Council **campground** (only one in Malindi). 1½ km south of town. Inappropriately named. Flush toilets, cold showers, drinking water, cafeteria. Camping: 5/– to 10/– per tent. Also fully equipped tents—32/50 or 35/–. Beach is somewhat messy.

Continuing on the highway straight through Malindi (Km 115–117), the paving runs out just past the golf club. Km 124: Turnoff (L) to Marafa 38 km and *Hell's Kitchen* (Marafa Depression), a very curious Grand Canyonesque sight with purple, tan, red, orange, yellow, white, and black sand and clay cliffs and pinnacles, some about 100 feet high, dating from the Pliocene.

Km 128: Turnoff (R) to *Mambrui,* a conservative, cotton-planting Arab town of 1,000 people whose celebration of the Prophet's birthday is second only to Lamu's on the coast. The town has narrow streets, an interesting modern mosque and some ruins, including a fallen-down pillar tomb that, at last report, still had 16th-century Ming bowls remaining in position.

Km 136: Turnoff to *Ngomeni,* a Bajun village with ruins of a fort or watchtower. Off Ngomeni, in Ngwana (Formosa) Bay are the Italian rocket-launching platform *San Marco* and the control platform *Santa Rita.* Part of a joint Italian-U.S. space program run with the cooperation of Kenya and various organizations, San Marco has sent off (as of 1974) six satellites, including one December 12, 1970, the *Uhuru,* which has provided the first indirect evidence of the existence of "black holes" in the universe. The lucky Italians here also run a tracking station on the beach.

Km 155: Turnoff (R) to ferry to *Robinson Island* (Fundisa or Kiny'ole), Box 16, Malindi; tel. 152. Here David Hurd and his wife serve up a Kenya coast lunch: coconut chips, oysters in half-shell, fresh crab, homegrown salad, *tewa* and *chausi* fish, Arab-Swahili curry called mango masala, Malindi melon, Arab coffee with pressed coconut cream—for 30/–, including boat passage. No lodging yet, but 30 beds are planned. Goggling off the island's five reefs.

Km 230: *Garsen* and Tana River ferry. The road from here to Witu is usually out April–July, November–December. Latest information from the Ministry of Works, Mombasa, tel. 26863, 26864. The Tana River, flowing from the Aberdares and emptying into the ocean at Kipini (see Km 272), is Kenya's biggest river, navigable by small launch for about 200 miles. Below Garsen on the west bank is a *heronry* where many large breeding birds are observable May–September. At Garsen, B8 goes north to Garissa 236 km while C112 goes right to Witu, Lamu, and north. Km 272: *Witu* and turnoff (R) on C567 to Kipini. Witu was for five years, 1885–90, a German protectorate and enclave within the British sphere of influence in East Africa. Down on the coast is *Kipini,* once headquarters of Tana River District but now a rundown Swahili fishing village. Three km east are the good ruins of three towns, *Ngwana, Shaka,* and *Mwana.* Mwana has a small mosque, the only surviving example of one built with a dome and barrel-vaulted roof instead of a flat roof. Ngwana, the largest town, was known to the Portuguese as Hoja; it is, says James Kirkman, who excavated it in 1953–54, "one of the most impressive of the ruined towns" of the region—50 acres of ruins including two Great Mosques, at least two smaller ones, some large houses and fine tombs, a town wall.

Lamu

Km 338: *Mokowe* and boat to Lamu Island 6 km. Sandy *Lamu* is the most important and populated island in the Lamu Archipelago (or Bajun Islands), including Manda Island and Pate (Patta) Island and several smaller ones. Manda town is the earliest known town on the East African coast, and Pate town was probably the most important politically for the longest time, but it is Lamu, not historically important, which has survived—and that is its value. Depending on your authority, Lamu is the most truly Arab, or the most Swahili, town on the coast, but there is no doubt it is a fossil, a living museum that today looks like all the other towns—early Mombasa, Malindi, Gedi, Kilwa—must have looked like hundred of years ago. Lamu town (pop. 7,403) may have been founded about A.D. 700 by Azdite fugitives from Arabia, but there may have been people here before that. The famous 1st-century guidebook *Periplus* mentioned the Pyralaon Islands, which may be Lamu, but the first certain reference was by the 15th-century Arab geographer Abu al-Mahasin. Lamu was always a trading town, but it didn't have an eventful history because it never attempted to assert itself, preferring to bend with the breeze and bow to the mighty. The most exciting event in its history was in the early 19th century when a Byzantine intrigue led to Lamu's victory over the soldiers of the Mazrui in Mombasa and of Pate in the Battle of Shella, outside Lamu town. Pate declined, Lamu rose and prospered, not without a little help from hundreds of slaves, for 75 years. It collapsed economically about 1900 and became a sleepy museum town in a British colony. It is now one of Kenya's hottest tourist destinations. Piped water came in 1965, electricity in 1969, but the island still has only one motor vehicle, a Mini-Moke used by the district commissioner. "It is refreshing," says Kirkman, "to find one place in the world that does not pretend to believe in progress or indeed in motion at all."

The town has a main street, a sea-front promenade, and innumerable little alleyways and streets, some not more than a yard wide, enclosed by one- to three-story coral-rag houses with balconies built over the street. Some houses have delightful carved doors, some have plaster-work from the 18th and 19th centuries. The women hurry here and there dressed in black *buibuis* covering all but eyes; down at the harbor, Bajun fishermen set out in their boats; Somali cattle sellers (wearing red and blue plaids) herd their lean cattle down to the Mombasa-bound cattle boat; mangrove poles are being stacked on the beach for shipment by dhow to the Persian Gulf. If you go there, don't rush around; sit back, or wander slowly, and let it all happen around you. If you feel energetic after three or four days, you can always go swimming off Shella's white beaches.

Not much archaeological work has been done in Lamu. Although some buildings apparently have ancient first stories or foundations, most of the town between the main street and sea front was built after 1850, with 18th-century stone houses here and there. Lamu has few historical monuments: the ruined *tomb of Sharif Mwana Tau;* a *fluted pillar tomb* behind Riyadh Mosque; the *Mosque of Mwana Lalo* with a *kiblah* dated to 1753; and *Pwani Mosque,* which may have a 1370 foundation. There are 23 mosques on the island; most of the 19 in town were built between 1821 and 1860. The biggest building in town is the *old fort,* started by the Mazrui about 1813, completed 1821. With a carved doorway and cannon facing the central market-place, the fort is now a prison (no photography). In the *market* Saturday mornings is an auction. In the fine 1891 sea-front mansion, formerly the D.C.'s house, is the *Lamu Museum,* opened in 1971 with a select collection including woodcarvings, ceramics, silver and gold work, and furniture. The prizes of the collection are a pair of ceremonial horns called *siwas.* The Pate *siwa,* dated to 1688, is beautifully carved ivory, 7 feet long, with two articulated joints; the Lamu *siwa* is a bit shorter, is made of brass, and is not as old. According to the Kenya Museum Society magazine, the horns may be the oldest musical instruments discovered south of the Sahara.

There is a movement to make all of Lamu a protected national monument because it is in danger of being changed too much by the 20th century. For instance, Museum Curator James deVere Allen says there were about 250 carved doors in 1963 but now only 66; the others were bought by rich visitors, mostly American. Eighteenth-century houses are being torn down, 18th- and 19th-century plaster-work is being allowed to deteriorate. (If you want a carved door, go to Ali Skanda's shop on the waterfront; the craftsmen will make a new one for 2,000/– to 4,000/–.)

Neighboring *Manda Island,* only sporadically inhabited because it has little fresh water, has Lamu's airstrip and some important ruins. Neville Chittick, who excavated here in 1966 and 1970, says Manda is the earliest known important townsite on the East African coast. Dating back to the 9th century, Manda town was settled by Persian Gulf traders and quickly became a prosperous town, but began declining about the 13th century, being replaced by Shanga on Pate Island. Some buildings were constructed of coral stone with mortar, others of mud and wattle, while others were burned brick—"the only such found on the . . . coast at any period," says Chittick. Walls against the sea were built of blocks of coral, some weighing a ton—"a massive form of construction found nowhere else in sub-Saharan Africa" until colonial times. The chief import was apparently pottery, the export ivory. Some coins and glass beads have been found. Iron was smelted here on a large scale. The Manda people were once called "the wearers of gold" and were renowned for their snobbery. They were arrogant enough in 1589 to tell the Portuguese that only the sun and the moon could get into their town; the Portuguese landed anyway, and the people ran into the bush. The ruins of Manda town, on the north tip of the island, cover 5 to 10 acres and include two mosques (one probably destroyed by the Portuguese) and the sea wall. Also on the island are the ruins of a 5-acre walled town called *Takwa* (opposite Shella on Lamu), including a large mosque, small houses, the town wall, outside of which is a cylindrical pillar tomb dated to 1682. On the southern peninsula of Ras Takwa is the *fort of Kitau,* a 19th-century redoubt with cannons (minus carriages) still in the embrasures. Nearby is the new *Ras Kitau Hotel* and beach.

On *Pate Island* is Pate town, founded in the 14th century and in the 17th and 18th in a position of dominance on the coast north of Kilifi and south of Juba in Somaliland, rivaling Mombasa and at one time controlling clove-rich Pemba Island. A civil war about 1763–73 destroyed Pate as a state, and it declined quickly. The 17th-century town walls are largely gone, the 18th-century sultan's palace in ruins, the Great Mosque torn down so a new one could be built. The more accessible town of *Faza* took Pate's place. At Faza are two ruined mosques. The third town, *Siyu,* has a picturesque fort built in the early 1860s.

Getting There, Getting Around

Lamu can be reached by air anytime, by road not during or immediately after the rains unless you take the bus and are willing to walk a muddy mile or canoe across the Tana. If the road is open you can drive all the way to Mokowe jetty, where you have to leave the car. A bus from Malindi takes 6 hours, costs 15/–, and runs during the rains only when possible. The New Mahrus Hotel has a minibus service from Mombasa; inquire Box 25, Lamu, or Box 81564, Mombasa, tel. 20816. Regular ship service to Lamu is only by Kenya Meat Commission cattle boat. Best way to get there is air charter to Manda airstrip. Daily Tic-Air service from Malindi costs 150/– per person, day-return. See package listings KP-27, 37, 42, 45, 48, 57. Once you're on Lamu you have to walk to get around. To get to Manda or Pate, dicker with fishermen, or ask about a taxiboat for 50/– per day. Note: Freaks, after a 1972 crackdown, are tolerated if they purchase bed and board somewhere; but the District Commissioner chronically complains about the great unwashed.

Accommodations

Petley's Inn, Box 4, Lamu; tel. 48; bookings to Box 46582, Nairobi; tel. 29612. Next to Lamu Museum. 11 dbls w/bath. Rates: FB: sgl— 175/–; dbl—300/–; also rates for residents. Newly renovated and respectable version of formerly dilapidated inn started by Percy Petley, indescribable character who once (allegedly) strangled a leopard with his bare hands; further, if he didn't like a guest, the guest was thrown out. Now owned by a couple of Texans who ranch near Mount Kenya. Ornate arches have been restored, swimming pool added. Each room is different, has Lamu furnishings. . . . *Peponi Hotel,* Box 24, Lamu; tel. 29; cable PEPONI. In Shella, 3 km from Lamu town. 1 sgl, 13 dbls, all w/shower, plus 6 beds in rms sharing bath. Rates: FB: sgl—150/–; dbl—250/–, incl tax, levy, service. Closed May–July. Peponi means "a place of rest and coolness." Govt. class B. . . . *Ras Kitau Beach Hotel,* bookings to Ahamed Bros., Box 40254, Nairobi; tel. 29467. On Manda Island; hotel boat will pick you up at Mokowe jetty or Manda airstrip. 15 dbls w/bath. Rates: FB: sgl—150/–; dbl— 240/–. 5-room cottages, lounge, bar, dining room in big makuti-roofed main building, stone's throw from beach. . . . *Lamu Leisure Lodge,* Box 89, Lamu; tel. 45. New offshoot of South Beach Leisure Lodge. . . . *New Mahrus Hotel,* Box 25, Lamu; tel. Lamu 1 or Mombasa 81564. Next to fort in Lamu town. Rates: B&B: dbl w/shower— 55/–; w/o shower—33/–. . . . *Furaha lodging house.* Bed in dbl overlooking sea—7/50; in back rm—5/50. . . . Houses, some owned by Europeans, furnished with old Lamu furniture, equipped with kitchen and servant, can be rented cheaply—say, 50/– a day. Ask around Nairobi or in Lamu (New Mahrus and Kandara Hotel).

Route K-3: Mombasa–South Coast

The South Coast is far less developed than the North Coast, and it is not as long. There are fewer tourists and fewer places of historical interest, but many say the beaches and atmosphere are far more appealing.

From the intersection of Kilindini Road, take Nyerere Road south to *Likoni Ferry* (toll charged for vehicles only is 2/25 to 2/75 return) to the mainland. On the southern shore are Likoni town and *Shelly Beach,* named for its shells. Reef is best reached at the northern end; there is seaweed to excess at the southern end. Immediately after the ferry are two left turnoffs to hotel **accommodations:** *Shelly Beach Hotel,* Box 96030, Mombasa; tel. 76221; cable JOLLOP. 46 dbls w/bath or shower, 10 sgls w/o bath. Rates: FB: sgl—68/–; dbl—130/– or 150/–. Credit: DC. The English language is more common here than German. Rooms are in a couple attractive tile-roofed blocks; new wing was added to 1948 original. Pool, library. Rating: 2d-class international, friendly. Govt. class B. . . . *New Sea Breezes Hotel,* Box 96022, Mombasa; tel. 76218. 2d-class local, old, inexpensive, unfancy. . . .

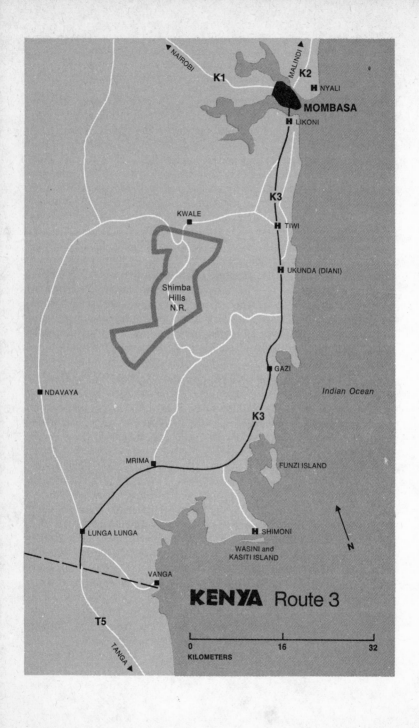

KENYA Route 3

Camping at Timbwani Camping Site, Box 96072, Mombasa. Fee: 5/– per adult, 3/– per child, or tents for hire at 30/– per day. Square, fenced campground, no shade, next to beach. Small store.

Shimba Hills

Km 9: Turnoff (R) on C106 to East Gate of *Shimba Hills National Reserve;* turnoffs also at Km 17 near Tiwi and Km 52 to Kidondo Gate. Usual admission charges. Established as a game reserve in 1963 and national reserve in 1968, the Shimba Hills (name from the Digo *shimba,* "lion," or *shambe,* "sable") are a forested plateau from 400 feet to 1,500 feet. The reserve is 47,550 acres (74.4 square miles). While the hills make a pleasant excursion through woodland and some deeply dark glades to a couple of viewpoints (Giriama Point and the Observation Post) over the South Coast, the hills' attraction is the

Sable antelope   Roan antelope

sable antelope, the most northerly in this part of Africa and the only ones in Kenya. Sable are superb large antelope with beautiful big scimitar-shaped horns; males are black or reddish black, females a chestnut-brown. The 60 indigenous sable were joined at Easter 1971 by a small herd of *roan antelope,* which resemble sable closely but are bigger, brown-gray in color, and have tufted ears and a blacker set of face markings. The roan were rescued from the Ithanga Hills near Thika and transported to this sanctuary. Though they prefer more open country, the roan are adjusting to the reserve and coexisting well with the sable.

Both are certainly worth looking for. Suitably warned that we might not see one sable, we went and saw not one sable. We are assured that the best chance is to go well before 9 A.M. for both sable and bird watching. The guidebook-map (cost 2/–) indicates most sable can be found around and between signposts 1 to 6—Makadara Forest, Longo Magandi Forest, Buffalo Ridge, Mwachomwana Valley. There are other animals—elephant, buffalo, leopard, duiker, waterbuck—but they are rarely seen; 90 species of birds were counted. Package tours rarely go to Shimba Hills; see listings KP-56 and 88.

Km 18: *Tiwi* area, location of several beach cottage colonies and a campground, turnoffs Km 19–20. The beach has an average gradient so that swimming is possible at high tide while reef walking is easy at low tide. **Accommodations:** *Maweni* self-service beach cottages, Box 96024, Likoni via Mombasa; tel. Tiwi 2Y5. . . . *El Capricho* cottages, Box 96093, Likoni via Mombasa; tel. Tiwi 2Y9. . . . *Tiwi Beach Bungalows,* Box 46008, Likoni via Mombasa; tel. Tiwi 2Y7. . . . (Note: Cottages rent for 55/– to 80/– and up per day.) . . . *Twiga Lodge,* Box 96005, Likoni via Mombasa; tel. Tiwi 2Y2. Self-service lodge has coral and makuti cottages. Rates per week: cottage for 4—315/–; for 5—350/–; for 6—385/–. Cottages are old with no real decor, but are comfortable. Small store plus cafeteria, large bar-lounge open to breezes. . . . **Camping** adjacent for 3/50 per person. Numbered campsites are on beach or hillside, most under good shade trees. Toilets, showers (cold, fresh water), water (potable). . . . *Moonlight Bay* cottages, bookings to Mrs. Gray, Box 30161, Nairobi; tel. Ruaraka (80) 263.

Diani

Km 27: *Ukunda.* Turnoff (L) on paved access road to *Diani Beach,* the most developed resort on the South Coast. No wonder, for Diani Beach is simply fantastic, with even a couple points of interest. Near the Trade Winds Hotel is a *famous baobab* said to be 500 years old; it measures 71 feet 2 inches around and is protected by order of President Kenyatta. Near the mouth of the Tiwi River is *Kongo,* with an 18th-century mosque still in good condition, and shaded by baobabs. Toward the southern end of the Diani road is the *Jadini Forest,* a place of tall trees, butterflies, and birds; look for the coastal variety of the black and white colobus monkey, which is different from other colobuses in having no white hair below the shoulders. Diani **accommodations** (turnoff at Km 27): *South Beach Leisure Lodge,* Box 84383, Mombasa; tel. Diani (82) 1, 2; cable LEISURELODGE Mombasa. 122 dbls (incl 5 suites) w/bath, a-c, sea view. Rates: FB: sgl—140/–;

dbl—200/–. One of the top 2 or 3 hotels on the coast, 1971–72 Leisure Lodge is uniquely situated on and in the coral cliffs immediately above the beach. Doubles all very nicely furnished, with a sea view from each. Lush inner garden opens into the Old Lamu Bar with Arab-chair replicas and bar incorporating old carved doors. Diani Room restaurant has good solid furniture, *kitenge* tablecloths, table d'hôte meals (lunch—18/–; dinner—18/– or 21/50 with dancing). Management has good taste and cares. Pool. Rating: Superior 1st-class international, bargain for the price. ★★★. . . . *Trade Winds Hotel*, P.O. Ukunda via Mombasa; tel. Diani (82) 8; bookings to African Tours & Hotels (p. 87). 61 dbls w/bath or shower. Rates: FB: sgl—90/– or 165/–; dbl—165/– or 234/–, incl tax, levy, service. Credit: BA, DC. Older, remodeled hotel with rooms in old, plain blocks or new wings with Dutch doors, woody interiors, balcony with sea view. Management is brusque. Draws mainly packages from Europe, U.S. Rating: 2d-class international but adequate. . . . *Two Fishes Hotel*, P.O. Ukunda via Mombasa; tel. Diani (82) 23. Being modernized from 1st-class local, to include East Africa's longest pool, meandering inside the hotel. . . . *Jadini Beach Hotel*, P.O. Ukunda via Mombasa; tel. Diani (82) 25. 2d-class international. . . . *Robinson Baobab Hotel*, with 300 beds, and built on a promontory, is to be open in 1975. Smaller 160-bed *Leopard Beach Hotel* was to be open earlier in 1975. . . . *Four° Twenty' South Beach Houses*, Box 14681, Nairobi; tel. 60960.

Km 43: *Gazi*, location of 1,000-acre coconut estate, one of the largest on the entire coast. Km 70: Turnoff (L) to *Shimoni* ("place of the hole"), a village with a minor coastal dhow trade and a series of caves, the first one near the turnoff to the *Pemba Channel Fishing Club*, which is 14 km from the highway. Address: P.O. Ukunda via Mombasa; tel. Gazi 5Y2; cable HEMPHILL Ukunda. 10 dbls w/bath or shower. Rates: B&B: sgl—91/–; dbl—182/–, incl tax, levy, service. Closed April 1–July 15. Favored by fishermen; club owner coauthored *Crash Strike!* (East African Publishing House) about coast fishing. Rooms are basic, breezy. Pool, bar, lounge, dining room with mounted fish and table d'hôte menu (breakfast—6/50; lunch—14/–; dinner—15/–). Rating: 1st-class local.

Off Shimoni is *Wasini Island*, with a huge reef on which shell sellers find many of their wares. *Kisiti-Mpunguti Marine National Park* was to be gazetted in early 1975. Km 101: Turnoffs (R) to *Lunga Lunga*,

border town; and (L) to *Vanga*. Immediately ahead, and marking the
end of the paved road, is the Kenya border post. The Tanzania border
post is another 6 km farther.

Route K-4: Taveta–Taita Hills–Voi

Beginning at the Tanzania border, you drive through *Taveta* (Km
5), a sisal-growing town that was captured by the Germans almost
as soon as World War I began; they held it until March 10, 1915.
Tsavo West was the scene of other fighting. Just past Taveta are turnoffs (L) to *Lake Chala* and (R) to *Lake Jipe*. Chala is an almost
perfectly circular and gemlike crater lake on the border to the north. Jipe
is a crocodile-filled lake 7 miles long, 2½ miles wide. Km 28: Mbuyuni
Gate into Tsavo West (L). Km 75: Turnoff (R) to Taita Hills Lodge
1 km, Salt Lick Lodge 9 km. *Taita Hills Game Lodge,* bookings to
Hilton Hotels (p. 87). 64 dbls (incl 2 suites) w/bath. Rates: FB:
sgl—200/–; dbl—300/–. Base for Salt Lick Lodge. The 1973 Hilton
lodge is designed uniquely, with 2 floors of rooms on concrete stilts,
in the form of a hollow square with one side open. Within the square
are a comma-shaped pool, garden. Rooms sizable, cozy, inviting, with
deep tufted-yarn rugs, overstuffed chairs, YMCA batiks. Enormous
lounge, big central fireplace, inside-outside bar, fully carpeted dining
room with decor based on the East African campaign of World War I:
German eagles, rifles on the wall. Rating: 1st-class international. ★★
for style, comfort. . . . *Salt Lick Lodge,* same address. 64 dbls w/
shower. Rates: FB: sgl—200/–; dbl—300/–. Salt Lick is the 4th
imitation Treetops. Access only through Taita Hills Lodge and at
certain hours; one-night tourist stands are the rule (see package listings
KP-15A, 40, 62). Children under 8 at manager's discretion. As a
Hilton creation, Salt Lick is architecturally unique, with rooms arranged
in 2-story thatched-roof rondavels on stilts (8 rooms per cluster of 4
towers), connected to main building by a bamboo-and-concrete walkway. Rooms are round, moderately large. Public areas are big, com-
fortable-to-plush. Whole complex forms a semicircle around the floodlit waterhole and mudwallow, and there are plenty of places to game-
view from. Though we had doubted the lodge's ability to attract game
quickly, Salt Lick by the end of October 1973 was able to compile a
weekly census that included 24 lions, 27 giraffes, 36 rhinos, 506 waterbucks, 211 impalas, 225 baboons, 439 elephants, and 1,245 buffalos.

Rating: 1st-class international. ★★. Both lodges are within the private *Ponderosa Game Sanctuary*.

Km 83: Turnoff (L) on Taita Hills circular route. Km 91: Mwatate and turnoff (L) on C104, paved road up into the *Taita Hills* to Wundanyi 15 km, whence a dirt road descends to Km 83 on the highway. The Taita Hills (pop. 61,446) are a small range of pretty, green hills that rise over 7,000 feet and provide the Taita tribe with sloping but fertile fields as well as a traditional refuge, with cliff pathways once easily defended against marauding Masai from the plains around. When the Taita captured some Masai, they shoved them off one of the higher cliffs. The hills are more accessible now, and a side trip up the good paved road, past perfect green valleys and terraced hillsides, to *Wundanyi* (pop. 4,385), Taita District HQ, is a very pleasant break from the monotony of the Nairobi–Mombasa road. At least one tour (KP-38A) goes into the Taita Hills. **Accommodations:** *Mwasungia Scenery Guest House,* Box 1026, Wundanyi; tel. 40. Rates: bed only: 10/– per person. Compact, barely furnished, very local guest house.

Km 114: Route ends at junction with Nairobi–Mombasa highway at Voi. Pick up Route K-1 at Km 323.

Route K-5: Namanga–Amboseli–Kajiado–Nairobi

This drive through Masailand includes Amboseli, a game park photographers like because Kilimanjaro provides a superb background for pictures of lions, giraffes, and rhinos.

The route begins at the Tanzania border at *Namanga,* a town unnoteworthy except for the presence of the *Masai,* the tourist's favorite tribe. No visitor to this part of East Africa will quickly forget the sight of a tall young Masai *moran* (warrior), standing on one leg, leaning against his spear, his lean body draped in rust-red cloth, his finely sculptured face, his intricately plaited, elaborately styled hair. This is old Africa and is not seen everywhere.

Conservative, abhorring change, clinging to tradition, the Masai are a living symbol of Kenya yesterday, resisting emotionally and actually most of the government's efforts to bring them into the 20th century. A Nilo-Hamitic (or Plains Nilotic) people, the Masai number 155,000 and are Kenya's eleventh-largest tribe. For hundreds of years, the tribe herded its cattle across vast areas of East Africa, raided as far as the coast, and gained a reputation as a fierce fighting tribe until brought low at the end of the 19th century by a series of misfortunes. Their herds were decimated by rinderpest in 1880, and a dozen years later three out of four Masai died in a smallpox epidemic. They had resisted Arab slavers and European explorers alike, but by the end of the century did not oppose the British colonizers. Masailand in Kenya, administered from Kajiado (Km 83 below) and Narok (on Route K-6), now covers 60,000 square miles between the Mara River and Tsavo National Park, from near Nairobi south into Tanzania.

When God divided heaven and earth, the tribe believes, He gave the cattle to the Masai, and around cattle the Masai world revolves. A Masai child may not know how old he is, but at an early age he will know some 70 words for cattle patterns and colors, 30 names of different kinds of grass. The Masai live largely on milk, supplemented with cattle blood, tea, and maize; cattle are slaughtered for meat only occasionally.

Masai males go through three stages in life: first they are boys, then *moran,* then elders. After a long, ritualized circumcision period, boys become full *moran,* with their duty to defend the people and herds against wild animals and human enemies. For eight years they live an unstructured life in a *manyatta,* a group of huts with no thorn-bush *boma* (the ordinary Masai village, encircled by a *boma,* is called an *enkang*). When moranhood ends, their heads are shaved and they are allowed to marry and settle down.

Photographing Masai: see p. 67.

Amboseli

Immediately after the border posts at Namanga is the turnoff (R) to Namanga Gate of *Amboseli National Park and Game Reserve.* The area around Ol Tukai swamp, free of Masai and their cattle, is the principal game-viewing area in the 1,259-square-mile park. Tourists will find the rest of Amboseli mostly dry, rocky, thornbush country. Overall, however, Amboseli is superbly scenic because of the photogenic mass of Kilimanjaro, most of which is in Tanzania.

First created a game reserve in 1948, Amboseli was the responsibility of the National Parks Trustees until 1961, when the colonial government experimentally turned this and other reserves back to tribal control. The Masai are no threat to wildlife, but their cattle do compete with plains animals for water and grass. The 303-square-mile Ol Tukai section in 1970 was declared off-limits to cattle, and 150 square miles was to be gazetted a national park in early 1975 on the completion of a water-and-forage scheme funded by the New York Zoological Society. The animals have a long, hunting-free corridor (Photography Block 72 and the Kitengela Game Conservation Area) between Amboseli and Nairobi National Park.

The ecology of the Ol Tukai area is interesting in that it is changing from yellow-barked acacia ("fever tree") woodland into a swamp and grassland because of the rise of the water table and the consequent alkalinizing of the soil. Two University of Nairobi researchers say there won't be any more fever trees by 1977, and the rhino, impala, vervets, baboons, and kudu in their woodland will have given way to antelope and other ungulates in a grassy savanna with umbrella acacias. One terrain feature which comes and goes is Lake Amboseli, which can be as big as 40 square miles.

Amboseli has a good variety of wildlife. In the Ol Tukai area can be found elephant, black rhino (including 70 earless rhino), lion, cheetah, buffalo. One species that seems very appropriate to the park is the *giraffe* (Swahili, *twiga*), which scarcely has to be described except for differing color patterns within the species. The common (locally, Masai) giraffe has dark spots with jagged, irregular outlines, with the overall color between the spots a yellowish buff. The other Kenya type, the reticulated giraffe, found in Samburu and Meru, has a well-defined network of narrow white lines separating the dark brown patches (picture, p. 254). The giraffe is the world's tallest animal—one bull of the subspecies *tippelskirchi* found in Kenya measured 19 feet 3 inches tall (it weighed 3,800 pounds). Giraffes are usually found in herds. Giraffes are not voiceless, but can utter low snorts and moans. They are equipped with a tough mouth that enables them to munch on thorny acacias. They drink by doing the splits with their front legs; a unique valve keeps the blood from rushing to the head. Giraffes walk and run (up to 35 mph) gracefully; when galloping, peculiarly, the back legs move outside the front ones. They defend themselves by kicking. The snakelike "necking" dance seen between two giraffes is actually sparring between males.

Amboseli birdwatching is excellent; John Williams counted some 421 species.

When to Visit

Amboseli is open all year but has the best weather in the dry season, December–February, when Kilimanjaro can be clearly seen.

Getting There, Getting Around

Namanga is the main gate (closes 5 P.M.); the other is Lemi Boti ("low table") Gate (closes 6 P.M.) on the road from Ol Tukai to Tsavo West (112 km from Amboseli Lodge to Kilaguni). Airstrips at Namanga and Ol Tukai. Game-viewing Land-Rovers are for hire at Amboseli New Lodge; with driver, 200/– half-day, 400/– whole day. Ranger guides can be hired for 10/– per day, and we recommend this for private cars. Many package tours, including from Nairobi and back in one day, go to Amboseli; see listings KP-18, 39–40, 61, 69–75, 79–88; and TP-29, 31. Note: Exercise care in taking the Lake Road across the bed of seasonal Lake Amboseli. What looks like an expanse of dried, cracked clay is sometimes wet, cracked mud, and you could get terribly stuck . . . as we did. Also, please don't drive off the roads and tracks; the ecology of the park can be affected when too many people do this.

Costs

Entry charge of 10/– per vehicle, 5/– per adult, 2/– per child; nonresidents the same.

Accommodations

Amboseli New Lodge and *Amboseli Safari Camp,* Box 20211, Nairobi; tel. 21273; cable MASAI. 54 dbls w/bath or shower in lodge plus 60 dbl "luxury" tents w/shower in camp. Rates for either: FB: sgl—227/50; dbl—295/75, incl tax, levy. Credit: DC. Lodge has a central table d'hôte dining room and lounge area looking over lawns, pool, bird feeders. Log and stone cottages are darkish, basic. Camp, a few hundred yards away (walking between camp and lodge *verboten*), consists of a long, curved row of heavy-duty tents, each a double with front porch, sleeping, and toilet/shower areas. Rating: Lodge is 2d-class international, pleasant but overpriced. It's a scandal the okay tented camp has the same high fee. . . . *Amboseli Serena Lodge,* bookings to Serena Lodges & Hotels (p. 87). Located 3½ km from Ol Tukai–Kilaguni road. 50 dbls w/bath. Rates: FB: sgl—215/–; dbl—323/–, incl. Aga Khan-initiated lodge, new in 1973, is designed like a Masai *enkang* or stockaded village, except it's not really stockaded, but cleverly designed for the same effect. Rooms are in humped square igloos. Ocher and clay colors, Masai motifs in the decor. Table d'hôte menu (breakfast—11/50; lunch—17/–; dinner—22/50). Pool. Rating: 1st-class international, welcome addition to Amboseli accommodations. . . . *Ol Tukai Lodge,* bookings to Game Dept. (p. 87). Self-service lodge 1 km from Amboseli New Lodge. 12 fully equipped dbl bandas. Rates: 40/– per banda. Built in late forties for the Gregory Peck movie *The Snows of Kilimanjaro,* Ol Tukai bandas have 2 cots, medieval furniture, simple bath; wood is splintering, plaster chipping and peeling. Bedding: 5/– per person. . . . **Camping** about 2 km from Amboseli New Lodge. 4 tent sites, no facilities. Fee: 5/– per person. Book with Amboseli Lodge (above). Camping area is grassy, near a thicket inhabited by vervets, guinea fowl, and flies. . . . *Namanga Hotel,* bookings to African Tours & Hotels (p. 87). Just off the main highway in Namanga—and far from the game-viewing area. 4 sgls, 9 dbls, 13 trpls, 1 qdrpl, all w/bath. Rates: B&B: sgl—57/– to 70/–; dbl—99/–; trpl—140/–, incl tax, levy, service. Credit: AE, BA, DC. Older highway hotel much used by package tours as tea stop or for overnights as alternative to park lodges. Singles and doubles are old, simple, adequate; triples are new, will do nicely. Plain dining room is table d'hôte (breakfast—10/50; lunch—16/–; dinner—18/–) plus snacks. Swimming pool and showers (charge for nonguests). Visits to a Masai manyatta can be arranged, and there are evening *son et lumière* shows. Rating: 1st-class local. Okay, but no chance of viewing wildlife. Govt. class C.

Km 83: *Kajiado* (Masai, "long river"), small district town (pop. 1,755). The *UNDP-FAO Range Management Program,* based here, is attempting to introduce modern methods of cattle husbandry and to end the Masai's seminomadic existence by introducing enclosure. Since 1963 the program has registered 15 group ranches, is registering 5 more, and has adjudicated 29 others.

About Km 108: *Isinya,* location of the *Masai Rural Training Centre.* Here you can visit the bead- and leather-working shops.

Km 130: Turnoff (R) to *Athi River* (pop. 5,343), a small industrial satellite of Nairobi. The Athi River has hippos and crocodiles. Km 132: Junction with A104; go left to Nairobi 26 km.

Route K-6: Nairobi–Masai Mara

Take Uhuru Highway–Chiromo Road–Waiyaki Way northwest out of Nairobi to Km 52; see Route K-10 for annotation. Km 52: Turn left off the highway onto B7, paved as far as Narok, dirt on to Masai Mara.

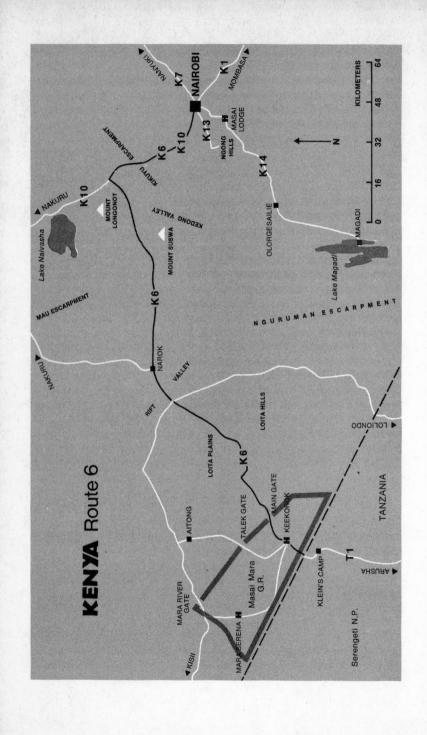

KENYA Route 6

Km 58: *Longonot Satellite Station,* a $4.3 million structure operated by East African External Telecommunications Company. The aerial tower with a 97-foot-diameter antenna has sent and received most of East Africa's international telephone, teletype, and facsimile since opening in 1970.

Km 65: Turnoff (L—at waterhole) on track to *Mount Suswa* (Masai, "place of the dusty plain"), a 7,732-foot volcano with a breached crater some 7 miles in diameter. The Masai call the crater Ol Doinyo Nyukie ("the lost land"), and it is, says naturalist Leslie Brown, "as savage a piece of country as one could hope to see." Suswa is easily climbed; see Robson's mountains guide.

Km 149: *Narok* (pop. 2,608), a district town which is the other capital of Masailand. **Accommodations:** *Narok Club,* bookings to D.C., Box 4, Narok. Banda lodgings but no bed linen; meals at the club. Charges: 10/– per person.

Km 165: Game Department checkpoint, after which you turn right to get to Keekorok Lodge. (Straight on B7 takes you to Mara River Bridge gate 97 km, Mara River campground 109 km, new Mara Serena Lodge 122 km, Kisii, Kericho.)

Masai Mara Game Reserve

From Narok on, you pass through the pretty *Loita Plains,* which are an extension (like most of Masai Mara) of Serengeti. Most of the area is protected as Photography Block 61. Novelist Robert Ruark described this as "country to make your mouth water . . . soft beautiful country . . . Hollywood Africa." Km 240: Main gate of *Masai Mara Game Reserve.* There doesn't seem to be much difference between this reserve and the land you just left behind: everything is still big, beautiful plains, acacia woodland, rolling hills—and, all around, wildlife in so much quantity. The Masai have never been hunters, so that here you can see wildlife in the numbers of a century ago. Masai Mara is about 700 square miles of plains and woodland bisected by the Mara River. The inner 200-square-mile Developed Area has had, since the Masai assumed control of the reserve in 1961, the status of a national park, with livestock and human population (except at lodges) excluded. The reserve is justly famous for its herds of zebra and wildebeest (the migration here is almost as impressive as in Serengeti), big prides of lion (30 lions or more), gazelle, Masai giraffe. You are more likely to see leopard here than anywhere else other than one of the game-viewing lodges in the Aberdares or Mount Kenya. Masai Mara is

Topi

also almost the only place in Kenya to see roan antelopes, and *topis* in particular are common here. Topis are big hartebeestlike antelopes that come in a rich deep rufous color with a satinlike sheen. *Buffalos* in large herds seem to like Masai Mara. The buffalo, or Cape buffalo as it is also known, does not resemble the American buffalo (bison) as much as an ordinary ox: it is a massive, blackish beast with a huge set of horns that look inappropriately like a mud-plastered hairdo that hugs the skull and drops down to the ears before recurving up a bit. The buffalo looks tremendously ill-tempered as it glares heavy-lidded at you, and it can be a fearsome opponent. As one of the Big Five, the buffalo has a reputation among hunters for revengeful savagery, especially when it is wounded, when it cunningly lays in ambush for the unlucky hunter. Birding is good in the reserve; John G. Williams has counted 421 species. An entertaining book about the park is Colin Fletcher's *Winds of Mara* (New York: Knopf, 1973).

When to Visit

Much of Mara is on black cotton soil, which becomes treacherous, bottomless mud during the rains. The reserve is liable to be closed altogether during the rainy seasons, April–May, October–December (roughly), though four-wheel-drive vehicles can negotiate the roads and nonroads then . . . perhaps.

Getting There, Getting Around

Mara is entered through any of three gates: the main one from Narok (at Km 240), a gate on the Talek River (road from Aitong), and a gate on the Tanzania border adjacent to Serengeti Park. Keekorok has an airstrip. Lodge has Land-Rovers for hire at 200/– per half-day with driver; a ranger-guide is 10/– or 20/– per day. A minibus rents for 3/– per km, Land-Rover at 2/– per km. Many "milk run" package tours include Masai Mara, and there are two- and three-day trips from Nairobi; see package listings KP-17, 33–37, 66–68, 76–88; and TP-31.

Costs

Entry fee into the Developed Area: 20/– per car plus 5/– per adult, 1/– per child; same for nonresidents. You gain entry to the Undeveloped Area by paying the camping fee (see below).

Accommodations

Keekorok Lodge, bookings to Wildlife Lodges (p. 87). 10 sgls, 15 dbls in cottages, 32 dbls in new blocks, 12 dbl tents; all rms w/bath. Rates: FB: sgl—200/–; dbl—260/–; tent accommodation—100/– per person. Credit: DC. One of the original game lodges, dating to 1961 when it was self-catering; main building and cottages added 1965, four new blocks and pool recently. Rooms pleasant, well decorated with batiks and wildlife photos, Maridadi drapes. Menu in cheerful, well-ordered dining room is table d'hôte. Rating: 1st-class international. ★★. . . . *Mara Serena Lodge,* bookings to Serena Lodges & Hotels (p. 87). Located west of Mara River in previously undeveloped Mara Triangle. 50 dbls w/bath. Rates: FB: sgl—180/–; dbl—270/–. New in 1973, Aga Khan-initiated lodge remotely resembles a Masai *manyatta,* with rooms in clay-colored, domed structures, Masai designs and colors here and there. Meals are set (breakfast—11/50; lunch—17/–; dinner—22/50). Pool. Rating: 1st-class international. . . . *Governor's Camp,* Box 48217, Nairobi; tel. 31871/2. Luxury tented camp on east bank of Mara River. 15 dbl tents w/shower. Rates: FB: 355/– per person for minimum 2 nights/3 days, incl game runs; from Day 3 on, sgl—270/–; dbl—380/–, incl service, not incl 120/– for "activities." . . . **Camping** is not allowed in the Developed Area around Keekorok, but seven parties may book to camp in the Undeveloped Area—two in Block A (west of the Mara River), five in Blocks B and C (the rest of the Undeveloped Area), with no restrictions as to actual camping site. Fees are high: 30/– per adult (15/– per person under 16) for nonresidents, 10/– per adult (5/– under 16) for Kenya residents. Book and pay in advance at Game Dept. (p. 87). Shower available at Keekorok.

Continuing the route from the Mara main gate: Km 250: Keekorok Lodge. Km 262: Kenya border post/Sand River Bridge/Tanzania

border. (Tanzania immigration and customs at Lobo or Seronera.)
The route here connects to T-1 to Arusha.

Route K-7: Nairobi–Nyeri–Nanyuki–Isiolo–Marsabit–Ethiopia

Route K-7 is one of the most traveled (at least as far as Samburu
Game Reserve) tourist routes, and one of the most interesting, going
from the heart of East Africa's largest city through farm and ranch
land and past craggy Mount Kenya into the middle of East Africa's
most desolate area, the Northern Frontier District (NFD).

Starting from Uhuru Highway, follow a map to the Globe Theater
traffic circle and up Murang'a Road to Muthaiga traffic circle (Km 6),
where there's a turnoff (L) on C64 (Kiambu Road) to the *Karura
Forest* (birdwatching) and *Kiambu* (pop. 2,776), settled by Europeans
in 1903, now HQ of heavily populated Kiambu District. From
Muthaiga traffic circle, continue along Murang'a Road to Thika Road.

Km 9: *Ruaraka,* a Nairobi industrial suburb which is the home of
Kenya Breweries (R), a million-cases-of-beer-a-month company
founded in 1923 by two brothers, one of whom was killed by an
elephant. This incident led to the naming of the first beer, Tusker.
Also in Ruaraka is the *Zimmermann taxidermy shop,* located half a
mile from Thika Road on Kamiti Road (bear left at first circle past
brewery). Visitors are welcome.

Km 12: Safari Park Hotel (L). Km 17: *Kahawa* (Swahili, "coffee"),
a town aptly named—this whole area is Kenya's main *coffee-growing
district.* Coffee is the country's most valuable crop and the No. 1 export, earning in 1973 almost $89 million. (Coffee is also the largest
single commodity in world trade, and 14 countries gain a quarter to
three-quarters of their earnings from it; half the world's coffee is
consumed in the U.S.) Most Kenya coffee is the "Colombian Mild"
variety, which the country has no difficulty selling (Germans are big
buyers). *Coffea arabica* is an exacting highland plant that prefers a
mean 70°F with swings neither too high nor too low, rainfall from 35
to 70 inches, and volcanic soil. The broad and gently rounded ridges
of deep red laterite soil in this area are almost perfect. Coffee bushes
must grow four years in the nursery and fields until a mass of sweet-
scented white blossoms appears against the deep and glossy green of
the foliage. When the flowers fade, clusters of green berries appear;
these turn brilliant red seven to nine months later. Then the planter
must quickly round up the labor to harvest in a short time. At the

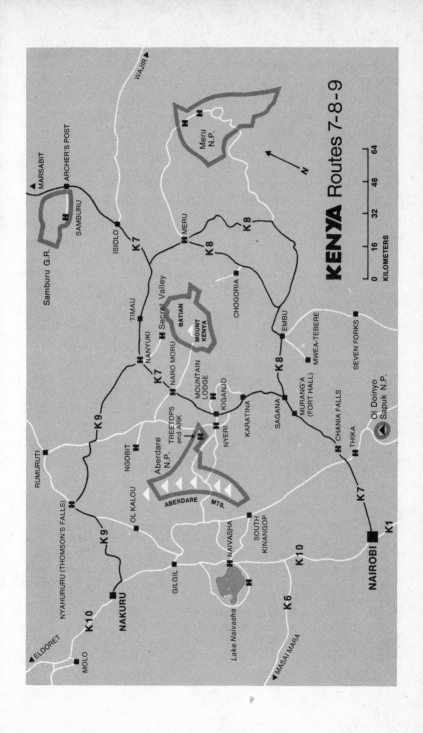

KENYA Routes 7-8-9

KILOMETERS
0 16 32 48 64

N

WAJIR ▲

MARSABIT ▲
ARCHER'S POST

Meru N.P.

Samburu G.R.
SAMBURU

ISIOLO

K 7

MERU

K 8

K 8

TIMAU

Secret Valley

BATIAN
MOUNT KENYA

CHOGORIA

NANYUKI

K 7

NARO MORU

EMBU

K 8

MWEA-TEBERE

SEVEN FORKS

K 9

MOUNTAIN LODGE

KIGANJO

MURANG'A (FORT HALL)

SAGANA

RUMURUTI

NGOBIT

Aberdare N.P.

TREETOPS and ARK

NYERI

KARATINA

CHANIA FALLS

Ol Doinyo Sapuk N.P.

THIKA

OL KALOU

ABERDARE MTS.

K 7

NYAHURURU (THOMSON'S FALLS)

K 9

NAIVASHA

SOUTH KINANGOP

K 10

K 1

NAIROBI

ELDORET ▲

GILGIL

K 10

NAKURU

K 6

MOLO

Lake Naivasha

MASAI MARA ▲

plantation, pulping machines take off the outer skin; then the slimy saccharine coating of the bean is removed by fermentation before the beans are washed and dried (by the sun or in mechanical dryers). Still in their hulls, the beans are sent to the KPCU Mills in Nairobi for hulling and machine grading. The coffee is sold at Tuesday morning auctions during the season at Kahawa House, Haile Selassie Avenue, Nairobi; visitors are allowed. Coffee was formerly a European monopoly, but since 1966 half of Kenya's coffee has been produced by 250,000 African small growers grouped in 155 co-ops, the other half by 306 coffee plantations.

Km 19: *Kenyatta University College* (L), a teacher-training school. Km 24: Ruiru (Kikuyu, "black"). Km 29: Turnoff (L) to *Gatundu* 19 km, President Kenyatta's country home. It was built for him with government funds in 1961 when he was allowed to return from exile after his release from prison, where he was confined for his alleged part in directing Mau Mau.

Thika

Km 41: Turnoff (L) on A3 to Thika 3 km, Fourteen Falls 23 km, Ol Doinyo Sapuk National Park 29 km, Garissa 326 km. *Thika* (pop. 18,387) is an industrial satellite of Nairobi. Off A3 east of the highway past Thika town you are in the most important sisal area in Kenya; coffee is grown on higher ridges. This is the land whose pioneer days Elspeth Huxley described in *The Flame Trees of Thika*. The area is important also for its pineapples and other produce and is the location of the National Horticultural Research Station. Kenya exports much horticultural produce and flowers to Europe by air cargo.

From the turnoff onto A3 go 20 km past Thika to a right turn toward *Fourteen Falls* and Ol Doinyo Sapuk. At a T-junction 1 km, go left 1.1 km to a track left to a big parking lot by the falls. Fourteen Falls are replaced by one wide waterfall when the river is in flood. They are not worth coming all the way from Nairobi to see. Keep a close eye on your car; ours was broken into here. Back at the T-junction, you would go right to get to *Ol Doinyo Sapuk National Park,* a 20-square-kilometer park (1969) around the 7,041-foot Ol Doinyo Sapuk (Masai, "the big mountain"). A motorable track goes nearly to the top, to which you then have to walk. On a shelf on the mountainside are buried the half-American (born in St. Louis) pioneer farmer Sir William Northrup McMillan (d. 1925) and his wife. Sir W. weighed some 336 pounds, and porters apparently could not carry his body as far as the summit for burial. McMillan Library in Nairobi is a better memorial to him anyway. Ol Doinyo Sapuk makes a pleasant excursion, and there's a good view from the summit. Watch out for ant-bear (aardvark) holes and buffalos.

Tana River Camps

Much farther along A3 from Thika you would bump to a halt at *Garissa* on the *Tana River,* along which will be established a national reserve by the Yatta Plateau. Plans are vague on this, but the river is scenic and has hippos and crocodiles and good birdwatching. At Garissa, which is North Eastern Province HQ, is the American Consolata Brothers' *Boys' Town,* set up to care for orphans of the *shifta* troubles (see p. 253), and run by an enthusiastic ex-nightclub owner from Denver or Detroit named Brother Mario. Fruit is grown on the 700-acre farm. North of Garissa is the *Sankuri-Tana River Tented Camp,* bookings to African & Alpine Safaris (p. 111). Luxury (Persian carpets!) tented camp. Rates: FB: sgl—1,078/– for 1 night, 1,398/– for 2 nights; dbl—1,333/– for 1 night, 1,833/– for 2 nights. Price includes Garissa airstrip transfer, canoe safari on the Tana River, game walk or drive, Koro Koro dancing, hotel tax, levy, and service. See package listing KP-47. New in 1973: *Saabduul Traditional Camp,* Box 63, Garissa, located 2 km north of town. Also new is *Ahamed's Elephant Camp,* bookings to Ahamed Bros. (p. 113). Rates for 2-night FB packages: air tour—455/– per person (min. 5); road tour—420/– (min. 6); your own transport—315/– per person.

Back on the main highway at Thika, you continue north to Km 43 turnoff (L) to the Blue Posts Hotel, good for a tea stop and a look at the *Chania* (Kikuyu, "noisy") *Falls,* an 81-foot drop in the Thika River to a muddy-brown pool below. The falls are on the grounds of the *Blue Posts Hotel,* Box 42, Thika; tel. 2241; cable BLUEPOSTS. 10 dbls w/bath, 4 w/o, 12 sgls w/o. Rates: bed only: sgl—55/–; dbl—60/– or 80/–. Dates to 1908 (see *Flame Trees* for some good anecdotes). As lodgings the hotel isn't much, but lots of tours stop here for coffee. Restaurant has simple à la carte menu (fried lake fish, grilled fillet) from 5/50 to 7/50. Rating: Not much better than 2d-class local. Govt. class C.

Km 55: Road forks here; go left on paving to Murang'a. Km 84: *Murang'a (Fort Hall),* a district town (pop. 4,750) established by Frank Hall in 1900 as an important extension of British authority into Kikuyuland. Hall, with John Ainsworth, was one of the original (and competent) administrators. Many Kikuyu resisted the British, however, and punitive expeditions were sent against parts of the tribe in 1902, 1904, and 1905. In the 1904 operation perhaps 1,500 Kikuyu were killed. At the *Church of St. James and All Martyrs,* a memorial to Kikuyu killed by the Mau Mau, is a series of black-white reversal murals by Chagga artist Elimo Njau showing a black baby Jesus in a Kikuyu manger, the Last Supper taking place in a banda in view of a giraffe and acacia tree, and African villages on the slopes of Golgotha. At the town you turn off the highway, go left up a hill then right at the PO, continue 16 km along a track, turn left, and go 3 km to *Mukuruwe wa Gathanga* or "Garden of Eden of the Kikuyu." The location was pointed out to the tribe's founder, Gikuyu, by Mogai (the Divider of the Universe)—see story at p. 247, Mount Kenya. There are three Kikuyu huts and a small museum with weapons and bead-work.

Km 95: *Sagana* and a major junction: right is B20 (our Route K-8) to Embu and Meru, left is B16 to Nyeri and Nanyuki; go left. Km 120: Karatina. Km 131: Turnoff (L) on B5, main paved access road to Nyeri 13 km, Aberdare National Park (Kiandongoro Gate 36 km, East Gate 34½ km), Outspan (for Treetops), Aberdare Country Club (for The Ark), Thomson's Falls (Nyahururu) 118 km, Nakuru 180 km, North Kinangop 67 km, Naivasha 100 km.

Nyeri

Nyeri (pop. 10,004), HQ of Central Province, is known as the capital of Kikuyuland though it is on the edge of it. Ironically, the town was founded as an administrative center by Captain Richard Meinertzhagen, who chose a campsite near Nyeri Hill while on an expedition against intransigent Kikuyu. In the middle of a coffee area spread over the foothills of the Aberdares, Nyeri has a pretty location. "The nearer to Nyeri the nearer to bliss," wrote Lord Robert Baden-Powell, founder of the Boy Scouts and co-founder of the Girl Guides. The "Hero of Mafeking" of the Boer War first visited East Africa in 1906, retired from the British army in 1907, started the scouting movement, and became Chief Scout in 1929. He returned to Kenya in 1935 and lived in *Paxtu Cottage* on the grounds of the *Outspan,* one of Kenya's famous old country hotels, founded in 1926. There Baden-Powell died on January 8, 1941, aged 84. The cottage has mementos of the Chief Scout and may be visited when not booked by a guest. Baden-Powell is buried at St. Peter's Church here (so is the famous big-game hunter Jim Corbett); Baden-Powell's grave, inscribed with the Scouts' circle-and-dot symbol ("gone home"), is visited by hundreds of Scouts each year. Kenya, which itself has 17,300 Scouts, hosted the 24th world conference in 1973. Also in Nyeri is the *Duke d'Aosta's grave.* The last Italian viceroy of Ethiopia, the duke was captured by the British and put in a POW camp here, where he died after the war. There is an *Italian Memorial Church* to the war dead, and in the middle of Nyeri's main street (to the right as you enter town) is a *stone cenotaph* dedicated "to the Memory of the Kikuyu Tribe who Died in the Fight for Freedom 1951–1957."

Accommodations

Outspan Hotel, Box 24, Nyeri; tel. 9, 257; bookings to Wildlife Lodges (p. 87). 28 dbls, 2 sets of connecting dbls, 6 suites, 5 sgls, all w/bath. Rates: B&B: sgl—85/–; dbl—150/–; cottage or suite—200/–. Credit: AE, BA, DC. Built 1928, extended 1946, hotel is base for Treetops but is also a fine country resort. Main building has several lounges, outdoor terrace, pleasant bar, Tudor-style dining room (standard menu plus à la carte; jacket and tie for dinner, please). Pool, squash court, riding, tennis, billiards, trout fishing, 70 acres of park and pathways, golf at nearby club. Rooms are uniformly nice, some are posh. Rating: 1st-class international. We give it ★★. Govt. class B*. . . . *Aberdare Country Club,* Box 448, Nyeri; tel. Mweiga 17; bookings to Percival Tours (p. 87). You can get there either via Nyeri 31 km, or by turning off highway at Km 149 to club 11 km. 5 dbls w/bath, expanding soon to 34 beds total. Rates: FB: sgl—115/– or 130/–; dbl—230/–; trpl—330/–; incl service charge and daily membership (otherwise 20/– per day). Credit: DC. Base for The Ark. Situated on a high grassy hill with long views in 3 directions, the 1,300-acre club used to belong to a gentleman farmer, whose 1936 stone house is the club's main building. Aiming to be a "relaxing upcountry resort," Aberdare CC is impeccably decorated, the 5 doubles stylishly and individually furnished (2 doubles have fireplaces). Menu is table d'hôte but would make a hungry chef kick his heels in delight. Rating: 1st-class international. ★★★ as a place of sure comfort and highest quality. Govt. class B. . . . *White Rhino Hotel,* Box 30, Nyeri; tel. 189. 7 sgls, 13 dbls, 1 trpl, 1 qdrpl (cottage), all w/bath. Rates: B&B: sgl—60/–; dbl—110/–. Built in the twenties, the badly built White Rhino teeters on three legs but, as the cost indicates, will charge you. Rooms are clean, cold; walls need painting. À la carte menu in wooden-floored dining room is mainly British. Rating: 2d-class local. Govt. class D, we agree. . . . *Village Dancers Hotel,* Box 783, Nyeri; tel. 2296; bookings to African Tours & Hotels (p. 87). On Ring Road 2 miles from P.O. 6 dbl rondavels w/shower. Rates: B&B: sgl—60/–; dbl—110/–, incl show. Newest stop on the Mount Kenya–Treetops tourist run. 1973 African-owned hotel has Kikuyu dancing, Kenya food or Continental menu (breakfast—10/–; lunch—15/–; dinner—15/–) and an "Activity Village" with a *muturi* (smith) and *mundu mugo* (medicine man). If you're not staying here, the show entry is 25/– without food, 30/– with Kenyan dishes, 35/– with complete lunch. . . . **Camping** at the Asian Community Rest House on Temple Road.

Nyeri is not only the capital of *Kikuyuland,* but it is also near what was the principal stronghold of the *Mau Mau,* in the forest and mountains of the Aberdares. A tribe with a somewhat homogeneous language and culture, and Kenya's biggest tribe (numbering 2.2 million in the 1969 census), the Kikuyu are the most important tribe in Kenya; it is no secret they dominate the government. The meat and muscle of the Mau Mau—now regarded as genuine freedom fighters—consisted of the Kikuyu and their close relatives, the Meru and the Embu. The Kikuyu's most famous son is President Jomo Kenyatta, born Johnstone Kamau Ngengi in Ichaweri; his official birthday is October 20, 1891. His book, *Facing Mount Kenya,* is an anthropological study of his own tribe.

It has been said that a tribe is a tribe because it feels like one. Like most other Bantu tribes, the Kikuyu have no central government or strong leader, but they have common traditions, customs, and beliefs which tie them together. The family is of primary importance, but a man assumes degrees of importance by his age status (seven age levels for males, five for females) and also by three institutionalized relationships in the tribe: clan, circumcision year, and generation. There are nine clans, but they are nonfunctional as units. More powerful are the tribe-wide *marika* groupings—age sets and generations—by which men circumcised at the same time are all closely related by common membership in an age set. These "regiments" are separated by periods when no circumcisions take place. A ruling generation (30 years long) is made up of married men with married sons whose sons are not yet adult, and the handing over of one generation to another was traditionally an important event. The 1931–32 handing-over was prohibited by the government, but grouping into age sets continued, and the keystone leaders of the Mau Mau were mostly members of the age set of 1940.

Aberdare National Park

Nyeri is the base for visiting *Aberdare National Park,* a 228-square-mile park that includes the high ground of the Aberdare Mountains, named by Joseph Thomson in 1884 for Lord Aberdare, the president of the Royal Geographical Society. The Kikuyu call the range Nyandarua, "drying hide"; it is also the name of the surrounding district. Of volcanic origin, the mountains have a height of more than 9,000 feet over a distance of more than 40 miles. The western slopes are steep; the eastern slopes descend gradually from moorlands through a forest belt to Kikuyuland's tiny *shambas* (farms). There is trout fishing in the numerous small streams. With permission from the warden of the Mountain Parks, Nyeri, you can climb any of the four main peaks in a day or less: *Ol Doinyo La Satima,* 13,120 feet, the northernmost summit; *Kinangop,* 12,816 feet, more impressive; *The Elephant,* 11,780 feet, a ridge with an elephant-shaped outline when seen from South Kinangop; and *Kipipiri,* 10,987 feet, standing apart from the others to the west. Details on climbing the peaks from Robson's Mountain Club guidebook.

As a game park, Aberdare has disappointed many. The forest harbors many solitary animals and small families—but forest animals rely on concealment rather than flight for protection, exceptions being the buffalo and the elephant. Aberdare wildlife is best seen at one of the world's famous hotels, *Treetops,* and its new competitor, *The Ark;* see listings below. On a random night about the time we day-visited both lodges, Treetops recorded 19 bushbucks, 48 waterbucks, 134 buffalos, 58 warthogs, 32 Sykes monkeys, 8 rhinos, 18 elephants, 2 genets, 2 white-tailed mongooses, 2 African hares, 3 hyenas, 5 giant forest hogs. The Ark had about the same, and on occasion has been hosting lions, a species rare in the Aberdares. The elusive bongo and leopard were not seen those nights at either lodge, though Treetops and The Ark are among the best places to see those animals.

The *leopard* comes in two varieties: the spotted one (spots in the shape of rosettes) and the all-black one, which is very rare and so is fully protected. Leopards hunt at night and sleep in the bush, in trees, or in rock outcrops during the day, so can easily be missed during an African tour unless you go to a lodge where leopard bait is put out; Secret Valley (see Nanyuki hotel listings, p. 252) specializes in leopards,

Leopard

and Samburu Lodge and Nairobi Park's Masai Lodge both bait for
leopards as well. John G. Williams observes that leopards are not
seen as frequently as the less numerous cheetahs. Though hunted and
poached everywhere for its valuable fur, the leopard in fact survives
nearly everywhere because of its habits, silence, and cunning—and also
because it will eat nearly anything: gazelle and small antelope, monkeys
and baboons, francolin, guinea fowl, even tortoises and insects.
Leopards often raid farms and ranches and carry off livestock. The
shy, silent, and mostly nocturnal *bongo,* a heavy, chestnut-red antelope
with vertical white stripes, is a real treat at the lodges when it ventures
near the waterholes. One animal easily seen there is the nocturnal *giant
forest hog,* which surprisingly was not even recorded until 1904, when
seen here in the Aberdares by Captain Meinertzhagen. A large (up to
500 pounds) black hairy animal with a huge snout, the giant forest
hog looks more like a bushpig than a warthog.

Elephants formerly had a well-used elephant walk from here to
Mount Kenya, but when the two parks were created in 1948, the
authorities decided to cut off this migration to protect the farming in
the middle. An elephant-proof ditch 5 miles long, 6 feet deep, and
6 feet wide (it takes 40 men all year to maintain) was constructed on
the eastern border of Aberdare Park. You will see this ditch when driving into Treetops or The Ark.

Two natural attractions in the park are *Karura Falls,* with a drop
of 894 feet in three steps, and *Gura Falls,* 791 feet in three stages.
Birdwatching is fair; Williams counted 203 species.

When to Visit

Treetops and The Ark are open all year, with access from the base
hotels into the park by four-wheel-drive vehicles. The cross-park road is
usually closed in the two rainy seasons, often at other times, too. See
the signboards at the White Rhino and the Outspan in Nyeri, and the
Naivasha Inn.

Getting There, Getting Around

You can drive across the mountains on a dry-weather road that climbs 4,000 feet in 22 km, up to 10,000 feet. You are allowed to drive 100 yards off the road. Numerous package tours include Treetops or The Ark (see listings KP-13, 28–36, 68, 78–79, 85–87) but for weather reasons rarely include a trip across the mountains (see KP-37).

Accommodations

Treetops, bookings to Wildlife Lodges (p. 87). Access only through the Outspan. 4 sgls, 30 dbls, all w/o bath, 2 suites w/shower. Rates: FB: 200/– per person (250/– in suite), not incl park fee; 2 nights at Outspan, Treetops—275/– per person. Credit: AE, BA, DC. No children under 10. What can you say about Treetops? Everybody who thinks of Africa thinks of Treetops, and everybody who comes wants to go there. It dates back to 1932, but the present 3-story structure (on stilts, not supported by trees or even obscured by them) was put up in 1957, replacing the one burned down by the Mau Mau in 1954. Princess Elizabeth stayed here the night of February 5–6, 1952, leaving the next morning as queen, since her father, George VI, had died in the night. The hotel overlooks a wide cleared area in the middle of which are a big waterhole and several blocks of salt. The rooms, frankly, are cubbyhole size, and showers and breakfast have to wait until your arrival back at the Outspan. You get tea and dinner at Treetops. Twenty thousand tourists a year stay overnight here, and they've worn the place out. The cost is far too high compared with quality. Given all this, Treetops is less a good hotel than an African experience, and that's something you may want to do, but not repeat. We favor The Ark for the money. Rating: 1st-class local. ★ for the experience only. . . . *The Ark,* bookings to Percival Tours (p. 87). Access only through Aberdare Country Club. 24 dbls, 11 sgls, all sharing central toilet-shower block. Rates: FB: sgl—200/– or 230/–; dbl—400/–, incl service charge, not incl park fee. Credit: DC. No children under 8. The Ark, opened in December 1969, is one of the best-designed and best-run game lodges in East Africa, outshining Treetops and lower. Surrounded by a thick sea of montane forest, it is indeed like the hull of an ark: a long gangplanklike walkway leads to the front deck; inside are two floors of small, ship-size, quiet double and single rooms. There are several good game-viewing spots, including "the dungeon," a round cellar at elephant-eye-level. The waterholes are lighted with 20,000 watts. Splendid lounge with fireplace, leather armchairs. Long, comfortable dining room (Craig Claiborne liked the food). You get tea, dinner, and breakfast (lunch the day before at the Aberdare CC). Rating: 1st-class international, excellent value, good experience. ★★★. . . . **Camping** at several streamside sites. Latrine at Queen's Cave. Camp fee: 5/– per adult, 1/– per child. . . . Self-service fishing lodge (book with Warden, Box 22, Nyeri).

On the Thomson's Falls road 29 km north of Nyeri is the *Solio Game Reserve,* a private game ranch surrounded by a rhino-proof fence.

Back on the main highway bypassing Nyeri, you continue north to *Kiganjo* (Km 144), where the other end of the Nyeri access road comes out. Kiganjo is the location of the Kenya Police Training College and, adjacent, the high-altitude (5,747 feet) camp where Kenya's medal-winning track team trained for the 1972 Munich Olympics.

Km 148: Turnoff (R) on D450 to Thego Fishing Camp 7 km, gate to Mountain Lodge 23 km, Sagana State Lodge. This road goes up into the forests on the lower slopes of Mount Kenya. The *State Lodge,* now a presidential residence, was built as the Royal Lodge and given to the then Princess Elizabeth and Prince Philip as Kenya's wedding present; it was returned at Independence. **Accommodations:** *Thego Fishing Camp,* run by the Fisheries Department, has two self-service rondavels renting for 5/– each. **Camping** for 5/– per tent. *Mountain Lodge,* bookings to African Tours & Hotels (p. 87). 9 sgls, 30 dbls, all sharing bath, plus 2 VIP suites (each a dbl w/bath). Rates: DB&B: sgl—250/– to 300/–; dbl—400/–, incl tax, levy, service; also low season rates. Credit: DC. This Treetopsy place on eucalyptus-trunk stilts has no base camp; if you're equipped with a voucher, you can drive almost up to the lodge in your own car (or tour minibus—see package listings KP-15, 28–31, 35), with entry between 4–6:30 P.M. We were given an unforgivably rude reception when we stopped in for a look and were prohibited from entering; a subsequent complaint to the head office went unanswered, so we cannot comment favorably on this lodge. The rooms, we understand, have washbasins, and the wood construction of the lodge results in much noise. Note: No kids under 8.

Km 169: *Naro Moru.* Km 170: Turnoff (L) on D448 to Naro Moru River Lodge 2 km, Ngobit Fishing Lodge 31 km. Turnoff (R) on D448 (Naro Moru Track) to Mount Kenya National Park. **Accommodations:** *Naro Moru River Lodge,* Box 18, Naro Moru; tel. 23. 12 full-board trpls, 5 self-service chalets (2 dbls, 1 qdrpl, 2 w/6 beds),

4-bed and 6-bed bunkhouses, and campground. Rooms and chalets have bath; bunkhouses, outside shower. Room rates: FB: sgl—80/– to 140/–; dbl—160/–. Chalet rates: 70/– for 2-bed 'chalet, 145/– for 4-bed chalet, 215/– for 6-bed chalet. Bunkhouse: 10/– per person. Lodge is admirably situated along the well-landscaped banks of the Naro Moru River, which flows cold off Mount Kenya and is stocked with trout (12/50 per day including tackle rental plus 5/– for a license). Friendly, informal main building has cozy bar-lounge, simple dining room. Menu is ad hoc, table d'hôte (breakfast—9/–; lunch— 13/–; dinner—15/–), awfully British and pretty awful. Lodge is virtually the headquarters for walking or climbing on Mount Kenya, so attracting a wide range of guests. Rating: 1st-class local but a must-stop for the individual traveler in this area. One of our favorites, despite the food, so it gets a ★. Self-service bunkhouses are a budget bargain. Govt. class C. . . . **Camping** is on lodge property about 1 km upstream. A little shade, also latrine. Fee: 5/– per person, incl lodge membership. . . . *Ngobit Fishing Lodge,* Private Bag, Naro Moru; tel. Ngobit 5; bookings to A. A. & Bunson (p. 86). 6 ron- davels, each a dbl w/bath. Rates: FB: sgl—143/–; dbl—231/–, incl tax, levy, service, membership. Run by Ngobit Trout Farms, lodge is primarily for fishermen (35/– per rod per day plus license) who have an eye on rainbow trout, catchable along 12 miles of Ngobit River.

Mount Kenya

The Naro Moru Track is the best-used road and climbing route up *Mount Kenya,* a 228-square-mile national park above the 11,000-foot level. Tall, craggy, snow-capped, infinitely grand when seen on a clear day, and a mountain walker's joy, Mount Kenya is at 17,058 feet Africa's second-highest mountain, conquered first by Halford Mac- kinder in 1899. The highest two peaks—*Batian,* the summit, and *Nelion,* 17,022 feet—are for advanced climbers, but anybody in moderately good shape and without climbing experience can walk up the third-highest peak, *Point Lenana,* 16,355 feet (it is now climbed by so many that it is called "Tourist Peak"). A number of organized climbing trips are available, including a four-day "round the peaks" tour that ends with a walk up Lenana. We took that trip, and in two ways it was the high point of our entire time in Eastern Africa.

Mount Kenya is a deeply dissected volcano in an advanced state of decay—it was once 6,000 feet higher. The crater has disappeared, and the peaks that you see (like jagged Mawenzi Peak on Kilimanjaro) were once part of the central core of the volcano. In volcanic action, as eruptions become less violent, lava may be thrust up into the vent, forming a plug. Since the plug cools slowly, it forms a rock much harder and more crystalline than the cone, and therefore may remain when the cone has eroded away. When Mount Kenya was 23,000 feet high about 10 million years ago, it must have looked like rounded, smooth Kibo Peak on Kilimanjaro. The peaks and spires area is a block a mile across. The Pleistocene's ice ages here coated the mountain with snow and hail, which formed into glaciers that were once as far down as 7,000 feet. There remain today 15 glaciers, most considerably smaller than when first photographed 75 years ago.

Going up the mountain, you pass several vegetation zones. The lower slopes of the dome on which the peaks stand are covered with original forest, then you pass through a belt of mountain bamboo at 8,000 to 8,500 feet, then enter the higher montane forest, which extends to about 10,000 feet. Topping this zone is what one naturalist has called "elfin forest"—open glades surrounded by *Hagenia* trees with their hanging orchids, old-man's-beard, and other moss, plus giant St.-John's-wort. Then the moorland begins, extending up to nearly 12,000 feet, sometimes to 13,500 feet. In a zone of less moisture and more frosty nights, plants have adapted in peculiar ways, with tussock grassland, giant heath (*Erica arborea*), giant lobelia, and giant groundsel (*Senecio*) giving the moorlands a strange appearance as a sort of alpine desert. There are two common species of lobelia, a tall, oddly rounded plant that looks something like a green-feathered cigar. One species has deep purple flowers, the other, "ostrich plume lobelia," has silky haired leaves that appear luminescent when caught by the sunlight. Giant groundsel comes in three species, one a brown-barked tree with one to three branches topped by dark-green rosettes; the flowers are purple. There is also the "cabbage groundsel," a ground-hugging white-rosetted species with yellow flowers. Giant heath is in France called *bruyère* and is used to make briar pipes. The higher alpine zone to 15,000 feet is more grassy, with isolated stands of lobelia and groundsel.

The Mount Kenya hyrax is the most commonly seen animal, although the game park and lower forest do have elephant, buffalo, leopard, bongo, bushbuck, duiker, zebra, and small mammals. Bird-life is not abundant (the Williams count is 127), but you will see an occasional sunbird in the moorlands; the forests below are much richer.

The origin of the name of the mountain, which became the name of the country, is as shrouded in mystery as the mountain is in mist. The Kikuyu called the mountain *Kirinyaga* or *Kere-Nyaga,* variously translated as "mountain of brightness" and "it is glorious" (both true!). The missionary Johann Ludwig Krapf, the first European to see the mountain, from Kitui in Kamba country on December 3, 1849, said the Kamba called it *Kima ja Kegnia,* "mountain of whiteness." Others have suggested the Masai *Erukenya,* "misty hill" or "mountain shrouded in mist," and the Kamba *Kiima* and *Kya Nyaa,* "hill of the cock ostrich," as the root words. The peak names are easily traceable: M'batian was a Masai *laibon* (medicine man) who died in 1890, Nelion was his brother, and Lenana his son (also a *laibon*). In any case, various tribes consider Mount Kenya important. In Kikuyu mythology it is the dwelling place of God (Ngai). As told by Kenyatta in *Facing Mount Kenya,* it seems that Mogai, the Divider of the Universe and Lord of Nature, made the mountain his resting place while on an inspection tour and as a sign of his wonders. He then took the man Gikuyu to the top to point out the beauty of the land he was giving him. Pointing out a grove of fig trees, Mogai told Gikuyu to establish his home there (see Km 84, Mukuruwe wa Gathanga), and added before parting that whenever he was in need, he should make a sacrifice and raise his hands toward Mount Kenya.

Dr. Krapf, when he reported seeing Mount Kenya, was laughed at by many educated Europeans, who knew practically nothing about "darkest" Africa but thought snow on the equator was a contradiction in terms. It wasn't until Joseph Thomson came through in 1883 that he confirmed Mount Kenya was on the equator and was covered with snow. Four years passed before anybody made an attempt on the mountain; Samuel Teleki von Szek reached 14,000 feet on the southwest moorland. After Count Teleki, three separate tries resulted in failure. The summit was finally reached in 1899 (ten years after Kilimanjaro) by Halford J. Mackinder, the founder of modern geography-teaching who was later knighted. From the railhead at Nairobi, Mackinder sallied forth with a large party that included six Europeans: a photographer, two Italian-Swiss (a guide and a porter) from Courmayeur in the Val d'Aosta, a botanist, and a taxidermist. After attempts from various directions, including one in which Mackinder and the Italian-Swiss, Cesar Ollier and Josef Brocherel, spent the night on the southeast face of Nelion, the three made a final try for the top of Batian, achieving it September 13, 1899. Remarkably, Nelion was not climbed until January 6, 1929, by P. Wyn Harris and Eric Shipton.

Climbing Mount Kenya

The mountain has now been scaled by many routes (11 on Batian, 6 commonly used ones on Nelion), and it is well mapped (see p. 90); climbers or walkers should get the Mountain Club of Kenya (MCK) guidebook (see p. 250). There are five approaches: Naro Moru Track (turnoff at Km 170), Burguret Track (Km 182), Sirimon Track (Km 206), Timau Track (Km 209), all on the west side of the mountain, and the Chogoria Route, on the east side; Naro Moru is the most convenient. Point Lenana is easily ascended by amateurs, but Batian and Nelion call for experience (Standards IV, V, and VI). The normal route up Batian takes 6–6½ hours from Top and Austrian huts (which are 1½ days from Naro Moru and the roadhead at 10,000 feet) while the normal Nelion route is 4½–5 hours from Top Hut. Many climbers do all three peaks in only a few days, and some of the minor peaks, all over 15,400 feet, can easily be added. Mount Kenya is a well-used mountain because it offers Everest conditions but is easily accessible. And, unlike Everest, there are two mountain rescue units which are in action every one to three days in December and January. Twenty-three climbers have been killed on the mountain (to March 1973), and mountain sickness or pulmonary edema (see p. 401) can be a hazard even if going up Point Lenana.

You can make all your own arrangements for huts (all owned by the Mountain Club of Kenya), porters, food and transport, or you can book a foot safari. Either way, you will be involved with the Naro Moru River Lodge, which handles all hut bookings and the local porter and guide service, as well as running a Land-Rover service to the Naro Moru Track roadhead, and accommodations at the base of the mountain and the main base camp at 13,500 feet; the lodge also rents equipment and operates three packaged foot safaris (see below). Write: W. D. Curry (address p. 244); Nairobi agent in Kearlines (p. 99). Sportsman's Arms in Nanyuki (p. 252) can arrange Land-Rover service up the Sirimon Track. Snowline Safaris (p. 112) has mule and zebroid pack animals available for 25/– per day plus 15/– per muleteer (one for two mules). Porters (arranged for at the Naro Moru Lodge) carry 35 pounds payload (their gear doesn't count) and cost a basic 20/– per day, 30/– per day if guiding as well; a nonporter guide is 25/– per day. Most African guides and porters belong to the Mount Kenya Guides and Porters Safaris Club (Box 24, Naro Moru; tel. 27) which can be contacted direct. Guides can climb Point Lenana but not the other peaks; professional guides for Batian and Nelion can be contacted at African & Alpine Safaris and Mountain Safaris (see p. 111—safari outfitters specializing in climbs on Mount Kenya, Kilimanjaro, and the Ruwenzoris.

Snowline Safaris runs horse and zebroid safaris up the mountain, with one day costing 425/– for each of two people; four days is 1,400/– each of two. Zebroids carry the load, horses carry you. Naro Moru River Lodge's three foot safaris are as follows: (1) two-day climb to Point Lenana, costing 450/– each of two, 400/– each of three to five; (2) three-day climb, with two nights spent at Mackinder's Camp; cost is 550/– each of two, 525/– each of three to five; and (3) four-day round-the-peaks tour with an overnight at Mackinder's, then Kami Hut, then Mackinder's, with the third day a rugged, highly satisfying one; cost is 800/– each of two, 650/– each of three to five. A day-trip foot safari starts at 200/– for one. We took the four-day trip and had a fantastic time, but we believe we could have done the same trip for less money if we had asked for separate hut bookings, porter arrangements, base accommodations, and transport to the roadhead, and then packed our own food, since the lodge's wasn't very good. Arranging a climb is not that complicated. Note: Bring as much of your own equipment and packaged dry or freeze-dried food from the U.S. as you can.

When to Visit

The mountain is regularly visible from the surrounding lowlands in January, February, and June; at other times, the peaks alone may stand out above the clouds. It is unwise to walk or climb on the mountain during the rains—mid-March to June, mid-October to middle or late December. Most reliable months: mid-January to late February, late August to late September. If you're climbing then, make bookings early. Early-morning weather is best; mist, rain, and snow, as on most high mountains, can come suddenly.

Accommodations

Mackinder's Camp, 13,500 feet in the Teleki Valley, has 2–3-man tents, is run by the River Lodge, costs 7/– per person for sleeping space. 9 huts are owned by the Mountain Club, are booked through the lodge, cost 5/– per night for nonmembers (2/– for MCK members). Among the huts on popular routes and at convenient places: *Austrian Hut,* 15,720 feet on the east side of Lewis Glacier, brand-new 3-room hut sleeping 30 in comfort, 60 in a pinch; water available. *Kami Hut,* at 14,564 feet, beside Kami Tarn (water), sleeps 8, has porter hut. *Teleki Hut,* at 13,500 feet in Teleki Valley, sleeps 12, has water. Note: We found sleeping easy at 13,500 feet, impossible only 1,000 feet higher. If you have time you can spend a day or more getting acclimatized at the new *self-service bandas,* about 10,000 feet high, at the park gate. **Camping** is permitted anywhere; the MCK guide lists good campsites. Camp fee of 5/– per adult, 1/– per porter, is payable to the park and is applicable even if you sleep in a hut. The usual park entry fees (pp. 136–137) apply also.

Information

Serious climbers and hikers will need *Guide Book to Mount Kenya and Kilimanjaro,* ed. by John Mitchell (Nairobi: Mountain Club of Kenya, 1971), available for 22/– in Kenya from MCK (Box 45741, Nairobi), outside Kenya from West Col Productions, 1, Meadow Close, Goring, Reading, Berkshire RG8 OAP, England. Maps, see p. 90. Other books and articles:

Benuzzi, F. *No Picnic on Mount Kenya.* London: Kimber, 1952; Nairobi: Longman, 1970. Heartbreaking story by an Italian POW who broke out of Nanyuki prison camp to make an attempt on Mount Kenya.

Mackinder, Halford J. "A Journey to the Summit of Mount Kenya, British East Africa," *Geographical Journal,* XV (1900), 453.

Shipton, Eric. *Upon That Mountain.* London: Hodder & Stoughton, 1937.

Watteville, Vivienne de. *Speak to the Earth.* London: Methuen, 1935.

Continuing north on the highway, you pass at Km 182 the turnoff to Nanyuki Airport, reaching 7 km farther the signposted *Equator* (the peaks of Mount Kenya are about 10′ south of 0°). Curio sellers hawk their carvings on the left; the entrance to the Silverbeck Hotel with its *Equator Bar* is on the right. You can take a picture of the equator signboard and snow-capped Mount Kenya. Km 190: Turnoff (R) to Home Farm and Snowline Safaris, alternate road to Mount Kenya Safari Club.

Nanyuki

Km 191: *Nanyuki* (pop. 11,624), a district town serving a wheat- and maize-growing, sheep- and cattle-ranching area. Nanyuki (Masai— Enkare Nanyuki, "red water") is a young town. Mackinder camped here, near Lone Tree in the middle of town, in 1899 before conquering the mountain. It was settled by Europeans in 1910, but the township wasn't started until 1920. The railway reached it in 1930. Besides being a base for seeing Mount Kenya, Nanyuki has two accommodation– destinations: the famous Mount Kenya Safari Club (see package listings KP-16, 28, 31–32, 35–37, 67, 78, 85–87) and Secret Valley (see KP-14, 28–31, 35, 87). Next to the Safari Club is the *Mount Kenya Game Ranch,* a private 1,260-acre game sanctuary set up in 1968; it has about 200 animals of 30 different species but no predators, elephants, or rhinos. A main purpose is to be a study center for professionals and for student members of the Wildlife Clubs of Kenya. Nanyuki **accommodations:** *Mount Kenya Safari Club,* Box 35, Nanyuki; tel. 2141/2; cable SAFCLUB; booking also to Nairobi office, Box 30493; tel. 20265; same cable address. Go north through Nanyuki town, turning right 1 block past the clock tower; then follow signs. 27 dbls in main bldg, 9 dbls in new wing, 12 cottages (each w/2 dbls), all w/bath. Rates: $1,000-yearly members get 20 percent off; nonmembers pay 35/– daily fee. High season: FB: sgl—150/–; dbl—260/–; 2 in cottage—560/–; 4 in cottage—700/–. Note: No children under 10 allowed. What can you say about the Mount Kenya Safari Club? Once past the pseudosnobbish atmosphere—the mock exclusiveness, an occasional laughable arrogance—you'll see it's actually a pretty good hotel, with rates not as high as you thought. It's got a beautiful location on a ridge on the lower slopes of the mountain. It's got activities aplenty: swimming, tennis, riding, golf, bowls, fishing, game viewing, walking, climbing. You can spend lots of money in the Safari Boutique, or photograph birds (crowned cranes, black swans, peacocks) up close, take a sauna or fly away to Lake Rudolf, talk to a countess (maybe) or a tourist from Indiana (more likely), try to find William Holden (last cottage along the ridge), eat fairly well, take pictures of the "famous Chuka drummers" who dance after lunch . . . or you can sit around complaining about how the place is not Africa, which is true. You can sup in either the Safari Tent grill room or the Hunters dining room. Table d'hôte lunch (buffet barbecue) for casual visitors is 31/–; standard dinner, about 26/–, includes items like tilapia filet à l'Orly and Iranian chicken kebab. À la carte menu (entrées—14/– to 40/–) features Parma ham, foie gras truffle, filet mignon, Dover sole meunière, smoked salmon. Rating: 1st-class international. A* in the govt. book, ★★★ in ours. . . . *Secret Valley Game Lodge,* bookings to Wildlife Lodges (p. 87). Located 45 minutes up the mountain, access only through Sportsman's Arms, Nanyuki, 1 sgl, 20 dbls, none w/bath. Rates: DB&B: 145/– per person. Opened in 1961, Secret Valley is a Treetops specializing in leopards, lured to spotlighted platforms by chained-down hunks of meat. Leopard are seen only 4–5 nights a week, however, and few other animals in the chilly, eerie bamboo forest (fantastic, dramatic location for the lodge) come to the waterhole below the lodge-on-stilts. Unfortunately, Secret Valley is tariffically a rip-off. A tourist couple is socked $41 for the dubious privilege of sleeping between grungy sheets in a stuffy, unclean cubbyhole, eating high school cafeteria-quality food, inhaling coal smoke in the only warm place there is or freezing while standing on the too-crowded viewing galleries, using a crowded, towelless, cold-water bathroom, and listening to everybody and his brother and *his* kids clumping around this plywood jerry-built lodge. The staff is friendly and tries hard, but the problem is too big. Rating: As a hotel, Secret Valley is 3d- or 4th-class local, and the government should force the owner to renovate or else close down. . . . *Sportsman's Arms Hotel,* Box 3, Nanyuki; tel. 25, 67; cable SPORTSMANS. In town. 31 dbls, 5 sgls, all w/bath. Rates: B&B: sgl—55/–; dbl—110/–. Modest hotel built in the late 1920s. Rooms, in blocks or cottages, are fairly pleasant but simple, too old. Main building has bar (with the last cold beer until Samburu or Marsabit), lounge, dining room with table d'hôte meals (awful, by reports) of an English variety. Rating: 2d-class local, only reasonably priced Nanyuki hostelry. Govt. class D. . . . *Silverbeck Hotel,* Box 20, Nanyuki; tel. 29; cable SILVERBECK. 2d-class local hotel built in the forties, perhaps not touched since. Rooms undelightful but reasonably clean. . . . *Home Farm,* Snowline Safaris, Box 82, Nanyuki. Accommodations in settler's house. Riding, walking. Rates: B&B: sgl—50/–; dbl—110/–. . . . *Nanyuki Youth Hostel,* bookings to Warden, c/o Emmanuel Parish Centre, Box 279, Nanyuki. Beds for 10. . . . **Camping** at Sportsman's Arms. Free, at last word.

The NFD

After Nanyuki you pass ranches that produce some of the best Merino wool in Kenya. The treeless plains roll dramatically past

Timau (Km 213) and the junction with B6 (our Route K-8 from Meru and Embu), finally rolling right over the Timau Escarpment down to *Isiolo* (Km 270), a small, dull road town marking the end of one kind of Kenya and the beginning of another, the *Northern Frontier District (NFD)*. The NFD is not merely a trackless waste; it is East Africa's Sahara, so is loved and hated. Hunter-author Robert Ruark wrote in *Uhuru:* The NFD is a "limitless sandy purgatory, which froze you at Maralal and drowned you in the Chalbi Desert and parboiled you at Baragoi . . . ruled by sun and rain, by heat and cold, by wet and dry . . . the filthy, fierce, treacherous, death-dominated, exasperating, scorching, freezing, mountainous, desert-wasted, forgotten by Allah and avoided by Shaitan, awful, terrifying, enticing, ugly . . . *lovely* Northern Frontier." See also John Hillaby's *Journey to the Jade Sea,* about a camel-and-foot trip of 1,000 miles. The NFD is Kenya's newest tourist frontier. Many short packages include Samburu Game Reserve; there are air safaris to Lake Rudolf and Marsabit and even to the Foreign Legion-like outpost of Wajir, also a camel and zebroid trek (Snowline Safaris), a Land-Rover-and-tented-camp safari (UTC), and a walking safari (Wilderness Trails). See package listings KP-45–46, 49–53.

The British were slow in establishing control over the NFD and its nomadic tribesmen, some of whom were formerly as quick to slice your throat as anything else. A commercial firm set up outposts here in 1908, the government following the next year. For several years to mid-1971, the NFD was closed to travelers except by special permit because of the *shifta* troubles. The *shiftas* were (still are) Somalis who recognize no map border and believe a good part of Kenya should be part of a pan-Somali nation. A state of emergency was declared here in 1963, and the army was sent to deal with the *shiftas,* who were raiding as far as Isiolo, Marsabit, and the Lamu coast. Peace talks in 1965 didn't conclude anything, but a 1967 agreement ended most of the fighting, and the two countries resumed diplomatic relations and trade. *Shiftas* still cause trouble; they killed a Meru Park ranger in 1973 and exchanged shots with police near Meru Mulika Lodge. The *shiftas,* however, are interested in guns, not tourists.

The paving ends at Km 272, where there is a turnoff (R) on C81 to Wajir 354 km, El Wak 454 km, Mandera 736 km, and Somalia. *Wajir,* a district HQ, has a battlemented Beau Geste fort (now a prison—no photos), camels, palm trees, a sandy main drag, whitewashed houses, two World War II blockhouses, and the ship-shaped

Gamir or Ngamia (Camel) Club, formerly the *Royal Wajir Yacht Club,* a famous institution fabricated by a British D.C. who thought it a wizard idea to have a yacht club in the desert. See package KP-45. *El Wak,* farther on, also looks like something out of the Sahara.

Samburu

Km 289: Turnoff (L) to *Samburu Game Reserve,* a game park rich in species you might not see anywhere else in Kenya: the thin-striped *Grevy's zebra,* the *reticulated giraffe* (for the difference between the reticulated and the common giraffe, see p. 227), and the *gerenuk,* a graceful, long-necked gazelle that browses high in tall bushes by standing on its hind legs (it is called the giraffe gazelle, and *gerenuk* is Somali for "giraffe-necked"). There is also the *Beisa oryx* with its distinctive black and white face markings and long, pointed, straight horns; a predator is unwise to attack an oryx. Also in the park: elephant, rhino, lion, leopard (baited for across from the lodge), cheetah, buffalo, hyena (two species), impala, dik-dik, baboon. Williams counted 363 species of birds—a bewildering abundance, he says. There are many tame, almost friendly birds around the lodge.

The park is small (128 square miles) and is officially two reserves: Samburu Reserve (run by the Samburu County Council) on the north bank of the Uaso Nyiro River, and Isiolo-Buffalo Springs Reserve (run by the Isiolo County Council) on the south bank. To go everywhere, you'll have to pay twice (see below). The animals have the additional protection of 400-square-mile Photography Block 55

Grevy's zebra

Reticulated giraffe

Gerenuk

Oryx

to the northwest. The Samburu part of the park seems to have more thornscrub, while the southern part, with umbrella acacias and champagne-colored savannah grass, is picture-postcard Africa. The Uaso Nyiro (Masai, "river of brown water"), dividing the reserves, looks very tropical, with crocs and hippos, and elephants coming to bathe. Buffalo Springs is a series of pools and streams and is inhabited by crocodiles.

When to Visit

The reserves don't close in the rainy season, but roads get wet and streams may swell, making crossing hazardous. Go during the dry season.

Getting There, Getting Around

The Samburu Reserve can be entered directly at Km 303 (Archer's Post) and on the west from Barsalinga and Wamba; Isiolo Reserve is entered at Km 289 and at Km 301 (MOW Camp). The two are connected at a bridge across the Uaso Nyiro near the lodge; you can best reach this crossing by taking the Km 289 turnoff. There's an airstrip 6½ km from the lodge (15/– for transfer). Land-Rovers and VW Buses at 200/– per half-day, or seats in one at 40/– per person, can be hired at the lodge. A game scout will accompany you for 10/– per day. Inquire about walking up to a hill lookout point. Packages KP-21, 30–32, 35–37, 43, 78–79, 87, go to Samburu.

Costs

Same as the national parks (p. 136), and if you want to enter the Buffalo Springs area, 10/– extra. Note: A four-wheel-drive station wagon is charged 20/–, a sedan 10/–.

Accommodations

Samburu Game Lodge, bookings to Wildlife Lodges (p. 87). 21 km from the main road. 8 sgls, 48 dbls, all w/bath or shower. Rates: FB: sgl—200/–; dbl—260/–; tent accommodation—100/– per person. Credit: DC. Built 1962–63, the Block-operated lodge is spread out along the banks of the muddy Uaso Nyiro River. Main building has a round, satellitelike lounge extending out over the riverbank; from here you can watch antelopes, even an occasional leopard, come to drink. Rooms are on either side of the main building: old, sizable doubles and singles in blocks of 4 rooms or less on spacious grounds, new small doubles all in one 2-story block, opened early 1973. Dining room is Spanish-on-the-savanna. Pool. Rating: Not quite 1st-class international, by no means a luxury lodge, yet quite comfortable in old rooms. The rates are far too high. ★. Govt. class B. . . . *Buffalo Springs self-service bandas,* bookings to A. A. & Bunson (p. 86). 8 bandas, each sleeping 4, equipped with bathroom, 2-burner stove (gas extra charge); bedding available. Rates: 35/– per adult; 15/– per child. . . . **Camping** at a couple of places: Buffalo Springs, which has 4 tentsites, and along Champagne Ridge, which seems to offer many sites. Fee at either is 5/– per person. Special riverside campsite available for 30/– per person. Campsite bookings to Game Department (p. 87). Champagne Ridge, about 6 km from the Km 301 gate, offers a real East African experience, and is our choice.

If you exit the park from the lodge to Archer's Post, you'll pass a picturesque Samburu village on a hill, perhaps a herd of humped cattle. The *Samburu* (from Masai, "butterfly") tribe, like their relatives the Masai, measure their wealth in cattle, have various age grades and a *moran* class of very proud warriors with ochered, elaborately styled hairdos, ivory ear rings. The nomadic Samburu numbered 54,796 in the 1969 census and range over a wide area from South Horr to Maralal to Archer's Post to Marsabit. Note: You probably won't be able to photograph the Samburu without paying.

Km 303: *Archer's Post,* hardly more than a row of *dukas.* Km 318: Turnoff (L) on C79 to Wamba 41 km, Maralal 139 km, Baragoi 232 km, South Horr 270 km, Loyengalani and Lake Rudolf 353 km. Along this road are the somewhat foreboding peaks of the hardly explored *Mathews Range,* whose peak, Wamba Mountain, is 8,820 feet. **Km**

365: Serolevi. Km 406: Merille River, with **camping** to left just north of bridge. Km 417: Laisamis.

Marsabit

About Km 450 you're in the *Kaisut Desert,* a black-lava stretch of frying pan. Keep going. Km 479: Boundary of *Marsabit National Reserve,* at which the scenery begins getting greener as it goes up to Marsabit town at Km 511. The 800-square-mile reserve is mostly desert except for the 50-square-mile forested oasis of volcanic *Marsabit Mountain,* which rises to somewhere between 5,531 and 5,993 feet—in any case, 4,000 feet above the surrounding plains. Elsewhere in the reserve are smaller volcanic craters, including Gof Redo, 8 km from town, and Gof Choba, which is 4,200 feet. The reserve (no entry fees yet) is less a game park than a nature reserve, but it is most famous for its long-tusked elephants (minerals may be the reason for the heavy ivory) and greater kudu. Its most famous elephant was Ahmed, a 55–60-year-old elephant who carried tusks weighing about 165 pounds each. After two American hunters bragged about going to bag Ahmed (outside the reserve), some 5,000 protesting postcards were sent to President Kenyatta, who then (1970) gave Ahmed presidential protection wherever he roamed. Ahmed died—of old age—in January 1974 and, again by presidential order, will be preserved in the National Museum. A Marsabit successor will no doubt trumpet his appearance, but there are other large-tusked elephants to see. You have little chance of seeing the other animals: reticulated giraffe (in the forest), striped hyena, aardwolf, various antelope including greater kudu. Birdlife is abundant (Williams counted 365 species), but you have to look while in the forest; water birds are obvious at Lake Paradise.

Marsabit has 30 miles of roads, with one leading from the town 10 km up to *Lake Paradise* (Gof Sokorte Guda), a mile-square crater lake made famous by Martin and Osa Johnson, who lived here for a time—see *Four Years in Paradise* (1939). From the lake (good birding), five tracks go down to the main road; no signposts, no map. You need four-wheel-drive or a good VW bus. The Marsabit Tented Lodge can provide directions to *Gof Redo Crater, Rhino Cave* (armed guide advisable), and *Boculy Waterhole.*

In and around the reserve live three tribes. The Moslem *Rendille* (pop. 18,729) are camel herders who live in pole-and-hide huts that look like Thermos Pop-tents and can be dismantled and transported on their camels, which carry flat wooden bells. The *Gabbra* are a wide-ranging, cattle-herding tribe formerly based near Lake Rudolf. The third tribe is the *Boran* (pop. 34,086), a Galla people whose land extends into Ethiopia. They herd a short-horned, humped, very hardy cattle which have been successfully crossbred with European breeds. All three tribes have lives oriented around waterholes and wells—one conveniently visited is *Oolanoola* (*Ula Ula*) *Well,* where camel trains water; well is located 5 miles south of town. The tribes' trading center is Marsabit town (pop. 6,635), a district HQ.

When to Visit

Dry season is best, but the road from Isiolo is now all-weather. The reserve is open all year.

Getting There, Getting Around

By road, travel self-contained north of Isiolo. Many people fly in and hire a Land-Rover (Tented Lodge—41/– per mile, minimum 50/– per hour; guide is 10/– per hour). See package listings KP-23, 43–44, 51.

Accommodations

Marsabit Lodge, bookings to KTDC (p. 87). Located inside the reserve at Sokorte Dika lake, not far from park HQ. 24 dbls w/shower. Rates: FB: sgl—200/–; dbl—300/–, incl. Prefabricated lodge opened in mid-1974 on edge of photogenic little lake, has bar-lounge, terrace, dining room (casual meals: breakfast—10/–; lunch or dinner—25/–). . . . *Marsabit Tented Lodge,* Box 125, Nanyuki; tel. 2175 or Nairobi 46826; bookings to A. A. & Bunson (p. 86). Located 2 km above town on Karantina Hill. 12 to 20 dbl tents; toilet tents separate. Rates: FB: sgl—140/– to 180/–; dbl—240/– to 300/–. John Alexander's *Karantina Tented Camp* under a new name is simple, clean, pleasant, and expensive. Cold beer. . . . **Camping** at two delightful sites: one in a grove of tall trees about a mile from park HQ, other actually on the shores of Lake Paradise 10 km away (four-wheel-drive or VW bus necessary to get up road). Pay at park office 5/– per person for forest site, 10/– at Lake Paradise. No facilities; drinking water from park office.

If you happen to be going to Ethiopia, the road is practically all-weather to Moyale. The terrain is inhospitable—north of Marsabit is the black-lava *Dida Galgalla Desert*—but there is rare birdlife. Km 514: Turnoff (L) on C82 to North Horr 177 km, Loyengalani and Lake Rudolf 262 km. This road has been recently improved and forms part of the Rudolf–Marsabit "circuit."

Km 751: *Moyale* (pop. 353) and Kenya border post, with Ethiopian post a mile north at Moiale.

Route K-8: Murang'a–Embu–Meru–Isiolo (East Side of Mount Kenya)

Route K-8 goes around the eastern side of Mount Kenya, an area far more populous, intensively cultivated, and greener than the western side.

Beginning at Murang'a (Fort Hall), you reach the main Sagana junction at Km 11; go right on paving. Km 29: Turnoff (L—after Kutas *dukas*) to *Thiba Fishing Camp* 18 km. Fee: 5/– per equipped, self-service rondavel. **Camping** for 5/– per tent. Nice, very green. Km 46: *Embu* (pop. 3,928), HQ of Eastern Province and Embu District, and capital of the *Embu tribe,* Kenya's thirteenth-largest (pop. 117,969). Famous for their dancing, the Embu are closely related to the Kikuyu. The market town has little of interest besides the flat-topped, pyramidal *Uhuru Monument* by Province HQ. **Accommodations:** *Izaak Walton Inn,* Box 1, Embu; tel. 28; bookings to KTDC (p. 87). 2 km north of town on main road. 18 dbls w/bath. Rates: FB: sgl—127/50, dbl—229/50, incl tax, levy, service. Credit: DC. 8½-acre inn grew up as a fishing lodge, now gets an occasional package tour. Rooms cheerful, opening onto central garden. Small woody bar, friendly dining room (breakfast—10/–; lunch or dinner—17/50). Fishing in the trout-stocked Rupengazi River (5/– for license; 5/– for tackle). Rating: 1st-class local, best hotel on this side of mountain.

On the plains below Embu is the *Mwea-Tebere irrigation scheme,* the largest in Kenya. At the town is the turnoff (R) to the *Seven Forks hydroelectric project* 54 km, on the Tana River near 440-foot Seven Forks waterfall. First phase of the project was the $20-million *Kindaruma Dam,* completed 1965, commissioned 1968. 24 km downstream is the $40-million second phase, *Kamburu Dam,* which when finished in 1974 is to be 2,925 feet long and hold back 161 million cubic yards of water. The Kindaruma lake has already attracted much wildlife; the area was made a game reserve in 1971, but you can get out of your car and walk around, which is nice. Seven Forks is also accessible from Thika on Route K-7.

Km 64: Ena and turnoff (L) on the Embu–Meru high road, a scenic but somewhat trying route full of U, W, and S curves. If you don't want to hassle that in your car, go straight on C92, the low road, coming out on this route at Km 173 at Meru. Distance and time: 108 km, 2 hours 45 minutes on the high road *vs.* 103 km, 1 hour 45 minutes on the newer, straighter road. The high road is one of the grueling, and famous, route sections of the *East African Safari Rally,* renowned as one of the world's toughest car rallies, run over Easter weekend, which is usually at the start of the rainy season. The 90–100 cars entered are supposed to maintain an average of 60 mph on the whole course, with sustained speeds of 115 mph on the better sections. The "worst" Safari was in 1968 when only 7 cars out of 91 finished. Should you think about entering your sedan in the 3,000-mile rally, be aware that it is not as hazardous as it is costly: Ford estimated it cost $22,000 to prepare each of four Escort RS1600s entered in 1972, and the company spent $60,000 for service vehicles and a plane; in 1974 neither Ford nor Datsun entered the Safari—too costly, they said. "East African Safari" is becoming a misnomer; the rally covered three countries in 1972, Kenya and Tanzania in 1973, Kenya only in 1974.

The pavement ends at Km 76; twisty dirt goes through Chuka (Km 98) and Chogoria (Km 123) to the next paved road, joining the lower road at Km 173: *Meru* (pop. 4,475), district HQ and capital of the Meru tribe, the sixth-largest with a population of 554,252. Center of a coffee, tea, and maize region, Meru town was established as a government station in 1908. Turn right at the Shell to get to *Nkeri Falls* 8 km; the falls are a modest 30 feet high but are pretty. The manager of the Pig & Whistle will direct you to other local sights: 101-foot-high *King Muhuru Tree* 5 km and *Sacred Lake* 22½ km. **Accommodations:** *Pig & Whistle Hotel,* Box 99, Meru; tel. 14. 5 sgls, 14 dbls, most w/bath or shower. Rates: B&B: sgl—70/–; dbl—110/–. Credit: DC. Dates to 1924. Two oldest rooms are nicest, with cool cedar walls. Shabby main building has bar, lounge, dining room (breakfast—7/50; lunch—12/–; dinner—13/–). Rating: 2d-class local, may improve with planned expansion; rooms overpriced. Govt. class D.

Meru National Park

Km 175: Turnoff (R) on D482 to Maua, Meru National Park (Murera Gate 78 km, Meru Mulika Lodge 82 km, Leopard Rock

Lodge 87 km, campsite 78 km). *Meru National Park* (320 square miles, may be expanded another 300 square miles) is on low, hot country that looks to the visitor like typical Africa. Appearances are deceptive, however, since the park is extremely well watered, with nine permanent rivers. The Rojwero River divides the park roughly into two sections: a dry northern area of open savanna with watercourses and swampy areas (Mulika, Leopard Rock swamps) marked by the doum palm and its peculiarly symmetrical branches; and a southern area with thick thornbush growing in sandy soil. Watch the black cotton soil in the north—it can bog even a Land-Rover.

Meru was established as a game reserve in 1959, as a national park in 1966. A year after establishment, a small herd of Uganda kob was transported to Meru, and a couple years later seven *white rhinos*— the first in Kenya—were imported from South Africa. One died after arrival and four are roaming free; two others are kept in a pen near park headquarters, where you can see them. The white rhino is so called from his wide lip (*weit* in Afrikaans), not from his color, which is the same gray as the *black rhino,* indigenous to Meru. The two species are different, however: the white rhino is much bigger and more massive, standing 70 inches at the shoulder and weighing 3½ to 5 tons, compared with the black rhino's 60-inch height and 1–1½-ton weight; the white has a longer head and the square lip, while the black has a pointed, triangular lip; the white grazes on the ground, the black browses on twigs, leaves, and bark; the white is a placid beast that you can approach rather closely, but the black is an ill-tempered, untrustworthy, and unpredictable creature that will charge for little reason (some say out of curiosity, since the rhino is dim-sighted); the white rhino will form parties, the black rhino is mostly solitary. Both types are threatened species, there being 11,000 to 13,500 head of black rhino in Africa, perhaps 4,000 head of white rhino. Incidentally, the white rhino is the largest living land mammal after the elephant.

Besides rhino, other big game includes lion, leopard, cheetah, elephant, hippo, reticulated giraffe, both Grevy's and common zebra, lesser kudu, gerenuk, Beisa oryx. John Williams reports the birdlife "abundant and colorful," and counted 341 species.

Meru has a certain fame as the one-time home of Joy Adamson's lioness *Elsa* and her cubs, not to mention *Pippa* the cheetah and her cubs. East of the park George Adamson today runs Kora Camp, where he continues lion rehabilitation. When Adamson, then a game warden, was forced to shoot Elsa's man-eating mother in the late

1950s, he had no idea he would be starting not only the so-called "Elsa cult" but a mini-industry in which everybody concerned with getting the lions back to nature seems to have written a book or made a movie or a TV documentary. One or the other Adamson has written *Born Free, Living Free, Forever Free, Pippa, Pippa's Challenge,* and *Bwana Game.* (They are just locations now, but you can visit Elsa's Camp south of signpost 80, exactly on the equator at the Ura River, and Pippa's Camp near signpost 13.) Elsa, by the way, died in 1961.

When to Visit

Because of the black cotton soil, it's best to see Meru in the dry season. Don't try to commute from Meru town, and do try to spend at least two full days in the park.

Getting There, Getting Around

The main entrance is Murera Gate; you can also enter at Bisanadi Gate on the road from Garba Tula, and at Ura Gate, which is some 46 km by poor road from the lower Embu–Meru road at Chiokarige. Until the lower road is paved, the easiest route from Nairobi is via Nyeri, Nanyuki, and Meru town, on the west side of Mount Kenya. Once you're in the park, there is a well-developed system of roads and tracks, well signposted. There are several airstrips, including Meru Mulika Lodge and Park HQ. Few package tours include Meru, since it's off the milk runs, but see listings KP-22, 37, 51. Game-viewing vehicles for hire at Meru Mulika.

Accommodations

Meru Mulika Lodge, bookings to KTDC (p. 87). Located 3½ km from Murera Gate. 50 dbls (incl 3 suites) w/bath or shower. Rates: FB: sgl—206/–; dbl—265/–, incl tax, levy, service; rate for Kenya residents—85/– per person. Meru Mulika (so named from the green, doum-dotted swamp behind the lodge) is 1973–new. After the current trend, the design is remotely like an African village, with rooms in round, thatched-roof structures, all painted a sort of muddy-gray color. Clean, comfortable, well decorated, the rooms are all too small. Bar-lounge is roomy, features central stone fireplace and attractive wall hangings by Danish artist Britta Bortelsen. The staff is most friendly. Pool. Casual meals: breakfast—10/–; lunch—20/–; dinner— 25/–. Rating: 1st-class international, with some reservations. ★. . . . *Leopard Rock Safari Lodge,* bookings to A. A. & Bunson (p. 86).

Located 14½ km from Murera Gate. Self-service lodge has 6 equipped dbl bandas, each with indoor bathroom, veranda, kitchen. Comfortable. Rates: 40/– per adult, 15/– per child. . . . Kenmare Lodge, shown on even the new Shell map, has been closed for some time. . . . **Camping** at several sites. Main, public campsite is on the Bwatherongi River 3 km downstream from Park HQ, and an exceptional place it is to camp, with running water, toilets, showers in a new block, lots of interesting birds all around, and grazing white rhinos (with armed guard). Fee: 5/– per adult. Also 3 nice new cabins with beds and table for those who are tentless. Fee: 10/– per adult. Other campsites have no facilities, are usually used by professionally led safaris but can be used by ordinary people, with permission (Warden, Box 162, Nanyuki).

Back in Meru town at Km 175, the route becomes rather pretty as it goes through the *Imenti Forest* and then rolling pasture and farmland before coming to the junction (Km 199) with B16 (our Route K-7) from Nanyuki. Go right to Isiolo 26 km.

Route K-9: Nanyuki–Nyahururu (Thomson's Falls)–Nakuru

This short route is not terribly scenic except after Nyahururu (Thomson's Falls), but it is well traveled by tourists since it connects the Mount Kenya area with Lake Nakuru. At Thomson's Falls begins the road north to the east side of Lake Rudolf.

At Nanyuki, take a turnoff on C76. The pavement ends at Km 3; the road to Nyahururu is well-engineered dirt, bumpy toward the end. Most of the land traversed is the *Laikipia Plateau*, one of the main beef cattle areas in Kenya, once a homeland of the Masai. Km 23: Hulme's Bridge. Km 53: Turnoff (R) to Rumuruti (also accessible from Nyahururu). Km 91: *Thomson's Falls* bridge and falls on the Ewaso Narok River. Depending on which source you consult, the waterfall—third highest in Kenya—is 76 feet, 100 feet, 237 feet, or 240 feet. The *National Atlas* says 237 feet, and we'll accept that. The falls are photogenic if you catch them at the right time of the day from the lawn of Thomson's Falls Lodge (entry: 2/– per adult) across the way. The first European to see the waterfall, Scottish explorer Joseph Thomson in 1883, named them for his father. Km 92: *Thomson's Falls* town in 1973 underwent a de-Briticizing name change to the mumbly *Nyahururu*, while the falls will apparently be called "the

Nyahururu." The town (pop. 7,602), HQ of Nyandarua District, was formerly a center of the White Highlands (altitude here is 7,743 feet) but is now an African farming center, since most of the district has been included in the *Land Settlement Program.* That is a polite term for shoving the Europeans off big farms (paying them off partly with British aid money) and settling landless African families (hereabouts, mostly Kikuyu) on them. Land settlement is vitally important to Kenya's future. The country is 140 million acres, but only 26 million acres can be cultivated—and Europeans owned some 7.4 million acres of the best mixed-farming and plantation land in addition to having a virtual monopoly on coffee and tea (the top two exports) and exclusive ownership in the Highlands. This arrangement even a Ku Kluxer might recognize as unfair, and the coin is now reversed. About 3 million acres had changed hands by 1973; the whole land settlement scheme will cost about $81 million. You will see one settlement scheme and farmers' cooperative society after another from Nyahururu south to Nakuru (the Laikipia Plateau stretch of this route is bordered on both sides by two to three King Ranch-size cattle spreads). **Accommodations:** *Thomson's Falls Lodge,* Box 38, tel. 6; bookings to Box 10530, Nairobi; tel. 24339. 32 rms and 3 cottages, all dbls; 20 w/bath or shower. Rates: B&B: sgl—50/–; dbl—80/–. Credit: DC. High-altitude American-owned lodge. Rooms in main building or 2-story cottages are simple; all have fireplaces to fight the evening chill. Bar, two woody but bare lounges, friendly dining room. Table d'hôte meals: breakfast—7/50; lunch or dinner—15/75. Riding, minigolf or 9-hole golf, fishing. Rating: 1st-class local. . . . **Camping** on either side of the falls, though not within view of them. Thomson's Falls Lodge has a fenced-in field next to a corral, with toilet, shower available. Fee: 7/50 per person. Across the bridge, on the grounds of the Forest Dept. office, is the High Altitude Camping and Picnic Site, with campsites above (best) and below the office. Latrine, picnic tables. Fee: 3/– per person. Campsite is so called because Kenya's medal-winning Olympic squad trained here in 1968.

At Thomson's Falls is the turnoff north to the eastern (Loyengalani) side of *Lake Rudolf.* This is one of three routes to the lake. Briefly, they are: (1) Thomson's Falls–Rumuruti–Maralal–Baragoi–South Horr–Loyengalani; (2) Isiolo–Marsabit–Chalbi Desert–North Horr–Loyengalani; and (3) Kitale–Kapenguria–Amudat (Uganda)–Lodwar–Eliye Springs–Ferguson's Gulf. In 1973 this third route was not being used because of the Uganda troubles, but the Kenya government is to build a road that skirts the border, going through Sigor and Lokichar to Lodwar. In the meantime, you can drive (four-wheel-drive necessary) to the eastern side but should fly to the western. From Thomson's Falls the first route goes through *Rumuruti,* a European cattle area (established 1905) where the Carr-Hartley big-game trapping farm is located (no longer open to the public), and on to *Maralal* (pop. 3,878), HQ of Samburu District and somewhat rich in wildlife (a local reserve is sanctuary for Grevy's zebra and other plains animals; common zebra and other animals graze on Maralal Lodge's lawn). The high, cool Maralal plateau is pretty; Americans will find the campsite reminiscent of the Sierra. Jomo Kenyatta was confined here between his exile in hot Lodwar and his triumphant return to Nairobi in 1961. **Accommodations:** *Maralal Safari Lodge,* P.O. Maralal; bookings to Box 10530, Nairobi; tel. 24339. 24 dbls w/bath. Rates: B&B: sgl—65/–; dbl—110/–. On a grassy rise. Rooms are in red wood cottages, are not fancy. Dining room serves standard meals (breakfast —7/50; lunch or dinner—15/–). Grounds ill-kept (but there is game viewing, and whole lodge could be neater. Rating: 2d-class local. . . . A new lodge is to be built with government financing. . . . **Camping** in a big, fenced-off hillside location (good views)ʿ just past the lodge. Free, as far as we know.

The Rudolf road continues through *Baragoi* (gasoline), with its Catholic church featuring carved doors and rose-quartz windows, then to the green Horr Valley and *South Horr,* a Samburu trading village overshadowed by *Mount Nyiru,* 9,030 feet, on whose high slopes the Samburu graze their cattle. From South Horr you drive over rough lava plains and descend an escarpment to Loyengalani. Non-four-wheel-drive vehicles have traveled this route, but not without damage. (For locations on the route to Eliye Springs and Ferguson's Gulf, see Route K-11.) From Loyengalani ("the place of the trees"), many people return to Nairobi by the second route, through North Horr to Marsabit; this also is a four-wheel-drive route, though a new road avoids a hazardous escarpment.

Lake Rudolf

Lake Rudolf, called the Jade Sea because of its greenish blue color, is a Great Rift Valley lake that is not only a rich source of fish (for commercial and sport fishing) but is one of Kenya's newest tourist attractions. The European discovery of the lake was made by Samuel Teleki von Szek, a Hungarian count of the Holy Roman Empire. Count

Teleki and Lieutenant Ludwig von Höhnel came upon Rudolf in March 1888, and the Austrian lieutenant described it as a "sheet of water set like a pearl of great price in the wonderful landscape beneath us." They named it after one of the expedition's patrons, Prince Rudolf, archduke and crown prince of Austria; in a famous tragedy in 1889, at Mayerling, Rudolf murdered his mistress and committed suicide.

Covering 3,500 square miles, Lake Rudolf, now surrounded by a frightening purple lava desert, was once much larger and was even connected to the Nile, which is why Nile perch live in it. The lake has several inlets but no outlet, so is mildly alkaline (it is the largest alkaline lake in the world). The western shore is somewhat sandy and less interesting than the eastern shore, which is dramatically volcanic to the south; Teleki's Volcano, still active, is on the edge. The lakeshore is rocky and arid on the southeast, sandy to the northeast. The Omo River delta at the Ethiopian north end is gentle if somewhat inaccessible. It is in the Omo River valley and on the northeastern shore above Allia Bay (in the new 900-square-mile *East Rudolf National Park*) that various archaeological expeditions, including one led by Richard Leakey, have made some momentous discoveries of early man (see below).

Rudolf is a fabulous tourist attraction partly because it is so unspoiled. The *Turkana* (who number 203,177) occupy the western shore and all of northwest Kenya. A nomadic Nilo-Hamitic tribe related to the Karomojong peoples of the Uganda-southern Sudan area, the warlike Turkana have not been much influenced by the outside world. The men wear elaborate hairstyles and ivory or wood lip plugs, carry around a small wooden stool, and are handy with their circular wrist knives. On the eastern side few people live. Around Loyengalani is the interesting *El Molo* tribe, a people who live off fish speared from the lake, occasionally hippo meat. Some sources say the tiny tribe is dying out, but naturalist Leslie Brown says they aren't; Teleki counted only 99 when he visited in 1888, but there were 197 in 1967.

Inhabiting the lake are unestimated quantities of fish: Nile perch up to 200 pounds, large tilapia up to 20 pounds, huge tigerfish up to a rumored 100 pounds. The feasibility of establishing a commercial fishing industry is being studied, but there's no doubt about fishing for sport. An estimated 22,000 crocodiles live in the lake but are not hunted much (and are as a result inoffensive) because their "button" skin growths make lousy ladies' handbags. The lake and its three islands (North, Central, and South Islands) support a delightful bird population, some 173 species including many northbound European migrants March to early May. The shores are bare of much wildlife except on the northeast, in the new national park. Near the shore there are zebras and topis in large numbers; inland are oryxes, Grevy's zebras, reticulated giraffes.

Since 1968 a large expedition of some 20 scientists and 50 African assistants has been based at Koobi Fora, midway between Allia Bay and Ileret in the northeast, surveying and digging in a 900-square-mile area rich in fossils. National Museum Administrator Richard Leakey, son of the late L. S. B. Leakey and co-leader of the expedition, announced in November 1972 the finding and reconstruction of the *oldest complete skull of early man*. An unnamed *Homo* specimen (it is known by the catalog name "1470 Man"), it is some 2.6 to 2.8 million years old. The skull and complete femur (thigh bone) are important for several reasons, not the least of which is that they are among some 90 specimens of early man found in dated horizons at Rudolf. More importantly, the skull has a cranial capacity of more than 800 cubic centimeters (cc), much larger than *Australopithecus*'s 500 cc. Further, the complete femur indicates that man began to walk upright far earlier—more than a million years earlier—than previously thought. What's more, because East Rudolf man is so much older than 1.5-million-year-old *Zinjanthropus boisei* found by Mary Leakey at Olduvai Gorge in 1959, Richard Leakey believes (but can't yet prove) that *Australopithecus* was not an ancestor of modern man at all, and that presently held evolutionary theories (and nomenclature of early man) will have to be revised.

There are more Eastern Africa fossil areas than just East Rudolf. Some major discoveries were made in the Omo Valley by teams from Kenya, Ethiopia, France, and the U.S.; fossils found were 1.8 to 3 million years old. "1470 Man" may not have been the first early man to walk upright, either. In early 1974, American paleontologist C. Donald Johanson of Case Western Reserve University announced the discovery, in the Hadar River basin in Ethiopia, of four fossil *Australopithecus* leg bones "in excess of 3 million years old," making them older than the "1470" skull, and pushing the origin of bipedal man further back.

Paralleling these recent finds in importance, in the *Australopithecus* scheme of things, was the 1967 discovery (announced in 1970) by a Harvard expedition of a 5.5-million-year-old jawbone with one molar in place. The expedition made the find at Lothagam Hill southwest of Lake Rudolf. The fragment is believed to have come from a hominid related to *Australopithecus* but is three times older than the Olduvai *Australopithecus,* which when found in 1959 was three times older than anything found before. The jawbone fills in part of the gap between *Ramapithecus* (man-ape; *Kenyapithecus*) and *Australopithecus.* (For more on prehistory, see Olduvai Gorge section in Tanzania chapter.)

When to Visit

Lake Rudolf becomes almost inaccessible by road during and after the rains, but you can still fly. Rains or not, Rudolf is blisteringly hot, and winds can roar through a campsite.

Getting There, Getting Around

The three road routes are described above. The East Rudolf National Park is currently almost impossible to get to unless you're someone important and the paleontologists let you use their airstrip—or even let you visit them. Mere mortals for the time being will have to content themselves with Loyengalani on the east, Eliye Springs and Ferguson's Gulf on the west; all three have airstrips. If you don't have a safari-equipped four-wheel-drive, better fly. See package listings KP-24, 36, 44, 50–51. The three lodges have cruisers for rent (up to 150/– per hour), motorized *sese* canoes (up to 60/– per hour), dinghies (40/– per hour), and sailing sprites (20/– per hour). Experience is necessary, since terrifying squalls in these waters can be sudden. Eliye Springs has VW bus or Land-Rover for 2/50 per mile.

Accommodations

Eliye Springs Lodge, bookings to African Tours & Hotels (p. 87). 10 dbls w/shower. Rates: FB: sgl—120/–; dbl—180/–, plus 10/– membership. Dinner, served on patio, can include guest-caught fish. . . . *Lake Rudolf Angling Lodge,* bookings to A. A. & Bunson (p. 86). 14 dbls. Rates: FB: sgl—201/65; dbl—346/60, incl tax, levy, service. Credit: DC. Bandas are grouped around a dining room–bar, whole club situated on a spit of land between the gulf and the lake. Pool. Fishing, birdwatching (hides nearby), visiting Turkana village. . . . *Oasis Lodge,* bookings to Northern Kenya Lodges, Box 43230, Nairobi; tel. 25856. 12 dbls w/shower. Rates: FB: dbl—391/–, incl tax, levy, service. New 6-cottage complex in Loyengalani replaces one burned down during the *shifta* troubles in 1965. 2 more cottages (4 more ˚rooms) will be added. 2 swimming pools. Bar-lounge, dining room—both with prices that angered solar eclipse watchers in June 1973. . . . **Camping** practically anywhere on the empty shore, and officially at Eliye Springs for 15/— per person.

Continuing the route (paved) from Thomson's Falls, you cross the *Equator* (signposted, for picture-taking purposes) at Km 97. At Km 104 you have a choice of going straight on C77 (paved) to Gilgil on the Nairobi–Nakuru road, or going right on C83 (dirt) almost directly to Nakuru. The paved route is quite scenic, passing much beautiful farmland; the dirt route is scenic toward the end. On the latter, the pavement resumes at Km 132. There are beautiful vistas over Lake Nakuru, Mau Escarpment, Menengai Crater, and the dramatic Rift Valley at Kms 128 and 138. You descend steadily, pass the Lanet (Nakuru) Airfield at Km 147, and in 1 km meet A104 (our Route K-10), at which you go right to Nakuru 8 km. If you take the paved roads, it is 53½ km to Gilgil, where you turn right to Nakuru 40 km.

Route K-10: Nairobi–Naivasha–Nakuru–Eldoret–Uganda

A main trunk route, this road is well used by tourists as far as Nakuru and its famous lake, but the whole length of it is quite scenic and has places of interest beyond Nakuru.

Part of the route overlaps Route K-12. Though K-10 is the main highway, the new Limuru road is far wider, better, and a more scenic way to the Escarpment.

Begin on Uhuru Highway, going northwest 3 km to Westlands. Km 3: Join *Waiyaki Way,* until 1973 called *Sclaters Road* after the captain who, in 1895–97, built this road from Kibwezi (near Tsavo) to Mumias near Lake Victoria. Km 6: *St. Austin's Mission,* off to the left, is where French Catholic missionaries grew the first successful coffee as a cash crop in Kenya, planting in 1901, harvesting in 1905. Km 17: *Zambezi Motel* (L), Box 44098, Nairobi; tel. 29651 or (83) 2143. 20 sgls, 25 dbls, all w/bath or shower. Rates: B&B: sgl—30/—; dbl—60/—, incl tax, levy, service. Zambezi is an old 2-story motel that's trying to get with it. Rooms are basic, unfancy. Rating: 2d-class local. Govt. class D.

Km 20: Turnoff (L) on C63 to *Kikuyu,* location of *Alliance High School,* founded 1926, the first high school for Africans in the coun-

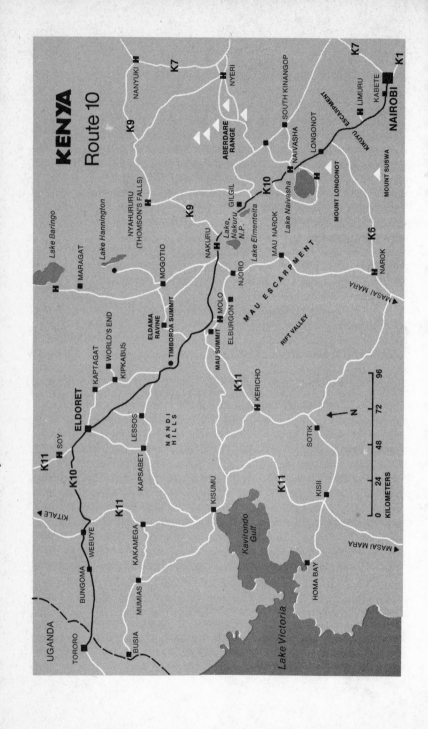

try; it has graduated many of Kenya's present leaders but now has a mostly Kikuyu student body. Km 22: *Muguga* and turnoff (L) to HQ of East African Agricultural and Forestry Research Organization (EAAFRO), a major scientific establishment with a variety of photogenic trees on the grounds. Km 34: Turnoff (R) on C62 (our Route K-12) to Limuru. Km 36: Turnoff (R) on old road to Limuru. Km 40: *Kikuyu Escarpment* and Rift Valley viewpoint (see Route K-12, Km 38 and following). Km 47: Turnoff (R) to Kijabe ("wind"). Km 49: Italian Chapel (R). Km 51: Floor of the Rift. Km 52: Turnoff (L) on B3 (our Route K-6) to Masai Mara Game Reserve.

Km 65: You are passing *Mount Longonot,* a 9,111-foot volcanic cone with a crater 600 feet deep, almost 4 km in diameter; there are steam jets on the bottom. Longonot (Masai, "mountain of the many spurs or steep ridges") is a popular day trip from Nairobi. It is a 45-minute walk to the crater rim; allow 2½–3 hours for a circuit of the almost perfectly circular crater. To get there, turn left off the highway onto a track just after the level railroad crossing (Km 66), go about 6½ km, then go left to the beginning of a good trail to the rim. Shortest route to the high point is counterclockwise. It is safest to leave your car at Longonot Station unless someone stays with it.

Lake Naivasha

Km 83: Turnoff (L) on D323 (South Lake Road) around *Lake Naivasha,* a fresh-water lake with superb birdwatching and several places to stay. Naivasha (from Enaiposha, Masai, "a lake") measures about 81 square miles in area and is about 55 feet deep, but it was once much larger (in 1917 it extended to the cliffs and railway line on the other side of the present highway), and at one time had a large outlet flowing out of Hell's Gate (Njorowa Gorge) when Lakes Naivasha, Nakuru, and Elmenteita were one. Around this lake lived our ancestors; the Leakeys turned up several prehistoric sites in this area (see below). Dr. Gustav A. Fischer, sent out by the Hamburg Geographical Society to find a route to Lake Victoria, recorded Naivasha in 1883, a few months before Thomson came by; *Fischer's Tower,* a photogenic spire of alkalite rhyolite lava near Hell's Gate, is named for him. To get to Hell's Gate, go about 15 km from the highway to a poorly signposted track to the left (if you get to Carnelley's Camp, you've gone too far). Several tracks cross farm and ranch land but most wind up at Fischer's Tower, and you continue on to *Hell's Gate,* which is 6½ km south of the lakeshore. At a certain point even four-wheel-drive vehicles can't go on, and you can then easily walk on a trail down through a rocky gully into the primeval forest at the bottom of the gorge. Continue on and you will find bubbling hot springs.

Lake Naivasha has hippos but no crocodile. According to Leslie Brown, the lake before the 1920s had no fish except for one species called *Aplocheilichthys antinorii;* all the others, including tilapia and large-mouthed and black bass, have been introduced. The lake is very popular with fishermen. Moreover, papyrus-fringed Naivasha is, like Nakuru, a birdwatcher's favorite. On 1½-square-kilometer *Crescent Island* (access through Marina Club: 5/– temporary membership; 10/– return boat trip) John G. Williams counted 147 species in one day, and over 300 have been recorded. More private is *Rima Island,* a 4-acre island on the west side of the lake, an hour from the Marina Club. Fishing and birdwatching there. Common birds at the lake: malachite kingfisher, great crested grebe, little grebe, fish eagle, white-necked cormorant, African marsh harrier, gray-headed gull, European swallow, white-winged black tern (migrant), red-billed duck, Hottentot teal, red-knobbed coot, purple gallinule, African lily-trotter, goliath heron, purple heron, African spoonbill, pelicans, ospreys, and egrets.

The pretty Naivasha area is often used as a movie location, and recently the TV series *Born Free* was filmed here.

When to Visit

April–June is definitely the off-season.

Getting There, Getting Around

Package tours to Nakuru often include a stop at Naivasha, and transport to the lake from Nairobi is easily arranged. See packages KP-9, 37, 78–79. The 58-km lake circular road (from the highway at Km 83, coming out at Km 99 above Naivasha town) has a couple of good viewpoints, and you can make a detour to Fischer's Tower and Hell's Gate, but otherwise the road is pretty far from the shore and is not a worthwhile circuit. Hotels have boats for hire (30/– per hour for 4-passenger motorized punt at Lake Hotel).

Accommodations

Hotel and other accommodations are all off South Lake Road. *Lake Naivasha Hotel,* Box 15, Naivasha; tel. 13; bookings to Wildlife Lodges (p. 87). 4 sgls, 29 dbls, all w/bath. Rates: FB: sgl—110/– or 150/–;

dbl—200/–. Credit: BA, DC. No children under 10, for some reason. The best hotel on the lake, first opened in 1925, renovated and expanded since. Clean, bright rooms. Birdwatching and tea on well-cropped lawn, shaded by fever trees. Semicircular lounge has hardwood floor, big fireplace; two-section dining room has table d'hôte meals featuring Molo lamb, Kinangop turkey. Rating: Superior 2d-class international. ★★. Govt. class B. . . . *Naivasha Marina Club*, Box 85, Naivasha; tel. 51Y2; bookings to A. A. & Bunson (p. 86). 32 dbls in cottages, 1 "superhouse" (suite), 10 cabins. Cottage rates: B&B: sgl—55–; dbl—100/–; cabin 50/– for 2. Day membership— 5/– per person, providing entry to Crescent Island. Marina Club was cabins-cum-campground until the *Living Free* film company set up here and a club developed around the shooting. Stone-walled rondavels and cottages have *marula* (papyrus) roofs, are new, furnished simply. Deep pool, boat-shaped bar, dining room with interesting wall hangings. À la carte menu has tilapia poached with anchovies, capers, and tomatoes, touched with garlic—10/50. Rating: 1st-class local. . . . *Safariland Lodge,* Box 72, Naivasha; tel. 29; bookings to African Tours & Hotels (p. 87). 32 varied dbls, all but tent dbls w/bath. Rates: FB: luxury cottage sgl—230/–, dbl—307/–; banda sgl—110/–, dbl— 175/–; nyumba (simpler than banda) sgl—77/–, dbl—142/–; incl tax, levy, service; also low season rates. Credit: DC. Lodge is situated on 106 acres sloping down to the lake and marina. 6 cottages are super in comfort, also in price; 12 cement-block bandas are like old American motel cottages; 4 nyumbas are white clapboard, have damp rooms with clammy bathroom; the 10 tents are raggy. Main building is pleasant. Large pool, riding, tennis. Rating: 2d-class international and local, everything overpriced. . . . *Rima Island Lodge,* bookings to Margaret Burke Ltd., Box 14040, Nairobi; tel. 61570. 2-story Danish-style house, furnished, on 5-acre island, with accommodations for 6 or 8; visitors bring own food. Rates: 100/– per person. 2 boats for use of guests. Access by boat from Marina Club or Fisherman's Camp. . . . *Carnelley's Fisherman's Camp,* Box 79, Naivasha; tel. 5Y2. 17 km from highway. Self-service camp with tents and cabins, and accommodations in a private home for 4 overseas visitors. Tents (at lake edge or 200 feet above) have hard floor, are furnished, rent for 40/– for large tent, 20/– for small tent. Fee in self-service cabin is 30/– per person. . . . *Naivasha Youth Hostel,* bookings to Warden, c/o YMCA Central, Box 30330, Nairobi; tel. 22217. 13 km from highway. Accommodations in rondavels; no meals available. Fees: 5/– for YHA members; 7/50 for nonmembers. . . . **Camping** at any of four places. At the Marina Club, sites are near the water below club grounds. Hot shower, drinking water, toilets, use of club pool, bar. Fees: 12/50 per campsite plus 5/– per person daily membership. Safariland's campground is nicely shaded with fever trees filled with squabbling black birds. Toilets, showers, use of club bar, pool. Fee: 10/– per adult. Carnelley's, by comparison, offers no facilities but a toilet, and it's hard to see the lake. Tentsites in green grass in deep shade. Fee: 5/– per person. Camping also at Youth Hostel.

Continuing on the highway, you come to Km 87: *Naivasha,* an uninteresting town started by railway surveyors, settled by many European farmers beginning in 1904. **Accommodations:** *Naivasha Inn,* Box 85, tel. 10. 6 sgls, 3 dbls; only 6 w/bath. Rates: B&B: sgl—38/–; dbl—76/–. Credit: DC. Mainly roadside refreshment stop; no reason to stay here. Rating: 2d- or 3d-class local. Govt. class D.

In town is a turnoff (R) on C67 to North and South Kinangop, Aberdare National Park, and Nyeri.

Km 99: Turnoff (L) on D323 (North Lake Road), the other end of the Lake Naivasha circuit road. About 9 km along, you turn right to get to *Mount Eburu* (Ol Doinyo Eburu or Opuru or Bura), 9,365 feet, a Pliocene volcano that has about 200 steam vents, mostly on the north slope. The government and the U.N. have committed $2.2 million for exploration and development of Rift Valley steam jets as a source of geothermal power. Farmers have long been condensing the steam into water.

Lake Elmenteita

Km 114: *Gilgil* (pop. 4,178), a farming center. The area to the east was the former location of the *Happy Valley Crowd,* a legendary bunch of British settlers whose high life in the 1920s and 1930s inspired the joke, "Are you married or do you live in Kenya?" Km 119: You are now passing *Lake Elmenteita,* a 7-square-mile soda lake no more than 6 feet deep, situated on private land in a lunarlike country of lava flows. On the western side the flows have created a series of bays and inlets and rocky islets where the greater flamingo breeds periodically (Lake Natron is the other known breeding place in East Africa). Ornithologists and others can be given permission to visit and camp at the lake by the owner, Arthur Cole Ltd., P.O. Gilgil. Km 121: Picturesque *Church of Good Will* (1949).

Kariandusi

Km 122: Kariandus diatomite quarry (L), then turnoff (L) to the *Kariandusi Prehistoric Site,* 400,000-year-old Stone Age campsite, with a small shelter protecting some stone tools, fossil bones, also some fault lines. The site was discovered by Dr. Leakey in 1928, excavated by the Leakeys 1946–47. Admission: 5/– for nonresident adult, 2/– for resident adult; 2/– and 1/– per child. The –/50 guide pamphlet is not very useful.

Km 132: You are now passing the *Soysambu* (Masai, "spotted rock") *Estate,* now almost the sole remnant of the vast estates owned by Lord Delamere, the pioneer farmer of the "White Highlands." (See Elspeth Huxley's superb two-volume biography, *White Man's Country.*)

Km 146: Turnoff (L) on D320 to Elmenteita town 19 km. Km 147: Lanet and turnoff (R) on C69 (our Route K-9) to Nyahururu (Thomson's Falls), Nanyuki.

Hyrax Hill

Km 152: Turnoff (R) to *Hyrax Hill Prehistoric Site,* an important Stone Age settlement found by Dr. Leakey in 1926. The stone circles, burial mounds, pit dwellings and mounds, and stone-walled fort on a hilltop were excavated by Mary Leakey 1937–38 and 1965. This is the most important known site of the Neolithic stone-bowl culture. The non-Negroid people who lived here were agricultural, had platters made of stone (this was the characteristic household utensil), buried their dead under cairns, and also played the *bao* game (see "Shopping" section, p. 132), with the board carved in rock. With a guide, you walk on a path from site to site. In the North-East Village are 13 sunken enclosures or pit dwellings; Pit D is open to public view. At the Iron Age Settlement are two large stone-walled enclosures and a hut circle adjoining, and two smaller hut circles built of loosely stacked rocks (they had grass or hide roofs). In the cemetery at the Neolithic Occupation Site were found 19 burial mounds (including 9 females) with grave goods such as platters and pestles. The stone-walled Hill Fort was probably built as a lookout post. Entrance fees: same as Kariandusi above. Visitor's guide for 1/– is not that useful. In the museum (formerly a settler's house) are artifacts from here, Kariandusi, Ol Kalou and Oleondo, Prospect Farm, Gamble's Cave, Nakuru Burial site, and the Njoro River Rock Shelter.

Menengai Crater

Km 153: *State Lodge* (R), the president's Rift Valley residence. Km 154: Turnoff (R) on Showground Road to *Menengai Crater*. Crater Climb road takes you 7½ km to the rim of the 7,475-foot caldera, which is more than 11 km across, 35 square miles in size, 2,000 feet deep. Menengai is Masai for "place of the corpses," and is so named for the time, about 1854, the Naivasha Masai shoved the losers of a battle, the Laikipia Masai, over the edge. There are good views in all directions, and on the rim a picnic shelter and latrine.

Lake Nakuru

Km 154: Just past the Menengai Crater turnoff, you come to the main traffic circle at *Nakuru*. Follow the signs to the left to *Lake Nakuru National Park* (gate 5 km), site of what Roger Tory Peterson has said is the "most staggering bird spectacle in my . . . years of bird-watching": more than a million flamingos (mostly of the lesser variety) feeding in the shallow waters of the soda lake. The pink spectacle almost obscures the fact that there are some 392 other species to be found; British naturalist Sir Peter Scott says it is "the finest bird lake I have seen."

The first national park in East Africa established (in 1961) to protect birdlife, Lake Nakuru park now covers 14,000 acres (10,000 acres is the lake itself) but this is being expanded after an international conservationist campaign focused attention on the land and population pressure on the lake. The Minister of Wildlife and Tourism announced in 1974 that 35,000 acres were to be added in early 1975. But one continuing threat to the lake is from pollution—sewage from Nakuru town (pop. 47,151) draining into a lake with no outlet—and the town garbage dump, next to the park entrance, causes smoke and attracts scads of marabou storks, which also prey on weaker flamingos.

A visitor to Kenya should not miss spending at least a couple of hours at Lake Nakuru. Binoculars are a must, as is a camera if you have a long lens (at least 200 mm) and patience to sit in a bird blind (there is at least one good blind near Hippo Point). The park roads go very near the northwest shore, which is the best place to see flamingos en masse. There is also a road on a narrow ledge between the rocky shore and Baboon Escarpment, a good vantage point to observe cormorants and other birds sitting in trees in the water, since you are hidden by bushes. Also, unlike the low-lying northwest shore, here you can get above flocks of flamingos, resulting in better pictures.

The lake is soda because it has no outlet, and all the minerals carried in by the three inlets have been stored and concentrated, resulting in highly alkaline water. This is the most favorable medium for the growth of the blue-green algae *Spirulina*, which is the primary food of the lesser flamingo. It is a perfect cycle: the flamingos eat about 150 tons of algae a day and deposit about 50 tons of droppings in the water; this decomposes into compounds used with sunlight by the algae to double their numbers in only a few hours, providing more food for the flamingos. The algae, incidentally, have a carotene pigment that turns the flamingo's white feathers pink. The flamingo feeds by filtering the algae out of the water by a complex set of lamellae, or thin flat scales, in the bill. Often seen on the outer edges, in deeper water, is the greater flamingo, which is bigger (56 inches as opposed to the lesser's 40 inches) and paler, and has a flesh-pink bill rather than a carmine bill. The greater flamingo feeds on insects and crustaceans rather than algae. Both species breed at Lake Natron in Tanzania, but the greater flamingo also breeds at Lake Elmenteita. Flamingos are to be found on nearly all the alkaline lakes in the Rift Valley, including in Ethiopia; half of the world's six million flamingos are in the Rift Valley. Incidentally, East African flamingos are not as violently pink-orange as those in the U.S.

Don't ignore the other birds. White and pink-backed pelicans are common (and you can get closer to them; flamingos edge away at the same speed you approach them). Also common are the long-tailed and white-necked cormorants. African darters (in dead trees), yellow-billed and marabou storks. Egyptian geese, African pochards, Cape widgeons, little and great crested grebes, African spoonbills, blacksmith plovers, Kittlitz sand plovers. Among European migrants: ruffs, little stints, ringed plovers, common and curlew sandpipers. The best bird list is in the 10/– National Parks booklet, but there are also checklists in Williams's field guide to the parks and in a pamphlet available at the Stag's Head Hotel.

In the lake live about 28 hippos, usually seen near Hippo Point, where the water is deep. Found in large herds are *Defassa waterbucks,* which differ from the *common waterbuck* in having white buttocks rather than a white ring. Both kinds are grayish brown and heavily built but friendly-looking and elegant, with large, furry ears, wet black

Waterbuck

Bohor reedbuck

noses, and crescent horns. You will also spot impala in the woodland, perhaps the *Bohor reedbuck,* a small, graceful, yellowish or reddish fawn-colored antelope with short, hook-shaped horns; when alarmed, reedbuck run like a rocking horse and make a shrill whistle. They graze in small groups in early morning and dusk and are never found too far from water. Compared with other Kenya game parks, reedbuck are quite common here.

When to Visit

European migrant birds are here September to April. The latter part of the dry season (February–March) can be very dusty and the lake reduced considerably in size, meaning the flamingos are feeding farther from the viewing road. December–January and May–June are good times.

Getting There, Getting Around

The main park road goes 20 km from the gate around to the mouth of the Nderit River, and from the gate a road goes along the northern shore a few km. Roads are passable in ordinary sedans all the time. Nakuru is on many package itineraries; see listings KP-8, 29, 32–35, 37, 79, 85–86. There is a Sunday bus service from Nakuru into the park for the benefit of the carless.

Accommodations

Inside the park there is camping only. A lodge may be built on a bluff in Baharini Wildlife Sanctuary near the northern lakeshore. **Camping** is at two sites: one, the Njoro River Campsite, is in a shady forest of yellow-barked acacias (fever trees—so called from the observed tendency of people in times past to come down with fever after camping near them—that is, near water, where mosquitoes breed). The other, Magadi Campsite, is more in the open amid dry, yellow grass near the lake. The first is shadier, but the second is nearer the lake, enabling you to hear the great waterfall-like roar of a million flamingos when you wake at dawn. Fee: 5/– per adult, 1/– per child, payable at the gate. Drinking water available. Also camping outside the park: in a large open field next to Nakuru Showground (no camping during annual mid-June show), 5/– per person; and on the rim of Menengai Crater for 3/– per adult. Both sites have latrine; Showground site has running water. Menengai site could be very windy, but the views are good. **Accommodations in town:** *Midland Hotel,* Box 257, Nakuru; tel. 2543. On main road. 25 sgls, 28 dbls, all w/bath or shower. Rates: B&B: sgl—80/–; dbl—103/–, incl. 1928 Midland is well kept, clean, unpresumptuous. Oldish rooms are quite well appointed. Dining room has table d'hôte (breakfast—6/–; lunch—10/–; dinner—12/50), some à la carte. Rating: 1st-class local, better deal than Stag's Head, though Lake Naivasha is a better place than Nakuru to stay. Govt. class B. . . . *Stag's Head Hotel,* Box 143, Nakuru; tel. 2516; cable STAGS. Kenyatta St., downtown. 34 sgls, 35 dbls, 3 trpls, most w/bath. Rates: B&B: sgl—100/– to 126/–; dbl—168/–, incl tax, levy, service. Credit: AE, BA, DC. Modest exterior with peeling paint, well-used lobby, poorly kept lounge-bar (renovation and new bar in early 1973), not bad dining room, unpretentious but roomy rooms. Rating: 1st-class local with rates too high. Govt. class B.

Nakuru

Compared with the national park, there's not much attraction to the town of *Nakuru* (Masai, either "swirling dust" or "little, bitter-water lake"). Kenya's third-largest city, and HQ of Rift Valley Province, Nakuru was established in 1900 when the railway reached the area. As Europeans settled, it became a farm center and then virtually the capital of the *"White Highlands,"* a 16,173-square-mile European farming reserve ("Native Lands" by the same 1950 definition took up 52,097 square miles). The White Highlands were not open to African ownership at all until 1960, and today all the European farms are being bought out. The town is still the farming capital of Kenya. The Kenya Farmer's Association, a nationwide co-op trading association, is headquartered here, and Nakuru is center of the *pyrethrum* industry.

Around Nakuru and elsewhere you will see fields of daisylike white pyrethrum flowers, the concentrate of which is a natural insecticide. Kenya is the world's leading producer of pyrethrum.

Attractions in town include the *Arboretum,* founded 1927; the *Bethany Bookshop* (run by the World Gospel Mission), which has the concession to collect discarded flamingo feathers, turning them into delightful "flowers" ($5 for a corsage by airmail, from Box 211, Nakuru); and *Nakuru Tanners,* on Ebrahim Estate, which tans sheepskin and makes sheepskin coats. South of the lake is *Gamble's Cave,* a Stone Age site occupied first about 30,000 B.C. Here were found skeletons of a Caucasoid people, buried in a contracted or fetal position, the earliest known indication of systematic religious practice. You can visit the cave by applying to the National Museum.

Continuing the route, drive through Nakuru on the main road. At Km 156, a traffic circle by the HQ of the Kenya Farmer's Association (KFA), there is a turnoff (R) on D365 to Mogotio, Lake Hannington 90 km, Marigat, and Lake Baringo (Kampi ya Samaki 110 km).

Lake Hannington

Lake Hannington is a different sort of lake. Very alkaline, measuring 13 square miles, with an inhospitable shoreline, and located in hot thornbush country, the lake is either very good or horrid. Along with flamingos (as many as 575,000), Hannington has hot sulfur springs, steam jets, and thermal geysers (where almost-boiling water erupts), which may be tapped to generate electricity. From Mogotio, go straight, avoiding the left fork to Marigat; go 4½ km to fork left along road signposted to Alphega, and about 4 km farther, fork right, then again 5 km later. Go 9 km, then fork left and go 20 km to the lake. About 82 km along the road, you'll reach a County Council barrier (5/– per car; 1/– per adult). At Maji ya Moto there's good camping near a hot springs, and a Land-Rover track to within a mile from the lake—or you can do the 2½-hour walk from the campsite. A proposed national park, the lake was first recorded by Bishop James Hannington, who was associated with the Church Missionary Society. He took Thomson's route through Masailand and was murdered at a Nile crossing by order of the Kabaka of Buganda in October 1885.

Lake Baringo

Lake Baringo is, like Naivasha, a fresh-water lake, even though it has no apparent outlet; in fact, there is underground drainage, with

the lake water coming out at Kapedo hot springs 50 km north (also
a hot waterfall there). The main attractions of the 50-square-mile lake
are birdwatching, fishing (boats for rent), *Jonathan Leakey's snake
farm,* the ruins of *Fort Baringo* (a halting place for caravans on the
way to Lake Victoria), and the *Pokot* (Suk) and *Njemps* (Ilchamus)
villages nearby. The road to Baringo goes through land occupied, and
overgrazed, by the *Tugen,* a small tribe whose most famous son is
Vice-President Daniel arap Moi. The Njemps, in the immediate vicinity of the lake, fish picturesquely from reed boats. Leakey's snake
farm, half a mile from Kampi ya Samaki, is the only commercial
snake farm in East Africa and is one of only 12 in the world where
snakes are milked for their venom, which is frozen and sent overseas
for processing into snakebite serum (antivenin). The antivenin is prepared by injecting increasingly larger doses of venom into a horse until the animal is immune because of the increase in antibodies. The
horse is then bled and the antibodies separated to produce antivenin.
Leakey's farm has between 1,000 and 1,500 snakes of nine species
in captivity. Admission: 10/–. Birdwatchers can visit *Gibraltar Island,*
where the largest nesting colony of goliath herons in East Africa is
located. Baringo **accommodations:** *Lake Baringo Lodge,* Box 1375,
Nakuru. 10 dbls w/bath. Rates: FB: sgl—220/–; dbl—400/– (East
African residents: 120/– and 200/–), incl daily membership. We
haven't been to this lodge, but we can scarcely believe the incredible
charges levied against nonresidents—it's the highest in Eastern Africa
except for suites in a few hotels. We hear the Spanish-style lodge, built
in 1968, is very homey, with oriental rugs on the walls, Georgian
silverware, lots of bric-a-brac. Pool. . . . *Lake Baringo Tenters Camp,*
bookings to Safari Air, Box 41951, Nairobi; tel. 556036, 556589. Luxury tented camp on Ol Kokwa Island opened in 1973 by Jonathan
Leakey, has 20 beds. Rates: FB: sgl—180/–; dbl—260/–, incl tax,
levy, service. . . . *Lake Baringo Self-Service Lodge,* bookings to A. A.
& Bunson (p. 86). 3 fully equipped houses with different rates: dbl
cabins—35/– per person; 3-dbl house—120/– for up to 6 persons.
. . . **Camping** waterside near the self-service lodge. Fee: 20/– per
tent. Free camping on lakeshore north of Kampi ya Samaki, where
the road peters out. . . . Note: Charter plane is the best way to get
to Baringo; see package listing KP-25.

From the KFA in Nakuru, continue north out of town, past the Industrial Area, and you will soon come to turnoffs (R) to Eldama

Ravine and (L) to Njoro and Elburgon, and farther down, Molo (best reached by a later turnoff from the main highway). At Njoro is a road south to Mau Narok and the Mau Escarpment and on to Narok and Masai Mara Game Reserve. The *Mau Escarpment* is the western wall of the Rift Valley, stretching from near the Tanzania border to Eldama Ravine. High points are *Mount Mau,* 10,002 feet, and *Melili,* 10,165 feet. Trout fishing in numerous streams; Kericho is a good fishing base.

Km 197: Turnoff (L) on D316 (our Route K-11) to Molo, Highlands Hotel. Km 205: Turnoff (L) on B1 to Molo (alternate), Londiani, Kericho, Kisumu, Lake Victoria (see Route K-11). Km 235: *Equator.* Km 237: *Timboroa Summit,* 9,320 feet. Km 243: Turnoff (R) to *Timboroa station,* 9,001 feet, the highest in Africa and the highest in the Commonwealth. The highest *point* on the railroad is 9,136 feet. Km 247: Turnoff (R) to Ainabkoi and scenic alternate road to Eldoret through Kipkabus and Kaptagat, beautiful farmland and quaint old railway stations.

Nandi Hills

Km 257: Turnoff (L) on C36 (Sclater's Road) to Lessos, Burnt Forest, Nandi Hills, Kapsabet, also scenic alternate from here through hills back to main highway at Km 286. The *Nandi Hills,* a tea-growing area partly settled by Europeans, are the center of the *Nandi tribe* (Nandi District HQ is at Kapsabet) and were once not quite so peaceful. The Nandi more than any other tribe in Kenya resisted British rule. Lugard reported in 1890 that no caravan "had ever yet dared to cross their hills," and when the railway came through a decade later, the Nandi attacked surveyors, stole entire lengths of iron rail and copper telegraph wire to make ornaments and weapons, committed other robberies up and down the line, killed *askaris* (African soldiers) and police, rail workers and traders. Forts were built, and the rail line was patrolled; and there was a big *baraza* (official meeting) in July 1905. But the Nandi Rebellion continued. Full-scale military operations in 1905–06 ended the rebellion with total Nandi losses set at 1,117 killed; 16,000 head of cattle and 36,000 sheep and goats were captured, and in the last drive, nearly 5,000 huts and grain storage bins were burned. The Nandi, like good American Indians, went to the new reserve, and by 1908 the British governor reported they had "settled down in the most exemplary manner."

Sharing the Nandi Hills are the *Ndorobo* (pop. 21,034, in scattered

Kenya locations), a bow-and-arrow hunting and collecting tribe who are among the survivors of the earliest inhabitants of Kenya. Nandi and Masai legends say that the Ndorobo were the original people in the world.

In the Nandi forests lives Kenya's Abominable Snowman or Loch Ness Monster, locally called the *Nandi Bear*. He has been described as "a very wise animal" that lives in a house with a hearth and hunts at night, killing people but not eating them. "But," says one local authority, "he likes to beat people with his stick, and so he has learned how to speak Kipsigis, Nandi, and Ndorobo. When he hears people from these tribes talking in the forests, slowly, slowly he creeps up to them, joins in their conversation and then jumps out on them and kills them." The Nandi say the bear likes to snatch people's heads. "It jumps at the head, gets hold of it, and runs away, leaving the body behind." One way to defeat the bear's impulse is, if you go out at night, to carry a round cooking pot on your head. Even the European settlers had stories featuring the Nandi Bear, something resembling a two-legged spotted hyena; the club in Nandi Hills town is named the Nandi Bear Club. The creature can be caught. A Kipsigis tribesman said that you have to sit up in a tree with a bow and arrow and say, "Come on." "Then it dances around at the foot of the tree and shakes its stick, but it can't get at you. So then you shoot it."

Km 276: Turnoff (R) to Kipkabus and *World's End* viewpoint over the Rift Valley. From the highway, go 15 km to Kipkabus station and proceed toward Kaptagat, turning right 1½ km at the Forest Department signboard. 2½ km later, fork right and go through the Forest Department barrier. Another 1½ km, turn left and then fork left, cross a dip, and take the second turn on the right onto a minor track. Go 3½ km and turn sharp right, then a bit less than 1 km to reach Kapchebelel Church (L). Walk 150 yards to the edge of the escarpment, and there's World's End.

Eldoret

Km 286: Turnoff (L) on D305 from Lessos (see Km 257 above). Km 308: Turnoff (L) on C39 to Nandi Hills, Kapsabet, Kisumu, Lake Victoria. You are now in *Eldoret* (pop. 18,196), center of the fertile mixed-farming Uasin Gishu Plateau, where wheat, maize, and most of Kenya's wattle (the bark used in tanning) is grown. The Plateau was until Independence the location of a colony of South African Boers, who have mostly trekked away. The town was first known

as "64" from the colonial postmaster general's choice of vacant farm
block 64 as the site of a post office. "64" was renamed Eldoret from
the river Eldore—the *t* was added because it was thought most Nandi
place names ended in *t*. Eldoret is well put together but has little attraction for the tourist. **Accommodations:** *New Lincoln Hotel,* Box 47,
tel. 2093. 7 sgls, 11 dbls, all w/bath. Rates: B&B: sgl—55/–; dbl—
90/–. 1927 hotel expanded in 1947. Rooms plain, functional. Rating:
2d-class local. Govt. class C (?). . . . *New Wagon Wheel Hotel,* Box
503, tel. 2753. 10 sgls, 10 dbls, only 2 w/bath. Rates: B&B: sgl—
45/–; dbl—65/–. Old hotel with barely acceptable rooms. Rating:
3d-class local. . . . **Camping** at the New Wagon Wheel for 10/– per
tent; bath is 4/– per person. You camp next to hotel, get noise from
train yard, hotel, dogs, crying babies. Try forests northwest of town.

Km 322: Turnoff (R) on B2 (our Route K-11) to Soy, Kitale,
Mount Elgon. Km 339: *Turbo,* small farm town in a reforestation
area. Km 371: Turnoff (L) on A1 (our Route K-11) to Kakamega,
Kisumu. Km 377: *Webuye* (formerly Broderick Falls), where the
$43-million Panafrican Paper Mills, the biggest single industrial project
in East Africa, is being built. It will be capable of producing two miles
of paper roll in four minutes. Km 401: *Bungoma,* a district town. Km
433: Uganda border at Malaba. Km 451: Tororo.

Route K-11: Western Kenya Circuit from Nakuru

This circular route takes you through part of Kenya that tourists
rarely see. From the floor of the Rift Valley at Nakuru, it ascends the
western wall of the Rift and goes through pretty Highlands to Kericho,
the center of the tea industry, and then down through fertile fields to
the humid shores of Lake Victoria. Our suggested route—a long
(900-km) journey—goes north from Kisumu to the neat farm town of
Kitale, near Mount Elgon, circles north of the pretty Cherangani Hills,
then turns south through the rugged picturesque and car-rattling Kerio
Valley, ending up at Nakuru. The road is mostly paved, but it is all
dirt from Kitale on; this part is best done in a VW bus or a four-
wheel-drive.

Because this is more of a made-up route, and because we did not
cover the last half of it, we adopt a different format in describing it.

Here are the rough kilometer distances: Km 0: Nakuru. Km 41:
Go left on D316 to Molo. Km 45: Molo. Km 55: Mau Summit. Km
57: Junction with B1—go left. Km 63: Turnoff (R) to Londiani 3 km,

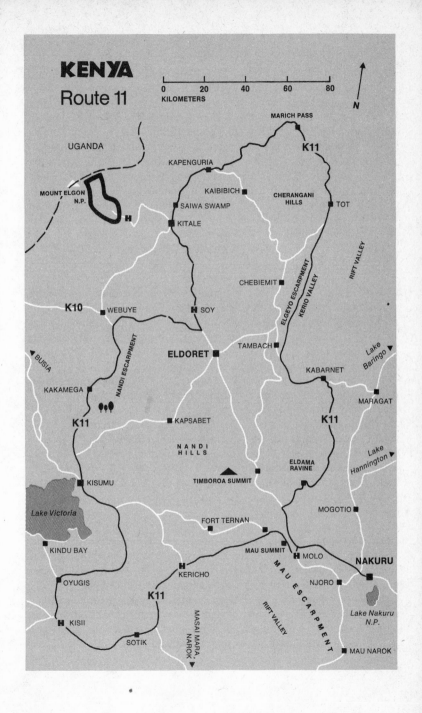

KENYA
Route 11

KILOMETERS
0   20   40   60   80

N

UGANDA

MARICH PASS

K11

KAPENGURIA

KAIBIBICH   CHERANGANI
                   HILLS

MOUNT ELGON
N.P.

SAIWA SWAMP   TOT

KITALE

CHEBIEMIT

ELGEYO ESCARPMENT
KERIO VALLEY
RIFT VALLEY

K10   WEBUYE   SOY

▲ BUSIA

TAMBACH   Lake
                     Baringo ▼

ELDORET

NANDI ESCARPMENT

KABARNET

KAKAMEGA

MARAGAT

K11   KAPSABET   K11

NANDI
HILLS

ELDAMA
RAVINE   Lake
                        Hannington ▼

TIMBOROA SUMMIT

KISUMU

MOGOTIO

Lake Victoria   FORT TERNAN

KINDU BAY

MAU SUMMIT   MOLO   NAKURU

OYUGIS   NJORO

KERICHO   Lake Nakuru
                                     N.P.
K11

KISII   MAU ESCARPMENT

MASAI MARA, NAROK

SOTIK   RIFT VALLEY

MAU NAROK

▼

Lumbwa, Fort Ternan 22 km. Km 108: Kericho. Km 110: Turnoff (R) on B1 direct to Kisumu—go left. Km 143: Junction with B7—left to Masai Mara, right to Kisii—go right. Km 161: Sotik. Km 206: Kisii. Km 296: Junction with B1 from Kericho. Km 326: Kisumu; go north on A1. Km 379: Kakamega and turnoff (L) to Mumias. Km 421: Junction with A104—left goes to Webuye and Uganda, right to Eldoret, Kitale; go right. Km 452: Turbo. Km 469: Turnoff (L) on B2 to Kitale; go left. Km 478: Turnoff (L) to Soy. Km 503: Moi's Bridge. Km 524: Kitale and turnoff to Mount Elgon National Park. Km 556: Kapenguria. Km 608: Marich Pass. Km 619: Sigor. Km 658: Tot. Km 745: Chebloch. Km 757: Kabarnet. Km 865: Eldama Ravine. Km 927: Nakuru.

Following are details on the main points of interest.

Molo

Molo (pop. 4,240) is in the middle of sheep country that on a cloudy day looks remarkably like the West Country of England, with high (8,000 feet), rolling, grassy hills. The Highlands Golf Club (at the hotel) boasts the "highest tee" in the Commonwealth—9,000 feet. **Accommodations:** *Highlands Hotel,* Box 142, Molo; tel. 50; cable GOLF. At Km 49, past town. 20 dbls w/bath. Rates: FB: sgl—105/–; dbl—210/–, incl tax, levy, service. Credit: DC. Charming country hotel dating to 1930s. Rooms nicely furnished; the oldest, coziest, have fireplaces and open onto the flower gardens. Bar, lounge, and dining room are warmed to a British tolerance by more fireplaces. Table d'hôte meals (breakfast—8/–; lunch—15/–; dinner—17/–) feature Molo lamb often. Golf, riding, tennis, driving excursions. In 1974 new owners began renovation. Rating: 1st class local, relaxing, pleasant, cool (bring warm clothes). ★. Govt. class C. . . . **Camping** near the hotel; inquire there.

Kericho

Kericho (pop. 10,144) is center of Kenya's tea industry. All around the town grow the vivid green tea bushes that produce $43 million worth of tea a year. Kericho gets rain almost every day, making the area, with its acidic soil and warm climate, perfect for tea growing. The plants are pruned regularly to form low bushes with spread-out foliage. Throughout the year, pickers with colorful rubberized aprons (to avoid catching on branches) move slowly through the green sea of bushes, plucking two leaves and a bud and throwing it over their shoulders into large wicker baskets. Once weighed, the tea is taken to a factory (the local Brooke Bond tea factory is 6 km east of town), where it is withered (dried), cut (macerated to release the flavor juices), fermented, dried, and sorted. You can tour the tea fields and the factory by contacting the Public Relations Officer, Brooke Bond Liebig Ltd., Box 20, Kericho; tel. 146; office is next to the factory, and arrangements are also made at the Tea Hotel.

Tea was first grown in Kenya at Limuru, with the first planting at Kericho in 1906. It was a minor industry until big companies began planting in the 1920s, and Kenya's first big tea factory was erected outside Kericho in 1927. This decade, small-holder production is expected to surpass estate production. Brooke Bond also owns *Kenya Fishing Flies* here, the largest fly-tying factory in the world. The 300 workers (180 tiers) produce more than 20,000 dozen flies a month from any of 2,500 different patterns, using some 2,000 different materials, including 30 different shades of green silk alone.

Kericho (from *kerichek,* an herb medicine), a district town, was established in 1902. It is the center of the agricultural *Kipsigis* tribe, Kenya's eighth-largest (pop. 471,459) and the second-largest of the Kalenjin-speaking group. Besides tea, of interest in Kericho is the *Arboretum,* with labeled trees and interesting birds, located on Chagaik Estate (inquire at Brooke Bond office). For package tours visiting Kericho, see listings KP-34–35, 85–87. **Accommodations:** *Tea Hotel,* Box 75, Kericho; tel. 40; bookings to A. A. & Bunson (p. 86). 20 sgls, 24 dbls, all w/bath. Rates: B&B: sgl—75/– or 85/–; dbl—115/– or 125/–. Suites or cottages with sitting rm: sgl—105/–; dbl—200/– or 205/–. Credit: DC. Charming hostelry on large, well-kept grounds, built (1952) and owned by Brooke Bond, which will at a moment's notice organize a tea tour for guests, or send them on any of seven other tours without charge. Rooms, all in main building, 2 annexes, and 4 cottages, are extremely nice; cottages have fireplaces. Big, well-decorated, wood-floored dining room (table d'hôte breakfast—9/50; lunch—15/50; dinner—18/50) is adjacent to smart barroom, residents' lounge, friendly lobby. Rating: 1st-class international, deservedly popular with safari operators, who book their clients (individuals, all) into this and other quiet, select hotels. ★★. Govt. class B.

Lambwe Valley Game Reserve, west of Kisii near the shore of Lake Victoria, is a 260-square-mile reserve protecting roan antelope, Jackson's hartebeest, topi, waterbuck, and other animals. The infrequently visited reserve may be expanded to include the Gwasi and Gembe hills, so far not much inhabited or farmed, and converted into a national park.

Kisumu and Lake Victoria

Kisumu (pop. 32,431), established in 1900, is Kenya's fourth-largest city and principal Lake Victoria port; the town is center of the *Luo,* Kenya's second-largest (pop. 1.5 million) and second most influential tribe. The Luo were originally pastoral but now cultivate the land and fish as well. The tribe is known for its rich culture (oral tradition, music, and dancing), even though they have adopted many Western habits, including style of dress. Luos do not circumcise, which is unusual for an East African tribe. The city of Kisumu, HQ of Nyanza Province, has few attractions for the visitor. The big lake port may be worth a quick look. All the big boats have been built abroad, transported in sections to Lake Victoria, and put together and launched. Two huge train ferries, the *Umoja* and the *Uhuru,* assembled and launched here in 1965–66, and the steamers *Victoria* and *Usoga,* are operated by East African Railways, which handles a quarter-million tons of lake cargo a year.

The most convenient place at Kisumu to see *Lake Victoria,* largest lake in Africa and second-largest fresh-water lake in the world, is at *Hippo Point,* where you may see hippos, crocodiles, and numerous birds. The government has some hopes to make the lake a tourist attraction, but, with bilharzia in the water (except off some of the uninhabited islands), endemic malaria, and a generally sticky climate, it will be difficult. **Kisumu accommodations:** *Kisumu Hotel,* bookings to KTDC (p. 87). Near Hippo Point on Impala Walk, is to open in late 1975, with a-c rms, pool. . . . *New Kisumu Hotel,* Box 1690, tel. 2520, 2652. 13 sgls, 27 dbls w/bath, 8 sgls, 9 dbls w/o bath. Rates: B&B: sgl—100/–; dbl—158/–, incl; a-c 15/–. Large 1940s structure with clean, well-kept rooms. Rating: 1st-class local. Govt. class C. . . . *YWCA* has a hostel for both sexes. Rates: B&B: 10/– per person in 4-bed room. . . . **Camping** at New Kisumu Hotel, 20/– per party. Drinking water, toilet, bath, free ice. Where to Eat: *Chateau Pereira,* Achieng' Oneko Road, tel. 2995. Credit: DC.

Kakamega, Western Province capital, was the center of a gold rush in the early 1930s that drew a thousand gold prospectors hoping to open up a new Klondike or Kimberley.

Kakamega and Kaimosi Forests, south of Kakamega town, are a peculiarity, since they are of the West African type, with a wide range of bird, animal, and reptile life. Kakamega Forest is, says John G. Williams, one of the best places in Kenya for birdwatching, and the two forests have many butterflies.

Kitale

Kitale (pop. 11,573), a railway terminus and center of the rich Trans-Nzoia maize, wheat, coffee, and sisal farming area, was known to early Arab slavers as Quitale. The tidy, European-looking town was founded in 1920, seven years after settlers began farming around it. Near Kitale is the *Forest Department nursery,* worth a visit for its birds; picnicking allowed. About 14 km from Kitale is the *Western Kenya Museum,* founded in 1926 by Colonel H. F. Stoneham and willed by him to the nation; the National Museum has now reopened it since the collection, mainly natural history and ethnography, has been reorganized. Kitale **accommodations:** *Kitale Hotel,* Box 41, tel. 41. Kenyatta St. in town center. 7 sgls, 9 dbls w/bath, 10 sgls, 10 dbls w/o bath. Rates: B&B: sgl—65/–; dbl—100/–. Credit: DC. 1920s hotel with newer rooms nice and light, old rooms dark and small. Rating: Less than 1st-class local. Govt. class C. . . . *Kitale Club,* Box 30, tel. 30. Rates: B&B: dbl—80/– and up. . . . **Camping** for 5/– per person at Greaves Farm, 3 km from main road, turnoff 11 km south of Kitale. Also here is 12-bed *Kitale Youth Hostel,* self-catering. Fee: 10/– per nonmember. Toilet, shower; hot water, eggs, milk available.

Mount Elgon

Mount Elgon National Park. Straight through Kitale 20 km brings you to a T-junction at Endebess; go left here to the gate into the national park 7 km. Mount Elgon, seventh-highest mountain in Africa, is a Pliocene volcano straddling the Uganda border, with the highest peak, Wagagai, 14,178 feet, in Uganda. There is a series of peaks 13,000 feet and higher on the edge of the crater, which is 4–6½ miles across and 2,000 feet deep. The mountain mass covers 1,800 square miles, making it larger than either Mount Kenya or Kilimanjaro. The national park, created in 1968, covers 37,500 acres in an hourglass-shaped segment on Kenya's side of the mountain. The name is not English; it is a corruption of the Masai name Ol Doinyo Ilgoon, "mountain shaped like breasts." Its other name is Mount Masaba, which is what Henry M. Stanley, possibly the first European to see the mountain, called it in 1875. The indomitable Thomson explored Elgon's caves in 1883, but the summit was not reached until 1890, by a party of three including Sir Frederick Jackson.

Like other mountains, Elgon has wildlife, but it won't be easy game viewing. Animals about are the forest elephant, buffalo, leopard, waterbuck, oribi, bushbuck, and red forest duiker. Some white rhinos have been imported and are kept in enclosures near Campsite No. 1.

The mountain offers pleasant walking in the open moorland (giant groundsel, lobelia, heath) and long views, though the lower forest, (cedar, olive, *Podocarpus*, bamboo) is unpleasant for walking. The paths are good, the going not steep. Elgon can be climbed any time, but the best season in the high parts is October–March, secondarily June–July. Of the three approaches, one is from Mbale, Uganda, one from Kimilili on a track high up the southern slope, the third from Kitale up through the national park to 10,000 feet. From Kitale you can drive to the roadhead, then walk 4 to 5 hours to Koitoboss peak or the crater rim. See Robson's guide to Kenya mountains. The park roads are fair but not easy to negotiate well unless you have four-wheel-drive, a VW bus, or other EPC (enterprising private car). Besides the forest and bamboo, both considerably eerie, there are a few viewpoints, but the most interesting attractions for those driving are the various signposted caves.

Accommodations

Mount Elgon Lodge, bookings to KTDC (p. 87). Converted mansion with a new wing, located near park, accommodates 50. Views over Cherangani Hills. . . . *Sasa Hut,* on Uganda side, owned by possibly defunct Mountain Club of Uganda. . . . *Mount Elgon Lodge* (*Youth Hostel*), single-room hut at 11,000 feet, 29 km from Kimilili Forest Station. . . . **Camping** is at a site near the rhino enclosures, about 3 km from main gate. No facilities. Fee: 5/– per person.

Saiwa Swamp

Saiwa Swamp, near Kipsoen Settlement Scheme a few miles from Kitale, is a sanctuary for sitatungas, antelopes that have developed especially elongated hooves, enabling them to walk on very soft ground or even floating vegetation without sinking through. Proposed as a national park, Saiwa Swamp is a valley bottom 6 km long, about 350 feet wide, with gallery forest on either side. There are several tree platforms for observing the sitatungas as they graze in the bulrushes, damp woods, reeds, and near the open water; best viewing is early morning and evening. You may also see deBrazza monkeys. Birding is good. **Camping** is allowed. Accurate directions to Saiwa Swamp (not the sitatunga sanctuary named on maps) from Greaves Farm (see Kitale accommodations), or Hon. Warden T. J. Barnley, Box 332, Kitale.

Cherangani Hills

Cherangani Hills, actually a major mountain range forming part of the Rift Valley's western wall, rise east of Kitale and Kapenguria. The hills differ from others in Kenya—they are of crystalline, not volcanic, origin. The highest peaks are Kamelogon, 11,540 feet; Kailelekalat, 10,991 feet; Songhang, 10,520 feet, all accessible by four-wheel-drive vehicles, followed by some tough walking through wild country. The hills are high enough to have moorlands with giant heath, lobelia, and groundsel, and there are good views all around to the Karapokot Hills and over the Rift. A cross-hills road goes from north of Kapenguria east to Kaibibich (spelled variously), then across to Chebiemit, giving access, says Leslie Brown, "to what is perhaps the finest hill scenery in Kenya."

Kerio Valley

Kerio Valley, Tot Escarpment. This area to the east of the Cherangani Hills is a rugged place of striking beauty. The road through it is poor but can be negotiated by EPCs, though damage to underparts is possible. This route is included in the East African Safari Rally as one of the most rugged sections possible. The Kerio Valley is inhabited by the Nilo-Hamitic Elgeyo and Marakwet tribes, who farm tiny terraced fields supplied with water by a complex irrigation system—which the Elgeyo say was there when they moved here. Some of the picturesque rocks—the *Sirikwa Rocks*—in the area fell from heaven, the tribe believes. In the valley are several archaeological sites, mostly connected with the somewhat obscure Sirikwa people; one site is a cemetery with 200 stone burial mounds. Farther south is the new fluorite (fluorspar) mining project, where the government hopes to produce 1,000 tons a day and earn $8.6 million a year. Fluorspar is used in the manufacture of aluminum, steel, and cement as a flux to promote fusion. **Camping** is possible anywhere, with good sites at the Weiwei River (after bridge, go right on track on Sigor side of river) and at Chebloch Bridge (riverside sites to left of bridge on Kabarnet side).

Tot Rest House, bookings to D.C., P.O. Tambach via Eldoret; has 3 beds, hard furniture. Fees: 10/– per adult; 5 /– per child.

Route K-12: Limuru High Country–Kikuyu Escarpment Excursion from Nairobi

This circular scenic route from Nairobi is one of the most worthwhile half-day excursions possible for those who want to see how the people—both Africans and Europeans—live and work the land.

Km 0: Muthaiga traffic circle, on the edge of which is a war memorial to the nearby exclusive *Muthaiga Club*'s war dead. Go out Muthaiga Road through Nairobi's richest suburb, home of government ministers, corporation presidents, diplomats. Km 3: traffic circle; go straight. 6 km farther, turn right into Banana Hill Road (D407). You ascend through Kikuyu *shambas* (farms), reach *Banana Hill* at Km 14, an area showcasing new African farming. The road continues into *Limuru* (Masai from *lemorog,* "wild apricot"), a high-altitude (7,300 feet plus) coffee area that has become more a tea region because of its coolness and frequent rain. In 1903 G. W. L. Caine planted Kenya's first tea bushes on what is today Brooke Bond's *Mabroukie Estate.* Caine subsequently abandoned the bushes, which are now large trees. Brooke Bond has about 3,000 acres under tea here. You can visit the Mabroukie estate and factory; tel. Limuru (738) 454. Limuru (area pop. 73,857) was first settled by Europeans in 1903, and the fact that they still live and grow tea and coffee here is seen in the very English houses and hedges.

Km 19: *Kentmere Club* (R), a rustic inn (★★) with beautiful gardens; good for lunch, tea, or dinner. See Nairobi restaurant listings. Km 23: *All Saints' Church* (R), 1940 English village church building. Turn right here 2 km to the *Farm Hotel* (★), actually Nairobi's best French restaurant. See Nairobi listings.

Rift Valley

Km 30: Turn left on C68 here at a railway overpass. (If you go straight you reach Limuru town, an unattractive place with an odorific Bata shoe factory, and, farther on, Uplands, location of a big bacon factory.) Km 32: At junction with new Limuru highway (C62) go right for 1 km to junction with the Nakuru road (A104—our Route K-10), and go right again. 6 km and many roadside curio sellers from here is the *Kikuyu Escarpment* with its fantastic, sudden views over

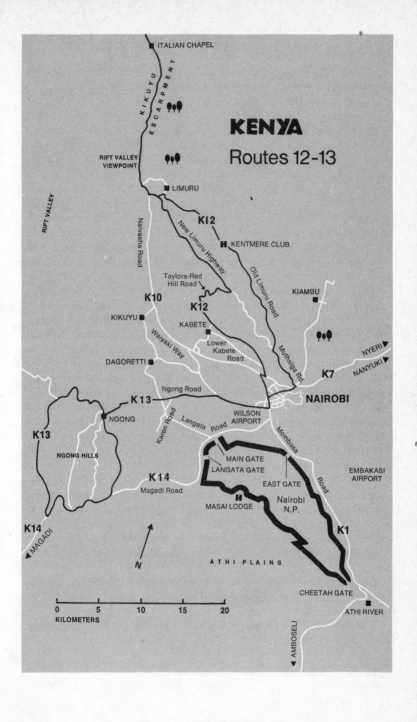

KENYA
Routes 12-13

ITALIAN CHAPEL

KIKUYU ESCARPMENT

RIFT VALLEY

RIFT VALLEY VIEWPOINT

LIMURU

Naivasha Road

New Limuru Highway

K12

Old Limuru Road

KENTMERE CLUB

KIAMBU

Taylors-Red Hill Road

K10

K12

KIKUYU

KABETE

Waiyaki Way

Lower Kabete Road

Muthaiga Rd.

NYERI

DAGORETTI

Ngong Road

K7

NANYUKI

NAIROBI

K13

WILSON AIRPORT

Mombasa Road

NGONG

Karen Road

Langata Road

MAIN GATE
LANGATA GATE

EAST GATE

EMBAKASI AIRPORT

K13

NGONG HILLS

K14

Magadi Road

MASAI LODGE

Nairobi N.P.

K1

K14

MAGADI

N

ATHI PLAINS

CHEETAH GATE

ATHI RIVER

AMBOSELI

0   5   10   15   20
KILOMETERS

the *Great Rift Valley*. There are periodic wide places to pull over on the narrow but well-engineered escarpment road (paved).

The Rift is a gigantic crack or fault that stretches all the way from Mozambique in the south to the Jordan Valley in the north. While there are places where an escarpment rises a mile almost vertically from the flat Rift Valley floor, the land is more generally lowered in steps so the Rift is not as dramatic as it is here. The rifting was not cataclysmic and sudden; it has taken some 15 million years for what you see to develop, and the average movement has been only a foot every 2,000 years. What happened was that in the Miocene epoch, at the same time primitive apes and grazing animals first appeared on earth, the earth here began to warp and rise, and the Arabian peninsula began pulling away and separating from the African continent. The warping caused parallel faults; between these faults, the earth's crust dropped, resulting in the formation of escarpments, a valley, and depressions that soon became lakes. Lakes Malawi, Tanganyika, George, Edward (Idi Amin Dada), and Albert (Mobutu Sese Seko) are in the Western or Central African Rift, while the longer Eastern Rift contains Lakes Manyara, Natron, Magadi, Naivasha, Nakuru, Hannington, Baringo, Rudolf, and the Ethiopian Rift lakes, and extends up through the Red Sea and Dead Sea. Simultaneous with the rifting was volcanic activity that made equally major changes in the earth: not only lava flows that in places are 10,000 feet thick, but also groups of volcanoes such as the Crater Highlands in Tanzania, and huge mountains that rise singly, dramatically from the surrounding plains, such as Kilimanjaro and Mounts Kenya and Elgon.

The giant sweep of the Rift is visible from here, and you can see such volcanoes as Suswa and Longonot. No lava is flowing now, but the Rift is still active underneath, as numerous hot springs, steam jets, and fumaroles show. The Kikuyu Escarpment runs from Kinangop south to the Ngong Hills; its counterpart, forming the western wall, is the Mau Escarpment, visible to the west. The highway snakes down the escarpment, then heads north by northwest up the Rift Valley floor to Nakuru before ascending the western side at Molo and Mau Summit.

Down the road, there is a turnoff (L) at Km 45 to a *Forest Department picnic site*. Good views from there, and as a bonus, many of the trees are labeled.

Km 48: *Italian Chapel* (R), a tiny Catholic chapel dedicated to

St. Mary of the Angels on Christmas Day, 1943. It was built by Italian prisoners of war after they finished constructing the escarpment road. Unless you want to see the floor of the Rift 2 km farther, turn around here and return 12 km to the left turnoff on the Limuru highway (C62) at Km 57. The highway passes some beautifully lush farmland, with greenery set off sharply against the brilliant red laterite soil, and making up in delight what the area lacks of the Rift Valley's brooding drama. At Km 74 turn right on Red Hill Road, passing banana and maize *shambas* for 4 km. At Km 78 turn right on Taylors Road and drive between rows of coffee trees. At Km 80, junction with Nyerere (formerly Marlborough) Road, go left on a winding road through green European suburbs, passing maize fields clinging to hillsides, and at Km 83, *Karura Forest* (good birdwatching). At Km 85 turn left on Lower Kabete Road to a traffic circle, where you go three-quarters the way around to head for Westlands traffic circle, where you go left, arriving in 3 km at Kenyatta Avenue and downtown. (For package tours visiting Limuru and the Rift Valley viewpoint, see package listings KP-7, 11.)

Route K-13: Karen–Ngong Hills Excursion from Nairobi

This route makes a delightful half-day excursion. Begin on Kenyatta Avenue at Uhuru Highway, heading away from downtown and passing the Panafric Hotel on the left. At the first traffic circle, go straight on Allen Road, and at the second, go right on *Ngong Road,* once part of the Cape-to-Cairo route and in the 1890s and 1900s the main road to Uganda. At Km 3, pass the *Royal Nairobi Golf Club,* a plush establishment which for some reason still retains its "royal." Another 1 km, off to the left, is *Kibera,* a suburb originally settled by Emin Pasha's Sudanese soldiers.

Km 7: At Dagoretti Corner, the ultramodern *Kenya Science Teachers College* (L), opened in 1968, funded by Swedish aid. The large tower is not some astronomical device but simply a stylish water tank. At the traffic circle here, bear left on Ngong Road. Km 8: Turnoff (L) to *Jamhuri Park* 1½ km, *Rowallan Camp* of the Boy Scouts 2½ km. At 296-acre Jamhuri Park is held the annual September *Nairobi Show* of the Agricultural Society of Kenya. First held in 1902, the show in 1972 attracted 120,000. In the park is the interesting *Cairn of Peace,* containing engraved stones native to some 44 donor countries.

Km 10: *Ngong Road Racecourse* (L), a track that attracts a cross section of Kenyan society most Sunday afternoons at 2:30 P.M. for eight races (totalizator betting, a daily double, sweepstakes on all races). Daily membership in the Jockey Club of Kenya (20/– for men, 10/– for women) will get you into the dining room and bar of the Members' Enclosure.

Past the racetrack you pass the *Ngong Forest,* which like other forests around Nairobi was not in times past cleared for cultivation because it served as a natural barrier against the Masai to the south. Good birdwatching; butterfly watching also.

Karen

Km 13: St. Francis' Church (L) and turnoff (L) on Karen Road to Karen Country Club and *Karen Blixen's house.* The *Karen* suburb, green, spacious, and elite, was once the 6,000-acre coffee estate of Baroness Karen von Blixen-Finecke; she farmed it from 1914 until financial difficulties forced her to sell in 1931. She returned to her native Denmark and in 1937 wrote the famous *Out of Africa* under the pen name *Isak Dinesen.* Her fondness for this land by the Ngong Hills is apparent on every page: The "landscape had not its like in all the world. There was no fat on it and no luxuriance anywhere; it was Africa distilled up through 6,000 feet, like the strong and refined essence of a continent." The views, she wrote, "were immensely wide. Everything that you saw made for greatness and freedom, and unequaled nobility." She first lived in what is today the dining room at the nearby Westwood Park Country Club (Km 15), then in *Bogani* or *Karen House,* which stands on 36 acres shared by the *Karen College of Home Economics and Nutrition.* Both house and college were Danish gifts—the house as an Independence present in 1963, the college in 1971. The house is open to visitors, but call Karen (88) 2366 before visiting.

Km 14: Traffic circle; go straight. Right is Dagoretti Road to *Dagoretti* (from Endakuleti, Masai term for a climbing plant), one of the original Imperial British East Africa Company outposts. Lugard selected the site in 1890, and a man named George Wilson established the station, promptly attacked by Waiyaki, a local Kikuyu chief, and burned after Wilson fled. It was revived as a government station in 1902. (Sclaters Road, named for the engineer who built it, was in 1973 renamed for Waiyaki.) Km 15: Turnoff (R) to Westwood Park Country Club. See Nairobi hotel listings.

Ngong Hills

Km 22: T-junction at *Ngong* (pop. 1,583), which dates back quite far as a caravan halting place and trading village between the Masai and the Kikuyu. Explorers knew it as Ngongo Bagas, a horrid mispronunciation of the Masai Eng-ong-e'-m-Bagasi (or Enkongu e Mpakasi), which means "eye or source of the Empakasi or Athi River." Towering over the town are the *Ngong Hills,* long a favorite destination of Nairobi residents on weekend afternoons—and a continual inspiration to Karen Blixen. The hills stick up like the knuckles of a closed fist and are a distinctive landmark on the ground or in the air.

There are at least three Masai myths on how the hills were formed, the most charming of which relates that a giant was running along and tripped over Kilimanjaro; in falling, his hand squeezed the earth into the shape of the Ngongs. The hills play another part in Masai lore: here, about 1640, they found their first *laibon,* or spiritual chief and medicine man, who is an intermediary between the Masai and God.

This route has you turn left in Ngong town and make a 49-km clockwise circuit of the hills; this is best for four-wheel-drive vehicles, VW buses, and enterprising private cars. Skirting the base of the hills, the road joins at Km 31 the Magadi Road (our Route K-14), at which you go right. In 5 km you pass over a cattle-grid into the *Ngong Reserve,* a 1,165-square-kilometer Masai-run game reserve. Exactly 1.1 km from there, a track goes right to the top of *Lamwia,* at 8,074 feet the highest of the Ngongs. Four-wheel-drives can make it to the top (5½ km up), others only halfway. The 360-degree view from the top is incomparable.

The route continues the circuit. At Km 45 turn right on Circular Road West into bush country where you will most likely see giraffes. Km 60: A rough road to Suswa 56 km goes left here. Km 71: Ngong town again.

If you're not up to the circuit but want a fine view, turn right as soon as you reach Ngong town at Km 22. In .2 km bear left, taking a one-lane paved road .7 km past a police barracks, then turn right on a dirt road. Go 3.2 km to a road barrier, then another 1.5 km to a radio beacon atop one of the four peaks. Beware of those who would break into your car while you're enjoying the views of the Rift Valley, the escarpment, Mount Suswa, Athi Plains, Kikuyu *shambas,* Nairobi, and on. The view is a lesson in geography—and perhaps meteorology as well. The wind blows quite strongly up here, so bring a sweater and ear protection for walking on the bare, grassy, Scottish Highlands-like hills. A footpath will take you to Lamwia peak at the other end of the hills in an hour or two. (For package tours visiting the hills, see listings KP-5, 6.)

Route K-14: Nairobi National Park–Olorgesailie–Lake Magadi Excursion from Nairobi

Beginning in Nairobi, this route ends up some 111 km later at Lake Magadi; past the Ngong Hills it is not quite an easy excursion like Route K-12 through Limuru to the Escarpment. Your car should be in good condition to go to Olorgesailie and Lake Magadi, which has some of the hottest temperatures in East Africa.

From the Kenyatta Avenue traffic circle, go south on Uhuru Highway to the fourth traffic circle along, turning right here on C58—Aerodrome Road–Langata Road. Km 4: *Wilson Airport* (L), for light planes. Km 6: The Golf Range (L). Km 7: Langata ("a plain") Road Barracks, home of the Seventh Battalion, Kenya Rifles, formerly the *King's African Rifles*. The famous KAR was formed in 1902,

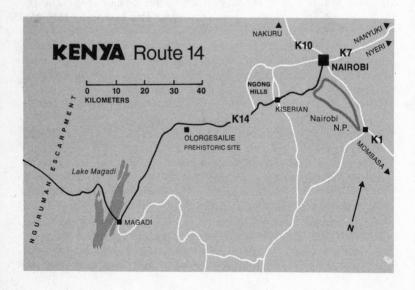

fought in the Ashanti War in West Africa; against German Gen. Paul von Lettow-Vorbeck in Tanganyika, Northern Rhodesia, and Mozambique in World War I; in British, French, and Italian Somaliland, Ethiopia, Madagascar, and Burma in World War II; against Malayan guerrillas—and against the Mau Mau. The four Kenya-raised battalions became the main part of the Kenya army in 1963. No photography here.

Nairobi National Park

Km 8: Main Gate (L) of *Nairobi National Park,* a perfect gem of a game park that no visitor to Kenya should miss—and few do, judging from the attendance figures. In a separate area on the edge of the park is the famous *Animal Orphanage,* founded in 1963 to care for young wild animals found deserted and unable to fend for themselves, to house (wild) pets of departing residents, to show animals usually not seen in the parks (such as the bat-eared fox), and to give professionals a chance to study wildlife in captivity. Many animals are later released in the park. The orphanage has occupied its present site since 1965, and in front of it is a 1973 stone monument, with a statue of a boy and a girl petting an antelope; this honors the children of seven European countries who raised a huge amount of pfennigs and pence to aid the game parks of Kenya. Feeding at the orphanage is prohibited; keepers feed the carnivores at 4 P.M. or so. This is more a zoo than not, so it may depress visitors who came to see animals in the wild; however, Nairobi children find it fun. Entry: 5/- for non-resident adults; 1/- for children. An interesting 3/- booklet has notes on 50 mammals, reptiles, and birds. Also at the main gate is a *Wildlife Education Centre* with some interesting displays designed for Kenya schoolchildren.

The 44-square-mile park is conveniently close to the biggest city in East Africa, yet it remains an almost completely natural environment for wild animals. There is a berm topped by a fence on the Mombasa Road side to keep animals and vehicles from interfering with each other, but otherwise the animals are free to wander in and out of the park and the adjacent *Athi and Kapiti Plains.* Part of the Athi Plains is included in the *Kitengela Game Conservation Area,* while the rest of it and a corridor all the way down to Amboseli are included in Photography Block 72. Preservation of 150,000 adjacent acres of wet-weather grassland is high on the list of priorities for the National Parks and conservation organizations, which fear not only the depreda-

tions of Nairobi-area poachers but also steadily encroaching settlement
all around the park. Dr. Bernhard Grzimek (*Serengeti Shall Not Die*)
believes Nairobi Park will disappear if surrounded by settlement, indeed believes it is "nearly too late" for Nairobi and Lake Nakuru
parks. Another threat to such a small park is vehicles making too
many tracks off the park roads; please don't go off the road without
good reason.

Commonest animals in the park, which has an amazing scenic variety, are the zebra, wildebeest, Coke's hartebeest (kongoni), Grant's
gazelle, Thomson's gazelle, eland, Masai giraffe, warthog, common
waterbuck, impala, baboon, bushbuck, and—as a very noticeable bird
—the Masai ostrich. There are many buffalos, which are not always
seen, and black rhinos (pop. 25–30) browse solitarily here and there.
Missing are elephants, oryxes, kudus. It is definitely easy to see lions
here (gate guards will tell you where), but it is difficult to find the
nocturnal leopards or the daytime cheetahs, which will, however, occasionally surprise visitors by using their vehicle as a vantage point.

It is impossible to enter Nairobi Park and not see *Coke's hartebeest,*

Coke's hartebeest (Kongoni)

which is commonly known by its Swahili name, *kongoni.* A sandy-
colored antelope, the hartebeest slopes from shoulder to rump, which
is white and looks naked; more peculiar-looking are its horns, which
jut out parallel to its ears before going up like a pair of brackets.
Hartebeests are social and congregate in small herds with zebra on the
open plains. Another antelope you will probably spot here is the
eland, a large and powerful fawn-colored animal with straight corkscrew horns, a black-fringed dewlap (piece of skin hanging from the
neck to the legs), a short brown mane, and a few thin white stripes. If
one of these leaps or bounds across the road in front of your vehicle,

Eland

you will not soon forget it. Elands can be semidomesticated and kept for their milk and meat; domestication experiments are being conducted at a nearby Athi River farm by research scientist David Hopcraft. A small relative of the eland (and the *kudu*) is the *bushbuck,*

Bushbuck

which you can find in the woods on the southern edge of Nairobi Park. While there are numerous races of bushbuck, they generally are darkish brown with scattered white spots and thin white lines. Small and delicate, bushbuck are found in pairs or small groups; they're browsers and generally nocturnal.

Because the animals in Nairobi Park are accustomed to man and vehicle, most will continue what they're doing—mainly eating—when you pull up. In this park you can easily take a picture of a *warthog,*

Warthog

which in many parks would be quick to trot off with tail straight up in the air like a warning flag. With its gray, sparsely haired body, powerful neck and head, and short, sharp-looking tusks, the warthog looks ugly and frightening. But it doesn't go around killing things; it grazes, often on its knees, and runs from danger. Its cousin, the *bushpig,* is hairy and reddish and nocturnal, so is rarely seen. Among animals which can be bold and vicious is the *baboon,* commonly the olive baboon, a heavily built, ground-loving, "broken-tailed" baboon seen in large troops in open areas or semiwoodland, very often in the company of impalas (the antelope's sense of hearing and smell complements the baboon's keen sight). With their sharp incisors and collective defense tactics, baboon troops keep predators at bay. Baboons feed mostly on grass but do eat insects and, occasionally, meat if they happen to find a bird or young gazelle hiding in the grass. There are usually baboons under the trees near the main gate; do not encourage them in any way—in fact, keep your window closed.

Jackal

Two predators easily seen are the lion and the jackal (the common black- or silver-backed variety). The *jackal* is big-eared and foxlike, and quite small; it is a scavenger and predator of small animals but also eats fruit and berries. If you see lions about, look for jackals, too. And what can we say about the *lion,* about which there are so many romantic stories, beliefs, and legends that a *New York Times* article recently named it the "king of myths." The biggest of the cats, lions are so naturally lazy that when they are full from eating—or gorging themselves—herds of their prey may graze quite close. Unadmirably, the king of beasts often lets the queen do most of the hunting. Lions hang about almost exclusively in family groups (prides) and will sometimes hunt together in a strategic operation. It has, however, been recently determined that lions more often than not will seize kills made by hyenas or wild dogs, rather than hunting their own food. What's more (to destroy another myth), a lion's kill is not the "clean" death accomplished by leaping on the prey's back and breaking its neck swiftly with the front paws. A lion kills by charging its prey from fairly close quarters, bringing it down with the claws, then slowly strangling it by biting its throat. If you prefer to keep believing in the king of beasts, you'll probably not want to know that lions will often kill for the fun of it—and will kill their own kind without remorse. Debunkers will want to read American biologist George Schaller's *The Serengeti Lion* (p. 318), and give the Elsa books to the kids. But no matter what you want to believe, in Nairobi Park you'll rarely see lions doing anything but lying about, probably surrounded by cars.

Typical of this small park is the world's largest bird, the *ostrich,* hereabouts the Masai ostrich. The male is black and white, the female a gray-brown. They can't fly, though they do flap their wings. They do not bury their heads in the sand. The male bird will roar something like a lion during the breeding season. The park is wealthy in smaller birdlife—you can see more species (400 plus) in 44 square miles than you can in the British Isles. John G. Williams cautions, however, that much depends on the rains and the time of year. Northern migrants come through in March and April.

When to Visit

The best game viewing is during the dry months of January and February when animals gather around the park's permanent water; other times the biomass is smaller as the plains animals drift south, out of the park. The best time of day for a visit is in the early morning; late afternoon would be fine if it weren't for the crowds of tour minibuses that spoil the view of lions and other popular animals. Early morning and late afternoon light is good for photography. The midday heat drives many animals into shade, and the tourist would do well to do the same. The park is open 6:30 A.M. to 7 P.M.

Getting There, Getting Around

Any kind of car can negotiate all the park roads in dry season; tracks, however, are not advisable if it has just rained. Since the park is small, you can see a variety of scenery and wildlife simply by entering one gate and exiting at another. Roads near the main gate are paved and have speed bumps to excess, so we'd recommend entering at Langata Gate and taking the good dirt roads through the woodland (impala, baboon, buffalo, bushbuck) to the Caltex Observation Hut (view of the whole park; the buildings in the distance off to the right are Masai Lodge, which is just outside the park in the Kitengela), then head across the park to Mbagathi Gorge and Baboon Escarpment, then back along Songora Ridge (signposts 16–19) to Lone Tree, then across the White Grass Ridge to Rocky Valley and two dams (many zebras, hartebeests, gazelles, warthogs, ostriches) to signpost 7, then out of the park at the East Gate (Mombasa Road). Also good is a day trip up through the park starting from Cheetah Gate at Athi River. The park map is good, and necessary. With a detailed topo map and a good vehicle, you can explore on your own in the areas next to the park. A new park gate, near Masai Lodge, opened in late 1973. For package tours visiting the park, see listing KP-2.

Accommodations

None inside the park, and no camping, but *Masai Lodge* (★★) is opposite the Leopard Cliffs across Mbagathi Gorge. Turn off this route at Km 16 to lodge 6 km off the road, or you can go through the park to exit at Masai Gate.

Continuing along Langata Road, you come to Km 10: *Bomas of Kenya* (see p. 171). At the same intersection, turn left on C58 (Magadi Road). Straight on Langata Road goes to Karen. On Magadi Road you pass Nairobi Park's Langata Gate (Km 11), Banda Gate (Km 13; usually closed), and the turnoff (L) to Masai Gate and Masai Lodge (Km 16), reaching at Km 24 Kiserian (Masai, "a good place") and then a turnoff (R) to Ngong town 10 km. Bear left and drive along the base of the Ngong Hills (see Route K-13); at Km 30 is a turnoff (R) on a rough track to the top of Lamwia peak. Continuing on, you descend into the Rift Valley at the same speed the mercury rises in the thermometer.

Olorgesailie

Km 63: Turnoff (L) to *Olorgesailie National Park* 1½ km. An important living site of hand-ax man, Olorgesailie was excavated by the Leakeys in 1943 and declared a national park in 1947 (today it is run by the National Museum). Left *in situ* and protected by thatched-roof shelters are isolated tools and fossils (an elephant humerus, for example) and literally thousands of hand axes, found scattered on the surface just as early man discarded them; paths and walkways now go around and over them. Interestingly, twelve groups of three stones were found; these may have been tied together and used, like bolas, for hurling at the legs of running animals. The campsite dates from the middle of the Pleistocene and is more than 100,000 years old. Guide by G. L. Isaac (who is co-leader of the East Rudolf expedition) is worth buying. Admission: 5/– per adult, 2/– per child for nonresidents; 2/– and 1/– for residents. **Accommodations** in 4 simple self-service bandas equipped with furniture. Fee: 5– per person. Bookings to Centre for Prehistory and Paleontology, Box 30239, Nairobi; tel. 22648.

Lake Magadi

From Olorgesailie you continue across the arid land, studded with euphorbia and whistling-thorn bushes, to a desert spectacle which is Kenya's most valuable mineral resource, *Lake Magadi* (Km 111). This is a "lake" of almost solid soda (trona) 30 miles long and 10 feet deep. The Magadi Soda Company removes the trona using a bucket dredger floating on an artificial pool, pumping it as a slurry to two large rotary kilns which break the trona down. The firm each year processes some 225,000 tons of soda ash (used for making glass, among other things) and 50,000 tons of salt for human and animal consumption. Total worth of the soda and salt is an annual $7 million. The Rift Valley lake is in a closed drainage area, so that there is a few million years' worth of accumulated soda from the leaching of the Rift's soda-rich volcanic rock in a low-lying basin that has no outlet. What is interesting is that the soda reserves are practically infinite: hot springs continuously supply alkaline water for evaporation, causing the trona to regenerate as fast as it is removed. The lake is the second-largest expanse of trona in the world; first in size is the Salton Sea in California. (Magadi, incidentally, is from the Masai *makat,* "soda.") A few soda water pools contain *Tilapia grahami,* a fish that survives the cruel, hot alkalinity, and lots of insects and algae, which in turn attract lesser flamingos (millions, on occasion) and other birds. The lake has a company town (pop. 5,000) but is a terrible place for humans. Come in the early morning to see, from a bluff 17 km distant, the pink, blue, and white surface of the lake.

A causeway crosses the lake to the *Nguruman Escarpment* about 40 km on. Four-wheel-drive is necessary.

TANZANIA

SOCIALISM AND TOURISM

Tanzania is a wide, long, expansive country touching on the Indian Ocean and on Africa's three largest lakes, crowned by the continent's tallest mountain, and protecting two of the world's largest game sanctuaries. Game viewing in Tanzania's superb national parks and reserves is an exciting experience, because the zebras, wildebeests, and gazelles number in the hundreds of thousands, because the elephants still trumpet their displeasure at your presence, and because the vast plains and high, lush mountains create dramatic backdrops. The tourist "milk run" in northern Tanzania from Serengeti Plains through Olduvai Gorge, into Ngorongoro Crater, to Lake Manyara, and past Kilimanjaro offers more contrast and intense beauty than any drive of similar length anywhere in Eastern Africa.

Tanzania also offers the traveler a chance to dig into man's long complex past by visiting one of the world's most important prehistoric sites, Olduvai Gorge. Whereas Kenya's significant and recent Lake Rudolf finds are still shut off to all but the directly involved scholars, Olduvai Gorge is on a well-beaten tourist track and is visited by thousands of people yearly. An on-the-spot museum and university-trained guides help spark or advance an interest in man's beginnings; and visiting Olduvai and other prehistoric sites, you begin to appreciate how long, or short, a time man has been around.

Tanzania is living history as well. Since its independence in 1961, the nation, under the leadership of President Julius Nyerere, has attempted to initiate and develop its own brand of socialism, with partial or total government ownership of the main means of production—banking, industry, agriculture, tourism, transportation, and so forth. While tourists may not normally see the grass-roots socialism, unless a visit to an *ujamaa* village (a sort of African *kibbutz*) is made, for example, you do feel the difference between capitalistic Kenya and socialistic Tanzania.

Like Kenya, Tanzania's history comes in two parts: the history of the interior, and the history of the coast including Zanzibar. The Leakeys' discoveries at Olduvai Gorge—1.7-million-year-old *Zinjanthropus boisei* in 1959 and *Homo habilis* in 1961—plus many other sites since excavated confirm that East Africa was where man was born. About 20,000 years ago there lived in the region Bushmen and Caucasian Hamites; both were mainly hunters. About 3000 B.C. men were settling in larger groups, keeping domestic animals, growing some crops, decorating their bodies, and painting on rocks and in caves. Starting about 1000 B.C. a black people living in the Sudan moved south, mixed with the Hamites, and thus formed the agricultural Bantu. The ancestors of today's more than 120 tribes (mainly Bantu) spread from the Great Lakes south and east, settling into the new areas including the coast by about A.D. 800.

Meanwhile, the coast was having visitors from distant points. The northeast monsoons from November to April carried boats from Egypt, Arabia, the Persian Gulf, and India to the East African coast, while the southeast monsoons from May to October took them back. In exchange for the glass, cloth, and metal, the coast tribes traded ivory, rhino horn, tortoise shell, wood, spices, and slaves. A few Arabs settled along the coast, planting coconut trees and sugar cane, cultivating trade. The 1st-century Greek mariners' guide *Periplus of the Erythraean Sea* mentioned a town called Rhapta (thought to be Pangani) and an island (thought to be Zanzibar).

After the Prophet Mohammed died in 632, more Arabs began immigrating to the East African coast. Some of them intermarried with the resident Bantu, creating the Swahili people, culture, and language. Settlements grew up on Zanzibar, Mafia, and Kilwa. Kilwa in the early 12th century seized control of the gold trade going north from Sofala port in Mozambique, and during its peak of wealth and power, the' Kilwa ruler built a grand palace with more than 100 rooms.

Vasco da Gama sailed up the East African coast in 1498, stopping at Mombasa and Malindi on his way to India. The Portuguese wanted to control the whole coast and thus the main trade route to India, so they proceeded to demand that the coastal settlements pay tribute. The struggle for coastal supremacy between the Portuguese and Arabs dragged on for centuries, but in 1698, when Fort Jesus in Mombasa fell to the Omani Arabs, the Sultan of Oman became the nominal master of the coast from the Rovuma River (on the Mozambique border) northward. By the 19th century, though, mainland Tanzania tribes were getting semiorganized within their separate domains, so that the Arab caravans, traveling inland in search of ivory and slaves to meet the growing demand, began to encounter strong, united tribes (such as the Gogo near Dodoma) who demanded *hongo* or payment for letting the caravans pass, and who raided weaker tribes to get fellow Africans to trade to the Arabs.

The real stimulus for expanding inland trade came when the Sultan of Oman moved his capital from Muscat on the Persian Gulf to Zanzibar in 1832. Seyyid Said strongly encouraged the planting of cloves on Zanzibar and Pemba, invited Indians to become financiers for the Arab ivory and slave caravans, and welcomed ships from the U.S. and Europe. While elsewhere the slave trade was generally on the decline, the trade on the East African coast reached its zenith under Seyyid with scores of thousands of slaves passing each year through Kilwa, Bagamoyo, Pangani, and Zanzibar.

It was during Sultan Majid's rule from 1856 to 1870 that many of the European explorers set off from Zanzibar on their great treks into the mainland in search of the lakes and the source of the Nile River. In 1848, Johannes Rebmann, from the Church Missionary Society near Mombasa, was the first European to see the snows of Kilimanjaro, a phenomenon disputed by many skeptics in Europe. The English in particular were very anxious to trace the enigmatic source of the Nile. The Royal Geographical Society in 1856 commissioned Richard Burton and John Speke to investigate reports of the East African inland lake or lakes. They were the first Europeans to see Lake Tanganyika, and while Burton lay ill, Speke marched north to Lake Victoria, which he guessed correctly was the true source of the Nile. Livingstone in 1866 left Zanzibar for his last long journey into the interior, and it was on a return visit to Ujiji that he was "found" by Stanley in 1871. Together they explored the north end of Lake Tanganyika and then went to Tabora, from where Stanley left for the coast, Livingstone for his eventual death in the heart of Zambia.

Sultan Barghash, Said's son, succeeded Majid in 1870. The British, who had been pressuring the sultans for decades to outlaw the slave trade in their domains, finally surrounded Zanzibar with warships to prevent any slaves from entering or leaving the island. Barghash unhappily signed a treaty on June 5, 1873, forbidding all export of slaves from the coast, and also closed the infamous slave market on Zanzibar. On the site of the slave market the Anglican Universities Mission to Central Africa (UMCA) built a church. After Livingstone's admonishments to Europeans to bring Christianity and honest trade to East and Central Africa, the Anglican UMCA and Catholic White Fathers started missions on Zanzibar, at Bagamoyo and Tabora, and along the great lakes, while the Lutherans later proselytized around Kilimanjaro and Mount Meru.

The Germans meanwhile were interested in the mainland. In 1884 the German Colonization Society secretly dispatched Karl Peters to the Tanzania coast. In three weeks he made twelve treaties with chiefs; these the Kaiser declared valid, and Sultan Barghash and the British were forced to accept a German Protectorate over the mainland. Tanzania's boundaries were generally fixed in 1890, with the Kaiser just barely getting Kilimanjaro from the British. Tanzania thus was first officially known as German East Africa (G.E.A.), while Zanzibar separately became a British Protectorate.

For the next 25 years the Germans proceeded to enforce the peace with the main tribes (not without bloodshed), spread the administration, and encourage white settlers, who established cotton and sisal plantations and coffee estates. A railway was started from Tanga to Moshi in 1896, another from Dar es Salaam to Tabora in 1905. That year a serious rebellion—the Maji Maji Rising—swept through southern G.E.A. A number of white settlers, administrators, and missionaries were killed, and thousands of German troops were called in as reinforcements. They carried out a scorched-earth policy, shooting the rebels and starving their supporters, so that by 1907 an estimated 120,000 Africans had died. The German government enacted some reforms—such as forbidding whips and prohibiting forced labor except for on public works.

When World War I started, G.E.A. automatically became Kenya's enemy, according to the way the lines were drawn in Europe, and black Africans found themselves fighting each other under mainly white officers. General Paul von Lettow-Vorbeck took command in G.E.A. with the intention of forcing Britain to divert troops from Europe in order to fight on the East African front. Vorbeck, his German troops, and his amazingly loyal African *askaris* defended Tanga from invasion, sabotaged the railway in Kenya, and then drew thousands of British, Belgians, Portuguese, and Africans into chasing them all over G.E.A. and Mozambique for three years. Finally, upon hearing officially that the war had ended, Vorbeck and his men reluctantly surrendered on November 12, 1918.

G.E.A. became a League of Nations mandated territory administered by Britain, which renamed it Tanganyika, after the lake. When the U.N. was formed, the country's status became that of a British trusteeship. Slavery was totally abolished in 1922, German farms were sold to other European and Indian settlers, more schools were opened, and dirt roads were built. As in Kenya, the British adopted a policy of "indirect rule," administering locally through provincial commissioners and "native authorities" or chiefs, with a Legislative Council advising the governor. During World War II, 92,000 Africans from Tanganyika fought in the King's African Rifles in Ethiopia, Somaliland, the Mediterranean, and Burma, developing a political awareness along with training.

Gradually Africans were appointed to the Legislative Council, and the British policy was that there would be eventual independence. Julius Nyerere, the first Tanganyika African to gain an overseas university degree, reorganized the former socially oriented Tanganyikan Association into the political Tanganyika African National Union (TANU), and its membership grew into the hundreds of thousands in the 1950s. In the 1958 Legislative Council elections, although there were two other parties competing, TANU won 30, or half, of the seats. The next step toward independence was *madaraka*, "responsible government." In 1960 elections TANU, with its moderate though firm policies, won every legislative seat but one. Nyerere was appointed chief minister, with TANU officials heading eight of eleven ministries. On May 1, 1961, Nyerere became prime minister, the Council of Ministers became the Cabinet, and the Legislative Council was renamed the National Assembly (later, Parliament). Independence came on December 9, 1961, with the official raising of the green, yellow, and black Tanganyika flag. Nyerere was elected president and was sworn in on December 9, 1962.

Meanwhile, Zanzibar had achieved its independence from Britain separately in December 1963. One month later the sultan was overthrown and exiled, and the Afro-Shirazi party assumed power. On April 26, 1964, Tanganyika and Zanzibar joined to form what was later called the United Republic of Tanzania.

Today Tanzania is essentially a one-party (TANU) republic within the Commonwealth with President Nyerere its twice-elected president. Advising President Nyerere is a Cabinet of Ministers, which includes two vice-presidents (the first vice-president, a resident of Zanzibar, is also president of Zanzibar, and there the Afro-Shirazi party is the sole party). The unicameral National Assembly has 107 elected members, all nominated by TANU and elected in their constituency by citizens over 21 years of age. The Assembly also has ten nominated members and a number of other nominated members to represent Zanzibar. Tanzania is divided into 17 regions, each in charge of an appointed regional commissioner. The regions in turn are divided into districts, each under an appointed area commissioner. At the end of 1973 the government announced that over a 10-year period the national capital would be transferred from Dar es Salaam to Dodoma in the center of the country.

Tanzania's domestic and foreign policies are basically Mwalimu ("teacher") Nyerere's creations. In February 1967 he made the famous Arusha Declaration, which outlined his ideas on African socialism, the method Tanzania was to use to "move the people of Tanzania and the people of Africa as a whole from a state of poverty to a state of prosperity." The government was to nationalize manufacturing, banking, tourism, import-export, etc.; while the people were to practice hard work, dedication, and self-reliance and to voluntarily organize themselves into *ujamaa* villages— *kibbutz*-like socialistic agricultural communes. This is in fact what has occurred, as Tanzania put Nyerere's theories into practice. Foreign assistance has been received from Britain, the U.S., Scandinavia, Germany, Eastern Europe, and the People's Republic of China, to name a few. Tanzania's foreign policy officially is one of nonalignment, though it leans more to the left than center. It openly supports and harbors guerrillas fighting the Portuguese in Mozambique and southern Africa. However, it was also involved in its own brief border battles in 1972 with Uganda and in 1973 with Burundi.

But basically Tanzania is a peaceful, beautiful country, and tourists need not worry about traveling through most of Tanzania.

Some Vital Statistics. Area: 364,943 sq. mi., smaller than Alaska but bigger than Texas, almost 2½ times as large as California.

Population of Tanzania (1974 est.) was: Tanganyika mainland, 14,350,000, Zanzibar, 411,782.

Cities: Dar es Salaam (est. pop. 477,000) is the capital, the largest port, and largest city. Tanga (pop. 61,058) is the second port. Other towns: Zanzibar Town (68,490), Mwanza (34,186), Arusha (32,-

452), Moshi (26,864), Morogoro (25,202), Dodoma (the future capital of Tanzania, 23,559), and Iringa (21,746).

Gross national product (1971): $1.411 billion ($103 per capita).

Currency

The basic unit of currency is the Tanzania shilling, which is pegged to the U.S. dollar. There are shilling currency notes in 5/–, 10/–, 20/–, and 100/– denominations; and coins of –/05, –/20, –/50, and 1/–. Abbreviations are: 20 shillings = 20/–; 1 shilling, 50 cents = 1/50; 50 cents = –/50. For the official-value conversion table, see p. 83.

However, you should know that the free market (Zurich) rate for the Tanzania shilling was 12/– to 20/– to the U.S. dollar. There is an active, though risky, black market in Tanzania, with the rate there about 10/– to 12/– to the U.S. dollar. Officially, the Kenya shilling is equal in value to the Tanzania shilling, but on the Tanzania black market the Kenya shilling is worth more—about 9 to 10 Tanzania shillings to 7 Kenya shillings. Dealing on the black market is strictly illegal.

Planning a Trip

What to See and Do

Most tourists are introduced to Tanzania through what is called the Northern Circuit (or in Kenya, "milk run") game parks: *Serengeti,* with its nearly 2 million plains animals; *Ngorongoro,* whose 5,500-foot-high caldera floor teems with wildlife; and *Lake Manyara,* famed for its tree-climbing lions. Usually, en route between Serengeti and Ngorongoro, a stop is made at *Olduvai Gorge,* the world-renowned prehistoric site. Other Northern Circuit parks slightly off the well-beaten path are *Tarangire,* where the river of that name draws many species in the dry season, and *Arusha,* which has unspoiled Ngurdoto Crater, the seven Momela lakes, and lofty Mount Meru. *Kilimanjaro*'s lush slopes can be included as a night stop between Arusha and Tsavo or Mombasa, though for the energetic and fit the five-day climb to the top of Africa's highest (19,340 feet) mountain will be the most memorable part of their trip to Tanzania. Any of these Northern Circuit destinations can be easily reached from Arusha or Nairobi on package tours, in charter plane, and by car. If you plan to visit East Africa only once, try not to miss Serengeti and Ngorongoro.

The Southern Circuit parks and beaches have *Dar es Salaam* as their jumping-off point, and the Tanzania government is trying to encourage tourists to see what this part of their country has to offer. One of the main drawing points is the gorgeous beaches, which have so far been developed mainly north of Dar es Salaam. The beach hotels offer a relaxing environment in which to unwind after an inland safari. Deep-sea fishing is particularly good off *Mafia Island*. *Zanzibar* still retains some Old World charm and intrigue, though it is quickly developing into a proletarian paradise. Big game abounds in southern Tanzania, protected in several parks and reserves. *Mikumi* is easily accessible via the new paved highway from Dar es Salaam, and has a good variety of bird and animal life. *Selous,* one of the world's largest game reserves, with more than 35,000 elephants, was a longtime haunt of professional hunting safaris, but has recently been opened up for regular ground and air tours.

Less accessible parks are *Ruaha,* west of Iringa and well populated with elephants, and *Gombe Stream* on Lake Tanganyika, especially gazetted for the resident chimpanzees though not yet open to visitors. Those with extra time on their hands at the coast can visit the old slave trading port of *Bagamoyo* or the Arab ruins at *Kunduchi* and *Kilwa,* or take a walking tour of Dar es Salaam. Good side trips to make en route elsewhere by private car include the *Usambara Mountains* west of Tanga, the *rock paintings* east of Kolo, the *Mbeya Range* and *Lake Rukwa* north of Mbeya.

How Long to Stay Where

These are our suggested minimum lengths of stay in some parks, towns, and areas:

Serengeti: Two nights, one at Lobo Lodge and one at Seronera Lodge or Fort Ikoma, with lots of game viewing during the two days.

Olduvai Gorge: At least three hours to spend looking around the excavation sites and the small museum.

Ngorongoro: A full day on the caldera floor, and two nights on the rim.

Lake Manyara: One night at the lodge or camping, a half-day game viewing.

Tarangire: One overnight, two half-days.

Kilimanjaro: One afternoon and night at a Marangu hotel is not too thrilling. To see the mountain, go on a five-day climb to the summit, perhaps spending a sixth night to recuperate in Marangu.

Arusha: A few hours for shopping, maybe an overnight in the town, a half or full day visiting Arusha National Park.

Dar es Salaam: One day for sightseeing and shopping.

Dar es Salaam Coast: Two nights to relax, two days to sunbathe, goggle, sail, etc.

Bagamoyo: A half-day sightseeing from Dar es Salaam or beach hotels.

Zanzibar: One day for sightseeing and shopping.

Mafia Island: For avid fishermen and water enthusiasts, one or two nights and days.

Kilwa: If flying round trip from Dar es Salaam, one day to hire a boat and explore the ruins.

Mikumi: If going by road round trip from Dar es Salaam, two nights and two days; by plane, one night and one day. Otherwise it can be an afternoon and night stop while driving along the Dar es Salaam–Tunduma highway.

Selous: Two nights and two days, because it's a long way in and a huge reserve.

Ruaha: Two nights and two days, for the same reasons.

Where to Stay

Since the government-owned Tanzania Tourist Corporation (TTC) built its big, new, expensive hotels geared to European and American package tours, Tanzania now has facilities for large groups in most of the Northern Circuit national parks, in Arusha, on the Dar es Salaam coast, and at Mikumi. The privately run hotels are on the whole not as well appointed as their TTC competition, and in fact Tanzania lacks the range of accommodations that Kenya has. Service charge at the hotels is usually 5 percent. There is a 12 percent government tax on accommodations only. Most hotels in Tanzania serve an English breakfast as part of the basic bed and breakfast (B&B) rate.

Since there are virtually no self-service accommodations, the usual alternative to staying in expensive hotels is to camp—and there are many beautiful campsites, particularly in the game parks and reserves. However, there is now a 20 percent tax on imported camping equipment; see p. 320. Camping fees in the national parks are 5/– per person per night, and most other sites charge about the same. The government maintains rest houses, usually in the district towns, but unfortunately they have little, if any, furniture, may or may not be clean, and cost about 7/– per person per night.

Booking Accommodations

The TTC hotels have a central booking office: New Africa Hotel, Azikiwe St., Box 9500, Dar es Salaam; tel. 28181; cable OVEROTEL. Bookings for Mikumi Wildlife Lodge, Mafia Island Lodge, New Africa Hotel, Bahari Beach Hotel, Kunduchi Beach Hotel, Lake Manyara Hotel, Ngorongoro Wildlife Lodge, Seronera Lodge, Lobo Lodge.

When to Go

Tanzania's climate, like Kenya's, ranges from a hot, humid coast to Kilimanjaro's thin, glacial, mountain air, with gradations in between. The best time to visit is during the dry seasons: June–September when the weather is also cool with mean temperatures in the seventies; and mid-December–February, when it is hot and dry. Late December–March is the high season for tourism, and hotel bookings are imperative. The times to avoid are the long rains in mid-March–May, when there are intermittent rains almost daily, and the short rains in November–mid-December, when there are showers several times weekly. Generally, though, the weather also depends on the altitude and inland position. The coastal strip and islands are tropical with temperatures 80°–95°F, about 78 percent humidity, and annual rainfall up to 76 inches. The coolest time to visit the coast is June–September; other times be ready to slow your pace, drink lots of liquids, and wear cool, loose clothing. The Central Plateau, which ranges from 3,000 to 4,000 feet in altitude and covers much of Tanzania, is hot and dry with rainfall of about 20 to 30 inches yearly, and temperatures in the eighties. The semitemperate highlands—which include Arusha to Ngorongoro, Kilimanjaro's lower slopes, the Usambara Mountains, and Iringa to Mbeya—have rainfall of 30 to 40 inches a year, and can get quite cool, especially at night. Around Lake Victoria there is rainfall all year, with the heaviest March–May.

What to Wear

Dress is casual but government regulations now forbid shorts, skirts ending above the knee, and wide-flared or skintight trousers.

Tourism Authority

The Tanzania Tourist Corporation (TTC), IPS Building, Azikiwe St., Box 2485, Dar es Salaam; tel. 27671. Representatives outside Tanzania: IPS Building, Kimathi St., Box 48610, Nairobi; tel. 26888.

11 Grand Buildings, Trafalgar Square, London WC2. There is also an office in Frankfurt. Zanzibar's tourism office is the Tanzania Friendship Tourist Bureau, Box 216, Zanzibar; tel. 2344; cable URAFIKI.

Maps

There are some good maps of Tanzania, Dar es Salaam, and the national parks. A general orientation map is the British Petroleum (BP) road map of East Africa (see below). Survey of Kenya produces some Tanzania maps which are available from the Public Map Office, Box 30089, Nairobi. Tanzania's map office produces a number of topographical, aerial, and township maps listed in their catalog of maps: Surveys and Mapping Division, Kivukoni Front, Box 9201, Dar es Salaam. Some maps are available through the Tanzania Tourist Center, Boma Road, Box 494, Arusha. If ordering by mail, include approximate cost of postage.

Tanzania, general: The BP road map of East Africa (cost 7/–) is good for drivers and others, showing most of the parks, main and secondary roads, scale 1:2 million. The Shell road map of Kenya shows most of northern Tanzania, and is useful for those doing the southern Kenya–northern Tanzania circuit by road. Tanzania Surveys' 1970 base country map (S.17) has a scale of 1:2 million, a cost of 5/–. The Surveys' 1968 *Atlas of Tanzania* has 20 sheets with descriptions and gazetteers (cost 120/–). *Tanzania in Maps,* published in 1971 by the University of London Press, is a good annotated atlas (cost 55/–).

Dar es Salaam: Surveys and Mapping prints a very detailed series, either 1:5,000 or 1:25,000 based on aerial photography. "The Map and Guide to Dar es Salaam," published by University Press of Africa (Box 43981, Nairobi), scale 1:5,000, is a foldout with lots of ads and an introduction printed in French, German, and English; the map proper is the best available for general use (cost 5/50). The same group prints the "Industrial Guide and Map to Dar es Salaam," which is useful for those with business to do in that area (cost 5/50). A small map of downtown Dar es Salaam is in the centerfold of *Karibu,* the free TTC magazine, and is handy for a walking tour of the city center.

Arusha and Moshi: General maps of each town are in *Kilimanjaro Country,* a 1968 commercial guide published by University Press of Africa, cost 8/–. Surveys and Mapping has detailed maps, scale 1:10,000, for both towns.

National Parks: The National Parks prints a series of excellent free brochures and booklets (price 5/– each) on Serengeti, Lake Manyara,

Arusha, Mikumi, and Ruaha national parks, and on Ngorongoro Crater. They are all available from the National Parks Office, Box 3134, Arusha; sometimes they are available in each park. The East African Wild Life Society shop in the Nairobi Hilton also sells the booklets for 7/– each. In each booklet is a very good description of the park's flora and fauna, and a centerfold map. Enlargements of the map are printed for Serengeti and Ruaha, available from National Parks. There are oblique Caltex maps for Serengeti, Ngorongoro, and Lake Manyara (cost 3/– each). *Olduvai Gorge:* An outline of the main discoveries and the Beds is in a free National Geographic Society brochure distributed at the Gorge, or write: The Secretary, Box 30239, Nairobi. *Kilimanjaro:* Tanzania Surveys and Mapping has 1964 contour maps, scale 1:50,000, price 5/– each. The most useful is No. 56/2, the central sheet covering Kibo, Mawenzi, and upper parts of the Marangu and some of the alternative routes. Southwestern slopes are in sheet 42/3, Shira Plateau in 56/1. A 1:100,000 map printed in 1965 by Surveys covers 2,000 sq. mi., is contoured per 100 ft., and shows all of Kilimanjaro. The Public Map Office in Nairobi has a 1:100,000 map, but is often out of stock.

Books to Read

(Also see this section under Kenya, p. 90.)

Freeman-Grenville, G. S. P. *The Medieval History of the Coast of Tanganyika.* London: Oxford University Press, 1962.

Fosbrooke, Henry. *Ngorongoro: The Eighth Wonder.* London: Trinity Press, 1972.

Gray, Sir John. *History of Zanzibar from the Middle Ages to 1856.* London: Oxford University Press, 1962.

Grzimek, Bernhard and Michael. *Serengeti Shall Not Die.* London: Hamish Hamilton, 1960; Fontana paperback, 1964.

Hatch, John. *Tanzania: A Profile.* New York: Praeger, 1972; London: Pall Mall Press, 1972.

Kimambo, I. N., and Temu, A. J., eds. *A History of Tanzania.* Nairobi: East African Publishing House, 1969.

Ministry of Information and Tourism. *Tanzania Today.* Nairobi: University Press of Africa, 1968; New York: International Publications Service, 1970.

Mosley, Leonard. *Duel for Kilimanjaro: An Account of the East African Campaign 1914–1918.* London: Weidenfeld and Nicolson, 1963.

Nyerere, Julius K. *Freedom and Unity*. New York: Oxford University Press, 1967.

———. *Freedom and Socialism*. New York: Oxford University Press, 1968.

———. *Ujamaa: Essays on Socialism*. New York: Oxford University Press, 1968.

Schaller, George P. *The Serengeti Lion: A Study of Predator-Prey Relations*. Chicago: University of Chicago Press, 1973.

Smith, William Edgett. *We Must Run While Others Walk*. New York: Random House, 1971.

Stahl, Kathleen. *History of the Chagga People of Kilimanjaro*. The Hague, 1964.

Tanzania Society. *Dar es Salaam: City, Port and Region*. Dar es Salaam, 1969.

———. *Kilimanjaro*. Dar es Salaam, 1965.

Tordoff, William, ed. *Government and Politics in Tanzania*. Nairobi: East African Publishing House, 1967.

Van Lawick-Goodall, Jane. *In the Shadow of Man*. Boston: Houghton Mifflin, 1971; Dell paperback, 1972.

Van Lawick-Goodall, Jane and Hugo. *The Innocent Killers*. Boston: Houghton-Mifflin, 1971.

Newspapers

The main English paper is the *Daily News* (Box 9033, Dar es Salaam), which is government-owned and carries mostly local news. Kenya papers, the *East African Standard* and *Daily Nation,* along with British papers, are available at big hotel newsstands in Dar es Salaam and Arusha.

Other Sources of Information

Information Services Division, Ministry of Information & Broadcasting, Haji Brothers Building, Azikiwe St., Box 9142, Dar es Salaam; tel. 29311. *Ministry of Commerce and Industries,* Commerce Division, Co-op Building, Lumumba St., Box 9503, Dar es Salaam; tel. 27251. *Tanganyika Association of Chambers of Commerce,* Kelvin House, Independence Ave., Box 41, Dar es Salaam; tel. 21893.

The Information Services Division publishes a booklet, *Who, What, Where in Tanzania,* which is dry but gives an official, general introduction to the country.

The Tanzania Society (National Museum, Box 511, Dar es Salaam) publishes twice-yearly journals and special long issues with scholarly articles on history, anthropology, etc.; membership is 30/– a year. The University's Historical Association of Tanzania (Box 9184, Dar es Salaam) publishes three papers a year; membership is 10/– regular; 2/– for students. The University's Department of Literature (Box 35091, Dar es Salaam) publishes a creative writing journal; subscription 10/–.

Entry Requirements

Immigration

American citizens entering Tanzania on tourist, business, or transit visas are required to have their passport; a visa; a ticket to leave; a vaccination certificate for smallpox and cholera and, if coming from an infected area, yellow fever; and, if asked, adequate means to support yourself during your stay. If you cannot prove you have enough money and a method of leaving, you may be required to pay a deposit of up to 5,000/–.

In September 1973 Tanzania announced a ban on visitors whose passports contained visa stamps for South Africa, Rhodesia, or any Portuguese territory. The prohibition was relaxed a few days later when it was announced members of package tours would be exempt, while individual travelers, especially if coming in by road, will still be barred. The problem can be avoided altogether by individual travelers simply by obtaining a second, restricted passport for the white countries; see p. 61.

On arrival you will be issued a visitor's pass, which is valid from two weeks to six months, and like a visa must be renewed whenever it expires. On each arrival into Tanzania, you will usually be issued a separate visitor's pass.

Commonwealth citizens and citizens of Norway, Sweden, and Denmark do not need visas.

To obtain a visa, go to the nearest Tanzania diplomatic mission (see list below) and submit your passport and one copy of the form, two photos, and $3.15 visa fee. The New York visa office processes visas in two days. Visas are usually valid for a single entry during a six-month period, but if obtaining a visa in Kenya you can get a multiple-entry visa (good only for three months). You can get a visa by mail by sending a stamped, self-addressed envelope for return by certified or registered mail.

Inquiries and renewals of visas and visitor's passes: Principal Immigration Officer, Immigration Division, Ohio St., Box 512, Dar es Salaam; tel. 27291.

Diplomatic Missions of Tanzania

Canada—Embassy, 124 O'Connor St., Ottawa. *Ethiopia*—Embassy, Africa Ave., Box 1077, Addis Ababa; tel. 448155. *Great Britain*—High Commission, 43 Hertford St., London W1; tel. 01-499 8951. *U.N.*—Permanent Mission, 800 Second Ave., New York, 10017; tel. (212) 972-9160. *USA*—Embassy, 2010 Massachusetts Ave., N.W., Washington, D.C. 20036; tel. (202) 872-1005. *West Germany*—Embassy, 53 Bad Godesberg, Friedrich Strasse 25. *Zambia*—High Commission, Woodgate House, Cairo Road, Box 1219, Lusaka; tel. 75811.

The immigration departments of Kenya (New Jogoo House, Harambee St., Nairobi; tel. 28411) and Uganda (35 Jinja Road, Box 7165, Kampala; tel. 31031) issue visas for Tanzania.

Tanzania also has embassies in China (People's Republic), Egypt, France, Guinea (Conakry), India, Italy, Japan, Mexico, Netherlands, Nigeria, Sweden, USSR, and Zaire.

Customs

Tanzania, as part of the East African Community, has the same customs regulations as Kenya and Uganda; see p. 93.

Tourists planning to travel through Tanzania on their own by road, carrying quantities of camping equipment, photographic supplies, typewriters, etc., may be required to have Transfer Traffic forms covering these items for entry to, transit within, and exit from Tanzania. At least, that's what customs officials in Nairobi told us. We got the forms, but were never asked for them, and we don't know of other campers who ever got the forms. What's more, in the fall of 1973 Tanzania abruptly imposed a 20 percent importation tax on the new retail value of camping equipment. At this, Kenya's camping safari firms canceled camping safaris into Tanzania. Before planning your own private camping trip into the country, contact the customs department or tourist authority to see if the tax is still in effect (before publication we understood negotiations were under way to lift the tax).

Inquiries: East African Customs & Excise Department, Customs

House, Box 90601, Mombasa; tel. 21244. Regional Headquarters, Box 9053, Dar es Salaam; tel. 26231.

Currency Control

You may import as much foreign currency—cash or traveler's checks—as you want, as long as you declare it. The amount of foreign currency you may take out depends upon how much you brought in, and how many days you stayed in Tanzania. For example, if an independent traveler enters Tanzania with $1,500, stays 10 days, and leaves with $1,500, a Tanzania customs official might justifiably ask, "Didn't you spend any money?"

You cannot import or export any Tanzanian shillings whatsoever. East African traveler's checks are the best way to carry local money, including Kenya shillings. Hotel bills in Tanzania usually must be paid in hard currency, but may be paid in Tanzania shillings if you show a bank exchange slip.

Although there is a fairly active black market in Tanzania, foreign currencies may legally be changed at the National Bank of Commerce and at some big hotels. As in Kenya, those dealing in the black market may be jailed if caught.

Vehicle Documents

If you are driving a car registered outside East Africa, you must have a Carnet de Passages en Douanes (triptyque) issued by a recognized motor club. The car will be stamped at the first frontier post in East Africa and the exit *souche* at the last border point. If driving an East Africa-registered car you don't need a carnet in Tanzania.

Private sedans seating five persons or less may circulate freely for up to 14 days, but for a stay of 15 to 90 days you must report to a Revenue Office and obtain a free permit. All other vehicles (other than private sedans seating five or less) *must* obtain a Foreign Commercial Vehicle License, before or immediately upon arrival at the Tanzania border. This includes private cars or station wagons seating more than five, all types of four-wheel-drive vehicles, all VW buses and campers, company vehicles of all types, trailers, and rental cars from Kenya or Uganda. The Foreign Commercial Vehicle License (form number G.P. DSM 21670/8780/30m) may be obtained from the following addresses: Tanzania Tourist Center, IPS Building, Kimathi St., Box 48610, Nairobi; tel. 26888. Licensing Officer, Regional Finance Office,

Box 222, Arusha. Licensing Officer, Box 400, Tanga. Licensing Officer, Box 100, Mbeya. The rates for the license vary according to the weight of the vehicle; examples for 14 days: not exceeding 1,100 pounds— 15/–; 2,200 to 3,300 pounds—45/–; 3,300 to 4,400 pounds—60/–. If you rent a car in Nairobi and plan to drive it to Tanzania, be sure to check whether you or the car-hire company is to obtain the Foreign Commercial Vehicle License. If your vehicle is stopped in Tanzania without this license, you may be subject to a 20,000/– fine and your car may be impounded.

Visiting drivers from the U.S. may use their state's driving license for up to 90 days. It is a good idea to have an International Driving Permit as well, though.

All vehicles must be covered by third-party liability insurance. Short-term insurance never seems to be purchasable at the border but can be bought in Dar es Salaam from the National Insurance Corporation, Insurance House, Independence Ave., Box 9264, Dar es Salaam; tel. 26561. NIC has branch offices in Mbeya, Moshi, Tanga, and other large towns.

All vehicles not registered in Tanzania should carry an approved nationality plate ("USA," "D," or whatever).

Firearms

To import a gun and ammunition, you must have an Import Permit which should be obtained prior to your arrival at the border. The permit is free and can be obtained by sending the particulars of the gun and ammunition to: Firearms, Import Licensing Section, East African Customs & Excise Department, Regional Headquarters, Box 9053, Dar es Salaam; or by writing to Central Police Station, Box 9140, Dar es Salaam.

Getting to Tanzania

By Air

Dar es Salaam International Airport is served by East African Airways (EAA), Aeroflot, Air France, Air India, Air Madagascar, Air Zaire, Alitalia, British Airways (BOAC), Egyptair, Ethiopian Airlines, KLM, Lufthansa, Pan American, PIA, Sabena, SAS, Swissair, and Zambia Airways.

From Europe: From London: British Airways 1Xwk, EAA 1Xwk.

From Frankfurt: Lufthansa 1Xwk. From Paris: Air France 1Xwk. From Rome: Alitalia 1Xwk. There are also flights 1X or 2Xwk from Athens, Geneva, Munich, Vienna, Zurich, Amsterdam, Copenhagen, Brussels, and Moscow.

From the U.S.: From New York: Pan Am 1Xwk.

From other African countries: From Nairobi: EAA 34Xwk (7Xwk nonstop). From Nairobi to Kilimanjaro International Airport: EAA 15Xwk. From Lusaka: EAA 3Xwk, Zambia Airways 2Xwk. From Blantyre: EAA 1Xwk. From Johannesburg: SAS 1Xwk, Swissair 1Xwk. From Cairo: Egyptair 1Xwk. From Addis Ababa: Ethiopian Airlines 1Xwk. There are also flights to Dar es Salaam from Mombasa, Kinshasa, Bujumbura, Tananarive, Majunga, and Mauritius.

From elsewhere: There are flights from Pakistan.

Sample fares, one-way economy/tourist class, valid for a year, to or from Dar es Salaam, are listed below (add 20% to get approximate early 1975 fares):

from/to Dar es Salaam	U.S. dollars	Tanzania shillings	other currency
Addis Ababa	192	1,368	E$397
Blantyre	89	634	MK71
Cairo	386	2,758	Eg. £167
Entebbe	109	780	U.shs. 780
Frankfurt	525	3,753	DM1,307
London	525	3,753	£210
Lusaka	131	937	ZK84
Nairobi	64	455	K.shs. 455
New York	643–693	4,329–4,665	
Rome	494	3,529	Lire 274,100

There are also flights on Kenya's Caspair (p. 101) from Nairobi to Mwanza, Musoma, and Bukoba, Tanzania.

Airports

Dar es Salaam International Airport, about 16 km west of city center, is the main airport. The terminal has a restaurant and bar, National Bank of Commerce, post and telegraph outlets, duty-free shop. Airport general inquiries: tel. Wageni 298.

East African Airways has a 5/– bus service to the downtown terminal at Tancot House, City Drive at Ohio St. Terminal, tel. 21251. Taxis should be not more than 25/– to a downtown location from the airport. Tanzania Tours Ltd. runs VW buses (minimum four people) to the downtown hotels, 25/– per person, and to the beach hotels, 60/– per person.

Kilimanjaro International Airport, new in 1971, is in the Sanya Juu plains, 39 km west of Moshi, 48 km east of Arusha. Its facilities include an outdoor observation deck, lounge, bar and restaurant and National Bank of Commerce.

There is an EAA bus to the downtown Arusha terminal. The Tanzania Tours VW bus (minimum four people) charges 80/– per person from the airport to Arusha.

Departure tax: Tanzania levies a 20/– departure tax on those leaving the country. Have this fee with you at the check-in counter.

By Boat

See Introduction for international ships sailing to Tanzania coastal ports.

East African Railway Marine Services has two ships steaming around Lake Victoria, stopping in Kenya, Tanzania, and Uganda. The lake cruise is a minor tourist attraction. The M.V. *Victoria* was built in Scotland in 1960, disassembled, and transported to Kisumu, from where it now makes its weekly voyage. It has room for 38 first-class, 54 second-class, and 600 third-class passengers, and also carries cars. The *Victoria*'s schedule is: Monday—Kisumu, Kenya, to Musoma, Tanzania; Tuesday—Mwanza to Bukoba, Tanzania; Wednesday—Port Bell, Uganda, to Bukoba; Thurday—Mwanza to Musoma; Friday—Kisumu. Meals cost: breakfast—7/50; lunch—11/–; tea—3/–; dinner —12/–. Fares without meals (first-, second-, and third-class fares in that order): Kisumu–Mwanza—67/–, 34/90, 20/10. Port Bell–Mwanza—67/80, 35/30, 20/40. The all-inclusive fare, first-class, round-trip Kisumu–Kisumu—422/60.

There is also twice-weekly service on the S.S. *Usoga* from Mwanza to Bukoba, and EARMS service from Port Bell to the Sesse Islands, Kisumu to Homa Bay, and Mwanza to Ukerewe Island.

EARMS operates the passenger-vehicle-cargo steamer S.S. *Liemba* on Lake Tanganyika on a twice-monthly schedule from its home port of Kigoma, Tanzania, to Mpulungu, Zambia, and back; the trip takes four days each way. There is room for 18 first-class, 16 second-class, and 350 third-class passengers. However, the elderly, German-built *Liemba* is temporarily out of service for $285,000 worth of renovations but was scheduled to be sailing again in mid-1974.

Inquiries address, p. 103.

By Train

East African Railways (EAR) tracks currently run into Tanzania only from Kenya. There are twice-weekly trains from Nairobi and Mombasa via Voi to Moshi, Korogwe, Tanga, and Dar es Salaam. The through trip from Nairobi or Mombasa to Dar es Salaam takes nearly 48 hours. There is first-, second-, and third-class service. Sample fares (first, second, and third class in that order): Nairobi–Dar es Salaam—169/30, 88/10, 30/60. Inquiries: see p. 103.

The completion of the Tanzania Zambia Railway, also called the Great Uhuru Railway (see p. 410), is projected for 1975. Then it may be possible to take a series of trains from Mount Kenya to Victoria Falls. Inquiries: Executive Officer, Tanzania Zambia Railway Authority, Kinondoni Hostel, Box 2834, Dar es Salaam; tel. 68661.

By Bus

There are long-distance bus services into Tanzania from Kenya, and connecting services from Zambia.

From Kenya: East African Road Services (see p. 103) has twice-daily buses: Nairobi–Arusha–Moshi, 6–8 hours; fare—12/50 to 17/–. Nairobi–Dar, 24-hour trip; fare—50/–. Mombasa–Moshi–Arusha, 7–9-hour trip; fare—14/– to 17/–.

Merali Bus Services (Box 42559, Nairobi; tel. 24814) has a daily service Nairobi–Arusha–Moshi. Fares to Arusha: 1st class 20/–, 2d class 12/50.

From Zambia: United Bus Co. (UBZ) of Zambia has daily services from Lusaka to Tunduma; the trip takes about 24 hours. Inquiries: see p. 553. From Tunduma, Tanzania Road Services buses run daily to Mbeya, where connecting TRS buses leave daily for Dar es Salaam.

By Car

There are two main paved roads into Tanzania, one each from Kenya and Zambia on the following routes: Lusaka–Kabwe–Mpika–Tunduma–Mbeya–Iringa–Dar es Salaam (Routes Z-1 and T-6), and Nairobi–Namanga–Arusha (Routes K-5 and T-2). Other routes are mostly dirt.

Secondary routes from Kenya are Voi–Taveta–Moshi (Routes K-4 and T-4), which has a dirt section between Taveta and Voi; Mombasa–Horohoro–Tanga (Routes K-3 and T-5), which is paved on the Kenya side; and Nairobi–Narok–Masai Mara–Seronera (Serengeti) (Routes

K-6 and T-1), which is mostly good dirt. All of these routes can be traveled in ordinary sedans.

It is not possible to cross directly from Malawi into Tanzania, because their borders are still officially closed to traffic. Therefore the best route from Malawi is Blantyre–Rumphi–Chitipa (Zambia)–Tunduma–Mbeya–Dar es Salaam (Routes Q-1 and T-6).

Trip times: Nairobi–Arusha, 4–5 hours. Mombasa–Tanga, 3–4 hours. Nairobi–Dar es Salaam, 2 days. Lusaka–Dar es Salaam, 3–4 days. Blantyre–Dar es Salaam, 4–5 days.

Gasoline: The mid-1974 price of gasoline in Dar es Salaam was about $1.30 per U.S. gallon (premium), a few cents higher in other localities. There is plenty on the routes from Kenya, though a jerry-can might prove useful Nairobi–Seronera. Lusaka–Tunduma and Blantyre–Tunduma you should try to get the gas tank filled as often as possible.

Border posts on the main routes: from /to Kenya—Horohoro, Lobo, Namanga, Sirari, Taveta. From/to Zambia—Tunduma, Kasesya. From /to Uganda—Mtukura. From/to Burundi—Kabanga, Manyovu, Mabamba, Nyaruonga.

Getting around Tanzania

Travel Agents

Some of the main travel agencies in Tanzania that make hotel, transport and car-hire, and tour bookings are as follows:

In Dar es Salaam: *Fourways Travel Service (T) Ltd.,* Independence Ave., Box 2926, tel. 22378. *Kassam's Travel Agencies,* Kisutu St., Box 20787, tel. 24199. *Kearsley Travel,* Kearsley House, Makunganya St., Box 801, tel. 20607. *State Travel Service* (subsidiary of TTC), Independence Ave., Box 21295, tel. 22657. *Sykes Travel Agents Ltd.,* Box 613, tel. 22197. *Takim's Agencies,* Odeon Cinema Bldg., Jamhuri St., Box 20350, tel. 23394.

In Arusha: *Emslies Ltd.,* Goliondoi Road, Box 24, tel. 2754. *Kearsley Travel,* Uhuru Road, Box 142, tel. 2542.

By Air

East African Airways serves 17 Tanzania cities and towns: Arusha, Dar es Salaam, Dodoma, Iringa, Kilwa, Lindi, Mafia Island, Mbeya, Mtwara, Mwanza, Musoma, Nachingwea, Pemba Island, Songea, Tabora, Tanga, and Zanzibar.

Sample services and fares (tourist class) are as follows: *Dar es Salaam–Arusha*—15Xwk, regular fare—350/– one-way; 630/–return; 380/– six day excursion, return. *Dar–Mafia*—4Xwk; regular fare—105/– one-way; 189/– return. *Dar–Zanzibar*—20Xwk; regular fare—60/– one-way; 108/– return; 70/– six day excursion, return. *Dar–Mbeya*—3Xwk; regular fare—410/– one-way; 738/– return. *Arusha–Zanzibar*—4Xwk; regular fare—335/– one-way; 603/– return; 370/– six day excursion, return.

Airline Offices

East African Airways has the following offices in Tanzania: Tancot House, City Drive, Box 543, Dar es Salaam; tel. 21251 (also city office in Kilimanjaro Hotel, Azania Front Road). Dar es Salaam Airport, tel. Wageni 321. Downtown Arusha, tel. 2587. Kilimanjaro Airport, tel. 2485. Majestic Cinema Building, Zanzibar, tel. 2181. Also Dodoma, Iringa, Kigoma, Lindi, Mombo, Moshi, Mtwara, Musoma, Nachingwea, Njombe, Tabora, and Tanga.

Other airlines with offices in Dar es Salaam are: *Air Zaire,* IPS Building, Independence Ave., tel. 20836. *British Airways (BOAC)*, Coronation House, Independence Ave., tel. 20322. *Ethiopian Airlines,* Holland House, Independence Ave., tel. 24174. *Pan American,* International Airport, tel. 82368. *Zambia Airways,* IPS Building, Azikiwe St., tel. 29071. Others with Dar es Salaam offices are Aeroflot, Air France, Air India, Alitalia, KLM, Lufthansa, Sabena, SAS, and Swissair.

By Air Charter

There are two air charter firms in Tanzania: *Tanzanair,* Box 364, Dar es Salaam; tel. 82249; cable TANZANAIR. *Tim Air Charters,* Box 804, Dar es Salaam; tel. 82234; and Box 685, Arusha; tel. 2423; cable both places TIMAIR.

Tanzanair flies Cessna twin- and single-engine aircraft (210, 310, and 402). Tim Air flies Piper Aztec twin engine (seats five, costs 5/– per mile), Cherokee 6 single (seats six, costs 4/– per mile), and Cherokee Arrow single (seats three, costs 2/80 per mile). Sample round-trip, one-day fares in a Cherokee 6 from Dar es Salaam: to Mikumi Park—1,160/–; to Selous (Behobeho)—1,260/–; to Serengeti—3,480/–. In addition there are landing fees, airport taxes, dropping charges, and night stop charges.

By Train

EAR train tracks currently run between two different areas of Tanzania. The Tanga Line runs Moshi–Korogwe–Tanga–Dar es Salaam. The Central Line runs Dar es Salaam–Kilosa–Dodoma–Tabora, and then splits and goes north to Mwanza on Lake Victoria, and west to Kigoma on Lake Tanganyika. All the passenger trains have third-class accommodations, most also have second and first class on the long runs. Sample fares without meals (first-, second-, and third-class fares, respectively): Dar es Salaam–Mwanza—191/30; 99/50; 34/30. Dar–Kigoma —195/–; 101/40; 34/90. Dar–Moshi—86/80; 45/20; 16/50.

The Dar–Mwanza/Kigoma trains depart daily and take about 63 hours. The Dar–Moshi trains leave 2Xwk and take nearly 24 hours.

For bedding and meal charges, see p. 98.

The Dar es Salaam train station is at the southwest end of City Drive at Railway St., about 1 km from the city center.

Inquiries: Chief Traffic Manager, Box 468, Dar es Salaam; tel. 26241.

By Bus

Thousands of Tanzanians ride the buses, which go to all major and many minor towns in their country. The basic routes are operated by East African Railways (Tanzania Road Services—TRS), East African Road Services (EARS), and Dar es Salaam Motor Transport (DMT).

TRS has daily buses on the following routes: Moshi–Arusha–Dodoma–Iringa, 16 hours. Mbeya–Tunduma, 4 hours. Mbeya–Lake Rukwa, 6 hours.

DMT has daily service from Dar es Salaam to Arusha, Tanga, Mbeya, Bukoba, Kigoma. Specimen fares: Dar–Arusha—35/–. Dar–Mbeya—42/50. Dar–Bukoba—60/–. The DMT terminal in Dar es Salaam is at the junction of Nkrumah and Pugu roads.

Inquiries: TRS, City Drive, Box 468, Dar es Salaam, tel. 25241. EARS, see p. 103. DMT, Bandari St., New Port Area, Box 872, Dar es Salaam, tel. 25011.

By Rent-a-Car

Car-hire rates are generally higher in Tanzania than in Kenya, and the range of models is not available. If you want to drive around southern Kenya and northern Tanzania, it is best to rent a car in Nairobi. If you just want to visit a couple of parks in northern Tanzania only, it might pay to rent a car in Arusha then. Be sure to get all the proper papers from the Nairobi car hire firms before bringing their vehicle into Tanzania (see p. 321).

ARUSHA CAR HIRE

Sample rates for one day, 100 km (with operators offering that model): *Fiat 850*—85/– (Victoria). *VW Beetle*—91/– to 115/– (Afro, Subzali, Victoria). *Ford Cortina*—108/– (Victoria). *Peugeot 404*—110/– to 155/– (Afro, Subzali, Victoria). *Mercedes 200*—165/– (Subzali). *VW Bus*—170/– to 235/– (Afro, Subzali, Victoria). *Land-Rover 109*—180/– to 255/– (Afro, Subzali, Victoria). Gasoline is included in the rates of Subzali, and a driver is included in the Afro rates and the Subzali VW bus and Land-Rover rates.

Arusha car-hire firms: *Afro Tours (T) Ltd.,* Box 1252, tel. 2055. *Subzali Tours & Safaris,* Box 3061, tel. 3681. (Takes DC card.) *Victoria/Chui Tours,* Box 1208, tel. 3585.

DAR ES SALAAM CAR HIRE

Sample rates for one day, 100 km (with operators offering that model): *Fiat 600*—90/– (Valji & Alibhai). *VW Beetle*—105/– to 110/– (Subzali, Takim's, Valji & Alibhai). *Ford Escort*—110/– (Takim's). *Peugeot 204 or Datsun 1600*—120/– (Valji & Alibhai). *Mercedes 200*—165/– (Subzali). *VW Bus*—170/– to 235/– (Subzali, Valji & Alibhai). *Land-Rover 109*—216/– to 255/– (Subzali, Valji & Alibhai). Gasoline is included in the rates of Subzali and Valji & Alibhai, and a driver in the Subzali VW bus and Land-Rover rates.

Dar es Salaam car-hire firms: *Subzali Tours & Safaris,* Upanga Road, Box 3121, tel. 25907. *Takim's Agencies,* Jamhuri St. in Odeon Cinema Building, Box 20350, tel. 23394. *Valji & Alibhai,* Bridge St., Box 786, tel. 20522.

Driving in Tanzania

Drive on the left, overtake on the right. Give way to traffic coming from the right, except when you are in a traffic circle, and then keep going.

Auto club: See p. 107. Emergency road service available for members in Dar es Salaam only. Headquarters: AA, Cargen House, Azikiwe St., Box 3004, Dar es Salaam; tel. 21965.

Vehicle servicing, repairs, spare parts: Servicing costs as much as in Kenya, and the quality ranges from very good to poor, depending upon the garage. Generally, try to have your car worked on by the dealer or authorized agent for it in either Arusha or Dar es Salaam. The following makes are handled: *VW, Land-Rover,* and *Audi* (Cooper Motor Corp. in Dar es Salaam; Marshall's Ltd. in Arusha and Moshi), *Ford* (Riddoch Motors Ltd. in Dar, Arusha, Tanga, Mwanza, Iringa), *Toyota* (International Motor Mart Ltd. in Dar, Arusha, Moshi, Tanga), *Mercedes* and *Datsun* (D. T. Dobie & Co. in Dar), *Morris* and *Austin* (U.A.C. Motors in Dar, Moshi, Tanga), and *Citroën* (M. K. Mithani Ltd. in Dar).

Tour and Safari Operators and Package Tours

There is a fairly good selection of tours around northern and southern Tanzania and some into Kenya starting from Arusha, Dar es Salaam, Zanzibar, and Tanga. If you want to see both southern Kenya and northern Tanzania, you should probably use a Nairobi tour or safari operator. However, Dar es Salaam tour operators are better chosen for touring southern Tanzania. On Zanzibar the only official authorized agency is the one listed. Below we list most of the Tanzania tour and safari operators. Addresses not listed below can be found in the "Rent-a-Car" section above.

In Arusha: *Afro Tours (T) Ltd. Kearline Tours,* c/o Kearsley Travel, Uhuru Road, Box 142, tel. 2542. *Subzali Tours & Safaris. Tanzania Tours Ltd.,* Box 1369; tel. 3300; cable WONDERLAND. *Thorn Tree Safaris Ltd.,* Mount Meru Game Sanctuary, Box 659, tel. Usa River 43. *Victoria Tours.*

In Dar es Salaam: *Kearline Tours,* Box 1638, tel. 20607. *Subzali Tours & Safaris. Tanzania Tours Ltd.,* Permanent House, Independence Ave., Box 9354; tel. 25586; cable WONDERLAND. *Africana Tours,* c/o Africana Hotel, Box 2802, tel. 81231. *Ker, Downey & Selby Safaris Ltd.,* Box 9370; tel. 68152; cable GAMEFIELDS.

In Tanga: *Tanga Touring Service,* Box 881, tel. 3075.

On Zanzibar: *Tanzania Friendship Tourist Bureau,* Box 216, Zanzibar; tel. 2344; cable URAFIKI.

Below we list many of the tours offered by Tanzania tour and safari operators. The most reasonable tours are the "seat in car" (SIC), those packages with a set itinerary that operate on a basis of two to seven people per minibus. Private car tours (PC) are more exclusive and expensive, because only two or so clients are using a car and driver with their own or a set itinerary. The tour itineraries are listed with their destinations, length, price range, and tour operators.

Note: The government-run Tanzania Tours Ltd. in 1974 was to begin offering a 20 percent discount to tourists flying into Kilimanjaro International Airport or Dar es Salaam, in an effort to draw tourists away from Nairobi operators.

PACKAGE TOURS AROUND TANZANIA

From Arusha:

TP-1: *Arusha National Park.* 5½ hours in park: 139/– each of 2, SIC (Thorn Tree). 1 day in park and Mount Meru Game Sanctuary: 120/– to 160/– each of 2 or 4, SIC (Tanzania Tours, Subzali).

TP-2: *Moshi and Kilimanjaro (Marangu).* 1 day with stop at Moshi, lunch at Marangu Hotel, return to Arusha: 185/– to 230/– each of 2 or 4, SIC (Subzali, Tanzania Tours).

TP-3: *Kilimanjaro Climb.* See Route T-4, p. 399, for details.

TP-4: *Tarangire National Park.* 1 day to and around the park: 231/– to 350/– each of 2 or 4, SIC (Thorn Tree, Subzali). 2 days: 561/– each of 2, SIC (Thorn Tree).

TP-5: *Lake Manyara National Park.* 1 day to and around the park: 240/– to 347/– each of 2 or 4, SIC (Thorn Tree, Subzali); 406/– each of 2 in PC (Afro). 2 days: 398/– to 578/– each of 2 or 4, SIC (Thorn Tree, Subzali); 518/– each of 2 in PC (Afro).

TP-6: *Ngorongoro Crater.* 1 day with a crater-floor tour in a TTC Land-Rover: 424/– each of 2, SIC (Thorn Tree). 2 days: 468/– to 655/– each of 2 or 4, SIC (Thorn Tree, Subzali).

TP-7: *Tarangire and Lake Manyara.* 2 days, one in each park: 550/– to 720/– each of 2 or 4, SIC (Tanzania Tours, Subzali); 700/– each of 2 in PC (Afro).

TP-8: *Lake Manyara and Ngorongoro.* 2 days, one in each park: 598/– to 762/– each of 2 or 4, SIC (Thorn Tree, Tanzania Tours, Subzali); 735/– each of 2 in PC (Afro). 3 days: 739/– to 946/– each of 2 or 4, SIC (Thorn Tree, Tanzania Tours, Subzali); 1,036/– each of 2 in PC (Afro).

TP-9: *Ngorongoro and Serengeti.* 4 days, including stop at Olduvai Gorge: 1,425/– each of 2, SIC (Subzali).

TP-10: *Manyara, Ngorongoro, and Serengeti.* A stop at Olduvai Gorge may or may not be included. 2 days: 450/– each, SIC (Victoria). 5 days: 1,474/– to 1,895/– each of 2 or 4, SIC (Thorn Tree, Tanzania Tours, Subzali): 1,967/– each of 2 in PC (Afro). 6 days including 2 nights at Fort Ikoma Lodge: 2,275/– each of 2, SIC (Subzali).

TP-11: *Tarangire, Manyara, Ngorongoro, and Serengeti.* 6 days including Olduvai: 2,415/– each of 2 in PC (Afro).

TP-12: *Arusha Park, Tarangire, Manyara, Ngorongoro, and Serengeti.* 7 days, with Olduvai: 2,530/– each of 2, SIC (Subzali).

TP-13: *Arusha Park, Manyara, Ngorongoro, Serengeti, and Dar es Salaam Beach Hotel.* 15 days, including Olduvai and 7 nights at a Dar beach hotel, but excluding air fare to/from Dar: 3,500/– each of 2, SIC (Subzali).

From Dar es Salaam:

TP-14: *Dar City Tour.* Usually includes harbor, Kariakoo Market, University, Village Museum, Oyster Bay, State House, National Museum; 2½ to 3 hours: 35/– to 65/– each of 2 or 4, SIC (Kearline, Africana, Tanzania Tours, Subzali).

TP-15: *Dar Shopping Tour.* Independence Ave. and Kariakoo Market. 3 hours: 45/– each of 4, SIC (Tanzania Tours).

TP-16: *Kunduchi Beach and Ruins, Village Museum, Dar Wood Carvers.* 1 day: 150/– each of 2, SIC (Kearline).

TP-17: *Bagamoyo.* Half-day: 50/– to 55/– each of 4, SIC (Africana, Tanzania Tours). 1 day: 60/– to 180/– each of 2 or 4, SIC (Tanzania Tours, Kearline, Subzali).

TP-18: *Zanzibar Island.* City and country tour usually includes Old Zanzibar Fort, Beit-el-Ajaib, People's Palace, Museum, harbor, Livingstone's house, Marahubi and Kibweni palaces, Persian baths, clove and other plantations. 1 day excluding Dar–Zanzibar air fare: 84/– to 135/– each of 2 or 4, SIC (Tanzania Friendship, Subzali, Kearline). Overnight excluding air fare: 135/– to 184/– each of 2 or 4, SIC (Tanzania Friendship, Kearline). Half-day including air fare: 380/– each of 3, SIC (Kearline). 1 day including air fare: 350/– to 390/– each of 2 or 4, SIC (Africana, Tanzania Tours). Overnight with air fare: 500/– each of 2, SIC (Africana). Tanzania Friendship also has short tours of the island, such as to Mangapwani or Uroa or Makunduchi beaches for an hour swim: 22/50 to 65/– each of 2, SIC; or to Jozani Forest for an hour visit: 40/– each of 2, SIC.

TP-19: *Mafia Island.* Includes air fare, deep-sea fishing, meals: 1 day: 430/– to 530/– each of 4 or 5, SIC (Tanzania Tours, Africana). 2 days: 575/– to 650/– each of 4 or 5 (Tanzania Tours, Africana).

TP-20: *Mikumi National Park.* 2 days to and around the park: 460/– to 850/– each of 2 or 4, SIC (Tanzania Tours, Africana,

Kearline, Subzali). 3 days: 680/– each of 4, SIC (Tanzania Tours).

TP-21: *Selous Game Reserve*. 1 day to and around: 520/– each of 5, SIC (Africana). 2 days: 1,005/– to 1,150/– each of 4 to 5, SIC (Africana, Tanzania Tours). 3 days: 1,450/– each of 4, SIC (Tanzania Tours).

TP-22: *Mikumi Air Safari*. 1 day to and from by air, around by car: 430/– to 520/– each of 3 to 5, SIC (Tanzania Tours, Africana, Kearline). 2 days: 785/– each of 4, SIC (Tanzania Tours).

TP-23: *Selous Air Safari*. 1 day: 510/– each of 5 (Tanzania Tours). 2 days: 930/– to 975/– each of 4 to 5 (Tanzania Tours, Ker, Downey & Selby). 4 days: 1,500/– each of 4, SIC (Ker, Downey & Selby).

TP-24: *Serengeti Air Safari*. 2 days: 1,500/– each of 4, SIC (Africana).

TP-25: *Lake Manyara and Ngorongoro Air Safari*. 3 days: 1,400/– to 1,650/– each of 4 or 5, SIC (Africana, Tanzania Tours).

TP-26: *Lake Manyara, Ngorongoro, and Serengeti Air Safari*. 2 days: 1,500/– each of 4, SIC (Tanzania Tours).

TP-27: *Dar es Salaam, Zanzibar, Arusha Park, Lake Manyara, Ngorongoro, and Serengeti*. Includes Dar es Salaam and Zanzibar city tours, but not air fares to Zanzibar and Arusha; 9 days: 3,100/– each, SIC (Subzali).

From Tanga:

TP-28: *Tanga and Environs*. Amboni Caves, Galanos Sulphur Springs, Tongoni ruins, Tanga; 1 day: 50/– each, SIC (Tanga Touring).

PACKAGE TOURS AROUND TANZANIA AND KENYA

From Arusha:

TP-29: *Amboseli Game Reserve*. 2 days: 680/– each of 2, SIC (Subzali).

TP-30: *Tsavo West National Park,* 2 days with overnight at Tsavo Inn: 690/– each of 2, SIC (Subzali).

TP-31: *Milk Run: Lake Manyara, Ngorongoro, Serengeti, Masai Mara, Amboseli, and Nairobi*. 7 days with one night in Nairobi: 2,716/– each of 2 in PC (Afro).

TP-32: *Lake Manyara, Ngorongoro, Serengeti, Arusha Park, and Mombasa Beach*. 15 days with 8 nights at Mombasa beach hotel: 3,500/– each of 2, SIC (Subzali).

General Information

Language

Swahili is the official language in Tanzania, though English is spoken in the cities, some towns and tourist areas. A Swahili glossary is on p. 124. Some Continental languages, especially German, are spoken at the major hotels, particularly those on the coast.

Time

Greenwich Mean Time plus three hours (see p. 126).

Weights and Measures

Tanzania uses the metric system officially.

Electricity

230 volts AC.

Holidays

Jan. 12—Zanzibar Revolution Day (overthrow of sultan's government, 1964). Good Friday. Easter Sunday and Monday. April 26—Union Day (Tanganyika and Zanzibar united in 1964). May 1—International Workers Day. May 24—United Nations Day. July 7—Saba Saba Day (seventh day of seventh month—anniversary of formation of TANU, the national party). Dec. 9—Independence and Republic Day (anniversary of both, 1961). Dec. 25—Christmas. Id-ul-Azha and Maulidi are observed by Moslems, while Hindus have several of their own holidays.

Hours of Business

Office and shop hours are generally 7:30 A.M. to 12:30 P.M., 2 P.M. to 6 P.M., Monday to Friday. Shops on Saturday are open until 1 P.M., then usually close for the weekend.

Banks are open 8:30 A.M. to noon, Monday to Friday; 8:30 A.M. to 11 A.M. Saturday.

Bars generally serve 10 A.M. to 2 P.M., 5 P.M. to 11 P.M., daily.

Banks

There is only one bank, the *National Bank of Commerce,* main branch, NBC House, City Drive at Azikiwe St., Box 1255, Dar es

Salaam; tel. 28671; cable NATCOMCITY. There are 9 branches in Dar es Salaam, 2 in Arusha, and 30 others throughout the country.

Diplomatic Representatives in Tanzania

All the following have offices in Dar es Salaam, with Zanzibar offices as indicated: *Burundi*—Embassy, 397 United Nations Road, tel. 22416. *Canada*—High Commission, Gailey & Roberts Building, Independence Ave., Box 1022; tel. 20651; cable DOMCAN. *Ethiopia*—Embassy, State House Ave., tel. 23941. *Great Britain*—High Commission, Permanent House, Maktaba St. at Independence Ave., Box 9200; tel. 29601; cable UKREP. *Kenya*—Visa Office, Tanzania Immigration Division, Ohio St., Box 512, tel. 27291. *Rwanda*—Embassy, 32 Upanga Road, tel. 2371. *USA*—Embassy, National Bank of Commerce House, City Drive, Box 9123; tel. 22775; cable AMEMBASSY. Consulate—83A Kelele Square, Box 4, Zanzibar; tel. 2118. *West Germany*—Embassy, NBC House, City Drive, Box 2590; tel. 23286; cable DIPLOGERMA. *Zambia*—High Commission, 442 Upanga Road, tel. 24175.

Other countries with diplomatic representation in Dar es Salaam include Algeria, Australia, Austria, Belgium, Bulgaria, China (People's Republic), Cuba, Cyprus, Czechoslovakia, Denmark, East Germany, Egypt, Finland, France, Greece, Guinea (Conakry), Holy See, Hungary, India, Indonesia, Ireland, Israel, Italy, Japan, Mexico, North Korea, North Vietnam, Netherlands, Norway, Pakistan, Poland, Rumania, Somalia, South Vietnam, Spain, Sudan, Sweden, Switzerland, Syria, USSR, and Yugoslavia.

Health

For a discussion of health, see p. 55. Tap water is safe in Dar es Salaam and Arusha; elsewhere inquire locally. Tourist hotels usually warn you if you cannot drink water from the tap.

There are fairly good doctors and hospitals in Dar es Salaam, and district and mission hospitals elsewhere. The two government-operated hospitals in Dar es Salaam are: Aga Khan Hospital, Ocean Road, tel. 23521; and Muhimbili Hospital, tel. 26211. The U.S. Embassy has the names of Dar es Salaam doctors and dentists. In Arusha there is the General Hospital, tel. 2318; and the Mount Meru Hospital, tel. 2233.

Most tourists join the Flying Doctors' Society, whose services extend to Tanzania; see Introduction, "Health Hazards and Precautions."

Mail, Telegrams

For postal rates within and from East Africa, including Tanzania, see p. 128.

The General Post Office in Dar es Salaam is on City Drive at Mkwepu St. In Arusha the GPO is by the clock tower in town center. Post office hours in Tanzania are generally 7:45 A.M. to 5 P.M. Monday–Friday, 7:45 A.M. to 1 P.M. Saturday; stamps are sold 9 to 10 A.M. Sunday.

Telegrams can be sent from post office branches during regular hours. See Kenya for cable rates.

Telephone Calls

For directions on how to use pay telephones, see p. 129. Coin phones in Tanzania also take –/50 pieces. Directory inquiries: 991 in Dar es Salaam, 791 in Arusha. English time announcement: 993 in Dar es Salaam. Emergencies (police, fire, ambulance) in most towns and all cities—999.

Shopping

The best items to shop for in Tanzania are wood carvings, Masai beadwork, gemstones, fabrics, and meerschaum pipes.

Wood carvings are done by two tribes: the Zaramo and the Makonde, both of whom use ebony from the 100-mile-wide coastal strip of that wood. The Zaramo are from the Dar es Salaam environs, and their work tends to be figures of old men, nude women carrying urns, or birds and animals, and walking sticks. The street sellers in Dar and Arusha sell the more stereotyped Zaramo carvings. The Makonde tribe originates from southern Tanzania near the Mozambique border, but many now live and carve around Dar es Salaam. Makonde carvings have fairly earned a reputation for being unique and often grotesque. A common Makonde theme is the "family tree," a tall, complex sculpture depicting struggling humanity. Other pieces look Picassoesque, with elongated, contorted limbs and bulging eyes. The best place to buy good Makonde sculptures at reasonable prices is the *National Arts of Tanzania* gallery on India Street in Dar es Salaam (Box 9363; tel. 29231). This TTC company has employed many Makonde carvers at their warehouse in the industrial area on Chang'ombe Road; you can visit them on the site and watch them carve. At the downtown gallery prices range from 20/– for a small piece, to 150/– for a medium-size family tree, to 500/— for a 5-foot-high screen panel with several figures in it. At the gallery, if you pay in hard currency you get a 10 percent discount, and you must pay in hard currency if you want to have things packed and shipped from there. Other shops which carry Makonde and Zaramo carvings of varying quality and prices in Dar es Salaam: *Serengeti Tourist Centre* on Azikiwe St.; *Museum of African Art* (actually a curio shop) and *Zanzibar Antiques,* both on Independence Ave. In Arusha, National Arts plans to open a gallery. Meanwhile, for carvings try *Tourist Kiosk, Arusha Tourist Center, Curios & Crafts, African Art & Curios*—all on Joel Maeda Road—and *Katen's* on Uhuru Road.

Masai beadwork is not only used by the Masai women as body ornamentation and status symbols, but now is also earning them cash. There is a noticeable difference between the "old" beadwork formerly done with softly colored Czechoslovakian glass beads and the "new" things made with brightly colored Hong Kong plastic beads. The best place to buy "old" Masai beadwork (plus shields, spears, and gourds) is in Arusha at the Tourist Kiosk. The owner, Mrs. Abrams, has been collecting good pieces of Masai work for the past few years, and she can tell you the name and use of many objects. Some of her prices: a large old *ilpusi* (stiff, multirowed bead necklace)—180/— to 250/—; small potent herb necklace—20/—; beaded leg decoration—25/—; "old" Masai spear—70/—; "new" Masai spear—20/— to 40/—.

Gemstones mined in Tanzania are rubies, sapphires, zircons, green tourmalines, moonstones, garnets, amethysts, topaz, beryl, tiger's-eye, agates, diamonds, and tanzanite. Tanzanite, a clear, blue stone, was discovered in northern Tanzania in 1967, and has been described by one gem expert as "like a sapphire, but softer." Gemstone shops in Dar es Salaam: *Peeras* and *Zanzibar Antiques,* both on Independence Ave., and *Silver Curio Shop* on Azikiwe St. In Arusha: *Tanganyika Gems,* on Joel Maeda Road.

Fabrics popular in Tanzania are the *khanga* and *kitenge.* The *khanga* is an almost see-through material which is manufactured in Tanzania in bright colors with bold patterns and political slogans. The *kitenge's* indigenous home is Indonesia, but it is also made in Holland, Belgium, West Africa, and Tanzania. It is heavier cotton than the *khanga,* and is also printed with bright colors and vivid designs. Two meters of fine Tanzania *kitenge* cost about 21/—. Some ready-made clothes of *kitenge* and *khanga* are women's dresses (short—40/— to 60/—; long—80/—·to 125/—) and men's shirts—20/— to 45/—. Dar es Salaam shops selling *khanga* and *kitenge* are *Rozana's* and *New Avenues,* both on Independence Ave. In Arusha, try *Katen's* on Uhuru Road.

Meerschaum pipes are popular items with male tourists. Meerschaum (German "seafoam"—it resembles that when floated on water) is mined in Sinya on the Tanzania side of the border by Lake Amboseli. This is the largest known deposit of it in the world. It is found in pockets or cavities in an upthrust limestone ridge 2 miles in length. After extraction the meerschaum is taken to a central cleaning area at the mine, then transported to the Tanganyika Meerschaum Corporation (Box 3151) factory in Arusha. There it goes through 80 distinct processes before its final inspection and packaging. The factory makes dozens of styles, ranging from the Caveman to the Townsman, from the Kiko Rough to the Kudu. It is possible to buy "seconds" and regular pipes from the factory showroom for less than in shops. Otherwise, in Arusha the *New Arusha Hotel giftshop* and *Soula's* sell pipes ranging in price from 25/– to about 100/–. In Dar es Salaam, the *National Arts Gallery* sells some beautiful hand-carved pipes starting at about 200/–.

For shopping on Zanzibar, see p. 359.

Wildlife and Game Parks

Until Tanzania's independence in 1961, game conservation was sketchy. The Germans during their rule established a game reserve near what is today Ruaha National Park. The British set aside Serengeti as a reserve in 1937, established a National Parks Board in 1951, gazetted Lake Manyara as a reserve and Ngorongoro as a special multifunctional conservation area.

After self-government in 1960 an International Wildlife Conference was held in Arusha, and Julius Nyerere issued the Arusha Manifesto stating that "wildlife is an integral part of our resources," and giving clear support for practical wildlife management schemes. Lake Manyara was gazetted a national park in 1960, Ngurdoto Crater in 1961, Momela Lakes in 1962, Mikumi and Ruaha in 1964, Gombe Stream in 1968, Tarangire in 1969, Arusha (incorporating Ngurdoto Crater, Momela Lakes, and Mount Meru) in 1970, Kilimanjaro in 1973 and Katavi in 1974. Twelve game reserves were also established, ranging from the immense 15,000-square-mile Selous in southern Tanzania with its more than 35,000 elephants, to the tiny 95-acre reserve on Saa Nane Island near Mwanza in Lake Victoria.

Conservation of wildlife in Tanzania received a great boost in February 1974 when the Tanzanian government declared that all hunting would be permanently banned. Generally Tanzania does not have as severe a problem of human population closing in on the game parks and reserves as does Kenya, though poaching is just as bad, especially around Serengeti, where an estimated 40,000 animals are poached yearly. To help Tanzanians understand why game conservation is important and to prove that the parks were not just established for "rich" people, the National Parks Board has produced films in Swahili to show all over Tanzania, particularly to tribes living around parks and reserves, and has opened hostels so schoolchildren can spend a night in their own parks. To train Africans to take over the staff positions in parks and reserves, the College of African Wildlife Management was started at Mweka near Moshi in 1963. The government also helps sponsor game research projects, such as the important Serengeti Research Institute employing 18 scientists from all over the world who are studying ecological problems in Serengeti.

To quote Norman Myers's book *The Long African Day:* "Tanzania started off independence with one park; now it has [eight], and it gives three times as large a share of its national kitty to its parks as the U.S. gives to its own, out of a total budget amounting to what New York spends on ice cream. . . . People complain the world is losing the world's heritage in Africa, but when Africans ask for help they hear how hard the world is finding it to make ends meet. . . . The parks of Tanzania need the cost of one destroyer to keep them going until today's child grows up. . . ."

If you wish to donate to Tanzania's parks, send contributions to The Michael Grzimek Memorial Fund, c/o Tanzania National Parks, Box 3134, Arusha. A worthwhile conservation group to join is the East African Wild Life Society; see p. 136.

Game Park Entry Fees

Entry to game reserves is free, but permission should be obtained from the Game Division, Lehmann's Building on Independence Ave., Box 1994, Dar es Salaam; or from the district or regional Game Division offices, whose addresses are listed under each reserve in our route.

Entry fees to Serengeti, Lake Manyara, and Ngorongoro Crater are 5/– per day for an adult Tanzania resident, 20/– per day for a nonresident adult. All the other national parks are 5/– for residents, 10/– for nonresidents. Children under 6 years of age enter free; those 6 to 18 are charged half-price.

Vehicle entry fees: For all the parks except Ngorongoro, all vehicles under 4,400 pounds cost 10/–, over this 60/–; there is also a special 20/– fee for commercial vehicles registered outside Tanzania. For Ngorongoro Crater the vehicle charges are 10/– for up to 3,000 pounds, 20/– for cars weighing more. Only TTC Land-Rovers are allowed onto the crater floor.

All entry fees are valid for exactly 24 hours from the time of entry. The park and reserve gates are generally open from dawn until dusk— about 6 A.M. to 6 P.M.

Birdwatching

Tanzania has hundreds of species of birds, and while the best places for observing them are in the parks and reserves, one Natural History Society member reported 130 species near her house in Korogwe in the east. The parks with lakes have the most varied birdlife, drawing many migrants in the European winter months. Both Lake Manyara and Arusha parks have about 380 species each, including visiting greater and lesser flamingos. The National Parks have compiled check- lists of the birds in most of the parks, and these, along with the in- dividual park guidebooks, are most helpful to use while touring in the parks.

See also this section under Kenya for bird books and societies.

Historic and Prehistoric Sites

Tanzania has 83 gazetted national monuments, of which about 27 are open to the public, including Olduvai Gorge, Kunduchi Ruins north of Dar es Salaam, Kilwa Island ruins south of Dar, Livingstone's one-time house in Tabora, the Mbozi Meteorite off the Mbeya–Tun- duma highway, and the rock paintings between Kolo and Kondoa. All of them are protected by the Antiquities Division of the Ministry of Education, which has published some very interesting and readable guide booklets on several of the monuments. Inquiries: Antiquities Division, National Museum, Box 9121, Dar es Salaam, tel. 21241.

Water Sports

Tanzania's water sports are concentrated along the Indian Ocean coastline and islands. The miles of white sandy beaches and protective coral reef make swimming and goggling safe and pleasurable, particularly north of Dar es Salaam and off Zanzibar and Mafia islands. TTC's Seafaris has equipment for hire at Bahari Beach, Kunduchi Beach, New Africa, and Mafia Island hotels; or through Box 9500, Dar es Salaam; tel. 28181; cable OVEROTEL. Goggling on a 24-foot twin-engine speedboat, up to six people: 70/– per hour. Goggling on a 14-foot single outboard, four people: 50/– per hour. Goggling equipment: 20/– per person per day. Sailboats for two: 20/– per hour. Water skiing: 40/– per half-hour. Round trip to Mbudya Island off Kunduchi Beach: 20/– per person.

Hotel Africana also has water sports. Goggling trips with equipment: 25/– per person (minimum of three) for two hours. Sailboat for one: 30/–. Water skiing for 4–5 minutes: 15/– per person. Pedal boats: 20/– per hour. Dory-17 for up to eight people: 90/– per hour. Round trips to Mbudya Island: 15/– per person.

Fishing

Tanzania has both sea and fresh-water fishing. Deep-sea fishing is excellent off the seacoast, with most facilities around Dar es Salaam and Mafia Island. During the northeast monsoons between October and March, migratory fish—marlin, sailfish, tuna, shark—swim down to the warmer waters. From May to October, the period of southeast monsoons, large local fish abound.

Mafia Island, very accessible to the Zanzibar Channel in which the big game fish hang out, is one of the best places for serious deep-sea fishermen. TTC's Seafaris operates a fleet of fishing boats from the Mafia Island Lodge. Their fishing boats include a 24-foot Coronet Twin—100/– per hour, 500/– for full day; 33-foot diesel-powered boat—80/– per hour, 400/– full day; and 24-foot diesel-powered boat—60/– per hour, 350/– full day. Fishing gear is included in price of the boat. Inquiries: Seafaris, Box 9500, Dar es Salaam, tel. 28181; cable OVEROTEL. A number of tour operators in Dar es Salaam who offer package tours to Mafia Island include deep-sea fishing in their itinerary; see Tanzania package TP-19.

Along the Dar es Salaam mainland coast, deep-sea fishing is available through Seafaris at the Kunduchi Beach, Bahari Beach, and New Africa hotels. Log Cabins, 29 km north of Dar es Salaam, also has deep-sea fishing boats renting from 35/– per hour. Hotel Africana's deep-sea fishing boats are 90/– per hour, with a minimum of three hours and a maximum of four people.

Fresh-water fishing is best in northern Tanzania in the streams flowing off Kilimanjaro and Mount Meru. On Kilimanjaro there are two fishable streams on the east side, two on the south side, and three on the west side. All of these have some trout in them from 5,000 up to 6,500 feet altitude. Low water is usually February to March, but otherwise the streams are clear year round. Licenses and arrangements for fishing can be made through the Kilimanjaro Tourist Association, Box 381, Moshi; or through the Revenue Officer, Box 109, Moshi, tel. 2211. License fees are 10/– per day, 30/– per week, 50/– per half-year; children under 16 are charged half-price. To fish in Mount Meru's two streams, it is necessary to get a license from the Arusha Information Bureau, Box 494, Arusha; tel. 2030. License fees are 5/– per day, 15/– per month, 25/– per half-year.

Fishing is also possible in Lake Tanganyika, especially from the piers at the port of Kigoma. There you can try for Nile perch, tiger-fish, yellowbelly, and tilapia.

Hunting and Photo Safaris

Although Tanzania had the reputation for being one of the best places in the world for big-game hunting, the government permanently banned all big-game hunting in February 1974. Rather than hunting with a gun, try a camera instead. Tanzania-based safari firms which once took out hunters and may now take out photographers are: *Tanzania Wildlife Safaris Ltd.*, Box 602, Arusha; tel. 2076; and Box 9270, Dar es Salaam; tel. 63352; cable WILDLIFE. *Ker, Downey & Selby Safaris (T) Ltd.*, Box 9370, Dar es Salaam; tel. 68152; cable GAME-FIELDS. *Mathews Safaris Tanzania*, Box 1314, Moshi; tel. 3096. *Mount Meru Game Sanctuary*, Box 659, Arusha; tel. Usa River 43.

Dar es Salaam

Dar es Salaam, with a population of about 343,911, is Tanzania's largest city, as well as its capital, its major port, and its industrial center. While new steel high rises are beginning to dominate downtown Dar (as it's called for short), the "Haven of Peace" still retains a beautiful harbor front and a number of charming old Arab, German, British, and Indian buildings in its city center, enough to make a walking tour worthwhile. Dar is not the cosmopolitan city that Nairobi is becoming, but has enough to occupy a visitor's time for a day or two, though accommodations are better at the beach hotels. As when visiting

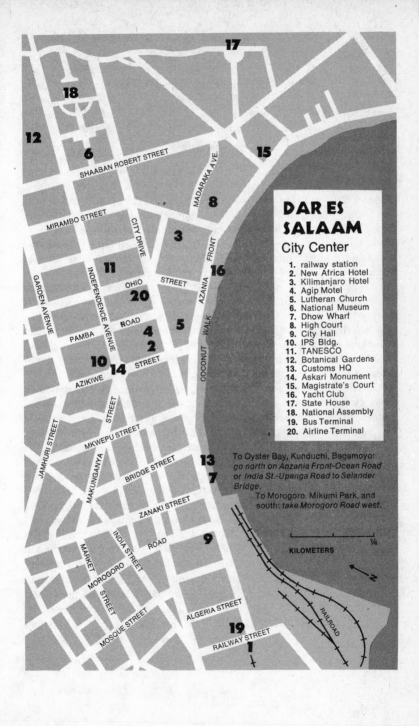

DAR ES SALAAM

City Center

1. railway station
2. New Africa Hotel
3. Kilimanjaro Hotel
4. Agip Motel
5. Lutheran Church
6. National Museum
7. Dhow Wharf
8. High Court
9. City Hall
10. IPS Bldg.
11. TANESCO
12. Botanical Gardens
13. Customs HQ
14. Askari Monument
15. Magistrate's Court
16. Yacht Club
17. State House
18. National Assembly
19. Bus Terminal
20. Airline Terminal

To Oyster Bay, Kunduchi, Bagamoyo: go north on Anzania Front-Ocean Road or India St.-Upanga Road to Selander Bridge.

To Morogoro, Mikumi Park, and south: take Morogoro Road west.

KILOMETERS ¼

N

Mombasa, a visitor to Dar should plan to take it slow and easy, and should seek out cool swims and drinks as often as possible.

Dar es Salaam (from Arabic *Dar Salaam*—"the house or haven of peace or salvation") was founded near a small fishing village by Seyyid Majid, Sultan of Zanzibar, in the 1860s. Majid chose the location because of its attractive, natural harbor, and he hoped by building a palace and encouraging trade to make Dar es Salaam the main caravan terminus, port, and commercial core of East Africa. Building of the sultan's city began in 1865–66, with streets planned, stone wells sunk, and the palace constructed; most of this activity was on the southwest end of the harbor front. The palace, which no longer stands, was a two-story building with slanted walls, the top story sunk back from a crenelated rampart in front. North along the harbor front were more buildings, such as the "Official Hotel," now thought to be the Old Boma. The expansion of Dar came to a rather abrupt halt when Sultan Majid died in 1870, possibly after a fall in his new palace. His half-brother and successor, Barghash, had no use for or interest in the newly developing mainland town, and building ceased for two decades. However, in 1877, under the inspiration of Sir William Mackinnon, a road from Dar to Lake Malawi was started, though like the Mackinnon road in Kenya, this one progressed only 83 miles southwest into Uzaramo by 1881 when the project was abandoned.

In 1887 the German East Africa Company established a station in Dar es Salaam, and four years later the town became the seat of administration, main port, and commercial center for German East Africa. Their buildings were focused at the eastern end of the harbor, with the previously Arab-built southwestern harbor area used for the port, warehousing, and commercial structures. The government offices went up along Azania Front, and behind them were built the German civil servant residences—airy, two-story, whitewashed stone villas with their overlapping open areas treated as one large botanical garden. Government House, the official German residence, was at the harbor's eastern end. It was heavily damaged during World War I, and its 1922 reconstruction by the British was larger and more ornate than the original German design. This is now State House and President Nyerere's official residence, but he doesn't like to use it for more than his office and resides with his family in a modest house north of Dar. This whole German-British administration area is now the center of the Tanzania national government, and the residential neighborhood still serves as such but also includes the Botanical Gardens, National

Museum, and Karimjee Hall (where Parliament meets). During the British era, residential areas expanded into Sea View by Selander Bridge, Regent Estate, Kinondoni, and Oyster Bay north of Selander Bridge.

West of Dar the industrial and dock areas spawned working-class neighborhoods, such as Chang'ombe and Kariakoo, around their edges. Some of them became tribal communities of Ngoni or Zaramo who had come seeking work and lived with those of their tribe. Many Africans lived and still live in "Swahili" houses, one-story houses with rooms for rent off either side of a central corridor, and a courtyard in the back. Big modern blocks of apartments, now being erected by the National Housing Corporation, appeal to the artisans and clerical workers.

One of the best ways to get a feel for a city is to take walks around it. Below are two suggested routes through downtown Dar es Salaam.

Dar es Salaam Walking Tour I

This is about 2 km long and takes in the harbor front, the government offices, and the National Museum.

Start your walk at the *New Africa Hotel,* City Drive at Azikiwe Street, which is considered city center. On this plot formerly stood the Kaiserhof, a German officers' club which was converted into the first New Africa. The new New Africa was built in 1968. Continue to the end of Azikiwe, passing the *Lutheran Church,* begun in 1898 and looking very Bavarian with its many little sloping tile roofs.

Cross the street and walk along the tree-shaded *harbor front,* taking an occasional footpath down to the water's edge to see some of the ships anchored in the harbor, or a dhow sail by on its way to the Dhow Wharf (see Walking Tour II). Pass the *Yacht Club* on your right, the large *Kilimanjaro Hotel* on your left. Turn left up Mirambo Street, and on your right is the *Magistrate's Court.* This is one of several German office buildings, dating from the 1890s, built in a classical style, with high ceilings, ground-floor masonry, and second-floor verandas with prefabricated carved beams and screens imported from Germany. Two blocks farther go right for one block on City Drive, then left onto Shaaban Robert Street. The National Museum is in a square block grassy plot on your right.

The *National Museum* is open daily 9:30 A.M. to 7 P.M., and admission is free. In the 1930s the British Governor MacMichael inspired the creation of a permanent museum, and the first building was opened in 1940. Still standing, it has an Arabesque theme, rounded horseshoe-type windows, and a curved entryway with a carved Zanzibar door dating from 1789; inside are two halls which display mainly ethnological collections of the tribes of Tanzania. The museum's modern front extension building was finished in 1965. It houses the prehistory collection (the real skull of *Zinjanthropus boisei* from Olduvai Gorge is kept safely in storage); an upstairs historical collection with relics of the slave trade, maps showing explorers' travels, Arab chairs, World War I rifles, and pottery fragments; and a series of main floor displays. The Information Desk sells copies of a number of interesting booklets and publications, including those of the Antiquities Division.

Coming out of the museum on Shaaban Robert Street again, turn right half a block to Independence Avenue. If you feel like some greenery, turn right again at Independence Avenue and go two blocks up to the *Botanical Gardens,* kitty-cornered across from *Karimjee Hall,* where Parliament meets. If you would rather head back, turn left down Independence Avenue, passing the *National Insurance Corporation Building,* new in 1972. Coming up on your left is the *Tanzania Electric Supply Company Building,* in front of which is an 80-kilowatt generating set, first used in 1932 at the Dar es Salaam Kurasuni Power Station, and later in Arusha and Bukoba, before being retired in 1967.

On the corner of Ohio Street is the *British Council Building and Library*. Two more blocks and you're at the *Askari Monument* traffic circle on Azikiwe Street at Independence, back at downtown city center. This life-size bronze statue was erected and unveiled in November 1927. Its English plaque wording, composed by Rudyard Kipling, says: "To the memory of the native African troops who fought: to the carriers who were the feet and hands of the army: and to all other men who served and died for their king and country in eastern Africa in the Great War 1914–1918." A plaque on the opposite side says the same in Swahili and Arabic. On the other side of the Askari Monument is the central shopping area along Independence Avenue. Otherwise, turn left down Azikiwe Street and you're back at the New Africa Hotel.

Dar es Salaam Walking Tour II

This tour is also about 2 km long and includes the other end of the harbor front, the Dhow Wharf, several of Sultan Majid's buildings, and colorful India Street.

Starting from the New Africa Hotel, go to the end of Azikiwe Street, passing the picturesque Lutheran Church (see Walking Tour I). Turn right on Azania Front—Azania being what the ancient Greeks called East Africa—and walk along the shaded harbor park strip. Azania Front runs into City Drive.

At the corner of City Drive and Mkwepu Street are two adjoining buildings dating from Sultan Majid's rule in the 1860s: the present *White Fathers' House* and the Seyyid Barghash Building (now *Customs Headquarters*). Both are two stories, having parapeted roofs and thick walls made of coral fragments mixed with lime and plastered white. One block farther, at Bridge Street and City Drive, is *St. Joseph's Cathedral,* built in a Gothic style during the German period from 1897 to 1902.

Another building standing since the 1860s is the *Old Boma,* two stories, built of coral and lime like its neighbors, with coral block floors laid over rafters and mangrove poles. The entrance door is carved wood with floral and geometric patterns. The Old Boma, which may have once served as the Sultan's "Official Hotel," looks very plain and aged, and one wonders how it managed to survive the corrosive, damp salt air so long. Farther down City Drive on the other side of the German-era *City Hall* (southwest corner of Morogoro Road) is the last of the buildings from the 1860s era: a three-story *commercial building* whose top floor and second-floor balcony were clearly added to the original structure.

Across the street from City Hall and the Old Boma is the entrance to the *Dhow Wharf.* There is a narrow driveway for wharf vehicles which you can walk down, turning left at the bottom. Check with the guards whether or not it is all right to walk in, and if so go out onto the piers for a look and perhaps some photos.

The term "dhow" is loosely used to describe the wooden sailing boats of any size or shape seen in the Indian Ocean, Persian Gulf, Red Sea, or inland lakes. While mistakenly thought to be an Arabic word, it more likely stemmed from the Portuguese word *ñao,* which referred to all small sailing craft seen in their early East African journeys; or from the Swahili word *dau* or *dau la mtepe,* an early sailboat with a single mast and square matted sail. According to Caroline Sassoon in a *Tanzania Notes and Records* article, "The Dhows of Dar es Salaam," the vessels seen at Dar Dhow Wharf can be divided into two categories: (1) local vessels which visit the East African mainland ports and islands, and (2) large foreign boats which arrive in the northeast

monsoon from December to April, having come from India's west
coast, the Persian Gulf, or the Red Sea. Both categories of these vessels
use the lateen, four-cornered, rhomboid-shaped sail on a single mast.

The local cargo-carrying boats include two types: the *jahazi* or
jolbot, which has a vertical bow, wineglass-shaped stern transom with
name and registration number perhaps painted on it; and the *jahazi*
from Zanzibar, which has a cutaway bow, usually square stern transom,
and horizontal lines painted lengthwise in white, green, red or white,
blue, and yellow.

The oceangoing dhows also vary in shape and decoration, with the
average weight 130 tons, and some have an auxiliary engine. They carry
Mangalore tiles from India, cotton piece goods, dates, dried fish, and
sometimes passengers from the Red Sea and Persian Gulf. Most carry
back mangrove poles. The Arab or Persian dhows come in two forms:
the *sambuk,* averaging 60 tons, with a high spoon bow boasting lots of
carving and paint, a squarish stern transom and more carving in the
pool deck supports; and the *būm* (or *boom*) reaching 250 tons, with
a high straight pointed box, perhaps a band of paint, and a canoe-
shaped stern. The Indian dhows also come in two varieties: the *kotia,*
100 to 200 tons, with a curved, birdlike stemhead solidly carved with
a circular motif, and a mushroom-shaped stern transom; and the *dengi*
(like English dinghy), which has a cutaway bow, canoe stern, and red,
green, white, and black painted lines above the water line. Whatever
vessels are in to view, each looks exotic and colorful, and gives you a
taste of old Dar es Salaam.

Coming back up onto City Drive from the Dhow Wharf, turn right
and then left onto Morogoro Road, the main road out of Dar going
northwest to Morogoro. Walk three blocks up to *India Street* and
turn right. This is the edge of the Indian or "Asian" bazaar area with
small shops and workshops, known unofficially as "Uhindini." When
first starting out, a family lived and worked in the same small building, but as more money was earned taller tenements and fancy façades
were added. There used to be neighborhoods of Hindus, Sikhs, Shiite
Moslems, Ismaili, Ithnasheri, and Bohora Asians, each around their
own temple or mosque, of which there are dozens in Dar es Salaam. But
the distinctions have blurred as more Indians move to the outlying
neighborhoods and suburbs.

Turn right onto Bridge Street for two blocks, then left onto Independence Avenue. This is the main tourist shopping street with small
stores on either side. Where Independence Avenue meets Azikiwe

Street is the *Askari Monument* (see Walking Tour I). Here turn right and you're back at the New Africa Hotel.

For a driving tour that starts in Dar and goes up the coast to Bagamoyo see Route T-7, which takes in the Village Museum, University, beach hotels, Kunduchi Ruins, and Bagamoyo.

Accommodations

The Kilimanjaro, Box 2802, tel. 21281; cable KILIMA. On Azania Front Road across from the High Court, about 6 blocks from city center. 200 dbls, all w/bath, a-c, balcony. Rates: B&B: sgl—170/–; dbl—265/–. The best hotel in the city of Dar, the Kilimanjaro is an 8-story block set back from the shore-line road along the harbor. Rooms, most with a harbor view, have pleasant semimodern furnishings. Lobby has airline offices, bank, beauty salon, tour operator, curio and stamp shops, newsstand, and boutique. Out back is the near-Olympic-size pool and terrace. Also 5 bars, 4 restaurants, 2 snack bars, nightclub/discotheque. Rating: 1st-class international, lots of amenities for your money. ★ for overall quality.

New Africa Hotel, Box 9314, tel. 29611; bookings also to TTC Hotels, Box 9500, tel. 28181, cable OVEROTEL. On Azikiwe St. at City Drive. 45 sgls, 55 dbls, incl 1 suite, all w/bath, a-c. Rates: B&B: sgl—130/– to 150/–; dbl—240/–. The New Africa dates back to 1909 but was completely replaced by the present building in 1968 as a tourist-class hotel drawing mostly business clientele. Rooms are quite pleasant with parquet floors, tasteful decor. Main dining room is the Bandari Grill, and the ground-floor coffee shop is well used by everybody in Dar. Front desk service sloppy. Rating: 1st-class international. Tariffs about the same as the Kilimanjaro but more amenities there for tourists.

Motel Agip, Box 529, tel. 23511; cable MOTAGI. On City Drive at Pamba Road. 12 sgls, 45 dbls, all rms w/shower and a-c. Rates: B&B: sgl—90/–; dbl—170/–. Credit: DC. In downtown Dar, elevated above the street by a parking ramp, the motel's rooms are newish, functional, and cool. Public area includes two lounges, a bar, dining rooms, and snack bar. Attracts lots of businessmen and officials. Rating: 2d-class international, central, though lacking personality.

Oyster Bay Hotel, Box 1907, tel. 68631; cable HOSPITABLE. About 5 km north of city center; after crossing Selander Bridge, take first right turnoff on Kenyatta Drive to Toure Drive; turn right to Oyster

Bay Road. 22 dbls, 1 sgl, incl 2 suites, all rms w/balcony, bath, a-c. Rates: B&B: sgl—90/–; dbl—134/–. Unfancy hotel in Oyster Bay suburb dating to 1968, more a restaurant-nightclub that looks most alive at night. Rating: 1st-class local, okay compromise between city and beach hotel, with swimming in Oyster Bay but better at Leopard's Cove or Ladder Cove, 3 km up the coast.

Twiga Hotel, Box 1194, tel. 22561. On Independence Ave., between Bridge and Zanaki sts., about 3 blocks from city center. Has 4 sgls, 26 dbls, all rms w/bath, a-c. Rates: B&B: sgl—100/–; dbl—160/–. Credit: DC. Twiga ("giraffe") is a 1960, 5-story downtown hotel whose guests are mainly local businessmen and politicians. Rooms are clean, comfortable. Although the entry—2 flights of ill-kept stairs—gives a bad first impression, hotel and public areas fine. Rating: 1st-class local, central and matter-of-fact.

Hotel Mawenzi, Box 3222, tel. 27761. On Maktaba Road at Upanga Road. 6 sgls, 42 dbls, all rms w/bath or shower, a-c. Rates: B&B: sgl—85/–; dbl—140/–. Credit: DC. Opened in 1971, the 3-story Mawenzi, named for a Kilimanjaro peak, is an unpretentious place that may suit middle budgets. Rooms have a peculiar odor but are tidy and plain. Downstairs restaurant, mostly for guests, has lamb chops, roast and BBQ chicken, fillet, other standards, each about 14/50. Rating: 1st-class local, generally okay.

Palm Beach Hotel, Box 1520, tel. 28891. On Upanga Road just before Selander Bridge, about 3 km from city center. 10 sgls, 21 dbls, 1 family rm; 17 rms w/bath, all w/a-c. Rates: B&B: sgl—65/–; dbl—130/–. Credit: DC. An older, family-style hotel, its rooms have cement floors, elderly furniture, maybe a bath. Public area has bar, lounge, and foliage-lined restaurant, serving table d'hôte and à la carte meals with dinners about 15/– to 17/50. Rating: between 1st- and 2d-class local, serviceable but aging.

Hotel Skyway, Box 21248, tel. 27601. On City Drive next to East African Airways terminal. Has 8 sgls, 72 dbls, all rms w/bath or shower. Rates: B&B: sgl—85/– to 90/–; dbl—135/– to 145/–. Credit: DC. Opened in 1970, the Skyway is a middling hotel without charm but with high charges. Rooms are adequate, not overly clean, and some have cracked or smudgy walls. Rating: 2d-class local and getting worse.

Hotel Afrique, Box 180, tel. 22695. Located on Karuta and Bridge sts. 6 sgls, 29 dbls; 24 dbls only w/bath. Rates: B&B: sgl w/o bath—65/–; dbl w/bath—125/–. Credit: DC. A central downtown, 4-story hotel, the Afrique has small, shopworn rooms, in which breakfast is served. Rating: 2d-class local, satisfactory if you just want an uncheap bed in Dar.

Airlines Hotel, Box 227, tel. 20647; cable SOAPKING. Occupies 2d to 4th floors of building at Bridge and Kaluta sts. 7 sgls, 18 dbls; 12 rms w/a-c, all w/shared bath. Rates: B&B: sgl—40/– to 55/–; dbl—75/– to 90/–. Simple, uncharming rooms good for middle- or low-budget travelers. However, pick an a-c room as far from the 1st-floor night-club as possible. Rating: 2d-class local.

Seaview Hotel, Box 542, tel. 22114. On Ocean Road just before Selander Bridge, about 3 km from city center. 10 sgls, 8 dbls, none w/bath. Rates: B&B: sgl—70/–; dbl—100/–. Vintage 1948, the Sea View is wearing down in the salt air, and its rooms are dank and dull. Main floor has bar, outdoor patio, and dining room with à la carte meals costing 6/50 to 12/50. Rating: 2d-class local, no deal, no delight.

Motel Oceanic, Box 1689, tel. 23094. Also on Ocean Road near the Sea View. 12 dbls, all sharing bath, all w/a-c. Rates: B&B: sgl—56/–; dbl—100/–. Built in 1969 as 4 apartments, the Oceanic has since been converted to an overpriced motel. Rooms are homely and uninteresting. Rating: 2d-class local, already showing its age.

Forodhani Hotel, Box 9181, tel. 21565. On City Drive next to Kili-manjaro Hotel. 16 sgls and dbls. Rates: B&B: sgl—60/–; dbl—90/–. Slovenly hotel with a highly suspicious management, recently taken over by the TTC. Rating: 2d-class local, may improve.

YMCA, Box 767, tel. 25167. On Upanga Road. Has rooms w/o bath for men, women, couples. Rates: Bed only: sgl—30/–; dbl—50/–.

The following hotels are downtown, are fairly cheap, and should be inspected before you check in: *City Guest House,* Box 1326, tel. 22987. On Chagga St. near Libya St. and Morogoro Road. Rates: Room only: sgl—22/–; dbl—26/– . . . . *Dar es Salaam Guest House,* Box 132, tel. 20949. Also on Chagga St. Rates: sgl w/tea—15/–. . . . *Zanzibar Hotel,* Box 20125, tel. 21197. On Zanaki St. Rates: Bed only: sgl—12/–.

For a listing of the beach hotels, including *Hotel Africana, Kunduchi Beach Hotel, Bahari Beach Hotel,* and *Silversands Hotel,* see Route T-7.

Camping

Basically, Dar es Salaam does not make life easy for campers. At the north end of *Oyster Bay* on the grassy shore-line park you can park and camp for free, but there are perpetual thieves about and no toilets after the public ones close at 6 P.M. The other sure site, an inconvenient 30 km farther north, is slovenly *Log Cabins:* 5/– per person. Check also at the Silversands Hotel, which occasionally allows camping.

Where to Eat

This section is divided into Continental restaurants, which are mainly hotel dining rooms, Indian and Oriental restaurants, and more casual coffeehouses and snack places.

CONTINENTAL

Simba Restaurant, 1st floor of the Kilimanjaro Hotel; tel. 21281. Open daily, except Sun., from 8:30 P.M. The poshest place to eat and dance in Dar proper. Its dining room has a circular dance floor, and the entertainment changes every two weeks. Samples from the long menu: sliced and garnished smoked salmon, Mchicha na Nyama (Tanzanian spinach and beef dish), roast young duckling "Tanga," châteaubriand for 2. Entrées: 14/– to 50/–.

The Summit, rooftop of the Kilimanjaro Hotel; tel. 21281. Open daily "from Moonrise till Midnight." This outdoor restaurant has the best view in the city of the harbor by night, and features grills, including prawns on a skewer, grilled lobster, filet mignon. Entrées 15/– to 25/–.

Bandari Grill, in the New Africa Hotel; tel. 29611. Open daily for lunch and dinner. Modern blue-green-white, main dining room of the hotel. Has table d'hôte lunch (17/50), dinner (21/–)—one dinner featured tournedos Rossini or Mikumi chicken. Also à la carte menu in Swahili with English subtitles: roast duck, sweet-and-sour lobster balls, châteaubriand for 2, steamed chicken with spicy sauce and coconut. Entrées 15/– to 45/–.

Rombo, ground floor of the Kilimanjaro Hotel; tel. 21281. Open daily, à la carte for lunch and dinner. The yellow and blue table d'hôte dining room serves breakfast—15/–; lunch—19/50; dinner—25/–. À la carte menu includes ravioli, tilapia with chips, filet mignon with mushrooms, with entrée prices 10/50 to 16/–.

Oyster Bay Hotel, tel. 68631. Bar and restaurant on the first floor are open to cooling breeze, with view of Oyster Bay and park—and the stars, too, through sliding roof over the dining room. Extensive à la carte menu includes grilled kingfish, crab Mornay, lobster thermidor, fillet steak, escalope Holstein, Bordelaise lamb. Entrées 12/– to 21/–.

Motel Agip Dining Room, tel. 23511. Open daily for lunch and dinner. Thankfully air-conditioned, with decor in blue and white. Sunday meals are table d'hôte. À la carte choices include prawn risotto, roast chicken, fillet steak, châteaubriand for 2, with prices for entrées 14/– to 40/–. Credit: DC.

Twiga Hotel Roof Garden, on the roof of same, tel. 22561. Open daily for dinner. In the cool of the evening, this is the à la carte eatery at the Twiga. Sample dishes: chicken and lobster soup, sweet-and-sour pork, prawns in oyster sauce, curries, fillet steak. Entrées: 13/– to 18/50. Credit: DC.

ORIENTAL AND INDIAN

Sheesh Mahal, India St. near Riddoch Motors. Open daily for lunch and dinner. Specialists in Indian foods, the Sheesh has two dining rooms, one wall with a Taj Mahal mural. Dishes, costing 10/– to 17/–, include prawns masala, beef or queema curry, plus sandwiches. Credit: DC.

Khalid Restaurant, Aggrey St., tel. 20192. Reputedly has good curries, though not much atmosphere.

Canton Restaurant, Nkrumah St., tel. 20422. Closed Mon. Chinese lunches and dinners.

COFFEEHOUSES AND SNACK PLACES

The Bruncherie, ground floor of the Kilimanjaro Hotel. Open daily. A pleasant, self-service cafeteria, the Bruncherie serves breakfasts, hot and cold sandwiches, daily specialty, and curry dishes, drinks. Entrées 7/– to 12/–; sandwiches 3/– to 10/–.

Duka La Kahawa, ground floor of the New Africa Hotel. Open daily from 7 A.M. to 11 P.M. The combination coffee shop and sidewalk café is one of the most popular sitting spots in Dar, the equivalent of Nairobi's Thorn Tree. Drinks and coffee 1/– to 2/–. Also diced steak with bananas and rice, burgers, sandwiches: 6/– to 10/– per dish.

Motel Agip Snack Bar. Open daily 9 A.M. to 11:30 P.M. A clean, well-lighted place for casual dinners, lunches. Hot dishes 6/50 to 8/–.

Mansons Confectionery, corner of Mkwepu St. and Independence Ave. Open daily, on Sat. until 2 A.M. Not very fancy, rather darkish with interior neon lights, semifunky. Various daily specials, plus omelet, spaghetti, sandwiches, hot and cold drinks: 1/50 to 6/–.

Tourist Restaurant & Bar, Independence Ave. at Bridge St. Barren place that echoes, has Indian and Tanzanian specialties on dog-eared menu. Seafood, curries, British and colonial dishes: 8/– to 11/–.

George's Grill, off Independence Ave., in driveway behind IPS Bldg. Informal place of no decor. Mostly short orders: hamburger steak, fresh sea fish fillet, chicken Sekela, kebab Hasusa; each 7/50 to 10/50.

Caffe Espresso, Independence Ave. Old and intimate, open 7 to 7 to serve café espresso, ice cream, for 1/20 to 3/–. Air-conditioned.

Wimpy, Makunganya St. If you must: Wimpys and cheeseburgers, about 2/50.

Getting Around

Taxis rank up outside the New Africa and Kilimanjaro hotels. Other-wise, numbers to call: White Cabs, tel. 23078; Ever Green Cabs, tel. 29246; Co-Cabs, tel. 20177. Taxis' standard fares are 5/– to 7/– within downtown city center, 10/– to 15/– within the city boundaries, 40/– to 50/– from the city center to the beach hotels, 20/– to 25/– to the airport. Buses also run all over the city.

Information Bureau

The Tanzania Tourist Corporation (TTC) has its main office in the IPS Building on Azikiwe St., Box 2485, tel. 27671. It is open weekday business hours and Saturday mornings.

"What's On . . ."

The TTC publishes a free little monthly magazine called *Karibu* ("welcome"), which has a handy map of downtown Dar and lists of restaurants, hotels, travel agents, sights to see, etc. It should be avail-able at most hotels or at the TTC office. For current happenings, check the *Daily News*.

Nightlife

Dar es Salaam does not exactly swing at night, but does have some action. The classiest place for a floor show and dancing is the *Simba Night Club and Restaurant* at the Kilimanjaro Hotel. The *Bahari Beach* and *Africana* coast hotels have discos nearly nightly. In town the *Sea View* and *Forodhani* hotels have discos. *Margots,* at the Airlines Hotel, has a band nightly except Sunday. Other local bands play at the *White Horse* on Mosque St., the *Green Garden* on Kassana St., and the *Princess Bar* on Libya St.

Cinemas

Town theaters: *Avalon,* Zanaki St., tel. 21556; *Empire,* Azikiwe St., tel. 20539; *Empress,* Independence Ave., tel. 20719; and the *New Chox.* Indian cinemas are the *Cameo* and *Odeon.* The *Drive-in-Cinema* is on Old Bagamoyo Road near Oyster Bay, tel. 67035. Occasionally the beach hotels will show movies, and nonguests must pay a cover charge.

The *Dar es Salaam Film Society* shows many of the same films that the Kenya Film Society does. Temporary membership is available for visitors: 10/– at the door.

Libraries

Tanganyika Library Service, Central Library, Azikiwe St. *U.S. Information Service Library,* Abdullah's Building next to Empress Cinema on Independence Ave. between Azikiwe St. and Pamba Road. *British Council Library,* Independence Ave. *University of Dar es Salaam Library,* on University Hill; open during the school term.

Religious Services

Anglican: St. Alban's, Upanga Road, tel. 22166. *Lutheran:* Azania Front Church, City Drive at Azikiwe St., tel. 68585. *Presbyterian:* St. Columba's, Ocean Road at Upanga Road, tel. 67450. *Roman Catholic:* St. Joseph's Cathedral, City Drive at Bridge St., tel. 22031; St. Peter's, off New Bagamoyo Road in Oyster Bay, tel. 67726. There are also Baptist, nondenominational, Mennonite, Quaker, Hindu, Moslem, Sikh, and Ismaili services. Saturday newspaper has times of services.

Shops and Services

Bakery: Gloria's, Independence Ave.

Books: Dar es Salaam Bookshop (Box 9030), Makunganya St. Tanzania Publishing House (Box 2138), Independence Ave. Both stores have lots of Swahili literature.

Camping gas: City Gas, Azikiwe St. by New Africa Hotel.

Groceries: Dewhursts, Independence Ave., next to Twiga Hotel.

Hairdresser: Salon Arcade Ladies Hairstylist, IPS Building ground floor, Azikiwe at Independence, tel. 26038.

Laundry, cleaning: Ritz Dry Cleaners, Independence Ave. by Empress Cinema.

Opticians: Jaff's & Greames Optical House, Independence Ave., next to USIS Library. Dar es Salaam Optical Co., Independence Ave.

Pharmacies: Mahen Pharmacy, and Elys Pharmacy, both on Azikiwe St. near New Africa Hotel.

Photo shop: Studio One, Azikiwe St. at Independence; Kodak sales and service, color prints done in Dar es Salaam in 4–5 days, color slides sent to Nairobi and take one week.

Secretarial services: City Secretarial Services, Independence Ave., tel. 26632.

Tailor: Janmahomeds Outfitters, Independence Ave. near Gloria Bakery.

Zanzibar

To many, the name Zanzibar conjures up images of narrow winding streets with carved Arab doors, dhows bobbing in the harbor, villages with piles of cloves drying in the sun, the old slave market where thousands were sold into bondage, and explorers preparing for their long expeditions. But today Zanzibar presents a new image: modern rent-free apartments for the Zanzibaris, Lenin Hospital manned with Chinese doctors, People's Park and People's Palace, and a strong African political party.

Zanzibar is officially made up of the 640-square-mile island of Zanzibar (pop. 190,494), 380-square-mile Pemba Island (pop. 164,321) 30 miles north of Zanzibar, plus the small islands of Tumbatu and Latham.

Zanzibar has a long, complex history with centuries of political and military tug-of-war between the Arabs, Portuguese, British, and Africans for control of the islands. Arabs from the Persian Gulf were probably the first outside settlers, attracted to the islands because of their ideal location in the midst of an expanding trade circuit along the East African coast, and between Arabia and India. During these early centuries of Arab influence Swahili developed as a lingua franca, combining Arab and Bantu words to make a new language with which to conduct trade; today experts say the purest form of Swahili is the Unguja dialect in Zanzibar town. The name Zanzibar is thought to be a combination of the Persian words *zang* ("black") and *bar* ("land") as "land of the black."

The Portuguese became very active on the East African coast in the

16th century, and Vasco da Gama made his first stop for one day at Zanzibar March 1, 1498. The Portuguese established their main center of activities in Mozambique, but on Zanzibar they built a trading post and church on the Shingani peninsula, where Zanzibar town had its origins. However, Portuguese power began to shrink in the 17th and 18th centuries, and after they lost Mombasa in 1729 for the last time, the Arabs took command again.

Zanzibar's golden age came in the 19th century. In 1832 the Sultan of Oman, Seyyid Said, decided to transfer his home and capital to Zanzibar. Though cloves had been grown on the islands before, Seyyid strongly encouraged planting on a wider scale. Today Zanzibar and Pemba produce nearly 90 percent of the world's supply of cloves, and three-fourths of that is grown on Pemba. With Indian financing, Seyyid sent more and bigger Arab caravans into the interior to the great lakes regions to bring out ivory and slaves. By the end of Seyyid's reign in 1856 it was said, "When they whistle in Zanzibar, the people dance on the shores of the great lakes." Not dance out of joy, to be sure. Seyyid established trade and diplomatic links with the United States in 1836, Great Britain in 1841, and France in 1844. The British brought pressure to bear on Seyyid to stop the lucrative but evil slave trade, and, reluctantly, he partially restricted it.

After Seyyid's death in 1856, his son Majid Said became sultan, and it was during his rule that Richard Burton, John Speke, and Dr. David Livingstone made their explorations of the mainland interior, using Zanzibar as their stocking-up and setting-off point. As Burton described the island in a two-volume work, Zanzibar port stank, the shore was a cesspool, corpses floated on the water, sea tides swamped the poorer areas of town, disease was rampant. Livingstone went so far as to call the place "Stinkibar." Sultan Majid must have wanted to escape the myriad problems himself, for he started a new town on the mainland in 1866: Dar es Salaam, "haven of peace."

Barghash became sultan in 1870. During his 18-year rule the British, through their consul, Sir John Kirk, worked on Barghash to stop the still-persistent slave trade. When the Sultan was obstinate, British warships surrounded Zanzibar, preventing any slaves from entering or leaving the island. On June 5, 1873, Barghash relented and signed a treaty making the slave trade illegal between all his ports, and soldiers were sent to close the slave market in Zanzibar. Upon its site the Universities Mission built its cathedral with the altar standing where the whipping post once stood. The Sultan's mainland possession dwindled rapidly in the 1880s, with the Germans establishing a protectorate by treaty and by purchase, until finally Zanzibar retained nominal rights only over Kenya's Ten-Mile Strip, ending in 1963.

In 1890 the British declared a protectorate over Zanzibar and Pemba, and the islands' affairs were from then on directed more from Britain, with the sultans as figureheads. The British instigated a number of reforms on Zanzibar, including the treasury, legal system, and port regulations. Garbage was collected from the streets, rats killed, anti-malaria precautions taken, milk pasteurized.

In 1925 a Legislative Council was established. For the next three decades the local people began to develop a political awareness, wanting civil service jobs and a system of elected rather than appointed seats on the Legislative Council. In 1955 the Zanzibar Nationalist party was formed, but it did not appeal to the majority, the Africans. However, the Afro-Shirazi party in 1957 did appeal to the blacks. The ASP won five out of six seats on the Legislative Council, and inspired the Zanzibaris to seek independence from Britain. On December 10, 1963, Zanzibar became independent with the Sultan still as the head of government, the Nationalist party as his voice. Barely one month later, January 11–12, 1964, there was a bloody revolution, the Sultan was deposed and exiled, and the Afro-Shirazi party installed under Sheikh Abeid Amani Karume and his Revolutionary Council. The same year in April, Zanzibar joined Tanganyika to form the United Republic of Tanzania. The Revolutionary Council was put in charge of Zanzibar's internal governing, and proceeded to redistribute land, build housing, health, and education facilities, nationalize industry, and invite Chinese advisers in to assist in the reorganization efforts. During this time tourists were closely watched and even followed, and were supposed to remain on an officially approved route when touring.

On April 7, 1972, Karume was gunned down by assassins, and Aboud Jumbe became leader of the ASP, president of Zanzibar, and Tanzania's first vice-president. Jumbe is generally considered more of a moderate than Karume was, and the atmosphere on Zanzibar has relaxed somewhat. The number of visitors has increased, new hotels are in the planning stages, and shops are supposedly better stocked with basic goods. In January 1973 the chairman of the Zanzibar Tourist Corporation said, "It is the Government's policy to encourage, by all means, tourists and visitors to make use of Zanzibar's hospitality."

Zanzibar Town

Zanzibar Town grew up from a tiny 16th-century fishing village to the hub of 19th-century East African trading to today's growing socialist city (pop. 68,490). While many of the old Stone Town Arab houses are crumbling and their stones being removed, there are still a few narrow streets with squares, shops, markets and two- or three-story whitewashed homes encircled by balconies and featuring those beautiful, brass-studded, carved teak doors, which incorporate several symbolic Arabic motifs in their design. The best place to admire the doors is in the streets around the Zanzibar Hotel, where the East Africa Tobacco Company has been assisting in their restoration.

While you are wandering in Zanzibar Town, there are larger buildings of historic interest to look for. In the vicinity of People's Park are the old *Arab Fort* built with round stone towers, the *People's Palace* (formerly the Sultan's Palace), and *Beit-el-Ajaib,* or the House of Wonders, built in 1883 by Sultan Barghash as a palace to outdo his other residences. It has three stories, each with a wide porticoed balcony, a central court, a wooden clock tower on top of the flat roof, and beautiful, massive, arched carved doors. Away from the harbor near Creek Road is the *Anglican Cathedral* built over the site of the 50-by-30-yard slave market, which was finally closed by Sultan Barghash in 1873 after thousands of slaves had been sold at its 4 P.M. sales. The *Museum,* on Museum Road, has exhibits of local wildlife, traditional carvings, dhow construction, and 19th-century relics of Livingstone, including his medicine chest.

Shopping is best in some of the quaint old Stone Town shops, in the modern cooperative stores by the post office, or at the Tanzania Tourist Friendship Bureau. Things to shop for include silverwork, local sweetmeats, baskets and mats, model dhows and outriggers, carved chests, and pomanders. A pomander (from French *pomme d'ambre*) is a ball of aromatic spices, such as cloves, tied in a cloth or gauze bag, and used as a fragrant sachet in a wardrobe or linen drawer.

Zanzibar Island

On greater Zanzibar there are a number of good beaches, interesting ruins, acres of clove groves, and offshore islands to explore, mainly by taxi, boat, or package tour. An excursion north has the most interest. Leaving Zanzibar Town via the road to Bububu, you pass the old dhow harbor and *Livingstone's House,* where the doctor stayed in 1866 while preparing for his last journey, now the head-quarters of the Clove Research Organization and closed to the public. Outside town about 6 km are the ruins of *Mtoni Palace,* with its courtyard and stone bath, built by an Arab merchant in the early 19th century. About 1½ km farther, on the left, is *Marahubi Palace,* Sultan Barghash's mango tree-lined abode for his harem. Farther along the Bububu road at Kibweni is the bright white summer palace of Zanzibar's last sultan. *Bububu,* about 15 km from town, was the ter-minus of one of the world's shortest railways, the 7-mile Bububu Rail-way, built by Arnold Cheyney & Company of New York in 1905. The railway shut down in 1927, and while the tracks were removed, some of the quaint stations and platforms remain. North of Bububu a track goes right through a coconut plantation to Kidichi and the domed *Persian Baths,* built of stone by Sultan Seyyid for his second wife. After *Mangapwani* village, about 24 km north of Zanzibar Town, the road ends, and there you take the path past the big house by the ocean to a coral cliff overlooking a small bay. To the right of the bay is the *slave hole,* now covered with stones, where slaves were penned while waiting secret shipment at night by dhow to Arabia and else-where.

An excursion south of east from Zanzibar Town includes clove plan-tations, ruins, and beaches. Directly south on the coastal road is Chuk-wani, where there are interesting coral cliffs. Taking the main road south toward Makunduchi at Km 35 by Pete is *Jozani Forest,* only 2 square miles in size but containing red colobus monkeys and leopards, among other animals. On Zanzibar and Pemba are the Sykes monkey, guenon, lemurs, bushpig, civet, genet, mongoose, forest duiker, Zan-zibar tree hyrax, Zanzibar *bdeogalo* (a mammal with only four toes on each foot), shrew mouse, elephant shrew, 30 species of snakes (5 poisonous), and 102 species of birds.

At Km 56 is a fork: left to Makunduchi, near which is an under-ground cave with stalagmites; and right to Kizimkazi. Going right, en route to the western coast you pass through villages drying cloves. *Cloves* (from French *clou*—"nail") are grown on a conical evergreen tree, *Eugenia aromatica,* that grows for fifty to sixty years up to 50 feet high. A mature tree, older than six years, yields 80 to 200 pounds of cloves a year, with the main harvests July–September and Novem-ber–January. It is the flower buds that are picked by hand when they are still reddish or greenish, unopened and undeveloped. Then, while drying in the sun, the buds expand, harden, and become dark brown and fragrant. Cloves are used whole or ground as a spice for food, and by Indonesians whole for flavoring cigarettes. Clove oil is used in perfumes, toothpastes, and mouthwashes, and in dentistry. In 1971 Zanzibar's clove exports totaled $25.57 million. A conviction for clove smuggling from Zanzibar is punishable by death.

Kizimkazi, Km 55 from Zanzibar Town, has an ancient mosque dating to A.D. 1107, restored in 1770. Around the mosque's north wall and *kiblah* run inscriptions, verses from the Koran, and dedications, all in Kufic, an ancient Arabic script.

As you leave Zanzibar Town by the road going east, at Km 18 is *Dunga,* where the ruins of the palace of Mwenyi Mkuu, built between 1845 and 1856, are supposedly haunted. *Uroa,* Km 40, has a fine beach.

Pemba Island may be featured as a tourist destination, but you should inquire at the Tanzania Tourist Friendship Bureau before making any arrangements to go there.

When to Visit

The northeast monsoon from December to March brings hot, dry weather with temperatures 77–91°F. The coolest months are June to October during the southwest monsoon, with days ranging 71–84°F. The heavy rains are in April and May, and are best avoided. Overall the humidity is a high 78 percent.

Getting There, Getting Around

EAA flies 20Xwk from Dar es Salaam, taking 20 minutes, and there are connecting flights via Dar from Mombasa, Malindi, Tanga, and Arusha. EAA also has flights 3Xwk to Pemba from Dar es Salaam and Tanga. There is a Zanzibar airport tax of 20/–. Steamships travel between Dar es Salaam and the islands; inquire in Dar. Package tours to Zanzibar are under TP-18, 27, and KP-89. The Tanzania Tourist Friendship Bureau, besides having its own tours, can help you hire taxis and boats for individual touring.

Accommodations

For all these hotels, bookings can be made directly or through the Tanzania Friendship Tourist Bureau, Box 216, Zanzibar; tel. 2344; cable URAFIKI. *Hoteli Ya Bwawani,* opened in January 1974, is the only first-class hotel on the island, a buff-and-white cube (designed by the late Sheik Karume) on the harbor near Livingstone's house. A journalist who stayed there (we have not seen it) described it as mostly air-conditioned, with big, attractive rooms (equipped with some of Zanzibar's new color TVs), pleasant bar and dining room. Rates: (bed only): sgl—160/–, dbl—230/–. . . . *Zanzibar Hotel,* Box 392, tel. 2777. Located on fringes of old Stone Town. 32 rms, some w/bath, some w/a-c. Rates: B&B: 35/– to 45/– per person. An interesting 3-story building, partly a former sultan's guesthouse, and though quite old it has been renovated. Rooms vary in size, with mostly Arab decor and ancient ant-proof mangrove poles in the ceilings. Also bar, table d'hôte dining room: breakfast—10/–; lunch—14/–; tea—3/–; dinner—15/–. . . . *Africa House Hotel,* Box 317, tel. 2552. 12 rms, some w/shower, some w/a-c. Rates: B&B: 35/– to 45/– per person. On the seashore with a public beach in front, and formerly the English Club, the Africa is also 3 stories and elderly. Large bar and library. . . . *Uwanjani Hotel,* Box 394, tel. 2804. 21 rms, all w/shower. Rates: B&B: sgl—35/– to 45/–; dbl—70/– to 90/–. Opened in 1970, the Uwanjani is 5 km from town near the 10,000-seat Amaan Sport Stadium. Has cots for beds. . . . *Victoria House,* Box 149, tel. 2223. Rates: B&B: sgl—15/–.

Route T-1: Serengeti–Ngorongoro Crater–Lake Manyara–Arusha

This is the most beaten tourist track in Tanzania, because of its beautiful variety of game and scenery, its fine facilities, and its accessibility. It takes in Serengeti Plains and Park, Olduvai Gorge, Ngorongoro Crater and Rim, Lake Manyara Park, and Arusha.

Serengeti

The route begins at the Kenya border post in Masai Mara and enters *Serengeti National Park* at Klein's Camp Gate at Km 28, exiting 157 km later at Naabi Hill Gate. Serengeti (from Masai *siringet,* "an extended area") is Tanzania's largest national park, stretching over about 5,700 square miles, from Masai Mara in the north to Ngorongoro Conservation Area in the south, from Masailand in the east to within 8 km of Speke's Gulf on Lake Victoria in the park's western corridor. This vast expanse consists of treeless central plains in the southwest, the central savanna with its acacias and kopjes (rocky outcrops), the riverine bush and forest in the north, and the mixed

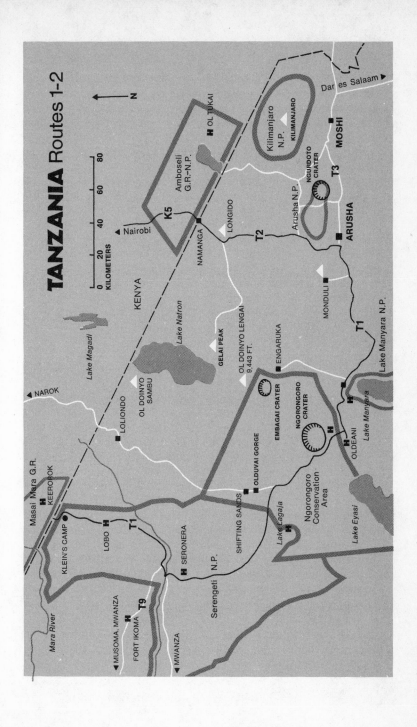

landscape of the western corridor. Serengeti is best and deservedly known for its huge herds of plains animals, particularly the wildebeest, gazelle, and zebra—estimated in 1973 at more than 2 million. The herds, and attendant predators, are constantly on the move, but their yearly mass migration (late May or early June) from the southern long- and short-grass plains to the western corridor and northern hills is one of the world's great natural spectacles. But because it lasts only a few short days, it is difficult to predict and to see unless you are right on the spot. Besides the 35 species of plains animals, there are large prides of lion, leopards, elephants, jackals, hunting dogs, bat-eared foxes, civets, genets, hyenas, caracals, black rhinos, hippos, klipspringers, baboons, and at least four species of monkeys. As can be expected, there is a profusion of birdlife, with about 407 species recorded, many of them European migrants which are present from October to April.

You should try to spend at least two nights in Serengeti. If your time is very limited, a drive around the Seronera valley to see lions, and perhaps leopards, is probably best. The park authorities say it is all right to get out of your car in open areas, but be on the alert for dangerous game. While touring, it is useful to have the official Seren- geti guide booklet (price 5/–) and the *Checklist of Birds* (price 3/–), both available at park headquarters at Seronera or perhaps at the park hotels.

Entering the park from Kenya's Masai Mara, you drive through the northern riverine bush and forest country. Watch particularly for elephants. By the Klein's Camp Gate is a turnoff to a track to the Mara and Bologonja rivers. The *Mara River,* 40 km of which is inside the park, is lined with a gallery forest of fig, mahogany, and *Podocarpus* trees in which live brightly colored touracos, kingfishers, and fish eagles, while crocodiles and hippos inhabit the river, and black rhinos, oribis, and gray bush duikers its environs. Wildebeest herds cross and recross the Mara River from August to November while searching for palatable grazing in the north, and up to 50 animals may drown when the herds surge across the river, which is 270 feet wide in places.

From Klein's Camp Gate the drive through the northern part of Serengeti includes the turnoff (Km 47) to spectacular *Lobo Lodge* (see below), worth stopping at just to admire the Dalgleish Marshall (Nairobi) architecture. Lobo is situated in a rocky outcrop 3 km to the west of the southern tip of Lobo Hill. A herd of about 1,000 buffalo is usually in the vicinity, and nearly 25,000 buffalo live in the northern part of the park. About Km 81, to the left of the road, is

Kilimafedha ("hill of wealth"). There is gold in the 2-to-3-billion-year-old quartz veins. Mining was begun by the Germans and continued until as recently as 1966. Into the deep disused shaft of one of the larger mines park rangers toss snares captured from poachers.

Impala

Banagi at Km 99 is the park's major junction. Near *Banagi Hill* can be found herds of buffalo, roan antelope, impala, and giraffe. The graceful *impala* (Swahili—*swala-pala*) has a rufous-fawn coat with a black stripe bordering the white rump patches. Impalas stand 33 to 37 inches at the shoulder and weigh 100 to 180 pounds. Only the male has the beautiful, long, slender, S-shaped, lyrelike horns. Impala are most frequently seen in riverine bush, grass-woodland, and grass-bush in breeding herds of a buck and his harem of females and young or in all-male groups of up to 100 animals. Their movements are quick, and they are capable of making huge leaps of up to 30 feet in length and 10 feet in height. Their main enemies are leopards, cheetahs, wild dogs, and, sometimes, lions.

Six km west of Banagi at *Retima Hippo Pool* you can watch hippos submerged in the muddy Orangi River. Continuing farther along this track you come to the main road out through the *western corridor,* which skirts the Grumeti River to Ndabaka Gate and Lake Victoria. During the dry months of June to October, poaching is at its worst in the western corridor and along the northwest boundary of the park. Poaching methods used include bows and poison-tipped arrows, deadly steel wire snares, pits, and traps. The poachers are mainly local people who poach perhaps more out of economic need than greed. More recently, however, very organized professional poachers have been using high-velocity rifles and hunting from four-wheel-drive vehicles at night. Poachers get about 1,050/– for a leopard skin, 35/– for zebra skin, and 70/– for a giraffe tail from illegal dealers. According to several authorities, including the *New York Times,* an estimated 40,000 animals are poached yearly in Serengeti. To combat poachers, the National Parks Field Force watches from outlying ranger posts and makes patrols by air and road. But the antipoaching work in all the parks is never-ending.

Go south from Banagi to the *Seronera Valley.* At *Seronera,* Km 119, is a small settlement that includes the park headquarters office, museum, Seronera Wildlife Lodge, an airstrip, the Serengeti Research Institute, and several campsites. The *Serengeti Research Institute* was organized in its present form in 1966 as a center for ecological studies of the park: animal behavior, vegetation changes, animal population and migratory habits, the effects of large mammals on habitats, grassland productivity, and so forth. Working at the institute is a permanent staff plus 18 visiting scientists of different disciplines from all over the world. Visitors are discouraged, however, because the institute is so busy.

In the immediate vicinity of Seronera Wildlife Lodge a number of birds and animals can be seen. Sometimes a pride of lions may amble through, and topis, hartebeests, gazelles, and, at night, hyenas and jackals are generally in the vicinity. *Hyraxes* (Swahili—*pimbi*) live in the rocky outcrops throughout the park, but can easily be seen near the lodge, where they are almost tame. The hyrax (or dassie), strangely enough, is thought by some to be the closest living relative of the elephant (the sea cow vies for that distinction). This rabbit-sized animal is dark brown, yellow, and/or gray, has no tail, and looks like a huge guinea pig. Hyraxes occur from 1,000 to 15,000 feet in altitude and are seen by climbers on Mount Kenya and Kilimanjaro. They are preyed upon by snakes, leopards, and Verreaux's eagles.

The Seronera Valley is renowned for leopards and black-maned lions. The large prides of lions resident in the valley feed on topis, hartebeests, waterbucks, and gazelles. Look for leopards in the branches of the yellow-barked acacia and "sausage" trees along the valley's rivers, where they often carry their prey to get it out of reach of lions, hyenas, and vultures, and to get out of the heat of the day.

Leaving Seronera and driving southeast toward Ngorongoro Conservation Area, you cross the expansive and beautiful *Serengeti Plains.* This vast open area is subdivided into the long-grass plains in the north and west and the short-grass plains in the south and east. The long-grass plains are studded with kopjes (Afrikaans—"small head"), technically known as inselbergs. Kopjes are very old granite rocks which have weathered with erosion but stand out dramatically over the flat surrounding plains. Hyraxes, dik-diks, spitting cobras, and puff adders like the kopjes' slightly damper, cooler environment. The long-grass plains and kopjes extend to Naabi Hill, beyond which the short-grass plains stretch past Olduvai Gorge well into the Ngorongoro Conservation Area.

Wildebeest

Both long-grass and short-grass plains are much favored by the huge herds of wildebeest, zebra, and gazelle during the wet season of November–May. The *wildebeest* (Afrikaans—"wild cattle") is the "clown of the plains." Also named the white-bearded gnu (or in Swahili *nyumbu*), once seen it cannot be mistaken. It is ungainly-looking with a dun-gray or brown humped back, buffalolike horns on both sexes, a long-haired black mane, and white chin beard. The mating season is usually in late May; the calves, born in January on the short-grass plains, can run almost immediately after birth. Predators, including lions, cheetahs, and wild dogs, are always on the watch, however, for weaklings who fall behind when the herds start moving. In 1973 the wildebeest population was estimated at one million in Serengeti.

Burchell's or *common zebras* (Swahili—*punda milia,* "striped donkey") look like short-maned, narrow-eared white ponies with broad black stripes (or vice versa), standing 50 to 55 inches at the shoulder, and weighing 500 to 700 pounds. It is thought that their stripes are a form of cryptic coloration intended to confuse an attacking predator—a sort of running, dazzling, black-and-white, psychedelic light show. The zebra community is composed of family units of from 5 to 20, each controlled by a dominant stallion. There are various species of Burchell's or common zebra in East Africa; the Serengeti

Thomson's gazelle   Grant's gazelle

type tends to have narrow gray shadow stripes in the white stripes on the rump.

The two gazelles which are often seen together and are tricky to tell apart are Thomson's and Grant's, which in 1973 were together estimated to number about one million in Serengeti. The *Thomson's gazelle,* or "Tommy" (Swahili—*swala tomi*), is smaller and redder than Grant's, and both sexes have a broad and strongly marked blackish horizontal side stripe. The Thomson's rump is white below the tail, and the black tail is perpetually in motion. Both sexes have upward and backward curving horns, though the female's are more slender and straighter. The *Grant's gazelle* (Swahili—*swala granti*) is pale fawn, with the white rump extending above the tail. The side stripe is more variable, in some races merely a slight shade darker than fawn, rather than black. Both sexes have horns, and the male's are particularly large and beautiful, curving up and out, then forward slightly at the tips. Both Grant's and Thomson's are preyed upon by lions, hunting dogs, hyenas, leopards, and cheetahs.

Cheetah (Swahili—*duma*) are most likely to be seen in the short-grass plains in Serengeti either alone or in pairs. While looking somewhat like a leopard, the cheetah is lighter-built, its overall tawny fur

Cheetah

has black spots, which are rounded rather than in rosettes, its tail tip is ringed, and its face has a distinctive long black "teardrop" from the inside corner of its eye to the corner of its mouth. The cheetah has several unfeline characteristics. Like the dog it cannot retract its blunt claws. It makes a chirping noise—but also purrs and growls. The cheetah can briefly sprint at 50–60 miles per hour in pursuit of its prey, but is *not* the fastest animal in the world. Even when cornered it usually does not attack man, unlike other wild cats. Cheetahs are widely distributed throughout East Africa but are not very easy to find.

There are two shallow saline lakes sometimes visited by flamingos in Serengeti: Lagaja and Magadi. Magadi means "soda" in Swahili, and is a common name for such lakes. These are rarely deeper than 6 feet at the height of the rains, and often dry up completely by the end of the dry season, when they glisten with a crust of salt, which looks like a mirage of snow from a distance.

When to Visit

The plains animals can best be seen November–May, especially January–February, when they are on the short- and long-grass plains in southwest Serengeti. Sometimes in November–December and March–May a four-wheel-drive is useful for the tracks in central Serengeti. Avoid the western corridor in the wet season because of the sticky "black cotton" soil; dry June–October is best there.

Getting There, Getting Around

Park entry gates are 317 km from Arusha, and 416 km from Nairobi via Masai Mara. Park roads, all dirt, are generally fair for Beetles and such. There are airstrips at Seronera, Lobo, and near the Grumeti River. Vehicles are for hire at both lodges for game viewing. Many package tours include Serengeti: see packages TP-9–13, 24, 26–27, 31–32, and KP-64, 66–68, 76–77, 79–88.

Accommodations

Lobo Wildlife Lodge, bookings to TTC Hotels (p. 315). Located 19 km from Klein's Camp Gate, 72 km from Seronera. 75 dbls, incl 1 suite, all w/bath. Rates: FB: sgl—176/–; dbl—286/–; also low season rates. The most spectacular TTC game lodge, Lobo is perched on a rocky promontory overlooking the northern area of Serengeti. Nicely decorated rooms have a view of the plains, though the wind rattles the windows. In the main building you cross a small stream with rock and cactus garden to reach the stone and wood bar, split-level lounges, and table d'hôte dining room (breakfast—10/–; lunch—17/50; tea—5/–; dinner—21/–). Also a pool. Rating: 1st-class international, with lots of style and sweeping view, though not many close-ups of the animals below. We give it ★. . . .

Seronera Wildlife Lodge, bookings to TTC Hotels (p. 315). Located at Seronera. 75 dbls, all w/bath. Rates: FB: sgl—264–; dbl—330/–; also low-season rates. The newest TTC game-viewing hotel. Seronera is at 4,590 feet altitude, amid some kopjes. The rooms are standard modern. Table d'hôte meals same price as at Lobo. Rating: 1st-class international, not as dramatic or isolated as Lobo but closer to the animals. Note: Seronera has a water supply problem that has forced closure at times. . . .

Grumeti Luxury Tented Camp, bookings to Ker, Downey & Selby Safaris, Box 9370, Dar es Salaam, tel. 68152; also to Thorn Tree Safaris, Nairobi (p. 114). Located in the western corridor, 70 km northwest of Seronera. Rates: FB: sgl—150/–; dbl—300/–. Camp is close to Kirawira airstrip, and is used frequently by Ker, Downey flying safaris. Camp is open December–March, June–October. . . .

Ndutu Safaris Lodge, bookings to George Dove Safaris, Box 284, Arusha, tel. 2147. Reached by a track starting outside Naabi Hill Gate and the park boundary, at Km 188. Go about 26 km along the dirt track toward Lake Lagaja. 12 dbl rms w/toilet and shower, 21 dbl tents w/o shower. Rates: FB: rooms, sgl—180/–; dbl—280/; tents, sgl—160/–; dbl—250/–. Near the lakeshore with views of it from rooms and tents. Table d'hôte dining room, bar, lounge, evening bon-fires, some electricity. Land-Rover for game viewing 3/– per mile. See also package tour KP-79. . . . *Ndabaka Gate Self-Service Cottages.* Rates: Bed only: sgl—15/–; dbl—30/–. Two double cabins furnished down to cooking utensils, but have no linens, food, staff, little water. Useful if entering or exiting via the western corridor. . . .
Camping is allowed at a couple of sites. The main camping area, 4 km from Seronera, has room for about 9 tents, has a latrine, water available from park office. Also some sites at Klein's Camp Gate, with stream water. Fee: 5/– per adult per night. Bookings should be made for December–May to: Warden, Serengeti National Park, Box 3134, Arusha, tel. 2335. Park officials suggest that campers keep their tent flaps shut, use a mosquito net, and leave a light on outside at night.

You leave Serengeti National Park through Naabi Hill Gate at Km 168, but the official boundary is at Km 185 where you enter *Ngoro-*

ngoro Conservation Area, a 3,200-square-mile area, two-thirds of which is lowlands and one-third of which is highlands. Included in it are parts of the southeast Serengeti Plains, ancient Olduvai Gorge, and a string of nearly a dozen volcanic mountains in the Ngorongoro Highlands. Formerly part of Serengeti National Park, it was made a conservation area in 1959 and has since been an experiment in multiple land use: Masai villages and grazing cattle, highland forest plantations, wild animal protection and study, and tourism.

Olduvai Gorge

At Km 215 is the turnoff left to *Olduvai Gorge,* a hot, desolate place that is probably the world's most famous prehistoric site. From the main road you travel 5 km over flat, rocky, thorny land. The gorge was "discovered" accidentally in 1911 by a German butterfly collector, Professor Kattwinkel, who found several fossil bones including those of an extinct three-toed horse. Dr. Louis and Mary Leakey, however, brought Olduvai into the spotlight. Their first expedition to the gorge was in 1931, and after patient and persistent excavation over 28 years, their really big discovery was made. In 1959 Mary Leakey uncovered fragments of a nearly complete skull of *Zinjanthropus boisei,* judged to be about 1.5 million years old and one of the best examples of *Australopithecus,* perhaps the first biped creature. In 1961 Jonathan Leakey, one of their sons, unearthed fragments from a child and an adult who were contemporary with *Zinjanthropus* but were hominids called *Homo habilis,* thought to be the first systematic toolmaker and probably the direct ancestor of modern man, *Homo sapiens.* Both of these "near-men" along with various small and large animals lived on the shore line of what for about 2 million years was a lake. As you come to the edge of the gorge you can see layers of different-colored earth forming what are called beds, which built up over 1.5 million years. Then severe earth movements and streams cut the gorge to about two-thirds of its present depth, and 30,000 years ago earthquake faults cut the gorge down to the lava layer on its bottom.

Olduvai and its layers of discoveries are understood through looking at the beds, which are sedimentary layers of history, each different and datable. The gorge is 200 to 500 feet deep and is subdivided into five widespread units called Bed I, Bed II, Bed III, Bed IV, and the Ndutu Beds. Bed I is the lowest and oldest, 40 to 130 feet thick, and it was in this bed that both *Zinjanthropus* and *Homo habilis* remains were found. *Zinjanthropus boisei* was nicknamed "Nutcracker Man" because of his large grinding molars, used in his mainly vegetarian diet. This *Australopithecus,* about 4 feet tall, had no forehead but a massive jaw and small brain (450–550 cubic centimeters versus as much as three times that for modern man). Fragments from about ten individuals have been found at Olduvai, and others at Lakes Natron and Eyasi. *Homo habilis* was a contemporary of *Zinjanthropus* but had a larger brain and different dental pattern, and was perhaps more advanced; thus he earned the name "Skillful Man." The hand bones of the *Homo habilis* child indicated that the hand, while not like ours, was capable of holding small objects with some precision. Also in Bed I was found a stone hut-circle and living floor, a rough circle of piled stones which seemed to represent man's early attempts to shelter himself from the elements. Near and within it were found various stone tools and animal fossils. The earliest known tools of human origin, called Olduwan tools, were choppers made from water-worn rock from which several flakes were struck off along one side to form a jagged cutting edge. These simple tools were used for chopping open bones and cutting branches off trees for spears. Sharp flakes from the stone were used for skinning animals and sharpening sticks, for example. Bed I "near-men" probably lived at the beginning of the Stone Age, a long period during which prehistoric tools were made primarily from rock.

Gradually Early Stone Age "near-men" developed practical hand axes, which became refined over 500,000 years, and are called Acheulean, after the place in France where they were first discovered in the 19th century. The Acheulean hand-ax industry spread over about one million years, lasting until about 60,000 years ago, and its artifacts extended from Bed II into Bed IV, with the best examples in the latter. Also found in the middle of 70- to 92-foot-thick Bed II were bones of huge extinct animals, including pigs the size of hippos with 3-foot-long tusks, a baboon the size of a present chimpanzee, and a gigantic horned beast called *Pelorovis* which had a horn span exceeding 6 feet. Bed III is the red bed, 20–35 feet thick, but few men lived in Olduvai during this hot, dry period, and few tools have been found.

Bed IV is divided into two parts—IVa and IVb—and it is in the lower IVa that Acheulean hand axes are most prevalent. The hand ax had a sharp edge all around with a point formed by the convergence of two sharp edges, and was a handy all-purpose tool. Other tools had also been developed by this time, including cleavers, scrapers, throwing stones, and knives. By about 750,000 B.C. the primary human type was *Homo erectus,* who had a larger brain (1,100 cubic centimeters) than his ancestors and a bigger skull to contain it, and whose face was still massive but looked more like ours. *Homo erectus* remains have been found in Africa, Europe, and Asia. Some of the best sites for Acheulean industry tools include Olduvai Gorge and Isimila in Tanzania, Kalambo Falls in Zambia, and Olorgesailie and Kariandusi in Kenya.

About 50,000 years ago man was busy adapting to his different environmental conditions, and *Homo sapiens neanderthalensis* appeared in western Europe while *Homo sapiens rhodesiensis* (Broken Hill Man, found in Kabwe, Zambia) spread throughout Africa. By this time fire was in use, and man used it in hunting animals and keeping warm. Smaller, more complicated, and specialized tools were made for working wood and bone, pounding plants, and skinning animals. The two main East African cultural traditions were the Sangoan-Lupemban, which were found in the more wooded areas where tools were for woodworking, digging up roots, and included adzes and chisels; and the Stillbay, found in the open country of the Rift Valley, where tools were small with distinctive leaflike points.

Modern man replaced the Neanderthal races about 40,000 to 30,000 years ago, and the oldest African fossils that belong to modern *Homo sapiens* were found at Kanjera near Lake Victoria's Kavirondo Gulf in Kenya, and in the lower Omo basin north of Lake Rudolf. For some of the latest East Africa discoveries, see Lake Rudolf section under Kenya.

At Olduvai Gorge is a small but very interesting museum explaining its formation and finds, and a number of Tanzanian university-trained guides who will gladly show you around on a short or long tour. A free, informative pamphlet has been produced on the gorge with the help of the National Geographic Society, which has funded and publicized the Leakeys' work for a number of years. Many package tours from Nairobi and Arusha include Olduvai Gorge on their itineraries; see TP-10–13 and KP-76, 80–87.

While you're at Olduvai Gorge, you can ask the guides to show you *Shifting Sands,* crescent-shaped dunes of black volcanic ash blown into the area from distant though still-active Ol Doinyo Lengai. The several dunes, standing on a grassy plain, are also called *barchans* (Arabic—"sand"). The wind rolls the sand grains up the gentle windward slope of the dunes, then grains drop down the steep leeward face, resulting in a dune that moves slowly downwind or in a circle.

The turnoff to Olduvai is also near the track north to remote *Lake Natron*, another of the Rift Valley soda lakes. Natron, whose main inlet is Kenya's Uaso Nyiro River, is the main breeding ground for the millions of greater and lesser flamingos. It is about 40 miles long and 15 miles wide, and though at 2,000 feet altitude is very hot and dry. Ol Doinyo Sambu (6,702 feet) is on its northwest side, Gelai Peak (9,653 feet) on its southwest side, and Ol Doinyo Lengai (9,443 feet) on its south end.

As you leave the Olduvai Gorge area and continue southeast, the *Ngorongoro Highlands* come into view. This is a large half-circle of eight extinct volcanoes, 5 million to 7 million years old, several of which are over 10,000 feet high. The road up to Ngorongoro's crater rim passes *Makarut* (10,276 feet), whose western flank slopes down to the plains below until cut by a scarp, and *Malanja,* whose floor is at 6,900 feet and whose south side is formed by the slopes of two extinct volcanoes, 9,400-foot *Satiman* (Masai—"newly castrated mature bull") and *Loroklukunya*. To the southeast of Ngorongoro is *Oldeani* (Masai—"bamboo"), a 10,460-foot, broad cone with a large crater on its summit and bamboo on its slopes. The northern Highlands have five extinct volcanoes. South of the Highlands is *Lake Eyasi,* a 400-square-mile soda lake with one inlet, the Sibiti River, and a 15- to 20-million-year-old wall of the Rift Valley on its west side.

Ngorongoro Crater

Having climbed up into the Highlands, by Km 244 you are on the rim of *Ngorongoro Crater* (pronounced EN-goro-EN-goro), a busy Garden of Eden visited by more than 55,000 people a year now. The average altitude of the crater rim is about 7,600 feet, and the sides and center of this volcano, once nearly 15,000 feet, collapsed inward hundreds of thousands of years ago, creating a 2,000-foot deep caldera with a lush 102-square-mile floor at 5,600 feet which is now teeming with animal and bird life. Ngorongoro is regarded as the world's largest unflooded, unbroken caldera. It is estimated that the wildebeest population fluctuates between 10,000 and 14,000, and that there are about 110 black rhinos and numerous zebras, elands, gazelles, harte-beests, and waterbucks. They attract the usual predators—lions, leop-ards, cheetahs, wild dogs, hyenas, and jackals. Elephants, buffalos, and hippos also live in the crater, but there are no giraffes, kudus, sables, roans, or crocodiles. At least 182 bird species have been counted in the crater itself and 291 in the Conservation Area. Some Masai also live in the crater, though the government is restricting their numbers and encouraging others to water their cattle at the boreholes outside the crater.

The first overseas visitor to Ngorongoro was Dr. O. Baumann, the German explorer. The spot where Dr. Baumann saw his first view of the crater on March 18, 1892, is marked by a board at *Baumann's Point* on the East Rim road. Also on the rim at Km 255 is a *memorial to Michael Grzimek,* who died in 1959 when his light plane crashed while he and his father Bernhard (*Serengeti Shall Not Die*) were pioneering ecological studies of Serengeti and Ngorongoro. The memorial reads: "He gave all he possessed including his life for the wild animals of Africa."

The Conservation Unit has published three very useful and interesting guide booklets, each costing 3/−: *Ngorongoro's First Visitor, Ngorongoro's Geological History,* and *Ngorongoro's Bird Life.* These are available at the unit headquarters (Km 249) and the lodges on the rim.

The trip down into the crater from the rim is by TTC four-wheel-drive vehicles only (see "Getting Around" below). The main route into the crater is Lerai Descent, next to the Wildlife Lodge at Km 254, while the exit road is near Windy Gap and comes up to the main rim road 6 km before our Km 244, near Lemagrut Mountain. The floor is mainly grassy plains, interspersed with fresh and salty lakes, pools and streams, with patches of forest and bumps of hills. There is a large circular road that goes through Lerai Forest around the large Lake Magadi, with smaller circuits off it to Engitati Hill, Lainai Forest, the Olijoronyuki River and drift areas, Engaitokitok Springs, and Hippo Pool. The plains animals—wildebeest, gazelle, zebra, hartebeest, cheetah, lion—spread out over the open grassland to the west and east of Lake Magadi. In the lakes and marshes look for hippos, waterbucks, rhinos, and lots of birds, including greater and lesser flamingos. In and near Lerai and Lainai forests might be seen baboons, monkeys, elephants, bushbucks, lions, and leopards.

Jane and Hugo van Lawick-Goodal previously published a layman's version of their studies—at Ngorongoro and in the Serengeti—of the doglike predators: hunting dog, jackal, and hyena, any of which you may see here. The *Cape hunting dog* stands 24 to 30 inches at the shoulder, has a 15-inch-long bushy tail, large rounded ears, and is black with uneven rufous and white blotches. He is diurnal and hunts zebra, gazelle, and wildebeest and other ungulates in small packs, quickly disemboweling the prey before its death.

There are two species of hyena: spotted and striped. The more common *spotted hyena* stands 27 to 36 inches at the shoulder, has a 12-inch-long tail, large rounded ears, big strong jaws, and is reddish brown to drab gray with dark spots on its fur. While hyenas are mainly nocturnal, they may be seen at dawn and dusk. Spotted hyenas live in Ngorongoro Crater, and according to the van Lawick-Goodalls the area is divided into eight different territories by the hyena clans, with each territory regularly marked with the scent from glands under the hyena's tail. Hyenas make a variety of noises, including whoops, growls, roars, chuckles, and giggles, and a common call of "ooooo-whup." They usually hunt in clans within their own territory, and when the prey—such as wildebeest, baby rhino, zebra—is caught, it is disemboweled very quickly and picked clean within an hour. Contrary to previous thought that hyenas frequently feed off lion kills, actually the reverse is often more true.

When to Visit

The crater can be visited all year, though the months of January–February are the warmest and driest. During the rainy seasons of March–May and November–December the crater may be rainy or very misty. June–September is cool and unpredictable, though generally dry. The night temperatures anytime are very cool, because of the near-8,000-foot altitude on the rim, so have some warm clothes.

Getting There, Getting Around

Ngorongoro can be approached by all-weather dirt roads from Serengeti and from Arusha; these roads are slippery when wet, especially on the hilly sections approaching the rim. The crater rim is 161 km from Arusha, 125 km from Seronera. The main airstrip is at Lake Manyara, but there's also an airstrip on the crater floor. Only TTC four-wheel-drive vehicles may go down into the crater itself. TTC Land-Rovers are for hire at the Crater Lodge and Wildlife Lodge: 300/– per 7-passenger vehicle, or 70/– a seat. Many package tours from Nairobi and Arusha include Ngorongoro in their itineraries; see TP-6, 9–13, 25–27, 31–32, and KP-63, 65, 69, 71, 74, 76–77, 79–88, 90, 92–93.

Accommodations

Ngorongoro Wildlife Lodge, bookings to TTC Hotels (p. 315). Located at Km 254 on the crater rim, 17 km from the main Arusha gate. 78 dbls incl 3 suites, all w/bath. Rates: FB: sgl—264/–; dbl—330/–; also low season rates. The TTC's Wildlife Lodge, designed by Zevit Architects of Nairobi, has superb views of the distant crater floor from the lodge terrace and from the four staggered layers of rooms. It is comfortable and well maintained, but does have slow service and high rates. Table d'hôte meals in the modern dining room: breakfast—10/–; lunch—17/50; tea—5/–; dinner—21/–. Rating: 1st-class international, fanciest hotel at a "must" tourist sight. . . .

Ngorongoro Crater Lodge, Box 751, Arusha; tel. 2193. Located at Km 251, 20 km from main Arusha gate. 2 sgls, 52 dbls, 4 trpls, all w/bath or shower. Rates: FB: sgl—240/–; dbl—330/–; also low season rates. Tent (sleeping 7): 80/– per person. Built in 1937 and expanded in 1967, the Crater Lodge looks like a Swiss mountain hotel with lots of flowers. Simply furnished rooms are in three 6-room blocks and in shingle-roofed log cabins. Main building has the bar, café, and table d'hôte dining room: breakfast—10/–; lunch—14/–; dinner—20/–. Rating: 1st-class local, cold, and scenic. . . .

Ngorongoro Forest Resort Lodge, bookings to Masailand Safaris (T) Ltd., Box 792, Arusha; tel. 2523. At Km 251, or 11 km from the Arusha gate. 23 dbls, none w/bath. Rates: FB: sgl—110/–; dbl—160/–. Though built in 1960 this place is cold, damp, dismal, and bad news. Rooms have sparse furnishings, no heat, no bath. Bamboo bar and red-and-white table d'hôte dining rooms are slightly more cheerful; breakfast—8/–; lunch—12/–; dinner—16/–. Rating: 2d-class local, not worth the money. . . .

Ngorongoro Crater House, c/o Conservation Unit, Box 6000, Ngorongoro. Self-service cottage for 6 people on the rim. Rates: 500/– per week. . . . Though the Youth Hostel is presently being used for tour drivers, travelers without tents can sometimes find a two-bed room for 15/– per person at Park Village. . . .

Camping is allowed at Simba Camp, Km 248, 18 km from the main Arusha gate. Facilities: toilet, water, wood-burning water heater for shower. Fee: 10/– per person per night. There are four special sites (20/– per person) on the crater floor; inquire at Conservation Unit headquarters.

The descent from the crater rim toward Arusha begins at Km 257, and you exit the Conservation Area at the main gate at Km 268. This side of the Crater Highlands is very moist, with the forest on Ngorongoro aiding in water catchment and soil preservation, and thus providing a vital service to the Iraqw (Mbulu) *shambas* growing mainly wheat.

At about Km 275 is the turnoff right to *Oldeani Residential Club,* Box 23, Oldeani; tel. 25. Located about 13 km from the turnoff. 3 dbls, 1 w/bath. Rates: FB: sgl—125/–; dbl—200/–. The club is at 4,900 feet altitude in the foothills of Oldeani Mountain and has simple rooms, a bar, indoor badminton, tennis, and a Land Cruiser for hire (300/– per day). Also near this turnoff is the signposted turnoff to *Ngorongoro Crater Farm,* bookings to Shezan Ltd., Box 25180, Nairobi, tel. 31859. Has rooms for about 12 guests. Rates: FB: sgl—180/–; dbl—260/–.

Km 303: Turnoff right to *Lake Manyara Hotel,* bookings to TTC Hotels (p. 315). Less than 1 km off the road. 100 dbls, incl 2 suites, all w/bath. Rates: FB: sgl—264/–; dbl—330/–; also low season rates. Spread out on top of an escarpment 1,000 feet above Lake Manyara, the sleek, modern lodge has good views of the park—you can see elephants and other large beasts at a distance. Long lounge leads into split-level dining room and bar, where service is slower than necessary. Pool. Table d'hôte meals cost breakfast—10/–; lunch—17/50; tea— 5/–; dinner—21/–. Rating: 1st-class international, only place to stay at Lake Manyara, but the cost is too high.

Lake Manyara

Km 309: Turnoff right to *Lake Manyara National Park.* The park, at 3,150 feet altitude, covers 123 square miles, about 88 square miles of which are lake, and contains a good variety of terrain and animal and bird life. The park includes part of the Rift Valley's western wall (on which is perched the hotel), a ground-water forest, an acacia woodland, areas of open grassland, the lake foreshore, a swamp, and part of the lake itself. The best-known animals at Manyara are the tree-climbing lions. Others to be seen are the buffalo, elephant, leopard, rhino, zebra, giraffe, impala, baboons, blue and vervet monkeys. Birdlife is prolific, with at least 380 species, some migratory and seasonal, recorded in the park so far.

The name Manyara is derived from the Masai word *emanyara,* which is the thornbush plant used for making the stock-proof hedge around a Masai *enkang* or circular living unit. Lake Manyara is one in the string of Great Rift Valley lakes formed 2 to 3 million years ago. Manyara's level varies: in 1961 during a drought it was completely dry, while in 1962 it rose so high it flooded many trees on its shore. Although it is an alkaline lake, catfish and bream live in it and are caught outside the park by local people with dugout canoes and gill nets.

There is only one park gate by which you enter and exit, this at Km 309 on the main Ngorongoro–Arusha road. By the gate is a small *nature museum,* where the National Parks' guide booklet on Manyara should be available (cost 5/–). Upon entering the park you are immediately in the *ground-water forest;* the trees here include wild fig, palm, tamarind, and baobab. Many of the trees and shrubs have been labeled with numbered tags; their numbers correspond to the names listed in the back of the guide booklet. Animals usually in the forest or marshy glades are elephants, blue monkeys, vervets, and yellow and olive baboons.

Taking the main road through the park, you cross the Marera River, and about 1 km later is a turnoff left to *Mahali pa Nyati* (Swahili—"place of the buffalo"), an open grassy area with a resident herd of about 400 buffalos. Beyond the Msasa River bridge is another track to the left leading to the *lakeshore,* which is teeming with birdlife, including the hammerhead stork, Egyptian goose, greater and lesser flamingos, yellow-billed stork, African spoonbill, and white and pink-backed pelicans.

Southwest of the Msasa River you enter acacia woodland, where those famous tree-climbing lions hang out. Several theories have been offered for why Manyara lions like to climb trees, unlike most lions elsewhere: to avoid the biting flies, to catch a cooling breeze, to get a better view, to keep out of the way of buffalo and elephant herds. Whatever their reasons, the manyara lions have made a name for themselves. Make sure you stay in your vehicle while around them.

In the Ndala River area is the *Elephant Research Camp,* which is studying elephants, about 350 of which live in the park. The end of the park road is at *Maji Moto,* the 140°F fresh-water hot springs which well up from a delta fan at the foot of the rift wall. There may be some biting tsetse flies in this area, but this species does not carry sleeping sickness. On your way back to the park gate, you can take numerous loop roads for a different route.

When to Visit

The park is open all year, though the circuit tracks in some sections may be closed after a heavy rainfall, especially November–December, March–May. Otherwise an ordinary sedan can use all the roads.

Getting There, Getting Around

The park is accessible via the all-weather dirt road from Arusha (114 km) and Ngorongoro Crater (47 km). Either way entry and exit is through the one main gate. The park's 37-km length can be easily driven in a morning or afternoon, though loop roads can make a drive of 100 km. A small airstrip is 1 km from the hotel, and vehicles are for hire there. Many package tours from Nairobi and Arusha include Manyara; see TP-5, 7–8, 10–13, 25–27, and 31–32, and KP-65, 68–69, 71, 74, 76–78, 80–88, 90, 92–93.

Accommodations

The *Lake Manyara Hotel* is described above at Km 303. . . . **Camping** is possible at three sites inside the park gate. Campers should be self-contained, and mosquito nets are useful. Fee: 5/– per person. Bookings, good idea December–March, to Warden, Lake Manyara National Park, Box 3134, Arusha; tel. 12.

Continuing along the road to Arusha, at Mto Wa Mbu, a small village at Km 310, is the turnoff left to the track to *Engaruka*, a rather mysterious Iron Age settlement covering about 10 square miles. The area includes stone-built ruins, circles, cairns, and terraces. According to 1964 excavations, it is thought that this was an ancient African community dating from the 4th to 16th centuries.

At Km 345 is a major junction. To the right the road goes to Tarangire National Park, Kolo, Dodoma, and Iringa (see Route T-8); but you turn left to go to Arusha. This is again Masai country (see also Route K-5), and the headquarters of Masai District is at *Monduli,* whose turnoff left is at Km 407. There are about 65,000 Masai in Tanzania, mostly living between Serengeti, Ngorongoro, Arusha, and the Kenya border, though some also live south of Arusha in the Masai Steppe. In the last few years the Tanzania government has been attempting to modernize the Masai cattle-keeping—and to get the Masai to wear pants. But the men persistently and proudly walk around with just a blanket or cloth slung over their shoulders. Also at Km 407 is the turnoff right south to *Naberera,* about 100 km, and *Ngasumet,* about 150 km, two important Masai watering holes in the Masai Steppe.

Arusha

At Km 415 is the turnoff left to the main road to Nairobi (see Route T-2). The end of this present route is at Km 423 in Arusha at the clock tower in the town center, junction of Boma and Uhuru roads. *Arusha,* with a population of about 32,450, is a pleasant town that sprawls at 4,600 feet altitude on the southern foothills of Mount Meru, and is the center of a busy agricultural region. It lies on the Great North Road and claims to be the halfway point between Cape Town and Cairo.

The three main tribes living in Arusha's environs are the Masai, Arusha, and Meru. The Arusha are related to the Masai and have similar dress, language, and customs, but are primarily agriculturalists, growing maize, beans, wheat, potatoes, and pyrethrum. The Meru (no close relation to Kenya's Meru tribe) are a Bantu tribe living on the slopes of Mount Meru, where they keep cattle and grow coffee, maize, and pyrethrum.

When the Germans began coming into northern Tanzania in the 1890s, they realized what a prime agricultural area this might be. The German administration was established with an army post at Arusha in 1899, and settlers moved in, planting coffee and lots of trees, many of which still beautify the area. After World War I the new British administration sold the formerly German farmland to British, South Africans, Indians, and Greeks, some of whom remain around Arusha. The railway line was extended from Moshi to Arusha in 1929. The missionary movement has been very active in the area, particularly the Roman Catholic and Lutheran churches, establishing schools, clinics, and hospitals.

Since Tanzania's independence in 1963, Arusha has become a busy commercial and administrative center. A decisive year for the town was 1967. In February, President Nyerere made his important Arusha Declaration that set Tanzania on its present socialist course, and in July the newly formed East African Community chose to make Arusha its headquarters, putting the buildings in the vicinity of town hall. The EAC succeeded other regional efforts. It operates such common services as the postal and telecommunications, East African Airways, Railway, Harbours, Customs, and scientific research organizations for its member states of Kenya, Tanzania, and Uganda. Despite occasional violent political difference among the states, all three presidents are sworn to keep the Community together. Arusha is now also a starting point for northern Tanzania safaris led by tour companies based in or near Arusha, as well as stopover for numerous tours swinging through from Nairobi and Mombasa.

Accommodations

New Arusha Hotel, Box 88, Arusha; tel. 3241; cable CENTRE; or bookings to African Tours & Hotels (p. 87). At the clock tower in the center of town. 17 sgls, 34 dbls, 18 trpls, 2 suites, all w/bath. Rates: B&B: sgl—100/—; dbl—155/—. Credit: DC. Modern (1965 and after) hotel with 5-floor main building and 3-story annex in spacious, grassy grounds. Rooms attractive, not plush, featuring, like rest of hotel, polished parquet floors. Big, pleasant dining room, plus 2 bars, snack bar, pool. Rating: a bit more than 2d-class international, best place in Arusha proper. . . .

Hotel Equator, Box 3002, tel. 3127. Located about 50 yards off Boma Road overlooking the Themi River, next to the City Council campground. 24 dbls, all w/bath, balcony. Rates: B&B: sgl—90/—; dbl—140/—. New in late 1972, all the Equator's rooms have a view of the gurgling Themi River. Also a bar, table d'hôte and à la carte dining room. Rating: 1st-class local. . . .

New Safari Hotel, Box 303, tel. 2325, cable FARIOTEL. On Boma Road half a block from the clock tower. 12 sgls, 28 dbls; only 19 rms w/bath. Rates: B&B: sgl—70/— to 80/—; dbl—100/— to 120/—. John Wayne may have stayed here during the making of *Hatari!* but the hotel is now old and crumbling, shabby and shopworn; the management is uninterested, negligent. Dining room and bar, though, are comfortably furnished with leather chairs. Rating: 2d-class local, may improve since TTC took over in late 1973. . . .

Arusha Inn (YMCA), Box 658, tel. 2765. On India St. behind the Safari Hotel. Rates: B&B: sgl—51/65; dbl—69/50, incl tax and daily membership. Rooms are spartan to bare, but clean. Dining room/ snack bar is practically in the lobby. Cost is incredibly high for what's offered. Rating: 2d-class local. . . .

Naaz Hotel, Box 92, tel. 2087. Rates: sgl—22/50; dbl—45/—. Rating: 2d-class local. . . . *Greenland Hotel,* Box 727. Rates: sgl—15/—; dbl—30/—. Rating: 3d-class local. . . . **Camping** is allowed off Boma

Road by the Town Council building on a grassy plot big enough for about 6 tents along the Themi River. Facilities: toilets, hot and cold showers, water. Fee: 5/– per person per night, 10/– per vehicle; payable to night watchman or to Town Treasurer's Department at Town Hall. For hotels between Arusha and Moshi, see Route T-3.

Where to Eat

New Arusha Hotel dining room, tel. 2345. The fanciest place in town for a bite. Table d'hôte meals: breakfast—10/–; lunch—15/–; dinner—20/–. Also à la carte lunch and snacks. . . . *New Safari Hotel dining room,* tel. 2325. Bar has old photos of hunters, and the table d'hôte meals are standard fare. Breakfast—8/50; lunch—14/50; dinner—17/50. . . . *Hotel Equator dining room,* tel. 3127. Has table d'hôte and some à la carte meals. . . . *Naaz Hotel dining room,* tel. 2087. Reputedly has good curries. . . . *Jambo Snack Bar,* on Boma Road near Safari Hotel. Looks like a funky soda fountain, but is the best place for a reasonably priced meal. Fillet, eggs and chips, chicken pili-pili—each about 8/50. . . . *Highway Restaurant,* on India St. Snacks but not much atmosphere.

Taxis

Taxis rank up outside the New Arusha and New Safari hotels, and charge about 3/– per mile, or 2/– per kilometer.

Information Bureau

The *Tanzania Tourist Center,* Boma Road, Box 494, can supply mostly information and maps about Tanzania in general but may have some local advice on Arusha.

Shops and Services

The main shopping street is Joel Maeda Road, with some stores also on Boma and Uhuru roads. *Books, magazines, papers:* New Arusha Hotel. Christian Bookstore, Boma Road. Kase Book Store and Corner Book Store, Joel Maeda Road. . . . *Central market:* Market St. off Uhuru Road, about 8 blocks from clock tower. . . . *Groceries:* Greengrocers, Joel Maeda Road Greengrocers and New Economy Store, Uhuru Road. . . . *Hardware:* General Hardware & Tool Mart, Uhuru Road. . . . *Photo shop:* Achelis Ltd., Uhuru Road.

Route T-2: Arusha–Namanga, Kenya

This is a connector route between northern Tanzania and southern Kenya. En route you pass through lush Arusha farmland and semi-dry Masai cattle country, in the middle of which is 8,500-foot Longido Mountain.

The route starts at Arusha's clock tower in the town center, from which you go north 2 km to the T-junction at the main Arusha–Moshi road; there go left to Nairobi. The turnoff to Lake Manyara, Ngorongoro Crater, and Serengeti is at Km 6 (see Route T-1). In this vicinity the country changes from coffee estates and green Arusha *shambas* to bare rolling hills with flocks of goats and sheep, and herds of cattle.

Km 38: To the immediate right on a slight rise along the road is the 1954 *Trek Monument,* a 15-foot-high obelisk with a stone torch on top, and an inscription: "Lord, guide us to a destiny worthy of their past," commemorating the Boers who trekked here at the beginning of the century. Considering Tanzania's present attitude toward South Africa, it is surprising this monument still stands.

Two km later at Km 40 is Dutch Corner, and the turnoff right to Arusha National Park (see Route T-3), 35 km via the north foothills of Mount Meru and the town of Ngare Nanyuki; and the road also goes to *Osirwa Safari Cottages,* P.O. West Kilimanjaro; tel. 5Y2; cable OSIRWA. About 77 km northeast from Dutch Corner on the northwest slopes of Kilimanjaro. Two large cottages, each w/3 dbls, 3 baths, sitting/dining room, kitchen, veranda. Rates: FB: 200/– per person, minimum of 4; also low season rates. Credit: DC. Located at 6,000 feet altitude on a wheat farm on Kilimanjaro's slopes with morning and evening views (weather permitting) of the mountain. Arrangements for bird shooting, riding, mountain strolling, and climbing. Expensive but private. See also package tour KP-73.

Leaving Mount Meru's foothills, the drive continues north; Africa's highest mountain, 19,340-foot Kilimanjaro, might be seen to the east, if its veil of clouds permits.

Km 89: Near here is a four-wheel-drive track to the left to *Gelai Peak* (9,653 feet) and *Ol Doinyo Lengai* (9,443 feet), both climbable for the determined and energetic. To reach both, turn left, go north of Kitumbeine Hill, then west to Gelai Meru-goi—about 77 km. Gelai Peak (from Masai *olgelai,* a tree which thrives on the mountain)

is an extinct volcano with a forested crater and extensive views of
Lake Natron and the Rift Valley. Ol Doinyo Lengai (Masai—"mountain of God") is another 50 km or so south over even rougher track,
and is East Africa's only active volcano. Its most recent eruptions were
in 1960 and 1966, and its bubbling mud pools and steam are pre-
liminary hints of its next soundoff. The whole mountain is coated with
slippery ash, and climbing it can be dry and hot. See Robson's *Mountains of Kenya* (p. 91).

Km 90: To the immediate right is *Longido* (from Masai *oloonkito,*
"place of the stone useful for sharpening knives"). This 8,625-foot
mountain is also climbable, and a prominent dead tree here at the
base marks a campsite favored by climbers. The climb is 5 to 6
hours; see Robson's guide.

The *Tanzania border post* is at Km 110, as is the *Kenya border post*
and *Namanga.* From here pick up Kenya Route K-5.

Route T-3: Arusha–Moshi–Dar es Salaam

This route is a long 643 km, and goes from northern Tanzania to
the capital city, Dar es Salaam. En route are turnoffs to Arusha National
Park, Moshi, sisal country, the Usambara Mountains, and three game
reserves—Mkomazi, Sadani, and Selous.

Leaving from the clock tower in central Arusha, at Km 2 you reach
the main Arusha–Moshi road, where you turn right. In this moist area
coffee is grown, one of Tanzania's three major crops, and estates line
the highway. The species grown here is *arabica,* introduced by German
missionaries in 1893. In 1971 Tanzania's total coffee exports amounted
to $32.4 million.

Km 11: *Tanzania Taxidermists,* turnoff to the left. Just a half km
farther is the turnoff right to *Lake Duluti,* 1½ km, a small crater lake
that is popular on weekends for fishing, boating, and water skiing.
Camping is at a lakeside site; bookings to Arusha Gymkhana Club,
Box 59, Arusha; tel. 2155. Facilities: toilets, bath. Fee: 5/– per person. Planned is the New Duluti Lodge, on the lakeshore.

Km 20: Turnoff left to *Mount Meru Game Sanctuary,* Box 659,
Arusha; tel. Usa River 43. Located just off the road. 6 dbls, 2 sgls, all
w/bath. Rates: B&B: sgl—115/50; dbl—220/–. On the lush green
grounds are a private zoo and small hotel, built in 1960 as the home
of Dr. Andreas von Nagy, a professional hunter and zoological collector. In closed and open cages are lions, leopards, cheetahs, baby ele-

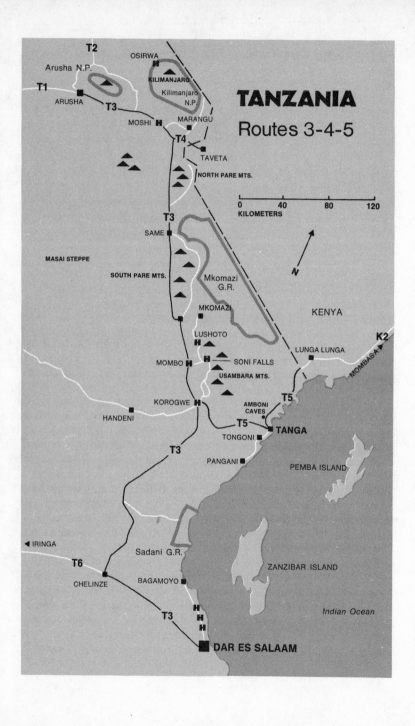

TANZANIA
Routes 3-4-5

T2
OSIRWA
Arusha N.P.
KILIMANJARO
T1
Kilimanjaro
ARUSHA   N.P.
T3
MARANGU
MOSHI H
T4
TAVETA
NORTH PARE MTS.

0   40   80   120
KILOMETERS

N

T3
SAME

MASAI STEPPE

SOUTH PARE MTS.
Mkomazi
G.R.

KENYA

MKOMAZI
LUSHOTO H
MOMBO H   H
SONI FALLS
USAMBARA MTS.
LUNGA LUNGA   K2

MOMBASA

T5
KOROGWE H
AMBONI
CAVES
HANDENI
T5
TANGA
TONGONI
T3
PANGANI

PEMBA ISLAND

IRINGA

T6
Sadani G.R.

ZANZIBAR ISLAND

CHELINZE
BAGAMOYO

T3   H H H

Indian Ocean

■■ DAR ES SALAAM

phants, chimpanzees, various bucks, buffalos, giraffes, and camels; there is a small charge to look at the animals. The guest rooms are homey, decorated with antiques, Persian rugs, some skins, while the main building has local artifacts and stuffed animals in nearly every square inch of the lounge and two intimate dining rooms. Casual meals: breakfast—9/–; lunch—12/50; tea—2/–; dinner—20/–. Thorn Tree Safaris has a Tanzania office here. Package tours including the Sanctuary are TP-1 and KP-83. Rating: 1st-class local, we give it a ★.

About .3 km down the highway is the turnoff left to *Hotel Tanzanite,* Box 3063, Arusha; tel. Usa River 32; cable TANZANITE. 30 dbls, all w/bath. Rates: B&B: sgl—115/–; dbl—155/–. A 1970 motel-modern place without much style, charm, or soul. Clean rooms (no bedspreads) in some 15 cottages scattered around large grassy grounds, with pool and tennis courts. Main building has schmaltzy music, bar, lobby, spacey lounge, big barren dining room with table d'hôte meals (breakfast—7/50; lunch—15/–; tea—1/–; dinner—17/–) plus some à la carte entrées: lobster thermidor, cheese omelet, vegetable curry, each 8– to 19/50. Rating: 2d-class international, but not extraordinary.

Arusha National Park

Km 21: Turnoff left to *Arusha National Park,* 8 km north. Arusha Park has three distinct areas within its 50 square miles: Ngurdoto Crater, a thickly forested caldera teeming with wildlife on its floor, which is closed to humans but which may be viewed from ten points on the crater rim; the Momela Lakes, a series of seven lakes varying in alkalinity and wildlife; and Mount Meru, Africa's fourth-highest mountain, officially called Socialist Peak, whose highest point is nearly 15,000 feet and which may be climbed. There are about 60 species of mammals you can spot including colobus and Sykes monkeys, bushbucks, buffalos, red forest duikers, hippos, rhinos, elephants, giraffes, reedbucks, leopards, and waterbucks—but there are no lions. About 380 species of birds have been recorded, and December–March there are many species of migratory birds from Europe and Asia.

Depending upon how much time you have, you can choose to see any or all of the park's three sections. A good little guide to follow during your drive is the National Parks' *Arusha National Park* booklet (cost 5/–). If you have a half-day, visit Ngurdoto Crater and the lakes, or Meru mountain. For a full-day visit or longer, you could take in everything.

Ngurdoto Crater was formed about 15 million years ago when the

Great Rift Valley took shape. The present caldera is about 1½ miles across and 4 square miles in area. The floor is closed to human traffic because it is a reserve within a reserve, protecting the quietude for the resident animals. From Ngurdoto Gate, where there is a small nature museum, take the road to the right up to the Ngurdoto Crater rim. There the road forks around both sides of the crater with five viewpoints on either side for seeing the caldera floor with its black rhino, buffalo, elephant, warthog, baboon, and monkeys, and for seeing distant Kilimanjaro and adjacent Meru. Since there is not yet a circular road, you must backtrack both ways.

Back at Ngurdoto Gate, follow the road north to Momela Lakes. At Boma la Megi is a turnoff to the left to Momela Gate and Meru Mountain, to the right to *Trappe's View* (named after the Trappe family, which owned Momela cattle ranch and started a game sanctuary), which overlooks the lakes. Going straight you come to the cluster of seven Momela lakes, each varying in alkalinity. The road around them is one-way going counterclockwise. *El Kekhotoito* is a favorite waterhole for hippos, rhinos, giraffes, bucks, and white and pink-backed pelicans. *Kusare* is surrounded by yellow-barked acacia trees, whose leaves giraffes find delicious, and October–April the lake is the home for numerous migratory birds from Europe and Asia. *Small Momela Lake* is quite salty by the islet, and sacred ibis, herons, and egrets live in the swamp. *Kinandia Swamp,* reached by a turnoff to the right, has a shelter with a view of an elephant bath. *Great Momela Lake* also is a destination of many migratory birds, and a flock of greater flamingos often feeds by the islet, on which Egyptian geese nest. The last bay on Great Momela has hides for birdwatchers and photographers, who should inquire about their use from the park warden. Between Small and Big Momela lakes is a turnoff to *Lake Tulusia,* which has a hide for watching lesser flamingos. There is a short circuit to *Lake Lakandiro,* and from its viewpoint can be observed many water birds and perhaps the herd of resident waterbuck. In order to reach the Meru mountain drive, you must go to Momela Gate.

Mount Meru (Masai, "that which does not make a noise") is a dormant volcano whose peak is at 14,978 feet, while a subsidiary peak, *Little Meru,* is 12,538 feet and the *Ash Cone* is 12,030 feet. Mount Meru would have been higher than Kilimanjaro, but about 250,000 years ago a series of violent explosions blew away the eastern wall of the formerly perfect crater and an avalanche of volcanic debris and liquid mud (lahar) covered the land. The Momela lakes were formed in hollows in the drying mud, and lahar still covers most of the greater Momela area. Since the original explosion and landslide, there has been repeated volcanic activity, which built the Ash Cone into its perfect shape. At least seven lava flows have erupted from the Cone's vent, the most recent in 1879. There are steam vents and hot springs which attest to Meru's dormancy, and the Jekukumia (Meru, "sometimes hot, sometimes cold") River flows alternately hot and cold owing to the volcanic activity.

After passing through Momela Gate you cross the Ngare Nanyuki River. A turnoff right goes to a falls on the Tululusia ("sentinel") River. The road climbs to 6,000 feet and comes to the *wild fig tree arch.* The wild fig, *Ficus thonningii,* produces seeds which are dropped by feeding birds, in this case into the branches of two trees which stood on either side of a path. The fig seed germinated and put out aerial roots which reached the ground, meanwhile strangling the two host trees and replacing them. Elephants find the fig roots tasty, and have nibbled on the roots in the center, making the large archway through which you can now drive. At Jekukumia you can walk down to the confluence of the *Jekukumia* and *Ngare Nanyuki* rivers, but en route watch for elephants, buffalos, colobus monkeys, and stinging nettles.

The main road ends at *Kitoto,* where you should park and continue by foot unless your vehicle is four-wheel-drive, in which case you can follow the track north. So as not to get lost while walking in the forest, it is a good idea to get a guide from the park office at Momela Gate. From Kitoto, Meru crater can be reached in a half-hour walk, and from there you can get good views of its cliffs, the peaks, and the Ash Cone. It is also possible to climb with a guide both the Ash Cone and the summit of Meru from inside the park, and Meru's summit from outside the park. For all climbing routes, see Robson's *Mountains of Kenya* (p. 91).

When to Visit

The park is open most of the year, but the best months are July through March, especially December. April–June is usually wet and misty.

Getting There, Getting Around

There are two ways to get to the park from Arusha by road. The faster way is to take this Route T-3, turning left 21 km from Arusha, then going 8 km to the gate. The alternate route is off Route T-2, turning right 38 km from Arusha, then going 25 km or so to the park's Momela Gate. Package tours including Arusha Park are TP-1, 12–13, 27, and KP-75, 83.

Accommodations

Momela Game Lodge, Box 535, Arusha, tel. 4505. Just outside the park's Momela Gate. Lodge has bungalows and thatched rondavels. Rates: FB: bungalow—65/– per person; rondavel w/bath—55/– per person. Besides bungalows and rondavels, there is a lounge with a blazing fire when it's cold. . . . *Mountain huts,* three altogether, are available for climbers and campers. Fee: 10/– per person per day. Inquire and book through Park Warden, Arusha National Park, Box 3134, Arusha; tel. 2335. . . . **Camping** is allowed on the Momela Game Lodge grounds. Fee: 10/– per tent. Also several sites scattered throughout the park; most have water and firewood. Fee: 5/– per person per night. Good idea to make bookings with the Park Warden.

Moshi

Back on the Arusha–Moshi highway, at Km 43 is the turnoff right to *Kilimanjaro International Airport,* 6 km, in the middle of the Sanya Juu plains. Km 76 is the first traffic circle turnoff right to Moshi, and 1 km farther is the second and last turnoff into town. *Moshi* (pop. 26,864) is at 2,900 feet on the southern slopes of Kilimanjaro, and its agricultural prosperity is largely due to the energetic Chagga people, who live on and around the mountain's southern and eastern sides. If you have some time in Moshi, you might drop by the *Mwariko Art Gallery* on Mafuta Street (Box 832, tel. 2464). Omari Athmani Mwariko is a self-taught sculptor who brands his own work as "primitive." Each of his works is different, but they usually portray a story or idea from various Tanzania tribes in the form of a person or people looking anguished, happy, angry, or whatever, and are carved from many local types of wood. While he says his works are not for sale, he will quote prices—very high ones, such as 2,000/– or 6,000/–.

Accommodations

Livingstone Hotel, Box 501, tel. 3071; cable LIVTEL. On Rengua Lane. 21 sgls, 40 dbls, incl 5 suites; 31 dbls w/bath or shower. Rates: B&B: sgl—48/– to 56/–; dbl w/bath—128/– to 152/–. Credit: DC. This large white-elephant hotel looks like something out of the 1930s, with stark but clean rooms, and a ballroomlike dining room that serves table d'hôte and some à la carte, including fillet fish, Wiener schnitzel (!), and T-bone, each 9/– to 18/–. Rating: between 1st- and 2d-class local, but the best in Moshi. . . . *Coffee Tree Hostel,* Box 484, tel. 2787. On Old Moshi Road, in Kilimanjaro Native Co-op Union Building. 48 sgls, 10 dbls incl 1 suite; fewer than half with bath. Rates: B&B: sgl w/bath—45/–; dbl w/bath—90/–. Hostel is rather run down, and rooms are sparsely furnished though tidy. Rooftop bar and restaurant have loud music, à la carte food, and a good view of Kilimanjaro. Rating: 2d-class local. . . . *YMCA Hostel,* Box 965, tel. 2362; cable YMCA. On the Arusha–Moshi highway at Km 77. 45 sgls, 19 dbls, incl 2 suites, 1 flat; none w/bath. Rates: B&B: sgl—32/50; dbl—53/75. This 1968, 4-story dormlike building has a pool, several kitchens, a snack bar, small, tidy institutional rooms, and climbing packages for Kilimanjaro (see p. 401). Good for kids. Rating: 2d-class local. . . . **Camping** is allowed by the Town Council at the Jamhuri Playing Fields, 2 km toward Arusha from Moshi. Facilities: toilets, showers, kitchen, and wood. Fee: 5/– per adult, payable to site keeper.

Km 77, besides being the second turnoff right into Moshi, is also the turnoff left to the *College of African Wildlife Management* in Mweka. This unique institution was founded in 1963 with the purpose of training African game wardens, national park officials, and professional hunters to replace the Europeans and Americans. The students work toward a one-year certificate or a two-year degree and spend about 40 percent of the school year on safari and 60 percent in the classroom. Patrick Hemingway, son of Ernest and a former professional hunter, in 1973 was teaching a course in the techniques of taking an animal census.

Continuing east from Moshi, at Km 99 is a major junction: Kilimanjaro and Mombasa are straight on A23 (see Route T-4); Tanga and Dar es Salaam are right and south on B1; turn right. To the left of the highway are the *North Pare Mountains,* whose highest point is Kindoroko at 6,925 feet. From this area south and east to Tanga is Tanzania's main *sisal*-growing region. Tanzania is the world's leading sisal producer, and the fiber has accounted for 25 percent of the country's total exports since 1925, with $19.1 million worth exported in 1971. Sisal estates average 3,000 acres, are equipped with their own roads, railroads, workshops, factory, houses, churches, and shops, and attract laborers from all over Tanzania. In 1967 the Tanzania government nationalized 50 to 60 percent of the sisal-producing companies and created the Tanzania Sisal Corporation as their holding company. Marketing is done through the Tanganyika Sisal Marketing Association.

The sisal plant is propagated from nursery-grown bulbs which are transplanted to the field and cultivated in blocks. The first leaves are cut two years after transplant, and the life cycle of the plant is five to ten years. The cultivation is mechanized, though the planting, transplanting, and upkeep are manual and labor-intensive. Every day each cutter cuts, bundles, and carries 90 bundles of 30 leaves each to the feeder rail or truck, which takes them to the factory. There the harvested leaves are stripped and the fibers extracted in decorticating machines. Each machine needs 3,000 to 5,000 acres of sisal to keep it fully employed, and can turn out five tons of dry fiber daily, which necessitates a labor force of 120 to 150 men for cutting alone. After the fiber is extracted, it is sun-dried over wires, brushed by machines, graded, and baled, with four bales to a ton. Recently there has been stiff competition from synthetics, but there is still a demand for sisal for making rope, twine, and household items. The Sisal Research Institute in Mlingano, among other projects, is looking into possible new products, such as paper pulp, which might be produced from sisal.

Mkomazi Game Reserve

Km 188: Turnoff left to *Same* (alt. 2,815 feet), a small town along the railway line, and *Mkomazi Game Reserve,* 6 km. Mkomazi is 1,400 square miles of semidesert hills, valleys, and plains, east of the Usambara Mountains and adjoining the southern part of Tsavo West. Mkomazi has good concentrations of game including the elephant, black rhino, buffalo, lion, leopard, lesser kudu, gerenuk, oryx, zebra, and, reportedly, one albino giraffe. There are about 322 km of roads within the reserve accessible to four-wheel-drive vehicles, though a 56-km circuit near Ibaya Camp, 16 km from the main Same entrance, is all right for sedans except during the heavy rains. There is no charge for entry to Mkomazi, but a pass should be obtained from the Same Game Division, Box 54, Same; tel. 39. **Accommodations:** two small rest houses with 10 beds at Ibaya Camp. There is no charge, but check with the Game Division in Same.

South of Same on the left of the highway are the *South Pare Mountains,* separated from the North Pares by the Ngulu Pass; the South Pares' highest point is Shengena Mountain at 8,078 feet. Km 302: *Mombo* (alt. 1,355 feet), another small railway town. **Accommoda-**

tions: *Mombo Hotel,* Box 16, tel. 22. Turnoff left at Km 302. 3 sgls, 1 dbl, 1 trpl. Charges: B&B: 35/– per person. Spartan, decrepit, reasonably clean. Rating: 3d-class local.

Also at Mombo is the turnoff left to the *Usambara Mountains,* steep, green, and intensively cultivated by the Sambaa people, with narrow, stony, tortuously winding roads that are inevitably included on the annual East African Safari Rally. The Usambaras' highest point is rocky *Chambolo* (7,557 feet), also called Jiwe la Mungu ("stone of God"), from where there is a splendid view of the plains and valleys below. Chambolo is located at Shume, about 67 km from the highway and 34 km from the town of *Lushoto,* a former German government outpost. Lushoto is in a valley thick with eucalyptus, wild flowers, cedar, and wattle, is 33 km from the highway, and has two small hotels. *Soni,* 16 km from the highway, has a minor waterfall of the same name, and one rundown hotel. If you have time, curiosity, and a good car, an excursion into the Usambaras can be quite pleasant, though it is not advisable in the rainy season. **Accommodations:** *Lawns Hotel,* Box 33, Lushoto; tel. 5; cable LAWNS. Near Lushoto town. 4 sgls, 16 dbls, 4 rms w/bath. Rates: FB: sgl—78/– to 85/–; dbl—145/– to 165/–, including tax and service. Opened in 1910, not changed much since. Rooms are musty, peeling, threadbare, very modest. Bar-lounge and table d'hôte dining room: breakfast—7/–; lunch—14/–; dinner—16/–. Perhaps also billiards, tennis, riding. Rating: 2d-class local, but best in Usambaras. . . . *Oaklands,* Box 41, Lushoto, tel. 59. Has 3 cottages w/bath and 3 dbl rms w/bath. Rates: FB: sgl—68/–; dbl—136/–. . . . *New Soni Falls Hotel,* Box 20, Soni; tel. 27. 4 sgls, 6 dbls, 7 rms w/bath. Rates: FB: sgl—50/–; dbl—90/–. Perched on a hillside near Soni Falls, the "hotel's" view beats the accommodations, which are dilapidated, dingy, and dismal. Rating: 3d-class local; avoid it. . . . **Camping** is sometimes possible on the grounds of the Lawns Hotel; inquire there.

Back on the main road, at Km 341 is *Travelers Inn,* Box 127, Korogwe, tel. 117. Right on the highway. 3 sgls, 4 dbls, 1 trpl, all w/ bath. Rates: B&B: sgl—45/–; dbl—90/–. This hotel is best utilized as a drink stop while you motor down the road. The clean though dampish rooms are around the garden parking lot. Rating: 2d-class local. . . . **Camping** is allowed on the hotel grounds; fee is 2/– per person.

Km 342: Turnoff left to *Korogwe,* a railway town with a population of 6,675 or so. Km 364: Junction, with road A14 to Tanga straight (see Route T-5), the road to Dar es Salaam right; turn right. The route from here on is not very interesting and gets progressively hotter as you approach the coast. Richard Burton, while tromping through the scrub bush and steaming bog in this area en route from Bagamoyo to Tabora in 1856 wrote later of "miasmatic putridities," and you may agree, as the road seems endless, hot, and humid.

Km 459: Turnoff left to *Sadani Game Reserve,* 53 km. This is a new 100-square-mile reserve along the ocean. The Wami River flows through it into the Indian Ocean. There is no charge for entry, but a pass should be obtained from the Game Division in Dar es Salaam, Box 1994, tel. 27011.

Km 533: *Chelinze,* a highway junction with a settlement strung out along the road. Morogoro and Zambia are to the right (see Route T-6), Dar es Salaam to the left; turn left. This is the last stretch of the long drive from Arusha. At Km 572 you cross the Ruvu River, also called the Kingani, which flows into the Indian Ocean north of Bagamoyo. West of Dar, at about Km 620 the road goes through the Pugu Hills, whose highest point is about 1,250 feet. Greater Dar es Salaam now begins to come into view. Km 641 is the turnoff right to Dar es Salaam International Airport, 8 km. Continuing on what is called Morogoro Road, go to its end, or beginning, at the waterfront at Km 643 and turn left onto City Drive. The New Africa Hotel on Azikiwe Street at City Drive in the town center is the end of this route and a fine place for a cold drink. For details on Dar es Salaam, see p. 342.

Selous Game Reserve

At Dar es Salaam you go south on the Kibiti road to Selous Game Reserve. *Selous Game Reserve,* perhaps the world's largest game park, covers some 15,500 square miles astride a network of rivers that includes the Kilombero, Great Ruaha, and Rufiji. Its nearly untouched terrain is typically *miombo* woodland with patches of dense hardwood forest, and virgin bush and savanna. Here roam approximately one million head of game—35,000 elephants, and lions, leopards, buffalos, black rhinos, zebras, hippos, wildebeests, Lichtenstein's hartebeests, sables, greater kudus, and elands. The birdlife is similar to Mikumi National Park.

Selous was named after the big-game hunter Frederick Selous, who, when not hunting elephants on horseback (sometimes killing as many as 30 in a day), was an explorer, naturalist, soldier. His grave is in the very northern part of the reserve near where he died during World War I. The government's Tanzania Wildlife Safaris was assigned the task of opening up the huge reserve, and about six airstrips were constructed, and nearly 1,500 km of tracks cut for driving. These roads are now used by photo safaris, and by ordinary tourists who book tours in Dar es Salaam.

When to Visit

Because the only lodge closes during the rains, it's best to visit July–October, January–March. Otherwise you must be totally self-sufficient.

Getting There, Getting Around

The best way to get there and get around is to go on a tour or arrange with a private safari operator, either by road or by air. At Behobeho Lodge vehicles are for hire. Tanzania packages going to Selous are under TP-21. To go on your own, check with the Game Division in Dar es Salaam (Box 1994, tel. 27011) about getting an entry permit, and with Tanzania Tours about road conditions.

Accommodations

Behobeho Lodge, bookings to Ker, Downey & Selby Safaris, Box 9370, Dar es Salaam; tel. 68152; cable GAMEFIELDS. Has 20 beds. Rates: FB: sgl—150/–; dbl—300/–. Located near the Behobeho River, this was formerly the Capon (luxury tented) Camp, but in 1973 a lodge, rondavels, and a new name were added. Closed November to mid-December, April to mid-June during the rains.

Route T-4: Moshi–Kilimanjaro (Marangu)–Taveta, Kenya

Besides being a connector route between Tanzania and Kenya, this route includes Kilimanjaro.

The route starts on the main highway at Moshi at the YMCA traffic circle. Heading east, at Km 22 is the junction of B1 south to Korogwe and Dar es Salaam, and A23 east to Himo and Taveta; continue straight on A23.

Kilimanjaro

Km 25: Main turnoff left to Marangu, jumping-off place for *Kilimanjaro,* Africa's highest mountain, reaching an impressive 19,340 feet at its summit. Kilimanjaro, like Mount Kenya, is an anomaly—a perpetually ice-capped mountain only 3° south of the equator. And thus when first reported upon in 1848 by a missionary, Johannes Rebmann, many Europeans scoffed at the idea. But later explorers were to prove Rebmann right. Conquered in 1889, Kilimanjaro today has a stream of climbers: the Tanzania government reported 3,494 people trekked up and down the mountain's slopes in 1972. Most followed what is called the Tourist Route, and on their way passed small Chagga *shambas* or farms, wove through thick forest with chattering colobus monkeys, crossed moorlands and the Saddle, a wide alpine desert, and breathing heavily, struggled up rocky scree—to the top of Africa. For those who make it all the way to the summit, it is an unforgettable experience, to know that somehow you have done it, and to see below you, weather permitting, miles of Kenya and Tanzania.

Kilimanjaro is the world's fourth-highest volcano, surpassed only by three in the Andes. The mountain base covers a 50-by-30-mile area, or 1,500 square miles. There are three major volcanic centers: Kibo— 19,340 feet, in the center; Mawenzi—16,896 feet, in the east; and Shira—13,140 feet, in the west. *Shira,* the first to become inactive, is very eroded, and only its southern and western rims remain. Originally its cone might have reached to more than 16,000 feet before it collapsed to form a caldera, whose north and east sides were later covered by lava from Kibo. *Mawenzi* is actually a few feet higher than Mount Kenya and like it is a plug: it plugged up the volcano's vent, cooled slowly, and became hard, much harder than the surrounding cone, which eroded away, leaving the plug visible as jagged Mawenzi. Its western side is full of crags and pinnacles for the upper 2,000 feet, while the eastern side is precipitous for about 4,000 feet. To climb Mawenzi you need rock-climbing skills and equipment.

Kibo is a relatively young ash cone with an almost perfectly preserved shape in its upper part. However, its crater collapsed to form a caldera 1½ miles in diameter, and its interior is like a Chinese puzzle box. The outer wall drops off, on its south side 600 feet to the caldera floor, which consists of several concentric terraces, most slanting toward the crater. The first and largest terrace, called the "inner cone," rises to 19,000 feet and slants away from the center rather than toward it. This inner cone circles the "inner crater," which is 900 yards across and nearly 150 feet deep. The floor of this second crater has the "ash cone," 370 yards wide, 425 feet deep. Finally, the fourth and most central crater is in the bottom of the ash cone and is called the "ash pit." The "ash cone" and "ash pit" form the entrance into Kibo's volcanic depths. Fumarole gases escaping at various points inside Kibo attest to its continued activity, but it is debatable whether or not they signify that Kibo will erupt again. Kibo alone still has glaciers, with the lowest fingers of Penck reaching down to about 15,000 feet, and the moraine to below 12,000 feet. Owing mainly to climatic changes, the glaciers are slowly retreating and may one day totally disappear.

Kilimanjaro was first sighted and reported by a European on May 11, 1848, when the Mombasa missionary Johannes Rebmann saw its snows from the plains to the east. His reports in the *Church Missionary Intelligencer* were ridiculed—for how could snow lie so close to the equator? One man even wrote a whole book proving the mountain couldn't exist, but other travelers confirmed the fact. Baron K. K. von der Decken and Otto Kersten in November 1862 made the first attempt at Kilimanjaro's heights, reaching a height of about 14,000 feet before turning back. Another Mombasa missionary, Charles New, was the first to reach the snow levels on the Saddle in August 1867. The end of the near half-century of various exploratory climbs came with Professor Hans Meyer, a Leipzig geographer, who after attempts in 1887 and 1888 finally, on October 5, 1889, with the Austrian Ludwig Purtscheller, reached Kibo's summit; 10 days later they gained Klute Peak on Mawenzi. The first European woman to make Kibo's crater rim was Frau von Ruckteschell, who climbed up in 1914 with her husband.

In 1929 the Mountain Club of East Africa was founded, of which the present Kilimanjaro Mountain Club (Box 66, Moshi) is successor. On the Kenya side, the East African Outward Bound School was founded at Loitokitok, and the finishing part of each strenuous course is the ascent of Kibo. When Tanganyika achieved self-government in December 1961, the national flag was raised at Gillman's Point on Kibo, and moved the next year on Republic Day to the mountain's highest point, formerly Kaiser Wilhelm Point, then renamed Uhuru (Swahili—"freedom") Point. More recently, there have been a number of stunts attempted on Kilimanjaro, including, in March 1973, an ascent to Kibo's summit by a New Zealander on a motorcycle.

The origin of the name Kilimanjaro is uncertain. The Chagga living on the mountain's slopes have no name for the whole entity, but did name Kibo and Mawenzi. In Kichagga, Kibo is actually *Kipoo,* meaning "spotted," and refers to the black rock which stands out against the snow. Mawenzi, or *Kimawenze,* means "having a broken top" and describes its rugged, jagged appearance. While the name Kilimanjaro is not a Chagga name, its real origins are speculated by linguists as perhaps being combinations of Swahili, Masai, and Kamba words.

There are two interesting myths connected with Kilimanjaro. An old Chagga legend, as related in *Tanzania Notes & Record*'s special Kilimanjaro issue (March 1965), can be summarized as follows: One day the fire in Mawenzi's hearth went out, so he went to Kibo to get some fire. Kibo was busy pounding dried bananas, but he gave Mawenzi both fire and some bananas. Mawenzi's fire again went out, and Kibo gave him more fire and bananas. The third time Mawenzi's fire went out, Kibo got angry and beat Mawenzi, and that is why Mawenzi's peaks are so jagged.

Strangely enough, there is also a legend about Kilimanjaro and an Ethiopian ruler. King Menelik I of Abyssinia, son of King Solomon and the Queen of Sheba, after conquering what is now East Africa, camped on his return journey on the Saddle of Kilimanjaro. Feeling death near, he climbed up to Kibo's crater, disappeared into it with several slaves bearing his jewels and treasure, and there he sleeps forever. But an offspring of his family is supposed to arise and restore the old glory of Ethiopia, conquering all of the land south to the Rufiji River. En route he will ascend Kilimanjaro, find the jewels of Menelik I, among which will be the seal ring of Solomon, which the old king has upon his finger. This ring he will put on his own hand, and thereafter he'll be endowed the wisdom of Solomon and the heroic spirit of King Menelik.

Kilimanjaro has a succession of vegetation belts varying with altitude, and in them live different animals and birds. The *cultivated areas* range from 2,500 to 6,000 feet altitude, and on small irrigated plots thousands of Chagga grow *Arabica* coffee and numerous fruits and vegetables, and graze their cattle on clover and grass. Next is the *montane forest,* which starts about 5,500 feet and grows up to about 10,000 feet, featuring many species of tall trees, bramble, ferns, orchids, and lichen. Animals that have been recorded in the montane forest zone are shrews, bats, bushbabies, blue and colobus monkeys, leopards, lions, elephants, hyrax, black rhinos, bushpigs, giraffes, duikers, sunis, bushbucks, elands, buffalos, porcupines, squirrels, dormice, rats, and other mice. Through this forest level up to the summit is the newly gazetted 1,500-square-mile *Kilimanjaro National Park.*

The next level of vegetation is the *moorland,* ranging from the edges of the forest to about 14,000 feet, where grow various heaths, hairy legumes, forest groundsel, numerous grasses, and everlasting flowers (with which your guide makes a garland and crowns you if you climb to Kibo's summit). The upper regions of the moorland have the characteristic East African mountain plants of lobelia and giant groundsel (see Mount Kenya, p. 246). There are about 47 species of birds to watch for in the forest and moorland, including the green ibis, black duck, crowned hawk eagle, mountain buzzard, and Hartlaub's touraco.

The last level of vegetation is in the *alpine zone*, from 14,000 to 16,000 feet, above which flowering plants cannot survive, though some mosses and lichens do. The alpine zone looks like a desert and, owing to the cold and the lack of rain and surface water, is rather barren plantwise. However, giant groundsel and giant lobelia thrive up here, as do short grasses and a few wild flowers. Birds which may be seen up to this level include lammergeier, buzzards, Shelley's francolin, Cape quail, African snipe, alpine swift, hill chat, scarlet tufted malachite sunbird, yellow-crowned canary, and streaky seed-eater. Many animals wander up looking for food. A leopard was found frozen at the rim of Kibo Crater in 1926, and as Hemingway wrote in his famous epigraph in *The Snows of Kilimanjaro,* "no one has explained what the leopard was seeking at that altitude." Most likely the feline was really hungry, and was hunting hyrax, duiker, or klipspringer.

Climbing Kilimanjaro

There are several Tanzania routes for climbing Kilimanjaro. However, the only government-approved route is the well-traveled "Tourist (or Marangu) Route" starting from Marangu on the southeast slopes. Several hotels and organizations can arrange climbing expeditions up the mountain from Marangu, and their packages are outlined below. If this will be your first climb on the mountain, it is a very good idea at least to hire porters and a guide or to arrange a complete package deal, in order to better enjoy the strenuous climb.

The Tourist Route takes five days—3½ days up, 1½ days down—and covers about 63 miles (or 98 km). The first day you climb 11 miles from the Marangu area past *shambas* and through the montane forest to Mandara Hut at 9,000 feet, taking about 5 hours. In dry weather four-wheel-drive vehicles can follow a track up to within 5 km of Mandara Hut. Day 2 you climb 10 miles from Mandara to Horombo Hut, 9,000 to 12,000 feet or approximately 5 hours, through the heath and across the moorland and the southern slopes of Mawenzi.

Day 3 you cross the Saddle, or alpine desert, walking about 8 miles at 14,000 to 15,000 feet, and the altitude becomes oppressive. Here is where you would probably feel mountain sickness symptoms and should turn back if you are so affected (see "Health" below). Generally, even if you are healthy, you will need to catch your breath often, about every 5 to 15 minutes. At Kibo Hut (15,420 feet) you go to bed about 5 P.M. because you have to get up at midnight. The fourth day you make the rigorous ascent of Kibo Peak. After waking at midnight (you haven't slept much anyway at this altitude), you start the final 4,000-foot endurance test, resting every 5 minutes. Your guide urges you on in the dark with his lantern, and you drag your body up the slippery scree in zigzags with your trusty walking stick. This takes from 5 to 7 hours. The point of doing the climb in the dark is to avoid seeing how far you have to climb, to avoid the heat of the day, and to see sunrise from Kibo's rim. Just when you think you can't possibly go on—you're on the rim. After catching your breath for the two-hundredth time, you can congratulate yourself, admire the spectacular view, and choose whether or not you want to walk at least 2 more hours on the rim to and from Uhuru Peak, Kilimanjaro's summit at 19,340 feet. After your time on the top of Africa, you begin the trip down, first to Kibo Hut for a nap and meal, and then to Horombo Hut—so your total walk that day is about 12 miles. The fifth and last day is long—22 miles down from Horombo Hut to Marangu. If you wanted to split this long trip, you could spend an additional night at one of the huts on the way down, making it a 6-day tour.

The other climbing routes are explained in detail in the Mountain Club of Kenya's *Guide Book to Mount Kenya and Kilimanjaro* (see p. 250), which you should get if you intend to climb either mountain, especially by a nontourist route. These other routes are also about 5-day climbs, the recommended minimum length for adapting to the altitude. Because these other routes are mainly used by local, experienced climbers, you should inquire at the Tanzania Tourist Center, Box 381, Moshi, before setting off on one.

Health on the Mountain

Of the thousands of people who climb Kilimanjaro and Mount Kenya every year, the majority stay healthy and make it to their highest goal; the rest give up partway. To quote one American writer who did the climb up Kilimanjaro, Catherine Wright, "As mountains go, it is an easy climb. There is no need to use ropes, ice-axes, or pitons. Yet, men in good condition, army mountain rescue teams, determined hikers, and hotel guides fail to make it; chain-smoking ladies, hard-living newspapermen, beer-drinking game wardens, and ten-year-old boys do make it." Basically, to climb you should be physically fit and healthy. En route set a pace that is comfortable for yourself, and rest as often as you feel necessary.

When you reach the 14,000 feet level you may experience what is commonly called *"mountain sickness."* This is a form of oxygen starvation, which remains until your blood has built up enough red cells to counteract it. The general symptoms are headache, loss of appetite, nausea, and possibly vomiting. Sometimes if you spend a few days at the 14,000- to 15,000-foot level you will begin to adjust. You might take some aspirin or travel sickness tablets (e.g., Dramamine). Otherwise, when you descend to a lower altitude the symptoms should disappear with no aftereffects.

A more serious, and sometimes fatal, mountain illness is *pulmonary edema.* This is a condition in which liquid passes from the blood into the lungs, and it can cause suffocation. It often occurs between 12 and 36 hours after arrival at altitudes of about 10,000 feet. The symptoms are: shortness of breath, general weakness, tightness in chest, loss of appetite, nausea, and vomiting (all which may mean "mountain sickness" instead); hacking cough producing white or pink spit or blood; bubbling sounds in the chest; rapid pulse (120–160 per minute); rapid, then shallow, breathing; blue lips, nails, and tongue; pale face; fever. The climber should immediately receive treatment and be quickly carried off the mountain even if in the middle of the night. If oxygen cylinders are available, 4–5 liters per minute should be administered. Medical attention, including X rays, should be received as fast as possible.

Climbing Packages

There are four organizations offering package climbing trips up Kilimanjaro: the Marangu Hotel, Kibo Hotel, Moshi YMCA, and Kilimanjaro Guides and Tours. If you have the money, we recommend the Marangu Hotel. Generally the tour costs are inclusive of hut bookings and fees, guide and porters with their food and equipment, climber's food and water, cooking and eating utensils. Clothes and equipment can be rented (e.g., heavy socks—5/– to 7/–). The Marangu Hotel provides sleeping bags and blankets, and special warm clothes (parka, mittens, goggles, balaclava, scarf). The YMCA charges extra to provide food. The porters each carry about 30 pounds of your things. Here is a comparison of prices:

	Marangu Hotel	Kibo Hotel	YMCA	Kilimanjaro G&T
One climber	900/–	850/–	–	780/–
Two climbers	840/– each	700/– each	–	680/– each
Three climbers or more	800/– each	600/– each	747/– each*	600/– each
Any extra day	190/– each	170/– each	–	150/– each

* 200/– each additional climber.

You can also arrange your own trip up the mountain through the hotels and Guides & Tours. You make hut bookings, bring your own food and equipment, hire guide (150/–) and porters (120/– each), all of whom must be over 18 years old. Either way you climb, it is a good idea to have your own warm, comfortable hiking boots, and preferably your own warm clothes and bedding, though all can be hired. Addresses: Kibo and Marangu Hotels, see below; Moshi YMCA, p. 391; Kilimanjaro Guides and Tours, Box 7, Moshi, tel. 2957.

When to Visit

Climbing and general visiting are best January to mid-March and mid-June to October during the dry months.

Getting There

East African Airways flies to Kilimanjaro Airport from Nairobi 15Xwk, and from Dar es Salaam 9Xwk. From there you can take a taxi directly to Marangu, though it probably would be fairly expensive unless you split the fare with other passengers. By road you can go all the way to Marangu on paving from Nairobi, Arusha, and Dar es Salaam, and most of the way on paving from Mombasa. Some package tours from Nairobi and Arusha have a Marangu hotel on their itineraries; see TP-2 and KP-70, 72–75, 82, 84, 87, 91, 93.

Accommodations

Marangu Hotel, Box 41, Moshi; tel. Himo 11Y1; cable LANYHOT. Located 10.4 km from the turnoff on the Moshi–Taveta road. Has 27 dbls, 2 sgls; 22 rms w/bath. Rates: FB: sgl w/bath—85/–; dbl w/bath—160/–. Built as a home about 1905, the cozy hotel's rooms are now in bungalows, rondavels, comfy cottages, and blocks. The large grounds are lushly lined with flowers and trees, a pool, and tennis court. Trout fishing, hiking, climbing. Rating: 1st-class local. . . . *Kibo Hotel,* Private Bag, Moshi; tel. Himo 2; cable KIBOTEL. Located 3.2 km above the Marangu Hotel. 12 sgls, 30 dbls, all but 4 sgls w/ bath. Rates: FB: sgl w/bath—80/– to 90/–; dbl w/bath—170/– to 180/–, incl tax and service. Operating since 1928, the Kibo is old, cold, rambling, but has lots of character, and the rooms are solidly furnished. Rating: less than 1st-class local. . . . *Mountain Huts.* Marangu (Tourist) Route: *Mandara Hut,* 9,000 feet, built of stone in 1924 and sleeps 24 on bunks with mattresses; lots of water and wood. *Horombo Hut,* 12,000 feet, 2 pre-World War I huts with 11 bunks, plus 1963 double hut with room for 24; stream water but scarce firewood. *Kibo Hut,* 15,420 feet, old 1932 hut sleeps 4 on bunks, while newer 1959 hut sleeps several but has no furniture; no water or fuel. There are also 6 huts on the other nontourist routes. All huts cost 5/– per person per night, and they should be booked well in advance, if you plan to climb on your own, through "Hut Bookings," Tanzania National Tourist Board, Box 381, Moshi. . . . **Camping** is allowed at the back of the Marangu Hotel on a long, narrow grassy plot big enough for about 6 tents. Facilities: toilets and cold-water shower. Fee: 5/– per person.

Back on the main highway to Kenya, the small town of *Himo* is at Km 27. Then the *Tanzanía/Kenya border* is at Km 36; from here pick up Kenya Route K-4 to Voi.

Route T-5: Lunga Lunga, Kenya–Tanga–Junction with Arusha–Dar es Salaam Highway

This is primarily a connector route, but it has several things of interest along the way, including Amboni Caves, Tanga town, and, off the route, Tongoni ruins on the coast and Amani in the Usambaras.

Starting at the Kenya border post at Lunga Lunga (see Kenya Route K-3), the Tanzania border post is at Km 6. The drive to Tanga is on a 1½-lane sandy dirt road that passes small villages set amid the palm trees. At about Km 60 the large *Amboni Sisal Estates* start to line either side of the road; tours of an estate can be arranged by contacting the head office, Box 117, Tanga; tel. Tanga 2245. See also T-3, p. 391.

About Km 63 is the turnoff left to *Galanos Sulphur Springs* 1 km, an enclosed pool of warm sulfur water, with rest rooms for changing. Near here is the turnoff also to *Amboni Caves,* which are supposed to be signposted through Kiomoni village to the caves. The biggest, Mabavu, has an entrance nearly 60 feet high, and a cold-water stream, the Mkurumzi, runs through the middle of the caves. Local inhabitants believe the caves have living spirits, and people frequently leave offerings of goats, chickens, coins, and beads at the entrances. Inside the caves are bats, stalactites, and stalagmites, occasional holes in the roof, and about 300 circuitous underground passages.

Tanga

Tanga town is reached at Km 71. Tanga (Swahili—"a light"), with a population of about 61,000, is Tanzania's second-largest town and port. It has wide streets with small shops along Independence Avenue and Market Street, and two parks—Jamhuri and Amboni—overlooking the harbor and Toten Island. Toten (German—"the dead") Island has three well-overgrown 18th- and 19th-century Arab mosques, and an old German cemetery, hence the name. In 1896 the Germans started the first railway line in German East Africa from Tanga to Moshi, and this line made it possible for crops grown inland to be brought and sold on the coast. Several of the spacious, old, two-story buildings in Tanga were built by German settlers, and a monument at Jamhuri Park commemorates the visit of the V.S.M.S. *Leipzig* in 1889. During World War I the German General Paul von Lettow-Vorbeck correctly ascertained that the British would try to invade German East Africa through Tanga, and thus he employed most of his troops in defending the town. On November 2, 1914, the British ship H.M.S. *Fox* and a small squadron dropped anchor in Tanga harbor, and Commander Caulfield announced to the German district commissioner that unless Tanga surrendered, it would be attacked. Not having received any message of surrender by the next day, the British and Indian troops were ordered to attack the town, but they were frustrated by the shore line's thick bush, swarming mosquitoes, leeches, tsetse flies —and by the German troops and African *askaris* firing on them with machine guns. By November 5 the British troops finally had to retreat to their ships and admit defeat with a truce the next day. Altogether the British had 800 dead, 500 wounded, and hundreds missing or imprisoned; the Germans had 69 dead, but gained 12 machine guns, hundreds of rifles, 600,000 rounds of ammunition, and lots of supplies. The Tanga town cemetery has many of the dead from this battle. But

the British came back after their troops had Vorbeck's men on the
run all over G.E.A. and occupied Tanga on July 7, 1916.

Since then things have been more quiet, with the sisal industry
dominating Tanga and the Tanga Line railway. The town is now the
headquarters of the Tanga Region. The Tanga Touring Service has a
package tour of the town and environs; see TP-28.

Accommodations

Sea View Hotel, Box 249, tel. 2041. On Independence Ave. 5 sgls,
5 dbls, all w/a-c, 3 w/bath. Rates: B&B: sgl w/bath—55/– or 65/–;
dbl w/bath—110/–. Best place in Tanga, with a sea view from the
terrace, and table d'hôte meals. Rating: 1st-class local. . . . *Tanga
Hotel,* Box 625, tel. 2081. On Eckenforde Ave. 1 sgl w/o bath, 15
dbls w/bath, all w/a-c. Rates: B&B: sgl w/o bath—65/–; dbl w/bath
—120/–. Rooms are clean though a bit worn, and there's also a main
floor bar, lounge, dining room, and patio. Rating: 2d-class local. . . .
Palm Court Hotel, Box 783, tel. 3162. Off Hospital Road, turn left at
YMCA sign. 2 sgls, 5 dbls; 2 dbls w/bath, all w/a-c. Rates: B&B:
sgl w/o bath—50/–; dbl w/bath—95/–. This must date from the
German era at least. Cement-floor rooms have long windows, bare
furnishings. Some à la carte meals on the patio. Rating: between 2d-
and 3d-class local. . . . *Planter's Hotel,* Box 242, tel. 2071. On
Market St. 3 sgls, 12 dbls; 4 rms w/bath. Rates: B&B: sgl—40/– to
55/–; dbl—80/– to 110/–. Pretty dismal and decrepit but fairly clean.
Rating: 3d-class local. . . . **Camping** sites are available by asking the
Town Clerk, Tanga Municipal Council.

Where to Eat. The dining rooms of the Sea View, Tanga, and Palm
Court hotels have table d'hôte or à la carte meals from 6/50 to 17/50.
. . . *Restaurant Afrique,* Market St. next to Planter's Hotel, has
snacks and Indian foods, such as curries and samoosas, –/50 to
6/50. . . . *Maimun Cake Shop* on Market St. has just snacks and
drinks.

Tongoni Ruins

From Tanga there is a small coastal road going south to Tongoni
ruins, Kigombe painted village, and Pangani town. *Tongoni ruins,*
about 23 km south, include a mosque and a large group of pillar
tombs dating from the 14th and 15th centuries. The mosque has two
aisles with a central arcade of four pillars, with rooms running the
whole length that may have been used for a school. The tombs cover

a half-acre; three tombs have square towers and four have octagonal towers. What pottery pieces were left were identified as 15th- to 16th-century Islamic, and 14th- to 19th-century Chinese. Tongoni used to be the center of the old state of Mtangata, whose rulers were usually hostile to Mombasa and friendly to the Portuguese. After 1728 the site was abandoned for a while, and then resettled in the late 18th or 19th century.

Kigombe, about 35 km down the dirt coastal road, is a small sisal workers' village with scenes of Tanzanian life painted as murals on the building walls, originally by Ali and Maya Panga. *Pangani,* approximately 51 km south and near the mouth of the Pangani or Ruvu River, may have been the ancient town of Rhapta shown on Ptolemy's 1st-century A.D. map of Azania (East Africa) and mentioned in the *Periplus*. By the 19th century it was a busy slave trade port, like Bagamoyo, with slaves brought from the interior and shipped from here to Zanzibar. It has a number of 19th- and early-20th-century Arab buildings, and some good beaches.

Leaving Tanga on the main highway west, at Km 104 is the turnoff right to *Amani,* 35 km, a 3,000-foot-high town in the Usambara Mountains, in the midst of rain forest and tea estates and featuring an arboretum. At Km 131 is the *Hale Power Station,* which harnesses the power of the Ruvu River and supplies electricity to Tanga. The route ends at Km 138 at the junction: straight ahead to the north are Moshi and Arusha, to the left and south is Dar es Salaam; from here pick up Route T-3.

Route T-6: Dar es Salaam–Mikumi National Park–Iringa–Mbeya–Tunduma–Zambia

Formerly called the "Hell Run" because it was such an endlessly rotten road, this 915-km-long route from Dar es Salaam to Tunduma is now the best highway in Tanzania and is very scenic as well. The new road was built 1971–73 with USAID funds and is smooth, wide, two-lane blacktop, with a dotted white line down the middle. To leave the highway and go south, especially between Iringa and Tunduma, you must have permission from the Second Vice-President's Office, Box 3021, Dar es Salaam.

The first 110 km, from Dar es Salaam city center to Chelinze, are the same as those covered in Route T-3, Km 533–643, though in re-

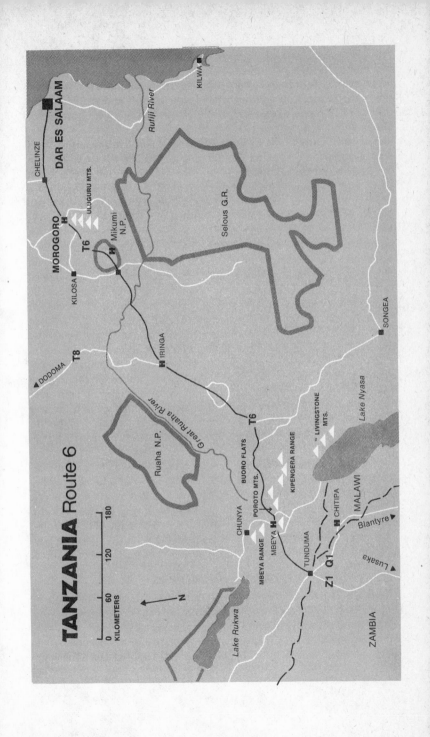

verse. At Chelinze is the turnoff right to Tanga and Arusha. Through this area the road cuts through large sisal estates, and the Morogoro district is Tanzania's second most important sisal-producing area after Tanga.

Km 196: Turnoff left to *Morogoro,* the regional headquarters town with a population of about 25,200 and an altitude of 1,634 feet. In the 19th century near here was the site of *Simbamwene,* the "Lion City" built by the Zigua chief Kisabengo. The town had high stone walls, a watchtower, and beautiful carved wooden gates, according to the explorer Henry M. Stanley, who visited it in 1871. At Morogoro is an agricultural college which in 1971–73 was the center for research into a biological warfare weapons system against the tsetse fly; it was being led by a U.S. Department of Agriculture team. The team's main objective was to release sterile male tsetse flies, which it was hoped would mate with female flies; since no offspring would result, the fly population would eventually shrink. There are about 20 species of tsetse fly, though the most widespread and dangerous is *Glossina morsitans.* The tsetse fly is a vector or carrier of parasites which cause the dread disease of sleeping sickness in humans. In cattle the parasites cause weight loss and general debility and low milk production. Tsetse fly infestations make normal agricultural life impossible through a belt of 22 African countries and 4.5 million square miles on both sides of the equator. One former method of dealing with the tsetse fly was to slaughter indiscriminately all wild game thought to serve as hosts. In areas where this was the policy, such as in Malawi, the game is still recovering.

Morogoro **accommodations:** *Acropol Hotel,* Box 78, Morogoro; tel. 2341. On Dar es Salaam Road. Rates: B&B: sgl—42/– to 52/–; dbl—80/– to 90/–. Serves table d'hôte meals. . . . *Savoy Hotel,* Box 35, Morogoro; tel. 2345. On Church St. 17 dbls, 2 sgls; 10 dbls w/bath. Rates: B&B: sgl w/o bath—35/– to 50/–; dbl w/bath—70/– to 90–.

Also at Km 196 is the turnoff right to Dodoma, 297 km. As you continue down the highway, the Uluguru Mountains are to the south.

Mikumi National Park

Km 262: *Mikumi National Park* lies astride the highway, with its approximately 450 square miles spread over flat flood plains and forested hills, riverine thicket, and open savanna. Named after the spindle-shaped *mikumi* (Swahili) or borassus palm, Mikumi is the national park closest to Dar es Salaam and is easily visited. The highway, bisecting the part from northeast to southwest, divides the park ecologically. To the east the slopes of the Uluguru Mountains are covered in deciduous *miombo* woodland; to the west are open flood plains or tree-dotted savanna to the north-flowing Mkata River and the Kilosa–Mikumi railway, then hilly and wooded slopes again west of the river and rail. Resident animals include the elephant, Masai giraffe, common zebra, impala, warthog, wildebeest, lion, greater kudu, black rhino, cheetah, leopard, common waterbuck, bohor reedbuck, Lichtenstein's hartebeest, and sable antelope. There are about 318 species of birds, many of which are not found in the northern parks.

If you have only an overnight or a day, the areas around the airstrip and the Hippo Pool offer the best game viewing. With more time, drive to Chamgore, along the river, or on the Hill Drive for variations in vegetation and game. You may get out of your car in open areas, but be aware of where game is at all times, and stick close to your car. A useful guide to follow en route is the National Parks' *Mikumi National Park* (price 5/–).

When to Visit

The dry months, August–October, when the wildlife drinks at the Hippo Pool, the waterholes, the main river, or the spring below the hotel, are the best for game viewing and driving. The short rains November–December and the long rains March–May are good times to avoid Mikumi's dirt tracks.

Getting There, Getting Around

The park's main gate is at Km 292 along the Dar–Tunduma highway. The airstrip is by park headquarters near the main gate. Vehicles are for hire at the Wildlife Lodge and Wildlife Camp. Package tours from Dar es Salaam visit Mikumi by road and air; see TP-20.

Accommodations

Mikumi Wildlife Lodge, bookings to TTC Hotels (p. 315). Located at Km 286 turnoff left off the highway, 6 km from the park's main gate. 50 dbls, all w/bath. Rates: FB: sgl—170/–; dbl—280/–. This TTC lodge sits at 2,500 feet altitude, curved on a spur overlooking a valley frequented by wildlife. The rooms are modern and pleasant, though in the rainy season the croaking frogs can nearly keep you awake. Table d'hôte dining room serves breakfast—10/–; lunch—17/50; tea—5/–; dinner—21/–. Also a pool. Rating: 1st-class international. . . . *Mikumi Wildlife Camp,* bookings to Oyster Bay Hotel, Box 1907, Dar es Salaam; tel. 68631; cable HOSPITABLE. Located just in from the main gate. Rates: DB&B: 70/– per person. Camp has 15 makuti and bamboo bandas or tents, each holding 3–4 people. Casual meals: breakfast—10/–; lunch—15/–; dinner—17/–. Land-Rover trips: 100/– per hour. . . . **Camping** is at one site, big enough for 3 parties, 1 km from the highway turnoff at Km 294, south of the main gate. Latrine; water available at Wildlife Camp. Fee: 5/– per adult.

The highway exits Mikumi National Park at Km 305, and 5 km south is the town of Mikumi. Here you can begin to see some of the activity going on around the building of the Tan-Zam Railway, or Great Uhuru ("freedom"), Railway, being built primarily to move tons of copper from and imports to landlocked Zambia. China has given a $406 million interest-free loan to Tanzania and Zambia, with the repayment stipulations including the purchase of $16.8 million of Chinese consumer goods by each country yearly. In 1973 an estimated 20,000 to 50,000 Chinese workers were helping in the building: from Mikumi south to Zambia's Copperbelt their large workcamps along the road are signposted in Swahili and Chinese, and their gray vehicles hurry up and down the USAID-built highway. As of April 1974 the railway was progressing rapidly through Zambia, and the projected date for reaching Kapiri Mposhi, to link with Zambia Railways, was the end of 1974. There will be passenger service eventually, so theoretically you could ride the rails all the way from Mount Kenya to Cape Town, politics permitting.

Km 311: Turnoff right to Kilosa, 77 km; and left to Ifakara, and southern Tanzania. This whole southern region of Tanzania was the scene in 1905–07 of what was called the *Maji Maji Rising,* in which thousands of Africans fought German settlers, missionaries, and soldiers. Africans became furious and frustrated because they were required to work on the German cotton plantations, where they received little if any pay, were overworked and whipped by hated Arab overseers, and in addition were expected to grow their own other cash crops and pay taxes. In 1904 a medicine man on a tributary of the Rufiji River convinced others that his *maji maji* or "magic water" from a nearby river pool would protect Africans against evil, and bullets would become mere water. By July 1905 the Africans were agitating for rebellion, and an incident in which a few workers rooted up some

German cotton shoots sparked off the movement. In about six weeks all the European centers were attacked and several whites killed, with the revolt spreading from its inception west of Kilwa throughout southern Tanzania. Governor von Götzen ordered troop reinforcements from Germany and the Pacific, who by November 1905 began systematically repressing the movement, using a scorched-earth policy, burning all the countryside's crops so the rebels could not find food and the people would starve and tire of fighting. By late 1905 things had quieted down, though pockets, such as Songea, still simmered and martial law continued until August 1907. As a result of the scorched-earth policy, southern Tanzania had a three-year famine. Perhaps as many as 120,000 Africans died during the fighting and famine. The Maji Maji Rising today symbolizes to Tanzanians their struggle against white and foreign domination, which they eventually overcame through political independence.

Continuing down the paved highway, the road climbs into a hilly area, with the Rubeho Mountains to the north. The highway for a while follows the Great Ruaha River, crossing it at Mbuyuni at Km 383, and then skirts its tributary the Lukosi River. This is a very scenic drive of about 140 km, one of the prettiest areas that the highway goes through. On either side of the road are scores of cacti and near-forests of baobab trees, which when in bloom in July color the hillsides with pink and yellow bouquets.

The road levels out as it nears Km 488, the turnoff right to Iringa 5 km, Ruaha National Park, 118 km, and Dodoma and Arusha via the Great North Road (see Route T-8). The turnoff left at Km 488 goes to the *Dabaga Highlands loop road,* 77 km of rolling moorland dotted with pockets of rain forest and wild flowers.

Km 499: Turnoff right to *Tosamaganga Mission,* 5 km, an Italian Catholic community founded at the end of the 19th century by Consolata fathers. The parish church dominates a group of sturdy brick buildings, including five schools and a seminary, all built in the Italian style. The Italian nuns have taught their female students how to embroider, and reportedly things can be made to order (Box 167, Iringa).

Isimila

Km 509: Turnoff left to *Isimila Prehistoric Site,* 1 km. This is a rich site of Acheulean, or Old Stone Age, tools. A guide booklet called *Short Guide to the Isimila Paleolithic Site,* by Neville Chittick, is published by the Antiquities Division (cost 1/–). About 60,000 years ago the area was covered by a small shallow lake, probably a mile long, half-mile wide, which was fed by a stream from the east. Stone Age man made his tools by the lakeside while he camped there, and then when he moved he left behind many tools, and flakes struck off in making them. What can be seen today are hand axes, cleavers, spherical stone and picklike tools, all from a variety of rocks. Fossil bones have also been uncovered: those of elephants, a type of antelope, several varieties of pig including an extinct giant one, an extinct member of the giraffe family having antlers and a shorter neck, and a type of hippo whose eyes were set in periscopelike projections.

Km 540: Ulete, and the turnoff right to Wasa via the *Rumile Hills,* in which are terraces with Iron Age remains dating back to about the 17th century. It is thought that the ruins—terraces, graves, old roads, fortifications stretching across the Lyandembera valley from Ulete to Ifunda 13 km north—were built by Bantu people.

Km 599: Turnoffs both left and right to the *Southern Highlands* or *Mufindi loop roads,* 79 km to the left, 47 km to the right. This area lies at about 6,000 feet altitude, and since the 1930s has been a tea-growing region.

At Km 588 is the settlement of Igawa, and the turnoff right to *Buhoro Flats,* a plains area south of the Great Ruaha River which July–November has herds of topi, zebra, buffalo and elephant; white giraffe and spotted zebra have also been reported.

Km 729: Turnoff left to the *Chimala Escarpment road,* which has 52 hairpin curves as it climbs into the Poroto Mountains. Another and more main road through the Porotos to Lake Ngozi, Rungwe, and Tukuyu is at Km 801, turnoff left. The *Porotos* are of volcanic origin, and their highest point is Chaluhangi at 9,623 feet. Through them flow several trout streams, and there are two fully furnished fishing camps; contact the Mbeya Trout Association, Box 108, Mbeya. *Lake Ngozi,* a crater lake 2 km long and dotted with islands, is about 2 km beyond the town of Isongole and is accessible by a track and a two-hour climb. Near Rungwe are Mount Rungwe (9,713 feet) and a signposted natural bridge, called *God's Bridge* locally, over the Kiwira River. Tukuyu, 45 km, is the district headquarters, and is surrounded by acres of tea and coffee planted by the Wanyakyusa tribe. The northern tip of Lake Malawi can also be reached via Tukuyu, but before traveling to any of these points south of the highway, get permission (see p. 406).

Mbeya

Km 811: Turnoff right to *Mbeya* (altitude 5,700 feet), the regional headquarters with a population of about 12,500, the last place of any size before Kabwe, Zambia, 975 km to the south. Founded as a government station in 1927 because of the interest in the Lupa gold fields to the north, Mbeya is now the main town in an agricultural area rich in coffee, tea, wheat, tobacco, pyrethrum, cocoa, vegetables, and fruit. Mbeya Peak (9,272 feet) and Loleza Peak (8,765 feet) form the backdrop to the town, and both can be climbed.

Accommodations

Mbeya Hotel, Box 80, tel. 20. At junction of Karume and Kaunda avenues. 13 sgls, 14 dbls, 3 family rms, most w/bath. Rates: B&B: sgl—60/–; dbl—110/–. Built in the 1930s, it was bought by East African Railways in 1957. Basic rooms are in 6 blocks around a garden, while the main building has a bar, lounge, and table d'hôte dining room. Rating: between 1st- and 2d-class local, nice enough. . . . *Mbeya Guest House,* Box 153, tel. 42. On a hill—the signposted road is on the right as you enter town. 4 sgls, 7 dbls, 2 family rms, some w/bath. Rates: B&B: 42/– per person. Friendly place though well worn everywhere. The lounge is homey and cluttered, dining room small and simple, rooms old-fashioned, rose garden nice. Rating: 2d-class local. . . . **Camping** at the Guest House, on the small terrace hillside above the kitchen. Fee: 5/– per person, plus 5/– each to use the bathtub.

A road north through Mbeya goes to Chunya, Lupa, and Lake Rukwa. The *Chunya Scarp* is the name of the first part of this scenic drive through the edge of the Mbeya Range, with the road climbing up to 8,050 feet. About 13 km out from Mbeya is the turnoff left to the 16-km-long, four-wheel-drive track, ending at the path to *Mbeya Peak,* reached in an hour's hike. At Km 21 on the Chunya Road is Forest Camp and the turnoff right to the track and path to *World's End,* a viewpoint and picnic site overlooking the Usangu Plains and the Rift Valley. *Chunya* (pop. 2,398) is about 72 km north of Mbeya, and west of it are the *Lupa Gold Fields,* whose gold can no longer be found in riverbeds but must be mined. *Lake Rukwa,* 151 km from Mbeya via Chunya, is a shallow, slightly alkaline Rift Valley lake which when wet covers 1,042 square miles. Around most of the lake is *Uwanda Game Reserve,* which protects the hippo, crocodile, fish, and birdlife; albino giraffes and black zebras have been reported on the rather inaccessible west shore. There is no charge for entry into Uwanda, but a pass must be obtained from the Game Division in Mbeya (Box 63, tel. 2206).

Going south from Mbeya on the highway to Tunduma, at Km 827 is another alternate turnoff left to Tukuyu, 58 km, and to the *Songwe Guano limestone caves,* about 20 km; again permission from the second vice-president's office is needed to go here. Also at Km 827 is the turnoff right to *Utengule walled village.* In 1879 when the Hehe tribe near Iringa was expanding, Chief Merere of Utengule Usangu, who had been driven out of the plains east of Mbeya, expelled the local chief and built a stone walled village as a defensive. Ruins of the wall are on both sides of the road, 3 km from the turnoff.

Km 865: Turnoff left to *Mbozi Meteorite,* 13 km via a loop road, and all right to visit without permission from the government. Mbozi is a 12-ton iron meteorite measuring 4 feet by 5 feet by 11 feet, one of about eight such that have landed in Tanzania. It was found by a private surveyor in 1930 with only its top visible. A trench was dug around it to determine its size and a concrete plinth built under it. Though it has been protected since 1931 and is now an official monument, people have persisted in cutting off pieces as souvenirs; please don't. *Guide to Mbozi Meteorite* by Hamo Sassoon is published by the Antiquities Division (cost 2/–).

Km 895: Turnoff right to Lake Tanganyika, 160 km (see Route T-9), and *Katavi National Park,* 335 km. Katavi covers miles of plains and swamps, contains large herds of buffalo, hippo, elephant, plus reedbuck, topi, eland, roan antelope, waterbuck, lion, and leopard. Best entry via road from Tabora and Mpanda. Camp sites will be established.

Km 914: *Tunduma,* and at Km 915 the *Tanzania Border Post.* After crossing into Zambia, you can go south on Z-1 to Lusaka or southeast to Malawi.

Route T-7: Dar es Salaam–Beach Hotels–Bagamoyo

This is a pleasant day's excursion from Dar es Salaam city center past the Village Museum and the various beach hotels and historic ruins on the north coast, to the old port of Bagamoyo.

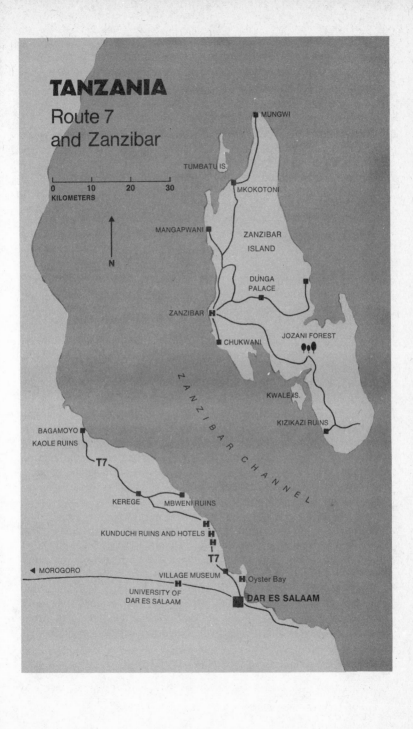

TANZANIA
Route 7
and Zanzibar

MUNGWI

TUMBATU IS.

MKOKOTONI

0   10   20   30
KILOMETERS

N

MANGAPWANI

ZANZIBAR
ISLAND

DUNGA
PALACE

ZANZIBAR

JOZANI FOREST

CHUKWANI

KWALE IS.

Z A N Z I B A R   C H A N N E L

KIZIKAZI RUINS

BAGAMOYO
KAOLE RUINS

T7

KEREGE   MBWENI RUINS

KUNDUCHI RUINS AND HOTELS

T7

◄ MOROGORO   VILLAGE MUSEUM   Oyster Bay

UNIVERSITY OF
DAR ES SALAAM

DAR ES SALAAM

Leaving Dar es Salaam's city center the quickest way to Selander Bridge is via Azikiwe Street and Upanga Road. A slightly longer and more scenic drive is beside the water along Kivukoni Front and Ocean Road. Either way Selander Bridge is reached about Km 3.

Just on the other side of Selander Bridge is a turnoff right to *Oyster Bay*, the fashionable residential suburb. If you wind through the neighborhood streets about 2 km you come to the grassy and palm-fringed park that lines the length of the curved beach, and which is popular with early-morning dog walkers and Indian families evenings and Sundays (and thieves perpetually). The *Oyster Bay Hotel* (see Dar listings) is located midway along the drive.

Km 4: Turnoff right to *St. Peter's Catholic Church*, its 1962-modern lines featuring a concrete barrel-vaulted roof, towering bell tower, and decorated panel. Quite close to it is Dar's *Little Theatre*, which has frequent amateur productions.

Farther up the highway, called New Bagamoyo Road, is the turnoff right at Km 8 to the *Village Museum*, open daily 9:30–6:30, admission: adults—2/–; children and students—1/–. This is the National Museum's attractive and interesting display of houses built by some of the different tribes in Tanzania, including Masai, Haya, Hehe, Fipa, Zaramo, Rundi, Chagga, Myakyusa, Nyamwezi, and Gogo. You can walk into each house, carvings and crafts are for sale, and dances are performed occasionally on Sunday afternoons.

Km 10: Turnoff left to the *University of Dar es Salaam* 5 km. Started in 1961 as part of the University of East Africa, it located at its present Observation Hill site in 1964 and became an independent institution in 1970. It has faculties of law, medicine, science, agriculture, arts, and social science, and institutes of education, Swahili research, economic research, and statistical training.

Beach Hotels

Km 17: Turnoff right to *Hotel Africana Vacation Village*, Box 2802, Dar es Salaam; tel. 81231; cable KILIMA. Hotel is 5 km on gravel road from highway. 200 dbls in standard chalets w/shower or luxury chalets w/bath. Rates: FB: standard sgl—154/–; dbl—210/–. Day visitors charged 6/– to 10/– for entry; 20/– for entry including table d'hôte lunch. The Africana imitates the Club Mediterranée style, with lots of activities—water sports, safaris, riding, nightly (except Monday) disco dances, tennis, basketball—payments for drinks with poppit beads, and highly informal dress. Beautiful white beach attracts pale Scandinavians and Germans like a magnet. Built in 1969–71, the bungalows are clean-cut and bright (though hot) hexagonals, while the dining areas include the table d'hôte room and Malaika specialty restaurant with Chinese Monday, Spanish Tuesday, etc. (15/– for guests; 25/– for nonguests). Rating: 2d-class international, ★ for exuberance.

Km 19: Turnoff right to Kunduchi Beach with its historic ruins and three beach hotels. *Kunduchi Beach Hotel,* bookings to TTC Hotels (p. 315). 3.6 km from the highway. 100 dbls plus 2 suites, all w/bath and a-c. Rates: FB: sgl—170/–; dbl—280/–; also low season rates. The TTC spent a lot of money on this starkly dazzling white Moorish-modern hotel, opened in late 1970. Entrance doors are hand carved, lobby floor is green Arabic tile, lobby desk looks like solid white marble, long lounge has colorful overstuffed chairs, etc. However, in the low season you may feel like you're rattling around Kubla Khan's Xanadu pleasure dome all alone. The beach is gorgeous and the pool equally inviting. The rooms are airy, split-level, and have a fine view. Red-stone-floored dining room is heavy on fish for table d'hôte and à la carte. Rating: 1st-class international, among the sleekest in East Africa. But try to go during the busy season, December–March. We give it ★. . . . *Bahari Beach Hotel,* bookings to TTC Hotels (p. 315). 4.8 km from highway turnoff. 100 dbls, incl 2 suites, all w/bath or shower, a-c, balcony. Rates: FB: sgl—160/–; dbl—280/–; also low season rates. Built with an African village in mind, Bahari Beach is a collection of 25 two-story rondavels, each with 4 doubles, spread over lawns along the sand. The rooms are modern, with cool coral and tile. The makuti roof of the main building looks like a huge upside-down boat, and the lounge, bar, and sunken dining areas are airy and colorful. Both table d'hôte and à la carte meals are served. Excellent beach, pool, fishing, boating, gift shop, and disco. Favored by higher-priced German package tours. Rating: 1st-class international, friendlier in style than the Kunduchi Beach Hotel, deserves ★ also. . . . *Silversands Hotel,* Box 20318, Dar es Salaam, tel. 81311. 4.3 km from highway turnoff. 48 dbls, all w/bath, 9 w/a-c. Rates: FB: sgl—65/– to 75/–; dbl—130/– to 150/–. Modest, somewhat weathered beach hotel with comfortable, unplush rooms, big dining room with dance floor, fine piece of Kunduchi beach. Haunt of low-cost German package tours. Rating: 1st-class local, best on Dar coast for middle budgets.

There are conflicting reports as to whether **camping** is allowed on the Silversands grounds; inquire at the hotel.

Kunduchi Ruins

Kunduchi Ruins are to the left of the driveway into Kunduchi Beach Hotel, 3.6 km from highway turnoff. The old site in all may cover 20 acres, but the main portion consists of a large cemetery and 100 yards north of it a ruined mosque. The mosque is oldest, thought to date from the late 15th or early 16th century. The mosque's south wall with an arched doorway and six pillars still stand, built originally of coral stone and lime. The tombs date from the 18th and 19th centuries when the Arab coastal settlements began to thrive again. Two of the tombs are of the 18th-century phallic pillar style, and four of the tombs have inscriptions, all referring to the family of al-Hatimi al-Barawi. One of the purposes of the pillars was to display the Arabian and Chinese porcelain bowls with which the dead person was honored; most of these have been stolen, though some were purposefully removed and taken to the National Museum in Dar es Salaam. The National Museum publishes a 1/– guide booklet to the ruins. Package tours going to Kunduchi Ruins are under TP-16.

Back on New Bagamoyo Road, about Km 40 is the turnoff right to *Mbweni Ruins,* 10 km, consisting of a ruined mosque divided into two aisles by three rough octagonal pillars, and a large cemetery with tombs decorated by plasterwork thought to be 17th to 19th century.

Karege Ujamaa Village is along New Bagamoyo Road at about Km 42, shortly after the paving ends. *Ujamaa* is a Swahili word meaning "familyhood," and was picked by President Nyerere to define the ideal of agriculture under Tanzanian socialism. *Ujamaa* villages are voluntary, socialistic communes, sort of African versions of Israel's kibbutzim. When villagers decide they want to join together into an *ujamaa* village, the government handles the technical training and supplies, and TANU the political ideology. Every day in the national newspapers there are success stories of various *ujamaa* villages meeting their projected goal, improving their production, learning new techniques, etc. In mid-1972 it was estimated that 1.5 million people were participating in 4,400 *ujamaa* villages throughout Tanzania. In Karege —which we describe merely as an example—the villagers have built a school, small clinic, TANU office, water tower, carpentry shop, dairy, barn, and cashew nut "factory."

Bagamoyo

New Bagamoyo Road reaches its goal at Km 67 in *Bagamoyo,* "place where the heart lays down its burden," so named by the caravan porters who knew that Bagamoyo was their final destination and there they could finally relax for a while. This quiet picturesque town (pop. 5,100) was once one of the mainland starting and ending points for the inland Arab caravans which brought tons of ivory and thousands of Africans in chains overland from the areas around Lakes Tanganyika and Victoria, and then shipped the tusks and the surviving slaves to Zanzibar to be sold. Most of the explorers stopped off in or near Bagamoyo on their way from Zanzibar to their discoveries: Burton and Speke in 1857, Speke and Grant in 1863, Stanley in 1871 and 1874. In 1868 the Society of Holy Ghosts under the leadership of Father Horner established a mission in Bagamoyo for the purpose of liberating and educating slaves, and then sending them to inland agricultural villages. The *Holy Ghost Mission,* a three-story building with arched windows, was built slowly from 1873 to 1903 and still stands, as does their two-story *church tower,* which in 1872 was the first Roman Catholic church structure on the mainland of East Africa. It was to this church on February 24, 1874, that Susi and Chuma, Livingstone's ever faithful servants, carried the explorer's body, having walked overland with it more than 1,000 miles, before finally accompanying it to Westminster Abbey for burial. The mission has a small *museum,* open weekdays 4–5 P.M., Sundays 10 A.M.–noon, 4–5 P.M.

The Germans also left their mark on Bagamoyo. The German East Africa Company made Bagamoyo its first capital in 1887. In 1888 there were battles between coastal Swahili and Arab people, led by Abushiri bin Salim al Harth, and the German officials and missionaries. German, Sudanese, Turkish, and Zulu troops led by Major Hermann von Wissmann finally recaptured the coastal towns, and Abushiri was betrayed and hanged at Bagamoyo on December 15, 1889. There are a few German buildings standing, including the district office built in 1889, an old storehouse and customs office, and the cemetery, which has the graves of some officers who died in the 1889 campaign.

The Arabs, besides leading the wretched slave caravans, left the tradition of their beautiful carved doors, which still adorn some of even the humblest houses in Bagamoyo. The present prison was probably one of the first Arab houses in town, and was enlarged upon orders from Seyyid Barghash, Sultan of Zanzibar (1870–88). The oldest Arab ruins, though, are those located at *Kaole,* reached by a dirt track that hugs the shore, about 5 km to the south. Here are two mosques and more than 20 tombs, all of different ages and states of disrepair. Near the beach is supposed to be a *plaque* commemorating the spot from which Burton and Speke set off in June 1857 on their way to explore Lakes Tanganyika and Victoria.

Package tours which include Bagamoyo are listed under TP-17.

Route T-8: Arusha–Tarangire National Park–Dodoma–Iringa

This 678-km-long route follows much of Tanzania's section of the Great North Road, though in this case it goes south. Its high points include Tarangire National Park, Kolo rock paintings, Dodoma, Iringa, and Ruaha National Park. Most of the road is very corrugated, two-lane dirt—miles and miles of it—and much of the drive is tiring and seems endless. Unless you have an avid interest in rock paintings or in central Tanzania, we advise taking the longer, paved road—our Routes T-3 and T-6—from Arusha to Iringa. The two national parks are at either end of this long route, and both can be reached without having to travel its entire length.

Begin at Arusha's clock tower, going south out of town. The first part of the route overlaps Route T-1, Km 345–423, though in reverse.

Tarangire National Park

Km 105: Turnoff left to *Tarangire National Park,* Tanzania's third-largest national park, which at 4,457 feet altitude covers about 1,000 square miles of acacia woodlands, savanna, and swamp watered by the Tarangire River and Lake Burungi. The park is particularly popular in the dry season when animals from the arid Masai Steppe come for the water, but most of the year it contains elephants, black rhinos, buffalos, oryxes, common zebras, elands, hartebeests, wildebeests, lesser kudus, impalas, waterbucks, lions, cheetahs, and leopards. More than 260 species of birds have been recorded, and watching is good during the rains in April–May. Tarangire is still comparatively undeveloped and, like Ruaha, gives you a feeling of being in the "wilds" of Africa. The best areas for game viewing are along the banks of the saline Tarangire River, on the park's eastern boundary at the swamp, and at Lake Burungi. One definite disadvantage is the presence of the tsetse fly, so have a strong fly swatter handy and wear long sleeves and pants.

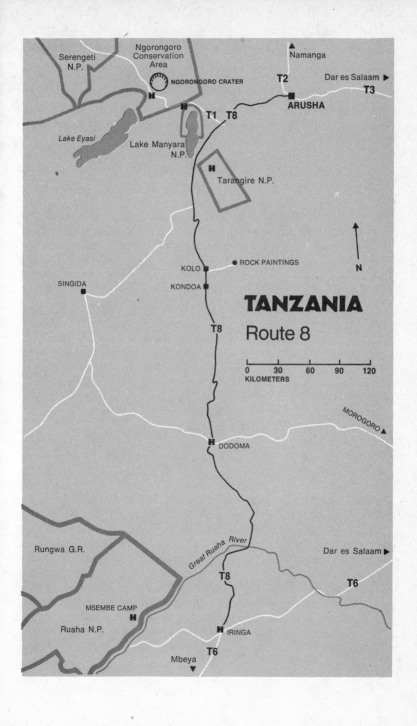

When to Visit

For game viewing the dry season of June–October, especially September, is best, because the animals come into the park in search of water.

Getting There, Getting Around

The road from Arusha is all paved up to the park turnoff, some 105 km, and is easily traveled by any car. The roads within the park are good dirt, and four-wheel drive is not necessary. An airstrip 1½ km from the tented camp is suitable for two-engine planes. Some tour operators are now including Tarangire on their itineraries; see TP-4, 7–8, 11–12, and KP-68, 78–79.

Accommodations

Tarangire Safari Camp, Box 1182 (Boma Road), Arusha, tel. 2504; cable TARANGIRE. A voucher from Arusha is a necessity. Tented camp is 13 km within the park from the gate. 30 dbl tents, each w/shower, toilet, electricity. Rates: FB: sgl—175/–; dbl—280/–. The camp is on the high bank of the Tarangire River overlooking a popular animal watering spot. The main permanent building contains the dining hall, bar, shop. Nearby airstrip and gasoline pump. . . . **Camping** at several sites with water and firewood. Book with Warden, Tarangire National Park, Box 3134, Arusha. Fee: 5/ per person.

Leaving Tarangire, the paved road ends at Km 109, and the corrugated two-lane dirt begins. Km 141: Turnoff right to *Mbulu,* district headquarters at 5,640 feet altitude, and the *Yaida Valley,* an area east of Lake Eyasi which is one of the few places left where the primitive Hadza or Bushman people live. Peter Matthiessen, in *The Tree Where Man Was Born,* describes the Hadza as having small, thick, and very dark bodies. They live primitively and primarily by hunting with poisoned arrows and by gathering plants, they speak a "click" or Koisan language, they may have once done rock paintings similar to those found near Kolo, and they are likely to be forced to assimilate with surrounding tribes. In the small village of *Yaida Chini* live diverse people from the Bantu Isanzu tribe, the Barabaig herdsmen, the agricultural Mbulu, and the Bushmen Hadza. This area is the only place in all of Africa where the four basic linguistic groups—the Bantu, Hamitic or Cushitic, Nilotic, and "click" or Koisan—come together in one spot, according to historian J. E. G. Sutton.

Km 166: Babati. South of Babati, the road climbs and winds up into the *Pienaars Heights* (up to 5,600 feet alt.), which are dotted with hillside *shambas* growing bananas and maize. This area can be quite pretty but is slippery during the rainy season. Km 206: Bereku.

Kolo Rock Paintings

The road continues to twist and turn down to *Kolo* (alt. 4,800 feet) at Km 244, location of some of the most important rock paintings in East Africa. Here to the left is the office of the Antiquities Division's guard/guide. He will sell you a 3/– guide booklet and will accompany you to any of the 14 rock paintings covered in the booklet. While there may be more than 1,000 sites, just visiting 2 of the 14 can occupy one to two hours, because each is in a different location reached first by car and then uphill on foot. At least a dozen painting styles have been distinguished, dating from 3,000 to 200 years ago, with the latest layers on top. The paintings are somewhat of an enigma, because precisely who did them and for what purpose is unknown. It is thought that people of Bushman stock might have done them, as was the case in southern Africa, because they merely enjoyed painting or because they thought that painting an animal would assist them in catching it for food. The paints were made from various organic substances; for instance, red and yellow from ocher, maybe mixed with egg white or yolk, gum, lime, oil, honey, ear wax, or other mediums. The pictures are often difficult to distinguish at first, and are not very vivid. But between the guide and the booklet, things begin to come into focus if you sit down and study the paintings on the spot. They usually portray wild animals—zebra, giraffe, elephant, eland—humans, and abstracts—circles and radarlike grids. One of the best sites to visit is Cheke III, A.17, which is 16 km east of Kolo.

Km 267: *Kondoa,* a district headquarters at 4,650 feet altitude. **Accommodations:** Two Government Rest Houses. South of Kondoa, after the small town of Haneti, are the *Chenene Hills,* whose highest point is 5,948 feet, and in which is a forest reserve about Km 352.

Dodoma

Km 420: *Dodoma* (pop. 23,559), on the Central Plateau at 3,717 feet altitude, and nearly in the center of Tanzania, is the headquarters for the agricultural Dodoma Region. At the end of 1973, after country-wide discussion, the government decided to make Dodoma the new national capital; the move from Dar es Salaam will be over a 10-year period. The most interesting thing about Dodoma now is its flourishing wine industry. In the late 1950s Italian missionaries brought Barbera vine stocks from Italy for a small plot at Kondoa, and a Kondoa cutting planted at Bihawana Mission, about 10 km southwest of Dodoma, took root and formed the basis for a new industry. Today thousands of cuttings are planted on more than 2,000 acres in *ujamaa* villages. Barbera grapes produce a rich, dry red wine, which an ad once called "subtle as a charging rhino." In August 1972 a new rosé wine produced from Aleatico grapes grown in Dodoma was judged as having a nice bouquet and taste. Both wines sell for about 10/– a bottle in Tanzania.

Accommodations

Dodoma Hotel, Box 239, tel. 21. Opposite the railway station. 8 sgls, 19 dbls; 15 rms w/bath. Rates: B&B: sgl—60/–; dbl—110/–. Run by East African Railways and built in 1948, the Dodoma has a terrace, quiet and well-worn bar, wood-paneled lounge, and airy, aging rooms. The menu is table d'hôte (breakfast—7/50; lunch—9/50; dinner—12/–), though also some à la carte snacks. Rating: between 1st- and 2d-class local, a welcome rest stop.

At Dodoma are also the trunk dirt road turnoffs to Morogoro 297 km, and to Singida 249 km. You are now in an area of funny names: Fufu, Hoho, and Hehe (if Ruaha isn't enough). The Great North Road continues south, climbing the slight Fufu Escarpment and then crossing the Fufu River at Km 494 and the Great Ruaha River at Km 552. Thereafter the road climbs 1,250 feet through the scenic Hoho Escarpment into the Iringa area.

Iringa

Km 651: Turnoff left to Iringa Airport. Km 664: *Iringa* (alt. 5,365 feet, pop. 21,746), which in the Hehe language means "a fence to discourage the entry of wild animals." It is a rather pleasant town with a tree-lined main street and an interesting history. The Hehe (pronounced HAY-hay; so called because of the way they expressed excitement—"He! He! He!") are the dominant tribe around Iringa. Up to the 1850s they were in about 30 separate groups until united under strong chiefs in the late 19th century. A small *Hehe museum* is at Kalenga, about 14 km west of Iringa. There is also a mausoleum housing the skull of Mkwawa, a famous 19th-century Hehe leader who led revolts against the Germans until 1898, when rather than be captured he shot himself. His head was sent to Germany, but it was formally returned in 1954.

Accommodations

White Horse Inn, Box 48, Iringa; tel. 30; cable CONTENTED. On Hill St. in the town center. 6 sgls, 25 dbls; 18 dbls w/bath. Rates: B&B: sgl w/o bath—40/–; dbl w/bath—110/–. The unappealing old main section of the White Horse dates from 1937, the satisfactory new annex over the Total station from 1969. Public area includes a bar, two lounges, and table d'hôte dining room (breakfast—7/–; lunch—12/–; dinner—14/–). Rating: between 1st- and 2d-class local. . . . **Camping** is possible about 3 km from the town center. Go north toward Dodoma, turn right 1.7 km from town at Sportsman Cigarettes sign, go along paved road 1.1 km to overgrown grassy field on right. Doorless latrine, no fee.

Ruaha National Park

Continuing south through Iringa town toward the Dar es Salaam–Tunduma highway, at Km 666 is the turnoff right to Kalenga 11 km (see above), and to *Ruaha National Park* 113 km. Ruaha is Tanzania's second-largest national park, well-wooded undulating plateau country covering approximately 5,000 square miles, most at an average of 3,000 feet altitude. Only the eastern central area of about 700 square miles has been opened to visitors, but this includes a 50-mile stretch of the Great Ruaha River as well as the Mwagusi and Mdonva sand rivers. The park is rich in all forms of wildlife except some of the typical plains animals. Animals which may be seen include the elephant, greater and lesser kudu, waterbuck, sable and roan antelopes, giraffe, zebra, baboon, jackal, hippo, rhino, lion, cheetah, leopard, hyrax, warthog, hartebeest, eland, and buffalo. There are over 350 species of birds, and according to John Williams this is one of the few places in Africa where you might see the rare raptorial Eleanora's falcon (in December–January migrations). Ruaha is almost completely unspoiled African wilderness with limited traces of man. Much of the park is plagued with tsetse flies, which explains why the land was largely uninhabited, but the area open to the public is fairly free of the pesty, nasty flies, though have a swatter handy anyway.

The Germans established the Saba River Game Reserve in the early 1900s in the western part of what is now Ruaha. In 1951 the British declared the *Rungwa Game Reserve,* twice as large as the present park. Ruaha National Park was excised from Rungwa in 1964, but the game reserve still exists to the north and is quite large, covering 3,500 square miles. It contains most of the same animals as Ruaha Park, but is less accessible. Permission for entry into Rungwa should be obtained from the Regional Game Officer, Box 148, Iringa, tel. 2687.

After you have entered Ruaha Park by the manually operated pontoon ferry at Ibuguziwa, it is a good idea to head to the right 6 km to the park office at Msembe, where you can get a map, the helpful *Ruaha National Park* guide booklet (cost 5/−), and the *Checklist of Birds.*

From Msembe you might first take the river drive downstream along the *Great Ruaha.* The name Ruaha is a corruption of *Luvaha,* which means "great" in the Hehe language. The most numerous and obvious animals along this drive are elephants, which you'll see mainly in cow/calf family units or as mature bulls, usually alone but sometimes with other bulls. These elephants are not as used to humans as the ones in other game parks, so approach them cautiously. They are particularly fond of the acacia seed pods, which look like dried apple rings. Recently they have also been stripping the bark from the acacias, eventually killing them. Though the elephants help distribute the acacia seeds after having digested them and thus aid in their regeneration, the landscape is beginning to look rather ravaged. Other animals to watch for along the Great Ruaha are troops of baboons, and possibly cheetahs and warthogs.

At the north end of the river drive you can return to Msembe on an inland drive or turn left onto the *Mwagusi sand river* drive. Watch for rhinos, giraffes, elands, and in the thick bush lesser kudus. *Lesser kudus* (Swahili—*tandala mdogo*) are gray antelopes standing about 40 inches at the shoulders with 13 to 14 vertical white stripes along the barrel of the body, conspicuous white throat and neck patches, and a short white mane down the back of the neck, top of the shoulders, and along the back. The horns, present on the male only, grow in three graceful spirals. When lesser kudus run away (they are very shy), their bushy tail curls over their back, showing the tail's white underpart.

Taking the road back toward Mwembe you come to the *Mdonya sand river* drive. At the west end of this river drive is a turnoff to the left to *Makindi,* where there is a permanent springs in a swampy area

and where the land rises and turns into *miombo* woodland. Near Makindi buffalos, zebras, and klipspringers are likely to be seen.

Back at Msembe you can also go upstream west along the Great
Ruaha, and the river tends to be more rocky and boulder-filled. The
dry bush along the river is a good place to watch for *greater kudus*
(Swahili—*tandala mkubwa*), which look like larger, bolder versions

Greater kudu

of their cousins, the lesser kudus. They stand about 5 feet at the shoulder, and a bull weighs up to 700 pounds. Compared to the lesser kudu,
they don't have the white throat and neck patches; their ears are
larger and more rounded; they have a more developed neck fringe;
their horns are much thicker, longer, and more widely set; but they
have similar distinctive narrow, white, vertical stripes along their body.
The bulls are seen in all-male groups or alone, except when they join
the females for breeding during the rainy season until June–July.

When to Visit

The best months are July–November. Avoid going January–March,
when Ruaha is very wet.

Getting There, Getting Around

You can drive or fly to Ruaha, but you must bring your own food
supplies with you. It is 113 km from Iringa to Ruaha along a semi-
corrugated, poorly signposted, 1½-lane dirt road. Allow about three
hours and have plenty of gasoline, though there is usually some at
park headquarters. There's a small airstrip at Msembe, and park headquarters has a Land-Rover for hire for 2/50 per mile.

Accommodations

Msembe Camp, c/o Ruaha Park Warden, Box 369, Iringa; or c/o Tanganyika Farmer's Association, Box 530, Iringa. Located on the banks of the Great Ruaha near Msembe. 6 rondavels w/water, firewood, beds and bedding; 5 dbls, one for 6 people. Rates: 20/– per adult. Elephants are frequent visitors. . . . **Camping** along the Great Ruaha is truly exciting. Our official site under the riverbank acacias was an elephant walk. No facilities, but lots of quadruped action. Fee: 5/– per adult.

Continuing along the route and leaving Iringa, you go south down the escarpment road to the junction at Km 678: Dar es Salaam is to the left, Mbeya and Zambia to the right. From here pick up Route T-6.

Route T-9: Seronera, Serengeti–Fort Ikoma–Lake Victoria– Lake Tanganyika–Gombe Stream National Park

This 1,112-km-long route goes from the middle of Serengeti west and south to Africa's two largest lakes, Victoria and Tanganyika. Up to Fort Ikoma the route is on the main tourist circuit, but thereafter not many foreign visitors travel in these parts unless they have their own vehicle, or they ride the trains and buses. We did not personally cover this route.

Seronera, Serengeti, is the starting point, and from there head north, passing the turnoff left to the western corridor at Km 8. At Banagi, Km 20, take the middle road going northwest. The road leaves the park about Km 57.

Km 67: Turnoff right to *Fort Ikoma* 10 km, a unique lodge but formerly an active fort. It was built in 1906 by the Germans in the style of a kind of knight's castle, a big square with two towers at opposite corners. It was used as an outpost against marauding Masai from Kenya and as a staging post for the line of supply and defense running throughout German East Africa. During World War I German and British troops fought it out here, and the old stone turrets still have the bullet scars. *Fort Ikoma Lodge,* Box 751, Arusha; tel. 2193. 60 dbl cottages w/bath and porch. Rates: FB: dbl—330/–. Also a few luxury tents, dbl—270/–. The lodge is built in and around the old restored fort: the baronial dining room is on one edge of the courtyard, the bar is in a parapeted tower, a long terrace runs the length of the front

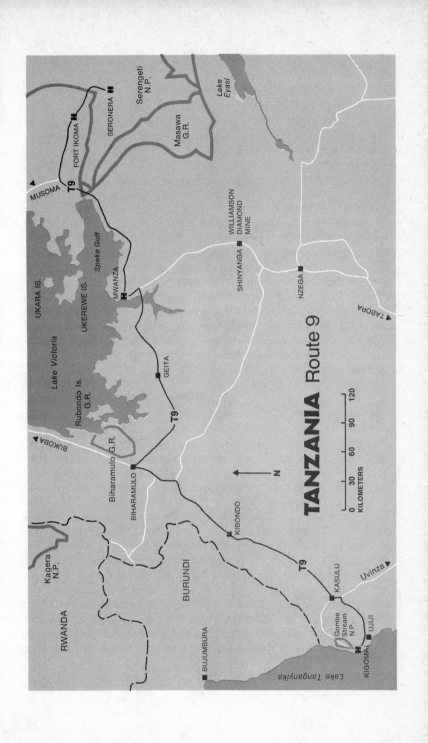

wall. The cottages have red river-stone mosaic floors, local wood furniture, a sunken bath in an ebony floor. Activities: swimming pool, game viewing in Serengeti (vehicle hire 3/50 per mile), early morning game walks, exploring old gold mines, "meet the people safari" on local bus to Musoma. Sounds very imaginative.

Back on the main dirt road, at Km 255 is a junction: Turnoff right to Butiama 13 km, Musoma 16 km, and the Kenya border; and left to Speke Gulf, Mwanza, and western Tanzania. Go left. *Butiama* is the village in the vicinity of President Julius Nyerere's birthplace. Born on a very rainy day in March 1922 to Nyerere Burito, the chief of the Zanaki tribe, and his eighteenth wife, Mugaya, he was named Kambarage after an ancestral spirit who lived in rain, though he took the first name of Julius when baptized at age 20. The agricultural, cattle-keeping Zanaki tribe is one of Tanzania's smallest, numbering only about 40,000. A good biography of Nyerere is William Edgett Smith's *We Must Run While Others Walk. Musoma* (pop. 15,400) is a district and regional headquarters, and a port of call for the East African Railways boat service. **Accommodations:** *Musoma Hotel,* Box 272, Musoma; tel. 64. All rms w/o bath. Rates: B&B: sgl—35/–; dbl—70/–. Table d'hôte meals.

Lake Victoria

At the junction going south, at Km 308 is the turnoff left to Ndabaka Gate into Serengeti's western corridor. To the right the road begins skirting *Speke Gulf* on *Lake Victoria.* The first white man to see Lake Victoria was John Hanning Speke on August 3, 1858, after he had left Richard Burton temporarily ill in Tabora following their explorations of Lake Tanganyika. Speke marched 16 days to search for this northern lake, which he actually saw from the village of Mwanza. He wrote, "The pale blue water of the Nyanza burst suddenly upon my gaze. . . . The distant sea-line of the north horizon was defined in the calm atmosphere, between the north and west points of the compass, but even this did not afford me any idea of the breadth of the lake. . . . I no longer felt any doubt that the lake at my feet gave birth to that interesting river [Nile] the source of which has been the source of so much speculation and the object of so many explorers."

Speke was the first European to see the largest lake in Africa, and the third largest in the world after the Caspian Sea and Lake Superior. It covers 26,828 square miles, about 250 miles in length and 200 miles in width. In its deepest point it is 270 feet, and more rain falls in its center than on its shores. Unfortunately bilharziasis, malaria, and sleeping sickness are endemic around its shores, except off a few uninhabited islands, so it is not as big a tourist attraction as it could be if swimming and boating were safer. Of the 208 species of fish in Victoria, the main commercially caught fish are two indigenous species of *Tilapia.*

Km 427: *Kisesa,* a small town with the Sukuma Museum. The Sukuma number over 1.5 million and are the largest tribe in Tanzania. They are Bantu cultivators and cattle owners, with their traditional lands spreading over 20,000 square miles south of Lake Victoria. They grow most of the cotton that is Tanzania's No. 1 export—$35 million worth in 1971. The *Sukuma Museum* (free admission) has historical items and handicrafts from 35 chiefdoms, arranged in four pavilions. After Saba Saba Day in July, the Sukuma have an *ngoma* or festival at Kisesa, with dances and exhibitions.

Mwanza

Km 445: *Mwanza,* with a population of 34,186, is Tanzania's largest Lake Victoria port, as well as the terminus of the northern branch from Tabora of the Central Railway Line. EAR boats make Mwanza one of their main ports of call for both passengers and cargo. Mwanza covers about 5 square miles on a narrow stretch of land just above the lake at the entrance to Mwanza Gulf. At the lake's edge is a leaning group of protruding rocks called *Bismarck Rocks;* the Germans are said to have had a beer garden on top of the tallest. A half-mile offshore from Mwanza, and accessible by a 1/– motorboat ride, is *Saa Nane Island Game Reserve,* a 95-acre sanctuary where nondangerous game—wildebeests, waterbucks, zebras, hartebeests, and other antelopes —are allowed to roam freely, while rhino and buffalo are fenced off from the public. There is no charge for entry, but permission should be obtained from the Regional Game Officer, Box 85, Mwanza, tel. 3196. **Accommodations:** *New Mwanza Hotel,* Box 25, tel. 3031. On Kenyatta Road. 69 rms, incl 3 suites, all w/bath, a-c. Rates: B&B: sgl— 80/–; dbl—150/–. Replacing the Mwanza Hotel, the large New Mwanza opened in late 1972. Main-floor Brunchery serves breakfast and à la carte meals, the 1st-floor Kipepeo ("butterfly") Grill à la carte. . . . *Lake Hotel,* Box 910, tel. 3216. 23 rms, all w/bath or shower. Rates: B&B: sgl—52/–; dbl—104/–. . . . *Hotel Deluxe,*

Box 1471, tel. 2411. On Uhuru St. 53 beds. Rates: B&B: sgl—56/25; dbl—99/–. . . . *Jaffries Hotel,* Box 647, tel. 2420. Rates: sgl—28/–; dbl—36/–.

Leaving Mwanza by the road going south, at Km 468 is Usagara. One road continues south to Shinyanga and Tabora; go right to the Busisi Ferry and Geita. Shinyanga, 145 km, is the closest town to the *Williamson Diamond Mine* at Mwadui. Diamonds are Tanzania's second-largest export, with $29.8 million worth sent out in 1971. Most of the stones found at Mwadui are clear colorless gems, or small green or pink gems. One of the best found was a rose-colored piece in 1947 weighing 54½ carats (142 carats to the ounce), which was presented to then Princess Elizabeth upon her marriage. The Tanzania government now owns 50 percent of the Williamson Diamond Mine. Tours of the mine can be arranged by writing Williamson Diamonds Ltd., Private Bag, Mwadui, Tanzania.

Tabora

Tabora, 345 km from the turnoff, a district and regional headquarters at 3,930 feet altitude, with a population of 21,000, used to lie on the main ivory and slave caravan route from the coast to the inland lakes. Ruins of the Arab traders' houses can be seen, as can a reconstruction of the house where Livingstone and Stanley stayed on and off in 1871–72 before the doctor set off on the last leg of his last journey. The modern town was laid out in its present form by the Germans, who once intended to make Tabora their capital. The Nyamwezi, Tanzania's second-largest tribe, live in the Tabora region, raising tobacco, honey, goats, vegetables, and groundnuts. The Central Line railway comes from Dar es Salaam and in Tabora branches out north to Mwanza and west to Kigoma. **Accommodations:** *Tabora Hotel,* Box 147, tel. 47. 14 rms w/bath, 11 rms w/o bath. Rates: B&B: sgl—50/– to 60/–; dbl—90/– to 110/–. Table d'hôte meals.

Back at the turnoff and going right, at Km 481 are Kikongo and *Busisi Ferry* across the Mwanza Gulf to Busisi. At the junction at Km 510, turn left and continue west. Km 707: Junction, right to Biharamulo Game Reserve and Rubondo Island, straight to Bukoba and Uganda, left to Biharamulo town and Lake Tanganyika. *Biharamulo Game Reserve,* 38 km to the northeast, is 450 square miles large and protects the common reedbuck, steinbuck, Sharp's grysbok, and Lichtenstein's hartebeest. There is no charge for entry, but a pass should be obtained from the Regional Game Officer, Box 671, Bukoba, tel. 349. Twenty miles offshore from Biharamulo is 85-square-mile *Rubondo Island Game Reserve.* There are plans to make a large open sanctuary with rhinos, gorillas, sitatungas, okapis, chimpanzees, colobus monkeys, buffalos, roan antelopes, elephants, and lots of birds. No charge for entry, but permission is necessary (see above). *Bukoba,* 177 km north, is a port town of about 8,100 set in a valley of seven hills. The Bukoba area is lush and green, with *robusta* coffee indigenous to the steep surrounding slopes. **Accommodations:** *Lake Hotel,* Box 66, tel. 237. 5 dbls w/bath, 9 rms w/o bath. Rates: FB: sgl—55/– to 85/–. . . . *Coffee Tree Inn,* Box 5, tel. 412. Rates: B&B: sgl—50/–. West of Bukoba about 200 km is *Rumanyika Orugundu Game Reserve,* 300 square miles of mostly high mountain rain forest in the Kishanda Valley, with rhinos, elephants, buffalos, lions, leopards, elands, roans, and small species. Again, permission for entry is necessary (see Biharamulo above). North of Bukoba 80 km are the Tanzania/Uganda border posts at Mtukura.

Back at the junction at Km 707, turn left and left again at the second junction at Km 711. Km 742: Turnoff right to Rwanda 135 km, and Burundi 112 km, both small, hilly, tribally torn countries west of the Kagera River. Km 859: Kibondo. About Km 910 you drive through the Lugeti Hills, and to the west are the Malagarasi River and Burundi. Km 1008: Kasulu. Km 1021: Junction—left to Uvinza 64 km, Mpanda 258 km, and Tunduma 679 km; right to Ujiji and Kigoma; turn right.

Lake Tanganyika

Km 1076: Turnoff left to Ujiji and *Lake Tanganyika. Ujiji* is the place where Stanley "found" Livingstone. Commissioned by the New York *Herald* to search for and find Dr. Livingstone, who hadn't been heard from in seven years, Stanley set out from Zanzibar in early 1871. After 7½ months he was in Tabora. Stuck there during a local war he heard conflicting stories about Livingstone. Finally, on November 10, 1871, Stanley and his caravan marched into Ujiji with an American flag in the lead and a Zanzibar flag in the rear. When Stanley at last saw Livingstone standing under a mango tree, he took off his pith helmet and said his four famous words: "Dr. Livingstone, I presume?" The reply was, "Yes." Today by the lakeshore the *Living-*

stone Monument marks the spot (or proximity) where the famous meeting took place.

Thirteen years prior to the Livingstone-Stanley meeting, Richard Burton and John Speke had "discovered" Lake Tanganyika at Ujiji. After a six-month delay in Zanzibar, they finally began their expedition in June 1857 under commission to the Royal Geographical Society to search for the two or three mysterious inland lakes. Their travels were long, arduous, frustrating, and fraught with illness and strife, but they reached Tabora on November 7, 1857, where Burton learned from the Arab traders that there were two inland lakes, one to the north and one to the west. Burton guessed (wrongly) that the one to the west was the true source of the Nile River, and he decided to explore that. Finally, on February 13, 1858, they looked upon and later explored part of *Lake Tanganyika,* the world's seventh-largest and second-deepest lake.

This Rift Valley fresh-water lake covers some 12,700 square miles, and is 420 miles long and 4,710 feet deep, or 2,300 feet below sea level at its maximum depth. Its main inlets are the Ruzizi River in the north and Malagarasi River in the east, and its main outlet, contrary to Burton's hopes, is the Lukuga River in the west (which is, though, one of the sources of the Zaire or Congo River). On the floor of this deep lake are great unseen mountains and huge masses of dead, lifeless "fossil" water never circulated by currents. But living in its upper waters is an astonishing variety of endemic species of fish: 160 different species, of which 125 are found nowhere else. The most common are tilapia, yellowbellies, Nile perch, and tigerfish, many of which can be caught from boats, piers, or wharves. Tiny sardinelike fish called *dagaa* (*Stolothrissa tanganyikae*), migrate to the surface at night to feed on microscopic organisms, and are themselves caught. Native netsmen in canoes shine a light that attracts the fish; one fisherman madly beats a drum, causing the frightened fish to huddle into a mass and then be easily netted. More than 8,000 tons of *dagaa* are caught in this way each year, with some exported to Zaire and Zambia. The name "Tanganyika" is said to mean "a meeting place or mixture of the waters" in the language of the people living around the lake. When the British were given the mandate to rule German East Africa as a trusteeship after World War I, they changed the name to Tanganyika, and this is still used to refer to the mainland of Tanzania.

North of Ujiji at Km 1088 is *Kigoma* (alt. 2,538 feet), the docking headquarters for the EAR steamer *Liembe,* and the terminus of the

Central Line railway branch from Tabora. **Accommodations:** *Gold Lion,* Box 18, Kigoma. Rates: B&B: sgl—40/−; dbl—80/−.

Gombe Stream

And 24 km north of Kigoma at about Km 1112 is *Gombe Stream National Park,* a 25-square-mile reserve of mountain, forest, and meadow created especially to protect the resident chimpanzees, who were the subject of Jane van Lawick-Goodall's fascinating book *In the Shadow of Man,* which is documented with excellent photographs by Hugo, her husband. Chimpanzees vary in size according to subspecies, sex, and age, but a male standing upright is about 3½ feet tall and weighs around 100 pounds; a female is slightly smaller. The Gombe chimp has a heavy, robust body, overall black coat, rounded head with noticeable ears, powerful limbs and especially long arms, and pinkish hands whose fingers are flexed in order to support its fore-weight on the knuckles when it walks on all fours on the ground. Chimps in Gombe have been observed to eat 90 species of tree and plant food including 50 types of fruit; three species of ant, two of termite, and one of caterpillar; bird eggs and fledglings; honey; soil thought to contain salt; and, contrary to previous belief, meat—usually the young of bushbucks, bushpigs, baboons, and monkeys. They have also been photographed by Hugo van Lawick-Goodall modifying, among other things, grass stems to use for fishing for termites in their mounds—a form of tool manipulation, rather than simply tool use (which even some birds do). Chimps have not yet succeeded in using one tool to make another, though, which man does. Jane van Lawick-Goodall says that the chimpanzee's brain structure resembles man's more than any other living mammal's, and that it may not be too dis-similar to that of ape-man's millions of years ago. Chimps' behavior and gestures are also similar to man's: reaching out to another for a touch of assurance, smiling when nervous or frightened, patting and kissing and hugging each other when happy, waving arms or throwing stones or kicking or biting or pulling another's hair when very angry. Their sounds vary tremendously: barks, screams, squeaks, whimpers, "pant-hoots," grunts, pants, and a loud "wraaaa." At Gombe now is the Gombe Stream Research Center, of which the van Lawick-Goodalls are directors. As a park, though, Gombe is still undeveloped for tourism, and visitors are strongly discouraged. There are plans to build a viewing island for visitors, so that they will be able to observe the chimpanzees without disturbing or passing any diseases to them.

Kilwa Ruins

South of Dar es Salaam 317 km is the island *Kilwa Kisiwani,* or "Kilwa on the island," where the most interesting Arab/Portuguese ruins in Tanzania are protected monuments. This is the "Quiloa" of Milton's *Paradise Lost.* On the northwest end of the island are the extensive ruins spread out over about one mile along the coast. The ruins include two palaces, five mosques, five cemeteries, numerous houses and foundations, and a large fort. An excellent description of Kilwa is *A Guide to the Ruins of Kilwa* by Neville Chittick, published by the Antiquities Division (cost 2/50).

Written chronicles record a tradition that about the 11th century the Sultan of Shiraz, in Persia, left home with his six sons, each in his own ship, and that each settled at a different place on the East African coast, including Mafia, Kilwa, and Pemba. The Shirazi dynasty developed Bantu-populated Kilwa into a Moslem community, erected the early part of the Great Mosque and other buildings, and increased trade with imports of Islamic earthenware and indirectly Chinese porcelain.

Sometime before A.D. 1300 a new dynasty known as Abu'l Mawahib took power at Kilwa and the island rose to its apex of trade, building, and prosperity. Kilwa was essentially a maritime power, with little influence over the mainland. It gained control, however, of the important Mozambique port of Sofala and thus of the gold trade, 900 miles to the south. During this peak of power the 100-plus-room grand palace of Husuni Kubwa was built, perhaps the largest pre-European building in equatorial Africa. Copper coins were minted, and more than 10,000 pieces have been found on Kilwa, Mafia, and Zanzibar. The second half of the 14th century saw a decline in wealth, but during the early part of the 15th century building continued, with the Small Domed Mosque erected and the Great Mosque rebuilt.

Then the Portuguese entered the picture. Pedro Cabral called in 1500, and Vasco da Gama in 1502, demanding that the sultan pay tribute to the king of Portugal. In 1505 the payment of tribute was denied, and a fleet of ships under Francisco d'Almeida landed, occupied and pillaged the town, and in 20 days built a fort, the Gereza, on foundations already constructed by the Kilwa inhabitants. The Portuguese left a garrison behind and sailed on to Mombasa. The fort was abandoned in 1513, and few Portuguese remained. But Kilwa's heyday was over because the Portuguese wanted to control all the coastal trade themselves, especially the gold exiting at Sofala. The sultan in 1520 did, however, order the *Kilwa Chronicle* to be written documenting the city's historical, and mythical, past; copies of it still exist.

Later in 1589 the Kilwa residents were further harassed when the Zimba, a tribe cannibalizing their way up the coast from the Zambezi, stopped long enough to eat some Kilwa residents before moving on. The 17th century was one of poverty, though the 18th century improved somewhat with the arrival of Arabs from Oman. During this time Kilwa's wealth depended upon trade with the interior and the export of slaves. In about 1784 forces led by the Imam of Muscat occupied Kilwa with a governor and garrison, though the sultanate was perpetuated mostly in name. By 1830 the Kilwa residents moved to Kilwa Kivinje, 28 km north, and in 1843 the governor moved there and Sultan Seyyid Said of Zanzibar deported the last sultan of Kilwa to Muscat. Thereafter Kilwa as a kingdom or sultanate was through.

As you approach Kilwa from the mainland by boat, the most prominent building is the *Gereza* (Swahili for "prison" or "barracks," from Portuguese *ingreja,* a "church"). It is almost square with circular towers at its northeast and southwest corners, and contains various two- and three-story buildings within it. The original structure was built by the Portuguese in 1505, but the visible remains with details like spy holes date from 1800 when the Imam of Muscat seized control of Kilwa.

The *Great Mosque* or *Friday Mosque* lies about 600 feet inland southwest of the fort, and is the largest mosque of this period on the East African coast. Recently partially reconstructed, it was first built in the 12th century, with alterations four different times over six centuries, the greatest about 1421–30. The mosque has two distinct parts, the northern roofless section being the oldest. In the final reconstructed version there were an amazing 22 small lime concrete domes and one great dome, all supported by scores of pillars of cut stone and rubble set in mortar.

Removed from the main cluster of buildings and cemeteries, and off to the east about ¾ mile are Husuni Kubwa and Husuni Ndogo. *Husuni Kubwa* is the largest building at Kilwa, with more than 100 rooms. This was probably built by Malik al-Mansur ("the conquering king"), who ruled 1310–33 at Kilwa's apex. It is shaped like a rectangular frying pan with a handle of rooms out of its northeast end. There are three large courtyards with rooms on all sides, and one

enormous Great Court with storerooms for supplies. A particularly interesting feature is the octagonal open-air swimming pool to which
water was hand-carried from wells, and from which water was drained
by holes in its west end.

Actually there are also two other Kilwas. *Kilwa Kivinje,* "Kilwa of
the casuarina trees," was built in the 1830's by former Kilwa Kisiwani
residents, and is now a dhow port. *Kilwa Masoko,* "Kilwa of the markets," is directly across from Kilwa Kisiwani on a promontory, is the
district headquarters, and has an airstrip.

Getting There, Getting Around

If driving, go in the dry season, when the coastal road is open.
Otherwise, EAA flies from Dar es Salaam 4Xwk to Kilwa Masoko,
from where boats can be hired for the trip to Kilwa Kisiwani. You
should allow a day to get there and explore the ruins, with the Antiquities Division *Guide to the Ruins of Kilwa* in hand.

Accommodations

There is no place to stay on the island. You can stay at rest houses
at Kilwa Kivinje and Kilwa Masoko, but bring your own food. Permission to stay at either should be obtained from the Area Commissioner, P.O. Kilwa Masoko.

Mafia Island

Mafia Island lies about 130 km southeast of Dar es Salaam on the
edge of the continental shelf, and according to Ernest Hemingway and
others has some of the greatest deep-sea fishing in the world. Fishing
in the Mafia Channel is best from December to March when the big
migratory sailfish and swordfish run, though the whole season stretches
from September to March. Some of the bigger catches include a 100-
pound sailfish, 75-pound dolphin, 148-pound dogtooth tuna, and 500-
pound rockcod. Fishing equipment and boats can be hired through
Seafaris at the Mafia Island Lodge (also see "Fishing," p. 341).

The main island itself covers some 170 square miles (there are several tiny offshore islands), and has a population of about 16,700,
mostly of the Wambwera tribe. Besides deep-sea fishing, there's excellent scuba diving, water skiing in the lagoon, sailing, and swimming,
especially in Chole Bay on the east side. Mafia has Arab ruins, these

on the island's west side at Ras Kisimani. Unfortunately much of the ruins are underwater at high tide.

"Mafia" seems to be an alien name for the island; the Swahili name is Chole, after a species of fish and also a species of bird.

Getting There, Getting Around

EAA has 40-minute flights 4Xwk from Dar es Salaam to the airstrip at Kilondoni. Package tours going to Mafia are under TP-19. Guests of Mafia Island Lodge will be met at the airport for 10/−.

Accommodations

Mafia Island Lodge, bookings to TTC Hotels (p. 315). 30 dbls, all w/bath and a-c. Rates: FB: sgl—240/−; dbl—300;−; also low-season rates. Lodge is on the east side of Mafia Island, nestled among the palms and coral in Chole Bay. Rooms are cool and modern. Lots of coral and wood incorporated in bar, lounge, and table d'hôte dining room (breakfast—10/−; lunch—17/50; dinner—21/−). Seafaris rents boats, fishing and diving gear. Rating: 1st-class international.

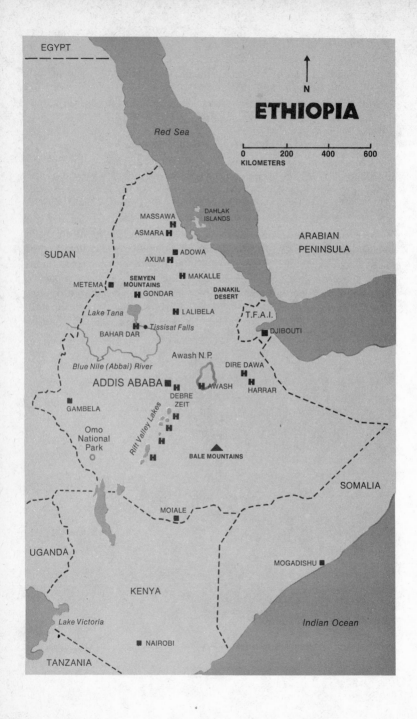

ETHIOPIA

THE HIDDEN EMPIRE

Ethiopia is different. First, unlike the other countries of Eastern Africa, it does not owe its nationhood to European colonizers. It is not a collection of tribes held together by an infant government within whimsical borders drawn by foreign mapmakers. It is not a republic; it was until recently a rigid monarchy headed by the world's last official emperor, Haile Selassie, who in 1974 was forced to surrender his power to a military junta. The country's people are black, to be sure, but the typical Ethiopian does not resemble a Kenyan or Zambian in physical features. The majority of highland Ethiopians are not animists or relatively recent converts to some Western religion, for the country has had its own brand of Christianity since the 4th century.

For the tourist, Ethiopia is therefore a different experience. You do not go to Ethiopia mainly to see wild animals, though rare and delightful creatures there are. You go to see what the tourist organization calls "the Hidden Empire," with its ruins of the ancient empire of Axum, associated with the Queen of Sheba; rock-hewn churches at Lalibela and some of the 15,000 churches elsewhere in the country, many never seen by foreigners; and 17th-century castles at the former imperial capital of Gondar. A lumpy-crescent-shaped mountainous country, Ethiopia has fabulous scenery—rugged mountains like the 15,000-foot Semyens; flat-topped *ambas,* which are like Arizona mesas except that there's likely to be a church or a monastery on top; blue Rift Valley lakes in a daisy chain on the map; escarpments with corkscrew roads like that between Asmara and Massawa; and, not least, Victoria Falls' seasonal rival, Tissisat Falls near the source of the Blue Nile, navigated fully for the first time in 1968. At the foot of the steep, cool mountain plateaus—highlands to which Ethiopia owes its centuries-old independence—are the hot, dry lowlands and deserts, inhabited by various Nilotic tribes and Somalis.

This fascinating country has an incomparable history—long, rich, full of drama and events, invasions and massacres, bloody battles and court intrigue, adventurers and saints, mad emperors and enlightened ones. The secretiveness with which a faceless group of thirteen military men staged a creeping coup in 1974 against the world's last remaining emperor—Haile Selassie I, 225th in a line stretching back to Solomon and Sheba—is perfectly in keeping with the style of Ethiopia's history.

Early man knew Ethiopia, as excavations in the lower Omo Valley on the Kenya-Ethiopia border and in the Rift Valley south of Addis Ababa have shown. But no civilization was evident until sometime after 1000 B.C. when the Sabeans, from the south Arabian kingdom of Saba or Sheba (revolving around San'a in present-day Yemen), came across the Red Sea and moved into the Ethiopian Highlands. These people, who had a written language and definite agricultural techniques, founded Yeha and the port of Adulis, both now isolated ruins. Their descendants founded the great Axum Empire about 500 B.C., building cities at Axum, Matara, Coloe (Cohaito), Agula, and elsewhere. Soldiers and traders, the Axumites spread as far west as Meroe on the Nile, and across the Red Sea.

An epic occurrence was the conversion of Axum in the 4th century to Christianity, then an infant religion. While sailing in the Red Sea, a young Syrian named Frumentius barely escaped capture by pirates and found his way to the Axumite court, where he was made treasurer and secretary to the emperor. On the emperor's death, Frumentius took charge of the education of the young Emperor Ezana and converted him. The Patriarch of Alexandria later made Frumentius the first bishop of the Axumite Empire.

Axum went into decline at the beginning of the 10th century, perhaps because of ecological deterioration, too many wars and the consequent decrease in trade. Additionally, tradition states that a pagan Queen Judith or Yudit revolted against the emperor at Axum and destroyed that city and numerous churches in the empire, this perhaps being the reason that women are not allowed in some Ethiopian churches to this day. The Axumite Empire ended in the 10th century, and 100 years later the Zagwe Dynasty temporarily seized the imperial throne. A Zagwe king, Lalibela, was responsible for the incredible rock-hewn churches in Lalibela in the 12th to 13th centuries. The Zagwe line ended about 1270, the Solomonic Dynasty was restored, and Ethiopia entered into more enlightened times, with imperial power growing, Christianity thriving, and literature flourishing.

Ethiopia (or Abyssinia, as it was also called) became a subject of increasing interest to Europeans because it was the only Christian country outside Europe, ruled, they thought, by one Prester or priest John. But Europeans didn't know much about the land, since no one went there to report on it until the 15th century, when the Italian Pietro Rombulo went to live in Ethiopia, and no coherent report was produced until Francisco Alvarez's *Narrative of the Portuguese Embassy to Abyssinia,* which was in 1520. Ethiopia was not at the ends of the earth, but Gibbon in 1788 did not exaggerate much when he noted that the Ethiopians, "encompassed on all sides by the enemies of the religion . . . slept near a thousand years, forgetful of the world by whom they were forgotten."

The Middle Ages in Ethiopia were a bloody time, with constant wars between the Christian highlanders and the Moslem lowlanders to the east. The ruler of Harrar, Ahmad ibn Ibrahim Gragn (or Grañ, meaning "the left-handed"), invaded Ethiopia in 1527, defeated Emperor Lebna Dengel, and overran most of the plateau, ransacking towns and everywhere destroying Christian churches before being defeated and killed on the shore of Lake Tana in 1543 by Emperor Galawdewos or Claudius, who had the help of the Portuguese Christopher da Gama (son of the explorer Vasco da Gama) and 400 soldiers. This began a period of great Portuguese influence, during which a large Jesuit mission eventually succeeded in converting two emperors to Catholicism, though they failed to convert the mass of the people and were eventually expelled in the 1630s by Emperor Fasiladas.

This coincided with the physical withdrawal—and, later, emotional retreat—of imperial power into the isolated mountains north of Lake Tana and the building of Gondar's famous castles. The empire disintegrated as the power of the regions, each headed by a *ras,* increased; the time from the mid-1700s to mid-1800s is called the Mesafint, or "time of the judges or princes." Civil war was accompanied by much destruction, and eventually Gondar was left in ruins as Axum was.

The empire was revived by the half-mad Emperor Tewodros or Theodore II (1855–68). His victory over one *ras* at Ayshel ended the chaotic Mesafint, and in the next decade Tewodros brought the provinces under control, unifying much of the central plateau. But now others were interested in empire, and Ethiopia's history becomes full of British, Egyptian, Sudanese, and Italian invaders. Through a misunderstanding when a letter Tewodros sent to Queen Victoria went unanswered, the emperor seized a number of Europeans, and the British sent an expedition against him in 1867. Defeated in battle in 1868, Tewodros committed suicide; his crown was sent to England.

The next emperor, Yohannes, defeated the Egyptians in 1875 and 1876, the Italians in 1887, and the Mahdist dervishes from the Sudan in 1889, but was killed in this last campaign. Then began the reign of one of Ethiopia's most famous emperors, Menelik II. He made peace with the Italians, but a ridiculous dispute over the Italian versus Amharic wording of the treaty led to another Italian invasion from Massawa, which the Italians had held since 1885. In a shrewdly conducted campaign, Menelik decisively defeated an Italian army at Adowa March 1, 1896, and Ethiopia was acknowledged by Europe as an independent entity, with several diplomatic missions established at the new capital of Addis Ababa. Menelik then brought more of Ethiopia under central control and took the first steps toward making it a modern country.

Menelik died in 1913 and was succeeded by an emperor who was so unpopular he was overthrown and replaced by Menelik's daughter Zawditu in 1917. Heir to the throne and regent was one Ras Tafari Makonnen, who led Ethiopia into the League of Nations, recovered Tewodros's crown from the British, and began work on a friendship treaty with Italy before he became Emperor Haile Selassie I in 1930. His reforms, such as the abolition of serfdom, the writing of a constitution, and the opening of a Parliament, continued after his coronation.

Italy had not yet given up hope of an African empire, however, and in 1934 Mussolini forced an incident that led to the full-scale invasion from Italian Eritrea into highland Ethiopia the next year. The big powers did nothing to help Ethiopia, the League of Nations proved powerless, and the Fascists occupied Addis Ababa May 5, 1936. Haile Selassie went into exile in Britain while the Patriots continued the struggle locally. The emperor's pleas for assistance in liberating his country went for naught until the formal beginning of World War II. After a brief campaign, Allied troops defeated the Italians, and Haile Selassie returned to the capital in triumph May 5, 1941.

But after the war, Ethiopia continued to be a basically medieval country with an unrepresentative government, and power, land, and money were concentrated in the hands of a very few, including royalty, the aristocracy, and the church. In 1960 there was a bloody attempted *coup d'état,* with Emperor Haile Selassie's son implicated and quickly deported to Europe. Things simmered for another fourteen years. Then in 1974 there was a "creeping coup." Disgusted with the corruption in government, a central military committee arrested hundreds of rich nobles and landowners, talked of establishing a constitutional monarchy and redistributing the land to the tillers, and finally on September 12 deposed and arrested the emperor. Predictions for the future included calling back from Switzerland the ailing Crown Prince Asfa Wossan, Haile Selassie's exiled son, and making him a figurehead king with no authority. Change is coming to feudalistic Ethiopia, and the "Hidden Empire" is perhaps going to fully enter the twentieth century.

Some Vital Statistics. Area: 492,557 square miles, tenth largest country in Africa, twice as large as Kenya, France, or Texas.

Population: 25,930,000 (est. 1972), more than California. Population density: 52 per square mile.

Cities: Addis Ababa (pop. 851,610) is the capital. The second city is Asmara (pop. 232,550). Other towns: Dire Dawa (63,670), Harrar (45,840), Dessie (45,731), Gondar (36,570), Debre Zeit (29,200), Makalle (29,180), Debre Marcos (27,170), Massawa (19,820), Axum (12,810). Ethiopia is 9.6 percent urban.

Gross National Product (1971): $2.031 billion ($79 per capita).

Currency

The basic unit of currency is the Ethiopian dollar (abbreviated E$). It is divided decimally, with copper coins in values of 1, 5, 10, and 25 cents. Currency notes are printed in denominations of 1, 5, 10, 20, 50, 100, and 500 Ethiopian dollars.

As of early 1974 the official value of the U.S. dollar was E$2.07, or E$1 equals about US$.4830. Here is a rough conversion table:

$$E\$100 = US\$48.30$$
$$E\$50 \ = US\$24.15$$
$$E\$20 \ = US\$9.66$$
$$E\$10 \ = US\$4.82$$
$$E\$5 \ \ = US\$2.41$$
$$E\$1 \ \ = US48¢$$
$$E50¢ \ = US24¢$$
$$E25¢ \ = US12¢$$
$$E10¢ \ = US4¢$$

The easy way to convert is divide or multiply by two to give an approximation. We abbreviate Ethiopian cents this way: E$.20 to E20¢.

Planning a Trip

What to See and Do

The scenery, history, and religion, often intertwined, provide most of "the Hidden Empire's" tourist attractions. By good fortune, most of the interesting places are along one major road route between Addis Ababa and Asmara, and the same places are served by daily Ethiopian Airlines service each way. This, of course, is the *Historic Route*. The principal attractions are *Bahar Dar* on the shore of *Lake Tana*, from which you make a side trip to *Tissisat Falls* on the Blue Nile; *Gondar*, the former imperial capital with its 17th- and 18th-century castles and churches; *Lalibela*, a mountain town virtually inaccessible except by air, with a dozen incredible churches carved in the 12th century from living rock; and *Axum*, seat of an ancient empire that at its height extended from Arabia to the Nile. Bahar Dar, Gondar, Lalibela, and Axum can all be visited in a five-day air tour from Addis Ababa ending in Asmara, or vice versa. Each is definitely worth a one-day visit, but you can profitably spend two days exploring Gondar and Lalibela, and perhaps Bahar Dar and Axum if you make local transport arrangements beforehand.

The next most popular major excursion is east of Addis Ababa to *Harrar*, a walled, mainly Moslem city, known for its bustling market, intricately woven baskets, and the "hyena man." Harrar is a two-day air excursion, three-day rail, car, and plane trip.

Addis Ababa, a sprawling city dating to the late 19th century, is the travel center. Stay, sightsee, and shop for at least one whole day, perhaps part of a second. Excursions from the capital that can each be done in a day trip are *Debre Zeit* with its crater lakes, and *Koka Dam;* the monastery of *Debre Libanos* and the *Blue Nile Gorge;* and the mineral hot springs at *Ambo* (Hagere Hiwot) and *Wollisso* (Ghion), if taking the waters is your idea of what to do in a foreign country. Two-day excursions can be made east to *Awash National Park* or south to the chain of *Rift Valley lakes*.

The second city, *Asmara*, is not worth a special visit but is a useful starting or stopping point for the Historic Route. A trip down the winding escarpment road to *Massawa* on the Red Sea is a popular excursion from Asmara. For the hardy, Asmara is a convenient base for trips to the ruins of *Adulis, Cohaito* (Coloe), and *Matara,* perhaps *Yeha* and *Axum* as well. Near Axum is the famous battlefield of *Adowa,* where the Ethiopians trounced the Italians in 1896, but there is little to see there. Males with energy (no women admitted) can visit the *monastery of Debre Damo,* a Mount Athos-like religious retreat on a flat-topped *amba* south of Asmara.

The very curious and the fit can use *Makalle* as a base for walking, hiking, scrambling, and climbing to Lalibela-like rock churches in Tigre Province. Similarly adventurous sorts can consider *mule trips* from Debarek into the *Semyen Mountains,* an extraordinarily wild, rugged area of savage beauty, or from the main Addis-Asmara road west into the hills to Lalibela.

Where to Stay

There are international-class hotels in Addis Ababa and Asmara, Dire Dawa, and Massawa; new Hilton lodges will open in the four Historic Route towns in late 1975. Elsewhere the hotels are 1st- or 2d-class local (though the prices don't always reflect the lower quality). Bookings as far in advance as possible, especially for November–February.

Generally, the only alternative to staying in hotels is camping, since there are no rest houses or self-service accommodations. There are few official campgrounds; a campsite is where you find one. We did not camp in Ethiopia, so can only pass on the U.S. State Department's warning that camping there has proved dangerous with the comment that the State Department is not an adventurous organization.

When to Go

The best time to visit Ethiopia is October to mid-February, then May to mid-June. The rainy periods are mid-February to April, mid-June to September. A when-to-travel consideration other than weather is the number of religious holidays (see p. 467).

Most of Ethiopia lies on a high plateau, with the fringes semiarid to arid land. The temperature during the dry seasons averages 60°F in the highlands, 70°F in the lower parts of the country.

The slogan "13 Months of Sunshine" is not a calendrical exaggeration (see p. 467) but an actual one, for the rainy seasons are wet, cold, and gray, although the sun will appear from time to time. Eighty percent of the rain falls during the "big rains" mid-June to September.

Massawa and the Red Sea Coast, as well as the Danakil Depression, are extremely hot all year.

Tourism Authority

The Ethiopian Tourist Organization and Ethiopian Airlines are the official government agencies for the promotion of tourism to Ethiopia. ETO publishes many excellent, free, colorful, and educational brochures, and a monthly news tabloid. Their offices are quite willing to answer questions. Ethiopian Airlines acts more as the overseas publicity and marketing body, and has many of its own bright and interesting brochures.

Offices of ETO: Ras Makonnen Ave. near Maskal Square, Box 2183, Addis Ababa, tel. 447470; cable ETHIOTOURISM. Haile Selassie (abbreviated H.S.I.) Ave., Box 1010, Asmara, tel. 112999. Box 22, Gondar, tel. 110022. Box 23, Axum, tel. 50. Box 194, Dire Dawa, tel. 113040.

U.S. offices of EAL: 200 East 42d St., New York 10017, tel. (212) 867-0095. 6290 W. Sunset Blvd., Los Angeles 90028, tel. (213) 466-8830.

Maps

There are some pretty good maps of Ethiopia, Addis Ababa, and the historic sites and parks. The Ministry of Land Reform and Administration publishes detailed maps, which are available from the ministry office on Menelik II Ave. across from the Hilton, Box 884, Addis Ababa, tel. 448445; the map catalog is free. Include approximate postage when ordering maps.

Ethiopia, general: Mobil Oil and ETO publish a "Road Map of Ethiopia" with a scale of about 1:3 million, and a map of Addis Ababa on the back; available from ETO and in bookstores (cost E$1). In commemoration of the tenth anniversary of the OAU, the ETO published a map with the country on the scale of 1:4 million on one half, Addis Ababa at a scale of 1:20,000 on the other half; available from the ECA bookshop in All Africa Hall (E$3). The Ministry of Land Reform has a general relief map, scale 1:2 million (E$1.75). They also have eight topographical maps (series 1501) covering the country, scale 1:250,000 (E$2 each).

Addis Ababa: See the Mobil–ETO map mentioned above. The Ministry of Land Reform has a huge six-color map of Addis, scale 1:10,000 (E$2.50). A handier-size foldout map for daily use is in the back of *What's Best?* available free from ETO or from Executive Promotions, Box 2691, Addis Ababa, tel. 153232.

Asmara: The free ETO booklet on Asmara has a sketchy map of the city in the back. An Italian map called "Pianta di Asmara" shows all the streets and *vias,* scale 1:6,000; available for E$4 from Monaci Derna Bookshop, 4 Fit. Melles Ghebrezghi St., just off Haile Selassie Ave., Box 1218, Asmara.

Axum, Lalibela, Gondar, Harrar: The ETO publishes excellent color booklets with centerfold maps of each of these places. They also have miniature foldouts of the maps and brochures that are handy to carry around with you. The sets are free at ETO. ETO also has a color booklet on *Makalle* and the churches of Tigre, and a miniature brochure on *Bahar Dar and Lake Tana,* both with outline maps, both free.

National Parks: The *Semyen Mountains* are covered in an ETO booklet with a small map, and the Ministry of Land Reform has a scale 1:50,000 map of the Semyen Mountains National Park, cost E$1. *Omo National Park* and river valley are described in an ETO booklet that has a small map of the area. Mobil Oil and the ETO publish a large annotated map of *Awash National Park,* scale 1:100,000 (cost E50¢).

Books to Read

Bidder, Irmgard. *Lalibela: The Monolithic Churches of Ethiopia.* Cologne: M. Du Mont, 1958.

Gerster, Georg. *Churches in Rock: Early Christian Art of Ethiopia.* London: Phaidon Press, 1970.

Greenfield, Richard. *Ethiopia: A New Political History.* London: Pall Mall Press, 1965; New York: Praeger, 1965.

Jager, Otto A. *Antiquities of North Ethiopia: A Guide.* London: Kegan Paul, Trench, Trubner & Co., 1965.

Jones, A. A. M., and Monroe, Elizabeth. *A History of Ethiopia.* New York: Oxford University Press, 1965.

Last, Geoffrey, and Pankhurst, Richard. *A History of Ethiopia in Pictures.* New York and Addis Ababa: Oxford University Press, 1969.

Lord, Edith. *Queen of Sheba's Heirs.* Washington, D.C.: Acropolis Books, 1970.

Moorehead, Alan. *The Blue Nile.* New York: Harper & Row, 1962, 1971. Dell paperback.

Nicol, Clive W. *From the Roof of Africa.* New York: Knopf, 1972.

Nolen, Barbara. *Ethiopia.* New York: Franklin Watts, 1971.

Pankhurst, Richard. *Economic History of Ethiopia, 1800–1935.* Evanston, Ill.: Northwestern University Press, 1970. *An Introduction to the Economic History of Ethiopia from Early Times to 1800.* New York: International Publications Services, 1961.

Shell Ethiopia. *Shell Guide to Ethiopian Birds. Shell Guide to the Wildlife of Ethiopia.* Both available from ETO.

Ullendorff, Edward. *The Ethiopians: An Introduction to Country and People.* 2d ed. New York and London: Oxford University Press, 1965.

University Press of Africa. *Ethiopia: The Official Handbook.* Nairobi: University Press of Africa, 1969.

Wolde-Mariam, Mesfin. *An Introductory Geography of Ethiopia.* Addis Ababa: Berhanena Selam H.S.I. Press, 1972.

Newspapers

The English language daily is the *Ethiopian Herald,* a six- or eight-page, full-size paper with foreign and local news. It is published by the Ministry of Information, Box 1074, Addis Ababa, and costs E10¢. There are also dailies printed in Amharic, Italian, and French.

Other Sources of Information

The *Ministry of Information,* Box 1020, Addis Ababa, publishes booklets on Ethiopia, such as *Facts and Figures* (latest edition, 1960). Their quarterly magazine is called *Ethiopian Mirror.* The *Ethiopian Chamber of Commerce,* Mexico Square, Box 517, Addis Ababa, publishes *Trade Directory and Guide Book to Ethiopia,* cost E$6, available at bookstores. *Executive Promotions,* H.S.I. Square, Box 2691, Addis Ababa, publishes *What's Best?,* a bimonthly, free little guide with some addresses and useful information.

Entry Requirements

Immigration

American citizens and citizens of all other countries entering Ethiopia on tourist or business visas are required to have their passport; a visa; a ticket to leave; a vaccination certificate for smallpox and cholera, and for yellow fever if coming from an infected area. For those in transit for a flight from the same airport within 24 hours, no visa is required.

Visas may be obtained on arrival at Addis Ababa or Asmara airports, with all the proper documents listed above, for E$10 (US$5); no photos are required. Otherwise, to obtain a visa before arrival in Ethiopia go to the nearest Ethiopian diplomatic mission (see list below), submit your passport, two copies of the application, two photos, yellow WHO card, and US$5. The New York visa office processes visas in about 24 hours. Visas are usually valid for one year from issue for a three-month stay. If you stay longer than 30 days, however, you must register with the Immigration Office and get an identity card, which requires two photos and E$15. Exit visas are issued automatically for visitors who stay in Ethiopia less than 30 days. But if you have stayed longer, you must surrender your identity card to Immigration before being issued your exit visa.

Diplomatic Missions of Ethiopia

Great Britain—Embassy, 17 Princes Gate, London SW7. *Kenya*— Embassy, State House Ave., Box 45198, Nairobi, tel. 23941. *Somalia* —Via Benedetti, Box 455, Mogadishu. *Sudan*—Block 11A, St. No. 3 New Extension, Box 844, Khartoum. *U.N.*—866 United Nations Plaza, New York 10017, tel. (212) 421-1830. *USA*—Embassy, 2134 Kalorama Road, Washington, D.C. 20008, tel. (202) 234-2281; Consulate General, 465 California, Calif. 94104, tel. (415) 397-2222. *West Germany*—Embassy, Brentano Strasse I, Bonn D53.

Ethiopia also has embassies or consulates in Aden, China, Czechoslovakia, Djibouti, Egypt, France, Ghana, Greece, Haiti, India, Israel, Italy, Ivory Coast, Japan, Jordan, Liberia, Mexico, Morocco, Nigeria, Saudi Arabia, Senegal, Sweden, Turkey, USSR, Vatican, Yemen, Yugoslavia, and Zaire.

Customs

Tourists may bring in, duty-free, their personal effects, including clothing, jewelry, toilet articles, and cameras intended for personal use; one liter (about one quart) of alcoholic beverage; 100 cigarettes, 50 cigars, or 250 grams of tobacco.

Currency Control

Tourists may import any amount of traveler's checks and foreign currency, though they may export no more foreign currency than they imported. A maximum of E$100 may be imported or exported by each visitor.

Vehicle Documents

To drive a car into Ethiopia you need a certificate of ownership, but a Carnet de Passages en Douanes is not necessary. Your car may circulate for six months, but thereafter duty must be paid on it. However, if customs officials at the border think you may sell your car surreptitiously, they may require that you post a refundable bond to ensure that you export the car or that you don't sell the car without paying the high import duty.

Firearms

Visitors are allowed to import firearms (excluding automatic and self-loading weapons) and 120 rounds of ammunition per firearm. However, permission must first be obtained prior to import from the Public Security Department of the Ministry of the Interior, Mesfine Harrar St., Box 105, Addis Ababa, tel. 110855. There is a fee of E$22. All imported weapons and remaining ammunition must be exported.

Getting to Ethiopia

By Air

The Addis Ababa International Airport is served by Air France, Air India, Alitalia, British Airways (BOAC), Air Djibouti, Ethiopian Airlines (EAL), East African Airways (EAA), Lufthansa, El Al, Middle East Airlines (MEA), Egyptair, and Sudan Airways. Asmara is served by Alitalia, Air Djibouti, Yemen Airways, Egyptair, Ethiopian Airlines, Sudan Airways, Saudi Arabian Airlines.

From Europe to Addis Ababa: From London: BOAC 1Xwk, EAL 3Xwk. From Frankfurt: Lufthansa 1Xwk, EAL 1Xwk. From Paris: Air France 2Xwk, EAL 4Xwk. From Rome: Alitalia 2Xwk, EAL 6Xwk. From Athens: Lufthansa 1Xwk, Air France 1Xwk, EAL 6Xwk.

From Europe to Asmara: From Frankfurt: EAL 2Xwk. From Paris: EAL 4Xwk. From Rome: Alitalia 1Xwk, EAL 7Xwk. From Athens: EAL 5Xwk.

From other African countries to Addis Ababa: From Nairobi: EAA 4Xwk, EAL 4Xwk, Air France 1Xwk, Sudan Airways 1Xwk. From Dar es Salaam: EAL 2Xwk, Air France 1Xwk. From Entebbe: EAL 2Xwk. From Djibouti: Air Djibouti 2Xwk, EAL 2Xwk. From Khartoum: Sudan Airways 1Xwk, EAL 2Xwk, MEA 2Xwk. From Cairo:

MEA 2Xwk, EAL 2Xwk. From Seychelles: BOAC 1Xwk. There are also flights to Addis Ababa from Accra, Douala, Lagos, and Mogadishu.

From other African countries to Asmara: From Khartoum: Sudan Airways 2Xwk, EAL 3Xwk, MEA 1Xwk. From Djibouti: Air Djibouti 1Xwk, EAL 1Xwk. From Cairo: EAL 3Xwk. There are also flights to Asmara from Jeddah, Aden, Accra, and Lagos.

From elsewhere: There are flights to Addis from Peking, Shanghai, Bombay, Aden, Jeddah, and Tel Aviv.

Sample fares, one-way, economy/tourist class, valid for a year, to or from Addis Ababa and Asmara, are listed below (add 20% to get approximate early 1975 fares):

from/to Addis	U.S. dollars	Ethiopian dollars	other currency
Athens	335	697	Dr. 10,077
Blantyre	264	550	MK226
Dar es Salaam	191	397	T.shs. 1,368
Djibouti, TFAI	60	126	Dj.Fr. 10,800
Entebbe	171	356	U.shs. 1,226
Frankfurt	449	935	DM1,122
Khartoum	125	260	S£43.500
Lagos	346	721	Naira 229
London	457	953	£184
Lusaka	274	570	ZK398
Mogadishu	119	248	Som.shs. 746
Nairobi	119	248	K.shs. 855
New York	608–659	1,320–1,430	
—14/45-day excursion fare (round trip)	871–959	1,803–1,985	
Paris	449	935	FF2,078
Rome	401	836	Lire 223,800
from/to Asmara			
Rome	336	701	Lire 187,700

Airports

Addis Ababa International Airport, built in 1963 and extended twice since, is about 8 km south of the city and is the main airport in the country. The terminal has the Skyway Restaurant, bar, snack bar, Commercial Bank of Ethiopia, post and telegraph facilities, VIP lounge, and King Solomon's Mines—one of the best duty-free shops in the world that's open to both incoming and outgoing passengers (articles purchased will be held until you leave).

Ethiopian Airlines has a bus service to the town hotels, and the fare is E$2. Town offices, tel. 447000, or 116503, or 447444. Taxis usually charge E$5–7, but you can get the fare down if you bargain.

Asmara has the small Yohannes IV International Airport, about 7 km from town, with a snack bar, post office, Commercial Bank, and duty-free shop. Ethiopian Airlines bus service into town costs E$2 to any hotel. Town office, tel. 112166/7. Taxis should cost about E$5 into Asmara. Addis and Asmara airport embarkation tax—E$3 per person.

The smaller airports at places like Gondar, Lalibela, and Axum usually just have a small EAL office, a dirt or grass landing strip, and perhaps taxis.

By Train

The Franco-Ethiopian Railway has service between Djibouti (TFAI), Dire Dawa, and Addis Ababa. Express passenger trains leave Djibouti 3Xwk at about 8:45 P.M. and arrive in Dire Dawa early the next morning. About an hour later the train leaves Dire Dawa for Addis Ababa, arriving about 6 P.M. that evening.

Sample fare, 1-way, Djibouti–Addis Ababa: 1st class—E$66; 2d class—E$39.45; 3d class—E$15.80.

Inquiries: Compagnie du Chemin de Fer Franco-Ethiopian (CFE), Beyene Aba Sebsib St., Box 1051, Addis Ababa; tel. 447250.

By Car

The best road to Ethiopia is from Kenya, and this is still in the building process between Marsabit and Moyale. On the Ethiopian side of the border, the road between Moyale and Dilla is quite rough, though VW Beetles and other small cars make it through in one piece. At least four or five days should be allotted for a straight drive from Nairobi to Addis Ababa, but once the two-lane engineered dirt highway is completed in both Kenya and Ethiopia, the Nairobi to Addis Ababa drive should take three to four days.

From Sudan the best-traveled route is Khartoum–Gedaret–Metema–Gondar, though the roads in Sudan are frequently flooded during the rains. From TFAI the route is Djibouti–Dire Dawa–Addis Ababa, though the stretch between the TFAI border and Dire Awas is rough. Somalia and Ethiopia are not on the best of diplomatic terms, and travel between the two countries is not advised.

Gasoline: It's advisable to carry gasoline in southern Ethiopia, since that is the less developed area. Elsewhere, the major towns have gas.

Border posts on the main routes: from/to Kenya—Moyale. From/to Sudan—Nasir, Sudan/Gambela, Ethiopia; Gallabat, Sudan/Metema, Ethiopia; Kassala, Sudan/Tessenei, Ethiopia; Kerora. From/to TFAI: Djibouti/Dikhil, Ethiopia.

Getting around Ethiopia

Travel Agents

The following travel agencies in Ethiopia make hotel, transport, car-hire, and tour bookings:

In Addis Ababa: *Adulis Travel,* Papassinos Building on Ras Desta Damtew Ave., Box 2719, tel. 153150; cable ADULIS. *Sheba Travel Service,* opposite H.S.I. Stadium on Ras Desta Damtew Ave., Box 3422, tel. 443901; cable SHEBA TRAVEL.

See also the list of travel agency tour operators in both Addis Ababa and Asmara, p. 459. The American Express representative is ITCO Travel & Tourist Agency.

By Air

Ethiopian Airlines flies to an amazing 43 cities and towns within Ethiopia: Addis Ababa, Arba Minch, Asmara, Asosa, Assab, Axum, Baco, Bahar Dar, Beica, Bulchi, Debre Marcos, Debre Tabor, Dembidollo, Dessie, Dire Dawa, Finchaa, Gambela, Ghinner, Goba, Gode, Gondar, Gore, Hosana, Humera, Jimma, Kabri Dar, Kelafo, Lalibela, Maji, Makalle, Massawa, Masslo, Mendi, Metema, Mizan Teferi, Mota, Mui, Nejjo, Nekempt, Soddu, Tippi, Waca.

Sample services and tourist-class fares: Addis Ababa–Asmara—E\$122. Addis–Axum—E\$97. Addis–Bahar Dar—E\$52. Addis–Dire Dawa—E\$65. Addis–Gondar—E\$68. Addis–Lalibela—E\$63. Round-trip fares are double. Historic Route services: Addis Ababa–Bahar Dar–Gondar–Lalibela–Addis Ababa (daily)—E\$166. Addis–Bahar Dar–Gondar–Lalibela–Axum–Asmara–Addis (daily)—E\$170 (20-day excursion fare). Addis–Bahar Dar–Gondar–Lalibela–Axum–Asmara (daily)—E\$169. Asmara–Massawa–Asmara (5Xwk)—E\$28.

Airline Offices

Ethiopian Airlines has the following offices: Addis Airport, Box 1755, Addis Ababa, tel. 152222. Also city offices at H.S.I. Square,

Piazza, Ghion and Hilton hotels. Africa Hall. Asmara: 8 Fessehaye Kifle Ave., Box 222; tel. 111266. EAL has town offices also in Gondar, Dire Dawa, Assab, Massawa and Gore. EAL otherwise has small offices at the airstrips at which it lands in Ethiopia. Overseas offices, p. 448.

Other airlines with offices in Addis Ababa: *Air Djibouti,* 123 Wavel St., tel. 110177. *Alitalia,* Ras Desta Damtew Ave., tel. 154400. *British Airways (BOAC),* Tesfaye Kadjiela Building, Ras Desta Damtew Ave., tel. 445836. *East African Airways,* Tesfaye Kadjiela Building, Ras Desta Damtew Ave., tel. 443018. *Sudan Airways,* Mesfine Building, Ras Makonnen Ave., tel. 440900. *Pan American,* H.S.I. Theatre Building, Churchill Road, tel. 444288. Others with offices in Addis Ababa are Air France, Air India, Egyptair, El Al, Lufthansa, KLM, SAS, and Swissair.

Airlines with offices in Asmara are Air France, Alitalia, Egyptair, and Saudi Arabian Airlines.

By Air Charter

The two firms with planes for hire in Ethiopia: *Aircraft Co. of Ethiopia,* Yohannes IV International Airport, Box 1051, Asmara, tel. 114447; and Ras Abebe Aregay St., Box 3448, Addis Ababa, tel. 445927. *Axum Air,* H.S.I. International Airport, Box 159, Addis Ababa, tel. 446453.

Their planes for hire include Piper PA–28 single-engine (seats 3, costs E60¢ per km), Cessna 185 single (seats 5, costs E80¢ per km), Piper PA-32 single (seats 5–6, costs E80¢ per km), Cessna T207 single (seats 6, costs E90¢ per km), Aero Commander 680E twin (seats 6, costs E$1.10 per km), Piper Aztec "C" twin (seats 5, costs E$1.10 per km), Piper PA–23 twin (seats 5, costs E$1.20 per km), and Dronier Skyservant twin (seats 10, costs E$1.70 per km).

Sample round-trip fares from Addis Ababa by Cessna 185: to Awash National Park—E$230.40; to Gambela—E$742.40; to Lalibela —E$524.80.

By Train

Northern Ethiopia Railways usually operates trains between Massawa–Asmara–Keren–Agordat. Trains leave Massawa early in the morning and arrive in Asmara about noon. There is only one class of seats, and the fare is about E$3 Massawa–Asmara. Inquiries: Box 218, Asmara.

Franco-Ethiopian Railways operates within Ethiopia between Dire Dawa–Awash–Addis Ababa. Trains leave Dire Dawa daily (except Saturday) for Awash and Addis Ababa in early morning or late evening; they leave Addis Ababa daily (except Tuesday) for Awash and Dire Dawa mornings or evenings. Either way the through ride is about 10 hours. Fares, one-way, Dire Dawa–Addis Ababa: 1st class—E$40.85; 2d class—E$24.35; 3d class—E$9.80. Inquiries: see p. 454.

By Bus

General Ethiopian Transport has buses traveling all over the country from Addis Ababa. At night buses stop in towns, where passengers stay in cheap local hotels at their own expense.

Going east: Addis Ababa–Debre Zeit–Nazareth–Awash–Dire Dawa–Harrar; through-ride takes a day, costs E$10.50. Going northwest: Addis Ababa–Debre Marcos–Bahar Dar–Gondar; through-trip about 1½ days, costs E$15. Going northeast: Addis Ababa–Debre Berhan–Dessie–Makalle–Asmara; through-trip 3 days, costs E$20. Going south: Addis Ababa–Debre Zeit–Awassa–Dilla; through-trip about 1 day, costs E$8. From Dilla there is supposed to be a 1Xwk Land-Rover service to Moyale on the Kenya border, a 2–3-day trip that costs about E$25, if and when it's running.

Inquiries: *General Ethiopian Transport,* Ras Abebe Aregay Ave., Box 472, Addis Ababa, tel. 448340. The main bus station in Addis Ababa is in the Mercato or New Market area, near Prince Makonnen High School. In Asmara it's on Menelik Road.

By Rent-a-Car

Rent-a-cars are not cheap in Ethiopia. For one day, 100 km, a VW Beetle costs an average of US$12.70 in Nairobi, US$18.20 in Addis Ababa. The Fiat 124 is comparatively less expensive—US$17.90 in Addis Ababa versus US$14.13 in Nairobi.

Following is a list of the most available car models, with the price range for one day, 100 km, in Ethiopian dollars, then the car-hire firms renting that car in order of relative expense.

Fiat 850—E$20 to E$38 (Lion Travel, ITCO, NTTA, Lion of Judah, Axum Travel, Avis). *Fiat 124*—E$28 to E$45 (Ras, Lion Travel, Axum Travel, ITCO, Lion of Judah, NTTA, GEITA, Avis, Forship). *VW Beetle*—E$31 to E$45 (NTTA, Lion of Judah, Axum Travel, GEITA, ITCO, Lion Travel, Avis, ETTC, Forship, Hertz). *Peugeot 404*—E$36 to E$55 (Ras, Lion of Judah, GEITA, NTTA,

Lion Travel, Axum Travel, Avis, Forship, Hertz). *Mercedes 200—* E$50 to E$67.50 (Lion Travel, Ras, GEITA, ETTC, ITCO, Hertz). *VW Minibus—*E$60 to E$87.50 (ETTC, Lion Travel, GEITA, Hertz, Forship, Ras). *Land-Rover 109—*E$75 to E$90 (ETTC, Avis, Forship, Ras, Axum Travel).

Other models for hire in Addis Ababa are Fiat 125 and 127, Renault 6–12, R6, and R16, Opel Kadett and Rekord, Peugeot 304, 504, and 404 wagon, Ford Taunus, Mercedes 250, Land-Rover 88, and Toyota Land Cruiser. Fewer models are available in Asmara and rates are higher.

Rent-a-cars are insured automatically, but the driver must pay the first E$150 to E$250 in case of accident damage claim. However, full collision protection is available for E$2.50 to E$5 extra per day.

Car-hire firms pay for oil and other running costs but only Hertz and Forship include gasoline for self-drive.

Car-hire firms in Ethiopia are listed below in alphabetical order. Addresses not given here can be found under "Tour Operators and Package Tours," p. 459.

ADDIS ABABA

*Avis—*Eastern Travel & Tourist Agency (ETTA). *Axum Travel Agency. Ethiopian Tourist Trading Co. (ETTC),* Maskal Square, Box 5640, tel. 448967. *Forship Travel Agency. General Ethiopian International Travel Agency (GEITA). Hertz—*United Touring Co. (UTC). *ITCO Tourist & Travel Agency. Lion of Judah Tour Agency. Lion Travel & Tourist Agency. National Tourist & Travel Agency (NTTA). Ras Rent A Super Car,* Varnero Building, Ras Makonnen Ave., Box 2180, tel. 555150.

ASMARA

Angelo Bandini, H.S.I. Ave. No. 7, tel. 110531. *Pietro Manera,* Tafari Yazew St. No. 29, tel. 112841. *Teaghes Ghebrewold Car Hire,* Tegulet St. No. 5, tel. 113737. *Ufficio Viaggi.*

Credit card acceptance: Avis (ETTA)—AE, DC, Avis. Hertz (UTC) —AE, DC, Hertz. ITCO—AE. Pietro Manera—AE. Ufficio Viaggi— AE, DC.

Driving in Ethiopia

Drive on the right, overtake on the left, just like in the U.S. Most cars sold and driven in Ethiopia are left-hand drive. Speed limits:

40 kph in towns and cities, 60 kph on highways, 30 kph in game parks.

Roads in Ethiopia vary from good pavement in and around the cities and larger towns, to two-lane engineered dirt on the main Addis Ababa–Asmara highways via Gondar and Dessie, to extremely rough tracks around some of the game parks and in other remote areas. To quote an ETO brochure on the Omo region, "Such roads as exist are primitive tracks, ranging in difficulty from unlikely to unbelievable." So unless you are really prepared with a four-wheel-drive vehicle, spare parts, and lots of food, water, and gas, it's best to stay on the main roads, or use a tour or safari operator, or hire mules or horses.

Vehicle servicing, repairs, spare parts: Addis Ababa and Asmara have several car dealers, servicing agents, and garages that can work on most makes, including the following: *Land-Rover and Fiat* (Mitchell Cotts & Co., Dejatch Wolde Michael St., Box 527, Addis Ababa; tel. 447160; also Dire Dawa, Gondar, Jimma, Massawa, Bahar Dar); *Toyota, GMC, Oldsmobile, Pontiac, Opel* (Moenco, Ras Abebe Aregay Ave., Box 1767, Addis Ababa; tel. 151300; also Asmara); *Volkswagen, Audi* (Seferian & Co., Mexico Square, Box 64, Addis Ababa; tel. 448100; also Asmara); *Chevrolet, Peugeot* (Paul Ries & Sons [E] Ltd., Wavel St., Box 3659, Addis Ababa; tel. 110233; also Asmara, Dire Dawa, Dessie); *Ford* (Amropa Motors Ltd., King George VI St., Box 263, Addis Ababa; tel. 110833). There are also agents for BMW, Mercedes, Renault, and less-known makes.

Auto club: Automobile Club Eritrea, Via Liusno De Jacobnis N-4-6-8, P.O. Box 1187, Asmara.

Tour Operators and Package Tours

There is a surprising number of all-inclusive package tours around Ethiopia, mostly starting from Addis Ababa, some from Asmara. A dozen tour operators offer 65 different itineraries (some differ only slightly). With the listing below, you and a travel agent can put together an interesting tour all around Ethiopia, which you can hardly get by purchasing a package starting in New York. Make your bookings as far in advance as possible.

Ethiopia tour operators, all in Addis Ababa except for one in Asmara, are as follows: *Adulis Travels,* Papassinos Building, Ras Desta Damtew Ave., Box 2719, tel. 153150. *At-Your-Service* (*Ethiopian Tourist Trading Co.—ETTC*), Maskal Square, Box 5640, tel. 448967. *Axum Air Service,* H.S.I. Airport, Box 159, tel. 446453; cable AXAIR.

Axum Travel Agency (*ATA*), Lion Insurance Building, Ras Desta Damtew Ave., Box 636, tel. 447831; cable AXTRA. *Eastern Travel & Tourist Agency* (*ETTA*), Kidane Beyene Building, Ras Desta Damtew Ave., Box 1136, tel. 444594; cable ETTA. *Forship Travel Agency,* H.S.I. Ave. (opposite International Hotel), Box 957, tel. 111493; cable FORSHIP. *General Ethiopian International Travel Agency* (*GEITA*), Geita Travel Agency, Empress Zawditu Building, Box 974, tel. 119100; cable GEITA. *ITCO Tourist & Travel Agency,* Eresco Building, Churchill Road near railway station, Box 1048, tel. 444334; cable INTRA. *Lion of Judah Tour Agency,* Getahun Berhe Building, Ras Makonnen St., Box 2465, tel. 153883. *Lion Travel & Tourist Agency,* Piazza (Gen. de Gaulle Square), Box 1294, tel. 112243; cable LITRA. *National Tourist & Travel Agency* (*NTTA*), Maskal Square, Box 1944, tel. 448717; cable NTTA. *United Touring Co.* (*UTC*), Afsol Building, Churchill Road, Box 3092, tel. 151122; cable OVERTOURCO.

In Asmara: *Ufficio Viaggi,* 20–22 Gennet Heroes St., Box 877, tel. 110659. *ETTA* has an office at 39 Haile Selassie Ave., tel. 114648.

Credit card acceptance: Adulis—DC. ETTA—AE, DC. ITCO—AE. UTC—AE, DC. Ufficio Viaggi—AE, DC.

Below is a list of most of the packages available, with prices in Ethiopian dollars (divide by 2 to get the U.S. dollar equivalent). "Seat in car" (abbreviated SIC) tours are the least expensive, but are offered to popular destinations only. Tour operators offer other tours on different bases. A per-person price with the notation "minimum 2" doesn't necessarily mean the same as a private-car (abbreviated PC) tour. Note: Lalibela is closed July, August, and September to Ethiopian Airlines flights, but air charter (e.g., Axum Air) can still fly in. Axum is also subject to weather closing.

Tours below begin in Addis Ababa and return there and all are by road, unless otherwise specified. The second, shorter part of the list includes Asmara tours.

FROM ADDIS ABABA

EP-1: *Addis Ababa City Tours.* There are several different tours offered in this category: half-day tour of modern Addis, half-day of historic Addis, full-day tour of both parts, and half-day tours with no modern or historic orientation. Historic and modern tours (UTC,

ITCO, Axum Travel, and Lion Travel) cost E$12.50 to E$14 SIC; E$20 to E$25 each of 2 in PC. The other operators offer morning and afternoon tours at the same prices. Full-day tours (UTC, NTTA, ITCO, Axum Travel, GEITA, ETTA, Lion of Judah, Forship, Lion Travel, and Ufficio Viaggi) cost E$22 to E$28 SIC; E$34.50 to E$50 each of 2 in PC, but may not include lunch.

EP-2: *Addis Ababa Shopping Tour*. 3 hours to Empress Menen Handicraft School, Mercato, jewelry and antique shops: E$16 SIC; E$28 each of 2 PC (ITCO).

EP-3: *Addis Ababa Religious Places Tour*. 3 hours to Trinity Cathedral, St. Mary Church, St. George Cathedral, Grand Mosque: E$16 SIC; E$28.50 each of 2 PC (ITCO).

EP-4: *Addis Ababa by Night:* 3–5 hours, including dinner, drive up to Entoto Ridge, nightclub visit—and for groups, a folkloric show by arrangement: E$25 to E$46 per person (min. 2); E$33 to E$42 each of 2 PC (NTTA, ITCO, GEITA, Lion of Judah, Forship, Lion Travel, Axum Travel).

EP-5: *Debre Zeit and Crater Lakes*. Half-day: E$28 to E$30 SIC; E$27 to E$50 each of 2 PC (UTC, NTTA, ITCO, Forship, Lion Travel, Axum Travel, GEITA, ETTA, Lion of Judah).

EP-6: *Debre Libanos Monastery and Blue Nile Gorge*. 1 day: E$75 to E$95 per person (min. 2); E$85 to E$185 each of 2 PC (Lion Travel, Forship, Lion of Judah, ETTC, GEITA, Axum Travel, ITCO, NTTA, UTC).

EP-7: *Sabata and Wollisso* (*Ghion*). 1 day: E$50 to E$62 per person (min. 2); E$54 to E$63 each of 2 PC (NTTA, ITCO, Lion of Judah, Ufficio Viaggi).

EP-8: *Ambo* (*Hagere Hiwot*). 1 day: E$46 to E$62 per person (min. 2), E$53 to E$72 each of 2 PC (Ufficio Viaggi, Lion of Judah, ETTA, ITCO, NTTA).

EP-9: *Debre Zeit, Crater Lakes, Koka Dam, Galila Palace Lunch, Hippo Pool, Wonji Sugar Estate, Nazareth*. 1 day: E$70 SIC; E$51 to E$65 per person (min. 2), E$65 to E$120 each of 2 PC.

EP-10: *Menagesha Forest*. Half-day: E$41 to E$65 each of 2 (ITCO, ETTA). 1 day: E$54 each of 2 PC (Lion of Judah).

EP-11: *Awash National Park*. 2 days: E$175 to E$225 each of 2 (Lion Travel, Lion of Judah, Axum Travel, ITCO, NTTA). 3 days: E$220 per person (min. 2) (ETTA).

EP-12: *Awash by Air*. 1 day: E$153 each of 2 (Axum Air). 2 days: E$145 per person (ETTA).

EP-13: *Rift Valley Lakes.* Usually overnight at Awassa on 2-day tours, and usually view Lakes Zwai, Abiata, Langano, Shalla, Awassa; 3-day tour goes to Lake Shamo and Arba Minch. 2 days: E$161 to E$175 per person (min. 2); E$164 to E$295 each of 2 PC (NTTA, ITCO, GEITA, ETTA, Axum Travel, Lion of Judah, Lion Travel). 3 days: E$450 each of 2 PC (ITCO).

EP-14: *Debre Zeit, Koka Dam, and Rift Valley Lakes.* 3 days: E$176 to E$230 per person (min. 2); E$263 to E$375 each of 2 PC (UTC, NTTA, Axum Travel, Lion of Judah, Forship, Lion Travel, Ufficio Viaggi).

EP-15: *Koka Dam, Rift Valley Lakes, and Awash National Park.* 4 days: E$499 each of 2–4; E$549 to E$624 each of 2 PC (Lion of Judah, NTTA).

EP-16: *Dire Dawa and Harrar by Air.* 2 days: E$60 to E$150 per person, plus air fare of E$130 (GEITA, ETTA, Lion of Judah, Forship, UTC, NTTA, ITCO, Axum Travel, Lion Travel). E$369 each of 2 on 1-day Axum Air charter tour.

EP-17: *Dire Dawa and Harrar by Train and Road* (*Return by Air to Addis Ababa*). 3 days: E$113 to E$213 per person (min. 2); E$164 to E$224 each of 2 PC, plus E$37 first-class train fare Addis Ababa–Dire Dawa and E$65 airfare Dire Dawa–Addis Ababa (Lion of Judah, Ufficio Viaggi, NTTA).

EP-18: *Awash National Park, Dire Dawa, and Harrar.* 3 days: E$375 per person (min. 3) (Lion Travel, Axum Travel). 3 days including air return to Addis Ababa: E$520 each of 2 PC (ITCO). 4 days: E$325 per person (min. 3) (GEITA). 5 days including air return to Addis: E$648 each of 2 PC (UTC). E$421 each of 2 on 2-day Axum Air charter tour.

EP-19: *Lake Shamo Nile Perch-Fishing Trip by Air.* 1 day: E$367 each of 2 (Axum Air).

EP-20: *Gambela, Baro River, Godere by Air Charter.* 2 days: E$720 each of 2 (Axum Air).

HISTORIC ROUTE TOURS (FROM/TO ADDIS ABABA UNLESS NOTED)

EP-21: *Bahar Dar by Air.* Day trip: E$75 per person, plus E$104 air fare (ITCO).

EP-22: *Gondar by Air.* Day trip: E$99 per person plus E$130 air fare (ITCO).

EP-23: *Lalibela by Air.* 2 days: E$50 to E$110 per person plus

E$136 air fare (UTC, ETTA, GEITA, ITCO, NTTA, Axum Travel, Lion of Judah, Forship, Lion Travel).

EP-24: *Bahar Dar and Gondar by Air*. 3 days: E$100 to E$225 per person, plus E$138 air fare (Lion of Judah, Forship, Lion Travel, Ufficio Viaggi, UTC, NTTA, ITCO, GEITA, Axum Travel). E$501 each of 2 on 2-day Axum Air charter tour.

EP-25: *Bahar Dar, Gondar, and Lalibela by Air*. 4 days: E$157 to E$220 per person plus E$168 air fare (UTC, Lion Travel, ITCO, GEITA).

EP-26: *Bahar Dar, Gondar, Lalibela, Axum, Asmara by Air*. 5 days, ending in Asmara: E$223 to E$314 per person plus E$169 air fare (Ufficio Viaggi, Lion Travel, Forship, Lion of Judah, ETTA, GEITA, Axum Travel, ITCO, NTTA, UTC).

EP-27: *Bahar Dar, Gondar, Axum, Asmara by Air*. 4 days, ending in Asmara: E$191 to E$210 per person plus E$139 air fare (ITCO, Axum Travel, Ufficio Viaggi).

EP-28: *Bahar Dar, Gondar, Lalibela, Makalle, Axum, Asmara by Air*. 7 days, ending Asmara: E$240 to E$375 per person plus E$126 air fare (Axum Travel, ITCO, GEITA, Lion Travel). If flown during wet season, skipping Lalibela, E$290 land cost.

EP-29: *Bahar Dar, Gondar, Axum, and Lalibela by Air Charter*. 2 days, returning to Addis Ababa: E$674 each of 2 (Axum Air).

EP-30: *Bahar Dar, Gondar, Axum, Asmara by Road*. 5 days, ending Asmara: E$850 to E$1,130 each of 2–3 PC (UTC, ITCO, Axum Travel, GEITA, Forship, Lion Travel).

EP-31: *Bahar Dar, Gondar, Axum, Asmara by Road plus Lalibela by Air*. 6 days, ending Asmara: E$930 to E$1,155 each of 2 PC plus E$60 each air fare (ITCO, Axum Travel, GEITA, Lion Travel). 7 days, ending Asmara: E$1,220 each of 2 PC plus E$60 each air fare (UTC). 10 days, ending Asmara: E$1,178 each of 2 PC plus E$60 each air fare (NTTA).

EP-32: *Tissisat Falls, Gondar, Lalibela by Air Charter*. Day trip: E$425 each of 2 (Axum Air).

EP-33: *Makalle, Desert Market, Dallol Depression, Axum, Lalibela by Air Charter*. 2 days: E$714 each of 2 (Axum Air). Desert market Monday–Tuesday only.

EP-34: *Lalibela and Makalle by Air Charter and Dallol Depression by Road*. 2 days, for those in good condition: E$782 each of 2 (Axum Air).

EP-35: *Desert Market and Lalibela by Air Charter.* Day trip: E$447 to E$475 each of 2 (UTC, Axum Air).

EP-36: *Scenic Route to Asmara: Debre Berhan, Debre Sina, Dessie, Lake Haik, Lake Ashange, Makalle, Wokro, Adowa, Axum, Asmara.* 4 days: E$1,299 each of 2–4 (NTTA).

EP-37: *Grand Tour of Ethiopia by Road: Addis City Tour, Debre Zeit, Rift Valley Lakes, Awash Park, Dire Dawa, Harrar, Addis, Bahar Dar, Gondar, Lalibela (by air), Axum, Adowa, Yeha, Asmara, Massawa, Asmara.* 18–19 days, ending Asmara: E$2,755 each of 2 PC (NTTA), E$2,089 each of 2 PC (Lion of Judah).

FROM ASMARA

Historic Route tours ending in Asmara are also run the other way, ending in Addis Ababa, at similar prices; see above. All trips listed below are by road unless otherwise specified.

EP-38: *Asmara City Tour.* 3 hours: E$8.80 to E$16 (Ufficio Viaggi, UTC, ITCO, GEITA, ETTA, Axum Travel, Forship, Lion Travel).

EP-39: *Massawa and Red Sea.* Day trip: E$50 to E$144 per person (min. 2); E$68 to E$95 each of 2 PC (Ufficio Viaggi, UTC, ITCO, GEITA, ETTA, Forship, Lion Travel, Axum Travel).

EP-40: *Keren.* Day trip: E$46 per person (min. 2), E$55 each of 2 PC (Ufficio Viaggi).

EP-41: *Cohaito, Senafe, Baraknaha, Matara, Yeha, Adowa, Axum.* 3 days. Overnight 1st night at Bisserat Berhe Inn, not the most comfortable. E$220 each of 2 PC (Ufficio Viaggi).

EP-42: *Axum.* Day trip: E$81 per person (min. 2), E$99 each of 2 PC (Ufficio Viaggi).

General Information

Language

There are scores of complex languages and dialects spoken in Ethiopia, but the official language is Amharic. English, French, and Italian are also spoken by many people in Addis Ababa and Asmara, and in the bigger towns. Amharic does not use the Roman alphabet; thus words and place names may have different spellings (e.g. Dilla, Dila) because transliteration methods differ. To pronounce the transliterated Amharic words listed below, use this key:

> *a*   as the *a*   in father
> *e*   as the *e*   in set
> *i*   as the *i*   in ship
> *o*   as the *o*   in hot
> *u*   as the *oo* in boot
> *gn* as the *gn* in campagne (French) or
>   *ñ* in señor (Spanish)

English	*Amharic*
hello	tenayistilligne
how are you?	tenayistillign?
fine (or it is good)	tiru no
thank you	ameseghinallehu
you're welcome (all right)	menemaydel
please	ebako
please bring me . . .	ibakeh ametaligne . . .
I want . . .	efelegalehu . . .
food	migib
coffee	bunna
tea	shay
water	wuha
beer	bira
milk	wetet
bread	dabbo
meat	siga
fish	asa
salt	chew
sugar	sequar
hot/cold	muk/kezekaza
big/small	tillik/tinnish
yes/no	awon/aydellem
slowly (do it slowly)	kess yikelu
quickly (please speed up)	befetenet
where is . . .	yetenew . . .
a hotel?	hotelu yetenew?
a telephone?	selek yetenew?
a garage?	gargeu yetenew?
a druggist (chemist)?	medhanit bet yetanew?
the American Embassy?	ye American Embassy yetenew?
a police station?	polic tabia yetenew?

the bus station?	yawtobus tabia yetenew?
the market?	gebeya yetenew?
a toilet?	shint beit yetenew?
how much? (what is the price?)	wagaw sent no?
I don't understand	alegebagnme
left/right	gera/kegne
one	and
two	hulet
three	sost
four	arat
five	amest
six	seddest
seven	sebat
eight	semmint
nine	zetegn
ten	asser
eleven	asra-and
fifty	amsa
hundred	meto
two hundred	hulet meto
Mr.	Ato
Mrs.	Woizero
Miss	Woizerit

A man takes his father's Christian name as his surname but is known by his own Christian name; e.g., Makonnen Asfaw is addressed Ato Makonnen. Women do not change their names after marriage. They also are addressed as Woizero (or Woizerit) plus their first name.

Time

G.M.T. plus 3 hours (see Kenya, p. 126).

Weights and Measures

Ethiopia uses the metric system.

Electricity

200 volts, 60-cycle A.C.

Ethiopian Calendar

Ethiopia follows its own calendar, rather than the Western Gregorian one, and the dates are now running seven years and eight months behind the West. So New Year's Day 1975 in the West is dated September 11, 1967, in Ethiopia. Furthermore, when Ethiopians boast that they have "13 months of sunshine," they are correct, at least as far as the 13 months go. Their calendar is divided into 12 months with 30 days in each, plus a thirteenth month with the 5 leftover days (or 6 in leap year). Their year begins on what is our September 11, and their months are all named differently—such as Maggabit (March 10–April 8). Businesses in Addis Ababa and Asmara use both the Ethiopian and the Gregorian calendars in their correspondence, as do the English-language newspapers.

Holidays

Ethiopian religious holidays are times of great feasting, dancing, and pageantry, especially those of Timkat and Maskal. While there are scores of saint's days, the main holidays that come on fixed dates in the Gregorian (Western) calendar are: Jan. 7—Christmas Day. Jan. 19—Timkat (Feast of the Epiphany). Jan. 20—Feast of St. Michael the Archangel. Feb. 19—Martyrs' Day (in 1937 thousands of Ethiopians were killed in Addis Ababa after an attempted assassination of the Italian viceroy failed). March 2—Commemoration of the Battle of Adowa (1896 victory against Italian invasion). Good Friday. Easter Sunday. Easter Monday. May 5—Liberation Day (1941 return of Emperor Haile Selassie to Addis Ababa after expulsion of Italians). Aug. 22—Feast of the Assumption. Sept. 11—New Year's Day; also return of Eritrea (1952); also Feast of St. John the Baptist. Sept. 27—Maskal (Feast of Finding of the True Cross). The new regime may replace those holidays that honored Haile Selassie (July 23 and November 2).

Hours of Business

Shops are generally open 9 A.M. to 1 P.M., 3 P.M. to 7:30 P.M., daily except Sunday, though in Asmara they may stay open until 8 or 8:30 P.M. Government and business office hours are usually 9 A.M. to 1 P.M., 3 to 6 P.M. Monday to Friday; 9 A.M. to 12 noon Saturday.

Banks are open 9 A.M. to 12:30 P.M., 3 to 4:30 P.M. Monday through Friday.

Banks

The largest is the *Commercial Bank of Ethiopia S.C.*, main branch at H.S.I. Square, Box 255, Addis Ababa; tel. 115500. Also H.S.I. Ave., Box 219, Asmara; tel. 111844. CBE has branches in most towns throughout Ethiopia. *Addis Ababa Bank S.C.*, Ras Desta Damtew Ave., Box 751, Addis Ababa; tel. 448285. Also L. Tazaz St., Box 245, Asmara; tel. 113233. *Banco di Roma Ethiopia S.C.*, Wavel St., Box 1642, Addis Ababa; tel. 110366. And Itegue Menen Ave., Box 228, Asmara; tel. 110629.

Diplomatic Representatives in Ethiopia

All the following have embassy offices in Addis Ababa, with Asmara offices as indicated: *Canada*—African Solidarity Insurance Building, H.S.I. Square, Box 1130, tel. 448335. *Egypt*—Near Yekatit 12 Square, Box 1611, tel. 113077. *France* (for TFAI)—Kabanna District, Box 1464, tel. 110066. *Great Britain*—Fikre Mariam Aba Techan St., Box 858, tel. 113055. *Kenya*—Fikre Mariam Aba Techan St., Box 3301, tel. 120033. *Malawi*—Ras Desta Damtew Ave., Box 2316, tel. 448295. *Somalia*—Africa Ave., Box 1006, tel. 443264. *Sudan*—Near Mexico Square, Box 1110, tel. 446946. *Tanzania*—Africa Ave., Box 1077, tel. 448155. *Uganda*—Africa Ave., Box 5644, tel. 153088. *USA* —Asfaw Wossen St., Box 1014, tel. 111066. 32 Franklin D. Roosevelt St., Asmara, tel. 110855. *West Germany*—Kabanna District, Box 660, tel. 110433. *Zambia*—Old Airport Zone, Box 1909, tel. 448015.

Other countries with diplomatic representation in Ethiopia: Argentina, Austria, Belgium, Bulgaria, Burundi, Cameroon, Colombia, China (People's Republic), Cyprus, Czechoslovakia, Egypt, Equatorial Guinea, Finland, France, Ghana, Greece, Guatemala, Guinea, Holy See, Hungary, India, Indonesia, Iran, Israel, Italy, Ivory Coast, Jamaica, Japan, Korea, Liberia, Malaysia, Malta, Mexico, Morocco, Netherlands, Nigeria, Poland, Rumania, Rwanda, Saudi Arabia, Senegal, Sierra Leone, Southern Yemen, Spain, Sweden, Switzerland, Thailand, Trinidad and Tobago, Tunisia, Turkey, USSR, Venezuela, Yemen, Yugoslavia, and Zaire.

Health

For a discussion of health, see Introduction, p. 55. Do not drink tap water in Ethiopia, and even go so far as not to use it to brush your teeth or as ice cubes. Instead, buy bottled mineral water (e.g.,

"Ambo"), which is bubbly but perfectly safe. Some clean but low-budget hotels are unfortunately afflicted with fleas. No big problem—just get the management to spray between your bed sheets.

The good hospitals are in Addis Ababa and Asmara, with smaller clinics elsewhere. The U.S. Embassy and Consulate have the names of Addis Ababa and Asmara doctors they recommend.

Mail, Telegrams

Airmail letters to the U.S. cost E90¢ for each half-ounce, an airmail postcard is E50¢, an aerogramme E65¢. Telegrams are handled by the post office.

The main post office (GPO) in Addis Ababa is on Churchill Road near H.S.I. Square in the tall office building. Hours in Ethiopia: 8:30 A.M. to 7 P.M. Monday–Friday, 8 A.M. to 1 P.M. Saturday. There is a Poste Restante service, and mail should be addressed to you c/o Poste Restante, Main Post Office, Addis Ababa, or wherever.

Telephone Calls

For a strictly local call from an ordinary phone, dial as you would in the U.S. From a coin phone, see directions for Kenya, p. 129. Pay phones use E10¢ for local calls. An international call to the U.S. is E$30 for the first three minutes, and calls must be booked beforehand through the operator.

If using the phone directory, the name to check under is what is apparently (but not really) the person's first name; i.e., Mr. (Ato) Makonnen Asfaw is listed under M. Similarly a European might be listed under what is actually his first name.

Emergency numbers in Addis Ababa: fire—112222 or 111331; police—91; ambulance—112446 or 111882; inquiries—97; wake-up call—99.

Emergency numbers in Asmara: fire—111288; police—112811 or 113505; ambulance—111933; inquiries—97; wake-up call—99.

Shopping

Ethiopia has a multitude of indigenous handicrafts and arts that are both religious and secular. If you plan to go on the Historic Route or otherwise tour the country, buy items en route in their specialty area where the prices are usually better than in Addis Ababa. However, the large Mercato or New Market, covering acres in northwest Addis Ababa, has vast quantities of just about any Ethiopian item you might desire: Wednesday and Saturday are traditional market days when there's the most activity. The Mercato's small indoor and outdoor stalls have baskets full of old and new silver neck crosses, walls lined with rugs, paintings by the dozen. Bargaining, a lost art in the U.S., is the rule of the day. When shopping in Ethiopia, after you inspect and admire something, ask the price, then exclaim and say you'll pay the equivalent of 15 to 20 percent of that, and work up from there to reach a mutually satisfactory price. If you're still not happy, walk away and usually the price will drop closer to your level. In the fancier shops in Addis Ababa and Asmara the prices are generally set.

Besides the Mercato in Addis Ababa, we suggest you try these shops: *Tresors D'Ethiopie,* Ras Desta Damtew Ave. by the Ghion Hotel. *Ethiopian Souvenirs Sales Center,* by the ETO office off Maskal Square. *Empress Menen Handicraft School,* Ras Abebe Aregay St. across from Ghion Hotel; where you can watch Ethiopians weaving rugs, etc. *Prester John's,* Hilton Hotel lobby. *Ethio Crafts* and *ECA Shop,* both in All Africa Hall, Menelik II Ave. *Ethiopian Ceramic Workshop,* Africa Ave.; where young potters are learning new and improving old techniques.

In Asmara there is a colorful central market off Ethiopia Square between H.S.I. Ave. and Menelik II Ave., where everything from spices to crafts is sold; it's best on Saturday. These shops on H.S.I. Ave. also have Ethiopian items: *Novis di Alberto Frezza, Giocattoli Peleteria,* and *Girmai Goldsmith.*

In Axum there is nearly a score of tiny shops selling crafts and religious relics, but the very best is the one on the far right across from the Touring Hotel called the *Ethiopian Ancient Hand Craft Shop.* There is also the *Axum Garment Industry* on a side street (ask directions at the hotel), where beautifully handmade cotton clothes are made, and you can watch people spin, weave, and sew. Harrar, Gondar, and other towns also have lively Saturday markets. The big market in Makalle is Monday.

Below are descriptions of some of the indigenous items that may be found in Ethiopia.

Neck and hand crosses. It has been said that after the conflict between Islam and Ethiopian Christianity started in the 6th century A.D., an Ethiopian emperor issued an edict stating that all his subjects should wear a cross to prove their faith. In any case, there seem to be hundreds of thousands of silver neck crosses worn in Ethiopia today, and their shapes and styles vary according to the region or town of manufacture. Today new crosses are still made, but their workmanship lacks the quality of the old crosses. To recognize an old cross (which will eventually become more rare), check the edges, back, and front to see if they look really smooth and worn; then examine the circular loop, which should be noticeably worn thin from years of use on a chain or string. Pay E$2 to E$6 for old crosses (the heavier the more expensive), less for new crosses. Also used in the Ethiopian churches are wood, brass, and other metal hand crosses that vary from simple to elaborate in their design and symbolism; prices range from E$10 to E$50. Shop for crosses in Axum, Lalibela, Asmara, and Addis Ababa.

Painting has been an integral part of Ethiopian religious life, though secular art has also flourished to a lesser degree. (Church paintings can usually be photographed, using a flash, fast ASA film, and/or a tripod.) Old Bibles handwritten in Ge'ez, the ancient liturgical language, and illustrated with pictures, and old goatskin scrolls, can be bought for E$3 to E$150, as can tiny triptychs, which fold out to show saints inside. More readily available are oil reproductions of the popular historical themes, such as the legend of Solomon and Sheba, or the Battle of Adowa, which in Addis Ababa start at about E$10 for a 2-by-4-foot oil painting done in the comic-strip style.

Wood carving is traditionally done in the forest country of Kaffa Province in the southwest, though it has also been done in other provinces as well. Items carved for centuries include the *jimma,* a three-legged squat stool carved in one piece from the *sholla* tree; the *inchet tiras,* a wooden stool or headrest; plus a multitude of other household utensils including cowbells, combs, coffee urns, and prayer beads. Statues of people and wooden masks are also carved today, but they are not as common as in Kenya and Tanzania.

Baskets are woven all over Ethiopia, though the most famous center is Harrar. The workmanship is very fine and the patterns quite complicated, so basketry is more expensive in Ethiopia than elsewhere. The largest piece is the *messob,* the round, covered, table-size basket upon which the national food and drink—*njera, wat,* and *tej* (see p. 65—are served; the large version of the *messob* is about E$150, though as the size gets smaller so does the price. Other baskets are made for storing food, for picnics, and for hotpads; these are usually under E$10 each.

Rugs are woven of wool and cotton in geometric patterns, often with a lion motif, especially in Dessie Province north of Addis Ababa.

Small squares, about 1½ by 1½ feet, good for a child's room or to hang on the wall, cost about E$1.50 to E$3 each, though if washed the colors may run. More plush rugs are woven at the Empress Menen Handicraft School in Addis Ababa, where six to eight women may work for four months to make beautiful, colorful, large, expensive rugs.

Pottery is another old craft dating back to pre-Axumite civilizations. The potter's wheel was only recently introduced into Ethiopia, so most of the work done was all by bare hands. Utilitarian pots used for cooking or storing liquids and foods are made in several places: Addis Alem, about 46 km west of Addis Ababa; Wollamo and Kambata, both south of Addis Ababa; and the Sambo Tree Monastery, in northeastern Ethiopia. The Falasha, a people near Gondar who practice an ancient form of Judaism, are the only Ethiopian craftsmen who traditionally fashion human and animal statuettes; they are very stylized but fascinating, and some have the Star of David incorporated in them; in Gondar they sell for about E$1 to E$5 per piece. One problem with all Ethiopian pottery is its fragility. Because the pots and pieces are fired mostly over relatively coolish, open wood fires, they tend to crack and crumble very easily, so are difficult to transport.

Musical instruments are used for both religious and secular gatherings and festivities. The *krar,* a lyre-type, five- or six-stringed instrument with a round wooden or tin base covered with calfskin or sheepskin, sounds like a guitar and is often played by women. The secular *masenk'o* has one horsehair string, a diamond-shaped sound box covered with skin, is played with a bow, and is associated with the *azmari* or troubadour. In the churches are used the *ts'nats'el* or sistrum, which has a brass frame mounted on a wooden handle, and from which metal disks slide on wires to produce a jingling sound (like a tambourine) when shaken; the *kabaro,* a tall slender drum, and the *dbi,* a type of kettledrum, both made of a hollowed tree section and covered with ox hide.

Wildlife and Game Parks

Ethiopia entered late into awareness of game conservation, when in 1963 it invited a UNESCO Mission headed by Sir Julian Huxley to analyze what should be done. The Mission recommended the establishment of a Wildlife Conservation Board and Department, which was done. The next year the Mission proposed a three-year plan for wild-

life in Ethiopia, including the establishment of three national parks—
Awash, Semyen, and Omo, two of which have since been gazetted,
while eight others are in the proposal or approval stages. This was
rather in the nick of time to protect several species unique to Ethiopia:
Walia ibex (a wild goat of which only about 150–200 exist, all in the
Semyen Mountains), mountain nyala, Gelada baboon, and the Semyen
fox.

Roughly speaking, the main areas of wildlife are in the western half
of the country, especially the Omo River (proposed national park)
and Gambela regions in the southwest, and the Semyen (Mountains)
National Park in the northwest. East of the main north–south mountain axis stretching down through Ethiopia, the wildlife is less plentiful, though in the east are Awash National Park and the proposed Bale
Mountain National Park. About 13 game reserves in various parts of
the country have been proposed (one established), including Gambela
Reserve and Harrar Elephant Sanctuary. A good booklet is the *Shell
Guide to the Wildlife of Ethiopia,* which describes all the rare species
plus others.

Birdlife is prolific, with approximately 830 species recorded so far
in the varied landscape, though many of the indigenous birds have
been little studied or described. The possibility of discovering new
species exists, especially in some of the remote forests. Ideal locales
for birdwatching are the Rift Valley lakes, where thousands of migratory birds join the resident species from November to March. The best
booklet describing 123 bird species, 13 native, is the *Shell Guide to
Ethiopian Birds.*

Game Park Entry Fees. Presently only Awash National Park and
Bale Mountain (proposed national park) have entry fees: adult—E$2;
child (5–12 years)—E$1.

Sports, Water Sports, Fishing

Addis Ababa and Asmara have tennis, golf, riding, bowling, and
pool swimming. There's water skiing through the hotel on the Rift
Valley's Lake Langano. Around the Red Sea port of Massawa you can
swim, skin-dive, and go deep-sea fishing. There's also fishing in the
Rift Valley lakes of Awassa, Abaya, and Shamo, and the trout-stocked
streams in the Bale Mountains. Riding and/or hiking are near-neces-
sities in order to see the Semyen and Bale mountains. Mountaineers
might try scaling 15,150-foot Ras Dashan in the Semyens or 12,782-
foot Batu and 14,208-foot Tullu Dimtu in the Bales.

Historic and Prehistoric Sites

Besides the more famous historic sites at Gondar, Lalibela, and Axum, there are interesting ruins at Yeha, Matara, Adulis, and Cohaito (Coloe), among other places. The Archaeological Institute of Ethiopia is conducting excavations at Matara and elsewhere. The Antiquities Department, Box 1907, Addis Ababa, is in charge of most of the larger historical sites, and collects admission fees through their local offices.

Prehistoric excavations have been and are being carried out in the Omo Valley, the Malka Contoure, the Errer Valley, and elsewhere, with more than 100 Stone Age sites yielding traces of early man. The National Museum in Addis Ababa has exhibits of historic and prehistoric finds in Ethiopia.

Hunting

Those interested in hunting in Ethiopia can write to the ETO or directly to these professional hunters: Lieutenant Getachew Tefera, Box 22476, Addis Ababa; George P. Myriallis, Box 1853, Addis Ababa; Thomas Mattanovitch, Box 2444, Addis Ababa; and Major Gezaw Gedele Giorgis, Box 1003, Addis Ababa. Nairobi safari operators can also outfit and escort you.

Addis Ababa

Addis Ababa is the largest city, the seat of national government, and the commercial and cultural center of Ethiopia. On the foothills of the encircling Entoto Mountains, Addis (as it's called for short) has a bustling population of more than 850,000 that spreads out over a vast area the size of Paris, with "old" Addis about 500 feet higher than 8,000-foot-altitude "new" Addis. There seems to be no city center (or city planning) per se, but rather about seven big traffic circles (called squares) with tall buildings and modern shops interspersed with low-level, tin-roofed shanties. Addis is truly a city of contrasts: imperial palaces versus hovels, two- to four-lane paved roads versus muddy dirt alleys, Cadillacs and Mercedes versus donkeys and goats, busy well-dressed Organization of African Unity (OAU) delegates and government officials versus beggars in the streets.

Founded in the early 1890s, Addis Ababa is only a decade older than Nairobi and Lusaka, though unlike them had more regal be-

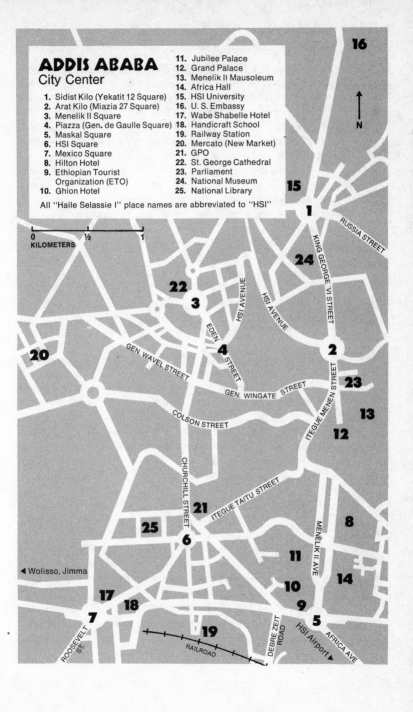

ADDIS ABABA
City Center

1. Sidist Kilo (Yekatit 12 Square)
2. Arat Kilo (Miazia 27 Square)
3. Menelik II Square
4. Piazza (Gen. de Gaulle Square)
5. Maskal Square
6. HSI Square
7. Mexico Square
8. Hilton Hotel
9. Ethiopian Tourist Organization (ETO)
10. Ghion Hotel
11. Jubilee Palace
12. Grand Palace
13. Menelik II Mausoleum
14. Africa Hall
15. HSI University
16. U. S. Embassy
17. Wabe Shabelle Hotel
18. Handicraft School
19. Railway Station
20. Mercato (New Market)
21. GPO
22. St. George Cathedral
23. Parliament
24. National Museum
25. National Library

All "Haile Selassie I" place names are abbreviated to "HSI"

0   ½   1
KILOMETERS

N

ginnings. In 1830 King Sahle Selassie of Shoa rode up into the Entoto hills and, surveying the beautiful view, said, "O land . . . one day my grandson will build here a house and make you a city. . . . In this place, my children and generations to follow will be crowned and will reign." Half a century later, in 1878, his grandson Menelik II built a palace and two churches high in the Entotos, while his wife, Empress Taitu, preferred the hot springs in the lower, warmer area called Filwoha, and there she built a house. Menelik II agreed with her choice and in 1892–94 built a palace, around which Addis Ababa ("new flower," as named by Empress Taitu) grew, spreading over the slopes, so that in just a few years thousands inhabited the new city.

By 1917 the railway from Djibouti reached Addis, and in 1929 the railway station house was finished. The next year was full of pomp and circumstance, as Haile Selassie was crowned emperor and the ceremonies attracted dignitaries from all over the world. In honor of this, streets were paved, police were dressed in uniforms, beggars were removed, and a fine equestrian statute of Menelik II was raised in a square named for him.

In 1936, just six years after his coronation, Haile Selassie had to make a hurried, unhappy exit from Addis in order to plead Ethiopia's cause before the League of Nations after Italy's invasion. On May 5, 1936, three days after the emperor's escape, the Italians moved in and occupied Addis Ababa as temporary conquerors. In February 1937, in an attempt to emulate the former emperors, the Italian viceroy made a show of distributing gifts to the poor outside one of the palaces. During this display, two Patriots, as the anti-Italian Ethiopians were called, threw several grenades in an attempted assassination of the viceroy. The Italian troops fired into the crowd, killing many old and poor plus some dignitaries. Then the Blackshirts were turned loose in Addis and proceeded to savagely kill thousands, burn and destroy homes and churches, smashing St. George Cathedral as one target. This is commemorated today as Martyrs' Day on February 16. On April 6, 1941, the Italian troops themselves fled from Addis and the British raised the Union Jack and then the emperor's standard. Haile Selassie ceremoniously and triumphantly returned to Addis Ababa exactly five years after he had been forced to flee, and on May 5, 1941, resumed his position as emperor.

Since World War II, Addis Ababa has grown up somewhat randomly near its squares and along its main arteries leading out to the provinces, and embassies from scores of countries ring its outskirts. In 1958 Addis was chosen as the headquarters of the U.N. Economic Commission for Africa (UNECA), and in 1963 as the headquarters of the Organization of African Unity (OAU), both of which bring visitors to the capital. Also in the past ten years Addis has started attracting tourists, usually on their way to or from East Africa. Addis offers a taste of Ethiopian history and culture with its palaces, museums, and restaurants, though after two days or so the traveler should also seek out other parts of the Hidden Empire to appreciate better its complexities and beauty.

Addis Ababa Driving Tour

Since Addis is so far-flung, it is best to have or hire a car, join a tour, or grab taxis to get between the distant points. Below is outlined a 15-km-long driving tour that leaves Maskal Square and goes up Menelik II Avenue and King George VI Street to H.S.I. University on Arat Kilo, over to St. George Cathedral, the Piazza and then the Mercato, down Churchill Road to H.S.I. Square, Mexico Square, and ends back at Maskal Square.

Leaving Maskal Square, where the ETO is headquartered, and where the airport road (Africa Road) ends and Menelik II Avenue begins, take the latter north uphill, passing *Stefanos Church* (R), a modern, cube-shaped, domed Ethiopian church with murals of the martyrdom of Stefanos inside. The road divides, and the center strip is planted with pines, grass, and flowers. *All Africa Hall* (R) is a seven-story structure built in 1963 for the first annual OAU meeting (conference hall seats 715) and to house the UNECA. Inside is a stunning stained glass window portraying Africa's past struggles, present freedoms, and future progress, designed by the Ethiopian artist Afewerk Tekle. The building is open Monday–Friday, 9 A.M. to 1 P.M., 2:30 to 6 P.M., Saturday 9 A.M. to 1 P.M.

Back on Menelik II Avenue, opposite All Africa Hall, are the grounds of *National Palace,* built in 1955 to commemorate the first 25 years of Emperor Haile Selassie's reign. The richly carved and decorated, spacious palace is in a parklike setting with its own private zoo, and used to be the official residence of the emperor. ETO can arrange tours for groups of ten or more, or you can join a tour that is going.

Continuing up Menelik II Avenue, you pass the *Addis Ababa Hilton* (R) and offices for the Ministry of Foreign Affairs and Ministry of Agriculture (both L). At the top of the divided avenue, the road changes to Itegue Menen (Itegue means "empress") Street and curves around the hill on which sit the Grand (Menelik II's) Palace, Menelik II Mausoleum, and Kidane Mihret and Gabriel churches. They are reached by a street turnoff (R) from Itegue Menen Street north of the hill. The *Grand Palace* of Menelik II was erected by him in 1892, though was recently relandscaped and remodeled with banquet and reception halls for grand entertaining. The *Mausoleum of Menelik II,* which has a church upstairs, was built in 1911 by Empress Zawditu, is of gray stone with a dome, and has four corners with cupolas, four entrances with two sculptured lions each, and three concentric walls. Valuable manuscripts, royal souvenirs, and historical objects are deposited in the vaults lining the mausoleum. Between the palace compound and mausoleum is *Kidane Mihret Church,* whose interior paintings depict Menelik II's family and his reign; to the south is Gabriel Church, another round Ethiopian holy sanctuary.

Now, on what has become King George VI Street, there is another immediate turnoff (R) that goes to Parliament and also Holy Trinity Cathedral. The *Parliament* building was completed in 1934, enlarged and redecorated in 1941 and again in 1948. At its gate are two golden Lions of Judah mounted on pillars, the front of the building has a mural of St. George slaying the dragon, and inside are the Chamber of Deputies, Senate Chamber, and Joint Assembly Hall. Visits can be made when Parliament is in session (Nov. 2 to June 30); contact the ETO. *Holy Trinity Cathedral,* set in expansive grounds at the end of the street, was built by Haile Selassie after his return to Addis in 1941. It has a large dome, tall ornate towers, stained glass windows with Biblical scenes, wood carvings on the ceiling, and mosaics. It is the crypt of the present dynasty. In the yard is the tomb of Sylvia Pankhurst, an English author of numerous books on and a staunch supporter of Ethiopia.

Next point of interest on King George VI Street is *Arat Kilo* (or *Miazia 27 Square*—this being the month and day in the Ethiopian calendar that the Emperor returned to Addis in our year 1941). In the center is an Axumite-style obelisk with images of Justice and War in the base and a Lion of Judah at the top. On the southwest corner is the Ministry of Education, on the northeast the faculties of science and engineering of *Haile Selassie I University.* The *Natural History Museum* on this campus can be visited by calling tel. 113177. Continuing up George VI Street, you pass the *National Museum* (L); for hours and exhibits, see p. 487.

At the end of the street, at *Sidist Kilo* (or *Yekatit 12 Square*), is a central, three-sided obelisk dedicated to those who died on and after Yekatit 12 (Feb. 19, 1937) following the attempted assassination of the Italian viceroy. The brass bas-relief and stone obelisk was designed by a Yugoslav artist, Anton Augustincic. On the southeast corner is the *Imperial Lion House,* where more than 20 felines live. On the southwest corner is the large *Haile Selassie I Hospital,* founded in 1924. Spreading out to the west and north is the main campus of *Haile Selassie I University,* whose core was the old *Genet Leul* ("gates of paradise") *Palace,* a gray stone structure set in large, beautiful gardens and donated by the emperor in 1961 for use as a university. The grounds are pleasant to walk around, and a visit to the *Ethnological Museum* (see p. 487) is well worthwhile.

Leaving Arat Kilo, take Atse Tesodros Street southwest to H.S.I. Avenue, turn right, cross Kechene Stream, and turn right onto Hailu Kebede Street, which brings you to *St. George Cathedral.* Built by Menelik II in 1896 soon after his victory at Adowa, it has been used since as the coronation place for Ethiopia's rulers. It is in the typical Ethiopian octagonal style with a central sanctuary, and after World War II Afewerk Tekle painted many murals during its restoration.

The cathedral is just off *Menelik II Square,* which has a fine equestrian statue of that emperor. Heading south, you come to the *Piazza,* which has a marble monument for the 1930 coronation of the emperor; the Piazza was renamed in 1966 *General De Gaulle Square* in honor of the French president's visit, though the former name is more commonly used. This is somewhat the center of "old," higher-altitude Addis, and around it are shops, local-class hotels and *pensiones,* taxi and bus stands. Taking Cunningham Street and then Abuna Petros Street, go west about 2 km to the *Mercato* or New Market area, which with its acres of outdoor stalls and indoor shops is reputedly the largest market in Africa; for shopping and bargaining hints, see "Shopping," p. 469. Give yourself time to wander and "window-shop." The busiest, most colorful days are Wednesday and Saturday, when people from miles around come in to sell their multitude of things.

Leaving the Mercato area, head east to Colson Street and then to Tewodros Square on *Churchill Street.* This wide, straight, 3-km-long avenue goes from the railway station in lower, "new" Addis up to three pointed star-shaped City Hall in upper, "old" Addis. On the way downhill you pass (L) the tall, new *General Post Office Building,* and reach spacious *Haile Selassie I Square* (abbreviated H.S.I. Square). On its northwest corner are the *Commercial Bank*'s contemporary round central branch and tower office building. Behind them a couple of blocks is the *National Library,* which has a good collection of books and manuscripts. On the southwest corner is a fine stylized *Lion of Judah statue,* erected in 1965 and now proudly overlooking H.S.I. Square's activity; sculptors were Bureand Etudes and Henri Chomeife. Near it is the 1,500-seat *Haile Selassie I Theatre,* completed in 1955 to encourage the performance of Ethiopian drama, dance, and music; it is also used as a cinema.

Going southwest on Ras Abebe Aregay Street, about 1 km from H.S.I. Square and across from the Wabe Shebelle Hotel is the *Empress Menen Handicraft School,* where traditional crafts, such as rug and *shamma* weaving, are taught and the end products sold in the show-room. South of Mexico Square about 1 km is the *OAU Headquarters* office building. Completing the tour, go east on Ras ("head" or "prince") Makonnen Street, past Churchill Road (railway station to the right), H.S.I. Stadium, Debre Zeit Road, and end up back at Maskal Square and the ETO office.

Accommodations

Addis Ababa Hilton, Box 1164, tel. 448400; cable HILTELS. On Menelik II Ave. above Jubilee Palace. 245 dbls, all w/bath, a-c, balcony. Rates: Bed only: sgl—E$38.90 to E$47.65; dbl—E$47.65 to E$52.55. Credit: AE, DC. A 10-story block opened in 1969 and set in 15 acres of gardens, the Hilton is the plushest hotel in Ethiopia. The slick red and gold lobby has travel and car-hire agencies, bank, florist, EAL office, boutique, jewelry and craft shops, beautician, bookstand. Rooms have pleasant, colorful decor, and depending upon price a fair or good view. Also three bars, Harrar Grill, Kaffa House, cross-shaped pool, tennis court, health club. Rating: 1st-class international, expensive but top-notch. Deserves ★.

Ghion Imperial Hotel, Box 1643, tel. 447130; cable GHIONS. Off Ras Desta Damtew Ave. about 1 km from Maskal Square. 65 sgls, 51 dbls, 7 suites, 19 bungalows, all w/bath. Rates: B&B: sgl—E$34; dbl—E$48. Credit: AE, DC. The Ghion ("river full of life"), whose gardens overlook one side of National Palace and the Royal Stables, was built mainly in the 1940s with new wings added 1963 and 1970. Ethiopian Wing (1970) rooms are most modern and are decorated with local crafts and carvings. Also two bars, casino (after 8 P.M.), Ghion Imperial restaurant, sauna, Olympic-size semiclean mineral-water pool, tennis court, EAL and car-hire offices, curio shops. Rating:

less 1st-class international than the Hilton, more rambling, older, and less plush.

Ethiopia Hotel, Box 1131, tel. 447400; cable ETHIOHOTEL. On Yohannes Ave. just off H.S.I. Square. 74 sgls, 25 dbls, 11 suites, all w/bath or shower. Rates: B&B: sgl—E$27; dbl—E$33, incl. Credit: AE, DC. Built in 1963 for the first OAU conference, the 6-story Ethiopia is central though lacks distinctive character. Spacious rooms have sharp-edged modern furniture. Main-floor restaurant is popular. Rating: 2d-class international, a pleasant enough place to stay.

Harambee Hotel, Box 3340, tel. 155400; cable HARTEL. On Ras Desta Damtew Ave. near Yohannes Ave. 21 sgls, 28 dbls, 1 suite, all w/bath or shower. Rates: Bed only: sgl—E$20 to E$30; dbl—E$35. The urban, 8-story Harambee (Swahili—"let's all pull together") opened in 1973 for the tenth anniversary of the OAU. Rooms are quite cramped though modly decorated with French flowered wallpaper and bright furniture. Also lounge, Fanfan Tavern, and Le Rimbaud restaurant. Rating: 2d-class international, swinging but a bit slipshod, more room for the money elsewhere.

Wabe Shebelle Hotel, Box 3154, tel. 447187; cable WABESHOTEL. On Ras Abebe Aregay Ave. near Mexico Square. 100 dbls, incl 30 suites, all w/bath or shower, balcony. Rates: B&B (Continental): sgl—E$22 to E$28; dbl—E$33 to E$35. Credit: AE, DC. The 12-story Wabe was built in 1968 and is popular with tours and businessmen. Lobby has tour and car-hire firms and souvenir stand; out front are more shops and offices. Rooms are modern and medium-sized, though under-furnished. Also ground floor and rooftop lounge-bar, 1st-floor restaurant. Rating: 2d-class international.

Hotel D'Afrique, Box 1120, tel. 447385; cable HOTAFRIC. On Dejatch Wolde Michael Road about 1 km from Mexico Square. 4 sgls w/ shower, 70 dbls w/bath and shower (incl 6 suites). Rates: Bed only: sgl—E$14 to E$19; dbl—E$27. The 7-story D'Afrique opened in 1967 and is frequented by businessmen and German package tourists. Rooms have modern, unmemorable furnishings, maybe a view. Also three TV lounges, two bar/lounges, snack bar, restaurants with Continental and Ethiopian cuisine. Rating: 2d-class international, the least expensive in this range, and though less central a fair deal.

Ras Hotel, Box 1632, tel. 447060; cable RASHOTEL. On Churchill Road just off H.S.I. Square. 32 sgls, 66 dbls, 3 suites, most w/bath or shower. Rates: B&B: sgl—E$22.50; dbl—E$39. Credit: AE, DC. The oldest of the Ras hotels, this dates from 1948 with later annexes and renovations. Rooms have oldish furniture, full carpets, usually a small bath. Also ground-floor bar and lounge, 1st-floor restaurant, top-floor nightclub. Rating: 1st-class local, central, good for middle-budget travelers.

Itegue Hotel, Box 7, tel. 113240. Near the Piazza on Serategna Sefer St. 88 sgls, 40 dbls, 24 w/bath or shower. Rates: Bed only: sgl—E$6 to E$16; dbl—E$10 to E$22. Built about 1907, the Itegue is Addis's oldest hotel and rambles accordingly with annexes. Better rooms are in original building, cheapest in the annexes; all are clean though have only occasional hot water. Unexceptional table d'hôte meals: breakfast—E$1.75; lunch or dinner—E$2.75. Rating: 2d-class local.

Plaza Hotel, Box 2718, tel. 116580. On the Piazza above the EAL office. 6 sgls, 18 dbls, none w/bath. Rates: Bed only: sgl—E$6; dbl—E$10. Freshly painted inside in 1973, the Plaza is central, functional, basic. Rating: 2d-class local.

There are numerous low-cost *pensiones* in Addis, which offer a bed and that's about it (check for fleas—endemic in Ethiopia—between the sheets). Rates: E$3 to E$6 per person per night. To list a few: *Lombardia Hotel* (above restaurant), Box 20, Ras Abebe Aregay Ave, across from Wabe Shebelle Hotel; tel. 446388. *Villa Verde Hotel* (next to restaurant), Box 3047, off Debre Zeit Road; tel. 444760. *Gondar Pensione,* Dej. Jotte St. next to Itegue Hotel; tel. 112392. *Shoa Hotel,* Box 1542, Dej. Jotte St. below Piazza; tel. 116419.

Where to Eat

For Addis Ababa this section is divided into Continental restaurants and hotel dining rooms; Italian; Oriental and Middle Eastern; Ethiopian; snacks and coffee.

CONTINENTAL

The Cottage, Ras Desta Damtew Ave. between Ghion and Harambee hotels; tel. 443479. Open daily for lunch and dinner. Set back from the road, the Cottage is in just that, with a timbered ceiling, brick bar, red tablecloths. Samples: French onion soup, snails Bourguignonne, braised duck, beef Stroganoff, Red Sea lobster. Entrées about E$3 to E$12. Credit: AE, DC.

Au Vieux Logis, Mesfine Harrar St., about 4 km north of St. George Cathedral and Menelik II Square, and set back from the road; tel. 118109. Open daily. In a house that has lots of provincial

French atmosphere and reputedly excellent food. Shrimp cocktail, Russian caviar, escargots, coquille St. Jacques, tournedos, filet mignon —each about E$6 to E$10.

Harrar Grill, in Hilton Hotel; tel. 448400. Daily for lunch and dinner. Four central pillars, an open-top dome, soft orange and brown chairs, traditional musical instruments on the wall, dance floor and nightly band. On the menu: Massawa lobster in suprême, Ethiopian pepper pot, red snapper "Dahlak Island," châteaubriand for 2, roasted Lidetta duckling. Entrées E$6.50 to E$18.75. Credit: AE, DC.

Ghion Imperial Restaurant, in Ghion Hotel; tel. 447130. Open daily for lunch and dinner. This is the hotel's main restaurant, and off it are two bars, an elevated coffee lounge in the shape of a round *tukul,* and the casino. Cheerful yellow and orange decor and an à la carte menu with at least 130 Continental and Chinese items: crabmeat salad cardina, Russian caviar on toast, turtle soup, ravioli à la Genovesi, fried rice dishes, sautéed shrimps Jambalaya New Orleans, châteaubriand bouquetière for 2, Chinese duck. Entrées E$3 to E$12. Credit: AE, DC.

Ethiopia Hotel Restaurant; tel. 447400. Pleasant, with wall paintings and hangings, fresh flowers, high ceilings. Table d'hôte lunch and dinner—E$6. À la carte, E$2 to E$18: crab cocktail, bouillabaisse, filet mignon "Henry IV," lamb cutlets and chops "provincial style," beef fondue Bourguignonne. Credit: AE, DC.

Kokeb Restaurant, at top of Africa Star Building next to All Africa Hall on Menelik II Ave.; tel. 448903. A glass elevator takes you up to the good view, central fireplace, split-level lounges and dining rooms decorated with Ethiopian objects. Quick lunch E$4 or E$7. À la carte entrées E$4 to E$14: Asmara baby lamb, "G'schnätzlets," beef fondue, flaming chicken in whiskey. Credit: AE.

Le Rimbaud, in Harambee Hotel; tel. 444482. Dark blue, white, and gold with hanging table lamps and French wall lithographs. Menu in French: hors d'oeuvre wagon, bouillabaisse Marseillaise, châteaubriand Béarnaise, escalope de veau cordon bleu. Entrées E$3 to E$9.

Skyway Restaurant, at H.S.I. International Airport; tel. 155558. Open daily. Orange and gray, overlooks the runway. Sandwiches— E$1.75 to E$2.50. Hot entrées and grills (shrimp on skewer, pepper steak)—E$3.50 to E$5.50.

Ras Grill, in Chamber of Commerce Building near Mexico Square; tel. 444182. Open daily. Big glass windows, a large Ethiopian wool rug, and lawn tables for outdoor diners. Hot entrées (shrimp, spaghetti) —E$1.50 to E$3. Sandwiches—E$1.50 to E$2.

Ras Hotel Restaurant; tel. 447060. The casual ground-floor circular dining area serves the same à la carte as the fancier 2d-floor restaurant. Hot entrées (pastas, steaks, fish, veal)—E$2.50 to E$5. Table d'hôte lunch or dinner—E$5. Band on Friday and Saturday nights. Credit: AE, DC.

Hotel D'Afrique dining room; tel. 447385. Black and white, uncozy dining room with nice tile mosaics of Ethiopian history. Table d'hôte lunch or dinner—E$4.50. À la carte includes mixed grill American, chicken and rice, breaded veal, steaks: E$4 to E$6.

Wabe Shebelle Hotel dining room; tel. 447187. Top-floor lounge (good view) and 2d-floor dining room both serve à la carte: veal, pork, chicken, and beef entrées E$3.50 to E$18. Ethiopian folk dancing in the ground floor lounge/bar Thursday night, regular band Tuesday–Saturday nights. Credit: AE, DC.

ITALIAN

Villa Verde, about 3 km from Maskal Square out Debre Zeit Road, then left at signpost and over railroad tracks; tel. 444760. Everybody's favorite, very homey and cheerful. À la carte includes shrimp cocktail, asparagus à la parmesaine, veal scallopine Villa Verde, cordon bleu, spaghetti à la carbonara; each E$1.50 to E$3.

Castelli's, just below the Piazza near Churchill Road; tel. 111058. Open daily. In an old house with a series of bright green and white dining rooms off a hallway. Good antipasto. Select 1st- and 2d-course dishes: E$2.50 for one course plus dessert and coffee; E$4 for two courses. Extra "express" dishes E$1 to E$8 besides flat rate.

La Taverna, off Debre Zeit Road—turn at signpost; tel. 449069. Open daily. In a house with casually hung burlap, salamis, bottles, scales, pitchforks, and nice wood floors, fireplace, and fresh flowers. Italian table d'hôte plus à la carte: lobster Taverne, charcoaled shrimp, young veal brains, coquille Taverne. Entrées E$3 to E$12.

Lombardia Restaurant, on Ras Abebe Aregay St. across from Wabe Shebelle Hotel; tel. 446388. Open daily. Very plain, with a little bar in front. Three-course lunch or dinner—E$3.

ORIENTAL AND MIDDLE EASTERN

China Bar, on Ras Desta Damtew Ave. below Ghion Hotel; tel. 443044. Closed Sunday, holidays. Has a splendid imported dragon tile ceiling and the best Chinese cook in Addis. Quick lunch—E$4. Small-portion dishes: soups, noodles, and dumplings—E50¢ to E$5.50, seafood, chicken, beef, pork, or lamb dishes—E$2.50 to E$8. Sizzling rice shrimp—E$6.50. Peking duck (order in advance)—E$30. Credit: DC.

Hong Kong, off Churchill Road below H.S.I. Square; tel. 444275. Open daily. Chinese lanterns and screens, 10-foot-long dragon mural. Quick lunch with 3 choices—E$3.50. Small portions E$1 to E$6. Peking duck (preorder)—E$25.

Omar Khayyam, on Dej. Jotte St. below the Piazza; tel. 112259. Open daily. Middle Eastern and Mediterranean, cozy, exotic decor and food. Mezzes (10 varieties of tidbits), hummus (spicy chickpea dip), yogurt kebab, couscous royal, rice pilaf with tas kebab. Each entrée E$1.25 to E$2.50. Credit: AE.

Chung Hwa, on Abebe Damte St. off Ras Makonnen Ave.; tel. 446904. Usual Chinese lanterns and murals, mediocre food too hastily prepared. Quick lunch—E$3. Small portions: E$1.50 to E$7.50.

Sangam, on Africa Ave. near Mobil station. Serves Indian dishes, some baked in the *tandoor,* a huge clay pot oven.

ETHIOPIAN (see p. 65)

Maru Denbiya, on Wingate St. about 4 blocks from Churchill Road and below the Piazza; tel. 117701. In a cottage with several rooms decorated with Ethiopian crafts; frequented by tourists and others wanting to sample the local, spicy food and drink. Lunch or dinner— E$2.75.

Addis Ababa, on Weatherall St. near Sylvia Pankhurst St. above Menelik II Square; tel. 113513. Also a favorite of overseas tour groups wanting to sample Ethiopian hospitality and food.

Ethiopian National Food Restaurant, on a side street off Patriots St.; tel. 120726. Open daily. E$2.50 for dinner, E$2 for a bottle of *tej.* Has a nice little cavelike coffee cellar.

SNACKS AND COFFEE

Kaffa House, in Hilton Hotel; tel. 448400. Bright and cheerful but expensive, and the service is snail-slow. Soups, salads, sandwiches, desserts—E$1.75 to E$6. Also an outdoor poolside barbecue lunch for about E$6.

Fanfan Tavern, in Harambee Hotel; tel. 444482. Shiny red, white, and blue. Soups, appetizers, sandwiches, grills, desserts—E$1 to E$4.50.

Roof of Wabe Shebelle Hotel; tel. 447187. Good view. Salads, sandwiches, hot dishes, desserts—E50¢ to E$4.

Finfinne Rendez Vous, in round building at Maskal Square. Circular,

black and white. Burgers and sandwiches, grills, soft drinks and coffee
—E35¢ to E$3.

Post Rendez Vous, on ground floor of PT&T building above H.S.I.
Square. Indoor and outdoor café, popular at lunch. Pastries, cold and
hot drinks, sandwiches, burgers, and hot snacks—E30¢ to E$2.25.

Oroscopo, on General Wingate St. below Piazza. Serves pizzas,
snacks, and good ice cream.

Getting Around

Places in Addis Ababa are usually located by their nearest square or
landmark rather than by the street name—such as "near the Piazza"
or "by Maskal Square." Streets and so forth named after Haile Selassie I
àre abbreviated H.S.I. (Some or all will change in the future.)

Expensive taxis rank up outside all the tourist-class hotels. When
using them determine the price before setting out, and if you want to
be picked up, for instance after dinner, say that you'll pay the driver
on the return trip, in which case he will be there.

Otherwise, there are literally dozens of dark blue and white Fiat
taxis ("taxi" license on back) buzzing up and down Addis. The custom
is to flag one down, inquire if it's going to your destination, and if so
hop in, with the perhaps one to three other passengers going in that
direction. The fare for a short distance, say from Maskal Square to
H.S.I. Square, should be E25¢. From "upper" Addis, e.g., around the
Piazza, to "lower" Addis, e.g., near H.S.I. Square, should be no more
than E50¢. However, all taxis stop running about 8 P.M.

Buses run up and down and across Addis. The standard fare is E15¢,
and to find out which bus number to take, ask English-speaking
Ethiopians at a bus stop. The Piazza is a good place to catch buses,
and other bus stops are marked with signs. Buses also stop running
about 8 P.M.

Information Bureau

The ETO staff can help you find your way around Addis, can tell
you what's happening, sign you up with a group for a Jubilee Palace
tour, and what not. Their office is at Maskal Square; tel. 447470.

"What's On . . ."

The free bimonthly guide that comes closest to being like Nairobi's
What's On is called alternately *What's Best* and *What's New*. However,

it's more useful as a source of addresses than for events. To find out movies and happenings, check the daily *Ethiopian Herald.*

Nightlife

Most of the classier action revolves around the hotels. The *Ghion Hotel* has the only *casino* in the city, and the wheel starts turning after 8 P.M. The Hilton's *Harrar Grill* has a dance band nightly, as does the top-floor lounge of the *Ras Hotel.* The *Chamber of Commerce Building* at Mexico Square has a band Friday and Saturday nights on the top floor. The *Wabe Shebelle Hotel* has a band Tuesday through Saturday nights, Ethiopian folkloric show Thursday 9–11 P.M. A popular nightclub per se is *La Fiesta,* on Ras Desta Damtew Ave. near the Ethiopia Hotel; it has a band and floor show. Credit: DC. Otherwise, latish dinners and a movie fill evenings.

Cinemas

Located near the Piazza: *Adwa,* Cunningham St., tel. 111421; *Empire,* H.S.I. Ave., tel. 115244; *Ethiopia,* on Piazza, tel. 111495; *City Hall,* Municipality Building, tel. 111495. There's also the *Ambassador,* Ras Desta Damtew Ave. near the Ethiopia Hotel, tel. 441935; and the *H.S.I. Theatre* by H.S.I. Square, tel. 446347. The *Drive-in Cinema* is on Dessie Road.

Libraries

National Library, Ras Tesemma Sefer, off H.S.I. Square, tel. 446247. *Kennedy Memorial Library,* tel. 110844, and *Institute of Ethiopian Studies Library,* tel. 119469, both at H.S.I. University by Sidist Kilo. *USIS Library,* Patriots St. near Piazza, tel. 113377. *British Council Library,* H.S.I. Ave., tel. 110022.

Museums

The *National Museum* on King George VI St. between Sidist and Arat Kilos, is open Monday–Saturday 9 A.M. to 1 P.M., 3 P.M. to 6 P.M., and Sunday 2–6 P.M.; admission is E50¢. Among other things, it has a prehistory collection of finds from the Omo and Awash river valleys, pottery and sculpture from Axum and Matara, the coronation throne of Emperor Haile Selassie, and modern paintings by Afewerk Tekle; photographs are allowed. The *Ethnological Museum* is in a yellow and green building in the center of the H.S.I. University campus by Sidist Kilo. It is open Monday–Friday 8:30 A.M.–12:30 P.M.,

2:30–5:30 P.M., Saturday and Sunday 9 A.M.–1 P.M. Admission is E50¢, though students enter free; tel. 119469. Several rooms contain processional crosses, ceremonial dress, triptychs, jewelry, crafts, furniture, weapons, tools, and other Ethiopian creations; photography is not allowed.

Religious Services

Ethiopian Orthodox: There are scores of churches; first services begin at 6 A.M. on Saturday, Sunday, and holidays. St. George Cathedral, above Menelik II Square. Stefanos, on Maskal Square. Trinity Cathedral, near Arat Kilo behind Parliament. *Greek Orthodox:* St. Frumentios Church, on H.S.I. Ave. near Ras Makonnen Bridge. *Anglican:* St. Matthew, Queen Elizabeth St. near the YMCA; tel. 112623. *Presbyterian:* American Presbyterian Mission, Patriots St. opposite Central Laboratories; tel. 110288. *Lutheran:* International Lutheran Church, from Mexico Square past and behind Mitchell Cotts; tel. 449331. *Roman Catholic:* Catholic Cathedral, off Wavel St. south of Piazza; tel. 111667. *Jewish Synagogue:* Shalom Sholemay, in Benin Sefer near Piazza; tel. 111725. *Mosque:* The Grand Mosque is in the center of the Mercato area.

Shops and Services

Routine shopping involves going to several different areas to collect basic things.

Beauty salon: Paris Coiffure, Cignarella Bldg., on Churchill Road by Ras Hotel; tel. 150665.

Books: G. P. Giannopoulos, Churchill Road at GPO, Box 120, tel. 446546. International Press Agency, Churchill Road near Ethiopia Hotel, Box 120, tel. 446546. Menno Bookstore, Gandhi St., Box 1236, tel. 112719; also on King George VI St. by German School.

Camping gas: Afrique Gas Supply Co., H.S.I. Ave., tel. 117500.

Freight forwarders: Compagnie Maritime Auxiliare D'Outre Mer, H.S.I. Square, Box 1230, tel. 448420. Maritime & Transit Services, Ras Abebe Aregay Ave., Box 1186, tel. 448763.

Groceries: Bambis Supermarket, Jomo Kenyatta Ave. near ETO, tel. 444441. Economy Supermarket, Ras Desta Damtew Ave., tel. 446781; also Churchill Road, tel. 116567.

Laundries: New Laundry, Churchill Road, tel. 443662. Stadium Laundry, Ras Desta Damtew Ave., tel. 443131.

Pharmacies: There are at least 43 in Addis. Broussalian Varouge

Pharmacy, Piazza, tel. 112694. Emmanuel Pharmacy, Ras Abebe Aregay Ave., tel. 447715. Ghion Pharmacy, Ras Desta Damtew Ave., tel. 448606.

Photo shops: Mac Ltd., Wavel St., tel. 115794. Sunderji Kalidas & Sons, Haile Selassie I Ave. opposite Cinema Empire, tel. 111916. Vaghi di Franco Celeste, Churchill Road near H.S.I. Square, tel. 446787. Photolite, Churchill Road opposite Ras Hotel, tel. 446456.

Photocopying: Tecnocopy, General Hailu Kebede St., tel. 117863. NCR, Maskal Square, Finfinne Bldg., tel. 443862.

Taxidermist: Svante Pohlstrand, Jimma Road, Box 754, tel. 447674.

Historic Route

Most of Ethiopia's prime tourist attractions are, conveniently, located in a corridor between Addis Ababa and Asmara. An airline route connects the "Big Four"—Bahar Dar, Gondar, Lalibela, and Axum—and a highway connects all but Lalibela. For those taking a road tour there are a number of minor attractions, such as Debre Libanos Monastery, the Blue Nile Gorge, and various ruins between Axum and Asmara.

Mainly as a driving route, the sites between Addis Ababa, Asmara, and Massawa have been strung together as the "Historic Route."

Debre Libanos, Blue Nile Gorge

Debre Libanos Monastery, 104 km north of Addis Ababa on the Historic Route road, makes with the Blue Nile Gorge a popular day trip from the capital (see package EP-6). The premier monastery in Ethiopia, dating to the 13th century, Debre Libanos of Shoa is on a slope overlooking a spectacular gorge. The founder of the monastery was St. Tekla Haymanot, who is shown in paintings with six wings and only one leg—the other fell off when the saint stood on one leg for seven years while meditating in a cave. Only male visitors are allowed into the refectory; they can see some tombs, a holy well, a sacred spring. More modern is the domed new church, built by Emperor Haile Selassie to fulfill a prophecy.

Blue Nile Gorge, which is included with Debre Libanos Monastery on excursions from Addis Ababa, is best seen not from the bridge that crosses the river but from 3,000 feet above it on a sheer cliff. The road toward Debre Marcos (pop. 27,170) follows along the edge of the plateau past a 300-year-old Portuguese bridge, then drops down the escarpment to the Blue Nile, which is actually quite brown. See package listing EP-6.

Bahar Dar, Lake Tana, and Tissisat Falls

Lake Tana is Ethiopia's largest lake, stretching 52 miles in length and covering some 1,400 square miles in western Begemder Province. At 5,700 feet altitude it is nearly surrounded by chains of extinct volcanic mountains. Dozens of small streams feed Tana, including the Tenish Abbai or Little Blue Nile, which originates in a swamp called Ghish Abbai, about 85 km southwest of the lake. Some say that this swamp is the actual source of the Abbai or *Blue Nile,* which is Tana's main outlet. Others (including Alan Moorehead) say that as the White Nile has Lake Victoria as its source, the Blue Nile has Tana as its primary source. In any case, both the swamp and the lake were first seen by a Portuguese priest, Pedro Paez, about 1618, but were not brought into the limelight until viewed by the Scottish explorer James Bruce in 1770. They both saw the beginnings of the Blue Nile, which flows quietly from the southern end of Lake Tana, later dramatically drops 140 feet at Tissisat Falls, then winds southeast, west, and north, cutting deep gorges into the Ethiopian highlands en route to flat, hot Sudan, and finally at Khartoum joins the White Nile to form the mighty Nile River.

Lake Tana's waters are dotted with about 30 islands, on some of which are a total of 20 old churches and monasteries used in earlier centuries as refuges as well as places of detention and exile; many of these can be visited by charter boat. Tana is teeming with fish (and with bilharzia), with some catfish weighing up to 30 pounds. Birds also abound, especially pelican, ibis, stork, cormorant, fish eagle, kite, hornbill, starling, and weaver species.

Around the lake grow brushwood, giant trees, and papyrus thickets. The latter is particularly used by the Waitos, who bind together bundles of papyrus stalks to make their long, narrow boats called *tankwas,* which formerly were used for attacking hippos (to kill one was a qualification for marriage—this partially explains why there are few hippos left on Tana today). You can see the Waitos propelling their *tankwas* around the lake using the bladeless pole of *shambako,* a sort of bamboo, and about 6 P.M. each evening the boats are lifted out onto the shore to let the papyrus dry overnight.

You can watch the Waitos near *Bahar Dar,* the lake's largest town, situated right on the southeast shore. With a population of about

25,000, Bahar Dar does not itself have a lot to offer tourists other than its picturesque market and its excellent view of the lake and head of the Abbai (Blue Nile) from the Imperial Villa 8 km east of town.

The biggest attraction, however, is nearby *Tissisat* (or *Blue Nile*) *Falls,* which are about 35 km due south of Bahar Dar via a dirt road and then a track. En route you pass typical *tukuls,* round huts whose walls are made of cow dung, grass, and clay (good for ten years) and whose pointed roof is formed from strong Sudan grass (good for two to three years). You stop at a gate to register, then take the bumpy track past the hydroelectric plant (which diverts water from the river) to the Italian stone bridge. Park, then cross the bridge over the Abbai or Blue Nile, which here below the falls is concentrated into and surges through a narrow gully of black basalt rock. Follow the 1-km-long path, made especially for Queen Elizabeth's visit in 1965, up the hillside to reach a viewpoint opposite *Tissisat Falls* (from *ch'ees issat,* "smoke fire").

After Bruce saw the falls in 1770, he wrote "The river had been considerably increased by rains, and fell in one sheet of water, without any interval, above half an English mile in breadth, with a force and noise that was truly terrible, and which stunned, and made me, for a time perfectly dizzy. A thick fume, or haze, covered the fall all round. . . . It was a magnificent sight." However, the falls best live up to their reputation during September–December, after the heavy rains have swollen the lake and river. The falls' three cataracts together do stretch half a mile across, and the divided river bed plunges down in two stages nearly 140 feet, creating, indeed, when the river is high, a deafening, "smoking," misty waterfall. In the distance are the chains of mountains forming a beautiful backdrop, and lush vegetation lines the riverbanks and gorge sheltering pythons, monkeys, and colorful birds.

Lake Tana's second attraction is its 30 or so islands with their churches and monasteries. Most of Tana's monasteries were founded in or just after the 14th century, several under Emperor Amda Tseyson (1314–44). The monasteries protected the libraries and treasuries of the imperial churches, especially during the invasions of the Moslems led by Gragn ("the left-handed") from Harrar. Gragn was killed by a Portuguese soldier near the lake in February 1543. The imperial court settled near the lake during the 17th century, and Gondar, about 100 km north, flourished as the capital until the mid-18th century, when political power began to be decentralized to the point of regional fighting. In the late 19th century the Tana region was overrun and devastated by the Mahdist dervishes from Sudan, and by then the power center had shifted eastward toward Addis Ababa. During the centuries many kings, princes, and their families were buried on the islands, especially on Daga, Rema, and Metraha.

Today several of the islands can be visited and their churches and treasures admired, though on some women are unfortunately forbidden entrance. The island monastery closest to Bahar Dar is *Debre Mariam,* built during Amda Tseyson's reign, rebuilt by King Tewodros II (1855–68). Now a large but unimpressive straw hut, it was once a famous monastery with 50 churches under it. The church owns a manuscript of the Tetra-Gospels, one of the oldest hand-illustrated Ethiopian manuscripts, that dates between 1360 and 1380.

Kebran Gabriel Island is about 40 minutes by chartered boat from Bahar Dar, and is one of those closed to women. The church, first built in the early 14th century, was reconstructed in red stone in the late 17th century by Iyasu the Great "for love of the Angel Gabriel because he had been his guardian angel since his infancy." The cubed sanctuary, which inside has many different painting styles, on the outside is encircled by 12 stone pillars, each symbolizing an apostle. Nearby is the tower of *Iqa-Biet,* which houses a 50-volume library, including another manuscript of Tetra-Gospels, this one dating from about 1420 and containing 36 illuminated pages about the Four Evangelists, 13 pages of the Canons of Eusebius, and 19 pages on the life of Christ.

Zeghie peninsula, 1½ hours by water from Bahar Dar, has a good Friday market, coffee and *gesho* (used to make *tej*) growing wild, and *Uhra Kidane Mehret,* a 17th-century monastery church, with its vivid "recent" paintings. The large island of *Dek,* 3½ hours from Bahar Dar, has several churches and the semimummified remains of King Fasilidas and his infant son in an open sepulcher. One church, *Arsima Sematat,* named after St. Ripsime, a virgin martyr who was stripped naked and beheaded along with her 27 companions by order of King Dertades, has a manuscript from 1430. On nearby wooded *Nargha Island,* which is joined to Dek's western shore in the dry season by a stone walkway, is *Selassie Church,* built by Queen Mentuab in 1746 and featuring a portrait of her lying at the feet of the Virgin Mary. Also near Dek is *Daga Estafanos Island* with its perfectly conical hill and its monastery of Daga on top—no females *of any species* are allowed near.

Mariam Ghemb Sysenyos peninsula is an hour west of Gorgora, Tana's northern town, and at its crest are the ruins of the castle and cathedral, built along the lines of a European convent for the Portuguese Jesuits during Emperor Sysenyos's reign (1607–32). *Debre Sina* is in Gorgora near the landing pier, and its paintings have been preserved since commissioned by the queen of Iyasu the Great (1682–1706).

When to Visit

The best time to visit Bahar Dar and its environs is September–December after the long rains, when the lake and river are at their fullest and Tissisat Falls at their height. Seeing the falls at their low point during May–June is a disappointment.

Getting There, Getting Around

By road Addis Ababa to Bahar Dar is 578 km, Asmara 699 km, Gondar 170 km. EAL has flights daily to Bahar Dar from both Addis Ababa and Asmara. If arriving by plane, you usually can (for a fee) join a tour group or hire a vehicle from the Ras Hotel to get out to the falls. See packages EP-21, 24–32, 37. Scheduled boats used by local people leave Bahar Dar 1Xwk (Sunday), pass through Delghi and Esey Deber islands, overnight at Kunzula Island, stop at Zechie Island, and reach Gorgora; cost E$2.75. The boat leaves Gorgora 1Xwk (Thursday) and returns to Bahar Dar. However, to see the islands with churches, you have to charter a boat for E$20 or more per hour from Bahar Dar, E$50 per hour from Gorgora; fares are reduced for more than two to three hours. Inquire at the Ras Hotel or at the UTC office at the airport in Bahar Dar. Better yet, arrange ahead of time to charter a boat through a tour operator or through Navigatana, Box 1630, Addis Ababa, tel. 444500.

Accommodations

Ras Hotel, Box 5, tel. 1; or c/o Ras Hotels, Box 1632, Addis Ababa; cable RASHOTEL. On the shore of Lake Tana about half-km from Bahar Dar. 30 dbls w/bath or shower. Rates: FB: sgl—E$30; dbl—E$50. Credit: DC. Though overpriced, the Ras has a beautiful lake view, excellent birdwatching from the dining porch, and some nice old shade trees on its lawn. Rooms are semimodern, comfortable, clean, and thankfully screened in against the ever pesky flies. Somewhat tasty table d'hôte meals: breakfast—E$2.50; lunch or dinner—E$4.50.

Rating: 1st-class local. . . . *Blue Nile Spring Hotel,* Box 21, tel. 38. On the lakeshore in Bahar Dar. 20 dbls w/shower. Rates: FB: sgl— E$14–16; dbl—E$18–20. Built in 1966 as a yellow one-story group of blocks with plain, functional rooms around a small garden. Table d'hôte, unfancy dining room by the lake: breakfast—E$2; lunch or dinner—E$3.50. Rating: 2d-class local. . . . To open in late 1975: Hilton Lodge, 64 rooms, with restaurant, bar, swimming pool.

Gondar

Imperial capital of "the Hidden Empire" for 200 years, Gondar is known to tourists for its 17th-century castles. Nestled in the hills north of Lake Tana, and 300 years ago quite isolated, Gondar was purposely chosen as an easily defended place. Emperor Lebna Dengel had fallen back into the northwest before the Moslem invader Gragn, of Harrar. When Gragn was defeated and killed at Gragn-Ber on Lake Tana's shore in 1543, the emperors were faced with Galla incursions from the south and southeast, and so decided to remain in the mountainous district.

Sartsa Dengel (1563–97) built a Portuguese-style turreted castle at Gouzara, but it was Fasiladas (1632–67), also called Fasil, who chose isolated Gondar as the official capital in 1636. There had been a previous settlement on the site (some of Gondar's churches predate Fasiladas), but the emperor began the important constructions which can still be seen. Though the architecture was undoubtedly influenced by the Jesuits whom Fasiladas expelled from the country, Gondar is the work of local builders, apparently with the help of an Indian craftsman. Fasiladas erected the first, biggest, and best-preserved castle. More castles, palaces, and buildings for special purposes (lion cages, a bridal dressing hall) were constructed by later emperors—Yohannes I (1667–82), Iyasu I the Great (1682–1706), Tekla Haimanot (1706– 16), Dawit III (1716–21), Bakaffa (1719–30), and Iyasu II the Lesser (1730–55).

In its heyday, Gondar was the center of imperial power as well as the economic and cultural center of what was then Ethiopia. It had a population variously estimated at 80,000 to 100,000 (now about 36,500), and there may have been schools of law, theology, and sacred music. The capital fostered a literary and artistic revival. But as the emperors withdrew emotionally as well as physically from the rest of Ethiopia, the court, wrote historian Richard Greenfield, "gave itself up to pleasure and intrigue. Ethiopian and European sources alike provide a picture of decadence where political assassinations, more than once of monarchs by their own sons, were commonplace." The Scot James Bruce, who arrived at Gondar in 1770 and later journeyed to the source of the Blue Nile, wrote in his *Travels to Discover the Sources of the Nile* (1790) of the trials and executions, tortures and murders, treachery and plain old intrigues of the court. "Nothing occupied my thoughts but how to escape from this bloody country."

Gondar was by then far into its decline, begun during Iyasu the Great. The Ethiopians call the period from the mid-18th to the mid-19th century the Mesafint, a chaotic "time of the judges" when the empire withered and regions grew stronger, when powerful princes disputed the isolated emperors. Natural and political forces led to the destruction of Gondar. A serious earthquake in 1704 toppled the castle tower of Jan Tekel; civil wars led to periodic ransackings of the palaces. Emperor Tewodros II (1855–68), who began to reunite the country, sacked and abandoned Gondar in 1866 when he moved to the fortress capital of Amba Magdala. Gondar remained a provincial town, was burned by Mahdist dervishes (soldiers) from the Sudan in 1888 (churches were their special target), was captured by the Italians in 1936, then underwent bombing in 1941 when the Allies liberated Ethiopia. Gondar, naturally, has many ruins. The destroyed castles (some partially restored) and the remarkable paintings in Debre Berhan Selassie church are the town's main attractions, though tourists also go to a village of the Falashas, Ethiopia's "black Jews."

From the Itegue Menen Hotel, walk down a driveway and into a piazza to the wall around the *imperial compound,* containing most of the castles. Go around to the right toward a spreading fig tree and enter the compound through the *Gate of Princess Inkoye.* Walk straight toward the biggest building, the handsome *castle of Fasiladas,* a two-story, turreted, wooden-balconied castle started by Emperor Fasiladas after the founding of Gondar in 1636 but finished by Yohannes and Iyasu I, restored in this century by the Italians. Resembling a European castle, its fortress appearance is modified by curved doorways and windows bordered by purplish blue stones. You go up an outside set of steps and into a large central hall used by several emperors as a throne room. A spiral staircase goes down to the ground floor and up to the terrace, where there is a vaulted chapel, and from the terrace you ascend a steep outside staircase to the battlements. From here you have a view of the imperial compound, the town, hills, Debre Berhan Selassie church, and Kusquam abbey.

Below Fasiladas's castle is a sunken pool, probably a cistern, and next to the palace is the ruined *castle of Iyasu the Great,* with only the walls still standing. Also called "the castle of the saddle" from the shape of one of the towers, the palace is said to have been the scene of tremendous orgies as well as tortures. Just north of the castle of Iyasu is a small ruined castle attributed to Fasiladas. Walking around the gardens you will come to a restored two-floor building housing offices, the library of *Tsadik Yohannes,* whose yellowish colored walls (resulting from a paint diluted with *noug* oil) are characteristic of Gondar historical constructions. Next to the library is the *chancellery of Tsadik Yohannes,* of which only the walls remain of the arcaded room on the ground floor where trials were held. Many minor buildings built by Fasiladas, Yohannes, and Iyasu have disappeared.

Going to the northern half of the compound you see buildings built by Dawit, Bakaffa and his part-Portuguese wife Mentuab, and Iyasu II. The first ruins are perhaps those of the house of Fasiladas's lionkeeper, then the *House of Song of Dawit III,* also called the House of Chants or the Debbal-Gemb, a rectangular building notable for its corner turret; only the walls remain of the building where feasts and celebrations took place during what was a "refined epoch." East of this are the ruins of *Dawit III's Nuptial House,* or House of Khol, where brides were dressed for royal weddings. North of this are the remains of the walls of Fasiladas's lion cages and some one-story buildings, also in ruins, including the *castle of Iyasu II,* decorated by Smyrna craftsmen (there was a room entirely paneled in ivory, another paneled in ivory and Venetian glass).

You are now near the northern wall, along which is the long, low, battlemented *castle of Bakaffa* to the left, and the *palace of Mentuab* to the right. At Bakaffa's castle is a reception room gallery that overlooks Gondar's main square outside the wall, and forming a courtyard in front of the castle is a one-story arcaded stable. Mentuab's palace, with its curved stone windows, ornamented façade, and complicated layout, is one of the most distinctive Gondar buildings. Mentuab, Bakaffa's queen who later was regent for young Iyasu II, was apparently one of the most beautiful and one of the wisest of Ethiopia's queens.

Also within the compound, but with independent access points, are the church of Attami Kiddus Mikael, Ilfis-Giorgis Church, and the church of Gemjabiet Mariam. *Attami Kiddus Mikael* (St. Michael the Beautiful), reached through the Gate of the Chiefs, or through the ruins north of the Nuptial House, was built by Dawit III but has partly fallen into ruin and been disfigured by hasty renovation. But it is still one of the most characteristic examples of the religious architectural styles seen also in the basilica of St. Mary of Zion at Axum. Behind the church is the round *Ilfis-Giorgis Church,* dating back to Fasiladas and containing six small paintings of St. George and the dragon. *Gemjabiet Mariam* (Gift of the Virgin Mary), reached through the gate of the same name, was originally built by Fasiladas, but that has been replaced by more recent constructions. Inside are some interesting paintings, supposedly portraits of Gondar's emperors. In the woods behind this church is hidden the grave of Walter Plowden, an English adventurer who became British consul for Abyssinia in 1848 and became a close friend of Tewodros II. In 1860 Plowden was killed by tribesmen near Gondar, and in retaliation the emperor massacred some 2,000 of the culprits—"a holocaust," observes Alan Moorehead, "exceptional even for Ethiopia."

Gondar's other attractions are outside the compound, some a distance away. Just north of the compound, the *castle of Ras Mikael Sehul,* built toward the end of the 18th century, was restored to serve as Haile Selassie's residence when he was in Gondar; it is partially furnished in the style of its period. Permission to visit must be obtained from the governor-general, whose villa is within the grounds. Nearby is the *church of Medhane Alem,* originally built by Fasiladas but rebuilt several times (the present building dates from the 19th century); it was one of a few of Gondar's 44 churches to survive the 1888 sacking by the dervishes. The modern paintings in the church are traditional in style.

A km from the city, on a hill, is the *church of Debre Berhan Selassie,* the best religious construction of Iyasu the Great. The rectangular church, with a well-preserved entrance pavilion and square tower, houses a choice collection of Ethiopian religious paintings. The dervishes who tried to destroy the church were, according to tradition, driven off by a swarm of bees. The remarkable paintings, which are the church's main interest, comprise large numbers of scenes from the Bible and Ethiopian hagiography. On the south wall are scenes from the life of the Virgin Mary, also portraits of monks and nuns. On the east wall are pictures of patriarchs, judges, kings, high priests, and prophets from the Old Testament. On the north wall are portraits of the martyrs and illustrations of the various tortures they underwent. On the church's 12 pillars are the 12 apostles, and at the tops of the pillars the 12 archangels. The ceiling is decorated with rows and rows of angels' faces. Only men are allowed inside during the services (the morning service begins at 6 A.M.); the priest emerges later to read the scriptures to the women outside. Otherwise, during tours, women can enter.

Two km east of Gondar is the so-called *Bath of Fasiladas,* a pleasure pavilion behind a thick wall studded by six towers and a square turret. The 227-by-130-foot rectangular bath, dry most of the time, has at one end a battlemented pavilion, supported by strong vaults above the basin. A double-arched bridge joins the ground floor of the pavilion to the shore. The original use of the building is not known, but a later Gondar emperor, Solomon II, converted it into a church honoring Fasiladas. Outside the wall is a dome supported by six arcades, said to be the tomb of Tsadik Yohannes's horse Suviel.

Farther east is the *abbey of Kusquam,* named for a place in Egypt where the Holy Family was said to have stopped. Empress Mentuab built Kusquam as a place of retirement after Bakaffa died, and it was the center of court life when James Bruce visited Gondar. In one enclosure are the ruins of Mentuab's private residence, her circular chapel, and the walls of a palace used for receptions. In the adjoining enclosure is the partially ruined church of Debre Tsehai (Abbey of the Sun).

About 10 from Gondar is a *Falasha village* that tourists are usually taken to. Except for a mud-and-stick *tukul* synagogue with a Star of David on top, and the fact that some of the people wore the same symbol, the village looked to us identical to other Ethiopian villages. The Falashas are by tradition the descendants of a Lost Tribe of Israel, though are probably the descendants of Cushites converted by Yemeni immigrants to pre-Talmud Judaism. Some unique, interesting, but extremely fragile pottery, in the form of birds, animals, and humans, is made in the village and sold for E$1–5.

When to Visit

October to January are the best months, but you can visit temperate Gondar anytime.

Getting There, Getting Around

Ethiopian Airlines serves Gondar twice daily, once in each direction between Addis Ababa and Asmara. The Historic Route road goes from Bahar Dar to the south, past Lake Tana to Gondar, thence on a very scenic section through the Semyen Mountains to Axum. See package listings EP-22, 24–32, 37.

Costs

E$1 is charged at Debre Berhan Selassie, E$6 at the imperial compound; these are already included in package tour costs. To join UTC's tour, if you arrive in Gondar independently, costs E$22 including entry fees. Taxi from the airstrip is E$5–6.

Accommodations

Itegue Menen Hotel, Box 106, Gondar; tel. 110153. On hill above the main street in town. 19 sgls, 21 dbls; 2 rms w/bath and toilet, 4 rms w/shower only. Rates: FB: sgl—E$24; dbl—E$30–34. Old hotel within walking distance (half-km) of the imperial compound, the Itegue's rooms, spread out on two floors and an annex, are dull and old-fashioned. Yellow dining room serves basic table d'hôte: breakfast—E$2.50; lunch or dinner—E$5. Out back are patio, vegetable garden, and perhaps-filled pool. Rating: Less than 1st-class local and very much overpriced, but the only tourist-class hotel in town. . . . *Fasil Hotel,* Box 1, tel. 110221. In Gondar on Medhane Alem St., the road to Asmara. 6 sgls, 2 dbls, none w/bath. Rates: Bed only: E$4 per person. For low-budgeters; cleanish rooms (though check for fleas), communal bath. Ground floor has pool table, bar, and restaurant serving chicken, *wat,* spaghetti, or eggs—each plate about E$1. Rating: 3d-class local. . . . *Prince Makonnen Hotel,* Box 75, tel. 110040. On Piazza. 16 rooms. Rates: Bed only: sgl—E$10–12; dbl—E$15–18. . . . A *Hilton Lodge* with 64 doubles, a dining room and bar, and pool, is to open in late 1975.

Lalibela

Lalibela, an isolated picturesque town with two-story, round *tukuls* clinging to the hillsides of the Lasta Mountains in central Ethiopia, has a near-dozen hand-hewn rock churches that are truly amazing, and are well worth the trip to this remote area to see. In fact, if you only have a two- or three-day stopover in Ethiopia, put Lalibela above all other places to visit.

The first European to see Lalibela's churches, the Portuguese priest Francisco Alvarez, in about 1520, wrote a factual description, then added, "it wearies me to write more of these works, because it seems to me they will not believe me if I write more." Other early visitors called Lalibela a "New Jerusalem," a "New Golgotha," and the "Christian citadel in the mountains of wondrous Ethiopia."

Historically, after Axum was burned and ransacked in the 10th century by the semilegendary Queen Judith and her troops, the Zagwe dynasty seized power from the Axumite Solomonic dynasty and established their capital high in the Lasta Mountains in Roha (later to be called Lalibela). The Zagwe claimed a rival ancestry to the Solomonic kings of Axum: they said that the Queen of Sheba's handmaiden also had a son fathered by King Solomon, and that this boy was the ancestor of the Zagwe dynasty. In any case, about 11 Zagwe kings ruled from the 11th to 13th centuries, until a famous priest, Tekla Haymanot, convinced them to abdicate so that a descendant of the old Axumite dynasty could rule.

However, it was during the early 12th century that the rock churches were supposed to have been carved, all in a matter of about 24 years during the Zagwe King Lalibela's rule. According to the Ethiopian Royal Chronicles, a dense cloud of bees surrounded the boy at his birth, and his mother, claiming they represented the soldiers that would serve her son, called him Lalibela—"the bees recognize his sovereignty." Lalibela's ambition was to build a "New Jerusalem" in Ethiopia, and 11 rock churches on either side of the River Jordan were quickly completed—thanks, a royal chronicler notes, to the angels who worked alongside the stone masons and also twice as hard at night. Lalibela was later canonized, and the town of Roha renamed in honor of him.

In Ethiopia there are three types of rock churches: (1) built-up cave churches, i.e., a regular structure inside a natural cave (e.g., Mekina Medhane Alem near Lalibela); (2) rock-hewn cave churches cut inward from a near-vertical cliff face, sometimes using an existing natural cave (e.g., Abba Libanos in Lalibela); (3) rock-hewn monolithic churches cut in one piece from the rock and separated from it all around by a trench (e.g., Bet Medhane Alem, Bet Mariam, Bet Giorgis, and others in Lalibela).

Most experts think that in sculpting, or more precisely in excavating, the Lalibela churches, the workers sank a rectangular trench in the pink, brownish, or green volcanic ash ("tuff") and cut free an oblong block of stone. Then the stone masons chiseled out the church, shaping the outside and hollowing out the inside, probably working downward from the top to the bottom, removing the unwanted stone and, in so doing, sculpting the pillars, beams, and arches. The architectural styles used seemed to have been derived from the typical

Axumite layered wood and stone effect (see p. 512); and from the Greek basilica, which featured the Holy of Holies facing east, an assembly hall with a flat ceiling, a central aisle or nave, and two or more other aisles. Typical of Ethiopian churches, some of the Lalibela churches have exactly three external doors, and three openings to the Holy of Holies, the innermost sanctum that is accessible only to priests celebrating Mass and to the emperor.

Experts think that the Lalibela rock churches were built at different times, though probably all during the Zagwe period. The interior paintings were mainly done later, in the 15th, 17th, and 18th centuries. The ETO has a superb detailed booklet on Lalibela and environs, plus a small foldout pamphlet and map, both of which you should inquire about.

Lalibela's dozen churches are divided into two groups and one solitary structure on either side of the River Jordan. If you start from the Seven Olives Hotel, the first group is reached by a half-km downhill walk or drive to the village square and then a walk to the left over the rise to the cavities sheltering the churches.

Bet Medhane Alem (Church of House of the Savior of the World) is a freestanding monolith and is the largest church of all, measuring approximately 108 by 78 by 37 feet. You first glimpse the roof, beautifully decorated with relief crosses enclosed by arches. Around the outside of the building is a row of square pillars, some of which collapsed and were restored or rebuilt through the Ethiopian Committee for the Restoration and Preservation of the Churches of Lalibela, which was organized by one of Haile Selassie's granddaughters, the energetic Princess Hirut Desta. Inside Medhane, 28 square pillars divide the interior into four aisles with flat ceilings and a nave with a barrel vault. The windows let in a little light through their carved patterns of swastikas (an ancient adaptation of the classic square Greek cross); inside there are some carved decorations but no paintings. In the trench walls outside are holes in which the bones of pilgrims and others were found buried.

Taking a short tunnel west from Medhane, you come to a large courtyard with a complex of churches. *Bet Mariam* (Church of the Virgin Mary) is the most beloved by the Lalibela clergy and by the thousands of pilgrims who flock to its courtyards on high holy days, and King Lalibela is said to have attended Mass there daily. The church measures about 32 by 29 by 29 feet, and outside has horizontal moldings, porches with Axumite-style carved doors, and a lower row of windows that have a rich variety of forms of crosses—Latin, Greek, swastika, loop, etc. Inside Mariam is a cloth-wrapped central pillar called the *and* ("one"), symbolizing the unity of faith. The priests explain that Christ touched the pillar when appearing to King Lalibela in one of his visions, and the past and future are written on the pillar, kept covered because man is too weak to hear the truth. Paintings richly decorate the inside of Mariam's walls, columns, and arches, with many referring to the life of Mary, to whom the church is dedicated. Outside in the courtyard is a cistern or well containing water which is said to have healing powers, and into which people jump on holy days.

Bet Maskal (Church of the Cross) was carved in a bulge in the northern wall of the Bet Mariam courtyard, and measures 35 by 11 feet. Its walls, pillars, and floor are chiseled with numerous crosses in high relief. *Bet Danaghel* (Church of the Virgin) juts out at the south end of the courtyard and is quite small, about 27 by 11½ feet. According to legend, it honors 50 young Roman maidens, nuns and novices who were murdered by order of the emperor Julian in the 4th century A.D.

Leaving the Bet Mariam courtyard by a trench to the west, you come to two squeezed-together churches, a chapel, and a tomb. *Bet Debre Sina* (Church of Mount Sinai) is semimonolithic, measuring 30 by 27 by 9 feet, and has three doorways, the northern one leading to the next church, Bet Golgotha. Debre Sina's interior is divided by cruciform-shaped pillars into a nave and two aisles with five bays each. *Bet Golgotha* (Church of Golgotha), dedicated to the passion and death of Christ, is the northern twin church of Debre Sina, and is best known for its rare figurative wall reliefs of the "tomb of Christ" behind a wrought-iron grille, and of seven saints in arched niches in the walls. From Golgotha a doorway to the east leads to the *Selassie Chapel* (Chapel of the Trinity), which is closed to all but a very few priests and is completely imprisoned in the rock.

Outside Bet Debre Sina again in a deep trench is a big block of stone called the *Tomb of Adam,* with a cross its only decoration. Inside its upper hollow floor is a hermit's cell, while carved below is the entranceway to the back of the first group of churches.

The second stop made on the west side of the River Jordan is at *Bet Giorgis,* the well-known cross-shaped monolithic church dedicated to the national saint of Ethiopia, St. George, and standing by itself in its deep pit apart from the other two groups of churches. Legend says that upon the near-completion of these other two groups of churches,

King Lalibela was reproached by St. George, who rode up on a white horse in full armor and then supervised the building of the church himself; the monks today will show the supposed hoof marks of St. George's horse. The church is almost a perfect cube from which sections were hewn to give it the shape of a classic square Greek cross. On its roof are carved three concentric crosses following the shape of the building. Doorways protrude on the west, north, and south sides. The church is reached through a tunnel, since the nearly perpendicular sides of its deep pit have no stairs. Inside, the cruciform plan is followed, though the eastern arm has a domed sanctuary decorated with crosses in relief.

The other group of churches is on the opposite bank of the River Jordan, and is approached by road by going back through the town and then south. This group is practically surrounded by an 11-foot-deep outer trench, and then dissected by a central trench. Usually the first church approached by crossing a small log bridge over the central trench is *Bet Gabriel-Rufa'el* (Church of Gabriel and Raphael *or* of the Archangels), which may once have originally been part of the Zagwe dynasty court, since its floor plan is labyrinthine and confused. Inside are three angular halls with pillars and pilasters, all squeezed between two courtyards.

The second church visited is *Bet Emanuel* (Church of Emmanuel), considered by art historians to be the finest and most impressive church in Lalibela. It is the only truly monolithic structure in this group, and measures about 58 by 38 by 38 feet. Stylistically it is an almost classic example of Axumite architecture with its exterior receding and projecting horizontal and vertical bands, and around the three entrances a framework of protruding beams; there are also three rows of windows, with the bottom ones cut in the shape of Greek crosses. Inside, though, the true basilica plan is followed with a central vaulted nave, two outer aisles, and an east–west orientation. From the right-hand aisle a 150-foot-long passageway leads eventually to *Bet Lehem* (Chapel of Bethlehem), which may have been the hermit cell of King Lalibela and/or the bakery for eucharistic bread, but which in any case is closed to the public.

Bet Mercurios (Church of Mercurios) honors this non-Ethiopian saint who proudly declared his faith and so was condemned to be beheaded by Roman emperor Julian, like the 50 maidens commemorated by Bet Danaghel. This church may originally have been used for a jail, since ankle shackles have been found in its trenches. Today the part used as a church is at the eastern end of the subterranean hall that opens onto a courtyard. Beautiful paintings used to hang on the walls, but they have been removed to and can be seen in the National Museum in Addis Ababa.

Bet Abba Libanos (House of Abba Libanos) is dedicated to one of the most famous monastic saints of the Ethiopian Church. According to legend, Lalibela's wife, Maskal Kebra, with the help of angels built this church in just one night. It is a good example of a cave church, because though its roof is not separated from the rock, its three other sides are detached by a tunnel. Inside, the aisles and nave run east–west. In the middle of the altar wall is a little light that priests tell you shines day and night by its own power—perhaps it is a piece of phosphorescent stone.

Outside Lalibela are a number of churches: Yemrehanna Krestos (Christ Show Us the Way), Arba Insissa (The Forty Animals), Bilbala Giorgis (St. George in the Bilbala District), Bilbala Cherqos (Kyrikos in the Bilbala District), Sarsana Mika'el (St. Michael of the Sarsana District), Makina Medhane Alem (Redeemer of the World in Makina), and Gennata Mariam (Paradise of Mary). All of these can be visited by long mule rides, and/or by a few long, vigorous walks.

Dr. Georg Gerster's *Churches in Rock* is an excellent book about the churches of Lalibela and elsewhere.

When to Visit

Because the mountainous Lalibela area gets incredibly heavy rains from July through September, the airport closes (to Ethiopian Airlines' planes but not to charter planes), the hotel is closed, and access by road is nearly impossible as well. Plan to visit between October 1 and June 30.

Getting There, Getting Around

By road, Addis Ababa north to the Weldiya turnoff is 521 km; then a rough four-wheel-drive track goes west 125 km to Lalibela. From Asmara the turnoff at Kobbo is 511 km south, then the four-wheel-drive track goes west 140 km to Lalibela. EAL has flights daily to Lalibela from both Addis Ababa and Asmara. See also package tours EP-23, 25–26, 28–29, 31–35, 37. From the dirt air-landing strip it is a 11-km drive by Land-Rover up 2,000 feet into the mountains to 8,500-foot-high Lalibela town. The first group of town churches described in the text above can be easily reached on foot by just walking downhill from the hotel, while the other churches are farther and are better visited by vehicle, then by foot. Be sure to wear comfortable, sturdy walking shoes, as there is plenty of walking involved. Have something handy to swat the flies with, because they seem particularly tenacious and ever present in Lalibela. Bring a flash attachment and/or fast ASA film to photograph inside the churches, since they are quite dark.

Costs

Transport from the airstrip is E$7.50 one way, E$15 round trip. To visit the churches (closed noon–3 P.M.) you can join tours leaving the Seven Olives Hotel in the Land-Rovers at 9 A.M. and 3 P.M. It costs E$10 for entry into all ten of the churches, and usually nothing is charged for Land-Rover transport. Mules can be hired at the hotel gate for treks to the outlying churches and hills; cost is about E$2–3 and up per person for a close-by church.

Accommodations

Seven Olives Hotel, bookings to Adulis Travels, Box 2719, Addis Ababa; tel. 153150; cable ADULIS. On a hillside overlooking Lalibela town. 2 sgls, 43 dbls, all w/bath or shower. Rates: FB: sgl—E$33; dbl—E$54. Built in 1966 with a new wing added in 1970, the Seven Olives rooms are cool, comfortable, though you must have the water heater turned on when you want a hot shower. Sometimes water itself gets scarce and is rationed. Dining room shaped like a round *tukul* with a colorful straw roof and Ethiopian wall murals, serves good table d'hôte meals: breakfast—E$3; lunch or dinner—E$7. Drinks and extras are very high—E$1 for a Coke or Ambo water. Closed July 1–September 30 during the heavy rains. Rating: 1st-class local. . . . In late 1975 the Seven Olives will be superseded by a brand-new, 64-room *Hilton,* with bar and restaurant and, apparently, a freshwater swimming pool, despite Lalibela's water supply problem. . . . **Camping** is possible, though you should be totally self-sufficient with water included. It is best to ask the hotel staff or the police where to camp.

Makalle

Makalle, with its big Monday market and castle-hotel, is a secondary Historic Route attraction, and generally replaces Lalibela on package-tour itineraries during the big rains July–September. Former imperial capital (1872–89) before Addis Ababa, and now capital of rugged Tigre Province, Makalle (pop. 29,100) is also gateway to many rock-hewn churches, some built in the face of perpendicular cliffs, others slightly more accessible.

On hilltops and facing each other across the town are two of Makalle's attractions, *Abraha Castle,* now a hotel, and the *Palace of Yohannes IV,* the emperor who designated Makalle as capital. The handsome palace, built of stone, is partly the residence of the provincial governor-general and partly a provincial museum with the beginnings of a collection of old church manuscripts.

The central square is the location of a daily *market* (the main market day is Monday). Available here is everything from blocks of salt brought by camel from the Danakil Desert, firewood, and food to baskets and leather baby-carriers decorated with cowrie shells. Other attractions in Makalle include the *Monastery of Debre Genet* with the two churches of Medhane Alem (no women allowed) and Kidane Mehret; and the hilltop *Fort of Enda Yesus,* near which the Italians were repulsed before the great Ethiopian victory at Adowa in 1896.

Tourists who are curious, interested, and energetic can use Makalle as a base for seeing some of the 130 known rock churches in Tigre Province, which was the heartland of the Axumite Empire (1000 B.C.–A.D. 1000). The ETO booklet *Makalle—Gateway to Rock-hewn Churches of Tigre* has details of three circuits of different lengths and difficulty, one circuit possible in an ordinary car, the other two by four-wheel-drive. The first circuit includes seven churches close to the main Addis Ababa–Asmara highway between Wokro and Adigrat; these can be visited in two days with an overnight at Makalle or Adigrat.

Getting There, Getting Around

Makalle, easily reached by twice-weekly EAL flights, is just off the main Addis–Asmara highway. See package tours EP-28, 33–34, and 36. There is a daily bus from Axum, frequent buses to Asmara, Dessie, and Addis Ababa. Permission to visit the churches must be obtained from the Abuna's office in Makalle; prepaid entrance cards can be purchased (E$1 each) from the Abraha Castle Hotel, which can arrange for guides, interpreters, and mule skinners (E$2 per day) and has one Land-Rover available (E75¢ per km plus E$5 for the driver).

When to Visit

You can visit Makalle anytime, but don't plan a church-climbing camping trip for June–September, February–March.

Accommodations

Abraha Castle Hotel, Box 82, Makalle, tel. 62. 30 dbls, some w/ bath. Rates: B&B: sgl—E$9.50 to E$10.50; dbl—E$17 to E$19. Built 80 years ago by a cousin of Yohannes IV, Abraha Castle fell into ruin, was restored for use as a hotel 1965–66, has a new, modern interior, bar, lounge, dining room (breakfast—E$1.50; lunch or dinner —E$3), broad terrace with view over town in basin-valley below. . . . *Green Hotel* is a small, new hotel serving breakfast only. . . . Many local hotels. . . . At Quiha, on the Addis–Asmara road, is the *Touring Hotel,* tel. 5. Rates: B&B: sgl—E$16; dbl—E$26; lunch or dinner— E$5.

Semyen Mountains

Semyen Mountains National Park, about 160 km northeast of Gondar, contains some of Ethiopia's most spectacular mountain scenery. The area is an awesomely rugged volcanic highland mostly exceeding 10,000 feet, with the Empire's highest mountain, 14,901-foot Ras Dashan, aloofly soaring in the center, and giant hills severely separated by 2,000-foot-deep canyons. The scenery is supposed to equal the Grand Canyon's, and owing to its extent and altitude well deserves the name "Roof of Africa." The 88-square-mile park itself is a segment of the mountainous region but encompasses the whole dramatic Northern Escarpment.

However, the Semyen Mountains and park remain somewhat remote for the average tourist, because there are no roads yet and to get into the mountains requires a mule trek from the Gondar–Axum road town of Debarek. You can either make a long, large circuit around the Semyens in four to six weeks of rough travel, or you can make a shorter, easier circuit that takes only about five unrushed days. A good booklet describing the two circuits, renting of mules, scenery, and animals is the ETO's *High Semyen,* which you should read before contemplating the trip. (Clive Nicol's *From the Roof of Africa* chronicles his time as a game warden in Semyen.)

Protected within the Semyen Park's boundaries are the Walia ibex, Semyen fox, and Gelada baboon, all unique to Ethiopia and usually seen above 7,500 feet altitude. The *Walia ibex* is one of two species of wild goat or ibex that occur in Africa; the other is the Nubian ibex, found in the hot, barren hills of northern Eritrea and Sudan. The Walia ibex is very rare, with an estimate given by the naturalist Leslie Brown of 150 to 200 goats left, all in the Semyen escarpments. The Walia ibex, usually seen on precipitous crags, is a sturdily built animal, 3 feet high at the shoulder, weighing up to about 250 pounds, and having an overall thick chocolate-brown-colored coat, with pale white on the belly and underlegs. Mature males have a beard on the chin, and heavily ringed, massive, backward-curving, arched horns; females have smaller bodies and shorter, thinner, lightly ringed horns.

The *Semyen fox* is bright sandy red with white undermarkings and has a long bushy tail with a black tip. Its prey is mainly mountain rodents, though it probably eats birds, rabbits, and hyrax.

The *Gelada baboon,* seen in troops of up to 400, is quite large and is covered with thick, silky chestnut-brown hair. The male has an enormous mane or ruff sprouting out around his head, so that sometimes he may be mistaken for a lion. The baboon's nickname "bleeding (or sacred) heart" derives from the heart-shaped patch of naked, bright pink skin in the middle of its chest, on both females and males.

Resident birds in the Semyens include the augur buzzard, Verreaux's eagle, kestrels and lanner falcons, lammergeier, choughs, wheatears, and chats.

When to Visit

The best months for mule trekking are September–February, and in May. It is not advisable to attempt treks in the rains March–April or mid-June–August, because the mules slip too much and it is very wet. Do have coolish clothes for the warm days, warm clothes for the cold nights.

Getting There, Getting Around

The base camp of Debarek is about 162 km from Gondar and 270 km from Axum on the main Gondar–Axum road. You could fly to Gondar, then rent a taxi to take you all the way to Debarek. If you have your own car, you can leave it at the police station in Debarek. Pack donkeys and mules, and riding mules or horses, can be hired in Debarek. The ETO suggests that the rate to bargain for is E$2 per day per mule, and E$1.50 per day for a drover (muleskinner) for every two to three pack animals. A caravan leader expects about E$3 per day. Bring all your food, though you can find thin chickens (E$1), sheep (E$9–10), goats (E$7–8), eggs (3 for E10¢), plus the non-alcoholic mountain village drink of *korifi*, which is made from cereals, looks like liquid mud, but can taste okay. Also bring all your own camping equipment, and warm clothes.

Accommodations

The only tourist-class hotels are in Gondar and Axum. There are supposed to be a couple of small, very local hotels at Sankober, Geech, and Chenek, which cost E$3 per night. Otherwise, come equipped with all camping gear and food.

Axum

Axum, a town of 12,810, is a quiet place, but it was once the capital of an empire whose power stretched from Arabia to the Nile. Established about 160 km inland from the Red Sea, Axum was said to be the residence of the semilegendary Queen of Sheba, whose brief union with King Solomon led to the birth of Menelik I, from whom Haile Selassie claimed direct descent. Axum reached its apex in the 4th century A.D., and at that time there were nearly 100 tall stone steles and large castles for the Axumite kings. The 4th century also saw the conversion of King Ezana to Christianity, and Axum has long been considered the holy city of Ethiopia.

The legend of Solomon and Sheba is a romantic one, and is directly interwoven with Ethiopian history and culture. There are many versions of the legend, one being that about 980 B.C. the Queen of Sheba (also called Queen Makeda) ruled over northern Ethiopia from her capital at Axum, where she lived in a castle and worshiped the sun. She had heard of the wisdom of King Solomon, and decided to test for herself how wise he might be. So with a huge retinue she set off to Jerusalem, bringing gifts of gold, spices, and jewels. She was immediately impressed with Solomon's wisdom and with Judaism. Her visit is referred to in the Bible (1 Kings 10:1–13, and 2 Chronicles 9:1–12), in which King Solomon was said to give Sheba "all her desires, whatsoever she asked." However, just before she left he tricked her into sleeping with him, according to Ethiopian legend. He fed her a very spicy meal and then said that if she insisted on sleeping alone, she could take absolutely nothing belonging to him. When she awoke in the night with a tremendous thirst and took a sip of water from the glass beside her bed, Solomon, watching her, reminded her of her promise, and Makeda, rather than break her word, slept with him. On her return journey, the Ethiopian story continues, a son, Ebna Hakim ("son of the wise") was born to Queen Makeda. When he came of age, she sent him to Solomon, and upon his return he brought with him the Holy Ark of the Covenant to strengthen Judaism in the country. The son succeeded to the throne, and was then given the name Menelik I. It is from him that the Solomonic line, until recently the oldest surviving monarchy in the world, was said to descend, with Emperor Haile Selassie the 225th in the line. The Solomon and Sheba story is the subject of traditional, comic-strip-like paintings, a good shopping buy; see p. 471.

Historically, around 1000 B.C. there were migrations of Sabean Semites from southwest Arabia to northern Ethiopia. They belonged to two groups: the Habashat ("a mixture of races," from which the word Abyssinia comes) and the A'gazi ("one who migrates," from which the name Ge'ez, the ancient Ethiopian liturgical language, comes). To the indigenous Hamitic peoples, the migrants brought with them their knowledge of irrigation canals and dams, terraced planting methods, property laws, animal husbandry, civil administration, urbanization, and a religious worship of the sun, moon, and stars (overthrowing the old animal worship—represented in Solomon and Sheba paintings by the slaying of the dragon). Gradually they moved from the coast into the highlands of Tigre and Eritrea, building their capital at well-forested, well-watered, 7,800-foot-high Axum. By the 1st century A.D. the Axumite kingdom emerged, and commerce expanded with ivory brought from the Nile regions through Axum to the Red Sea port of Adulis. The *Periplus,* a 1st-century A.D. guide to the Indian Ocean, mentions "the city of the people called Axumites," where "all the ivory is brought from the country beyond the Nile," and which is governed "by Zoscales, who is miserly in his ways and always striving for more but otherwise upright and acquainted with Greek literature."

The first Axumite king about whom much is known is Ezana (A.D. 325–350), and it is under him that Axum reached its height of power and fame. His quest for fame and empire, stretching to today's Khartoum on the Nile, led him to record his military and political achievements in three languages on stone thrones and steles that still exist in Axum. The greatest event during his reign, though, was his official conversion to Christianity. According to Ethiopian tradition, Ezana was influenced by a Syrian monk named Frumentius, who had served as regent of Axum until Ezana's manhood, and later became the first bishop of the Ethiopian Coptic Church and converted Ezana to Christianity sometime after A.D. 340. The coins minted by Ezana in his early years are still pagan, while his later ones include the words: "By the might of the Lord of Heaven who in Heaven and on Earth has power over all." Also during his reign, great building activity went on in Axum, with dozens of stone steles raised, including one over 100 feet high.

The second and last great Axumite king was Kaleb (514–542), who was famous for his military campaigns into Arabia. Under the inspiration of the Byzantine emperor Justinian and with some of his ships, Kaleb led 100,000 soldiers against Dhu Nuwas, the Jewish king of Himyar (Yemen), who had apparently been persecuting Christians there. Kaleb reestablished Axumite rule in southwest Arabia (as had been the case about A.D. 200). However, this second climax in Axum's role as a great empire in the Red Sea was brief. Persian armies conquered Axumite territories in south Arabia, and Arab armies conquered Palestine and Egypt, cutting Ethiopia from the rest of the Christian world. In the 8th century pirate raids launched from Eritrea against Jeddah, the Moslem port, led to the Moslems' capturing Axumite ports and burning Adulis. This destroyed Axum's commercial power on the Red Sea, and Axum's decline gained momentum. In the 10th century supposedly a non-Christian queen called Judith or Yudit from the rebellious Agau tribe led a revolt against the Axumite dynasty, killing hundreds of the ruling class and ransacking and burning Axum. According to tradition only one prince survived, and he settled in Shoa Province. A century later the new Zagwe dynasty emerged in Lasta and established their capital in what was to become Lalibela. After more than 1,000 years, the Axumite kingdom was through, and the power center shifted southward.

Today Axum is a fairly quiet, moderate-sized town to which tourists are drawn to see the evidence of its past glories: stelae, tombs, and ruins. Starting a driving-walking tour at the Touring Hotel, you come to a fork in the road with a small triangular park in the center. This *Garden of the Stelae* contains monoliths, capitals, and other examples of early Axumite architecture, the most important of which is the 3-foot-high, 4th-century stele of King Ezana. It has inscriptions in Greek, Ge'ez, and Sabean referring to Ezana's exploits against Beja tribesmen, and calls him "King of Axum, of Himyar, of Raidan, of Saba, of Solchin, of Siryamo, of Beja, and of Kaso, King of Kings, son of the unvanquished Area. . . ." Though pagan, the inscription shows the Christian influence by mentioning Ezana's kind treatment of prisoners captured.

To the right of the road and just off it is the *Tomb of King Bazen*, who is thought to have ruled 7 B.C. to A.D. 10. At the south end of the tombs a stairway cut into the stone descends to a chamber with several tombs cut in the walls. Another chamber leading off from this has four tombs cut in the walls.

Continuing up the road going north, you come to the focal point in historic Axum: on one side of the square are the new and old St. Mary of Zion churches, on the other side the *Park of the Stelae*. It is thought that there were no fewer than 100 stelae in Axum, 7 of them giant granite monoliths standing together, perhaps marking the graves of kings. The largest of this group now lies in huge pieces on the ground, but when upright measured about 105 feet high and weighed 500 tons. The second-highest stele, measuring about 83 feet, was removed by Mussolini's Italians in 1937 to Rome, where it still stands near the Arch of Constantine; Emperor Haile Selassie hoped to get it back during his state visit to Italy in 1970, but the Italians would still not relinquish it. The highest stele left standing measures 73½ feet above the ground, and 9½ feet below the ground. The other four tall stelae, including the "Stele of the Lances," which has a pair of lances in relief at the top, lie in ruins scattered around the area. All seven stelae date from the 3d or 4th century A.D., are made of immense single pieces of granite, and have very similar decoration. Each was erected in the middle of a step platform of stone on a terrace of polished limestone, and at each stele's base was a rectangular offering table or stone altar with bowl-shaped cavities, perhaps for sacrificial offerings to the dead. Each stele resembled what might be called a small skyscraper with multiple fake stories. At the bottom was carved an imitation doorway with a bolt and lock in a square framework of fake timber. Above this a row of low windows was followed by a series of tall ones separated from each other by round ends of imitation wooden beams that seem to support each window story. This layered, wood crossbeam and long window effect is the typical indigenous Axumite style, and is imitated in churches in Lalibela and elsewhere. At the top of the stele was an arc which perhaps symbolized the cosmic universe.

Besides the speculation that the mainly pre-Christian stelae marked the graves of kings, other theories are that they represented the stairway by which the "soul" of the deceased ascended to the celestial heights, or that they served as imaginary houses of the spirits of the dead. Looking at the immense stelae, one wonders how they were transported from the quarry (about 4 km out on the Gondar road) and then raised. Richard Pankhurst and Geoffrey Last suggest in their *History of Ethiopia in Pictures* that a stele was pulled forward on rolling logs, pulled up an earthen ramp, and then tilted down into a hole below the ramp by using the edge of the ramp as a fulcrum. The many workers (perhaps slaves) could then raise the stele to an upright position, secure it in the hole, and remove the ramp.

Across the street from the Park of the Stelae is the *new Church of St. Mary of Zion,* topped by a 24-foot-high cross. Greek architects designed it, using the hand-hewn rock churches of Lalibela as an inspiration, while the bell tower with its grilling imitates the stelae. It was dedicated and opened in 1965 by Haile Selassie with Queen Elizabeth of England in attendance. Crowns of Ethiopian emperors and other relics are displayed inside.

To the right of the new church is the *old Church of St. Mary of Zion,* which stands on the site of a 4th-century Axumite church that was destroyed first by Queen Judith in the 10th century, rebuilt, then destroyed again by the Moslem Gragn in the 16th century. It is closed to women. Only the platform and wide stone steps leading to the original church still remain. The present church was possibly built during the reign of Emperor Fasiladas of Gondar (1632–67), and is rectangular with a center aisle supported by pillars, the Holy of Holies in the rear, and a number of paintings depicting Ethiopian religious tradition; by tradition, in its inner sanctuary is the Ark of the Covenant, brought from Jerusalem by Menelik I. On the left side of the church is the *Treasury,* also closed to women. In it are manuscripts and paintings, gold and silver crosses, and crowns of Emperors Yohannes IV (1868–89) and Menelik II (1889–1911). A priest will bring the crowns and some crosses out into the Treasury's back garden so that women in a tour can see and photograph them through the metal fence.

Out in front of the old church is a row of 12 stone platforms, said to be the remains of the *Thrones of the Judges,* and while once they may have had statues of pagan gods they were later utilized in the kings' coronation ceremonies. To the left of them stood the king's *Throne of David,* now marked by four pillars which may have supported a canopy; here kings were crowned until the Middle Ages.

Leaving the area of the churches and going back past the stelae, you come to the *Mai Shum reservoir,* a large, sunken, open pool that is also called the Queen of Sheba's Bath. In ancient Axum it was the source of an irrigation system, while today women and children climb down into it to fill their pottery jugs and big tin cans. On Timkat it may be used for baptismal ceremonies. Continuing up this road for about 2 km to the top of the hill, you come to the I-shaped, connected remains of two edifices and two tombs. These are traditionally identified as those of 6th-century Emperor Kaleb on the left and his son Gebre-Maskal on the right. *King Kaleb's tomb* inside has three rooms side by side, and the stonework definitely shows a high mastery of the art of construction. In *King Gebre-Maskal's tomb* are five rooms: the one directly across from the stairs has three lidless coffins, two rooms have two stone coffins, and two others have crosses carved into the walls.

As you go back through town and take the Gondar road about 1 km out, the road bisects the ruins of *three castles* dating back to the Axumite empire, though now only the foundations remain. Their outline suggests that they were square, with a square tower at each corner, and two to four stories high. They are now named Enda Mikael, Enda Semeon, and Taeca Mariam, so either the original buildings were converted into churches or churches were built on the site of the old palaces.

Five km (or about two hours' walk) north of Axum is the *Church of Abba Pantaleon,* founded in the 6th century by one of the "nine saints" of the Ethiopian Church who came on a pilgrimage from Syria and settled in a hermitage on the present church site. On the hilltop is the old church (closed to women) which was the sanctuary for the saint. In a hole excavated in the rock the saint is reputed to have stood upright with his arms uplifted for 45 years praying for the success of King Kaleb in his military mission to prevent the persecution of Christians in southern Arabia. King Kaleb is also said to have used the church as a hermitage for 12 years, leaving his throne to his son Gebre-Maskal; the paintings of the church relate Kaleb's life. At the foot of the cliff is a new church open to women, with traditional paintings inside.

When to Visit

Axum is generally open all year, although during the heavy rainy season of July–September the airstrip may be closed temporarily to EAL planes.

Getting There, Getting Around

Axum is 178 km south of Asmara by road, 1,005 km north of Addis Ababa. Daily buses run from Asmara (about 4 hours); other buses run from Addis Ababa via Gondar. EAL has daily flights from both Addis Ababa and Asmara. Tour operators with packages are under EP-26–31, 33, 36–37, 41–42. VW buses from the Touring Hotel visit the ruins and stelae in the morning and/or afternoon; to join a tour is E$3 for transport, E$9 for admission fees. A very good local government-approved guide to ask for is Ato Brhane Meskel Zelelew.

Accommodations

Touring Hotel, Box 21, Axum; tel. 5. Bookings also to Navigatana S.A., Box 1630, Addis Ababa; tel. 444500. 8 sgls, 29 dbls, all but 6 dbls w/shower. Rates: FB: sgl—E$33; dbl—E$54. Built in the mid-1950s as one-story yellow buildings with corrugated red tin roofs, its plainish though comfortable new wing rooms were added in 1972. There are plans to add 42 more rooms and a pool by 1974. Round dining room has Ethiopian murals and serves delicious Italian table d'hôte meals: breakfast—E$2.50; lunch or dinner—E$6. Rating: 1st-class local. . . . *Ras Mengesha Hotel,* tel. 17. 20 rooms. Rates: Bed only: sgl—E$4; dbl—E$8. For the rockbottom budgeter. . . . Planned for the end of 1975 is a *Hilton Lodge,* with 64 double rooms, bar, dining room, pool.

Adowa

Adowa (Adua), a stop for road travelers on the Historic Route 25 km from Axum, was the site of the Ethiopians' decisive victory over the Italians on March 1, 1896. Led into war because of a dispute over an important article in the 1889 Treaty of Wuchale, Menelik II at Adowa fielded a force of 100,000 riflemen and 40 cannon against General Oreste Baratieri's 14,500 soldiers and 56 cannon. With superior strategy and a few tricks (planner Ras Alula led the Italians to believe there would be a mass pilgrimage from Menelik's army to Axum that day), Ethiopian soldiers in Adowa's rugged terrain wiped out the three Italian columns (each major general commanding was also killed). The Italian humiliation, celebrated as a big Ethiopian holiday, resulted in Italy's abandoning its claim to an Ethiopian protectorate, and the European powers acknowledged Ethiopia's independence. The battlefield, unmarked by any memorial, can be visited by a lengthy walk (with guide) over difficult terrain. Points of interest near Adowa town are the churches of *Enda Selassie,* built by Yohannes IV, with good wall paintings depicting the legends of saints, and *Adowa Tsion* and the old monastery of *Enda Abba Gerima.* **Accommodations:** *Assem Wenz Hotel* and the new *Yared Hotel,* neither the best lodging. See also package tours EP-37, 41.

Yeha

Yeha, 28 km from Adowa, has the ruins of Ethiopia's oldest town, perhaps predating Axum by 1,000 years. It was founded by Sabeans from the south Arabian kingdom of Saba (Sheba), who built a city here which was the political center of the north. By some local traditions, Yeha was the Queen of Sheba's capital and there was a temple faced with gold. Still standing is a *pagan temple* dedicated to a moon-god called Almuqah. Built about 500 B.C. of polished limestone slabs fitted together without mortar, it is the oldest surviving building in Ethiopia. In front are some interesting stelae, which are grave markers, and to the left of the temple is a church with a bas-relief frieze depicting a row of ibexes (wild goats), also an excellent inscription in ancient Sabean. A number of graves were excavated, and the burial goods and other finds, including pottery and bronze agricultural tools, are at the National Museum in Addis Ababa. A Christian city was built on top of the Sabean city in the 6th century and the temples converted into churches. Access: A 5-km track to Yeha village goes left 23 km from Adowa, 7 km past Enticcio if going toward Adowa. See also tours EP-37 and 41.

Debre Damo

Debre Damo is very much like Greece's Mount Athos—it is a barely accessible monastery perched on a flat-topped *amba* and is forbidden to all females, a tradition in some Ethiopian religious places that apparently dates from 10th-century Queen Judith's burning of Axum and its surrounding churches. Located 10 km north of the Adowa–Adigrat road, holy Debre Damo is reached by a footpath crossing several ravines, a long scramble up, then a climb up a Jacob's ladder—a 50-foot plaited-leather rope. The medieval church is in the Axumite style, built with layers of wood and stone. The monastery has been in continuous use since the 6th century. Though visitors are shown few treasures, they are given refreshment at the abbot's guesthouse.

Matara

Matara ruins, just south of Senafe, 135 km south of Asmara on the Addis Ababa road, are being extensively excavated by the Institute of Archaeology, which has been working here since 1959. Though mainly an Axumite city, the ruins show three levels of building: Ethio-Sabean period (5th to 4th century B.C.), an intermediate period (3d century B.C. to 1st century A.D.), and the Axumite period (1st to 10th centuries A.D.). The excavations at what has been described by historian Richard Greenfield as a "little Babylon of the sixth century" have uncovered six groups of buildings: *A* includes what is perhaps the house of a lord, constructed with alternating projecting and receding sections, characteristic of Axumite builders. *B* building, better conceived, has a stairway down to a small empty crypt, with a stone lintel inscribed with an Axumite cross. *C* and *D* groups have halls laid out without any apparent plan. *E,* on a privileged site on high ground, includes some excavated graves. *F* site has the ruins of a small basilica (early Christian church) and, to the east, a baptismal font. Nearby is the obelisk of Matara, a monolith about 17 feet high, the top decorated with a crescent mounted on a disk (the symbol of a great south Arabian divinity), the middle with an inscription in ancient Ethiopian. At the National Museum in Addis Ababa are some of the treasures found at Matara, including a 1st-century B.C. bronze oil lamp of great artistry, a blue glazed vase, gold Byzantine crosses of the 8th century A.D., and Roman coins. Getting to Matara is easy. Take a track left off the highway 1 km south of Senafe. See EP-41 tour listing. An ETO pamphlet on Matara includes a map. **Accommodations,** at Adigrat: *Ethiopia Hotel* and *Welwallo Hotel,* neither tourist class.

Cohaito

Cohaito, 132 km from Asmara off the Addis Ababa road, and not far from the Matara ruins, are the remains of the ancient Axumite city of Coloe, visited in the 1st century A.D. and described in the *Periplus.* Not much excavated, the ruins include a pre-Christian, Sabean reservoir, some foundations of Axumite buildings with some excellent pillars, and the Egyptian Tomb, in which were found the remains of 70 bodies wrapped in skins. Nearby, at the plateau cliff, are some remarkable cave paintings. Access: An 11-km track passable by four-wheel-drive leads left off the main road about 122 km from Asmara.

Asmara

Ethiopia's second city, and capital of Eritrea, is Asmara (alt. 7,541 feet), an Italian-looking city in a high, barren land that, just north-east of town, suddenly drops 7,500 feet down to Massawa on the Red Sea. With palm tree-lined Haile Selassie I Avenue, a couple of churches and museums, a Roman-style evening gaiety, and a warm, sunny climate with cool nights, Asmara ("forest of flowers") is a minor tourist attraction; most Historic Route tours begin or end here.

The Italians occupied the village of Asmara in August 1889 and established the colony of Eritrea (named from the Erythraean Sea—Mare Erythraeum of the ancient geographers) in 1890, but ran the colony from hot, low Massawa for a decade before moving up to cooler Asmara. The town grew under Mussolini and, at the invasion of Ethiopia in the mid-1930s, became a big military base. Fifty thousand Italians crowded into the city, doubling the population to 100,000 by 1940. The Allies liberated Asmara April 1, 1941, and Eritrea came under a British Military Administration.

In 1947 the Big Four were unable to agree on the future of Eritrea, but in 1950–52 the U.N. decided the area should be semiautonomous but connected to Ethiopia. On September 11, 1952, Eritrea federated with Ethiopia, but its own parliament ran Eritrea's domestic affairs. In 1962 the parliament realized the economic and political unviability of the area, dissolved itself, and Eritrea became an integral part of Ethiopia—a fact the Eritrean Liberation Front still disputes with occasional violence.

The population of 232,550 still includes 3,500 Italians, along with 2,000 Americans connected with the big Kagnew communications base, which is to be phased out. The city is somewhat quiet during the day but comes alive in the evening with hundreds of strollers along Haile Selassie I Avenue, seeking a place for the traditional late dinner and perhaps shopping (stores are open until about 8:30). Industry is growing, but compared with Addis Ababa, Asmara is stagnating. "The departure of many thousands of Italians," says Ethiopia authority Edward Ullendorf, "has left it an empty, at times almost eerie, place, a white elephant, a Turin or Perugia in the Alps of Ethiopia."

Besides the two museums, *Asmara Archaeological Museum* and

Museum of the Collegio La Salle (description below), the tourist can visit the three principal churches. *St. Mary's,* the Ethiopian Orthodox Church, on Menelik II Avenue, is built on the site of a church that collapsed in 1916 during the rains. The façade of the present church has large, colorful mosaics depicting religious figures, but the interior is simple, with only a series of eight paintings on the life of Christ. At the entrance to the St. Mary's compound is a small church built in 1917 after ancient Ethiopian models, with the Axumite-style imitation horizontal layers of wood and stone, with protruding beams. The red-brick *Roman Catholic Cathedral* on H.S.I. Avenue was built in 1922. Its tall Gothic bell tower is a landmark on the city skyline. A few blocks north of the municipal building on H.S.I. Avenue is the Arabic-Roman *Grand Mosque,* designed by an Italian architect and opened in 1937. Women are not allowed inside, and men must remove their shoes.

There are many local markets, including one specializing in used clothes, another in spices; the big market area is spread out near Ethiopia Square between Empress Menen and Menelik II avenues. Excursions can be made to Keren, the "garden city," to Massawa and on to the ancient port of Adulis, south to the ruins at Cohaito (Coloe), Matara, Yeha, and Axum, the famous battlefield of Adowa, and farther south to Makalle and the surrounding rock churches. Asmara city tours include a drive to Dorfu on the spectacular "corkscrew" road down to Massawa, and to the village of Aas-Aas. The more adventurous can make the steep climb from Nefasit, 24 km from Asmara, up to the monastery of *Debre Bizen* for a superb view of the coastal desert and the Red Sea.

Accommodations

Nyala Hotel, Box 867, tel. 113111; cable NYALA. On Queen Elizabeth Ave. about 1 km from H.S.I. Ave. and city center. 66 dbls, incl 12 suites, all w/bath, balcony. Rates: Bed only: sgl—E$18–23; dbl—E$33–38. Credit: AE, DC. Built in 1969 with 9 stories, the Nyala since added a 15-floor extension to make a total of 150–170 rooms in 1974. Rooms are semimodern and most have a view. Also several bars, 1st-floor table d'hôte dining room, top-floor à la carte restaurant, curio shop, airline, car-hire, and tour offices, babysitting service, parking. Rating: 1st-class international, although leaning toward the plastic. Popular with American package tours.

Imperial Hotel, bookings to Campagnia Italiana Alberghi Ciaao,

Box 181, tel. 113222; cable CIAAO. On 30 Dej. Hailu Kebede St. about ½ km from city center. 49 dbls, incl 4 suites, all w/bath or shower, balcony. Rates: Bed only: sgl—E$22–25.50; dbl—E$35–41. Credit: AE, DC. Built in 1968, the Imperial's gold and white lobby has nice marble floors and large lounge. Brown and white rooms are semi-modern but could use carpeting. Cheerful pink breakfast room, plus main table d'hôte and à la carte restaurant. Tour operators book packagers here, too. Rating: a little less 1st-class international than the Nyala, but nice nevertheless.

CIAAO Hotel, same booking address as the Imperial. On 62 Menelik II Ave. in a quiet residential area about 1½ km from city center. 34 sgls, 29 dbls, most w/bath or shower. Rates: Bed only: sgl—E$12.50–17; dbl—E$27–30. Credit: AE, DC. The CIAAO (pronounced "chow") was built in the late 1930s but has been kept up nicely. Its lobby features beautiful Verona marble, and its rooms are oldish but clean and ordered. Dining room serves mainly Italian table d'hôte and à la carte meals. Also a TV lounge, bar, and banquet room. Rating: 1st-class local, good for reasonably priced package tours or middle-budget travelers.

Albergo Italia, tel. 110740. About 4 blocks north of H.S.I. Ave. on Itegue Menen Ave. 13 sgls, 15 dbls; 6 rms w/shower. Rates: Bed only: sgl—E$16; dbl—E$18. Centrally located and older, the Albergo is quite tidy. Rooms are respectably clean, and some have fancy window-frame plasterwork. Restaurant is one of the best Italian ones in town. Rating: between 1st- and 2d-class local, good for budget travelers.

White Hotel, tel. 112844. About 2 blocks from the Albergo Italia and 6 blocks from H.S.I. Ave., on Said Abid St. and up some stone stairs. 11 sgls, 19 dbls; 7 rms w/bath or shower. Rates: Bed only: sgl—E$10–12; dbl—E$16. Owned by the Albergo Italia, the White is very Italian and most of the staff speak that more than English. Rooms are clean, modest, and matter-of-fact, but spray between the sheets for fleas. Central and quiet. Rating: 2d-class local.

Axum Hotel, Box 986, tel. 115044. 50 sgls and dbls, some w/bath or shower. Rates: Bed only: sgl—E$8; dbl—E$17. A well-built building with rooftop terrace but in the middle of the Babylon (bar) district so may be noisy at night. Rating: 2d-class local.

There are also a number of *pensiones* that offer unfancy, cheap lodgings. Rates: about E$3 for sgl, E$5 dbl, bed only. Check for fleas. Some of them are: *Pensione Africa,* 10 Haramat St. off Haile Selassie

Ave. *Pensione Diana,* 26 Welye Bitul St. *Pensione Lalibela,* Asfa Wossen St., tel. 114855.

Where to Eat

This section is divided into Continental (including Italian) and Ethiopian restaurants and dining rooms.

CONTINENTAL

Nyala Hotel Restaurant, tel. 113111. The 1st-floor dining room serves table d'hôte lunches and dinners—E$6.50. Top-floor restaurant, with a good view and a band nightly (except Monday), has à la carte: soufflé of artichokes or spinach, scampi picador, cordon bleu, filets de poisson Andalusie. Entrées E$5 to E$6. Credit: AE, DC.

Imperial Hotel Restaurant, tel. 113222. Modern blue and orange dining room serves table d'hôte lunch and dinner—E$6. Also à la carte: smoked salmon, asparagus omelet, shrimp U.S. style, grilled sirloin. Entrées E$2.50 to E$3. Credit: AE, DC.

CIAAO Hotel Restaurant, tel. 110933. Ground-floor dining room has Italian table d'hôte lunches and dinners with 3 course choices plus dessert and coffee—E$5; extra side dishes—E$1.75 to E$2.50. Credit: AE, DC.

Albergo Italia Hotel Restaurant, tel. 110740. High-ceilinged dining room serves good Italian à la cartes: hearty soups, spaghetti or macaroni, omelets, chicken, veal, and beef. Entrées E$1.50 to E$3.50.

Rino's Restaurant, at 10/14 Ali Osman Buri St. by ETO office; just off H.S.I. Ave.; tel. 111695. More good Italian à la carte fare served in a pleasant, unfancy atmosphere: pizza neapolitan, minestrone, fried shrimp, veal scallopini, chicken in rice suprême sauce. Entrées E$1 to E$3.

San Giorgio Restaurant, at 32/34 Fessahaye Kiffle St. by EAL office; just off H.S.I. Ave. Three-part yellow dining room serves prawn cocktail, filet mignon, beef fondue, fish fillet; entrées E$1.50 to E$3. Two-course table d'hôte: E$2.50. Specialty is "chicken in clay" (order a day in advance).

ETHIOPIAN

Sport Restaurant, 7 Melles Ghebrezghi St. off H.S.I. Ave., and the *Abeba Restaurant,* Ras Alula St. near the U.S. Consulate, both serve traditional Ethiopian food for about E$1 a meal.

There are also dozens of small, usually clean bar/cafés lining H.S.I. Ave. and other streets serving soft and hard drinks, coffee and tea, cakes for about E15¢–50¢ each.

Getting Around

Expensive taxis rank up outside the major hotels and charge at least E$2 to go somewhere within the central city. Determine the price before accepting the ride. There are also horse-drawn *gharis* (carts holding 3) which should cost E25¢–50¢ a ride within city center—set the price before riding. Buses run all over Asmara, and the standard fare is E15¢. Inquire with an English-speaking Ethiopian as to which bus to take to your destination. Note: "H.S.I." is a common written abbreviation for streets, etc., named for Haile Selassie I; some or all these names will change. Some old street signs still have "Via . . ." instead of ". . . Street." And some hotels, car-hire firms, etc., do not have P.O. box numbers but instead use their street address. Buses and taxis stop running about 8 P.M.

Information Bureau

The ETO office on H.S.I. Ave. at Ali Osman Buri Street can give you a free booklet on Asmara and help you find your way around.

Nightlife

The main form of entertainment until about 8:30 P.M. is promenading up and down Haile Selassie I Avenue looking at all the shops and choosing a place to eat a late dinner. Otherwise, there's not a lot happening in Asmara at night. The *Nyala Hotel*'s top-floor restaurant has an Italian band nightly except Monday. The *Mocambo Club* at 23 Itegue Zehaitu St. off H.S.I. Ave. has a band and an occasional cabaret. *Piccadilly Club* at 167 H.S.I. Ave. near the Impero Cinema also sometimes has a floor show. Most of the Ethiopian bars are in the "Babylon" district in the side streets south of H.S.I. Ave.

Cinemas

The *Odeon* at 6 King Mikael St., tel. 111544, specializes in English-speaking films. The *Roma* at 93 Queen Elizabeth Ave., tel. 111787, and the *Impero* on H.S.I. Ave., tel. 110162, have Italian films, sometimes with French and Arabic subtitles.

Museums

The *Asmara Archaeological Museum,* at the Liceo Scientifico "F. Martini" at 13 Dej. Hailu Kebede St. off H.S.I. Ave. is open Monday–Saturday mornings and late afternoons. It has a good collection of historical items from pre-Axumite and Axumite periods found at sites in Eritrea and Tigre provinces, including statues, pottery, columns, and pillars and woodwork from the ancient church that once stood at the present site of the St. Mary's Orthodox Church in Asmara. The *Museum of the Collegio La Salle* at 26 Abuna Kesate Berhan St. has a collection of ancient items found around Asmara by the avid amateur Italian archaeologist Sr. Giuseppe Tringali in the 1950s and 1960s.

Shops and Services

All the below are on Haile Selassie I Avenue unless otherwise indicated.

Books: Monaci Derna Bookshop, 4 Fit. Melles Ghebrezghi St., Box 1218, tel. 110672.

Dry cleaner: Seferian & Co.

Florist: Artico de Regalo.

Groceries: CASA.

Pharmacies: Farmacia Asmara. Adulis Pharmacy. Impero Pharmacy.

Photo shops: Bini Raffaello, Ras Desta Damtew Ave. Foto M. Zubeir.

Tailors: Tessuti Confezioni Silvestri. Sartoria Guidice Tessuti.

Massawa

Massawa (pop. 19,820) is Ethiopia's blisteringly hot Red Sea port, only 112 km from Asmara but fully 7,500 feet lower, and reached by a spectacular escarpment drive or ride on the railway. Built on two flat islands connected to the mainland by a short causeway, Massawa is a fairly popular tourist day trip from Asmara, and there is swimming, water skiing, skin diving and coral hunting, deep-sea fishing, and yachting in the Red Sea.

The seaport is quite old, being mentioned in 9th-century writings, perhaps founded as the successor to the Axumite port of Adulis. Massawa was conquered by the Ottoman Turks in the 16th century and held by them for nearly 300 years (Turkish buildings and ruins are scattered around) before being displaced by the Egyptians about 1850. The Egyptians used Massawa as a springboard into the interior but were defeated at Gura in 1875. The British took over the port in 1884 but sold it (what cheek!) to the Italians the next year, and it was a base of operations for Italy's campaigns in Ethiopia until the country was liberated in 1941. Most of the present city was built during the Italian colonial period.

Besides the *souk* or market, the tourist can visit the *salt pans*— shallow troughs of sea water between the causeway dikes where evaporation quickly creates salt fields that produce 100,000 tons of salt, which by weight is Eritrea's biggest export. The main beach is *Gurgusum Beach,* 15 minutes north; excursions can be made to *Isola Verde* ("green island"), which has a yacht club with pool, and to the Dahlak Islands (see below).

When to Visit

We quote from the ETO's Asmara brochure: "Massawa is world-famous for being one of the hottest inhabited places on earth. In the hot season, from March to September, the temperature often soars to 60° C. (140°F.). The coolest months are January and February. Light clothing is advisable."

Getting There, Getting Around

Getting there is most of the fun. There's the breathtaking, ear-popping, 7,500-foot drop down the winding, cliff-hanging escarpment road (a 3-hour drive; bus takes 4 hours). Small outdoor bars and *alberghi* en route. Don't drive it at night. The second way down is the Northern Ethiopia Railways' Eritrean railway, 73 miles from Asmara to Massawa, running through 30 tunnels (18 in a 6-mile stretch) and over 65 bridges as it zigzags its way down. Daily 4-hour *littorina* service each way, fare E$3 one way. See package listings EP-37, 39. Aircraft Company of Ethiopia has Chris-Craft and other boats for hire in Massawa.

Accommodations

Red Sea Hotel, Box 21, tel. 552544. 50 rooms w/bath, a-c. Rates: Bed only: sgl—E$25; dbl—E$40. Credit: AE. New (1967), first-class, modern, glaring-white hotel, all a-c, with sea view, swimming pool. Table d'hôte meals: breakfast—E$2 or E$3; lunch or dinner— E$6. . . . *Luna (New Ghedem) Hotel,* Box 91, tel. 552272. 23 rooms w/bath, a-c. Rates: Bed only: sgl—E$7; dbl—E$14. Meals: breakfast —E$1.50; lunch or dinner—E$2.50. Tourist-class motel with sea view. . . . *Corallo Hotel,* Box 109, tel. 552430. 18 rooms, some w/ bath, a-c. Rates: Bed only: sgl w/bath—E$10; dbl w/o bath—E$16. Meals: breakfast—E$2; lunch or dinner—E$4. Tourist class. . . . Also several small, cheap hotels and cheaper *pensiones.*

Where to Eat

Good seafood at the *Corallo.* Meals on the veranda at the *Regina Restaurant.* Many open-air cafés, also the *Trocadero* and *Cabaret* nightclubs.

Dahlak Islands

The *Dahlak Islands* have been proposed as a national park. They lie in the Red Sea right off Massawa, and include dozens of tiny, low-lying coral islands plus the larger ones of Dahlak-Kebir, Shumma, Nocra, Dissei, Dohul, Norah, and Kubari. Of the approximately 130 islands only 6 are inhabited by semi-Arab fishermen, who live in small villages and keep goats, sheep, donkeys, and camels, which compete with gazelles for the sparse vegetation. The Dahlak Islands offer beautiful white beaches, turquoise waters, exotic fish and coral reefs, boiling hot weather, and good birdwatching (reef heron, Caspian tern, tropic bird, osprey, Arabian bustard). There are no tourist facilities.

Adulis

Adulis, on the coast 48 km south of Massawa, is an ancient port, perhaps dating as early as 2400 B.C. when Egyptians seeking spices landed there, and flourished as one of the Sabean ports until apparently destroyed by Moslems from Arabia in the 8th century A.D. Excavations of sorts were conducted in 1868 and 1906, but the uncovered ruins mostly disappeared until recently when the Institute of Archaeology began digging.

Other Destinations

Other tourist destinations, off the Historic Route, are listed below alphabetically:

Awash National Park

Awash National Park, due east of Addis Ababa on the eastern edge of the Rift Valley overlooking the Danakil plains, stretches over about

450 square miles of mostly open plains covered with grass and thorn-scrub. In its southwest corner is the semidormant volcano Mount Fantalle, which rises to over 6,000 feet. Near the northern boundary is Filwoha, an extensive area of hot mineral-water pools fringed with palm trees. The southern boundary is partially formed by the Awash River with its waterfalls and gorges, and the Addis Ababa–Awash highway bisects the southern section of the park from west to east. Some of the animals recorded in the park are Beisa oryx, Soemmering's gazelle, greater and lesser kudu, hippo, Grevy's zebra, mountain reed-buck, bushbuck, lion, leopard, cheetah, bat-eared fox, caracul, aardvark, colobus and vervet monkeys, tortoise, hyrax, klipspringer, aardwolf, warthog, crocodile, spotted and striped hyena, and serval. More than 400 species of birds have also been seen in Awash.

There is a fairly good network of dirt tracks throughout the park, some accessible to ordinary sedans, a few only to four-wheel-drive vehicles. The ETO has an annotated outline map of the park with descriptions of five suggested game-viewing routes and many of the animals found in Awash.

When to Visit

So that the tracks will be passable, it is best to avoid the mid-June to September rains, and to visit October–May. But the park is open all year round.

Getting There, Getting Around

Awash Park is 225 km east of Addis Ababa by an all-weather road, about 99 km of which are paved. The Addis Ababa–Djibouti railway also runs through the park, stopping at Awash Station, which is about 19 km east of the park's main entrance gate. There is a small airstrip at park headquarters in the southern part of the park. However, we know of no vehicles for hire. Package tours going to Awash are EP-11–12, 15, 18, 37.

Accommodations

Kareyu Lodge, Box 3593, Addis, tel. 444482. Until the lodge is completed, accommodations are in single and double trailers. Rates: Bed only: sgl—E$14.50 to E$19.50; dbl—E$24.50 to E$29.50. Table d'hôte meals: breakfast—E$3; lunch or dinner—E$5 to E$7. . . . *Buffet de la Gare,* tel. Addis 444607. Awash Railway Station rooms. Rates: B&B: sgl—E$5 to E$10. Table d'hôte meals: breakfast—

E$1.50; lunch or dinner—E$2. . . . **Camping** along the Awash River
by park headquarters. Fees: adults—E$1; children (5–16 years)—
E50¢. Inquiries: Park Warden, Awash National Park, Box 386,
Addis Ababa.

Bale Mountains

Bale Mountains, east of the Addis Ababa–Nairobi highway, are still
in the proposal stages as a national park, though if established will
cover 654 square miles of mountain terrain. The main attractions of
the area are the camping and trekking in the highland forests, climbing
the two peaks of Batu (12,782 feet) and Tullu Dimtu (14,208 feet),
exploring the Omar caves, trout fishing, and seeing such rare animals
as the mountain nyala and the Semyen fox. The *mountain nyala,* unique
to Ethiopia, looks very much like its cousin the greater kudu, though
is not quite so large. It is overall grayish brown, with white markings
on the throat and chest, faint vertical white stripes on the flanks, and
a few spots on the hind. The male's horns (females have none) have
one and a half turns, and their surface is more or less smooth; the
record horn length is 46 inches.

The Bale Mountains are best approached from Shashamane, a town
154 km south of Addis Ababa on the Addis–Nairobi highway. From
here turn left (east) and skirt the northern edge of the mountains
155 km to Goba, the provincial capital. At Goba is an airstrip where
EAL lands once a week. Horses are for hire at Dodola, Adala, Goba,
and Dinshu for treks into the mountains. **Camping** is the only accommodation; campers must be self-sufficient. The entry fee for Bale is
E$2 per adult, E$1 per child, payable at park headquarters.

Danakil Desert

Danakil Desert or Depression, with the smaller *Dallol Depression,*
is a tremendous natural cauldron, one of the lowest (383 feet below
sea level) and hottest (140°F) places in the world. It is between the
Addis Ababa–Dessie–Asmara road and the Red Sea. Along with large
areas of rocky wasteland, sand, and desert, there is a region of active
volcanoes that fume and smoke; two salt lakes, one below sea level;
the 2,000-square-mile Plains of Salt; a 9,900-foot-high escarpment
on the western edge; and the Dallol Depression, with extravagantly
colored and grotesque formations around salt and mineral springs.
Besides potash at Dallol, the economic importance of this desolate
region has been and still is salt, used in the past as a form of currency,

gaining in value the farther inland the camel caravans traveled. Caravans from central highlands towns still travel to the salt plains, and
spend day and night hacking out slabs and blocks of salt for sale at
the markets in Makalle and elsewhere. Access for the adventurous
tourist is not easy, and a guide is necessary. You can Land-Rover
170 km from Kombolcha (near Dessie), north-northeast to Lake
Afdera (Giuletti). From Agula (near Makalle) it is two days' drive to
Dallol or Lake Afdera. More comfortably, more expensively, you can
take a charter flight; Axum Air has a couple of tours including the
Danakil Depression; see listings EP-33–34.

Debre Zeit

Debre Zeit (pop. about 29,200), only 49 km east of Addis Ababa,
is a favorite short excursion; see tour listings EP-5, 9, 14, and 37.
Tourists head mainly toward two or three of seven small crater lakes,
principally Lake Bishoftu, which are very pretty after the rainy
season. Swimming, birdwatching. **Accommodations:** *Grand Hotel,*
bookings to Itegue Hotel, Box 7, Addis Ababa, tel. 113240. 24 dbls,
15 w/bath. Rates: B&B: dbl—E$24. Rooms fairly basic though dark-
ish. Patio, dining room that serves table d'hôte Italian along with
probably the best ice cream in Ethiopia. Rating: 1st-class local, okay
for car travelers.

Dire Dawa

Dire Dawa, commercial and transportation center of Hararge
Province, is 503 km east of Addis Ababa and has a population of
about 64,600. It is low, hot, French-provincial modern, and is not a
tourist town. Though you have to go to Dire Dawa to get to Harrar,
there's little reason to hang around. The *market* in the old city is
worth a visit. See tour listings EP-16–18, 37. **Accommodations:** *Ras
Hotel,* Box 83, tel. 3255; cable RASHOTEL. 19 sgls, 30 dbls w/bath, a-c.
Rates: B&B: sgl—E$20; dbl—E$30. Credit: DC. Modern 6-story Ras
is the tallest building in town, has roof-garden cafeteria (table d'hôte
breakfast—E$2; lunch or dinner—E$3.50), marble lobby, American
bar, swimming pool. . . . *Continental Hotel* is old and for low-budget
travelers.

Harrar

Harrar (pop. 45,840), the walled-city capital of Hararge Province,
is a favorite destination of package tours after those places on the

Historic Route. Perhaps originally a Christian city, it may have been taken over by a migrant colony from southern Arabia between the 7th and 9th centuries to become a Moslem political and religious center, playing an important part in the 16th-century holy wars. Much of the picturesque quality of Harrar results from the settling of large numbers of Galla tribesmen toward the end of the 16th century. Harrar was in the 19th century a forbidden city, and Sir Richard Burton at great risk disguised himself to gain entry (he later did the same thing to get into Mecca); the adventure is described in *First Footsteps in Africa*. The city was occupied by the Egyptians in 1875, came under the rule of the British in 1886, but a year later was taken by Emperor Menelik II, who made Ras Makonnen governor of the province. The Ras was the father of Emperor Haile Selassie, born in Harrar in 1892 (his childhood home still stands).

Two of the city's attractions are markets. The *daily market,* where sellers—mainly women—lay out goods, each in a 4-square-yard area, is just outside Shoa Gate. This is called the Christian Market and, as elsewhere, is a colorful scene with buying and selling of spices, fruit, and vegetables as well as glass and metalware, basketry and horn. Within the walls is the second market, the *megallah* or Moslem Market, consisting of open-fronted shops mainly along a narrow street south of Medhane Alem church. Here you can find the famous Harrar basket-ware, silver jewelry, *shammas,* velvet blouses, satin trousers, and gauzy shawls worn by Harrari women. Inquire about visiting a *basket factory.*

About three of Harrar's other attractions there are contradictions. One is *Menelik's Palace,* built for a visit the emperor never made. The two-story stone building is topped by an ornamental cornice. At the foot of Mount Ghirella south of the city, *Ras Makonnen's Mausoleum,* with a silver dome, was built by Haile Selassie for his father's remains—which are actually interred in the *Church of St. Mikael.* The third building is an ugly-charming chaletlike house in a compound where Harrar's most famous European resident, the French poet Arthur Rimbaud, lived in the 1880s. However, lest the reader think Rimbaud was inspired by Harrar to write epics or romantic poetry, let it be said he had already ceased writing poetry and was an agent for an Aden trading company, organizing his own caravans and trading guns and other things to Menelik II.

Other attractions: *Medhane Alem,* an octagonal Christian church which is Harrar's cathedral, has a richly decorated interior with religious paintings, but is kept locked and is visited with occasional difficulty. *Ras Makonnen's Palace,* gutted during World War II, has Indian-style carved door and window frames on the first floor, Ethiopian metal scrollwork in the upper windows, balconies all around. *Jami Mosque,* dating to the 16th century, may not be photographed, and women aren't permitted in the grounds. The high, stone *city wall,* with 5 original and 2 later gates (one now blocked up) and 25 towers, was apparently built less for protection than to outline the original city limits. The main street enters through the *Gate of the Duke* (1889); nearby is the former *House of the Duke of Harrar.* The street continues to the middle of Harrar, the *Faras Megallah* (which means either "horse market" or "area where horses are ridden"), a circular piazza from which streets lead to the other city gates.

Rather a grotesque tourist attraction is Harrar's *hyena man,* apparently unique in being able to call hyenas to be fed by hand. The spectacle is a nightly occurrence south of the city wall, with 40 gleaming-eyed hyenas in attendance.

The *Valley of Marvels,* 45 km east of Harrar on the Jigjigga road, is a dry valley with weirdly shaped granite pedestals and boulders, some balancing.

When to Visit

Harrar (alt. 6,000 feet) has a very mild climate with little rainfall. September is the best month; July and August are locally known as the "French Season," when the French of Djibouti flee that hot port for refuge in Harrar.

Getting There, Getting Around

Daily air service to Dire Dawa, 55 km away by paved road. Addis Ababa is 527 km west. One common way to get to Harrar is the thrice-weekly overnight train or the daily *littorina* from Addis Ababa to Dire Dawa. See package tours EP-16–18, 37.

Accommodations

Ras Hotel, Box 45, tel. 660027; cable RASHOTEL. Bookings also to Box 1632, Addis Ababa; tel. 447060. 42 rms, 70 beds. Rates: B&B: sgl w/o bath—E$12 to E$18; dbl w/bath—E$20 to E$30. Credit: DC. Located within the walls near the Imperial Palace, the old Ras (formerly the Grand Hotel) is lacking in modernity but is the only tourist hotel. Table d'hôte meals: breakfast—E$2; lunch or dinner—

E$3.50. . . . *Asfa Wossen Hotel* is an inexpensive, amenityless hotel for low-budgeters.

Koka Dam

Koka Dam (*and Lake*) is a resort 80 km south of Addis Ababa, with one of its two hotels being a former royal palace. Blocking the Awash River, the dam, completed in 1965, produces 110 million kilowatt hours, or 40 percent of Ethiopia's electricity. There is a *hippo pool* oft visited by tourists, and the drive to Koka includes the *Wonji Sugar Estate* and the industrial town of *Nazareth*. There's fishing in the Koka Dam lake. See packages EP-9, 14–15. **Accommodations:** *Galila Palace Hotel,* tel. 2; bookings to Ghion Hotel, Box 1643, Addis Ababa. 10 rooms w/bath. Rates: FB: sgl—E$24–30; dbl—E$40–56; entry is E$2 for day visitors. Profits go to charity. Modern former palace has pool, gardens, lake view. Table d'hôte lunch or dinner—E$7. . . . *Koka Hotel,* tel. 2; bookings to above. 8 rooms. Rates: FB: sgl— E$18; dbl—E$36. Managed by the Galila Palace, Koka is less expensive, though guests take meals at the palace. On a cliff edge overlooking the lake. . . . *Nazareth* **accommodations:** *Itegue Menen Hotel,* Box 133, tel. 112188. Rates: B&B: sgl—E$13–18; dbl—E$21–26.

Omo National Park

Omo National Park (shortly to be gazetted) is along the Omo River in a remote section of southwest Ethiopia, covers about 1,347 square miles on the west bank of the Omo, and is bisected east-west by the Mui River. The whole Omo Valley area, which covers both sides of the Omo River, over to Lake Shamo in the east and down to Lake Stefanie and the tip of Lake Rudolf on the Kenya border, is very rich in wildlife, fascinating lowland tribes (Hamar, Geleb, Bume, Caro, and Surma), and archaeology. For years the Omo has been a big-game hunting destination, and still is, though the park naturally will be off-limits to hunters. Animals in the area include elephant, buffalo, lion, leopard, cheetah, rhino, eland, giraffe, zebra, waterbuck, lesser kudu, tiang, Lelwel hartebeest, Grant's gazelle, ostrich, reedbuck, crocodile, and hippo.

Omo Park and region are, like the Semyen Mountains, more for those with enough time and/or money to get into this rather inaccessible area fully equipped and self-sufficient rather than for casual tourists. The ETO has an excellent booklet which describes the region, park, peoples, archaeological digs, and various routes for getting in overland. The ETO may start raft or boat trips down the Omo River; inquire in Addis Ababa at the ETO.

When to Visit

The climate in the lower-altitude area is hot. Avoid the very rainy months of March–May. Light rains may fall anytime, particularly September–November. June–August cool because the rains are falling on the highlands. December–February ideal with clear hot, dry days and crisp nights.

Getting There, Getting Around

The park and region are very primitive and best attempted by four-wheel-drive vehicle. For independent four-wheel travelers, though, Omo can present an excellent challenge. Routes: in the west via Jimma–Bonga–Shoa Ghimera–Maji; in the east via Suddu–Arba Minch–Jinka (or, June–August, Gidole–Conso–Sagan River–Tertale–Stefanie), or Dilla–Agere Mariam (Anghe)–Yabello–Tertale. Otherwise, contact a safari operator in Addis or Nairobi. EAL planes land at Baco (Jinka), Bulchi, Mui, Maji, Mizan Teferi, and Jimma, and there are airstrips in the park and nearby missions. No local transport is available.

Rift Valley Lakes

Rift Valley Lakes. South of Addis Ababa on either side of the Addis Ababa–Nairobi road is a string of lakes, with seven of them stretching down the Rift Valley; Lakes Zwai, Langano, Abiata, Shalla, Awassa, Abaya, and Shamo. Two of them are shortly to be gazetted national parks—Abiata and Shalla. All of them have a variety of animal and bird life, and some have good recreational facilities and accommodations; package tours from Addis Ababa visit several or most of the lakes. The ETO has a colorful booklet on the lakes, while the Wildlife Conservation Organization has a brochure on the proposed national park lakes.

Lake Zwai (or Zuai) is about 160 km from Addis Ababa on the left of the paved highway. Oval-shaped Zwai, about 16 miles long by 11 miles wide and 45 feet at its deepest, has bright blue waters studded with islands, some inhabited by farmers raising wheat, maize, and cotton. The shore line is swampy and reedy, though tall sycamores line the shore and plains of acacia surround the lake. Lots of water birds live at or visit Zwai, including storks, white pelicans, wild ducks, geese, and fish eagles. Where the Macchi River flows into Zwai's north end is wide Hippopotamus Bay, called such for its many hippo residents. The best way to see Zwai is by boat, and the best places to camp are on the western shore.

Lake Langano is about 195 km from Addis Ababa and also lies to the east of the road directly across from Lake Abiata. Soft brown in color because of its mineral content, Lake Langano has a shoreline of about 51 miles and is 90 feet deep in parts. At the Bekele Mola Hotel on the west bay boats can be hired for water skiing, which according to the ETO is safe here.

Lake Abiata, one of the two lakes in the proposed 308-square-mile Rift Valley Lakes National Park, can be approached by taking the track west before the Horacallo River at about Km 190 from Addis Ababa. Abiata, though small, attracts 300 species of birds to its alkaline waters, including flamingos, pelicans, maribou storks, sacred ibis, wild geese and ducks, fish eagles, egrets, and herons. The Bulbulla River flows into the lake on its western side, and the fresh water supports vegetation and birdlife different from the rest of the saline lake.

Lake Shalla is signposted turnoff right about 215 km from Addis Ababa, or 23 km beyond the Abiata turnoff, and the track runs through acacia and euphorbia woodland to the hot springs on the lakeshore. Shalla is a crater lake about 73 miles around, lined with irregular peaks and jutting rocks, and sinking to a depth of about 825 feet. Its waters, besides being very deep, are highly alkaline and, depending upon the sky, range in color from blue to near-black. On the southeast corner is the mouth of the Adaba River, and in the valley is a small forest with colobus monkeys and forest birds, such as hornbills and touracos. The islands in Shalla provide good nesting sites for birds that feed on Lake Abiata; one island supports a huge colony of great white pelicans, and their breeding takes place from November to April. While Shalla and Abiata were gazetted as a national park mainly to protect the birds, there are also small numbers of some mammals in the area including spotted hyena, jackal, olive baboon, warthog, klipspringer, greater kudu, Grant's gazelle, oribi, and mountain reedbuck.

Lake Awassa is the fifth lake in the string, located near the town of Shashamane, about 275 km south of Addis Ababa to the right (west) of the road. Its shore line varies from swampy bays interspersed with black volcanic rock in the north, to sand and rocky hills with nesting ducks and cormorants in the east, to a low plateau in the west and a low bay in the south. Awassa, like Langano, is popular on weekends with Addis residents who drive down for fishing (especially tilapia), boating, and relaxing at campsites or at the two hotels, the Awassa Bekele Mola and the Belle Vue du Lac.

Lakes Abaya (Margherita) and *Shamo* (Ruspoli) are the farthest lakes from Addis Ababa, and are approached from a dirt road turnoff west at Shashamane that goes the 256 km south to Arba Minch; or from the dirt track turnoff west at Dilla which forks left between the two lakes to Arba Minch or forks right to Didichu on Lake Abaya. At Didichu is a ferry boat that leaves mornings 2Xwk and crosses Abaya to Arba Minch, returning in the afternoons. The two lakes are surrounded by mountain chains, and the western peaks form the side of the Great Rift escarpment. In the mountains live greater kudus and mountain nyalas, while on the eastern side of the lakes are zebras, gazelles, lions, jackals, wild pigs, and monkeys. In the lakes live hippos, crocodiles, and many species of fish, such as Nile perch and tigerfish. Arba Minch ("forty springs") overlooks the two lakes on a separating mountain ridge called the "Bridge of Heaven." Camping is excellent along the lakes, though you should be self-sufficient.

When to Visit

The months of November–March are best for bird viewing because then the resident African birds are joined by thousands of migrant birds; also the road and tracks are driest then. But the lakes are open year around.

Getting There, Getting Around

All the lakes are accessible from the Addis Ababa–Nairobi highway, which is paved down to near Awassa, about 260 km south of Addis. EAL flies to Arba Minch and Soddu 3Xwk. The Belle Vue du Lac Hotel on Awassa is supposed to have cars for hire. Package tours from Addis are EP-13–15, 19, 37.

Accommodations

Maki Bekele Molla Hotel, c/o Box 1349, Addis Ababa; local tel. 4. At the Agip station in Maki town, north of Lake Zwai. 34 dbls w/shower, veranda. Rates: B&B: sgl—E$9.50 to E$11.50; dbl—E$18 to E$21. . . . *Zwai Bekele Molla Hotel,* c/o Box 1349, Addis Ababa; tel. 21. Near Lake Zwai. 15 dbls w/shower, veranda. Rates: sgl— E$9.50 to E$11.50; dbl—E$18 to E$21. Bar and table d'hôte meals:

breakfast—E$1.50; lunch or dinner—E$3. . . . *Langano Bekele Molla Hotel,* c/o Box 1349, Addis Ababa; tel. 3. On the west side of Lake Langano. 85 lakeside cabins, private villas, bungalows, all w/shower. Rates: B&B: sgl—E$9.50 to E$11.50; dbl—E$18 to E$21. Along the lakeshore with a sloping sandy beach; swimming, boating, water skiing. Terrace restaurant serves table d'hôte: breakfast— E$1.50; lunch or dinner—E$3. Also lighted **camping** area south of the hotel. . . . *Shashamane Bekele Molla Hotel,* c/o Box 1349, Addis Ababa; tel. 2. In Shashamane town, north of Lake Awassa. 40 dbls w/veranda. Rates: B&B: sgl—E$7.50; dbl—E$13. Table d'hôte: breakfast—E$1.50; lunch or dinner—E$3. . . . *Belle Vue du Lac,* Box 29, Awassa, tel. 29. On Lake Awassa's southern shore. 120 beds in rooms and bungalows, all w/shower. Rates: B&B: sgl—E$12; dbl—E$24. A good lake view, fishing, boating, riding, car-hire. Table d'hôte meals: breakfast—E$2; lunch or dinner—E$3.50. . . . *Awassa Bekele Molla Hotel,* c/o Box 1349, Addis Ababa; tel. 3. Also on Awassa's southern shore. 50 dbls and bungalow, most w/shower. Rates: B&B: sgl—E$9.50 to E$11.50; dbl—E$18 to E$21. Lake view and table d'hôte meals: breakfast—E$1.50; lunch or dinner— E$3. . . . *Arba Minch Bekele Molla Hotel,* c/o Box 1349, Addis Ababa; tel. 46. In Arba Minch to the west of Lakes Abaya and Shamo. 32 dbls w/shower, veranda. Rates: B&B: sgl—E$9.50 to E$11.50; dbl —E$18 to E$21. . . . **Camping** is possible at all the lakes along the shore line, and near the Langano Bekele Molla Hotel.

ZAMBIA IN THE SUN

Twice the size of California, Zambia is shaped like a lumpy hourglass lying on its side, pinched in the middle by the foot-shaped Zaire Pedicle. Most of it is on a high plateau, giving it a fair climate, and most of the plateau is covered with the famous African bush—the exquisitely boring bush. "During the brief spells of dawn and sunset," writes historian L. H. Gann, "the land is plunged into gold and purple, but becomes grim and oppressive under the white glare of the midday sun." The bush "frightens by its monotony"—but he adds that, with a long visit, the traveler sees Zambia in "sharper definition."

Glancing at the map, the traveler will suspect that the British, who ran Zambia as Northern Rhodesia until 1964, drew the borders to include all the bush and leave out everything else. Such is not the case. However, nearly all of Zambia's tourist attractions are on the edges and are divided by international borders. Zambia shares Kalambo Falls and Lake Tanganyika with Tanzania. Its 10 percent of the Nyika Plateau borders on Malawi's 90 percent. Rhodesia has two-thirds of Victoria Falls (where you can't cross directly) and half of Lake Kariba and Kariba Dam. But Zambia does have two big national parks—Kafue and Luangwa—to itself. And, though sharing the land with Zaire, Zambia has more than its share of a huge copper deposit near the pinched middle of the country—the Copperbelt, which makes Zambia far richer than most other African countries.

The history of the area before David Livingstone is sketchy. The Tonga and the Ila, the first of the modern peoples of Zambia (there are now more than 70 recognized tribes), came into the land from the northeast about A.D. 1200, settling near Victoria Falls and what is now Lake Kariba in the steamy Zambezi River Valley. But most of the major tribes—the Luvale, Barotse, Lunda, Lala, Lamba, and

Bemba—came between 1600 and 1750 from the lower Congo basin, from the Great Lunda-Luba Empire. The last major migration, that of the warlike Ngoni and Kololo, sent northward during Chaka's Zulu wars in southern Africa, was about 1835. Fifteen years later, preceded only by a few Portuguese traders, came Livingstone, who first saw the Zambezi ("How glorious! How magnificent! How beautiful!") in 1851. He explored in and around Zambia for the next 22 years, and he died south of Lake Bangweulu in 1873. As he blazed the European path, so he was followed, too quickly, by the missionaries, the traders, the concession seekers, administrators and soldiers and miners and farmers.

Zambia has its present shape largely as a result of the greed and ambition of one man, Cecil Rhodes. While Whitehall itself had no great interest in the "trans-Zambezia," Rhodes did. He wanted to see half of Africa, from the "Cape to Cairo," a British domain (the dream gave its name to Lusaka's main thoroughfare, Cairo Road). Following success in what is now Rhodesia in obtaining mineral concessions, Rhodes sought a royal charter to set up a company to administer the lands; this was granted in 1889, and the British South Africa Company was born. Men with dreams of gold had already crossed the river and closed in on one of the powerful monarchs of the area, Lewanika, paramount chief of the Barotse in what is now Western Province. Lewanika was half-cajoled, half-tricked, into signing, in June 1890, the famous Lochner Concession, the basis of BSA Company rule, and eventually worth millions of pounds in copper revenue. Lewanika later realized he had not been dealing with the queen's ambassador, but with Rhodes's man. The chief regained something when Barotseland eventually became a protectorate within Northern Rhodesia.

The BSA Company used this concession, and others it obtained by other dubious means, to start interfering in the area, then to start administering it and collecting taxes; soon there was a company police force, too. Then, in a sleight of hand, the borders of Lewanika's Barotseland were artificially enlarged so the company could claim jurisdiction over the Copperbelt, even as it whittled away at Lewanika's authority.

Simultaneously, the company, acting through Nyasaland Commissioner Harry Johnston, began seeking concessions and treaties in what is today northeast Zambia. By 1894 the area had an administrator, who devoted some time to defeating the Arab slavers around Lake Mweru. The Ngoni in the southeast were forcibly put down in 1897; the pow-

erful Bemba, who abetted the Arabs, were subdued in 1898, Kazembe's Lunda in the Luapula Valley the next year. The two areas
were separately governed as North Western Rhodesia and North
Eastern Rhodesia until united in 1911 with Livingstone as the capital
(Lusaka became the capital in 1935).

Then history slowed down in Northern Rhodesia; there were no
more dramatic events. The railway was pushed north to Broken Hill
(now Kabwe) in 1906, on to copper-rich Katanga in 1909. The presence of metal in the Copperbelt (a term used first in 1905) was known,
but the necessary technology was lacking and the price of copper too
low. Development began in the mid-1920s, and the first mine, Roan
Antelope in Luanshya, produced in 1931.

Though it now seems strange, the commercial company which
owned the mineral rights and much else also governed the country,
though it did so subject to final British approval. After having done
virtually nothing for the Africans (though it ended the slave trade and
instituted a cash economy), the company's rule ended in 1924 when
Northern Rhodesia became a protectorate with a crown colony government.

It was in the makeup of the Legislative Council that Zambian nationalism originated, for as soon as there was a government, Africans
wanted a say in how it worked. These stirrings were slow in beginning.
A European was not appointed to represent African interests in the
"Legco" until 1938, and no Africans were admitted until 1948. A signal development was the formation in 1923 of the Mwenzo Welfare
Association by four educated Africans, one of whom was David
Kaunda, father of President Kenneth Kaunda (born 1924). That
group lasted only to 1928, but more Native Welfare Associations appeared, and by 1932 there was even a move to merge them into a
national body. Inexplicably, there was a lull in African political activity in the late 1930s, until the government set up what were called
urban or representative advisory councils on the district level, a system which was, says Richard Hall, "to speed the penetration of tribal
areas by modern nationalistic thinking."

After the war, political activity increased when Africans realized
there was a real enemy to be fought—the whites who wanted "closer
association" if not outright union with Southern Rhodesia, even then
recognized in many quarters as being an entrenched white-supremacist
state. A group called the Federation of Welfare Societies was formed

in 1946, later becoming the African National Congress. But the ANC lacked muscle and influence, and over much black protest the ill-fated Federation of the Rhodesias and Nyasaland (which today is Malawi) was put together by white colonials in 1953.

Ironically, Zambia might today still be part of the federation if the white politicians had not become grabby and attempted to push a series of colonial secretaries in London into granting independence with white rule. For whenever this was noised about, or whenever there was a constitutional conference in London, the African nationalists raised their own voices loud—and louder. The Congress grew very muscular even as it totally boycotted Federation politics. The party's two leaders, Harry Nkumbula and Kenneth Kaunda, grew apart, and in late 1958 Kaunda and his friend Simon Kapwepwe broke away to form the party that later became the United National Independence party (UNIP). What touched fire to tinder was the sudden roundup and jailing in early 1959 of some 2,000 Africans in the Federation and the banning of African parties. From then on the Federal government was on the defensive and Nyasaland and Northern Rhodesia in a permanent state of turmoil, though there was relatively little violence. The parties resurfaced under new names, and the leaders were eventually released from jail. Nyasaland got a constitution guaranteeing African majority rule, and Northern Rhodesia's days as a colony were then numbered. In a hard-fought election in 1962, Roy Welensky's Federal party won fifteen seats in an electoral system favoring the whites, while Kaunda's UNIP won fourteen seats, and the ANC five. ANC formed a coalition with UNIP, and the government had several African ministers. The Federation quietly died in 1963 after Britain recognized the right of Nyasaland to secede from it. An election in December brought in a clear UNIP majority; Kaunda became prime minister in January 1964, and plans were made for Independence Day. Only on that day did the BSA Company, under duress, surrender its lucrative mineral rights to the government, for a mere $5 million.

After Independence, October 24, 1964, Zambia was led by UNIP, with the ANC a tiny minority party. In early 1970 Kapwepwe (who had coined the name Zambia) broke away from Kaunda and formed a new party, which was promptly suppressed and its leader tossed into jail. Zambia formally became a one-party state at the end of 1972, and Harry Nkumbula joined UNIP.

A republic, Zambia has a government headed by a popularly elected president; the cabinet has a prime minister and 16 ministers. The National Assembly is unicameral with 125 elected members and up to 10 nominated members.

As the third-largest copper-mining country in the world, Zambia's economy is heavy with the metal, which makes up 70 percent of the gross national product and provides nearly all its foreign currency reserves even though mining employs only 16 percent of the labor force. The population, 4.4 million, is 79 percent rural, and most of the rural people are engaged in subsistence agriculture.

The government's biggest efforts have been in reorienting the economy away from Rhodesia and South Africa. This became urgent after Rhodesia's Unilateral Declaration of Independence (UDI) in 1965, doubly so with the complete closure of the border with Rhodesia in 1973. The lifeline is now the route to Dar es Salaam, Tanzania. The paved "Hell Run" is now the major trunk road, and the parallel Tan-Zam Railway will soon be used to carry Zambia's copper exports. From Dar runs the oil pipeline. A new internal railway system was built almost from the ground up after 1967, the same year Zambia Airways was formed. Meanwhile, the country is beginning to produce more of its own coal and will soon generate its own electricity from the Zambian side of Kariba Dam and the new Kafue Gorge Dam. The country is under a strict austerity program, and imports are very restricted. It would be, said President Kaunda, a "tough struggle" to make Zambia independent, but the nation seems to be winning.

Some Vital Statistics. Area: 290,587 square miles, about the size of Kansas and Colorado combined, larger than France, Belgium, the Netherlands, and Switzerland put together.

Population: 4,420,000 (est. 1972), about the population of Missouri or Finland. Population density: 14 per square mile. There are about 70,000 Europeans in Zambia.

Cities: Lusaka, pop. 262,000 (est. 1972), is the capital. Other major cities and towns: Kitwe (199,800), Ndola (159,900), Mufulira (107,-800), Chingola (103,300), Luanshya (96,000), Kabwe (67,000), Livingstone (43,000). Zambia is far more urbanized than the other countries covered in this guide.

Gross national product (1971): $1.5 billion ($330 per capita).

Currency

Since Zambia decimalized its currency in January 1968, the basic unit of currency has been the *kwacha* (pronounced KWAH-chah; means "dawn"), abbreviated *K*. The kwacha is divided into 100 ngwee (pronounced enn-GWAY), abbreviated *n*. There are K20, K10, K5, K2, K1, and 50n notes, and 20n, 10n, 5n, 2n, and 1n coins. The old monetary unit was the pound, divided into 20 shillings, with K1 equal to 10 old shillings.

Since 1973's second dollar devaluation, K1 has had an *official* value of $1.56; or $1 equals 64n. Here is a rough conversion table:

$$
\begin{aligned}
K20 &= \$31.10 \\
K10 &= \$15.55 \\
K5 &= \$7.77 \\
K2 &= \$3.11 \\
K1 &= \$1.56 \\
50n &= \$.77 \\
25n &= \$.39 \\
10n &= \$.15 \\
5n &= \$.07
\end{aligned}
$$

You should know that the Zambian kwacha is overvalued about 90 percent, having a Zurich free-market value of only $.87. There isn't much of a black market within Zambia, however.

Planning a Trip

What to See and Do

The No. 1 tourist attraction in Zambia is *Victoria Falls,* to which hundreds of tourists make a long side trip from East Africa to see. A three-day visit to both Rhodesian and Zambian sides of the falls (if time and the complexity of travel arrangements allow this) and to *Livingstone* and environs is not at all excessive.

Luangwa National Park is the equal of any East African game park. But an added attraction is that Zambia, uniquely, allows game park walking safaris, ranging from a few hours (free) to eight days (at a very reasonable price). Your photos will be sharper and the experience longer remembered. *Kafue National Park* is quieter, perhaps more beautiful than Luangwa, but it doesn't have the sheer quantity of wildlife. Five- and eight-day walking safaris are possible here also.

Fishing is the draw to *Kasaba Bay* and *Nkamba Bay* resorts on Lake Tanganyika, both within *Sumbu National Park.* Nearby is *Kalambo Falls,* the second-highest uninterrupted waterfall in Africa. Fishing for tigerfish is also the attraction at the third largest man-made lake in the world, *Lake Kariba*, whose waters are held back by the mighty *Kariba Dam*.

If you have the money, you can go on a *hunting safari* for the Big Five, and more jet-set hunters may be doing this now that hunting has been prohibited in Tanzania. Or you can go out with a camera on a *photo safari* instead.

The capital city of *Lusaka* is worth a visit of a day or two. If you're in the *Copperbelt*, Zambia's economic heart, you can visit the *Nchanga open-pit copper mine*, third largest in the world.

Zambia has many small tourist sights, most of them visited by those driving their own cars. Among them are a number of national monuments of prehistoric importance, including the *Nsalu Hill Cave Paintings*, *Chifubwa Stream Rock Engravings*, numerous rock paintings near Chipata, *Kalundu Mound*, and the *Victoria Falls Field Museum*, which incorporates an actual archaeological excavation.

There are some national parks established to preserve a particular species. Two near Lusaka, *Lochinvar* and *Blue Lagoon*, are refuges for the Kafue lechwe, a handsome antelope with big, back-swept horns. Lochinvar has two prehistoric sites as well.

A major event is the *Ku-omboka pageant*, the yearly move by canoe-and-barge convoy of the Barotse paramount chief to high ground when the Zambezi floods the Barotse Plain. The Ku-omboka takes place about February. The annual *Agricultural Show* is held in July or August and alternates between Lusaka. Kitwe, and Ndola. The annual *Arts Festival* in Lusaka takes place in early June.

Increasingly, we think, Zambia will be attracting tourists—even taking some of them from East Africa. The 1972–76 development plan calls for $27 million in new hotel rooms and $13 million in other tourist infrastructure.

Where to Stay

Zambia is quickly reaching the point where it is a viable tourist country—that is, it has enough hotel rooms in Lusaka, Livingstone and Victoria Falls, and (at least) South Luangwa National Park, to host moderately large package tours. Luangwa now has 164 beds (128 in fully catered lodges) while Kafue Park has 104 beds (only 36 in a lodge). Large new lodges are projected just outside the boundary of both parks. A 200-room hotel is rising in Lusaka, a holiday village is planned at Lake Tanganyika, motels are being built or planned for the Copperbelt and up the Great North Road to Tanzania, and a 200-room hotel is to go up in Ndola. What is lacking everywhere is good middle- and low-budget accommodation, this being particularly missing in Lusaka.

Those with cars can, of course, camp (it's inadvisable only in the Copperbelt) and use the system of rest houses, which are fully furnished though guests must bring their own food for preparation by the rest house cook. Charges at all rest houses: single room—K1.60; sharing room—K1.35 per person; children (3–14 years)—75n per person. Camping at rest houses is permitted for 15n per person. The cook will prepare meals at a cost of 15n per meal.

Zambian hotels are classified by the government on a one- to four-star system, with many hotels "ungraded." The classification determines the maximum room rates. There is a 10 percent service charge (in place of tips) and a 10 percent sales tax.

When to Go

The general height of the land gives Zambia a more pleasant climate than most other tropical countries. However, the best time for a visit is the cool and dry season, May or June through August. The other seasons are the hot and dry period from September to November, which is the second-best time to visit, and the warm and wet season from December to April (roughly, East Africa's high season, but Zambia's low season). The latter part of the wet season is a terrible time to visit; it is marked by frequent heavy showers and thundershowers, with spells of bright sunshine. At the height of the rainy season, it can rain seven or eight days out of ten. The game parks are closed during the rains.

Even during the best season, daytime highs are 60–80°F, and morning and evening temperatures can dip to 40°, with occasional frost. Luangwa and Kafue valleys, being lower, tend to be warmer than the plateau areas.

Tourism Authority

The Zambia National Tourist Bureau is charged with promoting tourism and is the country's only major tour operator. Head office: Century House, Lusaka Square, Cairo Road (in walkway to right of ZOK department store), Box 17, Lusaka; tel. 75438, 72891 (game park bookings, tel. 73296); cable ZAMTOUR. Tours and game lodges can be charged on AE and DC.

ZNTB has branch offices as follows: Tourist Centre, Musi-o-Tunya Road (next to Livingstone Museum), Box 342, Livingstone; tel. 3534/5, 3014. Wilfrid Watson Bldg., Box 1520, Ndola; tel. 3588. There are these overseas offices and representatives: 150 East 58th St., New York, N.Y. 10022; tel. (212) 758-9450/1; cable ZAMFARI. 163 Piccadilly, London W1V 9DE; tel. 01-493 5552, 5482; cable ZAM-TOUR, c/o Zambia Airways, Hilton Hotel Arcade, Mama Ngina St., Nairobi, Kenya; tel. 24722; cable ZACAIR. Also Frankfurt and Rome.

Maps

Zambia, topographical: A detailed 1:1,500,000 map (1967–69) showing roads is at times available free from ZNTB, otherwise for K1 plus postage from Survey Department Map Sales, Box RW 397, Lusaka (catalog available). *Zambia, roads:* The AA of Zambia (Box 300, Lusaka) with Caltex Oil publishes a not very detailed 1½ inches = 100 km road map (cost 20n) showing all distances in kilometers, covering Zambia, Malawi, and Rhodesia. Also has a distance chart. A 1:1,500,000 outline road map (Metric Road Map EMR 29/1), published in 1970, with accurate distances in miles and kilometers, is available from the Survey Department for 50n. Shell Zambia Ltd. (Box 1999, Lusaka) has a small, pretty, free, but impractical road map. *Lusaka:* A somewhat primitive map of city center is in *Lusaka Calls* (p. 570) or in the city publicity brochure. A larger version of the same map is sometimes available from the Lusaka Information Centre. The Survey has a 1:20,000 street map (1970) for 45n. *Luangwa Valley and Kafue National Parks:* Large maps of the southern section of Luangwa (1:250,000) and all of Kafue (1:500,000) are free from ZNTB and travel agencies. *Victoria Falls and Livingstone:* A big, very attractive, but poorly detailed map (1970) showing both sides of the falls (but slighting the Rhodesian side), with a street map of Livingstone, is available for 60n from Survey Department or ZNTB. Rhodesia National Tourist Board (p. 12) has a free brochure with map detailing their side of the spectacle.

Books to Read

Brelsford, William V. *The Tribes of Zambia.* 2d ed. New York: International Publications Service, 1971.

Davies, D. H., et al. *Zambia.* (Africa in Maps series.) New York: Africana Publishing Corp., 1972.

Gann, Lewis H. *A History of Northern Rhodesia: Early Days to 1953.* London: Chatto & Windus, 1964; New York: Humanities Press, 1969.

Hall, Richard. *Zambia.* New York: Praeger, 1966; London: Pall Mall Press, 1965 (paperback). *The High Price of Principles: Kaunda and the White South.* New York: Africana Publishing Corp., 1970.

Kaunda, Kenneth. *Zambia Shall Be Free.* New York: Humanities Press, 1969 (paperback); London: Heinemann, 1962.

Rotberg, Robert I. *The Rise of Nationalism in Central Africa: The Making of Malawi and Zambia, 1873–1964.* Cambridge, Mass.: Harvard University Press, 1965 (paperback).

Sampson, Richard. *So This Was Lusaakas.* Lusaka: Multimedia Publications, 1960.

Newspapers

The two daily papers, the *Times of Zambia* (Box 69, Ndola) and the *Zambia Daily Mail* (Box 1421, Lusaka), are interesting sources of information if you are planning a trip.

Other Sources of Information

Zambia Information Services, Independence Ave. (opp. British High Commission), Box RW 20, Lusaka; tel. 50188. Ministry of Trade and Industry, Box 1968, Lusaka; tel. 73816, 74321. Industrial Development Corp., Box 1935, Lusaka; tel. 74051. *Z Magazine* is published monthly by Zambia Information Services; subscriptions, postpaid, $2.50 to U.S., £1 to Britain.

Entry Requirements

Immigration

American citizens entering Zambia as tourists, on business, or in transit are required to have their passport, a visa, a ticket to leave, and certificate of smallpox vaccination and of yellow fever vaccination, the latter if coming from an infected area. British, Irish, and Commonwealth citizens must have a passport and ticket to leave along with vaccination certificate. Requirements for citizens of other countries except South Africa and Rhodesia are the same as those for Americans.

To obtain a visa, go to the nearest Zambian diplomatic mission (listed below) or, if none is available, to the nearest British mission, submit your passport, two copies of the application form (photostats accepted), and the visa fee of K2.25 ($3.15), and vaccination certificate. No photos required. Visas usually allow for a single entry within three months of the date stamped in the passport, and visits are ordinarily allowed for three months. Extensions can be granted by the chief immigration officer. If applying for a visa by mail, include a self-addressed, stamped envelope (stamped if you're in the same country) for return by certified or registered mail.

Tourists may be issued a tourist visa for 30 days on arrival in Zambia, without prior application, provided they can satisfy the immigration officer regarding their financial resources and ability to leave Zambia (ticket to leave).

The Immigration Department suggests that "wherever possible, tourists should enter Zambia from the north." The border with Rhodesia is officially closed, as of early 1973.

Immigration officers at borders are authorized to accept only Zambian kwachas, pounds sterling, and U.S. dollars in payment for visas.

Inquiries: Chief Immigration Officer, Kent Building, Box 1984, Lusaka; tel. 51933.

Diplomatic Missions of Zambia

Botswana—High Commission, Box 363, Gaborone. *Ethiopia*—Embassy, Ras Lulsegged St., Box 1909, Addis Ababa; tel. 448015/6. *Great Britain*—High Commission, 7–11 Cavendish Place, London W1; tel. 01-580 0691. *Kenya*—High Commission, International House, Mama Ngina St., Box 48741, Nairobi; tel. 35972. *Malawi*—High Commission, Victoria Ave., Box 556, Blantyre; tel. 2826. *Tanzania*—High Commission, 442 Upanga, Box 2525, Dar es Salaam; tel. 24175, 23758. *United Nations*—Permanent Mission, 150 East 58th St., New York, N.Y. 10022; tel. (212) 758-9450. *U.S.*—Embassy, 2419 Massachusetts Ave., N.W., Washington, D.C. 20008; tel. (202) 265-9717. *West Germany*—Embassy, Mittelstrasse 39, 532 Bonn–Bad Godesberg 1. *Zaire*—Embassy, B.P. 1144, Kinshasa. Consuláte-General, B.P. 596, Lubumbashi. Zambia also has diplomatic missions in China (People's Republic), Egypt, Italy, Ivory Coast, Nigeria, and USSR.

Customs

You may import, duty-free, your own used clothing and personal effects, including camping and sports equipment, binoculars, cameras and lenses, 100 cigarettes or 250 grams (half a pound) of tobacco, one unopened bottle of wine or spirits. Tourists not entering by air are required to complete a customs declaration form, listing such items as cameras and typewriters but not clothing or other things. Inquiries: Controller of Customs and Excise, Custom House, Jameson Road, Box 595, Livingstone; tel. 2093.

Currency Control

You may import or export up to K10 in Zambian currency; any amount of foreign currency notes, provided you declare the amounts on the customs form at the border and take out no more than you brought in; and any amount in traveler's checks.

Vehicle Documents

If driving into Zambia you should have a Carnet de Passages en Douanes (triptyque) issued by a recognized motor club. If not, you may, under certain conditions, be able to get a customs importation permit at the border. Visiting drivers must also have the car ownership papers and an international driving permit; your national driver's license by itself is no longer valid. You must have third-party (liability) insurance meeting the minimum risks as required by ordinance. The insurance is sometimes purchasable at the border, otherwise from the Zambia State Insurance Corp., Ishuko House, Cairo Road, Box 894, Lusaka; tel. 73101; cable ZAMSURE. Cost is minor.

Firearms

You are required to get a tourist's import permit for firearms and ammunition before arrival in Zambia. If you are booking a hunting safari, the firm can arrange for the permit. Permits (cost K4) are issued by the Registrar of Firearms, Box RW 103, Lusaka.

Getting to Zambia

By Air

Lusaka is served by Zambia Airways (below, QZ), British Caledonian, UTA French Airlines, Alitalia, East African Airways (EAA), Air Malawi and Air Zaire.

From Europe: From London: QZ 3Xwk (from Heathrow), British Caledonian 1Xwk (from Gatwick), EAA 3Xwk (from Heathrow, transfer at Nairobi). From Paris: UTA 1Xwk. From Rome: Alitalia 2Xwk.

From East Africa: From Nairobi: EAA 4Xwk, QZ 6Xwk (4X nonstop), Alitalia 1Xwk (nonstop). From Dar es Salaam: QZ 2Xwk, EAA 3Xwk (all nonstop). From Entebbe: EAA 3Xwk (transfer at Nairobi).

From other African countries: From Blantyre: QZ 2Xwk, Air Malawi 3Xwk (all nonstop). From Lubumbashi: Air Zaire 1Xwk (subject to confirmation). From Francistown and from Gaborone, Botswana: QZ 1Xwk (nonstop). From Mauritius and Tananarive: QZ 1Xwk.

Zambia Airways has flights from Ndola to Nairobi 1Xwk, while Alitalia operates Ndola–Kinshasa 1Xwk. Livingstone is served 1Xwk from Francistown and Gaborone, Botswana; this facilitates the seeing of both sides of Victoria Falls (see p. 581).

Sample fares (rounded figures), one-way economy/tourist class, valid for a year, to/from Lusaka, subject to change without notice, are as follows (add 20% to get approximate early 1975 fares):

from/to Lusaka	U.S. dollars	Zambian kwachas	other currency
Addis Ababa	617	398	E$570
Blantyre	50–62	32–40	MK40–50
Dar es Salaam	131	84	T.shs. 937
Entebbe	209	134	U.shs. 1,143
Frankfurt	682	437	DM2,216
Gaborone	91	59	R62
London	534	344	£215
Nairobi	155	100	K.shs. 1,113
New York	858–912	548–580	
Paris	530	342	FF2,449
Rome	510	329	Lire 283,900

Airports

Lusaka International Airport, completed in July 1967 at a cost of $18 million, is 20 km from the city. Facilities: Barclays, Standard Banks, car hire, restaurant, bar, luggage deposit service, duty-free shop (if you're leaving). Airport tax is K2, payable in kwachas on departure. Airport general inquiries, tel. 74213. City terminal is at Farmers House, Cairo Road; tel. 74801. A taxi should cost K6 from airport to town. Zambia Airways bus is K1 per person to the major hotels. The Inter-Continental (tel. 51000) has a free bus service for its guests, and ZNTB can arrange group transfers (tel. 72891/5, 73926, 75438).

The recently reconstructed Ndola International Airport is 6 km east of the city on Airport Road. City terminal is on Chimwemwe Road, tel. 2761. There is no bus transfer; taxi should cost about K3.

The Livingstone Airport is 5km northwest of town (which is 9 km from Victoria Falls). Bus transfer is 50n per person to town terminal in Capital Bldg.; ZNTB also operates transfers.

By Boat

Zambia is landlocked, but you can take a lake boat some distance in getting there and disembark at Zambia's only port, Mpulungu, on Lake Tanganyika. East Africa Railways operates the steamer *Liemba,* carrying passengers and vehicles, from its home port at Kigoma, Tanzania, on a twice-monthly schedule, the cruise taking four days. As of this writing, the *Liemba* is out of service but was due to continue its operation; see p. 324.

By Train

Train tracks run into Zambia from Tanzania, Zaire, and Rhodesia, but as of this writing, the only through service is between Zaire and the Copperbelt. The 1,859-km Tan-Zam Railway from Dar es Salaam to Kapiri Mposhi (connecting to existing lines) may be finished in 1975, and passenger service will follow soon thereafter. Inquiries: Tanzania Zambia Railway Authority (TAZARA), Box 1784, Lusaka; Kinondoni Hostel, Box 2834, Dar es Salaam. Those coming from southern Africa can take the train as far as Victoria Falls, Rhodesia. There are trains 2Xwk from Cape Town, 3Xwk from Johannesburg, all going via Bulawayo. Inquiries: Rhodesia Railways, Box 596, Bulawayo, Rhodesia. South African Railways, c/o SATOUR, Private Bag 164, Pretoria.

By Bus

There are long-distance bus services into Zambia from Tanzania and Malawi. *From Tanzania:* East African Railways' Tanzania Road Services (address, p. 328) runs daily from Dar es Salaam (leaving in the morning) to Mbeya (arriving at dawn the next day). At Mbeya you can either take a local bus to Tunduma on the border (departures in midafternoon, trip takes 4 hours) or connect to daily services of the United Bus Co. of Zambia (UBZ), running to Lusaka and elsewhere. At its best, the Tunduma-Lusaka run is supposed to take only 24 hours over 1,000 km. *From Malawi:* United Transport (Malawi) Ltd. (address, p. 635) runs daily from Lilongwe to Chipata, Zambia, leaving about dawn, arriving about noon. Here you can connect with UBZ's daily bus to Lusaka. From northern Malawi there is 2Xwk service from Karonga on the lake to Chitipa (cost 77t) and 5Xwk service from Chitipa to Tunduma/Nakonde (cost 67t) via United Transport. Note: UBZ has luxury-coach service Chipata–Lusaka and Tunduma–Lusaka; see p. 553.

By Car

You can travel in an ordinary car on good paving (some dirt) into Zambia from Tanzania, Malawi, Zaire, and Rhodesia via Kasane, Botswana. Demons and others have done Nairobi–Lusaka in three to four days, but seven to ten is far better. Blantyre–Lusaka takes two tiring days, three reasonably comfortable ones.

Best routes: From Tanzania: Dar es Salaam–Iringa–Mbeya–Tunduma–Lusaka (our Routes T-6 and Z-1). From Malawi: Blantyre–Lilongwe–Mchinji–Chipata–Lusaka (our Routes Q-1 and Z-2). From Rhodesia: Bulawayo–Victoria Falls–Kasane, Botswana–Kazungula, Zambia (by ferry)–Livingstone–Lusaka. From Zaire: Lubumbashi–Kasumbalesa–Chililabombwe–Kitwe–Lusaka (Route Z-5). From Botswana: Kasane (Chobe Park)–Kazungula–Livingstone–Lusaka. You cannot enter Zambia from Angola or Mozambique or Rhodesia.

Border posts: A few Zambian immigration and customs posts are open 24 hours, but most only 6 A.M.–6 P.M. From/to Zaire: Kasumbalesa, Mokambo, Kipushi, Muliashi, Sakania, and Chembe (ferry—extra charge outside regular hours). From/to Malawi: Mwami, Nyala, Lundazi, Misale. From/to Tanzania: Tunduma and Zombe. From/to Botswana: Kazungula.

Getting around Zambia

Travel Agents

In Lusaka: *Leopold Walford Ltd.,* Cairo Road, Box 1280, tel. 75041. *Eagle Travel,* Cairo Road, Box 3530, tel. 75851. *Travellers Ltd.,* Luangwa House, Cairo Road, Box 2591, tel. 74372. *Zambezi Travel Bureau,* Cairo Road, Box 1010, tel. 75931. In Ndola: *Turnbull Gibson & Co. Ltd.,* Carswell Bldg., President Ave., Box 1698, tel. 4713. In Kitwe: *Thomas Hunter & Co.,* Permanent House, Kaunda Square, Box 97, tel. 2416. In Livingstone: *Victoria Falls Travel Bureau,* Mutual House, Musi-o-Tunya Road, Box 451, tel. 2311, 2285.

ZNTB will also make many of your arrangements—tours, game lodge bookings, etc.

By Air

Zambia Airways operates HS-748 prop jets on its internal routes, with BAC-111 jet service on some Lusaka–Livingstone flights.

From Lusaka: Kitwe 6Xwk, Ndola 16Xwk, Livingstone 8Xwk, Ngoma (Kafue Park) 2Xwk (seasonal), Mfuwe (Luangwa Valley) 4Xwk (seasonal), Chipata 6Xwk, Kaoma 2Xwk, Zambezi 2Xwk, Mongu 3Xwk, Kalabo 2Xwk, Lukulu 1Xwk, Solwezi 1Xwk.

From Ndola: Lusaka 16Xwk, Kitwe 6Xwk, Mansa 4Xwk, Kasama 4Xwk, Mbala 1Xwk, Kasaba Bay 2Xwk, Solwezi 1Xwk.

Sample fares, one-way, economy/tourist class, valid a year, are as follows, with three/seven-day excursion fares, return, in parentheses: To/from Lusaka: Kitwe—K13.50; Livingstone—K18.70 (excursion—K27.20); Ngoma—K11.50 (excursion—K16.70); Mfuwe—K23.30 (excursion—K33.80); Ndola—K13.50. To/from Ndola: Kitwe—K3.80; Kasaba Bay—K34.20 (excursion—K48.90).

Airline Offices

Zambia Airways has the following offices: Farmers House, Cairo Road, Box 2850, Lusaka; tel. 74801 (ticket office, terminal); 74301 (in-country flight reservations); 74309 (international reservations). Chimwemwe Road, Ndola; tel. 2761. Capital Theatre Bldg., Musi-o-Tunya Road, Livingstone; tel. 3152, 3162. Mutual Bldg., Kitwe; tel. 2216. Also in Chipata, Kaoma, Kasama, Lukulu, Mansa, Mbala, Mongu, Senanga, Sesheke, and Zambezi. Overseas offices: 150 East 58th St., New York, N.Y. 10022; tel. (212) 758-9450; also in London, Rome, Nairobi, Dar es Salaam.

Other airlines with offices in Zambia: *Alitalia,* Permanent House, Cairo Road, Lusaka; tel. 74317. Security House, Buteko Ave., Ndola; tel. 3636. *Air Zaire,* Design House, Dar es Salaam Place, Cairo Road, Lusaka; tel. 72345. Lusaka Airport, tel. 77963. 174 President Ave., Ndola; tel. 3165. *British Caledonian,* Gerry's Bldg., Cairo Road, Lusaka; tel. 72809. 69 President Ave., Ndola; tel. 2110, 2918. *East African Airways,* Chester House, Cairo Road, Lusaka; tel. 75891 (general); 75894 (reservations). Lusaka Airport, tel. 77960. *UTA French Airlines,* 6 Central Arcade, Cairo Road, Lusaka; tel. 72124. *British Airways,* Cairo Road, Lusaka; tel. 73187.

By Air Charter

Firms having small planes for hire include: *Prestonair Ltd.,* International Airport, Box 1502, Lusaka; tel. 73131/23; cable ENGINES.

Zamair Ltd., Ndola Airport, Box 23, Ndola; tel. 2864. *Prospair Ltd.,* Nkana-Kitwe Aerodrome, Box 1703, Kitwe; tel. 2237, 84846.

Prospair charges the following rates for a three-passenger Bonanza from Kitwe and return: Lusaka—K138; Livingstone—K301; Ngoma—K205; Kasaba Bay—K266; Mfuwe—K186. Prestonair's rates for a five-passenger Beechcraft Baron from Lusaka and return: Ngoma—K213; Mfuwe—K334; Kasaba Bay—K612; Livingstone—K299; Kitwe—K213; Ndola—K198; Salima (Lake Malawi)—K540; Blantyre—K612. Charge per kilometer: 38n.

ZNTB will handle air charter arrangements.

By Boat

The adventurous may wish to contact *Zambezi River Transport,* Box 177, Livingstone, for information on their road and river passenger services in Western and Southern Provinces.

By Train

You can travel along the present "line of rail" between Ndola, Kabwe, Lusaka, and Livingstone, with many stops in between, especially between Lusaka and Livingstone. There are two types of service: Daily Mixed, with first-, second-, third-, and fourth-class carriages; and Daily Railcar Service, with standard (between first- and second-class) and economy (between third- and fourth-class) accommodations. Some of the Daily Railcar fares: Livingstone–Lusaka: standard—K7.25; economy—K2.35. Lusaka–Ndola: standard—K4.95; economy—K1.60. Some of the Daily Mixed fares: Livingstone–Lusaka: first—K8.15; second—K5.40; third—K2.73; fourth—K1.60.

A Daily Mixed train leaves Livingstone about 6 A.M., arrives in Lusaka about 7 P.M., in Ndola about 6 A.M. the next day. Railcar service is a bit faster, with a 9:45 A.M. train from Livingstone arriving at Lusaka about 5 P.M., in Ndola about 8 P.M. Southbound Daily Mixed trains leave Ndola about 8 P.M., arrive in Lusaka about 5:30 A.M. the next day, Livingstone about 7 P.M. The Railcar leaves Ndola at 7 A.M., arrives Lusaka about 11:30 A.M., Livingstone about 7 P.M.

Booking offices: Box 400, Livingstone; tel. 2181. Box 1932, Lusaka; tel. 75945, 72276. Box 935, Kabwe; tel. 2680. Box 364, Ndola; tel. 2373. Railway HQ is in Kabwe. The Lusaka station is across the tracks from Cairo Road. The Livingstone station is off Musi-o-Tunya Road about five blocks south of the Tourist Centre.

By Bus

United Bus Co. of Zambia (UBZ) has many routes within Zambia, with long-distance buses originating in Lusaka and Kitwe to Livingstone, Kabwe, Chipata, Solwezi, Kasama, Chingola, Petauke, Mpulungu, Mongu, Kapiri Mposhi (the Tan-Zam railway terminus), Tunduma, and intermediate points. There is ordinary and luxury-coach service. On ordinary buses, which are not known for their comfort, fares are low: 50 km—60n; 100 km—K1.10; 200 km—K2.20; 300 km —K3.20; 400 km—K4.10; 500 km—K4.90; and so forth. There is ordinary service daily from Tunduma to Mbala and Mpulungu (6 hours) and 5 times weekly from Tunduma to Chitipa, Malawi, on United Transport (Malawi).

UBZ operates a luxury coach service twice daily between Lusaka, Kabwe, Ndola, and Kitwe; once daily to Chipata and Tunduma; and twice weekly to Mongu. There is service between Lusaka and Livingstone 4 times a week (ZNTB controls the Friday bus). Fares: From Lusaka: to Livingstone—K7; Victoria Falls—K8; Kabwe—K2; Ndola —K5; Kitwe—K6; Chipata—K11.75; Mongu—K10.50; Kapiri Mposhi—K3.50; Tunduma—K17.60. From Kitwe: to Ndola—K1; Kabwe—K4; Lusaka—K6; Livingstone—K13; Victoria Falls—K14.

Reservations for the luxury service should be made with Eagle Travel offices in Lusaka (p. 550), Kabwe (Freedom Way, tel. 2206), Ndola (Broadway, tel. 3395), and Kitwe (Permanent House, tel. 2324); and to UBZ in Chipata (tel. 444), Mongu, Tunduma, and elsewhere.

Inquiries: UBZ, Box 2404, Lusaka; tel. 74891/2. UBZ HQ, Box 187, Kitwe; tel. 2436. UBZ, Ndola, tel. 2346/7. UBZ, Livingstone, tel. 2975.

By Rent-a-Car

Zambia has the following car-hire firms: *Ridgeway Car Hire Service Ltd.*, Box 929, Lusaka; tel. 75361 (main office), 77970 (airport); takes AE and DC cards. *Streamline Car Hire Ltd.* (Isuzu Bullet, Fiat 128), New Africa House, Cairo Road (opposite National Milling), Box 3189, Lusaka; tel. 75728; takes DC card. *Metro Zambia Motors* (British Leyland passenger cars), Cairo Road (North End), Box 469, Lusaka; tel. 74911. *CAMS Ltd.* (VWs, Rover 2000), Cairo Road (South End), Box 672, Lusaka; tel. 73181. *Rent-a-Car (1967) Ltd.*, Savoy St. (opposite Castle Breweries), Box 2123, Ndola; tel. 2865,

2469. *Streamline Car Hire Ltd.,* 2d floor, Stansfield House (opposite Savoy Hotel), Box 1309, Ndola; tel. 2262; takes DC card. *CAMS Ltd.,* Broadway, Box 105, Ndola; tel. 2381, 3621/2. *CAMS Ltd.,* President Ave. (corner Kabengela Ave.), Box 1053, Kitwe; tel. 2390/1/2. *CAMS Ltd.,* Musi-o-Tunya Road, Box 57, Livingstone; tel. 3066, 3088. Ridgeway sample rates: small car—K8 per day (20 miles free), 15n per mile; Peugeot 404/504—K12 per day; luxury cars—K20 per day.

Driving in Zambia

Drive on the left, overtake on the right. Speed limits: 60 mph on 22-foot-wide paved roads, 50 mph on other roads. Limits in urban areas are posted in kilometers.

Auto club: The Automobile Association of Zambia membership fee is K8 per year, with a K4 entrance fee; spouses can join for K4 per year extra. The AA offers the usual services: mechanical aid, towing charge refund, road information, legal advice, publications. It also issues mimeographed reports on main road conditions in Zambia, Malawi, and Rhodesia. Inquiries: AA of Zambia, Dedam Kimathi Road, Box 300, Lusaka; tel. 75311/2; cable FANUM.

Vehicle servicing, repairs, spare parts: Servicing and repair costs are incredible. Lusaka and the Copperbelt towns do have the car dealers for servicing of many makes, but as of February 1973, the importation of all but ten car models was stopped to cut the outflow of hard currency and to ensure the supply of spare parts and proper servicing. The models allowed in: Toyota 1600, Datsun 1200, Galant 16L, Cortina 1600, Marina 1.8, and one model each of Peugeot, Renault, Volkswagen, and Holden, plus all Mercedes-Benz models with a higher duty. Land-Rovers and Fiats are assembled in Zambia, and Daimler-Benz is putting up an assembly plant.

Package Tours around Zambia

The Zambia National Tourist Bureau (p. 543) operates all of the following in-country package tours except for the Luangwa Valley walking safaris. ZNTB tours can be charged on AE and DC.

ZP-1: *South Luangwa National Park.* 9 tours of 3–8 days' duration, from Lusaka, departing for Mfuwe by air 4Xwk. Accommodation, meals, game walks and drives: 3 days—K38; 4 days—K55; 5 days—

K72; 6 days—K89; 8 days—K123. Air fare (3/7-day excursion, return)—K33.80.

ZP-2: *Luangwa Valley Foot Safaris*. Walking safaris are operated
by both ZNTB and the idea's originator, Wilderness Trails Ltd., Box
72, Chipata; bookings, respectively, to ZNTB and Eagle Travel (pp.
543–550). Wilderness Trails are rather more rugged: Just like old-
time Africa of the Clark Gable–Ava Gardner movies—a line of people
moving through the jungle, some with rifles, some with boxes on their
heads. Three 3–8-day walking safaris in South Luangwa, another 8-day
tour in the northern part, June–Oct. Groups number 6 only with each
safari leader. On longest tour, walk 5–7 miles a day on Days 2–7,
camping wherever. All camping equipment supplied; you bring change
of bush clothes, good footwear, and toilet items. Tours: 8 days (Sun.–
Sun.), ground cost—K186.70; 6 days (Sun.–Fri.)—K140; 3 days
(Fri.–Sun.), walking out from base camp only—K70.45; 8 days in
North Luangwa (Sun.–Sun.)—K209. In contrast, ZNTB's Luangwa
Tented Safaris utilize two established tented camps in South Luangwa
as well as the game camps and lodges, and there's game-viewing by
Land-Rover and on foot. Two departures from Lusaka. Ground cost:
4 days—K67, 6 days—K113.

ZP-3: *Kafue National Park*. Tours of 4–8 days from Lusaka or Livingstone and return to either city; departures 2Xwk May–Nov. Rates,
with accommodations at Ngoma Lodge, are the same as the Luangwa
packages in ZP-1. Air fare (3/7-day excursion, return) Lusaka–
Ngoma—K16.70.

ZP-4: *Safari Trails*. Kafue Park walking safaris, run July–Oct. by
ZNTB, are similar to the Luangwa Tented Safaris: there's not so much
walking, some game-viewing is by Land-Rover and river boat *Ulendo,*
and accommodation is at established game camps (rondavels). Six
tours of 3–8 days, with transport from Lusaka by road (except one
tour), short tours staying at Chunga Safari Village, others at Chunga
and other game camps. Costs: 3 days (Fri.–Sun.)—K43.40; 4 days
(Mon.–Thurs.)—K55; 5 days (Fri.–Tues.)—K85.25; 6 days (Tues.–
Sun.)—K106.70; 7 days (air-road tour, Mon.–Sun.)—K134.20 not
incl air fare; 8 days (Wed.–Wed.)—K150.25. Groups are restricted to
6 persons; no children under 12 except at Chunga; light luggage only
(transported by car).

ZP-5: *Lusaka–Livingstone–Victoria Falls "Safari Express."* Weekend coach excursion from Lusaka, departure Fri.; incl sightseeing to
Eastern Cataract, Knife Edge Bridge, Zambezi cruise, Musi-o-Tunya

Zoological Park, Maramba Cultural Centre, National Museum. Cost, transport and sightseeing only: single—K10; return—K16; children under 12—50 percent. Inclusive cost with accommodations at the Inter-Continental: K38.80 per person in dbl (K47.60 for sgl).

ZP-6: *Livingstone and Victoria Falls*. From ZNTB Livingstone office, tel. 3534/5. Eastern Cataract and Knife Edge Bridge (3 hours) —K3. Zoological Park (3 hours)—K3. Museum, Maramba Cultural Centre (2½ hours)—K3. Riverside Drive tour past Old Drift (2½ hours)—K3.

ZP-7: *Zambezi River Cruises,* on the *Makumbi* or the *Zambezi Queen*. Afternoon cruise (Sat., 2 hours)—K3. Sundowner Cruise (daily at 5 P.M., 1½ hours)—K3. Luncheon Cruise (Sun., 2 hours)— K5, incl lunch. Speedboat and driver—K10 per person per hour.

ZP-8: *Kasaba Bay and Nkamba Bay*. Tours of 4, 5, and 8 days to Lake Tanganyika fishing resorts, departures 2Xwk from Lusaka. Ground costs: 4 days—K34, 5 days—K44, 8 days—K74.

ZP-9: *Lusaka City Tour*. 2½ hours to Anglican Cathedral, YWCA Crafts Centre, Parliament, Zambia Gemstones, Luburma Market, Chilenje 394. Adults—K3, children under 12—K1.50.

ZP-10: *Munda Wanga Gardens and Chilanga*. 2½ hrs, from Lusaka ZNTB. Adults—K3, children under 12—K1.50.

General Information

Language

English is the official language and is widespread, making it more useful than any of the six major local languages—Bemba, Tonga, Lozi, Lunda, Luvale, and Nyanja—or 72 dialects. All are Bantu languages. Bemba is widely spoken in the Copperbelt, Northern, and Luapula provinces; Nyanja is common in the Eastern Province and in Lusaka. Tourists, even if motoring, need no local words to get along.

Time

Zambian time country-wide is two hours ahead of Greenwich Mean Time, one hour behind East Africa time. See p. 126.

Weights and Measures

Zambia is metric, though not everybody has completely changed over from the British system, and the use of such variable measures as a pile (of six tomatoes, for instance) seems to be the norm in the markets.

Electricity

220 volts single phase and 380 volts three phase, 50-cycle AC.

Holidays

Jan. 1—New Year's Day. Good Friday. Holy Saturday. Easter Monday. Labour Day (first Monday in May). May 24—Commonwealth Day. May 25—African Freedom Day. Whit Monday. Heroes Day (first Monday after first weekend in July). Unity Day (Tuesday after Heroes Day). Aug. 9—Youth Day. Oct. 24—Independence Day (sometimes Oct. 25 as well). Dec. 25—Christmas. Dec. 26—Boxing Day.

Hours of Business

Hours at offices and most shops are a standard 8 A.M.–5 P.M., with lunchtime closing from 1–2 P.M. Government offices go from 7:30 A.M.–4 P.M., with the same lunch hour. On Wednesday most shops close early at 1 P.M., and tourists will find it difficult to shop that afternoon. Businesses, shops, and markets are open Saturday 8 A.M.–1 P.M.; after that time, Lusaka takes on the appearance of a ghost town. Sundays are worse, but the big central market is open every day 6 A.M.–6 P.M. Some shops and department stores are open late Thursday and Friday, and some are open until 6 P.M. Saturday if Monday is a holiday. Hotel bars are generally open 10 A.M.–2 P.M., 5–11 P.M., sometimes later. Banks are open 8:15 A.M.–12:45 P.M. Monday, Tuesday, Thursday, and Friday, 8:15 A.M.–noon Wednesday, 8:15–11 A.M. Saturday.

Banks

Main Lusaka branches: *Barclays Bank of Zambia Ltd.,* Mutaba House, Cairo Road, Box 1416, tel. 74366; cable BARCLADOM. Has 6 Lusaka branches plus 28 branches and 26 agencies in the country. *Standard Bank of Zambia Ltd.,* Standard House, Cairo Road, Box 1934, tel. 75151; cable DERBY. Has 4 Lusaka branches, 43 branches and agencies elsewhere. Smaller banks are Grindlays, Commercial Bank of Zambia, and National Commercial Bank.

Diplomatic Representatives in Zambia

In Lusaka: *Botswana*—High Commission, Freedom Way, tel. 73668, 50804. *Great Britain*—High Commission, Independence Ave., Box RW

50, tel. 51122; cable UKREP. *Kenya*—High Commission, Kafue House, Cairo Road, tel. 75897. *Tanzania*—High Commission, Woodgate House, Cairo Road, tel. 51300. *U.S.*—Embassy, United Nations Ave. (corner Independence Ave.), Box 1617, tel. 50222; cable AMEMBASSY. *West Germany*—Embassy, 350 Independence Ave., tel. 51899. *Zaire*—Embassy, tel. 77232, 77245. Consulate-General, tel. 77245. Other countries with representatives in Lusaka include Austria, Belgium, Chile, China (People's Republic), Czechoslovakia, Denmark, Egypt, Finland, France, Greece, Guinea, India, Israel, Italy, Japan, Netherlands, Norway, Somalia, Sweden, Switzerland, USSR, Vatican, and Yugoslavia.

Mail, Telegrams

Airmail letters to the U.S. cost 25n for each 10 grams, an ordinary airmail postcard or aerogramme 9n. Surface letters to the U.S. go at the rate of 9n up to 20 grams, then rates are complicated.

The main post office in Lusaka is on Cairo Road (corner Church Road), tel. 73066. General post office hours: 7:30 A.M.–5 P.M. weekdays, 7:30 A.M.–12:30 P.M. Saturday. Lusaka's Ridgeway branch, Ndola, Kitwe, and Livingstone post offices open at 8 A.M. You can pick up registered mail, and post or pick up parcels, 8 A.M.–12:30 P.M. and 2–4 P.M. weekdays, 8 A.M.–12:30 P.M. Saturday.

The U.S. Embassy no longer saves Americans' mail, but sends it along to Poste Restante (General Delivery).

General rates for telegrams, which are handled by post offices: to U.S. and Europe except Britain—20n per word, minimum K1.40 for 7 words; night letter—10n per word, minimum K2.20 for 22 words. To Britain and Commonwealth—16n per word, minimum K1.12 for 7 words; night letter—8n per word, minimum K1.76 for 22 words.

Telephone Calls

Direct dialing to points in Zambia is possible from a large percentage of the phones in every city and town. Calls outside Zambia should be booked at least 24 hours in advance through the international operator in Ndola. A three-minute call to the U.S. costs K9, to Britain K6, to East Africa K3.

For operation of coin telephones, see p. 129. Lusaka has few public phones. There are three booths around the corner to the right of the main post office, also in the Ridgeway and Inter-Continental hotels.

From city phones, dial 999 for emergencies, 100 for the operator, 090 for international calls.

Shopping

Don't shop with the expectation of finding anything that looks *Zambian,* though here and there you will find some nice African-looking things to buy—and some merely nice things such as copperware, gemstones, woven material, cloth, blankets. If you want to be sure it was produced in Zambia, better ask. The squads of curio sellers in the Cairo Road center island sell almost nothing Zambian; it's all from Zaire and Kenya.

Copperware is not cheap because while the copper is mined and refined here, it is shipped elsewhere to be made into plate, which is then shipped back to Zambian workshops for making into trays, beer mugs, and candlesticks. Lusaka shops where copperware is sold: Kingston's (next to ZOK), ZCBC department store, Copper Boutique (in ZNTB office, also in Inter-Continental). Not much copperware is available in Livingstone. Among the better items available are copper jewelry (dangly earrings, brooches), mugs, wine and champagne "glasses," water goblets, candlesticks, ashtrays, salt and pepper shakers, trays, and miscellaneous dishes. Sample prices (at ZCBC store): glassbottom beer mug—K9.40; plain serving tray—K10.25; triangular candlestick —K9.25; salt and pepper shakers—K4.50; goblet—K6; vase—K5.75–7.95; napkin rings—K1.20 each.

Cloth in some bold, modern, or semitraditional designs, and more artistic prints, as well as some copied East African designs, is available in bolts as well as *chirundu* or *khanga.* One of the best places to see what Zambia's weaving is like is the Kafue Textiles showroom on Cairo Road (next to ZOK). Nothing is for sale there, but the department stores carry many of the fabrics.

Gemstones, especially amethyst, are the specialty of Zambia Gemstones, Panganani Road (located about three blocks to the left of the North End traffic circle), Box 1149, Lusaka; tel. 75308; branch in the Hotel Edinburgh arcade, Kitwe. Most of the amethyst is exported in bulk, but the Lusaka workshop produces 200 pieces of jewelry a week from amethyst and imported gemstones.

Traditional items, such as thumb pianos, musical instruments, functional household items (not Western ones, but African ones like *nsima* porridge servers), and straw containers, such things as Luvale Makishi dancers' fright masks (actually representing ancestral spirits and used in youth initiation rites), seem to be more available in Livingstone, at the Museum and Maramba Cultural Centre, and the two curio shops on Musi-o-Tunya Road.

Carvings are a special problem. Basically, there is little genuine traditional stuff, and whatever is genuine is not generally obtainable. In your quest for carvings of quality, good luck. "Curios" are available everywhere; try the middle of Cairo Road, Africa Art Studio (mid-Cairo Road) and the Safari Gift Center (Cairo Road opposite the GPO), the major hotels, the two curio shops in Livingstone, and the curio vendors near the Eastern Cataract at Victoria Falls. Prices indoors are fixed, outdoors negotiable; when in doubt, dicker.

Wildlife and Game Parks

If Zambia doesn't have the reputation among tourists as a wildlife country, it's not because there isn't any game. There is probably more wildlife in Zambia than all of West Africa; it's just not as visible as in East Africa, partly because most of the national parks are closed to visitors.

Like most African countries, Zambia was slow in starting a conservation program. Mweru Marsh was a game reserve as early as 1900, and tribal chiefs had set up private hunting preserves here and there. But nothing serious was done until 1931 when the colonial government invited the game warden of Uganda, C. R. S. Pitman, to do an extensive survey. His report showed wildlife decreasing at an alarming rate—except for elephants and buffalos. Some of his proposals were implemented in 1941, and the Game and Tsetse Department was set up in 1942. However, as in many countries, game was eliminated to eliminate the tsetse fly (it didn't work). The Game Preservation and Hunting Association (later the Wild Life Conservation Society of Zambia) was formed in 1953, but even by then the Game and Tsetse Department got very little money to do anything. On Independence, a Department of Wildlife, Fisheries, and National Parks was formed. Luangwa Valley, Kafue, and Sumbu, along with Victoria Falls, were given added protection as national parks. Then, in 1971–72, the government really started moving. In October 1971 a new system of 32 Game Management Areas (habitation allowed, hunting controlled) covering nearly a quarter of Zambia was declared, and in November Parliament approved a new system of 18 national parks (including preexisting ones) covering *8 percent of the country*. Seventeen of the parks were gazetted in early 1972; Blue Lagoon followed in 1973.

Eight of the parks are open to the public: Kafue, South Luangwa, North Luangwa (Wilderness Trails use only), Luambe (next to Luangwa), Nyika, Sumbu (Kasaba Bay), Lochinvar, and Musi-o-Tunya (Victoria Falls). The other nine parks are all undeveloped wilderness areas and not open to the public: Lukusuzi, Mweru Wantipa, Lusenga Plain, Isangano, Kasanka, Lavushi Manda, West Lunga, Liuwa Plain, and Sioma Ngwezi. The Department of Wildlife, Fisheries, and National Parks (Box 1, Chilanga) says that there are "strong possibilities" Kasanka, West Lunga, and Lukusuzi will be opened to the public, possibly for Wilderness Trails purposes (see package listing ZP-2), within the decade.

Conservation society: The Wild Life Conservation Society of Zambia (WLCSZ) publicizes the need for wildlife protection and, among other things, operates two school camps in Kafue and South Luangwa for schoolchildren. The *Black Lechwe,* named for a rare breed of antelope threatened with oblivion, is published quarterly. Annual membership is K4 (husband and wife—K5.50), with a K2 entrance fee; under-18s can join for K1. The magazine can be obtained by nonmembers for K2.50 for four issues (one year). Inquiries: WLCSZ, Concession House, Cairo Road, Box 255, Lusaka; tel. 72824. *Black Lechwe,* Box 9094, Kitwe.

Birdwatching

There are about 600 species of birds in Zambia, with about 400 of them found in Kafue Park. The Zambia Ornithological Society (Box 3944, Lusaka) has numerous activities, including social. Field guide: *Birds of Zambia,* by Benson, Brooks, Dowsett, and Irwin (London: Collins, 1971).

Historic and Prehistoric Sites

Zambia has 49 declared national monuments in three categories: A—monuments developed and open to the public; B—undeveloped monuments with access restricted (lack of roads, private ownership of land, etc.); C—monuments closed to the public. At present there are 12 in the B category, 9 in the C. The latter are closed for very good reason, such as the presence of Cave Sickness parasites at one prehistoric cave site. All monuments are protected by the Commission for the Preservation of Natural and Historical Monuments and Relics, Box 124, Livingstone. Guidebook: *The National Monuments of Zam-*

bia: An Ilustrated Guide, by D. W. Phillipson (published by the monuments commission, 1972).

Fishing

Fishing has always been a favorite outdoor recreational activity for Europeans in Zambia, and some tourists now do a bit of it between sightseeing at Victoria Falls and game viewing in Kafue or Luangwa. One favorite catch is the iron-jawed, razor-toothed tiger, a striped fish that will fight to the last ounce of its strength. Good eating fish include many species of tasty bream (tilapia). The best fishing areas are Lake Kariba and Lake Tanganyika, also the Zambezi above Victoria Falls, the Kafue River, Lakes Bangweulu and Chila, and the Luangwa, Luapula, and Chambeshi rivers.

Lake Tanganyika: Nile perch, up to 140 pounds, is the most common catch, but you can hook an 11-pound fighting tiger, giant catfish (locally, *vundu*), goliath tiger up to 70 pounds, lake salmon, *nkupi,* or, what Zambian anglers dream of, the glittering, pale-gold golden perch, the albino of the species—only one per year is caught, on the average. Best fishing: December–March.

Lake Kariba: Tiger, bream, chessa, *nkupi,* bottlenose, Cornish jack, barbel (catfish), electric barbel, Hunyani salmon, yellowfish, *vundu,* squeakers, silverfish, eels, lungfish. Best fishing: October–January.

Hunting

Those interested in hunting in Zambia can write to Amalgamated Safaris (merger of Luangwa Safaris and Zambia Safaris), Box 2955, Lusaka; tel. 715220, 715327.

Lusaka

Lusaka, Zambia's capital city with a population of 262,200 (est. 1972), has its location rather incidentally and its present appearance rather accidentally. In 1905, when Cecil Rhodes's "Cape to Cairo" railway was being laid from Victoria Falls to Broken Hill (Kabwe), the chief engineer had a siding built every 20 miles. One was built at Chipongwe, and the tracks pushed on. Twenty miles north, near a Lenje village, there was enough level land, so a siding was laid. It was named Lusaaka's, after the local headman, reputedly a good elephant hunter.

In 1908 someone put up a pole-and-daga shop at Lusaaka's siding, and a settlement began developing. The British South Africa Co. took notice of the place, set up a Village Management Board in 1913, and officially named it Lusaka. Geographer George Kay summed up the early history of the city: "It was born, survived, and grew in spite of its site, which had nothing to recommend it except the occurrence of the siding." There was little water in the dry season, too much in the wet season. It was dusty, it was muddy. And mosquitoes bred everywhere. BSA Co. president Starr Jameson visited Lusaka in 1914 and promptly said the place had been made a township in too much of a hurry.

What a surprise, then, that the colonial government decided to make the ugly duckling its capital.

When the administration decided to move from Livingstone, many towns clamored for the honor. An English city planner chose Lusaka not because it was that good but because every other place had a worse disadvantage. So, in July 1931, the decision was made to make Lusaka the capital. Lack of funds led the government not to compensate the established businessmen in the old town, which is why all the business activity is at the western extremity of the city, up and down *Cairo Road* (named for the Cape-to-Cairo idea). Some government offices were erected on the ridge 2 miles southeast of the old town, along what is now *Independence Avenue,* a street of spread-out government ministries and, farther out, the *State House* (formerly Government House, now President Kaunda's residence) and other large houses. European residential areas were plotted in the northeast; the "African compounds" were banished to the southwest. Half-completed, the new capital was declared open in May 1935, with everybody saying the decision to transfer the capital was "a blunder of the first magnitude."

But the spaces between the buildings were filled, and it now appears the planners had the right idea in spreading things out—though a car is necessary to get around easily, and the African housing areas are, as Kay says, "a blot on the landscape." Most of the older areas—some of which the tourist is especially taken to see during the ZNTB's city sightseeing tour—are fairly dismal collections of little boxes. When the tour microbus pauses by *Kamwala,* the guide will remind the visitor that the round, thatched-roof huts were built during the colonial regime and "we are not tearing them down in order to show to tourists." Nearby are such new areas as *New Kamwala* and *Libala Stage 2,* which have pleasant, simple, but uniform small houses.

LUSAKA

City Center

1. Information Center
2. High Court
3. Holy Cross Cathedral
4. Railway Station
5. Luburma Market
6. Government ministries
7. Ridgeway Hotel
8. Inter-Continental Hotel
9. ZNTB tourist office
10. Zambia Airways
11. General Post Office

0   KILOMETERS   ⅛

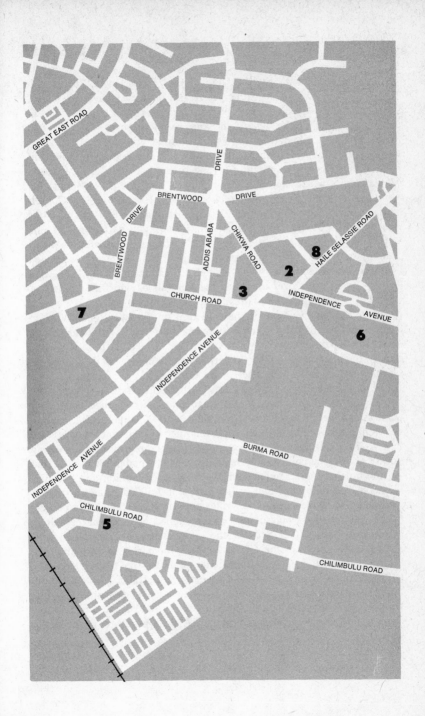

Despite its growth, Lusaka had a Town Management Board until 1953 when it became a Municipal Board. That became a Municipal Council the next year, and in 1960 Lusaka became a city, the first in Zambia. In 1970, the city limits were extended, expanding the city from 93 square kilometers to 360 square kilometers.

Today's nonbusiness visitor to Lusaka will find enough to hold him a day or so before continuing to one of the game parks or Victoria Falls, any of which are more fascinating. Among the photogenic sights in Lusaka is the Anglican *Cathedral of the Holy Cross,* on Church Road across from the colonial *High Court* building and the big glass headquarters of the *Anglo American Corporation,* part owner of one of the two big copper companies. The cathedral, a concrete, copper, and glass structure that soars even though it has no spire, was opened for services in 1962, with the formal dedication in 1970. There is a great copper cross over the altar; the top half of one wall consists of five huge panels of colored glass in a checkerboard pattern.

If you go to the right of the cathedral on Chikwa Road and then out Addis Ababa Drive, you will reach the *Great East Road,* which runs to Chipata and on to Malawi. Past the *Lusaka Turf Club* and the *Show Grounds,* on a hill to the left is the Parliament or *National Assembly,* opened in 1970. The square building has a big copper dome that has weathered to a brownish purple. Unfortunately, you can't enter the building unless you've made previous arrangements; you can usually get in if you take the ZNTB tour—though we did, and we couldn't. Across Parliament Road is another hill on which sits *Mulungushi Hall,* built as a conference center for the big three-day meeting of 54 nonaligned countries in September 1970. Though much criticized at the time, the government spent between $10.4 million and $20 million on the conference hall, which can seat 1,500 delegates around a massive oval table, and on 62 villas for the delegations. The conference was the third big summit of nonaligned nations. Farther along the Great East Road and on the right is the big, modern, well-landscaped campus of the *University of Zambia.* Still in an embryonic state at Independence, the university admitted its first students in 1966 and now has an enrollment of more than 1,500. It offers a wide range of degree courses, including law, medicine, and engineering. The first 27 students graduated in 1969, and 104 in 1970; these two classes alone just about doubled the number of African graduates in the whole country.

The ZNTB tour goes to the Chilenje Area B so that the simply furnished four-room house called *Chilenje 394* can be shown. Now behind a brick wall with an iron gate, and declared a national monument, the house was Kenneth Kaunda's residence from January 1960 to December 1962 while he directed the Independence struggle. Open daily 10 A.M.–1 P.M., 2–5 P.M., closed Monday afternoon, all day Tuesday.

Other stops on the sightseeing tour include the *Zambia Gemstones* workshop (see "Shopping" section); *Luburma central market,* Chilimbulu Road, off Independence Avenue, about 2 blocks east of the railway overpass, open 6–6 daily, where fruit and vegetables, meat and fish, clothes, and housewares are sold, along with coils of tobacco, big bags of charcoal, and such delectables as dead mice and dried caterpillars; and the big copper *Independence Arch* off Independence Avenue. Also of interest are the *tobacco auction floor,* in season; and *Twickenham Road Archaeological Site,* an 8-acre site in the Olympia Park suburb that yielded some fine early Iron Age pottery (the site may not yet be open, but plans are to construct a small museum).

Good day trips can be made to the following: *Munda Wanga Park and Gardens* and the *Department of Wildlife, Fisheries, and National Parks* in Chilanga and *Kafue Gorge* (see Route Z-1). With permission (inquire at ZNTB), you might arrange to visit the *Ayrshire Farm Rock Engravings,* a national monument located about 32 km southwest of Lusaka. The engravings include representations of ceremonial crescentic battle axes, hoes, *chisolo* boards, and an indeterminate beast. They are the best examples of Iron Age engravings known in Zambia.

Accommodations

Hotel Inter-Continental, Box 2201, tel. 51000; cable INHOTELCOR. On Haile Selassie Ave. 189 dbls, 12 suites, 9 sgls, all w/bath, a-c. Rates: B&B: sgl—K15.30; dbl—K20.15. Credit: AE, DC. The premier hotel in Lusaka, built 1968 by the government and Pan Am, has American comfort, style, amenities. Makumbi Bar on 8th floor, Luangwa Bar on ground. Lots of places to eat. Pool, public phones, telex service, newsstand, Copper Boutique, drugstore, hairdresser, Barclays Bank (8:30–10:30 A.M. Mon.–Sat.). A casino may be added. Rating: 1st-class international, ★. Govt. 4 stars.

Ridgeway Hotel, Box 666, tel. 51699; cable RIDGEOTEL. On Church Road just past Evelyn Hone College if you're coming from Cairo Road. 49 sgls, 80 dbls (incl 3 suites), all but 11 rms w/bath; some a-c. Rates: B&B: sgl—to K15; dbl—to K17.40. Credit: AE, DC. Just one notch below the Inter-Continental. Old wing 1953, new wing 1968–69. All rooms comfortable enough, the newest ones a bit sterile. 2 restaurants, 2 bars. Main lounge looks out onto lily pond and terrace. Rating: 1st-class international. Govt. 4 stars.

Lusaka Hotel, Box 44, tel. 73136. On Cairo Road. Was to be replaced with a brand-new building. Rates: B&B: sgl—to K8.75; dbl—to K11.70. Credit: DC. Govt. 3 stars.

Andrews Motel, Box 475, tel. 74966; cable ANDMOTEL. 8 km south of city on Kafue Road. 30 rms, all w/bath. Rates: B&B: sgl—K7.50; dbl—K9. Pool. Rating: Govt. 2 stars.

Barn Motel. Box 973, tel. 719420. 19 km from city on Great East Road, 5 km past airport turnoff. 8 sgls, 8 dbls. Rates: B&B: sgl—K4.50, dbl—K6. Pool, playground, bars, restaurant.

Bwacha Hotel and *The Annex* are scuzzy places (both ungraded by govt.) we wouldn't recommend to anyone. The *Evelyn Hone College Hotel,* Box 29, was to open in 1974.

The *Pamodzi Hotel,* an imaginatively designed hotel with 200 split-level rooms, is being constructed on Church Road, to open before 1976.

Camping at Makeni Caravan Camp, Box 1770, tel. 73285. Located at 3-Mile Peg on Kafue Road, next to Shell station. Best place for campers, hitchhikers. 2 big lots with green lawn, gardens, friendly dogs; 2 ablution blocks with hot shower, bath. Fee: 35n per person, incl use of all facilities.

Where to Eat

The Makumbi Room, 8th floor of Inter-Continental, tel. 51000. Poshest eatery in town. Reservations necessary even for lunch; tie and jacket (women—dress best) or national dress mandatory in the evening. You won't be overwhelmed by the bland decor, Pan Am's idea of the semi-African, but there's a nice view of the city. K2.50 lunch buffet Monday–Saturday; dinner starts at 8 P.M., band at 8:30. À la carte (entrées—K2–3) items include tender well-aged sirloin, Danish rainbow trout Grenobloise, East African rock lobster thermidor, traditional *nsima* (K2—outrageous), Kafue River bream Makumbi. Choice of 3 table d'hôte meals—K3.50–4. Credit: AE, DC.

Woodpecker Inn, tel. 62329. 6½ km from city center at end of Independence Ave. (at Gizenga Road). Big manor-style building housing 3 bars, restaurant, nightclub—the only cabaret in Zambia, showcasing Western talent mostly. Restaurant-nightclub is for diners only, otherwise a cover charge equal to the price of dinner. Dance band

6 nights. Entrées run K2–4.40, include beef fondue in a variety of sauces (tartar, tomato, béchamel, curry, chili), steak Diane, escalope of veal royale. Credit: DC.

The Ambassador, in the Ridgeway Hotel, tel. 51699. Decor nothing to get excited about, but do dress. Businessman's lunch—K3. Band nights. À la carte items include spaghetti Bolognaise, lobster mayonnaise salad, filet steak Rossini, baked Alaska for 6; entrées mostly K1.75–3. Credit: AE, DC.

Mutanda Coffee Hut, off lobby of Inter-Continental. Good snack bar, resembling an African Howard Johnson's. Standard lunch is K2.25, also à la carte items like hamburgers (K1!), grilled chicken Tikka with Punjabi salad, Reuben. Ritzy snack bar—even has a wine list. Open to 11:30 P.M. Credit: AE, DC.

Pool Terrace, at the Ridgeway. Charcoal grill, table d'hôte lunch, dinner.

Lutabo Hut, off Inter-Continental garden terrace. You pay K3 as you walk in, get a choice of grilled specialties: Punjabi kebab, T-bone, chicken, sirloin, churasco, spatchcock, pork chops. The smell in this place is delightful.

La Gondola, Katondo Road at Freedom Way, tel. 75581. Restaurant-nightclub has K2 table d'hôte lunch, K1 courtyard lunch, à la carte dinner with dance band and entertainment Tuesday–Saturday to 3 A.M.

Lotus Inn, toward the North End of Cairo Road, tel. 72641. Yes, a Chinese restaurant, with unassuming decor, somewhat dark atmosphere, bamboo-shoot wallpaper. Dishes from 50n–K1.50. Call up 24 hours in advance and you can have spare ribs in black beans for K1.50.

Kudu Inn, at Longacres shopping center, tel. 50970. New. Credit: DC.

Lunch Box, Freedom Way.

Au Mont Blanc, in arcade off Dar es Salaam Place, Cairo Road. Ordinary, nice lunch place.

Steakhouse, Chachacha Road, end of Central Arcade. Smoky, greasy air. Grilled dishes from K1.35–1.80; full lunch or dinner—K2.15. Band at night.

Zamby Snack Bar, in Mwaiseni department store. Local McDonald's, with the Zamby costing 25n; cheeseburger—35n; milkshake—25n. Open to 6 daily, which makes it about the only living thing on Cairo Road Saturday and Sunday afternoons. (A chain of Zambys is opening all over Zambia.)

Getting Around

Taxis are the only practical way to get around. Main cab rank is near Sergio's garage, Nkwazi Road (block west of Cairo Road), tel. 73232. Ranks at the major hotels. UBZ's Zamcabs are on call 24 hours; tel. 73145/6. Other taxis, tel. 72314, 73503. You will rarely be able to flag down a cab on the street. Taxis have 35n on the meter when you get in, go up 5n after a mile.

"What's On . . ."

The Lusaka Information Centre (located in the City Library, Katondo St., Box 1304, tel. 72584) publishes free the monthly *Lusaka Calls,* available at hotels and elsewhere. It has a map, a handy list of addresses, times of club meetings and church services, and no events. See the newspapers.

Culture

There isn't much cultural activity in Zambian towns. Lusaka has no museum or art gallery, but it does have a small orchestra, choral society, musical society, and Theatre Club (which performs at the Playhouse). The Anglo American Art Centre, ground floor of the Anglo American Bldg., Independence Ave., has periodic art displays.

Cinemas

20th Century, Tenzebantu Road (near ZCBC store), tel. 73512. *Lido Drive-In,* about 5 km south on Kafue Road, tel. 73593. *Plaza,* Chachacha Road, tel. 72278. 20th Century, Plaza, and *The Other Cinema,* are the first-run houses. *Cinema Petite* meets three times a month at the Playhouse, has classic movies; see Saturday papers for details. *Palace,* Bombay Road, tel. 74521, has old movies and skin flicks.

Libraries

Lusaka City Library, Katondo St. (down street from Lusaka Hotel). *USIS Library,* Central Arcade, Cairo Road. *National Archives,* Government Road (for Africana, Zambiana).

Religious Services

The faiths represented in Lusaka: Catholic, Jewish, Presbyterian, Anglican, Pentecostal, Quaker, Baptist, Lutheran, Seventh-Day Adventist, Church of the Nazarene, Apostolic Church, Christian Scientist,

Church of Christ, Dutch Reformed, Hindu, Moslem, and the United Church of Zambia. See *Lusaka Calls* and the newspapers for details.

Shops and Services

The main shopping street is Cairo Road, with very few nice shops on the parallel or cross streets. Because of import restrictions, many things are hard to find and expensive. Bring it with you.

Barber: Central Hairdressers.

Books: Kingston's, Anchor House (next to ZOK), Box 651.

Camping, hunting, fishing equipment: Standay Gerry, Box 1840.

Camping gas: Handigas, Nkwazi Road.

Department stores (the main places to shop for everything): ZOK, ZCBC, Mwaiseni.

Hairdressers: Ducali (tel. 72348), Antoinette's (tel. 72296), Coquette (in the Inter-Continental).

Laundry, dry cleaners: Lusaka Steam Laundry and Dry Cleaners (corner Chiparamba and Chachacha roads).

Optician: Klaus Rygaard Ltd.

Pharmacies: Lusaka Pharmacy (Central Arcade), Karibu Chemists.

Photo shop: Royal Art Studio.

Livingstone and Victoria Falls

Centuries ago the great River Zembre (or Zambere) was shown rising far inland from fantastic lakes. It wasn't until the last century that, in the far, far northwestern tip of Zambia, near the Kalene Hill mission, was found the tiny, tree-shrouded stream which is the source of the mighty Zambezi. The 1,700-mile river, the only important African river to flow into the Indian Ocean, begins its journey remarkably only half a mile from one of the sources of the Congo, which empties into the Atlantic. The Zambezi flows through a corner of Angola, then back into Zambia, picking up the water of a thousand tributaries along the way. Eight hundred miles from Kalene Hill the river is more than a mile wide when, all of a sudden, as a magnificent sheet of thundering water, it drops some 355 feet over a hard ledge at Victoria Falls.

The great waterfall, the greatest geographical spectacle in Africa, was known to generations of Africans who lived near the falls—but only to them. The European discovery of the falls was made by Dr. David Livingstone, who came upon them on November 16, 1855. He had heard of *Musi-o-Tunya* (spelling varies, but it means "the smoke that thunders") four years before from the Zambezi tribes. Livingstone was transported enough by the beauty of the river—"scenes so lovely must have been gazed upon by angels in their flight," he wrote in *Missionary Travels and Researches in Southern Africa*. On the day of discovery, Livingstone paddled toward the falls "in the care of persons well acquainted with the rapids," down to what is now called Livingstone Island, on the lip of the falls. He looked over the edge at what is "simply the whole mass of the Zambezi waters rushing into a fissure or rent made right across the bed of the river." He was there at low water, but still, "in peering down over the edge, we could see only a dense white cloud with two rainbows in it. A smart shower from the ascending column falls [*sic*] when the wind shifted eastwards and soon drenched us to the skin. . . . When the river is full the noise is said to be terriffic and the vapour seen ten miles off." He named it for England's Queen (the Zambian government seems to want to call it Musi-o-Tunya, and once was about to change the name of Livingstone town to Maramba).

Livingstone thought that the earth had been split here during some cataclysmic upheaval. Present-day geologists have not confirmed his theory, but have instead found that the Zambezi was just doing what all rivers do in the course of their lives—that is, finding their way to the sea by the shortest, lowest route, gradually over millions of years cutting gorges and valleys, smoothing corners until, in the words of G. Bond, "in old age the long profile [of the river] is a slow smooth curve fully adjusted to sea level below which it cannot excavate."

The natural history of rivers combines with the fact that the rock in the Victoria Falls region is a huge 1,000-foot-thick bed of volcanic basalt, laid down 150 million years ago, split by numerous cracks or joints formed when the lava cooled. Along one dominant series of joints are some zones of softer basalt. Geologists theorize that the upper Zambezi was diverted long ago by a gentle upward movement of the earth; the water headed for low ground eastward but then spilled suddenly down into what is now the Middle Zambezi (previously a different river from the Upper Zambezi). As a waterfall, the river cut the Batoka Gorge (downstream from Victoria Falls), and the cutting action of the water deepened the gorge as the line of the falls moved upstream. Eventually, the pressure of the water found the series of joints filled with the softer material; since the joints *crossed* the line of the river, the water scooped out the soft material and formed a broad waterfall.

A glance at a map shows a series of zigzag gorges below the present falls. The gorge into which the Zambezi now falls directly is at least the eighth fall line. The river may have always established a straight falls line, but the water always found a weak spot along the lip and began to erode it. Once the lip was lowered, more water concentrated at that point, thus increasing the force of erosion. More blocks of rock were weakened and washed away until the whole river was forced through the narrow fissure. This widened until a new, broad lip, at an angle to the old one, was formed. If you go below the falls to see the gorges, you will be walking on the old bed of the river; the northern edge of each gorge you see was once the lip of Victoria Falls.

You can see where the present lip may—not in our lifetime but in thousands of years—give way, forming a new line. Devil's Cataract, on the Rhodesian side, has cut deep into the lip; this is the cleft that will eventually form a short connecting gorge (like the present one near the Boiling Pot) back to the new line, which will be at one of two intersecting lines of weakness in the base rock (revealed by aerial photos).

How long has all this been happening? About 100 million years ago, there was the upward movement that diverted the river, setting up the conditions that formed the falls. The erosion of the Batoka Gorge downstream may have begun 1.5 million years ago, during the Lower Pleistocene. By the time of the Upper Pleistocene pluvial (wet period) about 40,000 years ago, the waterfall (or rapids) was at the present Songwe River Gorge, about 11 km below the falls. At the end of the Pleistocene about 10,000 years ago, the waterfall was at the present Fourth Gorge. It has taken that 10,000 years for the falls to erode the 2 km from the Fourth Gorge to the present line.

Statistics

The *width of the Zambezi River* at the falls is 1,850 yards. The *mean height of the falls* is 263 feet, with the mean height of Devil's Cataract 200 feet, Main Falls 273 feet, Rainbow Falls 326 feet, the Eastern Cataract 323 feet. The *greatest known flow of water* over the falls was 158,812,500 Imperial gallons per minute, measured March 7, 1958; the water in the Silent Pool rose 68 feet. The *mean maximum flow during the flood season* is 120 million Imperial gallons per minute. The *mean annual maximum flow* is 47.5 million Imperial gallons per minute, while the *mean annual flow* is 14.9 million Imperial gallons per minute. The *lowest known flow* of water, November 7–11, 1959, was a mere 2.3 million Imperial gallons per minute. To compare these statistics on the basis of annual flow, 38,400 cusecs (cubic feet per second) go over Victoria Falls, while 212,000 cusecs go over Niagara Falls and an incredible 470,000 cusecs over Guaíra, on the Brazil-Paraguay border, which is the world's greatest waterfall.

The Falls (Zambian Side)

For those tourists who are coming from Livingstone, 8 km from the Tourist Centre there is a signposted turnoff right to the Eastern Cataract. Take this turnoff; go less than ½ km to a T-junction. To the right is the *Falls Restaurant* on the bank of the Zambezi, the *North Bank Rest Camp,* and, more than 1 km away, the *record high-water-mark monument.* Go left at the T-junction past the entrance to the *campground* and the back garden of the *Musi-o-Tunya Inter-Continental* (entrance on the highway). You will come to a potholed parking lot; park here and proceed on foot, heading into the unkempt park on your right. Bear right toward the palm-frond-roofed shelter; past this and down some steps is a good viewpoint on the *Eastern Cataract,* the only part of the falls easily seen from the Zambian side. Some 304 yards wide, it is separated from adjacent Rainbow Falls by the *Armchair,* a 25-foot-wide depression in the lip that is filled with a deep pool of water in the dry season. From the shelter, walk toward the *War Memorial.* Bear to the right on a gravel path into a small *rain forest;* along this path are a couple of viewpoints toward the Eastern Cataract. Straight ahead through the trees you will come to the *Knife Edge Bridge,* a slender band of steel, usually drenched with spray, that was constructed at a cost of K32,000 for the International Year for African Tourism in 1969. The bridge, with a 4½-foot-high handrail, is 4 feet wide and goes 120 feet across the Knife Edge to a promontory opposite the left end of the Eastern Cataract. Crossing the bridge and circling around on the wet footpath, you will get a view down into the *Boiling Pot* (usually obscured by spray). This mad, terrible whirlpool is where all the waters of the Zambezi are forced through a 100-yard-wide gap between the promontory and Danger Point opposite on the Rhodesian side.

Going back across the Knife Edge into the park, turn right toward another shelter. Near here is a rough path and steps leading down 1 km through the tropical *Gwaula* or *Palm Grove* to a viewpoint over the Boiling Pot. The Palm Grove is said to be superior to the Rain Forest on the Rhodesian side. Inquire at ZNTB or the Zambian border post about access. Despite the existence of a footpath to the 657-foot-long *Victoria Falls Bridge* through *Baboon Park,* you will not be able to proceed past the Zambian border post since the border is closed.

Opposite the Eastern Cataract park is the small *Victoria Falls Field Museum,* built around the excavation of the Pleistocene gravels, from which numerous Stone Age implements have been recovered. J. Desmond Clark, for many years director of the Livingstone Museum and now teaching at Berkeley, excavated here from 1938 to 1950 and established the chronological sequence of several distinct Stone Age cultures. This sequence, says D. W. Phillipson, was "one of the cornerstones on which knowledge of Africa's prehistoric past was built up." The museum preserves a section of gravel, and there are displays showing how the falls may have originated and also the sequence of Stone Age cultures. The museum is open daily (except Wednesday and Thursday) from 10:30 A.M.–5:30 P.M. Admission: adults—10n; children—5n. Next to the Field Museum is a long open-sided shed which is the official area for the *curio sellers.* Most of the stuff sold here is airport art. For something on the sociology of Zambian wood carvers, read Bonnie B. Keller's fascinating booklet, published by the Livingstone Museum for 50n.

The Falls (Rhodesian Side)

Those travelers who are planning to see both sides of the falls will approach the Rhodesian side through the small town of Victoria Falls, reaching in ½ km the main gate into *Victoria Falls National Park,* which includes the whole of the south bank of the falls and extends upriver 48 km. Through a grass-roofed gate goes a walkway into the *Rain Forest* to the falls viewpoints. Bear left close to the edge of the falls to the *statue of Dr. Livingstone,* erected in 1934. As sculpted by Sir William Reid Dick, the explorer is photogenic, with his cane, captain's cap, and hand on hip, looking out over *Devil's Cataract.* This frightening channel, some 200 feet deep, angles down sharply where the water, moving at 100 mph at peak flood, has eroded the lip of the falls 20 to 30 feet below the rest of the lip. Next to Devil's Cataract is *Cataract Island,* 200 yards wide and split by a fissure which in time will become part of a new gorge being eroded by Devil's Cataract. Water sometimes pours over the island, but it can be visited by canoe during the dry season.

Start walking now on the path into the *Rain Forest* proper, which properly isn't a rain forest at all, but an extensive area of riverine or gallery forest. The trees in this junglelike area grow large because of the abundant water from the spray. In hot weather the Rain Forest can be steamy and sticky, and the asphalt walkway through the forest can get slippery. Every several yards there is a little path off to the left, offering one wet, stunning view after another from an incredibly close distance. From here you can see the *Main Falls,* a 573-yard-wide stretch between Cataract Island and Livingstone Island that carries most of the water during the dry season. *Livingstone Island* (called Namakabwa Island in Zambia) is where the explorer obtained his first view of the falls. Here he carved his initials on a tree (they are still faintly visible), writing in his journal later, "This is the only instance in which I indulged in this piece of vanity." Right from Livingstone Island extends the 600-foot-wide *Rainbow Falls,* obviously named for both the rainbows and double rainbows in the spray by daylight and the lunar rainbows at night. The left part of this waterfall is called *Horseshoe Falls.* Next to Rainbow Falls is the *Armchair* and then *Eastern Cataract.* As you walk along, the Rain Forest thins out and then disappears until you are in a drier, open, grassy area, which extends out to *Danger Point,* opposite which is the *Knife Edge* and below which is the *Boiling Pot.* From Danger Point you can see the railway bridge.

You have to return through the Rain Forest to the entrance. Back on the highway, you can take a 2-km walk through tropical vegetation along the riverbank past the Livingstone statue to *Big Tree,* a huge baobab almost 67 feet in circumference. If you continue on the circular drive which turns at Big Tree, you will come into the *town of Victoria Falls.* In addition to shops and the *Sprayview Restaurant* (there will be a *Tower Restaurant* near the Livingstone statue), there are two hotels, one of which is Rhodesia's only *casino,* an *information center, curio shops,* and the *Falls Craft Village,* a replica of a 19th-century Matabele kraal. Here you can watch craftsmen making pottery, beadwork, and elephant bone and soapstone carvings, which are for sale. A witch doctor will cast his bones and tell your fortune.

Livingstone

The tourist capital of Zambia, the town of Livingstone was founded in 1905 when the British South Africa Co. decided that Old Drift 10 km away at the principal Zambezi ford was too unhealthful for a European settlement. Surveying started in late 1904, several months after the railroad reached the south bank of the river at the falls. The Old Drift settlers moved up, and soon there was a flourishing town which, in 1907, became the capital of North Western Rhodesia (and during 1911–35 the capital of the whole colony of Northern Rhodesia). The first hotel in town was the *North Western,* built in 1904; three years later the hotel moved and the building became what is now called the *Old Government House,* the official residence of the colony's administrators and governors until 1935; it is now a government office (closed to the public). Today Livingstone is a pleasant, quiet town with a population of about 43,000, with some industry, notably a Fiat assembly plant.

The main road, called *Musi-o-Tunya Road,* comes into town from the north, passes the town park, *Barotse Gardens* (named for the dominant tribe of western Zambia, it has shady walks, tropical and exotic flowers, an aviary), many shops, banks, and the post office, then at a left bend in the road, the *Tourist Centre* and the *Livingstone Museum,* facing each other. The Tourist Centre is run by the ZNTB and arranges sightseeing and boat excursions around Victoria Falls. In the garden is a *stone monument* to Dr. Livingstone, who made the European discovery of the falls. The museum (admission free) is worth a two-hour visit. Founded in 1934, the present museum building opened in 1951 and the first new wing was added in 1960. The museum has carried out and continues extensive archaeological work around the country. Along with exhibits of Stone Age and Iron Age artifacts, tribal dress and symbols, slave trade relics, historical dioramas, and a scale model of a working underground copper mine, there is an extensive display illustrating Zambia's fight for Independence, and an exhibit of Livingstone's personal effects. Among them is a notebook open to a sketch of Victoria Falls with this note: "Mosioatunya bears SSE from Sekota islet after 20 minutes sail thence on 16th November, 1855, saw three or five large columns of vapour rising 100 or more feet." Remarkably, it was not until 1955, when the notebook was found, that it was known the date Livingstone first saw the falls. The museum has many publications for sale along with some interesting musical instruments and handicrafts.

The highway continues south past the modern cathedral and railway station; see below, "Drive outside Livingstone."

The town's facilities include curio shops (Zambia Gemcraft and Zambezi Game Skins) and bookshops (Kingston's, Livingstone Bookroom).

Drive outside Livingstone

This 30-km circular excursion starts from the Tourist Centre. Drive south on Musi-o-Tunya Road past the Motel to the *Maramba Cultural Centre,* 4 km south of town at the corner of Riverside Drive. Opened by the Livingstone Museum in 1960, this is the open-air museum "established to preserve the arts and crafts of old Africa." Along with gardens there are some 50 huts, granaries, and shrines, representing Zambia's five major tribes. In the huts, many craftsmen—blacksmiths, potters, wood carvers, maskmakers—work to produce salable handicrafts and curios. Makishi and other tribal dances (3 P.M. 5 days a week) are performed. Admission: 20n.

Turning right into *Riverside Drive,* you drive through somewhat thick bush with high trees (gallery forest closer to the river); 3 km from the crafts village is the *launch landing stage* from which the 152-passenger *Makumbi* leaves daily at 5 P.M. for the K3 "Sundowner Cruise" —a must for any visitor (you can get superb sunset pictures). The double-deck *Makumbi,* which has an air-conditioned bar, goes a short distance toward the falls, doubles back upriver a few km, then turns around again (at Kunkunka or Palm Island) so that the sun sets over the taffrail. Elephants are often seen on the shore, and there are small families of hippos. Drinks are available on board. Also used is the 50-passenger *Zambezi Queen.* Just past the landing stage is a turnoff right on Sichanga Road (once called the Royal Mile) back to the highway and to town; but go left here. Continuing along you will pass some nice picnic sites on the riverbank and, 4 km along, the main gate into *Musi-o-Tunya Zoological Park* (formerly Livingstone Game Park), a fenced-in area within Musi-o-Tunya National Park. It has about 400 non-predatory animals including the giraffe, zebra, warthog, bushpig, white rhino, and several species of antelope; in a fenced enclosure are a snake pit, crocodile pool, aviaries, and a cheetah. Park is open 8 A.M.–5:30 P.M. April–Sept.; to 6:30 P.M. Oct.–March. Admission: 25n.

About 1½ km past the park entrance is the site of *Old Drift,* marked by a monument. This was a village of the Toka chief Sekute, who guided Livingstone to the falls. Old Drift, so called from the river crossing (drift), became the first European settlement near Victoria Falls (which is 9 km downstream) when F. J. "Mopani" Clarke established himself as a trader, hotelkeeper, and forwarding agent here 1896–98. A missionary family arrived in 1898, and 5 years later the town had a population of 68—and a full cemetery, since flat, marshy Old Drift was not healthful (11 out of 31 settlers died of malaria and blackwater fever in 1903 alone). The pub was kept open all night if there were customers, and an American gambler ran a roulette table. By the end of 1905, everybody had moved to Livingstone. Nearby is the cemetery, with 21 graves (only 7 are known). 3 km farther on is a vehicle turn-around. Turn right on Katombora Road to Livingstone 7 km.

Excursion to the Gorges (*Zambian Side*). Following the 1973 border closing, visits to the gorges were temporarily suspended. If they are once again allowed, you can take Hubert Young Drive, also called Manjalide Drive, a circular road that goes to viewpoints over the Fourth and Fifth Gorges, with signposted stops at *Kopje's View*, a local high point; a lookout platform in a much-initialed tree, the *Baobab Tree Lookout;* another *lookout tower* from which you can see the "smoke that thunders"; *Candelabra Pool*, overshadowed by some candelabralike euphorbia trees; *Katonta Pool;* and the *Victoria Falls Power Station*, which has a capacity of 8,000 kilowatts, being expanded to 50,000 KW. Inquire at the gate about taking the *cable trolley* (25n) over the lip of the Third Gorge and down a 45-degree incline, giving a panorama of the Third and Fourth Gorges, to a stop near the *Silent Pool*. Off Hubert Young Drive is Arthur Brew Drive leading to *Songwe Gorge*, where you can look over into the green waters of the *Seventh Gorge*. Various Stone Age artifacts were found here. Picnic site overlooks the Songwe River.

Accommodations

Described below are accommodations on the Zambian side of Victoria Falls (at the falls and 9 km away in Livingstone) and on the Rhodesian side.

Zambian side: *Hotel Musi-o-Tunya Inter-Continental*, Box 151, Livingstone; tel. 2112; cable INHOTELCOR. 100 dbls (incl 7 suites) w/bath. Rates: B&B: sgl—K14.30; dbl—K19.15. Credit: AE, DC. Built 1968 by government and Pan Am, Musi-o-Tunya is a frequent haunt of package tourists, though occupancy falls short of capacity. Rooms are modern, standard, comfortable, clean, with an African motif here and there, and wall-to-wall carpeting. Couple of places to eat: Mutanda Coffee Hut, with snacks and short meals; and the Kuta Restaurant (Botswana steer T-bone, châteaubriand, Tanzania shrimp cocktail aurore), with a band at night. Bar, pool-terrace. Falls are out the back door. Rating: 1st-class international, ★. Govt. 4 stars . . . . *North Bank Rest Camp*, Box 86, Livingstone; tel. 2981. 1 km north of falls. 37 rondavels, mostly dbls, some trpls. Rates: bed only: adults—

K2.50; children under 12—K1.50; under 2—K1. Cooking utensils, crockery, etc., provided; you bring the food and cook it. Pleasant rest camp with simply furnished rondavels, outside bathrooms, outdoor fireplaces. . . . **Camping** at the campground next to the Inter-Continental. Access from riverside road. Fee: 30n per person (pay at Rest Camp). Ablution block has hot showers.

In Livingstone: *North Western Hotel,* Box 69, tel. 2255/6; cable NORWESTOL. Corner Libala and Queens Way. 19 dbls (incl 1 suite), 12 w/bath, all w/a-c. Rates: B&B: sgl—K8.75; dbl—K11.70. Credit: DC. Oldest hotel in Zambia, and was the best hostelry in the area until the Musi-o-Tunya Inter-Continental (which is at the falls). A big, 60-room, 3-sided wing and a pool are planned. Rooms have French doors opening into large inner garden with tall trees, pond with stone bridge, Chinese lanterns, aviary. Rooms are airy, bathrooms a bit damp. Housekeeping not A-1. Dining room is old-fashioned with a Victorian air—there's even a tiny, perfectly set table for one. Standard menu (breakfast—K1.20; lunch—K2.50; dinner—K3) is mostly British in taste. Rating: 1st-class local, with a few marks of age; we give this congenial, charming place a ★. Govt. 2 stars. . . . *New Fairmount Hotel,* Box 96, tel. 2066; cable FAIRMOUNT. Musi-o-Tunya Road at Mose St. 31 dbls (incl 2 suites), 4 sgls; 19 rms w/bath, some a-c. Rates: B&B: sgl—K8.25; dbl—K9.90, incl service charge. Originally built 1931, since remodeled at obviously little cost; best rooms are upstairs in old section. Housekeeping terrible. 2 bars and casino (3 roulette tables, 3 blackjack), restaurant with à la carte menu (buttered prawns on toast, T-bone); entrées—K1.25–1.95. Rating: Not very outstanding 1st-class local, and slipping. Govt. 2 stars. . . . *The Motel,* Box 105, tel. 3060. 3 km from town toward the falls. 26 dbls, 5 qdrpls, all but 6 rms w/bath, some a-c. Rates: B&B: a-c dbl—K7.70. Small, old-fashioned, with unlandscaped grounds, ill-kept buildings, rooms. Rating: 2d-class local, no bargain. Ungraded by govt. . . . *The Chalets Hotel,* Box 143, tel. 8655; cable CHALETS. Go 1 km past airport. 22 rms, most w/bath. Rates: B&B: sgl—K7; dbl—K9. Govt. one star. . . . *Maramba Govt. Rest House,* Box 48. Rates: sharing rm—K1.35 per person; sgl—K1.60; children 3–14 years—75n.

Rhodesian Side (all in the town of Victoria Falls): *Victoria Falls Casino-Hotel,* Box 90, tel. 275; cable CASINO. 102 rms (incl 6 suites), all w/bath, a-c. Pool. Rates: B&B: sgl—R$12, dbl—R$20. Credit: AE, DC. Rated L****. . . . *Victoria Falls Hotel,* Box 10, tel. 203; cable FALSOTEL. 180 rms (incl 6 suites), all w/bath, a-c. Pool. Rates:

B&B: R$9.50 per person. Credit: AE, DC. Rated L***. . . . *Peter's Holiday Motel,* Box 70, Victoria Falls; tel. 344; cable PETERFALL. 49 rms (incl 4 fam. rms), all w/bath, a-c. Pool. Rates: B&B: R$6.50 per person. Credit: AE, DC. Rated L**. . . . *A'Zambezi River Lodge,* Box 130, Victoria Falls; tel. 561; cable AZAMBEZI. 63 dbls, 15 fam. rms, all w/bath, a-c. Pool. Rates: B&B: $6.50 per person. New in 1973. . . . Cottage and chalet lodging and **camping** at Falls Camp in village 1½ km from Falls, also Zambezi Caravan Park (3 km) and Zambezi Camp (6½ km). Rates: chalet—R$1.50 per adult; cottage— R$2 per adult; campsite—R$.25 per adult; caravan-only site—R$1.50 per site plus R$.25 per person. Game reserve (open May 1–Oct. 31) entry—R$1 per vehicle.

Visiting Victoria Falls

The main problem facing the traveler of any nationality who wants to see Victoria Falls is seeing both sides of it. Zambia owns two-thirds but from there you can see only one-third; Rhodesia owns one-third, but has the most fantastic views of two-thirds of the falls. Between them is an invisible dotted line, a border guarded by soldiers and across which you cannot go directly. The border was officially closed, permanently, by Zambia in early 1973; the Rhodesian side is theoretically open. Since there is no direct air service or land transport between Zambia and Rhodesia, tourists have to take the roundabout way to see both sides of the spectacle. The choices, a couple of which have been adopted by package tour operators: (1) Drive from Livingstone to Kazungula (70 km), cross the Zambezi to Kasane, Botswana, then drive about 70 km to Victoria Falls, Rhodesia; ZNTB and the Rhodesian tour operators both route tourists this way. The Zambian road to Kazungula has been paved, and Botswana will pave the road on its side. The modern Kazungula Ferry will be joined by a new motel. (2) Take Zambia Airways' new Thursday flight from Francistown or Gaborone, Botswana (you would get there from Rhodesia or South Africa) to Livingstone; vice-versa on Tuesday; but the schedule is so arranged that Zambia tourists can go from Livingstone to Francistown on Tuesday and return on Thursday, in the meantime having seen the Rhodesian side of the falls. (3) If you have more time and want to see Malawi, fly the circle Victoria Falls-Salisbury-Blantyre-Lusaka-Livingstone.

Is it worth it? The road arrangement (No. 1 above) seems to be all right for package tourists and those with their own cars. Car-less freelance travelers may find the problem not worth solving, and settle on seeing only one side of the falls. In this case, we regretfully suggest that the Rhodesian side is the better of the two.

Crossing the border. The road or air passage to/from Rhodesia and Zambia via Botswana is not a difficult one as far as paperwork is concerned. Citizens of the U.S., Britain and Commonwealth countries, and several European countries do not need a visa to enter Botswana and Rhodesia (just passport and vaccination certificate). Those visiting both white and black countries, however, are advised either to obtain a second passport (restricted to white countries) or, taking a chance on refusal, to ask immigration officials in Rhodesia not to stamp in their passport but on a separate slip of paper.

Your safety. In May 1973, two Canadian girls were killed and an American man wounded by Zambian gunfire while they were sightseeing near the Fourth Gorge on the Rhodesian side. The official Zambian explanation is that border guards thought the tourists were saboteurs about to cross and destroy the Zambian power station. The bloody incident is not, in our opinion, likely to be repeated, but exercise caution while visiting either side of the falls: do not stray from accepted sightseeing walkways, do not act suspiciously, and do solicit local advice before touring the gorges or seeing the falls at night.

Getting to Victoria Falls

For details on getting to the falls, see our road route Z-3 from Lusaka, also the sections in this chapter on rail, bus, and air travel.

Getting Around

Package tours: For ZNTB tours to and around the falls and Livingstone, see listings ZP-5, 6, 7. United Touring Co. (UTC; Victoria Falls Garage, Box 35, Victoria Falls; tel. 267/8) is the principal operator on the Rhodesian side, with the following tours: Victoria Falls, including Big Tree and Crocodile Farm (3½ hours)—R$3.50 for seat-in-car (SIC), R$7 each of 2 in private car (PC). Launch Cruise (2 hours)—R$3 per person. Sundowner Cruise (1¼ hours)—R$4.50 per person (min. 12). Shangaan Musha Dancing (2½ hours)—R$7 per person (min. 12). Victoria Falls National Park and Crocodile Farm (2 hours)—R$3.50 SIC, R$5.50 each of 2 in PC. Flight of Angels (10-minute flight over falls)—R$4 per person, R$20 per 5-pax aircraft. Zambezi Sky Safari (1¼ hours)—R$14 per person, R$70 per 5-pax aircraft. Also tours to Westwood Ranch, Wankie and Chobe game parks. *Kazungula-Kasane transfers:* ZNTB operates the Livingstone-Kazungula section of the Zambia-Botswana-Rhodesia transfer; cost is K5 SIC, K10 in PC. *Car hire:* See p. 553 for Zambian car hire. UTC-Hertz (credit: AE, DC) is on the Rhodesian side; address above. Sample rate, for Datsun 1200 or Toyota Corolla—R$3 per day, R$.06 per mile, not incl gasoline. Also, Tilden/National Car-Hire, tel. 202. *Taxis:* Livingstone, tel. 2493, 2767.

When to Visit

Generally the best time to see the falls is when the river is at a good level and the weather cool: June–July. Views can be obscured by all the spray when the river is at flood March–May, during the rainy season, although the falls are at the most powerful then. The weather is very hot August–November, and it can be very humid. November is the worst time to go—the weather is too hot, and the water is usually so low that the Eastern Cataract becomes a few trickles of water if it doesn't dry up altogether (it did in October 1936 and November 1949). Incidentally, plan your visit to last at least a full day; 2 days is better, 3 days not excessive, if you can visit both sides.

Photography

The best time for seeing and photographing the Zambian side of the falls is in the morning, the Rhodesian side in the afternoon. You should take special precautions to keep your camera dry, especially in the Rain Forest and on the Knife Edge Bridge and promontory. Night photography (if nocturnal visits are permitted): The falls are subtly lit with floodlight on moonless nights. Lunar rainbows can be taken from 8:30 to 9:30 P.M. when the moon is rising—ask the ZNTB when this is. Fast film (ASA 400 or 500) should be used with a wide aperture and the highest exposure time possible for the movement of the falls. See instructions with the film you use.

Clothing

Do not wear anything you don't want to get wet.

Notes: Mosi-oa-Tunya: A Handbook to the Victoria Falls Region, ed. by D. W. Phillipson, was recently published and may be available in Livingstone bookstores. It supersedes the 1964 handbook and has long chapters on the origin of the falls, mammals and birds, and so forth. . . . Fishing is good around the falls, but because of the border situation, loitering on the riverbanks is inadvisable.

Route Z-1 (Great North Road): Tunduma, Tanzania–Mpika–Kapiri Mposhi–Kabwe–Lusaka–Chirundu, Rhodesia

Completely paved, this is Zambia's main trunk road and is part of the *Great North Road,* the grand trunk that starts in Cape Town and ends at Juba in the Sudan, somewhat short of Cairo. For Zambia it is an economic lifeline until the completion of the Tan-Zam Railway (Great Uhuru Railway); up this road from the Copperbelt to Dar es Salaam barrel huge trucks filled with copper, and down it come trucks with vitally needed imports.

For longer than anyone who drove it wants to remember, the Great North Road through Zambia was dirt, which was dust in the summer and mud in the rainy season. Not surprisingly, it was called the *Hell Run,* and it was a graveyard for cars, trucks, and freight. The scenery along most of the road in Zambia is famously dull; before it was paved in the late 1960s by Italian engineers, says historian Richard Hall, drivers in the wet season were known to "spin around several times in the mud and then drive for miles before realizing they were going back the way they had come."

Zambia is expecting enough of an increase in tourist traffic on the road to justify the planned building of several motels between Kabwe and Tunduma.

Km 0: *Tunduma/ border with Tanzania/ Nakonde.* Tunduma on the Tanzanian side has a gasoline station, last one until Km 110. Nakonde, a nothing place, was formerly called Fife, for the Duke of.

Km 1: Turnoff (L) on M14 to Chitipa, Malawi, 92 km. Km 7: Turnoff (R) on D1 (our Route Z-7) to Mbala, Kalambo Falls. Km 110: Turnoff (R) to *Isoka* 4 km. Gasoline here. **Accommodations:** *Rest House,* Box 1. 6 beds. Km 124: Turnoff (R) on D18 to Kasama 175 km, Luwingu 333 km, Mansa 514 km, Zaire Pedicle and Copperbelt (Mufulira 687 km).

Km 204: Turnoff (R) on D55 to Chinsali 13 km and *Lubwa Mission* 20 km, birthplace of President Kaunda in 1924. David Kaunda, his father, settled here after leaving Nyasaland at the turn of the century. A Nyasa who was educated as a preacher-teacher at Livingstonia, the elder Kaunda died when young Kenneth was 8. **Accommodations:** *Chinsali Rest House,* Box 1. 4 beds.

Km 223: Turnoff (R) to *Chipoma Falls* 7 km, a series of rapids and cascades. **Camping,** no facilities.

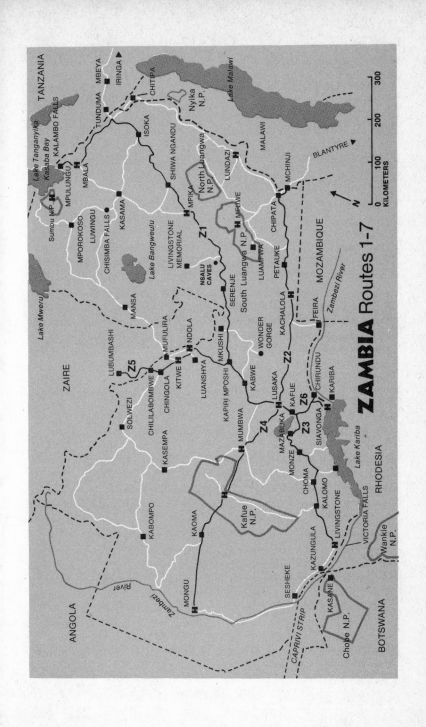

Km 283: Turnoff (R) on D53 to *Shiwa Ngandu* 12 km, which is the unlikeliest place you would expect to find an Elizabethan-style manor, but here it is. The house, called Lake of the Crocodiles after a nearby lake, was built by Lieutenant Colonel Sir Stewart Gore-Browne (b. 1880), an aristocratic artillery officer who served with the Anglo-Belgian boundary commission, first visiting Northern Rhodesia in 1911. He returned in 1921, walking and canoeing for 500 miles to get here (he was accompanied by a line of porters), purchased 25,000 acres, and started building the fabulous house. After two years the settlement thrived as a miniature welfare state, with steam power, a saw mill, a dispensary, an infants' clinic, a school, good housing, training programs for carpenters and bricklayers, and a vegetable oil plant. Gore-Browne, turning to politics in the 1930s, eventually was named to the Legislative Council of the colony to represent African interests. He gave way to the African nationalists in the 1950s and enlisted as an early supporter of UNIP and Kaunda. The estate is located near the "Mountains of Crying" and *"Hill of Boldness,"* which Livingstone climbed in early 1867 to find his bearings.

Km 342: Turnoff (R) to Mist Forest. Km 344: *Lacerda Monument* (R), a stone monument on the highway (good views from here) with a brass plaque commemorating the Portuguese explorer Dr. Francisco José Maria de Lacerda e Almeida, a half-caste Brazilian who was doctor of mathematics and the Astronomer Royal at Lisbon before becoming governor of the Rios de Sena in Mozambique. He became entranced with the idea of a *viagema a contra costa,* an overland journey from Mozambique to Angola, and he set out in July 1798. He had with him 400 slaves as porters, 50 soldiers, some officers, a chaplain, and 3 guides. The cumbersome expedition soon ran into trouble: porters vanished into the bush, food was difficult to find, and the people met on the way were hostile. It took two months to reach the plateau beyond the Muchinga Escarpment (north of Mpika, about where this monument is) and it wasn't until October 1798 that the expedition, bearing a fever-weakened Lacerda, straggled into Kazembe's, then located on the Mofwe Lagoon south of Lake Mweru. Lacerda died, and command was passed to Father Francisco Pinto, who led the remnants back to Tete. Lacerda's journal was luckily preserved and gives the first accurate account of the people and country of northeast Zambia.

Km 368: Turnoff (L) to *Mpika* 2 km, a district town. **Accommodations:** *Crested Crane Hotel,* Box 16, tel. 0145. Turn off highway at Km 376 to hotel 1 km away. 9 dbls, 4 w/bath. Rates: B&B: sgl—K4.50;

dbl—K6. Small, pleasant, well-kept government-run hotel with comfortable rooms of brick and stone. Standard menu: breakfast—K1;
lunch—K1.50; dinner—K2. Rating: 1st-class local. Ungraded by govt.

Km 371: Turnoff (R) on M1 to *Von Lettow-Vorbeck Monument* 127
km, located at the Chambeshi River Bridge on the site of the surrender
of the commander of German East Africa's forces, General Paul Emil
von Lettow-Vorbeck, to Mr. Hector Croad, D.C. of Mpika, on November 14, 1918. Although the war had ended three days earlier, the
general was unaware of it until told by the district commissioner. The
troops were marched to Mbala for formal surrendering. The monument includes an 1890 breach-loading artillery piece. Road continues
north to Kasama 211 km, Mbala 375 km, Kalambo Falls 406 km.

Nsalu Hill Cave

Km 446: Kalonje. Km 515: Turnoff (R) on D47 to *Nsalu Hill Cave
National Monument* 9 km. Go along the road (signposted) 14 km, then
turn south. The cave is locked (cave paintings visible through the
fence), and you must be accompanied by the caretaker, who is not on
duty Wednesdays. Fee: 25n. The cave, an important prehistoric site,
had been inhabited for a long period during the Stone Age and into the
Iron Age. Desmond Clark's excavations showed that Middle Stone Age
people lived here about 20,000 years ago, but most of the remains were
from the Late Stone Age—10,000 B.C. up to A.D. 1000. The blue
quartzite walls of the cave have a varied fresco of pseudogeometric or
schematic designs, done first with yellow, then red, then red and white,
finally gray and dirty white pigments, and are Iron Age in date. The
considerable collection (more varied than any other in Zambia) includes delicate grids, parallel lines, ladder designs, concentric circles and
loops, some bridge- and boat-shaped figures, lines of fine dots, and
one design consisting of two parallel lines in white with a line of red in
between. Among the last paintings are some crude copies of older ones,
plus suns with rays, human figures, snakes, and three designs that look
like stretched-out hides.

Kundalila Falls

Km 546: Kanona and turnoff (L) to *Kundalila Falls,* a national
monument with access by a good 13-km dirt road, making it an excellent detour for drivers on this route. The setting is beautiful. "Cooing
Dove" Falls drop vertically 208 feet, breaking into thin white veils
toward the bottom. With an hour and no skill you can walk around to

the left of the falls to the clear deep pool (swimming) at the bottom. **Camping** for 25n per car if the caretaker comes around to collect it. Latrine.

Livingstone Memorial

Km 567: Turnoff (R) to *David Livingstone Memorial* at Old Chitambo 89 km, considerably in the middle of nowhere. The memorial, a squat obelisk surmounted by a cross and bearing a plaque, is built on the site of the tree under which Livingstone's heart was buried May 1, 1873. The explorer's last journey began in 1866. After being "found" by Stanley November 10, 1871, on Lake Tanganyika, Livingstone journeyed back to the swamps around Lake Bangweulu "as though drawn by a fatal magnet," historian Richard Hall wrote. Wandering through the swamps in the rains, Livingstone received little help. His journal noted the innumerable, ridiculous delays. On his sixtieth birthday, March 19, 1873, he wrote sadly, "Thanks to the Almighty Preserver of men for sparing me thus far on the journey of life. Can I hope for ultimate success?" He pressed on south of Bangweulu, wading through the rainy season floods three feet deep or being carried because he was so weak from dysentery. The last entry in his diary, April 27, was that he felt "knocked up quite." He was borne to Chitambo's village where, after the incredible trials of 32 years of African exploration, his heart gave out. He was discovered dead on his knees in prayer. Two faithful servants, Susi and Chuma, buried his heart in a metal box beneath an *mpundu* tree while an African servant-preacher named Jacob Wainwright read the service; then Susi and Chuma left with the roughly embalmed body for a long journey to the coast 1,500 km away and on to England, where it was interred in Westminster Abbey. Chitambo's village eventually moved away; the dead, rotting tree was ordered cut down in 1902, and a Royal Geographical Society trust fund raised the present monument on the site.

Km 606: Turnoff (R) on D231 to *Serenje,* a district town. **Accommodations:** *Rest House,* Box 13. 8 beds. Km 679: Turnoff (R) to Mkushi River 1 km. Km 709: Turnoff (L) on D214 and 207 to Old Mkushi 97 km, Mita Hills Dam, *Bell Point,* and *Lunsemfwa Wonder Gorge* 160 km. The last section of the signposted route to Bell Point (via Old Mkushi) is passable only in the dry season, and four-wheel-drive vehicles are advisable. Bell Point overlooks Lunsemfwa Wonder Gorge at the junction of the Lunsemfwa and Mkushi rivers. Both have cut narrow gorges 1,000 feet into the Karoo sedimentary rock, creating what the Monuments Commission calls "one of the finest and most spectacular views to be found in Zambia."

Km 713: Turnoff (R) on D219 to Mkushi 2 km and Fort Elwes 42 km. *Mkushi* is a European farming area. **Accommodations:** *Mkushi Rest House,* Box 1. 20 rms. A very bad track not suitable for ordinary cars leads from Mkushi Boma northeast to *Fort Elwes National Monument,* a strongly built rectangular fort put up 1896–98 by a party of gold prospectors. There is a good view from the ruins.

Km 776: Turnoff (L) to Mkushi Copper Mine. Km 803: Main junction—right is T3 to the Copperbelt (our Route Z-5), left is T2 to Kabwe, Lusaka. Go left.

Km 808: *Kapiri Mposhi* ("hills of refuge"), a road-junction town that will be the Zambian terminal of the Tan-Zam Railway, a joint project of the two African governments with more than a little help from China. The $423 million, 1,778-km-long railway will go through 147 stations in Zambia and at Kapiri will join the existing Zambia Railways' 1,048-km line from Livingstone to the Copperbelt. It may be finished in 1975, and will have passenger service.

Kabwe

Km 871: *Kabwe* (formerly Broken Hill), pop. 67,000. Administrative HQ for Central Province, Kabwe is perhaps the transport center of Zambia, with the HQ of Zambia Railways and the big motoryards for Hell Run trucks. Kabwe also has mines producing high-grade lead, zinc, and vanadium worth $22.5 million a year. To the world, however, Kabwe is known as the place where the skull of Broken Hill Man (*Homo rhodesiensis*) was turned up in mining operations June 17, 1921. During blasting in No. 1 Kopje at Broken Hill Mine, a small cave was uncovered within a mass of lead ore, 65 feet below the surface. A Swiss miner named T. Zwigelaar spotted the skull first; the African laborers ran in terror. A few days later a mine doctor heard about it and had it sent off to the British Museum. Some of the bones found nearby came from the same skeleton, but the 27,000-year-old skull was enough to establish *Homo rhodesiensis* in the early Middle Stone Age. Although that prehistoric Zambian had little forehead, heavy bone ridges under his eyebrows, a large mouth, and a thick, short neck, the associated bones indicate that Rhodesian Man, contemporary with the European Neanderthals, was not as different from modern man as just the skull would indicate. He was about 5 feet 10 inches tall and stood erect. The skull—which has a hole in it, indicating violent death —is now in the Natural History Museum in London.

The *Broken Hill Mine* (owned by Nchanga Consolidated Copper Mines) was discovered in 1902 by an Australian who named the lead and zinc deposit Broken Hill for its resemblance to the Australian mining area. The railroad was extended from Victoria Falls north largely because of the mine, which began producing in 1906. In town is the *Big Tree,* a very large, magnificent fig tree which was the meeting place of townspeople in the early days. Nearby, on the lawn of the civic center, is a *monument to the discovery of Broken Hill Man.* The present town has a relatively modern, spread-out appearance, with two long shopping streets crossed by secondary streets. **Accommodations:** *Elephant's Head Hotel,* Box 410, tel. 32120. Freedom Way. 16 dbls w/bath. Rates: B&B: sgl—K7.50; dbl—K9. Some doubles were singles, so are a bit squeezed, but all pleasant enough. Nice patio, garden, pool, lounge. Big dining room has à la carte (grilled trout, T-bone, châteaubriand) with entrées running K2–2.50. Rating: Good 1st-class local, agreeable. Govt. 2 stars. . . . *Bwacha Rest House,* Box 914. . . . *Muchinga Motel,* tel. 2588. Rates: B&B: sgl—K4.50; dbl—K6. Ungraded by govt.

At Kabwe is a turnoff on D200 to Mulungushi Dam 64 km and on to Bell Point and Wonder Gorge (see Km 709 above).

Km 940: Landless Corner and turnoff (R) on M9 to Mumbwa, Kafue National Park, Kaoma, Mongu. Km 962: Turnoff (L) on D176 to Chisamba 22 km, a farm town. Km 1009: *Lusaka* at North End of Cairo Road. Turnoff (L) on T4 (our Route Z-2) to Chipata, South Luangwa National Park, and Malawi. At Kalundwe Road is turnoff (R) on M17 (our Route Z-4) to Mumbwa 161 km, main road into Kafue National Park and west; and to Blue Lagoon National Park 114 km.

Chilanga

Km 1027: *Chilanga,* home of a huge cement factory that got its start making cement for Kariba Dam. It is also the home of the famous *Munda Wanga Park and Gardens,* a picturesque and popular botanical garden with aviary and snake park. Open 9 A.M.–6 P.M. weekdays, 9 A.M.–6:30 P.M. weekends, holidays. Admission: adults—50n; children —30n. Extra charge to snake park: adults—20n; children—10n. In addition to some 300 species of exotic plants from around the world, including 45 types of bougainvillaea and 32 types of palm, Munda Wanga has a pool and wading pool, picnic area, playground, wildlife orphanage. Also in Chilanga is the HQ of the *Department of Wildlife, Fisheries, and National Parks,* which has a collection of game, including a baby elephant, tame eland, and red lechwe. See package listing ZP-10 for tour to Chilanga.

Km 1052: *Kafue* (pop. 5,000) is being planned to become Zambia's future industrial center. Already built are a K16 million fertilizer plant and a K7 million textile plant. There are plans for many more industries including a steel mill and a population of 100,000 by the year 2000. The Greek city planner Constantine Doxiades has a hand in the design of Kafue.

Km 1061: Turnoff (L) to *Iolanda* 5 km, a pleasant place to fish, picnic, and, by arrangement, camp. On the banks of the Kafue. Entrance: 50n per car. Km 1062: *Kafue River Bridge* allegedly once spanned the Thames. However, do not stop to look at it or take any pictures—there's an armed guard and a warning sign. Km 1064: Main turnoff (R) on T1 (our Route Z-3) to Livingstone, Victoria Falls, Rhodesia, and Botswana. Km 1071: Turnoff (L) on D396 to *Kafue Gorge* 21 km. Drive in about 20 km, then walk 1 km to the narrow gorge. Here is being built the $110-million *Kafue Gorge Dam,* which will produce 600 million watts with provision for another 300 MW. This was to have been the big project of the Central African Federation (1953–63), but the Salisbury-dominated government built Kariba Dam instead.

Km 1094: The winding road becomes steeper and more winding in going down the Zambezi Escarpment, straightening and flattening out on the valley floor about Km 1112. Km 1126: Turnoff (R) on M15 (our Route Z-6) to Ingombe Ilede National Monument, Siavonga, Kariba Dam, and Rhodesia. Km 1127: *Chirundu Fossil Forest,* on the right just past the turnoff to Siavonga and Kariba. The forest, a national monument, consists of several large chunks of fossilized coniferlike trees, measuring 6 to 9 feet long, that grew here 150 million years ago. Km 1144: *Chirundu/border with Rhodesia. Otto Beit Bridge* (1939) over the Zambezi. This and other Zambia-Rhodesia border posts may be closed to all traffic; inquire at ZNTB.

Route Z-2 (Great East Road): Lusaka–Luangwa Valley–Chipata–Malawi

The Great East Road is generally a scenic route, all paved two-lane, to Luangwa Valley National Park and on to Malawi. There are many nice "lay-bys" en route, most with picnic shelters and room to camp (free).

Beginning in Lusaka, go to the North End traffic circle and turn right. Km 13: Turnoff (L) to Lusaka International Airport 8 km. Km 140: Rufunsa (off road). Km 176: Turnoff (R) on D145 to *Feira,* a town with a Portuguese name because it used to be Portuguese, established in 1732 as a "fair" or slave market and trading station at the confluence of the Luangwa and Zambezi rivers. Feira was a somewhat dangerous outpost of the Portuguese empire but not very important compared with Tete. By the time Livingstone came by in 1856, Feira was in ruins. In 1887 a South African named J. Harrison "Changa Changa" Clark came here when it was still wild country; he made himself chief of the local Africans, married a real chief's daughter, levied taxes, and recruited a private army which he led in an invasion across the Luangwa to Zumbo to defeat the Portuguese half-caste slavers there. Clark ended up as the first beerhall manager at Broken Hill Mine. There is a *historical monument* in Feira. **Accommodations:** *Rest House,* P.O. Feira. 6 beds.

Km 213: *Luangwa River Bridge.* Armed guards will check your passport. Take no pictures. Km 262: *Kachalola.* **Accommodations:** *Kachalola Hotel,* Private Bag E20, Nyimba. 5 qdrpls, 8 dbls, all sharing bath. Rates: B&B: sgl—K4.50; dbl—K6. Built 1951, not fancy but functional, clean. Dining room has standard menu. Pool. Rating: Bit less than 1st-class local but a welcome stop on a hot road. Ungraded by govt.

Km 326: Nyimba. Km 402: Turnoff (L) on D138 to *Petauke,* district town. **Accommodations:** *Petauke Rest House,* Box 9. 6 beds.

Luangwa Valley

Km 449: Turnoff (L) on D134 to Lusangazi Gate, *South Luangwa National Park,* 97 km. Game-rich Luangwa Valley, gazetted a game reserve in 1938, was in 1972 formally divided into two national parks, separated by the Munyamadzi Corridor: South Luangwa (3,494 square miles), regularly open to the public; and *North Luangwa* (1,810 square miles), open only to Wilderness Trails foot safaris. Just northeast of South Luangwa is tiny *Luambe National Park,* for all intents and purposes part of Luangwa.

Millions of years ago, from about 200 million B.C. to 1 million B.C., some fabulous animals lived in Luangwa Valley, such as the saber-toothed tiger, a type of wolf, giant baboons, short-necked giraffes with big antlers, *dinotheres* with downward pointing tusks (one of the elephant's ancestors), and a reptile crocodilelike in appearance but akin to the earliest dinosaurs, with teeth 5 inches long. Today you will see what is merely a fabulous collection of modern-day African mammals, including thousands of elephants and thousands of buffalos, along with the wildebeest, hartebeest, impala, puku, waterbuck, kudu, roan, eland, zebra, hippo, black rhino, lion (some black-maned), leopard, hyena, wild dog, baboon, monkey, warthog. *Cookson's wildebeest,* common in the northern part of the valley and Luambe, is a variation of the ordinary blue wildebeest, the noisy, foolish-looking, dark-colored, bearded antelope with the crazy gallop. *Thornicroft's giraffe* is peculiar to the valley. Commonest on the left bank of the Luangwa River from Kakumbi Pontoon down to Lusangazi, the Thornicroft is distinguished by exceptionally dark brown spots with jagged edges.

But the unique thing about Luangwa is the walking safari. On a daily basis, park rangers suitably armed will take you out walking from the lodge. When we stayed at Luamfwa, our guard asked what we wanted to see. Thornicroft's giraffe, we said, and any cats. He took us on a grueling, interesting, and satisfying 10-mile hike, without a break, through the bush, and we saw Thornicroft and many cat prints. These ad-lib walks are available only from the catered lodges, Mfuwe and Luamfwa, but game guards at the game camps will accompany you in your vehicle. Game walks have been commercially developed into full-scale eight-day foot safaris during which you walk and camp in the bush most of the time. See package listing ZP-2.

Game walks to see the elephants cross the Luangwa River in the early morning are scheduled from Mfuwe Lodge, starting as early as 4:30 A.M. The elephants forage across the river during the darkness but return to the park in the morning because they have learned they are safe there. Relatively safe, that is. Like other parks, Luangwa is within the grasp of the poacher, but the elephants must leave the park some of the time to forage.

Like Kruger and Tsavo, Luangwa has an elephant overpopulation problem, evidenced by huge tracts of mopane woodland that have been converted into open grassland littered with dead and dying trees. With an elephant population somewhere around 23,000, and a breeding rate for females of once every four years up to age 55, conservationists in Zambia were forced in 1965 to begin a cropping program, which has become, as everywhere, a subject of controversy (see Tsavo National Park, p. 192. But there are plenty of elephants for visitors to see.

When to Visit

South Luangwa is normally open May 1–October 31, depending on the rains. Lodges usually open June, close in October; game camps operate July–October. Best time to visit is June–August when temperatures are cool; nights then can be quite chilly.

Getting There, Getting Around

Zambia Airways has flights four times a week in season (June–Oct.) to Mfuwe. Park staff will pick you up, and game drives and walks can be arranged from the lodges. See package listings ZP-1, 2. If you're driving, it's a grueling one-day trip, or an easy two-day trip, from Lusaka, the Copperbelt, or Blantyre. There are three roads into South Luangwa: one from Sinda (this route, Km 449), which may be impracticable for some vehicles immediately after the rains; another from Chipata (Km 577); and the third from Lundazi, entering through Luambe Park. The Sinda road saves much time; demand the current road condition from ZNTB, AA, or the wildlife department (tel. Chilanga 229, 277). Only Wilderness Trails groups can go into North Luangwa. Sixty miles of new all-weather game roads, to be finished in 1975, may enable South Luangwa to remain open all year.

Costs

There are entrance fees of 50n per person per entry plus K2 per car. Rates at Mfuwe and Luamfwa lodges: adults—K12.50; children under 12—K5; under 2—K1. Rates at self-catering game camps: adults—K4; children under 12—K2; under 2—free. Game viewing by Land-Rover: adults—K3.50; children under 12—K1.75. Booking (mandatory!) and fees to ZNTB.

Accommodations

At present (1974) there are three fully catered lodges and four self-catering game camps, and the new 150-bed Chinzombo Lodge is being built on a hilltop on the east bank of the Luangwa River opposite Mfuwe (just outside the park, in accordance with new policy). Facilities at the game camps include beds with linen and blankets, mosquito nets, lamps, crockery, cutlery, and all other essential equipment. You bring the food; the camp cook prepares it. All bookings to ZNTB. No camping. *Mfuwe Lodge* has 16 dbls in 8 chalets. Main building has bar, dining room, terrace, upstairs patio. Table d'hôte meals reasonably tasty. Bath water is coppery brown—from minerals; you won't turn that color, but it's unpleasant. Lodge otherwise comfortable. Pool. Located on Mfuwe Lagoon—antelopes, elephants, birdlife all around. . . . *Luamfwa Lodge* has 8 dbl rms in 4 chalets, modern main building with bar, dining room (table d'hôte), lounge, terraces looking over lagoon (resident hippos, frogs, birds). Lodge has water problem like Mfuwe. . . . New in mid-1974 is *Chichele Lodge,* with 40 doubles, overlooking the Luangwa River about 15 miles south of Mfuwe. The self-catering game camps: *Lion Camp,* 6 beds; *Big Lagoon,* 12 beds; *Nsefu Camp,* 12 beds; *Luambe Camp,* 6 beds. All have brown water problem, but the drinking water is okay. Big Lagoon, aptly named, was our favorite; you can sit all day by lagoon edge, binoculars and telephoto lens close by, and watch an elephant, then a pied kingfisher, then a puku, then a hippo, then a lily-trotter. The other three camps are on the river. Nyamaluma School Camp, run by the Wild Life Society, is where African schoolchildren come to learn about Zambia's wildlife heritage. ZNTB's Luangwa Tented Safaris use *Tundwe Safari Village,* on the opposite bank of the Luangwa River, as base camp.

Km 455: Sinda. Km 496: Turnoff (R) on D125 to *Katete* 6 km. **Accommodations:** *Katete Rest House,* Box 1. At nearby *Makwe Rock Shelter,* a national monument, is an important prehistoric site first occupied by Late Stone Age people about 6,000 years ago. The stone tools found here were of a previously unknown type. There are also some interesting rock paintings.

Cave Paintings

Km 515: Turnoff (L) to *Mkoma Rock Paintings* 5 km, national monument situated on the east side of a small rock outcrop on the Zambia National Service Farm. The shelter is fenced in, but the view is not obstructed. On the underside of the overhang are an elaborate knotlike grid and something that looks like a comet with long spreading tail, both done in dark purple and white. On the rear wall are paintings in white of men, animals, and metal tools. All are Iron Age in date, the white figures the most recent.

Km 543: Turnoff (R) to *Thandwe Rock Shelter* 9 km, national monument in the Thandwe Hills 13 km east of Kazimuli. Road to site is signposted; visitors must be accompanied to rock shelter (locked) by the caretaker, whose home 225 yards from site is signposted. Fee: 25n. Excavations by D. W. Phillipson in 1970 revealed a sequence of occupation from hunter-gatherer people in the Late Stone Age 2,000 years ago, through some farmer-ironworkers of the Early Iron Age 1,200 years ago to Later Iron Age. The Stone Age and the Iron Age met here, with the older culture obtaining pottery from the newcomers. The Late Stone Age did not end here until about 500 years ago. Later Iron Age inhabitants did ironworking and decorated the walls first with some animal figures in two colors, later with schematic designs (lines, dots), something like a dotted leopard skin, manlike figures, still later with schematic circular designs—and, in this century, a representation of a motor vehicle.

Km 577: Turnoff (L) on D104, main road to South Luangwa National Park's eastern gates. This is the best road to Luangwa, but for those coming from Lusaka is vastly longer than going via the Sinda turnoff (Km 449). From here, Mfuwe is 131 km, Big Lagoon 182 km, Chilongozi 195 km, Luambe 177 km, Nsefu 123 km, Lion 173 km, Luamfwa 200 km.

After 5 km is a turnoff (R) on M12 to Lundazi 181 km and Nyika National Park. About 29 km along this road is the turnoff for the *Zawi Hill Rock Paintings,* a national monument since 1953, located about 3 km down a rough track from the main road. At one site on the south side of Zawi Hill, above Kamukwe village, are some naturalistic paintings of a small eland and a large bird, possibly an ostrich, as well as some schematic designs in red and white. *Lundazi* has as perhaps its main attraction *Lundazi Castle Hotel* (Box 1, Lundazi), a Norman-style building with battlements and a couple of turrets, built by a former district commissioner—British, of course. It's the place you wouldn't expect to find in Zambia, unless, of course, you just came from Shiwa Ngandu (on Route Z-1). Set on a small hill among trees, the 12-bed hotel has its own 34-acre lake. Rooms don't have private bath, but there is a dining room, lounge, bar, pool. Rates: B&B sgl— K4.50; dbl—K6. Ungraded by govt., which owns it. For all details on *Nyika National Park,* a fascinating place to visit, see Malawi Route Q-1, Km 199.

Chipata

Km 579: Turnoff (L) to Chipata commercial center 1 km. *Chipata* (pop. 8,000), formerly Fort Jameson, was selected in October 1898 as

the capital of North East Rhodesia after British South Africa Co. forces defeated the Ngoni tribe. Like the Lundazi area to the north, this region was one of the two "states" of the belligerent Ngoni, a tribe that fled Natal before Chaka's Zulu warriors in the early 1830s. Chief Mpezeni declined to sign a treaty with the BSA Co.'s Alfred Sharpe and, like the Bemba chiefs to the north, lived to regret it. As had been the case with the Matabele in Rhodesia, the company started looking for trouble so the Ngoni could be blamed and put down formally. In December 1897 the chance came when Mpezeni's son Nsingu rose in revolt, attacking and besieging a German trader named Carl Wiese at *Fort Young* (or Loangweni, 34 km southeast of Chipata; turn east off the Chadiza Road after 24 km to the national monument), which was built 1896–97 as headquarters of the North Charterland Exploration Co., an extension of the BSA Co. Wiese called for help. He wasn't in danger very long, but Colonel William Manning and Nyasaland troops went ahead and attacked the Ngoni, dispersing and killing many, burning villages, seizing some 10,000 head of cattle, and capturing Mpezeni's village. The first battle was fought near *Old Fort Jameson,* some 32 km north of Chipata near Chumulu. Nsingu was court-martialed and publicly executed; Mpezeni was temporarily lodged in jail; the Ngoni were subdued. Some of the cattle were returned later. Fort Young was occupied until 1902, but the BSA Co. set up their *boma* in the village of one of Mpezeni's lieutenants, Kapatamoyo. It was renamed *Fort Jameson* after Dr. Starr Jameson, crony of Rhodes and leader of the infamous Jameson Raid into South Africa. The town was the capital of North East Rhodesia until the two sections united in 1911 with Livingstone as the capital. Many Europeans settled in the area to farm. A local boom in tobacco collapsed in the 1920s, and many of the old estates are now resettlement areas for small-holding African farmers. Tobacco is still an important crop, along with maize. *St. Paul's Church,* Anglican, is the oldest church building in Zambia.
Accommodations: *Kapata Rest House,* Box 20, tel. 52011. 25 beds. **Camping** at the rest house, also at a big lay-by with picnic shelter at Km 592. . . . *Crystal Springs Hotel,* Box 100, Chipata; tel. 0102. Turn off highway at Km 577; hotel is 9 km along. 11 dbls, 10 sgls, all w/bath or shower. Rates: B&B: sgl—K4.50; dbl—K6. Rooms simple, pleasant, clean to a fault. Small dining room has à la carte menu with standard items. New garden being planted, pool to be built. Rating: 1st-class local. Ungraded by govt.

Katolola Rock Paintings

Km 582: Turnoff (R) on D128 to *Katolola Rock Paintings* 14 km, located on former Rocklands Farm (way is signposted). Both rock shelters are fenced, but the view is not obscured. In one shelter at the base of Katolola Hill is a remarkable naturalistic painting of an eland in purple outline. About 5 feet long, the eland has a dewlap and mane defined, but the legs and head (weathered out) are very small. The eland strongly resembles the work of the Central and Northern Tanzania Art Groups, and more importantly was painted over a large schematic grid, thus postdating it. Naturalistic paintings are usually Late Stone Age, schematics Iron Age. Just to the northeast is a second rock shelter with several large geometrics and schematics. From one large grid emerge some ladder designs from which it appears rain is falling. The rock is covered with pits made by thrown rocks, and indications are that the rock throwing was part of rainmaking ceremonies.

Km 602: Zambia border post/border with Malawi. Km 612: Malawi border post. Km 614: Mchinji, Malawi. Note: Because a 103-km section of this road, from the Luangwa River to Nyimba, was paved after we drove the route, the distances will now be slightly different.

Route Z-3: Lusaka–Livingstone–Victoria Falls

This route is a very long, rather dull one ending in a bang—Victoria Falls, one of the world's great spectacles. The 478-km road from Lusaka to the falls is entirely paved, though when we drove it, there were two short sections of one-lane paved road (keep only two wheels on the pavement when passing someone, who will, hopefully, do the same). For drivers, the route is altogether too long and tiring. Carless tourists should remain that way, and fly.

Beginning in Lusaka, go straight south on the highway. The first part of the route overlaps Route Z-1, Km 1010–1065. Km 54: Turn right on T1 to Livingstone. Km 88: *Munali Pass* in the Munali Hills. At the summit, an *obelisk* marks where Livingstone first saw the Kafue River. Km 122: *Mazabuka* (pop. 9,400), founded in 1927, is a small but attractive ranching and farming center with a tree-lined main avenue. The nearby 7,094-acre *Nakambala Sugar Estate,* producing at a commercial level since 1968, provides Zambia with nearly all the raw sugar it needs.

Km 184: *Monze* (pop. 4,300) calls itself "The Capital of Zambia's Granary," since it is the center of a maize and tobacco region, with cattle and pigs also of importance. **Accommodations:** *Monze Hotel,* Box 41, tel. 202. Rates: B&B: sgl—K4.50; dbl—K6. Ungraded by govt. Monze is the turnoff north (R) on D365 to *Lochinvar National Park* 45 km. Lochinvar (unlikely name) was a private ranch that gave refuge to the red lechwe antelope, which was on the verge of being poached out of existence. The government bought the 100,000-acre ranch in the late 1960s, gazetted it as a national park in 1972. The park is generally open April 1–December 31. **Accommodations:** *Lochinvar Lodge,* with beds for 12 on a self-catering basis. Details from ZNTB. In the 410-square-kilometer park, the most important resident is the *red lechwe,* cousin to the equally beleaguered black lechwe of the Bangweulu Swamp. Highly aquatic, the lechwes graze in shallow water, retreating into the water and swimming when alarmed. They are very gregarious and found in large herds; the lechwe population of Lochinvar and the Kafue Flats was about 90,000 in early 1972. The animal has bright tawny chestnut back and sides, white underparts; the rump is higher than the shoulders. The male has large back-swept horns. Other mammals in the park: zebra, wildebeest, and eland mainly, also hippo, kudu, impala, oribi, vervet monkey, baboon, jackal, lion, cheetah, buffalo, hyena. But the main side attraction to the lechwe herds is some 400 species of birds.

In Lochinvar are two prehistoric sites, both national monuments. *Gwisho Hotsprings* are on the southern edge of the park, 1 km west of the lodge. Excavations of the low mounds by the springs, on the edge of the Kafue flood plain, in 1960 and 1963–64 showed the area to have been inhabited by Late Stone Age people during the 3d and 4th millennia B.C. Skeletons and much organic material, including grasses, twigs, fruit, nuts, and wooden tools, were well preserved. 1 km west of the hot springs is *Sebanzi Hill,* site of the oldest Tonga settlement in Zambia, occupied from A.D. 1100 to the 18th century. Displays of finds from both sites are in Lochinvar Lodge. The Lochinvar road goes on to M11 to Kafue National Park (Ngoma 186 km).

Km 185: Turnoff (R—at southern end of Monze town) to *Fort Monze* 16 km. The ruined fort was one of the earliest colonial police forts in Zambia, established by the BSA Co. in 1898, demolished in 1903. A cemetery is 1½ km away.

Km 203: Turnoff (L) on D375 to Gwembe 15 km and Chipepo 72 km. *Chipepo,* on Lake Kariba, is a fishing resort but the least developed of the three on the Zambian side. The original village is covered with water now. **Accommodations:** *Chipepo Rest Camp*, 4 beds. Gwembe will soon be linked by road directly to Siavonga, near Kariba Dam.

Km 218: *Pemba*, a farm town. Km 252: Batoka and turnoff (L) on D775 to Sinazongwe 69 km, Maamba 84 km. A washing plant for coal was completed at *Maamba* in 1970, and the coal mining in the area is largely cutting out Zambia's former dependence on Rhodesia's Wankie colliery for coal to feed the copper mines and refineries. On the lake is *Sinazongwe*, a fishing village on a wooded peninsula. A tigerfish contest is held here once a year. **Accommodations:** *Sinazongwe Rest House*, Box 1. Three chalets, each a simply furnished double.

Km 281: Turnoff (R) on M11 to Namwala 169 km and Kafue National Park (Ngoma 173 km). Km 282: *Choma* (pop. 11,300) is the largest town on the line-of-rail agricultural region between Lusaka and Livingstone. It was settled early by European farmers. Virginia and Turkish tobacco is grown along with maize; there are dairying and ranching. Choma is attractive and spread out 4 km along the highway. **Accommodations:** *Kalundu Motel*, Box 49, tel. 212. 18 beds in rms w/bath. Pool. Rates: B&B: sgl—K4.50; dbl—K6. Ungraded by govt. . . . **Camping** at Choma Dam 5 km away.

Km 340: *Kalundu Mound*, a national monument, is an Iron Age site discovered in 1957 when the highway was being realigned. The mounds at Kalundu (Tonga for "little hill") and *Isamu Pati* ("big tree"), both near Kalomo, were both sites of villages used over a 500-year period, the earliest about A.D. 300 with intensive occupation about A.D. 1000, being abandoned about the 12th century. Some mounds are 10 feet deep and give a good view of village life then. The 300-year-long culture, with its distinctive pottery, has been named the Kalomo Culture.

Km 344: *Kalomo*, pop. 3,100, a quiet farming center. Settled in the early 1900s by white farmers from South Africa and Rhodesia, Kalomo was the first capital of North West Rhodesia, starting in 1903 when Robert Coryndon, the BSA Co.'s first administrator (later governor of Kenya), put up the brick *Administrator's House*. The well-preserved building is now a national monument; it is the residence of the Kalomo district governor and is not open to the public. In 1903 the town had 15 officials and a hospital—which was put to a lot of use, since the area was swampy and unhealthful. Livingstone became the capital in 1907. A *monument* on the town green gives a brief history of the town. Amethyst is mined nearby. At the town is the turnoff (R) on D344, the major southern access road to Kafue National Park (Ndumdumwense Gate 73 km). Km 394: Zimba.

Km 470: *Livingstone,* the tourist capital of Zambia by virtue of its location 9 km from *Victoria Falls.* Details on the attractions of this area begin on p. 574. Following are some route notes from Livingstone to the Rhodesian border.

The highway goes through Livingstone as Mosi-oa-Tunya Road. At Katombora Road is the turnoff on the newly paved Nakatindi Highway to Katombora fishing village and *Kazungula* (70 km) on the Zambezi, where the borders of Zambia, Rhodesia, Southwest Africa (Caprivi Strip), Angola, and Botswana meet. A ferry here goes to Botswana (Kasane and Chobe National Park 69 km).

Km 473: The Motel (R) and turnoff on Sichanga Road (R) to launch landing stage, Musi-o-Tunya Zoological Park, and Old Drift. Km 474: Maramba Cultural Centre (R) and turnoff (R) on Riverside Drive to landing stage, park, Old Drift. Km 475: Turnoff (L) on Hubert Young Drive. Km 478: Turnoff (L) on Hubert Young Drive (or Manjalide Drive)—circular drive to gorges and on to Arthur Brew Drive to Songwe Gorge. Seeing the gorges may not be permitted.

Km 478: Turnoff (R) to Victoria Falls—Eastern Cataract, Knife Edge Bridge, and so forth. Km 478.5: Hotel Musi-o-Tunya Inter-Continental. Km 479: Zambia border post (closed).

Route Z-4: Lusaka–Blue Lagoon–Kafue National Park–Mongu

This long route, starting in Lusaka, takes a new Chinese-built highway through the big Kafue game park and deep into the western half of Zambia to Mongu. Past Kafue it is by no means a tourist route.

From Lusaka, turn at Kalundwe Road (M17) toward Mumbwa. Km 25: Turnoff (L) on D169 (to D534) to *Blue Lagoon* 90 km, a private game ranch which was gazetted recently as a national park. On the Kafue Flats north of the river, Blue Lagoon is the main sanctuary of the Kafue lechwe, a race of antelope distinguished by its particularly long, high, back-swept horns. Also resident in the park in small numbers are the buffalo, eland, roan antelope, wild dog, jackal, zebra, duiker, reedbuck, oribi. The wildlife department says Blue Lagoon, with no accommodations, will be open to day visitors only.

Km 162: Turnoff (L) on D180 to Namwala and direct to Ngoma

Lodge 190 km. Km 164: Turnoff (R) to *Mumbwa* 7 km, a district town. Many copper mines developed in the surrounding *Kafue Hook* region, so called from the abrupt changes of course of the southward-moving Kafue River. Two early European prospectors found 70 "ancient workings" and pegged 5 mines in the Hook before 1900. Development was started, but all except *Sable Antelope Mine* (37 km north of Mumbwa) closed in the 1920s. **Accommodations:** *La Hacienda Hotel,* Box 15, tel. 10. 9 dbls w/bath. Rates: B&B: sgl—K4.50; dbl—K6. Spanish-style La Hacienda is a long, low bungalow of white stucco with patios, big lawn, pool, dining room, lounge, bar. A stop-over for those on the way to Kafue Park. Ungraded by govt. . . . *Mumbwa Rest House,* Box 1.

Kafue National Park

Km 295: *Kafue Hook Bridge,* over the Kafue River, followed by turnoffs into *Kafue National Park,* the largest national park in East and Central Africa. At 8,650 square miles, it's as large as Wales and half the size of Switzerland. First declared a game reserve in 1925, Kafue's boundaries were extended several times until first proclaimed a national park in 1950. The Kafue River flows for 160 miles along the eastern boundary of the long park, and the tourist roads are in a network of loops on the left bank of the river. The vegetation ranges from teak forest to Kalahari sand country to open grassland. Tsetse flies will irritate you on game-viewing drives, but few are around the camps and lodge. Roll up your windows as soon as you stop, and keep a swatter handy.

As a game park Kafue is not as good as Luangwa or most of the big ones in East Africa. ZNTB's brochures to the contrary, the park is not terribly rich in exciting wildlife, and you might have to be content with pukus, hippos, impalas, more pukus, warthogs, Lichtenstein's hartebeests, waterbucks, a few greater kudus, and even more pukus. We saw, in a four-day June visit, not even the tail of an elephant—but we had an excellent time in Kafue anyway. The charmingly named *puku* is a medium-sized yellowish antelope related to, and resembling, the Uganda kob, except it has shorter, lyre-shaped horns (males only) and has no black foreleg markings. Gregarious grazers, pukus are found in groups of 3 to 15, though females and young will gather in groups of 50. Some of the other animals resident but possibly difficult to find: red lechwe, sitatunga, sable, roan, oribi, eland, wildebeest, blue and gray duikers, steinbok, Sharpe's grysbok, aardwolf, pangolin, buffalo, zebra, rhino, lion, leopard, cheetah. There are some 400 species of birds. Short game-viewing walks, accompanied by rangers, are not encouraged here, but there are three- to eight-day Safari Trails packages that include game walks, drives, and even a game cruise. See package listing ZP-4.

Because Kafue was formerly at least partly settled, it has some human history. On the road north toward Namwembwe Hill, across from Ngoma, is the *sacred tree,* about 21 km along at the end of the track. This tree, sacred to the Ila people, is a 100-foot-high mahogany which was, according to legend, planted by a witch doctor skilled in the medicines of war. Before a battle the warriors would hurl spears at the tree from about 20 paces. If his spear missed, the warrior would not return if he attended the battle. Make inquiries at Ngoma Lodge before visiting the tree. Outside the park boundary on a hill called Kapili ka Nakalomwe, near the Nkala River opposite Ngoma Lodge, are the ruins of a 1901–03 Barotse Native Police fort, *Nkala Fortified Camp,* a national monument. There is a good view from the site, where ruined walls on the hilltop indicate the fort's outline. Nearby are the ruins of the *Nkala Mission,* 1892–1930.

When to Visit

Park is usually open May 1 to mid-November, depending on the rains. Best time is June–August, when temperatures are cooler, though park is in a warm river valley; nights then can be very cool.

Getting There, Getting Around

Zambia Airways has 2Xwk flights from Lusaka to Ngoma in season. Park staff will pick you up at the airstrip. There are two game-viewing tours by Land-Rover daily. ZNTB has a number of packages to Kafue; see listing ZP-3. Seeing the animals is considerably more convenient if you're driving yourself. Three access routes are: this route (the best), paved from Lusaka on M17 via Mumbwa (if you're coming from the Copperbelt, you can turn at Landless Corner to Mumbwa); the second from the Copperbelt via Kasempa through Kabanga Gate into the northern part of Kafue; the third from Kalomo on the Victoria Falls road (Route Z-3) to Ndumdumwense Gate.

Costs

Park entrance fees: K2 per car plus 50n per person per day. Rates at Ngoma Lodge: adults—K10; children under 12—K5; under 2—

K1. Rates at self-catering camps: adults—K2.75; children under 12—
K1.50; under 2—free. Game drives from Ngoma by Land-Rover:
adults—K3.50; children under 12—K1.75. Transfer from airstrip to
Ngoma or Safari Village: adults—K1; children under 12—50n.

Accommodations

As of 1973 there were four self-catering game camps, one Wild Life
Society camp (Kafwala), one camp for Safari Trail groups (Chunga
Safari Village), one camp for schoolchildren (Ntwemwa School
Camp), and one fully catered lodge (Ngoma). When the Iteshi Teshi
("slippery hill") Dam on the Kafue River is completed 1974–75,
Ngoma Lodge will probably be replaced with a new one. In line with
new policy, it will probably be built outside the park; the other accommodations, similarly, will be phased out. A new Safari Village is also
planned. The game camp rondavels are fully equipped—but you bring
the food, which the camp cook prepares for you (often very well, too).
Camping only at Chunga, but inquire beforehand. *Ngoma Lodge* has
18 dbls in chalets and blocks, all sharing bath. Rates are so much higher
than the camps that it is simply not worth staying here if you do have
your own vehicle and food. Bar, dining room (reasonably tasty table
d'hôte) with large fireplace with copper hood. Pool. Game-viewing
tower and, 4½ km away, a bird hide. Rating: 1st-class local. . . .
The self-catering camps, all fully furnished, are *Ntemwa Camp,* 8 beds;
Moshi Camp, 6 beds; *Kalala Island Camp,* 6 beds; and *Nanzhila Camp,*
8 beds. Our favorite among these was Moshi Camp. It is built on a rise
overlooking a plain, and you can sup while watching pukus, impalas,
and occasional hippos grazing below you or in the distance. *Kafwala
Camp* is very nicely situated on the very tropical banks of the Kafue;
it is for WLCSZ members only (see p. 561). *Chunga Safari Village,* 40
beds, is just outside the park, across the river. It is catered.

To continue the route from Kafue Hook Bridge, the highway goes
straight through the park. Km 300: Park checkpoint gate (off road).
Here the park road goes south to Chunga 3 km, Kalala Island 97 km,
Safari Village 101 km, Ngoma Lodge 121 km, Nanzhila 192 km,
Ndumdumwense Gate 243 km, Kalomo 320 km, Livingstone 444
km; and north to Kafwala Camp 64 km, Lufupa 79 km, Moshi
108 km, Ntemwa 124 km, Busanga Plain 148 km.

Km 359: Leave Kafue Park at Tatetoyo Gate. Km 436: *Kaoma,* a district town formerly called Mankoya. **Accommodations:** *Rest House,* Box 10. 8 beds. At Kaoma is a turnoff (R) on D301 to Kasempa 240 km, Solwezi 428 km, Chingola (Copperbelt) 601 km. Km 454: Turnoff (L) on D305 to Mulobezi 298 km, Sesheke 399 km. Km 464: Turnoff (R) on D306 to Zambezi 257 km, Kabompo 262 km. Km 504: Sikalenge.

Mongu

Km 634: *Mongu* (pop. 10,700) is administrative HQ for the Western (formerly Barotse) Province. Not much happens in Mongu itself, but nearby is *Lealui,* the Barotse (Lozi) capital a few km west, where the annual *Ku-omboka pageant* takes place. This is the yearly move of the paramount chief of the Lozi from Lealui, on the Barotse flood plain of the Zambezi, to the high-ground capital of Limulunga, which is north of Mongu. *Ku-omboka* means "to get out of the water"; this is necessary because of the annual rains and Lealui's location: the capital was established on the flood plain by one Litunga (Paramount) several hundred years ago for unknown reasons. It starts raining about November, and by February, if the rains are heavy, water is lapping at the edge of Lealui knoll. It is time to move; fires are lit near the massive royal drums, and the royal drummers do their thing all night, alerting the people to the move. All over the valley the people pack their belongings up in canoes and gather in the morning at Lealui. To the beat of drums, the Litunga and his retinue proceed to the green-and-white-striped royal barge, the Nalikwanda (like Ku-omboka, a word from the legend in which a man named Nakambela paddled away during a flood in a boat made of palm leaves). Red berets with lion-mane tufts on their heads, and wearing kiltlike skin wrappings, 60 tribesmen paddle for five to six hours to move the Litunga (whose wife, the Moyo, has her own barge), accompanied by a tribal flotilla of canoes, to Limulunga, about 16 km away by drainage canals. The whole thing happens on a less grand scale about July when everybody moves back to Lealui and the other low-ground villages. The Ku-omboka usually happens in February, but the exact day is not known until a few days before. The newspapers will have an announcement, though in 1972 the government downplayed the whole event. In Mongu is a *Home Craft Center;* the Lozi make fine woven trays, baskets, mats. **Accommodations:** *Lyambai Hotel,* Box 193,

Mongu; tel. 271. On Queen's Drive. New hotel overlooks the flood plain. 22 beds in rms w/bath. Rates: B&B: sgl—K4.50; dbl—K6. Ungraded by govt. . . . *Mongu Rest House,* Box 20. 12 beds.

At Mongu is a turnoff (R) on M10 to Senanga 87 km, Sitoti 120 km, Sioma 171 km, Katima Mulilo 313 km, Sesheke 319 km.

Note: Because of the paving of the road, in progress, some of the distances on this route may be slightly changed.

Route Z-5: Lusaka–Copperbelt–Zaire

Because it stretches between the national capital and its economic heart, the Copperbelt, this route is the busiest in Zambia. It is by no means a tourist route—but neither is it without interest. The road is trunk route T3, good two-lane pavement all the way to the Zaire border.

Beginning in Lusaka, take the highway straight north out of town. To Km 206, the route overlaps Route Z-1, Km 803–1009 (in reverse). Km 138: Kabwe. Km 201: Kapiri Mposhi. Km 206: Turnoff (R) on T2 (our Route Z-1) to Tunduma, Tanzania. Go straight. Km 260 (approx.): Turnoff (R) to *Na Chitalo Hill* 49 km, a national monument 8 km from Msofu Mission, difficult to get to. Near the summit are two areas with some minor prehistoric rock paintings.

The Copperbelt

Km 287: Kafulafuta Junction. Left on M6 goes straight to Luanshya 44 km, Kitwe 71 km, Chingola 123 km, and on; straight on T3 goes to Ndola and Mufulira—and the other towns indirectly. Go straight. As you go toward Ndola you are heading into *the Copperbelt.* Although there's no mining in Ndola, it is a gateway and commercial and distributive center for the 120-km-long, 32-km-wide strip of land that is rich in copper, with 9 percent of the world's supply. For about 2,000 years, copper has been extracted from surface deposits in Zambia, and trading in copper has been carried out for the past 1,300 years. Two European prospectors pegged both Roan Antelope Mine at Luanshya and Bwana Mkubwa Mine near Ndola in 1902. Until the 1920s, however, almost all the mining outside Bwana Mkubwa was done 200 km away at Kansanshi (see Km 434) and in the Kafue Hook. By 1914, production at all mines had halted because of the drop in copper prices—and, besides, neighboring Katanga in the southern Congo had far better ore. It was not until the 1922 declaration by the

British South Africa Co. of the Nkana Concession (including Nkana, Mufulira, Roan Antelope, Chibuluma, and Chambishi mines) and the start of an extensive drilling program in the late 1920s that the Copperbelt's vast underground deposits were discovered. Roan Antelope started production in 1931, and others followed. Most quickly closed down at the start of the Depression, then started up again. By 1940, Zambia's production was more than 266,000 metric tons, rising to 686,000 tons in 1970. Today the eight mines of the Copperbelt comprise the world's most concentrated copper industry, and Zambia is the third-largest producer, after the U.S. and the Soviet Union. Most important for Zambia, copper earnings are about $1 billion a year (when the price of copper peaked, earnings were $1.1 billion in 1969, dropping to $910 million in 1970). Seventy percent of Zambia's gross national product comes from copper, and the metal is about 94 percent of the country's total export earnings.

On the Copperbelt, with 600,000 people in eight major cities and towns, more than 50,000 persons are employed by the mines, and there are more than 2,000 different job categories. Expatriates are still necessary, but all jobs are gradually being Zambianized from the bottom up, so that by the 1980s all the jobs will be held by Zambian citizens.

As of January 1, 1970, the government has owned 51 percent of two new companies, Nchanga Consolidated Copper Mines (NCCM, formerly Harry Oppenheimer's Anglo American group) and Roan Consolidated Mines (RCM, the old Roan Selection Trust group). NCCM and RCM produce, respectively, 52 and 48 percent of the copper, and the mines are operated by Anglo American and RST under management contracts. Further nationalization of the mines was proposed in 1973.

Copper is not found as the metal itself but as minerals scattered in rock. In all the mines but Nchanga, the primary sulfide ores are diffused through shale layers down to 3,000 feet; at Nchanga much enriched oxide ore has been deposited also, so that it can be mined in an open pit rather than by underground methods. On the Copperbelt about three-quarters of the copper comes from underground mining, which can be complicated and costly (Zambia is a high-cost producer). The mined ore, once on the surface, is crushed and milled with water down to a fine size; this is called *pulp*. Chemicals are added and the pulp is agitated with air, causing the copper particles to float to the surface, the waste materials to sink. The copper minerals, filtered from the water, form a *concentrate*. This is sent to a furnace, where it melts and separates into two layers. The *slag* floats to the top and is discarded (if approaching Kitwe you can see railcars dumping the molten slag from the top of the huge black slag heaps). The copper minerals form a liquid called *matte,* consisting of copper, iron, and sulfur, which sinks to the bottom of the furnace. The matte goes to a second furnace, where blown air removes most of the iron and sulfur. By now the copper is 99.4 percent pure and is called *blister,* from the surface blisters raised by residual gases. The molten blister goes to a third furnace for more refining, and excess oxygen is removed by "poling" the metal with green tree trunks. It is now 99.8 percent pure—but not pure enough for most manufacturing. Electrolytic refining reduces impurities to 15 parts per million. The 99.998 percent refined copper is melted down and cast into the shapes required by customers, mainly as *wirebars.* The copper industry here produces some 40 different products and exports them to about 30 countries, moving the copper out by the road to Dar es Salaam and other ports (the Tan-Zam Railway will be used when it is finished in 1975).

Copper mine tours: The copper companies are loath to give mine tours to everyone. RCM and NCCM cite the hazards involved, inadequate facilities, and the shortage of qualified personnel to guide tourists around. RCM says, however, that "we are always prepared to consider applications from individuals or small parties, provided we are given ample notice," and NCCM says that "the standard arrangement we have to date is that the tourist may visit the public observation points at our open-cast workings [that is, the huge Nchanga open pit at Chingola]." Addresses: NCCM Ltd., 74 Independence Ave., Box 1986, Lusaka; tel. 50899. RST Management Services Ltd., Kafue House, Nairobi Place, Cairo Road, Box 851, Lusaka; tel. 74070.

Km 311: *Bwana Mkubwa* ("big boss") is now a suburb of Ndola but is the location of the Copperbelt's original working mine (NCCM), now producing again.

Ndola

Km 321: *Ndola,* pop. 159,800 (est. 1972), is HQ of Copperbelt Province and commercial center for the region. Named for a small stream, Ndola's site was first selected in 1904. It became a municipality in 1932, a city in 1966—the third city in Zambia to be granted that status. It has an ever increasing number of industries and is the terminal of the *Tazama Pipeline,* said to be the longest pipeline in Africa. The

1,700-km, 8-inch diameter fuel line from Dar es Salaam was laid in only 17 months after Rhodesia's Unilateral Declaration of Independence made it imperative for Zambia to get her oil elsewhere. The $36-million *Indeni oil refinery* will make Zambia more independent.

As a city Ndola is not much to look at. It has a few busy streets and a small skyline, the two biggest buildings being the *Savoy Hotel* and the attractive eight-story glass-and-concrete *Mpelembe House,* with offices of RCM. Looking down President Avenue, you can see the stack of the enormous *copper refinery.* Near the intersection of Livingstone Road and Makoli Avenue is the *Slave Tree,* a very old *mupapa* tree with two species of parasitic wild fig. Swahili slave traders erected a stockade in what is now Ndola in the 1880s, and used the shade of this tree, now a national monument, as a meeting place and for councils of war. The slave trade was ended in the early 1900s. Another point of interest is *Lake Chilengwa* or Sunken Lake, a national monument 16 km east of the city and 3 km from Zaire (take the Bwana Mkubwa Road south for 5 km, turn north just before the copper refinery, go across the tracks to a signposted turnoff left about 5 km along). A craterlike lake some 45 yards wide situated near the top of a ridge of schist, it was formed when the schistose rock collapsed into a large sinkhole. The water level, which never varies, is 110 feet below the surrounding ground, and the water depth is about 70 feet. Don't get too close to the edge—a legend says an entire tribe was swallowed up by the lake.

Accommodations

Savoy Hotel, Box 1800, tel. 3771. Buteko Ave. 21 dbls, 51 sgls, 3 fam rms, 3 suites (dbl and sitting room, a-c). Rates: B&B: sgl—K7.50; dbl—K9. Built 1958 for a business clientele, 9-story Savoy is the second-best hotel in the Copperbelt. Average decor, atmosphere, cleanliness; repainting needed. Big à la carte menu in dining room, where band plays Friday, Saturday. Top-floor Casino open 8 P.M.–midnight Wednesday, 9 P.M.–3 A.M. Friday, Saturday; no informal dress. Rating: 2d-class international, not a memorable place. Govt. 2 stars. . . . *Coppersmith Arms,* Box 1063, tel. 2395. Vitanda St. 8 suites, each a dbl w/bath. Rates: B&B: sgl—K12; dbl—K16. Recently renovated hotel is a most pleasant place with a couple of courtyard-gardens and terraces. Suites colorful, cheerful, quite comfortable. Good à la carte menu; entrées—K2.20 and up. Rating: 1st-class local, ★. Govt. 1 star. . . . *Falcon Hotel,* Box 127, tel. 2355. Rates: B&B: sgl—K5.50; dbl—K7, incl service. Rating: Functional, inexpensive 2d-class local. Govt. 1 star. . . . *Rutland Hotel,* Box 1, tel. 2631. Rates: B&B: sgl—K4.50; dbl—K6. Ungraded by govt. . . . The 200-room *President Hotel,* with a pedestrian mall, shopping center, and civic center, will be built adjacent to parkland. . . . **Camping** at Trade Fair grounds. Be inside gate before 5 P.M. Fee: 50n per person.

Where to Eat

Besides the *Savoy* and the *Coppersmith Arms: Tudor Inn,* located 14½ km out Mufulira Road (tel. 70216), is a bar-restaurant with pool, big lawn with shade trees, flowering shrubs. Dining room in Elizabethan-style red-roofed building with latticed dormer windows. Standard businessman's lunch, à la carte dinner. Band nights. . . . *Golden Ray,* President Ave. Grills, snacks. . . . *Hong Kong,* President Ave. North, tel. 3951. Chinese.

Getting Around

UBZ has local buses around the Copperbelt, also operates Zamcab taxis, Ndola, tel. 3911, 4381/2. Rates are 10n per km plus 25n flag charge per trip; Kitwe to Ndola would cost K6.15. Other taxis, tel. 3000, 4360.

Mufulira

When you reach Ndola, the route goes left at Broadway and Kwacha Road, and in another 1 km, at Km 322, is the turnoff (R) on M4 to Mufulira 65 km. *Mufulira,* pop. 107,800 (est. 1972), a major town established in 1926, is home of *Mufulira Mine* (RCM). Two prospectors found the copper outcrops here in June 1923. The mine was ready to produce in late 1933. Now either the first or second largest, and the richest, underground copper mine in the world, Mufulira was expanding to 190,000 metric tons a year when, in September 1970, the bottom 2,000 feet filled with 2 million tons of mud and sludge, killing 89 men. This was a serious blow, since Mufulira Mine alone produced 20 percent of Zambia's foreign exchange. It took nine months to get back in production, and at the end of 1971 the mine was producing 8,000 tons a month. Mufulira town has the appearance of a medium-sized English town because is was designed as a Garden Town according to the popular planning style of the day. It has avenues of flowering trees and much open space. **Accommodations:** *Ipusukilo Hotel,* Box 340, tel. 2041. Rates: B&B: sgl—K4.50; dbl—K6. Ungraded by govt. . . . A new motel is planned.

Km 324: Turnoff (L) to *Monkey Fountain,* Ndola's zoo. Km 330: Turnoff (R) to *Dag Hammarskjold Memorial* 5 km. The memorial marks the site of the airplane crash on September 18, 1961, that took the life of the United Nations secretary-general while he was on a mission connected with the fighting in the Congo and Katanga Province. A small cairn topped by a symbolic globe is in the center of a nicely laid-out garden; there are benches scattered about under the trees. It is a sad place to visit. Access is through a forest plantation.

Luanshya

Km 340: Junction. Here M6 goes straight to Luanshya 11 km; M6 goes left back to Kafulafuta Junction 32 km, Kabwe, and Lusaka; and T3 goes right to Kitwe. Go right. *Luanshya,* pop. 96,000, is the home of *Roan Antelope Mine* (RCM), found in June 1902 in a famous incident. William Collier, in the area with Jock Donohoe looking for "native workings," shot a roan antelope buck for dinner; near the body Collier saw the telltale trace of malachite, the green copper-bearing ore indicating underlying deposits of sulfide ore. The story has become a legend and is commemorated in the *Collier Monument,* a copper obelisk about 8 feet high near the original outcrop. No development took place until 1925–27. In a race with Nkana Mine in Kitwe to produce the first copper, Roan Antelope produced concentrates in October 1931. The mine today has a capacity of 96,000 metric tons a year. The nearby *Baluba Mine* is being developed. By the end of 1973, total Luanshya output was to be 120,000 tons a year.

Kitwe

Km 379: *Kitwe,* pop. 199,800 (est. 1972), the hub city of the Copperbelt and location of *Nkana Mine* and *Rokana Division* (NCCM). The Nkana outcrop was discovered by a colonial official— after it was pointed out to him by a local African—in 1910. A firm called Copper Ventures purchased an option on the Nkana claims and in 1922 got the prospecting rights in a huge area including Nkana, Roan Antelope, and Mufulira. In 1924 Copper Ventures (associated with the Selection Trust) sold its Nkana Concession rights to Bwana Mkubwa Mining Co., in which Sir Ernest Oppenheimer's Anglo American Corp. had an interest, the first of many on the Copperbelt. RST thereby lost its opportunity to own the whole Copperbelt, and Nkana is now an NCCM mine. Nkana started producing in 1931, the Mindola mine in 1935. Second shafts have since been added to both, and in 1956 a third was opened 3 km away to work the South Ore Body (often called the SOB Mine). Mindola Mine is 3,200 feet deep, the other two more than 2,000 feet deep; there is also an open pit. Rokana Division now produces about 100,000 metric tons a year; it also smelts and refines the ore extracted by the other NCCM mines at what is the largest copper smelter in the world.

Despite the size of Rokana Division, the city of Kitwe is not dominated by it and the mine township the way other Copperbelt towns are. Now Zambia's principal industrial center, Kitwe didn't come into being until 1935. It was granted city status after Lusaka in 1960. Ten years later the city increased dramatically in size, from 45 to 700 square miles. Today, Kitwe, while not exactly bustling, seems a bit more like a city than Ndola and is more attractive.

Accommodations

Hotel Edinburgh, Box 410, tel. 2771; cable EDINBREW. Independence at Obote Ave. 4 sgls, 61 dbls (incl 3 suites), all dbls w/bath, all a-c. Rates: B&B: sgl—K8.75; dbl—K11.70. Credit: AE, DC. Best hotel on the Copperbelt, built 1961, has businessmen as main clientele. Singles, doubles nice, suites expensive. 3 bars, terrace, big restaurant with good menu; entrées—K2.50 and up. Dancing 6 nights. Rating: 1st-class international. Govt. 3 stars. . . . *Nkana Hotel,* Box 664, tel. 2410; cable HOTELAC. Independence Ave. 36 sgls, 23 dbls. Rates: B&B: sgl—K5–6; dbl—K7–8. Old 2-story hotel with a few graces left. Wide airy corridors, okay rooms—annex rooms are modern, best. Dining room reached through pleasant, palm-shaded courtyard. À la carte menu with entrées K1.85 and up. Rating: 1st-class local, fair if you're staying a while. Govt. 1 star.

Where to Eat

Mukuba Room, in OK Bazaars, Independence Ave. . . . *Lotus Inn,* Kabelenge Ave., tel. 3608. Chinese. Open except Saturday lunch, Sunday. Credit: DC. . . . *Ernie's,* near Rokana Cinema; tel. 4020. Best restaurant in Kitwe.

At Kitwe is the turnoff (L) on M7 to *Kalulushi* 14 km (pop. 24,000), home of *Chibuluma Mine* (RCM), whose ore body was intersected by drilling in 1939. Extraction began in 1956, and present capacity is about 24,000 metric tons a year. Km 395: Turnoff (L) on M16 to Kalulushi 15 km. Km 396: Turnoff (R) on M4 to Mufulira 24 km. Km 403: *Chambishi,* pop. 10,000, planned to grow to 40,000, is the Copperbelt's newest community, built for the workers of *Chambishi Mine* (RCM), an open-cast mine. Copper here was discovered in 1902, development began in 1927, and full production started in 1965. The mine's capacity of 24,000 metric tons a year was expected to double by 1973 with the development of underground mining.

Chingola

Km 431: *Chingola*, pop. 103,292 (est. 1973), is the location of *Nchanga Mine* (NCCM), the third-largest open-pit mine in the world. Chingola Division as a whole is the largest copper producer in the Commonwealth and second-largest in the world, with an annual production of 250,000 metric tons a year. The large oxide ore body was discovered in 1923. Production began in 1939. Nchanga overtook Nkana as the biggest producer in 1955. The two ore bodies are now mined in four open pits and also underground. **Accommodations:** *Nchanga Hotel,* Box 24, tel. 2246. 29 rms. Rates: B&B: sgl—K4.50; dbl—K6. Ungraded by govt. . . . A new motel is to be built.

Km 434: Turnoff (L) on T5 to Solwezi 170 km, Chifubwa Stream Rock Engravings 176 km, Kansanshi Mine 179 km. *Kansanshi Mine* (NCCM) was the biggest copper mining area before the Europeans arrived and was to reopen in 1973. At Solwezi go south for 6 km from town center to get to the *Chifubwa Stream Rock Engravings.* The engravings, some of which show signs of having been painted, played an important part in dating the rock paintings of East and Central Africa by their location in relation to the occupation layers. Excavation in 1951 found small microliths of optical quartz and bored stones of the Nachikufan I period, carbon-14-dated to about 4350 B.C., thus establishing a probable connection between the schematic engravings and the Late Stone Age people of Zambia. The engravings consist of lines, pits, and upside-down U shapes, executed by pecking and rubbing the granite-schist with a pointed tool of quartz. The engravings must be viewed from outside the fence. **Accommodations:** *Solwezi Rest House,* Box 1. . . . *Solwezi Hotel,* Box 17, tel. 6427. Rates: B&B: sgl—K4.50; dbl—K6. Ungraded by govt.

Km 439: The *Hippo Pool* on the Kafue River, astride the Chililabombwe Road, is a 400-hectare recreation area administered by the Forest Department. A national monument, it contains the Hippo Pool and a group of hot springs.

Km 454: *Chililabombwe,* pop. 40,000, was formerly known as Bancroft, and the Bancroft Mine is now part of *Konkola Mine Division* (NCCM). The copper outcrop was discovered in 1924, but the mine began production first in 1957, ceasing the next year because of falling prices and tremendous flooding problems. Konkola Mine has since progressed and is now producing about 50,000 tons of copper a year.

Km 470: Kasumbalesa and Zaire border. Km 576: Lubumbashi, Zaire.

Route Z-6: Lusaka–Siavonga–Kariba Dam–Rhodesia

Beginning in Lusaka and ending at Lake Kariba, this route overlaps Route Z-1, Km 1010–1126. After passing Kafue (Km 43) and the Livingstone turnoff (Km 55), you continue on T2 toward Chirundu. The road is good, straight, two-lane pavement to Km 84, after which there is a twisty, occasionally steep section through the Zambezi Escarpment to about Km 102. Km 117: Turn right on new paving (M15) to Siavonga and Kariba. Km 125: Turnoff (R) on D501 to *Chipepo* 162 km, *Sinazongwe* 254 km. These are minor Lake Kariba resorts; see Route Z-3 (p. 599) for details.

Km 131: Turnoff (L) to *Ingombe Ilede National Monument.* Ingombe Ilede ("the place where the cow sleeps") was an Iron Age village on an important trade route. Excavations in 1961–62 and 1968 revealed 46 graves; 11 persons, possibly traders, had been buried on top of the hill, and their burial goods were a rich selection of gold beads and bangles, iron tools, glass beads, seashells, copper bracelets, wood and leather amulets, copper-working tools, copper wire, cotton and bark-cloth clothing, pots, bowls, needles, and cross-shaped copper ingots weighing up to 8 pounds (used as currency in trading). Carbon-14 tests dated the first period of Ingombe Ilede to A.D. 680–900. Although a monument is at the site, there is little to see.

Kariba Dam

Km 180: Turnoff (R) to *Siavonga* lake resort 7 km; details below. Km 182: Zambia border post. Km 183: *Kariba Dam,* in 1962 said to be the biggest building project in Africa since the pyramids, was built in the narrow Kariba Gorge on the Zambezi between 1956 and 1961, when Zambia was part of the Central African Federation. The dam is a double-curvature concrete arch with a maximum height of 420 feet and a crest length of 2,025 feet. It carries a 40-foot-wide road, which now, because of 1973's border closure, may not be open. The

dam contains 1,275,000 cubic yards of concrete. There are six flood-
gates, each 30 by 31 feet, and their combined discharge of water
(which plunges 300 feet) is some 2 million gallons per second, more
water than flows over Victoria Falls at peak. Behind the dam is *Lake
Kariba,* the third-largest man-made lake in the world, the size of the
state of Delaware. When full, the lake holds more than 160 billion
cubic meters of water—or, measured another way, is about 149 million
acre-feet in size. From end to end, it is about 175 miles, with a maximum width of 26 miles and a total area of about 2,000 square miles.
The *Kariba hydroelectric plant* on the Rhodesian side, initially operated
in 1959, is the 27th largest in the world, with a present rated capacity
of 600 megawatts. Work is under way inside the face of the gorge on
the Zambian side to put in the $90-million second phase of the plant.
That unit's rated capacity is expected to be 900 megawatts. Electricity
generated presently goes to both countries despite the ill feeling between them.

The creation of the lake had a drastic effect on the lives of many
thousands of Africans. Displaced by the flooding were 28,000 Tonga
on the Zambian side and 23,000 Batoka, some persuaded with great
difficulty (several were killed at Chipepo when police attempted to
move villagers), since witch doctors spread the tale that the "great
snake" of the Zambezi would destroy the dam builders (actually, 86
men were killed, up to 1962, in constructing the $221-million dam);
Zambian nationalists sounded the theme that the white man was taking
away more ancestral lands. A sidelight of the flooding gained more of
the world's attention. This was the plight of the animals of the Zambezi Valley after the river was sealed in December 1958, flooding the
lower parts of the valley and creating several hundred temporary islands.
The Northern and Southern Rhodesian game departments launched
Operation Noah to rescue the marooned animals, including nearly
every species of Central African mammal and reptile. Equipped with
boats and trapping gear, game rangers went out and caught, tied up
or caged, and ferried to the mainland some 6,000 animals, including
hundreds of mambas, puff adders, and less harmful snakes.

As a recreational lake, Kariba leaves a lot to be desired. One
difficulty is the unattractive shore line (no sandy beaches). More
serious is that the shore waters are infected with bilharziasis, though
swimming and water skiing are safe about 100 yards out. Most of the
recreational activity is on the Rhodesian side (the government there
has invested heavily to make it attractive). Besides sightseeing (United

Touring Co.) to the dam, Crocodile Farm, and elsewhere, there's a cruise (The Ark), Kariba Game Park, and the hydroelectric plant. On the Zambian side there is an air of drowsy neglect.

Fishing is the big thing at Kariba. Especially if you stay on the Rhodesian side, you can easily hire boats and cruisers, or even rafts, and fishing tackle, and set off on a fishing expedition with all the advice and assistance you need. The most sought-after fish is the razor-toothed fighting tigerfish. Easier to catch but better eating are various tilapia (bream). Boats can be hired in Rhodesia at the Lake View Inn, Venture Cruises Motel, and Cutty Sark Hotel, all in Kariba town. In Zambia, at Point Pleasure and Joe's Boat Hire, Siavonga East.

As at Victoria Falls, the international border inconveniently runs through the tourist attraction. Ask ZNTB Lusaka about visiting the dam before you go.

Accommodations

Leisure Bay Motel, Box 15, Siavonga; tel. 23; cable LEISURE. 7 chalets, each w/2 dbls, all sharing bath. Rates: B&B: sgl—K4.50; dbl—K6. Tree-shaded hotel built 1961. Patio looks over lake. Restaurant has creeping ivy peeping through beams, garden inside, à la carte or table d'hôte. Chalet rooms ordinary. Rating: 1st-class local, an amiable place to stay. Ungraded by govt. . . . *Point Pleasure,* Box 14, Siavonga; tel. 62. 14 dbls. Rates: B&B: sgl—K3.50; dbl—K6.50. Day membership (incl 1 meal)—K2. Friendly Irish place with nice pool, noisy bar. Concrete-floored rondavels are modestly furnished, have lake view. Rating: 2d-class local but friendly air. Ungraded by govt. . . . Also, *Siavonga Rest Camp,* tel. 74, with 75 beds. . . . *Eagle Rest Chalets,* tel. 52, also for self-contained travelers. . . . **Camping** at Eagle Rest and Point Pleasure, on grounds amid rocks and gravel; 50n fee covers pool, membership. . . . **Accommodations** (Rhodesian Side): *Lake View Inn,* Box 100, Kariba; tel. 411/2. 56 rms w/bath, a-c. Rates: B&B: R$8.50 or R$9.50. Credit: DC. Rated L***. . . . *Kariba Heights Hotel,* Box 88, Kariba; tel. 364; cable SUNHOTEL. 18 rms w/bath, a-c. Rates: B&B: sgl—R$4.50, dbl—R$11. Rated L**. . . . *Cutty Sark Hotel,* Box 80, Kariba; tel. 321/2; cable CUTTER. 49 rms (incl 10 fam rms), all w/bath, a-c. Rates: B&B: R$5.05 per person. Rated L**. . . . *Bumi Hills Safari Lodge,* Box 41, Kariba; tel. 353. 60 km from Kariba Dam. 30 rms, 10 w/bath. Rates: DB&B: R$8.50 per person (R$12.50 w/private game-viewing porch). . . . **Camping** on grounds of Lake View Inn and at Mopani Bay Holiday Camp (Box 7, Kariba) for R$.50 per person.

Route Z-7: Tunduma, Tanzania–Mbala–Lake Tanganyika–Kalambo Falls

This route is interesting as far as its destinations, Kalambo Falls and Lake Tanganyika. Except for the initial 7-km stretch of pavement, the road is secondary dirt, and the road from Mbala to Kalambo Falls is rough and rocky and not easily negotiated in the wet season.

Begin at the Tanzania border at Tunduma, passing Nakonde and in 7 km turning right on D1. Km 46: Turnoff (L) on D3 to Kayambi 57 km, Kasama 197 km. Km 179: Junction—go right on M1 north to Mbala; left is M1 south to Kasama 150 km.

Km 192: Turnoff (L) to *Mpulungu,* Zambia's only port, located on *Lake Tanganyika.* Mpulungu is a port of call for East African Railways' steamer *Liemba* when it is in service, and is a center for commercial fishing. Since Lake Tanganyika is 2,515 feet above sea level, and Mbala is 5,400 feet, the Mpulungu Road drops 2,885 feet over 39 km. There is nice rugged scenery along the road and, about 20 km down, *Lunzua Falls* on the left. Two km east of Mpulungu is *Niamkolo Church,* a national monument which is the oldest surviving stone-built church in Zambia. Built 1895–96, it was used continuously until 1908 when, because of sleeping sickness, the local population moved 15 km inland. The church was afterward burned, and beams and thatched roof collapsed. The building deteriorated, but repairs made in 1962 restored the walls to full height with cement pointing and capping. The 48-foot-high square tower is a landmark for lake boats. Mpulungu **accommodations:** *Rest House,* Box 1, Mbala. 14 beds.

Lake Resorts

Mpulungu is one of the jumping-off points for the *Kasaba Bay* and *Nkamba Bay* resorts on Lake Tanganyika. The fishing resorts are within *Sumbu National Park,* a 780-square-mile thicket-covered park made a game reserve in 1942, a national park in 1972. Most of the commoner animals, including the elephant, buffalo, puku, bushbuck, warthog, blue and gray duikers, and bushpig, are well represented, and smaller numbers of waterbuck, hartebeest, reedbuck, roan antelope, hippo, Sharpe's grysbok, klipspringer, and yellow-backed duiker are also present. Sitatunga occur in a small, reedy swamp in the Nkamba Valley. But the park's main attractions are the scenic lakeshore and the fishing. Accessible by boat only is the *Good News Monument* on the Lufubu River 3 km from its mouth. A national monument, it was erected by one Robert Yule to commemorate the launching in 1885 at this site of the missionary boat *Good News,* the first steamship on Lake Tanganyika.

The surface waters of the great inland sea are calm, and the water is fresh; see Tanzania Route T-9 for the history of the lake. You don't have to fear crocodiles or bilharziasis, says the ZNTB, but you will be accompanied from the lodge to the beach by a game guard, since there are elephants about. Best fishing is for Nile perch, tigerfish, giant catfish, lake salmon, *nkupi.*

When to Visit

Sumbu Park is open all year, as are the resorts. Fishing is good November–March.

Getting There, Getting Around

Most people fly direct to Kasaba Bay (Zambia Airways operates 2Xwk from Ndola), and ZNTB has a package tour, listing ZP-8. Two land routes are: drive to Mpulungu and then take the launch (4 hours, 95 km); or drive via Mansa or Kasama and Mporokoso through Sumbu Park to Nkamba and Kasaba lodges. Motorboats can be hired to take fishermen to fishing grounds. Game-viewing walks or drives can be arranged.

Costs

Vehicle permit is K1. People pay 50n per day. Lodge charges: FB: adult—K10; child 3–11 years—K5, under 2—K1. Bookings and fees to ZNTB.

Accommodations

Kasaba Bay Lodge has 30 beds in dbl-rm chalets. Meals in dining room usually incl 1 or 2 courses of fresh lake fish. Afternoon tea served in a thatched *nsakka* under a giant winterthorn tree. Elephants not uncommonly wander around the lodge grounds—careful. Lodge is located on a small promontory, but the white sandy beach is 1 km away. . . . *Nkamba Bay Lodge,* located above the lake, about 24 km from Kasaba Bay, has a terraced garden sweeping down to the water; 14 beds and dining room. . . . The government has a 400-bed holiday village at Lake Tanganyika on the drawing board.

Km 193: *Mbala* (pop. 5,000), founded in 1893, was one of the original areas of European settlement in Zambia. Formerly named Abercorn (for the Duke of), Mbala was the center of a coffee-growing area—there were 12 big estates in 1937—but it declined with the coming of World War II. The agriculture now is mostly cassava and millet. Mbala is the headquarters of the International Red Locust Control Service and the Outward Bound Lake School. Besides that, its one claim to attention was the formal surrender here of Paul von Lettow-Vorbeck, military commander of German East Africa (Tanganyika), on November 14, 1918. The *war memorial* in town commemorates the cessation of hostilities. Von Lettow-Vorbeck, in 1916 pressed from both sides, proved his resourcefulness and led the Allies a merry chase through the bush of Central Africa and Mozambique. Toward the end he was moving toward Broken Hill when the Armistice came. Mbala has most facilities, including a club (visitors can get temporary membership) and a golf course near *Lake Chila,* in whose bilharziasis- and crocodile-free waters you can fish, maybe swim. **Accommodations:** *Grasshopper Inn,* Box 93, tel. 291. Near Lake Chila. 14 dbls. Rates: B&B: sgl—K4.50; dbl—K6. Often used by those going to Kasaba Bay. Ungraded by govt.

At Mbala, continue on D9, coming at Km 195 to a turnoff (R) on D7 to Tanzania; go left here, reaching at Km 230 *Kalambo Falls,* a thin stream of the Kalambo River (which forms the Zambia-Tanzania border here) falling 726 feet straight down—the second-highest uninterrupted waterfall in Africa and twelfth-highest in the world. During the September–November dry season, the width of the falls at the lip can be less than 6 feet; in the wet season it can be as wide as 50 feet. The deep gorge is more than 1,000 feet deep, and through it the river winds for 8 km to Lake Tanganyika. Berkeley Prof. J. Desmond Clark, who excavated here 1953–66, said the falls are "a single perfect example of the beauty that is to be found in falling water, in a setting of unsurpassed grandeur." A cliff path from the parking lot leads along the Zambian side of the gorge to a viewpoint opposite the waterfall and then on to another viewpoint (with picnic shelter) overlooking Lake Tanganyika. On ledges in the gorge nests a colony of marabou storks. Excavations in an area upstream (not open to the public), in a small basin that was once a lake, revealed evidence of habitation over a long period—Early Stone Age (60,000 years ago) up to A.D. 1580. Remarkably, the peat soil had preserved trees, leaves, seeds, wooden implements. Some hand axes were found vertically stuck in the ground, apparently undisturbed for 55,000 years. Also found were an Olduvai-like temporary windbreak, indicated by a circle of stones, and—most important of all—a hearth. Kalambo Falls was the earliest site in southern Africa where traces of fire were found. "There is," says D. W. Phillipson, "a strong likelihood that fire was unknown in this continent until the close of the Early Stone Age." A three-volume account by Desmond Clark of the excavation of the long succession of cultures is being prepared.

MALAWI

LAND OF THE LAKE

Malawi is a long, narrow, compact country with a selection of Africa's most beautiful scenery. From the tourist's point of view it might be said that on one side of the white sandy beach are the clear blue waters of Lake Malawi, and on the other side are the heights of Mulanje, Zomba, Vipya, and Nyika. The 365-mile-long lake, part of the Great Rift Valley chain of lakes, is the country's dominant feature. Virtually unpolluted and, according to tourist officials, free of bilharziasis in the tourist areas, Lake Malawi offers superb swimming, fishing, and boating—and there is even a comfortable passenger ship, the *Ilala,* that circumnavigates the lake.

The history of Malawi prior to Livingstone's arrival in 1859 is vague. Most Malawians today are descendants of various Iron Age Bantu agriculturalists who came into the country between the 14th and the 19th centuries, pushing out or assimilating a Bushman-pygmy people there earlier. The tribal group that was the best organized and established something of an empire was the Maravi or Malawi, who probably moved from the southern Congo basin in the 16th and 17th centuries. Portuguese explorers mention the Maravi empire with great respect, but in the 19th century—probably the nadir of the area's history—it was undermined by several devastating forces. The Yao, pushed out of southern Tanzania, immigrated to the east side of the lake, subjugating the Maravi there. Following close on their westward trail were the Arab slavers seeking lucrative new sources of black bodies. The Yao happily cooperated with the Arabs in capturing members of other tribes. Meanwhile, the warlike Ngoni, escaping from the Zulus in southern Africa, fought their way north, terrorizing the Maravi and other lake tribes.

Into this land drenched with blood and ringing with slavers' chains stepped David Livingstone. He made four journeys into the region from 1858 to 1863, naming Lake Nyasa in September 1859. Before his last trip he made a series of speeches in Britain about the need to bring "Christianity, civilization, and commerce" into Central Africa to rid it of the plague of the slave trade. Missionary groups were formed to follow his call. The first, the Universities Mission to Central Africa (UMCA) was unsuccessful in its first attempt in 1861–64. More successful was the Free Church of Scotland's Livingstonia Mission, founded at Cape Maclear in 1875, two years after Dr. Livingstone's death in what is today Zambia. The Established Church of Scotland founded Blantyre Mission in the Shire (pronounced SHEEREE) Highlands three years later.

The traders followed on the missionaries' heels, with the Glasgow-based African Lakes Company establishing itself as an influence. Under pressure from the Portuguese in neighboring Mozambique, the British missionaries and settlers asked for the English queen's protection. The government was reluctant, but it sent in its young Mozambique consul, Harry Johnston, to make some treaties with the chiefs. Conveniently, the brash and energetic Johnston also acted as agent for Cecil Rhodes's British South Africa (BSA) Company in obtaining concessions. When the European powers agreed that Nyasaland was within the British sphere of influence, Britain, after years of hesitation, declared the Nyasaland Protectorate in May 1891, with Harry Johnston as commissioner.

The African Lakes Company was taken over by the BSA Company. With money and troops, Johnston bought out one slaver, Jumbe at Nkhotakota, and defeated another, Mlozi at Karonga. Mlozi had fought a vicious little war for eight years with the ALC, and was finally captured in 1895 by a force of 400 Sikhs and Africans led by Johnston. Tried by a council of Nkonde chiefs, Mlozi was found guilty and was hanged.

The framework for an administration was established, a hut tax was imposed, and magistrates were sent in to govern districts. Europeans carved out large cotton, coffee, tea, and tobacco estates. A railway was built from Beira on the Portuguese Mozambique coast through Nsanje and Chiromo to Salima on the lake. In 1907 the country became a crown colony, and Nyasaland settled down to become a quiet backwater—the "Cinderella of the protectorates, poor but beautiful."

Beneath the placidity, revolt stirred. Africa had one of its earliest nationalist-martyr-heroes in John Chilembwe, an African preacher who staged a short but bloody armed rebellion in 1915. Two world wars into which Nyasas were dragooned as soldiers and carriers brought more political awareness. Becoming skillful at political activity, Africans formed "native associations" and, in 1944, the Nyasaland Congress party, which under a change of name was to lead the country to Independence 20 years later. Like the Africans in Northern Rhodesia, the Nyasas fought to prevent the formation of the Federation of the Rhodesias and Nyasaland in 1953, fearing that black majority rule and Independence would never come.

A key event was the 1958 return from overseas of Dr. Hastings Kamuzu Banda, who had spent 43 years studying and practicing medicine in the U.S. and Britain. In March 1959, on the pretext that violence was brewing, the colonial government declared a state of emergency in Nyasaland (and the other two colonies) and mass arrests were made. Dr. Banda was jailed and the Congress party banned. While Banda was in prison the Malawi Congress was formed, which Banda took over after his release in April 1960. That year he led a delegation to London, and a new constitution was agreed upon, which included direct election of the Legislative Council. In August 1961 the Malawi Congress won an overwhelming majority in the council. Another conference in November 1962 agreed to the phased granting of Responsible Government, with Dr. Banda becoming prime minister in 1963. On July 5, 1964, Nyasaland was granted full independence under the name Malawi, and the Congress won all 50 seats in Parliament.

Today Malawi is a one-party republic within the Commonwealth, with Dr. Banda as its life president since 1970. The unicameral National Assembly has 65 elected members, all nominated by the Congress and elected for five-year terms, plus 16 members nominated by the president. The country's three regions—Northern, Central, and Southern—are divided into 23 districts. Each district has a council and a president elected by universal suffrage, and the councils are primarily responsible for grammar school education and public services.

President Banda regards himself and Malawi as nearly synonymous, and resents his country's being called poor. He contends that the country is rich in land and people, and hopes that many agricultural schemes will improve the overall standard of living (the annual per capita income in 1971 was $89). As a landlocked country whose only rail outlet to the sea is two lines through Mozambique, yet also bordered by socialist Tanzania and rich Zambia, Malawi is forced by sheer necessity to tread a tightrope, getting along with both her black and her white neighbors. In 1967 Malawi became the first black African country to have diplomatic and trade relations with white South Africa, and since then trade with and aid from that country has leaped upward. President Banda was severely criticized by most black African leaders, but he defends his policy by saying, "I would do business with the devil to help the economic development of Malawi."

Some Vital Statistics. Area: 45,193 sq. mi., a little smaller than Alabama, almost four times the size of the Netherlands.

Population: 4,670,000 (est. 1972), a bit more than the Detroit metropolitan area, about the same number as Virginia or Zambia. Ninety-two percent of the people live in rural areas, with an average of 111 people per square mile. There are about 12,000 Asians and 8,000 Europeans in Malawi; 23 Europeans and 294 Asians are citizens of Malawi.

Cities: Blantyre (pop. 109,461) is the commercial center and most important city. The old capital is Zomba (pop. 19,666), being replaced by Lilongwe (est. 40,000).

Gross national product (1971): $406 million ($89 per capita).

Currency

Since the decimalization of the currency in February 1971, the basic unit of currency in Malawi has been the *kwacha* (means "dawn"), abbreviated *K*. The kwacha is divided into 100 *tambala,* abbreviated *t;* tambala means cockerel or rooster and is the national symbol of Malawi. There are K10, K2, K1, and 50t notes, and 20t, 10t, 2t, and 1t coins. The old monetary unit was the pound, divided into 20 shillings, with K1 equal to 10 shillings.

As of the middle of 1974, K1 has an average official value of U.S. $1.21; or $1 equals 82t. Here is a rough conversion table:

$$
\begin{aligned}
K10 &= \$12.10 \\
K5 &= \$\ \ 6.05 \\
K2 &= \$\ \ 2.42 \\
K1 &= \$\ \ 1.21 \\
20t &= \$\ \ \ \ .24 \\
10t &= \$\ \ \ \ .12 \\
5t &= \$\ \ \ \ .06 \\
1t &= \$\ \ \ \ .01
\end{aligned}
$$

No active black market exists in Malawi.

Planning a Trip

What to See and Do

Lake Malawi is the country's big drawing point. This long, narrow, crystal-clear, blue waterway is unusual for an African lake because, according to the tourist authorities, you can safely swim as well as fish and boat in the tourist areas without fear of bilharziasis. A three- or four-day visit to one or more of the lakeside resorts between Salima and Mangochi is a perfect way to relax. If you have a week, try the *Ilala,* the lake steamer which offers an ideal way to see the lake and its Malawi ports.

The three national parks are all quite different. *Lengwe National Park* is a small sanctuary for the graceful nyala antelope and other small game, and makes an excellent day trip from Blantyre. *Kasungu National Park* is the country's big park, although it is not as populated by quadrupeds as parks in Zambia or East Africa. A pleasant minivacation can be had at Lifupa game camp, however. *Nyika National Park* looks un-African with its Scottish Highlands-like grassy mountain plateaus. But the zebra, reedbuck, warthogs, and other game remind you that you are indeed in the highlands of Africa.

Zomba Plateau is the high, forested recreational area just one hour from Blantyre. Eucalyptus-lined *Zomba* town was the capital, now is the new University of Malawi campus. *Mount Mulanje,* at 9,847 feet the tallest in Central Africa, delights hikers and climbers.

Blantyre is Malawi's main city and tourist center and is worth a visit of a day or so. *Lilongwe,* à la Brasilia, is the newly designed national capital and in a few years will be the center of governmental activity.

Where to Stay

Malawi is equipped to handle its 10,000 tourists a year, but does not have the facilities for group tours unless they stick to Blantyre and the lake. The country's dozen tourist-class hotels are concentrated in those two areas, with ten, and Zomba Plateau and Lilongwe, with one each. Otherwise, in the isolated, beautiful Northern Region you must use the rest houses or camp. Accommodations at the game parks are self-catering and very pleasant.

The Department of Tourism operates a string of 12 rest houses, 4 in the Central Region and 8 in the Northern. We encourage tourists with cars to use these. The rest houses have beds with linen, hard furniture, crockery, cutlery, etc., but you bring the food, which the resident cook prepares for you. There are plans to offer a fixed menu, changed daily. Charges: adults—K2; children under 12—K1.

Camping is easy and enjoyable in Malawi. Camping is allowed at all rest houses for 50t per person, including use of all indoor conveniences. Other campsites are located at the lakeside and in the mountains.

When to Go

Malawi's climate varies from the fresh-to-chilly air of the high plateaus to the warm, dry weather by the lake. The dry season—the best time to visit—is during the "winter" from May to October, when the sun shines about 8 hours a day, there is little rain, and the average temperatures range between 53° and 72°F. October is the hottest dry month, with temperatures going as high as 85°. The wet season is November–April, when most of the 40 inches of average rainfall occurs. The humidity increases, and the temperatures go up to 65–80°.

Regional differences in climate are quite noticeable. The lower-lying areas, such as around Karonga in the north and in the Lower Shire River Valley, are hot and dry. The main tourist spots on the lake around Salima, Monkey Bay, and Mangochi have temperatures in the 70–80° range and can be recommended all year, except June and July, when it is cooler and windier. The water temperature is usually 75–82° —ideal for swimming and water skiing. Occasional southeast winds can result in the *mwera,* a gusting wind whipping up surflike waves of up to 10 feet on the lake.

The Shire Highlands, which include Blantyre and Zomba, and other medium-high plateaus, are warm and have a moderate rainfall (65–75°, 30–60 inches). The high plateaus of Nyika, Vipya, Zomba, and Mulanje are cooler and wetter, and warm jackets and sweaters are a must, with most temperatures below 65° and annual rain between 50 and 130 inches.

During the dry season, a *chiperone* might blow into Malawi. This is not a French-fried Italian noodle but a southeast wind bringing overcast, cold, and wet weather. It can last for several days or a week, and is particularly prevalent in the Shire Highlands (including Blantyre).

To best enjoy the whole range of climates in Malawi, bring both a bathing suit and a warm coat.

What to Wear

Informal dress is the norm in Malawi (see Introduction), but women are restricted to below-the-knee dresses except in resort areas and while in transit. The Malawi government publishes in all its tourist literature and on publicly displayed posters the accepted dress code, which explains that Malawi custom regards it as improper for a woman to "expose any part of her leg above the knee. There is therefore a restriction in this country on the wearing in public of dresses and skirts that do not fully cover the knee-cap when the wearer is standing upright. Another strongly held local convention is that shorts and trousers are unsuitable as women's attire." According to June 1972 policy, these restrictions "do not apply when the wearer is at any holiday resort on Lake Malawi, on the mountains of Zomba, Mulanje, Dedza, Vipya, and Nyika, and any hotel, airport, or railway station, if the visitor or wearer is in direct transit to a Malawi holiday resort, or to any other destinations outside the country."

"Men, too," the poster continues, "should be aware of certain local conventions on male attire and appearance. For instance, very short shorts and excessively tight shorts and trousers are frowned upon, as are manifestations of the unscrubbed, unwholesome 'hippie' image— beads, unkempt beards, ultra-long hair, and tight jeans."

Tourism Authority

The Malawi Department of Tourism is responsible for promoting tourism locally and abroad. Main office: Kanabar House, Victoria Ave. (at Glyn Jones Road, across from the Mount Soche Hotel), Box 402, Blantyre; tel. 2811; cable TOURISM. Representatives outside Malawi: c/o Air Malawi, Box 20117, Nairobi, Kenya. c/o Air Malawi, Box 2752, Salisbury, Rhodesia. c/o Air Malawi, Box 10424, Johannesburg, South Africa. c/o Hallway Hotels, 345 Sixth Ave., Suite 4402, New York, N.Y. 10019. c/o Malawi Buying and Trade Agents, 6 Victoria St., London SW1.

Maps

Malawi, topographical: A detailed 1:1 million map with all the land features, but lacking the new roads and mileages, costs 75t from the Department of Surveys, Victoria Avenue (near Delamere House), Box 349, Blantyre; tel. 8353. *Malawi, general:* A simple map showing the main roads, towns, tourist attractions, and mileages, called "Shell

Gazetteer Map of Malawi," is available free from the Department of Tourism. *National parks:* An Oilcom brochure has sketchy maps of Nyika, Kasungu, and Lengwe; available from the Department of Tourism. The wardens of each park have produced, or plan to, more detailed maps. *Lake Malawi:* The Department of Tourism has a free brochure outlining the tourist sights and accommodations. The Department of Surveys has a set of 16 navigation charts. *Blantyre:* A very good, detailed, 1:20,000 map is available for 75t from the Department of Surveys. A small Mobil street map is free from the Department of Tourism. *Lilongwe:* A topo development map, scale 1:25,000, costs 50t from the Department of Surveys. The new capital's zoning plan is free from the Liaison Officer, CCDC, Box 331, Lilongwe; tel. 2350. *Zomba Plateau:* The Department of Tourism has a free brochure with a good map showing roads and viewpoints.

Books to Read

Agnew, S., and Stubbs, M. *Malawi in Maps.* New York: Africana Publishing Corp., 1972.

Johnston, Harry H. *The Story of My Life.* Indianapolis: Bobbs-Merrill, 1923.

Pike, J. G. *Malawi: A Political and Economic History.* London: Pall Mall Press, 1969; New York: Praeger, 1968.

Pike, J. G., and Remmington, G. T. *Malawi: A Geographical Study.* New York and London: Oxford University Press, 1965.

Ransford, Oliver. *Livingstone's Lake.* London: John Murray, 1966.

Shepperson, George, and Price, Thomas. *Independent African: John Chilemwe and the Origins, Setting, and Significance of the Nyasaland Native Rising of 1915.* Edinburgh: University Press, 1958.

Newspapers

The twice-weekly *Times* (Box 458, Blantyre) and the *Malawi News* (Box 5699, Limbe) are local sources of information if you are planning a trip. Both are in English with a few pages in Chichewa.

Other Sources of Information

Besides the Department of Tourism, diplomatic missions abroad, and Air Malawi, there are these sources of information: Department of Information, Delamere House, Victoria Ave., Box 494, Blantyre; tel. 2811. Malawi Development Corporation, Development House, Victoria

Ave., Box 566, Blantyre; tel. 8961. Chamber of Commerce and Industry, Livingstone Ave., Box 258, Blantyre; tel. 2550.

There are these publications available from the Department of Information: *Vision of Malawi,* a quarterly feature magazine with many travel articles; subscriptions $2 per year postpaid to the U.S. *This Is Malawi,* monthly news (mostly economic and business) magazine; subscription $1 per year postpaid to U.S.

Entry Requirements

Immigration

American citizens entering Malawi as tourists, on business, or in transit are required to have their passport and a ticket to leave (no visa required). A certificate of smallpox, cholera, and yellow fever is advised, and required if you are coming from an infected area. Citizens of Britain, Commonwealth nations, most European nations, and South Africa also need the same documents. If asked by immigration officials, you should be prepared to show you have sufficient funds for your stay in Malawi.

Inquiries: Deputy Chief Immigration Officer, Victoria Ave., Box 331, Blantyre; tel. 8371, 8987. Visas can be issued here for independent Commonwealth countries except Rhodesia, Tanzania, and Zambia.

Diplomatic Missions of Malawi

Ethiopia—Embassy, Box 2316, Addis Ababa; tel. 48295/6. *Great Britain*—High Commission, 47 Great Cumberland Place, London W1; tel. 01-723 6021/3. *Kenya*—High Commission, Gateway House, Government Road, Box 30453, Nairobi; tel. 21174, 20435. *South Africa*—Embassy, 99 Burns St., Colbyn, Box 11172, Lynnwood, Pretoria; tel. 74-6361/2. *United Nations*—Permanent Mission, 777 Third Ave., New York, N.Y. 10017; tel. (212) 755-8470. *U.S.*—Embassy, 2362 Massachusetts Ave., N.W., Washington, D.C. 20006; tel. (202) 234-9312. *West Germany*—Embassy, 53 Bonn, Bonn-Center, HI 1103, Bundeskanzlerplatz; tel. 22 60 89/80.

Customs

You may import, duty-free, your own used clothing and personal effects, including camping and sports equipment, binoculars, cameras, jewelry, film, radios, tape recorders, musical instruments, typewriters, baby carriages, and boats, 200 cigarettes or half-pound of tobacco, one bottle of alcohol and one bottle of wine, and a reasonable quantity of food to meet your immediate travel needs. Souvenirs and curios are duty-free, as long as they are taken out of Malawi when you leave.

Inquiries: Controller of Customs and Excise, Head Office, Box 5057, Limbe; tel. 50522.

Currency Control

You can import or export up to K20 in Malawi currency, and any amount of foreign currency notes and traveler's checks, provided you get a customs certificate confirming the amount. Otherwise you may be restricted to taking out the equivalent of K20.

Vehicle Documents

If driving into Malawi, you should have a Carnet de Passages en Douanes (triptyque) issued by a recognized motor club. If you do not, a temporary import permit, valid for four months, will be issued by officials at border posts. Your car should be licensed in the country where it is owned and bear appropriate registration and nationality plates. Visiting drivers from the U.S. must have an international driving permit. Drivers from Britain, many European countries, and Commonwealth nations need their country of residence driving license. You must have third-party (liability) insurance meeting the minimum risks as required by ordinance. Short-term policies may be purchased at the border posts, or from the Commercial Union Assurance Co., Hardelec House, Victoria Ave., Box 661, Blantyre; tel. 2287.

Firearms

To import firearms, you must have a valid tourist firearms permit, which should be obtained in advance from the Registrar of Firearms, Box 41, Zomba. If you arrive with a firearm not covered by a permit, it will be impounded until a permit has been obtained.

Getting to Malawi

By Air

Blantyre (Chileka International Airport) is served by Air Malawi, Zambia Airways, British Airways (BOAC), East African Airways

(EAA), Air Rhodesia, South African Airways, and DETA Mozambique Airways.

From Europe: From London: BOAC 2Xwk. *From East Africa:* From Nairobi: Air Malawi 3Xwk, EAA 2Xwk. From Dar es Salaam: BOAC 1Xwk, EAA 1Xwk. From Entebbe: BOAC 2Xwk. *From other African countries:* From Lusaka: Air Malawi 1Xwk, Zambia Airways 2Xwk. From Ndola: Air Malawi 1Xwk. From Salisbury: Air Malawi 7Xwk, Air Rhodesia 6Xwk. From Beira: Air Malawi 1Xwk, DETA 1Xwk. From Johannesburg: South African Airways 6Xwk, Air Malawi 3Xwk. From Mauritius: Zambia Airways 1Xwk.

The new capital of Lilongwe will not be served from international points for a couple of years.

Sample fares, one-way, economy/tourist class, valid for a year, to or from Blantyre, are below (add 20% to get early 1975 fares):

to/from Blantyre	U.S. dollars	Malawi kwachas	other currency
Addis Ababa	264	226	E$550
Dar es Salaam	91	78	T.shs. 634
Entebbe	209	178	U.shs. 1,443
Frankfurt	680	579	DM2,211
Johannesburg	101	86	R73
London	506	432	£216
Lusaka	47–58	40–50	ZK32–40
Nairobi	146	125	K.shs. 1,113
Salisbury	38	32	

Airports

Chileka International Airport is 17 km from Blantyre. Facilities: National Bank, car hire, restaurant, post and telegraph, duty-free shop (if you're leaving). No airport tax. Airport general inquiries, tel. 204. City terminal is on Robins Road near Ryall's Hotel; tel. 2001. It should cost K3.50 by cab from Chileka to Blantyre. Air Malawi bus is 50t per person airport–downtown. In Lilongwe airport bus service is 50t, taxi K1.75 to downtown hotel.

At present there is a small airport in Lilongwe, but as the new capital grows, a planned Lilongwe International will eventually replace Chileka as the main air center.

By Train

Train tracks run into Malawi only from Mozambique. There are daily trains from Beira to Blantyre (539 km) taking third-class passengers (second-class also 1Xwk) on a 24-hour trip. A diesel train with first- and second-class cars runs 1Xwk, taking about 15 hours. A newly opened railway line has trains from the port of Nacala 3Xwk via Nova Freixo to Nayuci and Balaka, Malawi. Only third-class passenger service is so far available on this route.

From South Africa and Rhodesia: It is possible to travel by train from Cape Town to Salisbury, from there to Beira for connections by rail to Blantyre, but that's a lot of trouble. The Salisbury–Beira train runs daily, and the total trip to Blantyre is about 1,118 km. Inquiries: Mozambique Railways, c/o Information and Tourist Department, Box 614, Lourenço Marques, Mozambique. Malawi Railways, p. 634.

By Bus

Intercountry bus service into Malawi from Zambia, Mozambique, and Rhodesia is by United Transport (Malawi) Ltd. (address, p. 635). *From Zambia:* Three routes are served. The most popular run is Chipata–Mchinji–Lilongwe, daily 6-hour trip; fare is MK1.12. The Lundazi–Mzimba run is 2Xwk. The third route is Tunduma–Chitipa 5Xwk; fare is 67t. *From Rhodesia:* The twice-weekly service from Salisbury to Blantyre has been temporarily suspended because the route via Tete is "still not considered safe to travel on," according to bus company officials. The fare, when buses run, is K3.32. *From Mozambique:* Because the Tete–Blantyre route is closed, the only service presently is Quelimane–Blantyre, 2Xwk.

By Car

You can travel in an ordinary car by paved and dirt roads into Malawi from East Africa via Zambia, from Zambia itself, and from Mozambique. If you are a speed demon, you could do Nairobi–Blantyre in a hectic four or five days, but ten days would be more comfortable. Lusaka–Blantyre takes a bare minimum of two days.

Best routes: *From East Africa:* Dar es Salaam–Iringa–Tunduma–Chitipa–Blantyre (our Routes T-6 and Q-1). Do not try to cross directly from Tanzania into Malawi—the border is closed. *From Zambia:* Lusaka–Chipata–Mchinji–Lilongwe–Blantyre (our Routes Z-2, Q-1). *From Rhodesia:* Salisbury–Tete–Mwanza–Blantyre. However, this route is considered very risky owing to guerrilla activities—such as planting land mines—along it; go through Zambia by road instead.

From Mozambique: The best route was Beira–Tete–Blantyre, but until it is safe, the alternative route is Beira–Sena–Nsanje–Blantyre; check locally.

Border posts: Malawi border posts are open 6 A.M.–6 P.M. weekdays, and 6 A.M.–noon Saturday. Service outside these hours and on Sundays and holidays is available. From/to Zambia: Mchinji, Namizana, Chisenga, Chitipa, Katumbi, Kibwe, and Mqocha (Lundazi). From/to Mozambique: Chiponde, Marka Nyathando, Muloza, Mwanza, Nayuci, Nsanje, Biriwiri, Dedza, and Namizana.

Getting around Malawi

Travel Agents

Some of the agencies in Malawi are as follows: In Blantyre: *African Lakes Corp. Ltd.*, Mandala Road, Box 49, tel. 2011. *Airtour & Travel Ltd.*, Travel Centre, Osman Court, Box 112, tel. 2416. *Cory Mann George (Malawi) Ltd.*, Unit House, Victoria Ave., Box 146 and 383, tel. 2345. *International Travel & Tour Co.*, Victoria Ave., Box 477, tel. 2465, 2477. *United Touring Co. Ltd.*, Mount Soche Hotel, Box 176, tel. 8251. In Lilongwe: *International Travel & Tour Co.*, Box 247, tel. 2278. In Zomba: *International Travel & Tour Co.*, Box 300, tel. 375.

By Air

Air Malawi flies HS-748 prop jets and Viscount prop planes to the main cities and towns, and Britten Norman Islanders (9-passenger, twin-prop aircraft) to the smaller towns. Its internal services are as follows:

Northbound: Blantyre–Lilongwe 7Xwk. Blantyre–Salima 2Xwk. Lilongwe–Mzuzu 7Xwk. Blantyre–Club Makakola 4Xwk.

Southbound: Lilongwe–Blantyre 7Xwk. Lilongwe–Mangochi–Blantyre 1Xwk. Salima–Blantyre 2Xwk. Club Makakola–Blantyre 4Xwk. Mzuzu–Lilongwe 7Xwk.

Sample fares, one-way, economy/tourist class: Blantyre–Lilongwe—K14.70. Blantyre–Salima—K15.20. Lilongwe–Mzuzu—K15.60.

Airline Offices

Air Malawi has the following offices: Robins Road, Box 84, Blantyre; tel. 2001 (reservations, sales). Moir Road, Box 89, Lilongwe; tel. 2465. Mzuzu Airport, Box 78, tel. 341. Karonga, tel. 24. Offices outside Malawi: See under "Tourism Authority" above. Other airlines with offices in Blantyre are: *BOAC*, Hardelec House, Victoria Ave. (bookings through Air Malawi). *East African Airways*, Delamere House, Victoria Ave., tel. 2165. *South African Airways*, Delamere House, Victoria Ave., tel. 2151. *Zambia Airways*, c/o Air Malawi, tel. 2743.

By Air Charter

Two firms having small planes for hire are Leopard Air Ltd., Box 70, Thyolo; tel. 309 and Chileka 210; and Capital Air Services Ltd., Box 327, Blantyre; tel. 2723/4 and Lilongwe 2185. Leopard Air flies Beech Baron and Cessna aircraft, and charges 50t per mile. Capital has a fleet of Piper Aztecs, Cherokees, and Super Cubs. Capital's sample rates, return trip from Chileka by Cherokee: to Chelinda Camp, Nyika Park—K277; Likoma Island—K189; Salima—K105; Zomba—K27.

By Train

Malawi Railways daily service extends from Nsanje through Blantyre to Salima on Lake Malawi, and Balaka to Nayuci south of the lake. There are first-, second-, and third-class accommodations on the Nsanje–Salima route, only third-class on the Balaka–Nayuci run.

Trains leave Limbe and Blantyre every morning, arriving in Chipoka (connections with the *Ilala* and the *Chauncy Maples*) and Salima in late afternoon. Third-class passengers are carried daily, first and second class 2Xwk. In reverse, trains leave Salima and Chipoka every morning, arriving in Blantyre–Limbe in the evening; first and second class go 2Xwk.

An interesting and scenic rail-boat trip would be to take the train from Blantyre to Chipoka, where you catch the *Ilala* and circumnavigate Lake Malawi. Hitchhikers and low-budgeters can save money by going second or third class all the way. For style and comfort, go first class. A sample round-trip rail-boat fare from Blantyre to Kambwe (port near Karonga, north tip of Lake Malawi) and back, second-class train, first-class berth on *Ilala*, is K47, not including meals.

Inquiries: Transportation Superintendent, Malawi Railways, Box 5500, Limbe; tel. 50011.

The Blantyre railway station is at the junction of Haile Selassie Road, Kamuzu Highway, and Chileka Road, just off the latter; tel. 30896. In Limbe the station is on Churchill Road by the tobacco auctions; tel. 50011.

By Bus

Buses, being cheap, are the main means of four-wheeled transport for most Malawians. If you plan to take buses around the country, expect also to walk or hitchhike because the buses do not always go directly to the tourist destinations. The following is an outline of United Transport (Malawi) service to the tourist or scenic areas: Blantyre–Mulanje 3Xwk. Blantyre–Chileka–Mwanza 7Xwk. Blantyre–Zomba–Lilongwe 7Xwk. Blantyre–Lilongwe express 6Xwk. Blantyre–Zomba–Mangochi–Monkey Bay 7Xwk. Lilongwe–Kasungu–Mzimba 7Xwk. Lilongwe–Salima–Senga Bay 7Xwk. Kasungu–Nkhotakota 6Xwk. Mzimba–Mzuzu 7Xwk. Mzuzu–Nkhata Bay 7Xwk. Mzuzu–Rumphi–Katumbi 7Xwk. Rumphi–Chiweta 7Xwk. Chiweta–Chilumba–Karonga 7Xwk. Karonga–Chitipa 6Xwk.

Some sample one-way fares: Blantyre–Lilongwe—K2.20. Blantyre–Zomba—51t. Lilongwe–Salima—77t. Mzuzu–Nkhata Bay—34t. Chitipa–Karonga—77t.

Inquiries: United Transport (Malawi) Ltd., Box 176, Blantyre; tel. 30122.

By Boat

Seeing Malawi by boat is ideal. Malawi Railways runs two passenger boats—the *Ilala II* and the *Chauncy Maples*—on a weekly schedule. The *Ilala* carries 11 first-class, 26 second-class, and 320 third-class passengers, and 100 tons of cargo. Equipped with modern navigational equipment, it is a 620-ton, 172-foot-long, 10½-knot ship, launched in 1951, and named after the original *Ilala,* which served Livingstonia Mission until 1903. The *Chauncy Maples* carries third-class passengers only; it is an old boat (built in Glasgow in 1899, launched in 1901), formerly used by the Universities Mission to Central Africa station on Likoma Island, and named after the Reverend Chauncy Maples, who drowned in the lake in 1895. The two boats are based in Monkey Bay. The calmest months for lake cruises are March to May.

The *Ilala* makes a once-weekly trip around the Malawi ports on the lake. Its schedule going north is as follows: Friday—Monkey Bay, Chipoka; Saturday—Nkhotakota, Likoma Island, Chisumulu, Nkhata Bay; Sunday—Nkhata Bay, Usisya, Ruarwe, Mlowe, Thekero, Chilumba; Monday—Chilumba, Kambwe (Karonga). Going south: Monday—Kambwe, Chilumba; Tuesday—Chilumba, Thekero, Mlowe, Ruarwe, Usisya, Nkhata Bay; Wednesday—Nkhata Bay, Chisumulu, Likoma

Island, Nkhotakota; Thursday—Chipoka, Monkey Bay. There are rail connections at Chipoka, and road connections for bus service at Nkhata Bay and Monkey Bay. With prior arrangement, you can take your car on the *Ilala,* loading only at Monkey Bay, Chipoka, and Nkhata Bay.

The *Chauncy Maples* makes a circuit of the lake but goes only as far north as Nkhata Bay. The boat starts Wednesday from Monkey Bay, reaches Nkhata Bay, and turns around on Saturday.

Sample fare: Monkey Bay–Kambwe, first class, return, on the *Ilala* —K46.20, not including meals (breakfast—75t; tea—12t; lunch—K1, dinner—K1.25).

Inquiries: Marine Superintendent, Box 15, Monkey Bay; tel. 9. Transportation Superintendent, Box 5500, Limbe; tel. 50011.

By Rent-a-Car

Malawi has the following car-hire firms: *Automotive Products Ltd.* (VW, Mercedes), Ginnery Corner on Kamuzu Highway, Box 1222, Blantyre; tel. 30161. *Hall's Garage Ltd.* (Austin-Morris, Morris, Land-Rover), Box 368, Blantyre; tel. 2356, 2403; also Chileka Airport, tel. 961219, and Lilongwe, tel. 2447 (accepts DC card). *Mandala Motors Ltd.* (Ford), Box 467, Blantyre; tel. 33837; also Lilongwe, tel. 2242. *Patel's Garage,* Kamuzu Highway, Box 5134, Limbe; tel. 50930. *United Touring Co. Ltd.* (*Hertz*), Mount Soche Hotel lobby, Box 176, Blantyre; tel. 8251; also Lilongwe, tel. 2546.

Here are some sample car-hire rates computed for one day, 100 km (62 miles), so that the rates can be compared: Morris 1000 (Hall's Garage)—K7.33. VW Beetle 1200 (UTC)—K9.07. Ford Escort (Mandala)—K8.70. Ford Cortina (Mandala)—K10.44. Mercedes 220 (UTC)—K17.18. Land-Rover station wagon with chauffeur (Hall's)—K18.04.

Chauffeurs are available for K1.50–2.50 per day. Mandala Motors requires a deposit of K100. Drivers should generally be 25 or over, and under 65.

Driving in Malawi

Drive on the left, overtake on the right. Speed limits: 60 mph on 18-foot-wide paved roads, 50 mph on other roads. Limits in towns and cities are posted, or the limit is 30 mph.

Auto club: Automobile Association, Victoria Ave., Box 333, Blantyre; tel. 8170.

Vehicle servicing, repairs, spare parts: Servicing does not cost as much as in Zambia, because wages are lower, but parts are about the same—that is, expensive. Blantyre and Lilongwe have car dealers and garages for Land-Rover and Morris (Hall's Garage), Toyota (Mobile Motors in Blantyre), Fiat (I. Conforzi in Blantyre), Ford (Mandala Motors), General Motors (Central African Transport Co. in Blantyre and Zomba), Leyland (Leyland Motor Corp. in Blantyre), VW and Mercedes (Automotive Products in Blantyre). Daihatsu, Datsun, Volvo, Triumph, Renault, Peugeot, and Rover are less extensively sold and serviced.

Package Tours

United Touring Co. (UTC) offers short in-country tours to two national parks, Lake Malawi, and the cities. Air Malawi operates airfare-plus-land arrangements packages from Zambia, Rhodesia, and South Africa. Extremely few package tours from the U.S. include Malawi.

MP-1: *Mangochi Lakeshore* (UTC). 2 days to Nkopola Lodge: K84 for 1 person, K48 each of 2.

MP-2: *Mangochi Lakeshore and Blantyre* (Air Malawi). 10 days; arrive Blantyre, fly to Makokola, stay there or Nkopola, overnight in Blantyre on way out. ZK149 from Lusaka, R$123 from Salisbury, R242 from Johannesburg.

MP-3: *Blantyre, Mulanje, Zomba, and Mangochi Lakeshore* (Air Malawi). 9 days; incl city tour, Blantyre overnight, drive to Mount Mulanje, Zomba Plateau (Ku Chawe Inn overnight), thence Nkopola or Makokola. ZK168 from Lusaka, R$139 from Salisbury, R240 from Johannesburg. Extra days: ZK10, R$9, R9.

MP-4: *Zomba, Mangochi Lakeshore, and Blantyre* (Air Malawi). 10 days; from Chileka Airport direct to Zomba Plateau (overnight), then Nkopola or Makokola, then Blantyre (overnight). ZK162 from Lusaka, R$134 from Salisbury, R255 from Johannesburg.

MP-5: *Zomba, Mangochi Lakeshore, Blantyre, and Mulanje Self-Drive* (Air Malawi). 8 days; unlimited mileage on rent-a-car, but you pay for gasoline unless you pay extra for chauffeur and gas. Self-drive: ZK139 from Lusaka, R$112 from Salisbury, R283 from Johannesburg. Rates lower if another person shares trip.

MP-6: *Salima and Mangochi Lakeshore, Zomba, and Blantyre* (Air Malawi). 10 days; fly Chileka to Salima (overnight), thence Nkopola or Makokola, drive to Zomba Plateau (overnight), Blantyre (overnight). ZK175 from Lusaka, R$146 from Salisbury.

MP-7: *Salima Lakeshore and Blantyre* (Air Malawi). 9 days: ZK132 from Lusaka, R$106 from Salisbury.

MP-8: *Salima Lakeshore from Lilongwe* (UTC). 2 days: K52 for 1, K30.50 each of 2.

MP-9: *Zomba Plateau* (UTC). 1 day from Blantyre or Chileka Airport; lunch at Ku Chawe Inn if from Blantyre, tour of plateau in either case. K34 or K38 for 1; K17.80 or K19 each of 2.

MP-10: *Lengwe National Park* (UTC). 1 day from Blantyre; picnic lunch in park. K38 for 1; K19 each of 2.

MP-11: *Kasungu National Park* (UTC). 2 days from Lilongwe; overnight at Lifupa Camp, game viewing. K90 for 1; K50 each of 2.

MP-12: *Blantyre City Tour* (UTC). 2½ hrs, visiting central market, shopping areas, Soche Hill, residential areas, St. Michael's, Museum of Malawi: K8 for 1; K4 each of 2; K2.70 each of 3; K2 each of 4. Also 3½-hour tour from Chileka Airport: K20 for 1; K10 each of 2.

MP-13: *Blantyre and Tea Estates* (UTC). Half-day from Chileka Airport: K34 for 1; K17 each of 2.

MP-14: *Lilongwe City Tour* (UTC). 1½ or 2½ hours from Lilongwe Airport: K8 or K10 for 1; K4 or K5 each of 2.

UTC in 1975 began offering some extended tours, including a 12-day lake cruise and sightseeing package—about K300 for 1, K200 each of 2.

General Information

Language

English and Chichewa (the national language) are the official languages. Most Malawians, even in isolated areas, speak some English, but here are some Chichewa words that may come in handy:

greetings!	moni!
how are you?	muli bwanji?
I'm well	ndili bwino
thank you; excuse me	zikomo
good, fine, okay	chabwino
go well; good-bye	pitani bwino
yes	inde
no	iai
please	chonde

I want . . .	ndifuna . . .
I don't want . . .	sindifuna . . .
meat	nyama
chicken	nkhuku
fish	nsomba
lake "perch"	chambo
eggs	mandanda
potatoes	mbatata
fruit	zipatso
water	madzi
milk	mkaka
salt	nchere
sugar	suga
tea	tii
coffee	kofi
gasoline	petrol
how much?	mtengo bwanji?
where?	kuti?
when?	liti?
from . . . to . . . is how many miles?	kuchokera ku . . . kufikila ku . . . ndi mitunda ingati?
father (polite way to address a man)	bambo
mother (polite way to address a woman)	amai
sir	bwana
madam, Mrs.	dona
European	mzungu (plural—azungu)

Pronunciation is about the same as Swahili. See p. 123.

Time

Malawian time country wide is two hours ahead of Greenwich Mean Time, one hour behind East African Time. See p. 126.

Weights and Measures

Malawi uses a combination of the old British system (but the short ton of 2,000 pounds is in general use) and the metric system, though variables such as the pile (a pile of ten tomatoes, for instance) are also used.

Electricity

220/250 volts.

Holidays

Jan. 1—New Year's Day. March 3—Martyrs' Day (in honor of those killed in 1959 anticolonial activities). Good Friday. Holy Saturday. Easter Sunday and Monday. May 14—Kamuzu Day (in honor of the president). July 6—Republic Day. Aug. 7—August Bank Holiday. Oct. 17—Mothers' Day. Dec. 25—Christmas Day. Dec. 26—Boxing Day.

Hours of Business

Hours at offices and most shops are a standard 8 A.M.–4 P.M., with lunchtime closing from noon to 1:30 P.M. Some shops stay open during the lunch hour, some close at 4:30 or later on weekdays, and some are open Saturday and Sunday mornings. Sundays in Blantyre are quiet. Bars are open 11 A.M.–2 P.M., 4 P.M.–10 P.M. Monday–Friday, 10 A.M.–2 P.M., 4 P.M.–midnight Saturday, Sunday, and holidays. Banks in Blantyre and Zomba are open 8 A.M.–12:30 P.M. Monday, Tuesday, Thursday, and Friday, 8 A.M.–10:30 A.M. Wednesday, 8 A.M.– 10:30 A.M. Saturday. Banks in Lilongwe and Mzuzu are open 8 A.M.– 11:30 A.M. Monday–Friday, 8 A.M.–10:30 A.M. Saturday.

Banks

National Bank of Malawi, Henderson St., Box 945, Blantyre; tel. 8369; cable FOCAL. Has six Blantyre-Limbe branches plus 5 branches and 14 agencies elsewhere. *Commercial Bank of Malawi Ltd.,* Victoria Ave., Box 1111, Blantyre; tel. 50677; cable BANK. Has 3 Blantyre-Limbe branches plus 4 branches and 2 agencies elsewhere.

Diplomatic Representatives in Malawi

The following have offices in Blantyre as of this writing, but increasingly many will move their representatives to Lilongwe, the new capital. *Great Britain*—High Commission, Victoria Ave., Box 479, Blantyre; tel. 8301. *Portugal*—Embassy, Box 5596, Limbe; tel. 50255; consulate, Box 5599, Limbe; tel. 50532 (about the only place in black Africa you can get Portuguese visas). *South Africa*—Embassy, Delamere House, Victoria Ave., Box 1072, Blantyre; tel. 2061 (about the only place in black Africa you can get a South African visa). *U.S.*—

Embassy, 4th floor, Unit House, Victoria Ave., Box 380, Blantyre; tel. 2437. *West Germany*—Embassy, Kamuzu Highway, Box 5695, Limbe; tel. 50860. *Zambia*—High Commission, Victoria Ave., Box 556, Blantyre; tel. 2826. Other countries with representatives in Malawi include Austria, Belgium, China (Nationalist), Denmark, France, India, Ireland, Israel, Norway, Sweden, and Switzerland.

Mail, Telegrams

Airmail letters to the U.S. cost 28t for each half-ounce, an ordinary airmail postcard or aerogramme 12t. Surface letters to the U.S. go at the rate of 6t for the first ounce, 10t per additional ounce. Telegrams are handled by the post office.

The main post office in Blantyre is on Glyn Jones Road, tel. 8383. General post office hours: 7:30 A.M.–noon, 1–4 P.M. Monday–Friday, 7:30 A.M.–noon Saturday. Post offices in Blantyre, Limbe, Thyolo, Zomba, Lilongwe, and Mzuzu are open 9–10 A.M. Sundays and holidays for the sale of stamps and the acceptance of cables.

Poste Restante facilities exist at post offices throughout Malawi. Your mail should be addressed to Poste Restante rather than the U.S. Embassy.

Telephone Calls

For a strictly local call from an ordinary phone, dial as you would in the U.S. For a coin telephone, see p. 129. International calls cannot be made from coin phones and should be booked well in advance.

Emergency numbers are not uniform in Malawi. In Blantyre, Lilongwe, and Zomba, dial 0 for operator. In Blantyre, fire is 30014, police 2333, hospital and ambulance 30333, inquiries 991.

Shopping

The main items made and sold in Malawi are of straw, ivory, wood, beads, soapstone, and cloth. Certain areas specialize in a craft, and if you can find it and buy it at its source, it will be cheaper than in a curio shop in Blantyre.

Straw things are well made and inexpensive. The two main production areas are between Liwonde Barrage and Mangochi and between Chilumba and Karonga, where we purchased a handsome 3-foot-high laundry basket with a lid for only K3, while a similar one in a hotel gift shop was K7 (and the prices in Nairobi out of sight). The Malawi Arts and Crafts Center on Glyn Jones Road in Blantyre carries many straw products, mostly overpriced: small wastebasket—K1.50; hat K2; handbag—K1.75; 4-foot-round, thin rug—K2.50. *Ivory* is carved by craftsmen in their hut workshops outside Salima and Nkhotakota. Make sure you know whether you are getting elephant ivory or a hippo tooth. The Arts and Crafts Center has some ivory items, such as a simple ring for 85t. *Wood* articles are somewhat common. In the local markets you can cheaply buy plain *nsima* (stew) stirring or serving spoons. For fancier things look along Victoria Avenue in Blantyre. Arts and Crafts Center has such wood items as an ebony ring—65t; elephant—K11.50; comb tied with colored threads—65t; mask—K5; a variety of traditional musical instruments—K3–10. The curio sellers on Victoria Avenue have an abundance of Kenya carvings, some local work.

Beadwork is done mainly in Blantyre. Arts and Crafts was again overpriced but had a good choice range. Bead butterflies, which you can hang by thread from a window frame, or make into a mobile, each cost 65t—or go out to the street and get five for K1.25 instead. At the Center a necklace is K1.20; a well-made *nsenga* (straw fruit-holder, beaded on the lid and bottom) is K14 for a small one, K16 for a large one. *Soapstone* is locally carved, particularly by two artists named Brown and Mdoka, and the best products are snapped up by Blantyre shops. Prices range from K3.50 for a small bird to K25 for a large abstract rooster, up to K100 for a superb, complex figure. *Cloth,* finally, is primarily cotton, made into men's shirts, children's clothes, women's *chirundu.* The *chirundu* is a loose cloth which can be worn in different ways, such as a long skirt wrapped from the shoulders to below the knee. Off-the-rack skirts with top cost K15–24 at the Arts and Crafts Center, and a man's shirt is about K4.75. Handmade batik placemats— K9.25 (too much).

Wildlife and Game Parks

Malawi used to have a lot of game, but in the early 20th century the animals were killed off at a terrible rate. The first public stirrings came in 1947 when the Nyasaland Fauna Preservation Society was formed, with the declared object of "opposing the wasteful and destructive policy of wildlife extermination in the name of tsetse fly control," in the words of the Department of Information. Until 1963, however, no government body had the authority to protect game; that year a Department of Forestry and Game was organized from the Forestry Department, and since then game has slowly but steadily increased within the boundaries of five game reserves and three national parks—Kasungu, Nyika, and Lengwe.

The new National Fauna Preservation Society of Malawi (NFPS) continues to publicize the need for wildlife protection, and welcomes new members. Inquiries: Hon. Secretary, NFPS, Box 5135, Limbe.

Game park entry fees are uniformly K1.50 per vehicle and 25t per day visitor.

Birdwatching

Malawi has about 600 species of birds. The best areas for birdwatching include the Lake Malawi shore and the plateaus.

Historic and Prehistoric Sites

Malawi has about ten declared national monuments, which are natural, prehistoric, or historic. All monuments are protected by the Monuments Act of 1965 and the Monuments Advisory Council, c/o Department of Antiquities, Box 685, Blantyre. The Antiquities Department has published several monographs.

Fishing

In Lake Malawi, fish can swim practically the length of the country, and commercial and recreational fishing is possible everywhere.

Lake Malawi: More than 240 different species live in the deep blue waters of Lake Malawi, the majority of species existing nowhere else in the world. There are omnivores, predators, and foragers, and their sizes range from 3 inches (lake whitebait) to 6 feet and 110 pounds (catfish). The three main lake fish are varieties of catfish, perch, and carp, among which are the "lake tigerfish" and the "lake salmon," both incorrectly named but offering good sport and eating. The commercial fisheries on the lake net great quantities of *chambo* (tilapia) and *nchila* (labeo)—both very delicious and popular on the menus of lakeshore hotels. No permits are needed for lake fishing.

Shire River: The Shire River is divided into the upper and lower reaches by the 50-mile stretch of waterfalls called the Murchison Cataracts, which prevents fish from mixing. The upper Shire has many fish similar to those found in the lake—catfish, perch, and carp. The lower Shire has fish more similar to the Zambezi River varieties—tigerfish, sawfish, river shark, Indian Ocean tarpon, electric catfish, and lungfish (which really has a lung and can breathe). Fishing for indigenous species requires no license and is possible all year.

Rainbow trout are stocked in some streams by the government and can be fished under license in the open season, September 1–April 30. The three main areas for trout are the streams and dams on the Mulanje, Zomba, and Nyika plateaus. Another stocked fish is the large-mouth bass, which can be found in the private waters of Hynde Dam and Coronation Dam, both in Blantyre; permits are controlled by the Angling Society of Malawi, Box 744, Blantyre. Trout licenses cost K1.50 for one day, K4 for a week, and are available from the Treasury Cashiers in Blantyre and Zomba; from the Forester, Likabula, Mulanje; from the officer in charge, Chelinda Camp, Nyika National Park; and from the Ku Chawe Inn, Zomba Plateau. Inquiries: Director of Forestry and Game, Box 182, Zomba.

Hunting

Opportunities for hunting big or small game in Malawi are extremely limited, and there are no safari firms. Inquiries: Director of Forestry and Game, Box 182, Zomba.

Blantyre

Blantyre is Malawi's commercial center and has the distinction of being the oldest municipality in Central Africa, declared such in 1895. It was first chosen as a mission site by Henry Henderson, who, liking the location between the Nasolo and Likabula streams, in the bowl formed by the Ndirandi, Kabula, Soche, and other hills, led the Church of Scotland missionaries to it in 1876. After some early administration problems in the mission, the Reverend David Clement Scott was appointed in charge in 1881. Under his leadership, with self-taught architecture, the impressive Church of St. Michael's and All the Angels (see below) was built, with the mission forming the nucleus of the Blantyre community.

Commercial stimulus came from the Livingstonia Trading Co.—later called the African Lakes Corp. The ALC's first store, managed by John and Frederick Moir, was opened in 1879 in a mission bungalow, and their permanent headquarters was built on a hill now called *Top Mandala*. "Bwana Mandala" was the name given to John Moir by the Africans because his spectacles reflected the glint of the sun; Mandala later became the trading name of the company, which today imports and distributes technical products. The *Mandala Building* and the *manager's house* (oldest surviving building in Malawi) stand as a national monument on Mandala, overlooking Haile Selassie Road and the new city *central market* (which, incidentally, is far less picturesque than older markets).

In the 1880s a local chief named Kumtaja erected a brick house in imitation of the Mandala building. This house was later bought for £115, and materials from it were incorporated into the original *district boma building* in 1894; now occupied by Treasury officials, it is at the south end of Victoria Avenue by City Hall. Close by stand *three fig trees,* which grew roots from poles used in the stockade surrounding Chief Kumtaja's house; the trees are now preserved by the City Council.

The Blantyre township was formally created on July 14, 1894, taking its name from the mission, which had been named for Dr. Livingstone's Scottish birthplace. *Limbe* town grew up around the railway station and the Imperial Tobacco Co. plant and headquarters, with a township declared in 1909. The neighboring towns were amalgamated in 1956, and declared the City of Blantyre on Republic Day, July 6, 1966. The city has a population of 109,461 and covers an area of 83 square miles, with Blantyre (alt. 3,400 feet) and Limbe (alt. 3,800 feet) 5 miles apart but joined by *Kamuzu Highway,* along which are a host of new buildings and an expanding industrial area. Today Blantyre is the most modern city in Malawi, and it will probably maintain its position as the commercial-industrial-communications center even when Lilongwe is completed as the new capital.

If you enter Blantyre by road from Zomba, you will come to several intersections, and it seems as though the city, elusively, does not have a center. Continue straight on Kamuzu Highway (named for the president, Dr. H. Kamuzu Banda), going under *Independence Arch* (1964) and passing the *Malawi Congress Party headquarters,* the *Museum of Malawi* (see below), *Kamuzu Stadium* (seats 40,000), the *High Court, Malawi Broadcasting Corp., Police Headquarters, Malawi Polytechnic College* (built with U.S. aid in 1965), and *Queen Elizabeth Central Hospital,* and finally come to a main junction. Here Kamuzu Highway ends, and there is an intersection with Chileka Road (to the airport 16 km). Straight ahead is another big intersection: Haile Selassie Road to the left and Glyn Jones to the right, those two streets with Victoria Avenue forming the central business district triangle. At one end of Victoria Avenue is the Mount Soche Hotel and the Department of Tourism, at the other end is Delamere House, an eight-story building which is one of Blantyre's few modest skyscrapers. Along Victoria

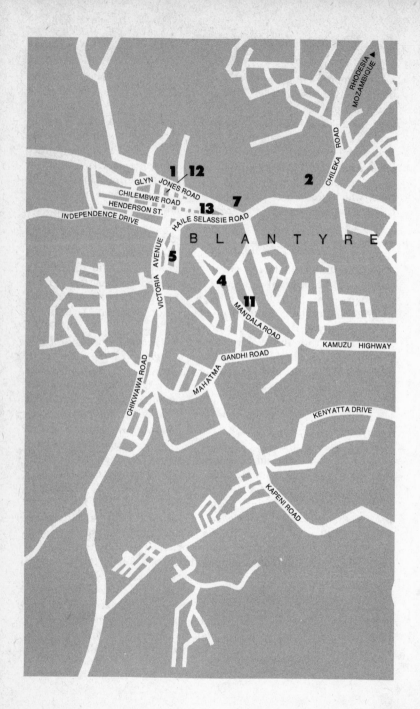

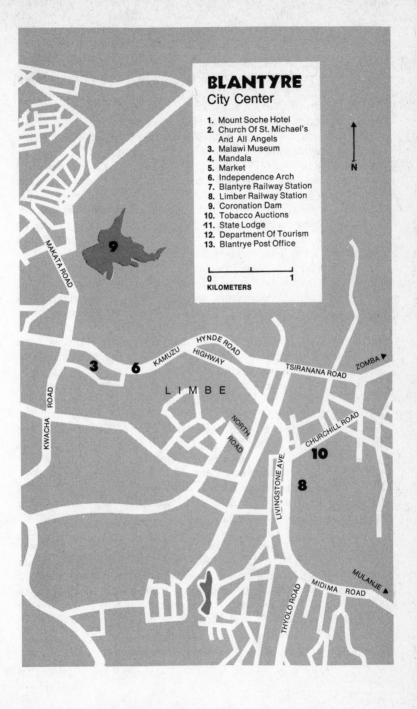

BLANTYRE
City Center

1. Mount Soche Hotel
2. Church Of St. Michael's And All Angels
3. Malawi Museum
4. Mandala
5. Market
6. Independence Arch
7. Blantyre Railway Station
8. Limber Railway Station
9. Coronation Dam
10. Tobacco Auctions
11. State Lodge
12. Department Of Tourism
13. Blantrye Post Office

0   1
KILOMETERS

N

MAKATA ROAD
KWACHA ROAD
HYNDE ROAD
KAMUZU HIGHWAY
TSIRANANA ROAD
ZOMBA ►
LIMBE
NORTH ROAD
CHURCHILL ROAD
LIVINGSTONE AVE.
MULANJE ►
THYOLO ROAD
MIDIMA ROAD

3   6

9

10

8

Avenue are the bank headquarters, embassies, and offices, miscellaneous shops, supermarkets, and curio sellers. It is a miniature downtown
district, compact but with a fair supply of amenities. Haile Selassie
Road is lined with Asian wholesalers and retailers, and on Glyn Jones
Road are restaurants, shops, and the main post office.

If you have a couple of days in Blantyre, there are a few places that
make good sightseeing stops: some are included in the UTC city tour
(see package listings MP-12 and 13). The *Blantyre Church and Mission,* on Chileka Road, about 1 km from the clock tower, is a must.
Started by a group of Church of Scotland missionaries in 1876, the
Church of Central Africa Presbyterian mission now embraces schools,
workshops, offices, a bookshop and printshop, and the noble *Church of
St. Michael's and All Angels.* Without a plan or sketch, the church
organically grew, incorporating 81 different molded brick designs,
made on site from clay dug from anthills by African workers, the construction guided by the Reverend Scott, the mission's head. The result
is in the form of a Latin cross, enhanced by a Moorish-domed bell
tower, an apse dome, arches, four flying buttresses, lancet windows,
and many intricate moldings. Inside are the paneled roof with paneled
mahogany ceiling, pillars with wooden carvings by Africans (one
representing the vision of Ezekiel), and the long Byzantine arcade of
multiple arches. It is well worth a close look.

The *tobacco auction floors* are in Limbe, on Churchill Road between
the railway station and the Shire Highlands Hotel. The time to visit is
mid-April to September, during the sales season. The huge building
housing the auctions is open weekdays, with the buying and selling
starting at 8 A.M. and ending at 11:30 A.M. (because the two halls
are specially designed to catch the morning light, tobacco is not sold
after 1 P.M.). In the cavernous halls are bales and bales of tobacco—
half a million pounds are sold daily, 700–750 per hour. For permission
to watch the auctions, check with the warehouse supervisor, whose
office is just inside one of the big doors.

The *Museum of Malawi* is off Kamuzu Highway; turn at Kwacha
Road and again at Kasungu Crescent. Museum is open daily except
Monday, 10 A.M.–4 P.M.; admission is 3t. Located in this building
since 1966, the museum has a small collection of Malawi arts and
crafts, prehistoric artifacts, and slave trade and early missionary
items. Outside is the steam traction engine used 1897–1907 by the
African Lakes Corp. to haul goods from the Lower Shire River to

Blantyre; it was retired when the railway was built. Complementing the museum is the Musuem of Lake Malawi in Mangochi.

Other places of interest in Blantyre: *President Banda's* residence (a national monument), *Rangely Gardens* and *Jubilee Gardens* on Chikwawa Road, *Coronation Dam* off Kamuzu Highway, and *Burn Dam* off Churchill Road (note: by British usage, a "dam" actually refers to the water behind the dam).

Good day trips can be made to the following: *Zomba Plateau, Mikolongwe Hill, Thyolo,* and *Mulanje Mountain* (all on Route Q–1), and *Kapachira Falls* and *Lengwe National Park* (all Route Q-2). Another side trip could include *Mpatamanga Gorge,* another of the series of falls in the Murchison Cataracts. This one rushes through a narrow gorge, and it makes an ideal picnic spot. Follow Chileka Road past the airport for 57 km from Blantyre; leave your car by the Shire River Bridge and walk in about 1 km.

Accommodations

Mount Soche Hotel, Box 284, tel. 2191; cable OVEROTEL. Glyn Jones Road at Victoria Ave. 96 dbls (incl 3 suites), 4 sgls, all w/bath, heat. Rates: B&B: sgl—K10; dbl—K15.75. Credit: DC. Only international-class city hotel in Malawi, Mount Soche (named after one of Blantyre's hills) has modern, tastefully furnished rooms; ones facing garden toward Nyambadwe Hill are best. Ground floor has Ndirande Restaurant and Kabula Bar (both named for other hills). Other facilities: telex, bookshop, UTC office. Rating: 1st-class international; except for a rather abrupt management, a convenient, pleasant hotel, ★.

Ryall's Hotel, Box 21, tel. 2856; cable RYALLS. Hanover Ave. at Glyn Jones Road. 42 dbls, 23 sgls, all w/bath; 40 rms w/a-c. Rates: B&B: sgl—K8–9; dbl—K12–14. Credit: AE, DC. Oldest hotel in Malawi, renovated 1969, with 28 new rooms and a pool added 1972. New-wing rooms (#30–57) are most comfortable. Uncozy dining room serves set menu (breakfast—K1.25; lunch or dinner—K1.50). Nicer is "21" cocktail bar and grillroom. Rating: 2d-class international, if you pick a new-wing double.

Shire Highlands Hotel, Box 5204, tel. 50055; cable HIGHTEL. Churchill Road in Limbe. 46 dbls and sgls, half w/bath. Rates: B&B: sgl—K7.50; dbl—K10.50. Credit: DC. 1950 Shire Highlands has old-fashioned charm as well as inconvenience. No central heating makes winter cooler inside than out. Large, airy, Iberian-Siberian doubles w/bath are best. Dining room serves mostly British, set menu (breakfast—K1.05; lunch—K1.25; dinner—K1.50); higher-priced eating in the Balmoral Room. Barbecue in beer garden daily at lunch. Pool, hairdresser. Rating: 1st-class local; despite the drawbacks, the best moderately priced hotel in town.

Nash's Hotel, Box 106, tel. 2689; cable NASHS. Chilembwe Roundabout, 2 blocks off Victoria Ave. 7 dbls (incl 2 family rms), 10 sgls; none w/bath. Rates: B&B: K3.55 per person. Small, friendly, homey, old-fashioned. Rating: 2d-class local, good bet for low-budgeters.

Hotel Continental, Box 5249, Limbe; tel. 50670. On Tsiranana Road, 6½ km from Blantyre going toward Zomba. 12 dbls w/bath. Rates: B&B: sgl—K4.45; dbl—K6.90. Plain, traveling-salesman-style hotel. Rating: Good 2d-class local, very functional. **Camping** on adjacent grounds.

There are two city rest houses, both government owned and operated, catering to local bus and train travelers: *Blantyre Rest House,* Chileka Road just past the clock tower. Rates: bed only: sgl—K1–1.25; family rm or dbl—K2; "VIP" rm—K3; bed in dorm—25t w/o bedding, 50t w/bedding. *Limbe Rest House,* off Churchill Road near police station. Rates: same as above except family rm—K2.50; bath only is 10 or 20t. **Camping** outside either rest house—20t each. Also permitted on the playing fields of Limbe Country Club, Churchill Road past the Imperial Tobacco factory (ITG). Temporary membership of 50t entitles use of indoor facilities, and there's a good 35t breakfast. Inquire first: Manager, CCL, Box 5031, Limbe; tel. 51022.

Where to Eat

Ndirande Restaurant, in the Mount Soche Hotel, tel. 2191. One of the few fancy restaurants in town, named for a city hill (means "sleeping man mountain"). Band 6 evenings. Table d'hôte (breakfast—K1; lunch—K1.60; dinner—K2.10) and à la carte (entrées—K2–5.50), including rainbow trout meunière, châteaubriand with sauce Béarnaise for 2, escalope of veal Sophia Loren.

Balmoral Restaurant, in the Shire Highlands Hotel, tel. 50055. The huge Continental menu (14 inches wide, 2 feet 9 inches long—the printing is big) features roast chicken with apricots, Hash Geisha in pineapple with rice and mushrooms, entrecôte Béarnaise, "drunk fillet Cinzana," lobster piri-piri, grilled *chambo* tartare. Entrées priced K1.40–3.75. Closed Sunday.

21 Room, in Ryall's, tel. 2856. Fairly intimate grillroom with cocktail bar, serves as à la carte annex of hotel. Menu offers fillets of sole, *chambo*, prawns, fillet steak, lamb chops, mixed grill—nothing very elaborate—for K1.50–3.

Maxim's Restaurant, St. Andrew's St., tel. 2305. Possibly the fanciest independent restaurant in Blantyre, with starched white tablecloths, low lighting. Long Continental menu has Asian and local additions: mushroom appetizer, rainbow trout, *chambo*, fillet steak with wine and mushroom sauce, and so on; entrées—K1.15–1.95.

China Bar & Restaurant, Glyn Jones Road, tel. 8039. Very nice Chinese place, clean and atmospheric, good deal. Large and small portions range 40t–K3. Quick lunch for K1.20—choice of 3 soups, 7 dishes, 3 side staples.

Riviera Restaurant, Churchill Road, Limbe. Blue, yellow, pleasant. Entrées K1.25–2.50, includes half-chicken, Portuguese steak, prawn curry.

Tahiti Restaurant, Kamuzu Highway near Churchill Road, Limbe. Clean, simple. Curry (K1.50–2.50) has good reputation.

Cafe Capri, Haile Selassie Road. Ordinary, functional, dishes K1–1.60.

Sands Restaurant, Haile Selassie Road. Diner atmosphere, greasy food.

Le Bistro, Dossani Arcade. Intimate little café that has handwritten Brillat-Savarin quotes on menu.

El Brazil, Henderson St. Coffee bar is friendly, cozy.

Apollo Cafeteria, Livingstone Ave. Big, clean, bright—for low-budget snackers.

Sun Flower Fish 'n Chips, Livingstone Ave. Fish—12t; chips—12t; Coke—7t, and that's it.

Getting Around

Blantyre's small downtown is easily walked. Taxis rank up outside the Mount Soche Hotel. Otherwise, call 2604, 8929, 8046, 50025, 30813 or 50930. Taxis are metered and charge 40t for first mile, 24t per mile thereafter.

Cinemas

Majestic, Citrona Ave. off Kamuzu Highway, Limbe; tel. 50555. *Apollo*, Livingstone Ave., tel. 8479. *Rainbow*, off Kamuzu Highway, Limbe; tel. 50379. *Queen's*, Hynde Road and Kamuzu Highway, tel. 50759. *Rainbow Drive-In*, Chikwawa Road, tel. 2216.

Libraries

Malawi National Library Service, Ginnery Corner on Kamuzu Highway. *USIS Library,* St. Andrew's St. *Kwacha National Culture Center Library,* Kwacha Road. *National Archives,* in Zomba (Africana, Malawiana).

Religious Services

The faiths represented in Blantyre: Presbyterian, Catholic, Lutheran, Anglican, Church of Christ, Baptist, Seventh-Day Adventist, Assemblies of God, Hindu, Moslem, Sikh. See the newspapers for times of services.

Shops and Services

Main shopping street is Victoria Avenue, with a few stores on the side streets and in Dossani Arcade.

Books, newspapers, magazines: Times Bookshop, Victoria Ave., Box 445. Central Bookshop, Dossani Arcade, Box 264. •

Central Market: Off Lower Sclater Road below Mandala.

Grocers: Kandodo Supermarket, Victoria Ave. PTL, Hardelec House, Victoria Ave.

Hairdressers: Elden Salon, tel. 8015. Letha of London, tel. 50330.

Route Q-1: Nyala, Zambia–Rumphi–Lilongwe–Zomba– Limbe (Blantyre)–Thyolo–Mulanje–Milanje, Mozambique

This route follows Malawi's trunk highway, M1, the whole length of the country. Half the route to Lilongwe is engineered one-and-a-half- or two-lane dirt; the second half from Lilongwe to the Mozambique border is paved. En route are two of Malawi's three national parks, Nyika and Kasungu, and the two cities of Lilongwe and Blantyre-Limbe.

Km 0: Nyala/border with Zambia. Km 10: Malawi border post. Km 11: *Chitipa,* northernmost border town in Malawi, and turnoff (L) on S6 (our Route Q-6) to Karonga 96 km. **Accommodations:** *Govt. Rest House,* P.O. Chitipa, tel. 2. Near the *boma* in the center of town. 4 beds. Rates: see p. 626. Km 53: *Chisenga.* **Accommodations:** *Govt. Rest House,* P.O. Chitipa, tel. 2. Near the *boma.* 4 beds. Rates: see p. 626. About Km 65, M1 crosses into Zambia. There is a Malawi border checkpoint. After the D111 turnoff (R) to Lundazi 194 km

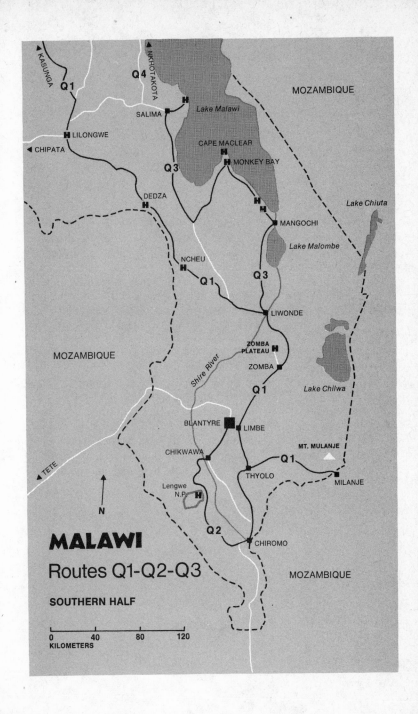

MALAWI
Routes Q1-Q2-Q3
SOUTHERN HALF

KILOMETERS
0   40   80   120

and Chipata 375 km, at Km 174, M1 continues back into Malawi to Katumbi (border checkpoint) at Km 187.

Nyika National Park

Km 199: Turnoff (L) to *Nyika National Park* 27 km, which is divided between Malawi and Zambia and is an unusual African park. Over 90 percent of the Malawi side of the Nyika Plateau's 360 square miles is rolling montane grassland, miles of undulations cut by deep valleys, and dotted with occasional clumps of trees or planted *patula* pine forests. The scenery is clean, golden, windswept, high. The headwaters of the Chelinda, Runyina, and North Rukuru rivers are in the park, hence the vernacular name Nyika, meaning "where the water comes from." Along with the adjoining 30.9 square miles of the Zambian Nyika National Park (both open all year round), the whole area's average elevation is over 7,000 feet, in some spots rising to peaks over 8,200 feet. The road network covers some 225 km, and excellent views toward Lake Malawi are seen from *Kasarambe Viewpoint* at the south end, and *Mondwe Viewpoint* at the north end of the park. You may find your car sputtering at the high altitudes, and because it will consume more gas than usual, have plenty in your tank before driving around (gasoline at Chelinda Camp).

Game viewing of herds of zebra, eland, and roan is facilitated by the clean-swept lines of the plateau. Reedbucks are most plentiful, while duikers, hartebeests, and bushbucks are less common. Predators around but not often seen are lions, leopards, hyenas, jackals, genets, servals, and caraculs. One small antelope which you may be lucky to see is the *klipspringer,* which is only 22 inches at the shoulder and weighs 30–40 pounds. It has a thick coat of long, brittle hair, and its overall color

Klipspringer

is olive yellow speckled with gray; its horns are short and nearly vertical. The klipspringer lives on rocky hills or in rocks, and when it runs away, it looks stilted, bounding along in a series of large hops.

Birdwatchers will be kept busy admiring the hundreds of species, including wattle crane, Stanley's bustard (near Chelinda Camp), Crawshay's francolin, hill babbler, and double-collared sunbird. Rainbow trout can be found in the dam and streams near Chelinda; licenses are obtainable in the park office. There are several archaeological sites near and on the plateau, the most important being *Fingira Cave National Monument,* a Later Stone Age site dating back to 3000 B.C., in which were found many microliths and tools, and ocher paintings; upon request, a game guard will accompany you to the cave, which is just south of the park entrance gate.

Getting There, Getting Around

At the time of writing, the only way to reach Nyika by road was via S10 from the Katumbi–Rumphi road. In mid-1972, 200 British Army engineers were building another Malawi road down the west escarpment out of the park; it will connect to a Malawi road going north to Chisenga in the future and will be entirely inside the Malawi border. There is an airstrip near Chelinda Camp, but no local transport is available.

Accommodations

Chelinda Camp, bookings to Director of Forestry and Game, Box 182; Zomba; tel. 797. Located 41½ km from park gate. Rates: adult— K2; child—K1. Spread out along the side of a small valley at the forest woodline, camp has 18 beds in 4 cozy self-contained chalets (1 with 3 dbls; 3 with 2 dbls) and 12 beds in a block of 6 dbl rms with a common dining room. Bring your own food, which will be cooked for you; camp store has some supplies. Camp is beautiful, very alpine, and if you have a chalet, you'll think it a perfect mountainside retreat. . . . *Zambian Govt. Rest House,* 24 km from park gate (access from Malawi only). 8 simply furnished dbls on a long corridor, all sharing bath, plus nice big living room with view to west, and dining room. Rates: sgl— K1.60; dbl—K1.35 per person; children 75t or 75n. Casual visitors and campers—15n or 15t per meal (bring own food). Cook-manager William is, on request, a baker, too. **Camping** permitted only outside the Zambian rest house for 15t or 15n per person.

Km 243: *Rumphi* is in a flat-bottomed bowl at the base of the Nyika Plateau. **Accommodations:** *Govt. Rest House,* P.O. Rumphi, tel. 7. 1 km from town center. 10 beds, very comfortable. Rates: see p. 626. Km 247: Junction—M11 (our Route Q-6) to Livingstonia 66 km, Karonga 156 km; and M1 to Mzimba. Turn right here. At Engucwini, Km 269, is the turnoff (L) onto M14 to Ekwendeni 22 km and Mzuzu 45 km.

Km 360: *Mount Hora* is an inselberg rising 1,000 feet above the Mzimba Plains. Seven rock shelters found in 1950 and 1967 excavations included two human skeletons, plus many schematic paintings, probably remains of the Nachikufan Culture—Late Stone Age hunter-gatherers. Mount Hora was also the scene of an 1879 massacre of the Tumbuka by the Ngoni, who slaughtered the rebellious Tumbuka who had fled here for refuge.

Km 400: *Mzimba* is a small town (pop. 4,000) near four junctions, with roads going north to Mzuzu or Rumphi, south to Kasungu or Lundazi. In the surrounding Mzimba Plains, Turkish tobacco is grown on small plots. **Accommodations:** *Govt. Rest House,* Box 8, tel. 6. Next door to the Road Motor Services garage. 10 beds, cozy sitting room, hot bath. Rates: see p. 626.

At Km 414 is a turnoff (L) to S44 (our Route Q-5) through the Vipya Plateau to Mzuzu 132 km. Km 419 is a turnoff (R) onto M13 to Lundazi, Zambia, 69 km. Km 470: You leave the Northern Region and enter the Central Region, passing the *Vipya Mountains* to the east; highest peak being Mount Champhila at 5,460 feet. The Central Region Plateau begins, covering some 9,000 square miles at 3,800–4,100 feet altitude, the largest continuous plateau surface in Malawi. Here is another turnoff (R) onto S49 to Lundazi 69 km.

Kasungu

Km 554: *Kasungu* town and turnoff (L) on S54 to Nkhotakota 125 km. Kasungu district was the birthplace of Malawi's president, Dr. Banda, and a large house is being built for him outside town on the way to Kasungu National Park. New tobacco estates are opening under the Kasungu Tobacco Growers Scheme, in which Malawi farmers are being taught the technique of growing flue-cured-type tobacco on a large scale. To tour an estate, make prior arrangements with the Project Manager, Kasungu Flue-Cured Tobacco Growers Authority, Private Bag, Lilongwe; tel. 00511. **Accommodations:** *Kasungu Inn,* P.O. Kasungu; tel. 8. Just off the Blantyre-Mzimba road, near the

Boma. New in 1973, this fancier government house has 10 dbls, each with shower. Charges: K4 adults, K2 child. . . . *Govt. Rest House,* P.O. Kasungu; tel. 8. Also near the Boma. 18 beds, comfortable. Rates: see p. 625.

Kasungu National Park

Km 559: Turnoff (L) to *Kasungu National Park* 44 km, Malawi's largest, covering approximately 800 square miles, open for visitors May 1–December 31. There are 300 miles of road within Kasungu. Most of the park is flat brachystegia country, with intersecting grass-land and a few hills and rocky kopjes. Three streams have their head-waters in the park, and game viewing along them is best. The range of game is the most varied in Malawi, although not very abundant. Elephants are the easiest to spot of the big game, while hippos and buffalos are less common. Other animals include the zebra, hartebeest, kudu, eland, roan, sable, reedbuck, waterbuck, and oribi. Occasionally seen are leopards, cheetahs, lions, and very rarely black-maned lions. Birdwatchers should spend time by the dam at Lifupa Camp or along the streams. Upon request at the park office, a game guard will take you to see the Later Stone Age and Iron Age rock paintings at the *Wangombe Rume Hills,* to the iron-smelting furnace on the Dwanga River, and to the view from the summit of Black Rock.

Getting There, Getting Around

Day trips are possible from Kasungu town and Lilongwe, although two days would be better from the latter. The main road in is D187. A *day visitors' camp,* including a dining shelter, barbecue-type cooking facility, and toilet, is located near Lifupa Camp. Airfield. Two-day package tour available from Lilongwe (see listing MP-11).

Accommodations

Lifupa Game Camp, bookings to International Travel & Tour Co., Box 247, Lilongwe; tel. 2278. 14 km from gate, overlooking Lifupa Stream. 12 red-brick rondavels, each a trpl with its own terrace. Main building has communal dining room, lounge, bar. Bring your own food, which the staff cooks. Pool. Rates: adults—K2; children—K1. Excellent for short game-viewing break.

Km 680: Turnoff (L) on M5 to Salima 111 km; and (R) to Mchinji 108 km via S11.

Lilongwe

Km 692: *Lilongwe* (est. pop. 87,000), slated as Malawi's new capital, is the center of a rich agricultural district, and has long been settled. It was selected as a district *boma* site in 1904 and, being at a crossroads, grew with the commerce. In 1947 it became a township. In 1964 Dr. Banda chose Lilongwe as the new capital site. Reasons given were that government ministry buildings were inconveniently divided between the Southern Region's Zomba and Blantyre, several government buildings were old and in need of expensive repairs; the Central and Northern regions needed economic stimulation; and centrally located Lilongwe had some structure to build on and sufficient land for expansion. The Master Plan is a scaled-down adaptation of a very expensive South African architectual consultants' design. In 1968, after Britain declined to give aid, Malawi announced a K8-million loan from South Africa, and the Capital City Development Corp. was established. Work began, with the new Lilongwe Designated Area of 50,000 acres including areas for the ministries and parliament on Capital Hill, commercial areas including a new City Center near the capital, more industrial areas, and a new presidential residence. There will also be areas for the army and the police, an ornamental lake with campsite, a 200-acre park, national stadium, another golf course, motel, possible K2-million hotel, and an international airport. The projections were that in 1975 seven ministries, the president's office, and all embassies would be functioning in the new capital, and by 1976 all the ministries will be installed. The population in 1974 was estimated to be about 87,000, rising to 500,000 in the year 2000, with one-fifth employed by government. Inquiries: Liaison Officer, CCDC, Box 125, Lilongwe; tel. 2350.

During our visit, things were just being laid out and the access route to Capital Hill will undoubtedly change. One suggested route: from Kamuzu traffic circle, take Procession Road north to Sharrar Road; turn right and continue for 4 km to Parliament Procession Way, which leads into the new capital area. There is a United Touring Co. tour (see listing MP-14).

Around Lilongwe will be the Land Development Scheme, financed by the World Bank. Half a million acres of land will be agriculturally developed to support an eventual 450 people per square mile, or 50,000 families. A feature of the plan is to have the small tobacco, maize, groundnut, and cattle farms individually owned by people and groups, rather than tribally or communally. Also in the new area is a Young Pioneers tobacco settlement scheme.

Accommodations

Lilongwe Hotel, Box 44, tel. 2461; cable OVEROTEL. Kamuzu Procession Road. 23 rms in new wing, 8 chalets, 9 *khonde* (old-wing balconied rms), all w/bath. Rates: B&B: sgl—K6–10; dbl—K9.80–14. Credit: DC. Lilongwe's only tourist-class hotel, dating from the 1930s; chalets built 1968, new wing 1972. Chalets are most pleasant, new rooms identically standardized modern. Dining room has table d'hôte (breakfast—K1; lunch—K1.60; dinner—K1.80) and à la carte (entrées—K1.40–2.50), including grilled *chambo,* baby chicken piri-piri. Outdoor dance floor, tennis court. Rating: Good 2d-class international.

Km 773: Turnoff (L) to Dedza 3 km and Chencherere Hill National Monument 14 km. Go ½ km to a signposted dirt road on your left; follow this about 13 km to *Chencherere Hill.* Here are several once-occupied rock shelters containing paintings, fortifications, and other evidence of Later Stone Age and Iron Age occupation. On the northwest side is a one-acre iron smelting site, and Iron Age pottery has been found all around the hill.

Dedza

Dedza itself is reached by continuing straight on the original turnoff road 3 km. The district's headquarters, Dedza is a peaceful town nestled beautifully amid tall pines at the base of 7,120-foot *Dedza Mountain.* Settled originally by the Maseko Ngoni in 1876, it is still an Ngoni neighborhood. Today the softwood timber industry has planted hundreds of acres of pine on the mountain slopes, with the predominant tree being the graceful *patula* pine. You can drive or hike to the top of the mountain; go to the center of town, turn at the "police" and "boma" signs opposite the hospital, go about 1 km, bearing left at a T-junction, passing the rest house on your right; follow the red, green, and yellow signs to Mountain Road and the radio station; the road winds 6 km to the top, where you can walk along a firebreak trail to the rocky outcrop by the radio station, where there is a sweeping view toward Lake Malawi in the east and Mozambique in the west. **Accommodations:** *Govt. Rest House,* Box 108, tel. 1. 6 beds, fireplace in sitting room, inside dining room. Worth staying a couple nights for a short, restful break from the road. Rates: see p. 626.

Km 777: The main road between Dedza and Ncheu runs right along the border with Mozambique, and at this point there is a turnoff (R) to the town of *Vila Coutinho* 43 km. At Km 789 is a turnoff (L) on S22 to Golomoti 39 km and the lakeshore road.

Diwa Hill Rock Paintings

Km 795: Turnoff (L) to *Mlanda* Dutch Reformed mission, perched on a hillside and surrounded by trees, and *Diwa Hill,* an important prehistoric rock shelter with excellent layers of paintings: the first and oldest layer has schematic circles, stars, ladders, gridirons, parallel lines, and other designs in red paint with some touches of white— these have been traced to the Akafulas (or Batwe), a Later Stone Age people. This layer is overlain with a seminaturalistic series of anthropomorphic or zoomorphic figures in white, probably dating from the Iron Age and connected with initiation rituals. The latest layer, geometric designs, was done in charcoal.

Km 844: *Ncheu* is that district's headquarters, and nearby is *Gomani Chikuse Memorial,* raised in memory of the paramount chief of the Maseko-Ngoni, who died in 1896. The stone obelisk is surrounded by mountain scenery and is a national monument. **Accommodations:** *Govt. Rest House,* Private Bag 1, tel. 1. Near the *boma.* 5 beds.

Km 879: Turnoff to *Murchison Cataracts* 50 km, a 50-mile series of rapids and falls in the Shire River. At Km 914 is the major turnoff (L) to Mangochi 69 km and Monkey Bay 142 km on Lake Malawi, via M3, the Lakeshore Road (our Route Q-3). Km 918: *Liwonde Barrage,* built on the Shire River about 50 miles downstream from Lake Malawi to ensure the necessary minimum flow of water into the modest hydroelectric plant at Nkula Falls on the Murchison Cataracts, which has an output of 25 megawatts. Good fishing along the barrage.

Km 943: Turnoff (L) to Lake Chiuta 169, a seasonal lake.

Lake Chilwa

Km 964: Turnoff (L) to Zomba Airfield 3 km and *Lake Chilwa* 20 km. The lake is in a shallow and saline basin covering 1,000 square miles, less than half of which is open water, 10 feet in depth. Weeds encircle the lake, choking the northern part, but forming protection for the fish in time of breeding and attracting ducks and geese. Birdlife is prolific, and a few crocodiles sometimes come down from Lake Chiuta in times of flood.

Zomba

Km 968: *Zomba* (pop. 19,666) has been the capital of Malawi since 1891, and was originally chosen for its scenic beauty. Like Dedza the town snuggles at the foot of a mountain, the *Zomba Plateau,* and the hilly landscaping of poinsettias, eucalyptus, and pine is lush and beautiful. In the early days of the protectorate, the area between Zomba and Lake Chilwa was used as a slave trading route, so from the capital the caravans could be kept under surveillance. The first permanent building on the site was the *Official Residency,* built by John Buchanan, the Scottish gardener for the Blantyre Mission. When Harry Johnston arrived in 1889, the Residency, then occupied by Consul Hawes, was the best house available, designed with terraces, a curved front, and hexagonal towers at either end—unusual but convertible into a fortress at any time. While Johnston occupied the house as commissioner, the back yard was filled with pets—leopards, cats, baboons, crested cranes, geese, and guinea fowl (one known as "the sergeant" attended parades with his master).

Across from the Residency, now a Government Hostel, is the large *Botanical Garden,* inspired by Johnston and planted under the green thumb of Dr. Whyte, an elderly botanist, who discovered the Mulanje cedar in his early days of exploration. This large garden is still well kept and pleasant to walk around in. Other buildings of interest in Zomba: *State House,* the official residence of Dr. Banda; *Parliament* building, where Malawi's legislative body meets; *Secretariat,* housing numerous government offices.

These and others occupied by the government were scheduled to be vacated by 1974, to be taken over by the University of Malawi, which is moving its campus to this idyllic setting. Of its five colleges, the university will have 600 students in three colleges here: Chancellor College (arts and sciences), the Institute of Public Administration (public administration and law), and Soche Hill College (education). Two other colleges, not moving here but connected with the university, are Bunda College (agriculture) in Lilongwe and the Polytechnic (business, health, technical subjects) in Blantyre. The move to Zomba will cost K2.4 million and is mostly financed by a British loan of K2 million.

Another place of interest in Zomba is the *Monument to the King's African Rifles,* located off the highway to the right. The KAR was a regiment of white-officered Africans who served in both world wars, including the battle with the Germans in Karonga in 1914.

Zomba Plateau

The feature of beauty above the town is the massive *Zomba Plateau.* The turnoff (R) for it is in the center of town, and an 8-km drive goes to the top through Zomba's residential areas, past the sawmill (production expected to be 500,000 cubic feet of wood in 1974), through the Mulanje cedar plantations, and up the one-way paved road clinging to the cliff. The Zomba Plateau, spread over 50 square miles, rises out of the Shire Highlands to an average height of 6,000 feet, with Malumbe peak reaching 6,837 feet. The western edge overlooks the Shire Valley, and Zomba town is nestled at the foot; the southeast rim looks toward the Lake Chilwa depression and Tuchila-Palombe Plain to Mulanje Mountain 40 miles away. The Domasi River (called the Mlunguzi Stream on the Plateau) has eroded the deep valley transversely across from east to west. Two dams, Chagwa and Mlunguzi, and the stream offer excellent trout-fishing opportunities, and licenses are available through the Ku Chawe Inn. Seven thousand acres of trees, particularly the *patula* pine, have been planted on the plateau and slopes, since the native-Mexican *Pinus patula* was first introduced in 1927 to Zomba. The pine gives not only aroma, coolness, and greenery to the high region, but also high-quality timber for the sawmill below. You can cross the lush plateau on a network of dirt roads, with a 24-km circular drive taking you around to the main areas; allow at least an hour for the excursion. The *Reserved Natural Area,* with occasional grass and occasional trees, looks like the Nyika Plateau, and is the location of *Chingwe's Hole*—a big circular cavity, descending 60 feet to a split in the rock below, allegedly an old burial place into which the dead were lowered. As you stand looking over for the hole, the pit as such is not obvious—it just looks like the side of the mountain. On a clear day you get a view from here of the Shire River, the Kirk Range, and Lake Malombe. Two other viewpoints worth visiting are *Emperor's View* (named in honor of Emperor Haile Selassie) and *Queen's View* (after Elizabeth the Queen Mother), both of which overlook Zomba town and on good days have perspectives of Mulanje Mountain, Palombe Plain, Lake Chilwa, and Chiradzulu Mountain. If you feel energetic you can take walks and hikes along footpaths throughout the plateau. When it comes time to go down again, follow the one-way road descending the mountain, back into town.

Accommodations

Ku Chawe Inn, Box 71, Zomba; tel. 403; cable CHAWE; bookings to Box 284, Blantyre; tel. 2191. At the top of the road from Zomba. 18 dbls, 10 w/bath. Rates: B&B: sgl—K5 to K10; dbl—K9 to K11. Credit: DC. The inn is perched on the edge of the plateau facing toward the town and Mount Mulanje. When it is a clear day, you can see for miles; when it is a foggy day, you can barely see over the porch. New rooms all have views, but the one rondavel with a fireplace is the best old room. Standard menu: breakfast—K1; lunch—K1.60; tea— 40t; dinner—K1.80. Rating: 1st-class local, worth coming up the mountain to stay here and enjoy the bracing mountain air and gorgeous scenery. ★. . . . *Government Hostel,* tel. 218, in Zomba town across from the Botanical Gardens, is a finer version of a rest house, complete with good table d'hôte meals served. Rates: FB: K5 per person. . . . **Camping** is at an official site on Zomba Plateau; as you reach the top of the road, there's a junction—go left about .6 km to another junction, then turn right and the campsite is almost immediately on your left. Delightful, double-terraced clearing among the pines, with small toilet/shower block (cold water), and barbecue pits (caretaker's children will bring firewood for sale). Warning: watch for biting ants. Otherwise it's a perfect Sierras or Rockies-like campsite. Free.

Km 1027: Turnoff (L) to *Chiradzulu* 15 km, a square-shaped mountain, 5,820 feet high, around which is one of the most densely populated rural areas in Malawi, with 900–1,000 people per square mile. The Universities Mission to Central Africa had its first mission station here briefly in 1861–62, at a spot near the village of Magomero.

Another mission in the shadow of Chiradzulu mountain was that of the Ajawa Providence Industrial Mission, started by Malawi's early rebel, John Chilembwe. His mission in 1912 attracted hundreds of African followers, who under the influence of Chilembwe became convinced that Europeans were mistreating Africans, especially using them as cannon fodder in World War I. On January 23, 1915, Chilembwe and his followers rose in armed rebellion and killed three white men. On February 3 Chilembwe and his nephew were shot near Mulanje after resisting arrest. A large number of Chilembwe's followers were arrested, some imprisoned, and some executed. The Chilembwe rebellion was more of an individual protest than an attempt to overthrow the government, but was to serve as a rallying point for later African leaders. A commemorative stamp was issued in Malawi on the 50th anniversary of the rebellion in 1965.

Km 1031: Junction: (L) on Churchill Road to Limbe and straight on Tsiranana Road to Blantyre. Turn left to continue the route through Limbe to Thyolo Road and Thyolo.

Mikolongwe Cave Paintings

Km 1034: Turnoff (R) to *Mikolongwe Hill and Cave National Monument,* also called Mwalawolemba ("rock of writing"), containing schematic paintings done by Stone Age artists 500 to 1,000 years ago. The drawings are a series of dots, circles, and loops whose meaning is not known. To reach the shelter, drive about 19 km along Midima Road, turn right at a signposted road which leads to Nandi School, where a guide will walk the 1 km with you up the hill.

Thyolo

Just before Tyolo is a turnoff (R) on M9 (our Route Q-2) to Chiromo 88 km. Km 1074: *Thyolo* (formerly Cholo) is in one of the biggest tea-producing districts in Malawi. Tea is the country's leading cash crop, providing over 30 percent of the export revenue and employment for over 30,000 people. The total acreage under tea is 35,000, making Malawi one of the largest producers in Africa. Environmental factors needed to grow tea, a perennial crop, are ample rainfall (at least 50 inches yearly) and a deep acidic soil. Small growers are encouraged by the Smallholders' Tea Authority, which sells 30-month-old stumps to owners of small holdings. To ensure proper growth, the Authority supervises the planting on terraced land with moderate or steep slopes and windbreaks of silver-oak trees. At four years of age the tea bush is old enough for the young shoots, two small leaves and bud, to be picked. Then, like the tea grown on plantations, the tea is taken to factories, where it is dried and rolled, packaged, and sold locally and exported.

By the junction with the road to Chiromo, near the *boma,* is *Mwalawanthunzi* ("rock of shade"), thought to have been an ancient rain shrine. Travelers passing frequently tap the stone with a pebble, which they leave there, to ensure themselves good luck. If you make the proper offering, it is said that rain clouds will gather over the rock to shade you—thus its name.

Km 1105: Turnoff (L) to *Fort Lister National Monument* 50 km. Named after Sir Villiers Lister of the British Foreign Office, the fort was built in 1893 as a civil administrative center and a military base for the Indian troops and African recruits to watch slave caravans and keep peace along the Mozambique border, but was used only until 1902. From the ruins is an excellent panorama of Mulanje Mountain and the plains below north to the Zomba Plateau. To get to the fort, take S40 to Phalombe, then S43 southeast for a few km.

Km 1119: *Mulanje* is the district headquarters amid the acres of tea at the base of Mulanje Mountain. The first successful tea growing was at a coffee plantation here called Lauderdale in 1888, started from a tea plant imported from Britain's Kew Gardens by the African Lakes Corporation.

Mulanje Mountain

Mulanje Mountain is the highest in Central Africa, peaking at 9,847 feet above sea level. The mountain rises abruptly from the southeast corner of the Shire Highlands (alt. 2,000 feet) near the Mozambique border, and the almost rectangular mass of syenite dominates the landscape around it. The massif has a series of peaks and plateaus, covering about 140 square miles. The outer slopes are steep and precipitous, rising to 6,000 feet, and mark the outer edge of a number of mile-wide, black-soil bench plateaus above them—Linje, Litchenya, Tuchila, and Mlosa.

Wedged in ravines or lining the steep slopes is wild Mulanje cedar, *Widdringtonia whytei,* named after botanist Dr. Whyte, the first European to discover them. These trees are relics of larger forests practically destroyed by burning, but now the whole area is protected as a forest reserve, so the trees are slowly regenerating. The Mulanje cedar is not botanically related to true cedars but resembles them in its softwood features, and has formed the bulk of Malawi timber production for more than 70 years. Also on these lower plateaus giant lobelias and wild flowers grow in profusion.

Above these are some higher plateaus, notably Chambe, at about 8,000 feet. The prominent peaks are *Sapitwa* (the main and highest— 9,847 feet), *Namasile* (8,815 feet), *Manene* (8,695 feet), and *Matambala* (8,667 feet)—all on the southeast flank by the Mozambique border— plus *Chambe* (8,390 feet), a ring whose inner core has been eroded down to form a large circular amphitheater at 6,000 feet.

It is possible to climb Mulanje Mountain from several different angles, approached from the road encircling the mountain. There are no roads up to the plateaus. Porters can be hired locally by applying a week in advance to the Forestry Officer, Box 50, Mulanje; tel. 218. The main starting points are Mulanje township for Lichenya Plateau (a 6-hour hike); Mini-Mini tea estate off M1 for Luchenya Plateau via a different path (also 6 hours); Likhabula, along S40 to Phalombe (6 hours), Chambe Plateau (3 hours) and Sapitwa Peak (no path, more difficult); Likulezi, also along S40 for Thuchila Plateau (4 to 7 hours); and Fort Lister on S43 for Sombani Plateau and Madzeka Basin (3 to 6 hours); there are also ways up from the Rhuchila and Malosa drifts.

The Department of Forestry and Game has huts on Lichenya, Chambe, Thuchila, Sombani, and Madzeka plateaus. They may be used by the public for 25t per person per night, and should be booked in advance with the Forestry Officer. The huts are sparsely furnished (no beds), have stoves or open firepits, wood, and water. The Mulanje Mountain Club has its own equipment locked up at each hut, and if you join one of their climbs or go with a member you can use their facilities. Inquiries: Secretary, Mulanje Mountain Club, Box 240, Blantyre.

The best time to climb Mulanje Mountain is after the rains, from mid-April to the end of September. Don't be surprised if there is frost at night, and beware of misty *chiperones,* during which climbing is risky.

Km 1144: *Malosa* and the border with Mozambique. The Mozambique border post is at Milanje, Km 1150.

Route Q-2: Blantyre–Lengwe National Park–Chiromo–Thyolo

This route goes south from the center of Blantyre down the Shire Highlands escarpment, across the Shire River, past Lengwe Park to Chiromo, then north to Thyolo. The whole road, excluding the first 16 km, is 1½ - to 2-lane dirt of varying quality.

Begin at Delamere House on Victoria Avenue and take Victoria 1 km to Chikwawa Road, then turn (R). Km 17–38: The road twists and winds down the wooded *escarpment* of the Shire Highlands, following in parts the original route taken to Lake Malawi by Dr. Livingstone.

This is the oldest roadway in Malawi, some sections dating from 1878. About Km 35 there are wide vistas of the Shire River snaking through the valley below, while to the far west the Kirk Range lines the horizon. At the junction at Km 38 to the left on S38 is Chiromo 103 km, to the right Chikwawa; turn (R).

Km 44: *Kamuzu Bridge* over the Shire River. Livingstone camped nearby in 1861 at Chief Chibisa's Village, which was also the site of the Universities Mission to Central Africa *mission of 1862–63,* now a national monument, with the graves of two missionaries, Dickinson and Scudamore.

Km 46: Turnoff (R) to Kapachira Falls 21 km. To visit them, go through the small town of Chikwawa and at its far side go left onto a signposted road leading to the cataracts. On the way, 16 km from town, is a fork to the right, which goes to the *grave of Richard Thornton,* a young geologist with Livingstone's Zambezi expedition who died of malaria in 1863; now a national monument, the grave is marked by a marble cross and an old baobab tree. Back on the road to the falls, go about 3 km farther—on the left is the gate to *Majete Game Reserve,* 70 square miles, with some elephants, elands, sables, kudus, waterbucks, klipspringers, bushbucks, common duikers, possibly lions, and leopards; not yet open to the public. On the right, the road to the falls goes into a parking area and a short walk takes you to a choice of viewpoints of *Kapachira or Livingstone Falls.* This is the southernmost cataract of the 50-mile-long series of Murchison Rapids, the beginning of the barrier that prevented Livingstone and others from navigating wholly by boat from the Indian Ocean to Lake Malawi.

Lengwe National Park

Back on the main road, at Km 68 is the turnoff (R) to *Lengwe National Park* 1 km, only 50 square miles but the place to go to be guaranteed of seeing the rare nyala antelope. The park is open from May 1 to December 31, and game viewing is best September–November. Lengwe was first declared a game reserve in 1928 to preserve the nyala, today found only in patches in Malawi and Mozambique and few other places. Then as now Lengwe was covered with open forest and large, dense thickets, and into these the nyala retreated when poaching was on the rise from 1939 on. A water borehole was drilled in 1964, and two years later there were enough nyala to open the park, with its 40 miles of roads, to the public. Lengwe was gazetted a national park in 1971.

The *nyala* is a striped antelope related to the kudu, sitatunga, and bushbuck. The male and female are so different that they almost look like different species. The male stands 42 inches at the shoulder and weighs up to 300 pounds. He has a dark gray body with faint vertical white stripes, long dark hair on the neck and underside, and a generally shaggy appearance. Only the males have lyre-shaped horns up to 32 inches long. In contrast the female is 36 inches at the shoulder, weighs only half as much as the male, has a very slender build, is light orange-tan in color, and has 11 to 13 conspicuous vertical white stripes. Nyalas feed from late afternoon to early morning, but do not shun the daylight. They can be seen and photographed on the circular drive at the edge of the thicket and at the four watering points (natural pans filled with water pumped from boreholes). Near the game camp is a hide overlooking a waterhole. A game guard will accompany you on a drive and escort you to the hide. Along with the 500 resident nyalas, there are some 50 buffalos, plus kudus, bushbucks, impalas, Livingstone's sunis (a tiny antelope standing 14–15 inches at the shoulder), Lichtenstein's hartebeests, Sharpe's grysboks, duikers, bushpigs, warthogs, baboons, blue samangos and vervet monkeys.

Getting There, Getting Around

The only way to see Lengwe Park is in a car—your own, a rented one, or as part of a tour. UTC in Blantyre has a one-day tour; see MP-10. For day visitors there are picnic tables and toilet facilities.

Accommodations

Lengwe Game Camp, bookings to UTC, Box 176, Blantyre; tel. 30122. Camp is 1 km inside the park entrance. It has 8 twin beds in 2 screened-in duplexes; separate toilet block. You bring your own food; the staff cooks it. Drinking water is slightly saline. Rates: adult— K2; child—K1.

Back on the road, at Km 81 is the turnoff (L) to *Sucoma Sugar Estate* in Nchalo 1 km, operated by the Sugar Corporation of Malawi in conjunction with the Malawi government. The estate opened in 1965 and covers 11,720 acres along the Shire River. Because the U.S. granted Malawi a sugar quota of 15,000 tons yearly starting in 1973, Sucoma will expand production to 60,000 tons to meet the demand, giving employment to 4,000 Malawians.

Km 120: To the west side of the road is *Mwabvi Game Reserve,* 60 square miles partly on the Rift Valley scarp and partly on the

Shire River plain. Established for protection of the nyala, the park also has rhinos, buffalos, impalas, and kudus; it is not open to the public.

Km 144: *Chiromo* is at the lower end of the 160-square-mile Elephant Marsh, at the confluence of the Ruo and Shire rivers. Chiromo was the experimental ground for the *Young Pioneers* Settlement Scheme. After independence Dr. Banda wanted to train the country's youth to become a disciplined corps of leaders in agricultural progress. Using Israeli rural development experts, intensive agricultural and general training started in 1964 at organized camps, which by 1971 numbered 20, most camps having 75–125 males, three southern camps also having 30 girls each. A youth can choose to return to his village to serve as a leader or can join a settlement scheme. The first settlement scheme was in 1966 at Chikonje Estate on the Ruo River near Chiromo. Here 2,000 acres of land, most of it still virgin bush and forest, were cleared for cotton by the 22 Young Pioneers, who were then provided with a plot of land and agricultural credit in cash and material. The Chikonje project proved a success, and by 1971 there were 15 settlement schemes growing cotton, tobacco, and irrigated rice all over Malawi. These cash crops bring the young farmers a yearly income of about K120, equal to that of an average Malawi urban worker. Inquire at the tourist office in Blantyre about visiting a Young Pioneer scheme.

Km 156: Turnoff (L) to Chikwawa 87 km. The turnoff (R) to Thyolo is reached at Km 228; here pick up our Route Q-1.

Route Q-3: Liwonde Barrage–Mangochi–Monkey Bay–Salima

This is the main southern Lake Malawi route, taking in the resort hotels along its shore. It begins at Liwonde Barrage, 50 km north of Zomba on the main paved highway. At Km 4, going north, is a junction: M1 continues north to Lilongwe, M3 turns right to the lake; go right. Km 24: Turnoff (L) on S55 to Balaka 28 km. The road to and along the lake, when completely paved, will be known as the Lakeshore Road, and should be a pleasant drive, although in few places will it actually be lakeside.

On your way to the Southern Lakeshore you pass villages with handmade straw things for sale (see "Shopping") and Yao people dressed in Moslem caps and white gowns known as *mikhanjo*. Km 27: Ulongwe.

Km 30: *Lake Malombe,* to the east, is a shallow body of water 18 miles long, 9 miles wide. It is filled by the Shire River from the outflow of Lake Malawi and once was part of that lake. Along Lake Malombe's shore are small fishing villages, which have roadside drying racks of small fish called *utaka* for sale. Just before the Mangochi turnoff, the road becomes paved and tall fan palm trees come into view.

Lake Malawi

Lake Malawi is one of the truly beautiful lakes in the world, and is Malawi's greatest attraction. Africa's third and the world's twelfth largest lake, it stretches as part of the Great Rift Valley chain of lakes 360 miles in length by 10 to 50 miles in width, or 8,900 square miles in area. The depth ranges from gently sloping shore lines at Monkey Bay, to 120 to 300 feet on either side of Cape Maclear, to an awesome 2,300 feet (750 feet below sea level) between Nkhata Bay and Chilumba in the far north. The eastern shore line forms the borders with Tanzania and Mozambique, and although Likoma and Chisumulu islands are much closer to the Mozambique shore, they are part of Malawi. Tanzanian and other maps may call it Lake Nyasa.

There are numerous rivers draining into the lake, but the only river outlet is the Shire, which first drains the lake's waters into Lake Chilwa, then flows 250 miles south to join the Zambezi on its way to the Indian Ocean. Lake Malawi has no tides or currents, but fluctuates seasonally between 3 and 4 feet. Occasional high southeast winds, called *mwera,* cause 6-foot waves on the lake, making boating dangerous and swimming risky in the pounding surf. But when the water is gentle, especially March to May, the lake is perfect for swimming, water skiing, boating, fishing, and other sports. Bilharziasis, the scourge of most African lakes, is, according to the Malawi Department of Tourism, absent from the resort areas around Mangochi, Monkey Bay, Salima, and Nkhata Bay.

Recorded history of the lake begins with the Portuguese; a trader on the Zambezi, Gaspar Bocarro, in 1616 reported seeing "a lake which looks like the sea" when he passed the present Mangochi area on his way to the Indian Ocean. The man to bring it into the spotlight, though, was David Livingstone, who in 1859 came up the Shire River and saw the lake twice from a distance. The third time Livingstone saw the lake in more detail, bringing a small sailboat with his party; for three hot months, September to November 1861, the men sailed around the lake enduring storms and fevers, taking soundings along the western shore, bereaving the Ngoni raiders' human destruction and Arabs' slave trading, and going just north of Nkhata Bay, where they thought the lake ended. The sad human sights along the shore made Livingstone exclaim, "O, when will Christ's Holy Gospel enter into this dark region!" However, on his final trip to the lake in 1866: "It was as if I had come back to an old home I never expected again to see; and pleasant to bathe in the delicious waters, again, hear the roar of the sea, and dash in the rollers."

This was the last time he saw the lake before his death in 1873, but on October 17, 1875, a boat (named the *Ilala* after the district where Livingstone died in Zambia) full of missionaries and settlers steamed onto the lake to fulfill the doctor's dreams to bring Christianity and legitimate trade to the lake. They started the Livingstonia Mission and circumnavigated the lake, naming the bays and mountains after relatives and friends.

Trade links were initiated in 1878 by the African Lakes Company, which opened a post at Karonga, chartered the *Ilala,* and steamed back and forth between the south and north ends of the lake. The company was dragged into a private war with the slaver Mlozi in Karonga in 1887, which the Protectorate administration inherited and won in 1895. The only battle to take place on the lake water itself, though, was in fact the first naval engagement of World War I. The Hotchkiss gun used by the H.M.S. *Gwendolen* in this swift battle, won by the British, is on display in Mangochi.

Boats used today on Lake Malawi include the ancient dugout canoes, graceful dhows, and practical cargo-passenger ships, the *Ilala II, Chauncy Maples,* and *Nkhwazi.* The dugout canoe, called *bwato,* is the principal transportation used by fishermen. The canoe is made in the forest from a tall, mature tree, using an ax and adze to hollow out the 12- to 25-foot-long log. The canoe, when completed, can roll almost 90 degrees over without taking water, and will last for several years. Early in the morning and evening a fishing fleet of dugouts may glide out from shore to haul in with nets large quantities of the small *utaka* fish, which are gutted and laid out to dry on racks. There are some 240 different species of fish in the lake, many unique to Lake Malawi.

Dhows, or *ngalawa,* are the other long-used boats, dating on the lake from the early 19th century, when the Arabs introduced them to transport first ivory and then slaves from Nkhotakota and Karonga to Losefa on the east shore, from where the captives were marched to the sea. Today dhows carry fare-paying passengers and cargo, particularly from Leopard Bay near Salima to Fort Maguire and Makanjila on the Malawi east shore, with occasional stops at Likoma Island.

Besides getting infrequent rides in dugouts and dhows, as a tourist you can have regular accommodations on the *Ilala*, which offers the best way of seeing the length of the lake and its Malawi ports. Pleasure boats are also on the lake, and are easily rented by the hour or day through the lakeshore hotels for kayaking, cruising, water skiing, or fishing.

Mangochi

Km 73: Turnoff (R) 2 km to *Mangochi* (formerly Fort Johnston), located on the west bank of the Shire River, about 5 miles from the southern tip of Lake Malawi. It was and is mainly inhabited by the Yao people. In 1891, the same year the Protectorate was declared, Fort Johnston was established nearly opposite Chief Mponda's village, an important Yao slave-trading post on the west bank of the Shire. Old Fort Johnston was considered one of the most unhealthful stations in the country, so in 1896 the present site on the west side of the Shire was chosen. Building started in 1897, and the new Fort Johnston was declared a township in 1899.

Following the death of Queen Victoria, the Town Council decided to erect a suitable memorial, which in 1903 took the form of the *clock tower,* standing at the end of the town's main street by the landing for the Shire ferry service. By the tower is a *memorial tablet* to those who died when the *Vipya* sank near Chitimba Bay in 1946. Here also is the *Hotchkiss gun,* used on August 13, 1914, in the lake's only naval battle, when the British gunboat *Gwendolen* captured the German gunboat *Hermann von Wissman*. When the war started, the British found there was no ammunition for the gun and no one knew how to operate it. A diligent search, though, turned up some ammunition in a government shed on the Fort Johnston wharfs, also a salesman named Jock in the Fort's African Lakes Corporation store who just happened to know something about such guns. Jock and the Hotchkiss were put to use, and following the quickly won bloodless battle, the London *Times* carried a headline reading "Naval Victory on Lake Nyasa."

Another attraction in town is the *Lake Malawi Museum,* worth a visit for anyone coming through Mangochi. To get there, turn right at the post office. The museum opened in April 1971; it is open daily 9 A.M.–5 P.M.; admission: adults—10t; children—5t. Exhibits include the compound steam engine with propeller from the steamer *Chauncy*

Maples (removed when the boat was converted to diesel in 1968); some Later Stone Age artifacts and Iron Age pottery; pictures and descriptions of all the important Lake Malawi boats and steamers; the steering wheel, compass, and engine-room signal from the *Gwendolen;* and a good display of traditional fishing methods on the lake.

Km 93: Turnoff (R) for *Nkopola Campsite* 2 km, Box 23, Mangochi. Camp has 10 simple, screened-in chalets, outdoor toilet blocks, space for camping, all on lakeshore. Day visitors—50t; campers—50t.

Nkopola Lodge

Km 95: Turnoff (R) 1 km. to *Nkopola Lodge,* Box 284, Blantyre, tel. 2191; cable OVEROTEL. 18 dbl rms, 8 dbl chalets, all/bath. Rates: FB: sgl—K7; dbl—K11. Credit: DC. Chalets, if self-catering—K10 for 2 adults, 2 children. Nkopola Lodge, built with government money and managed by Hallway Overseas, was opened March 1970, and is one of the sleekest lakeshore hotels. Rooms are in concrete blocks picturesquely scattered among boulders and ledges over the lake. Chalets, with small kitchen attached, are good for families. Main building has outdoor veranda, indoor lounge and dining rooms, and the table d'hôte menu is Frenchified: breakfast—K1; lunch—K1.60; tea— 40t; dinner—K1.80. Facilities: excellent beach, diving raft, marina, badminton, putting, donkey cart rides. Rentals per hour: rowboat— K1; minisailboat—K1.50; kayak/canoe—75t; fishing rods—25t; sailboat—K2; flippers and snorkel—25t. Rating: 1st-class international, one of the top two hotels on the lake. We'll give it a ★.

Situated between Nkopola Lodge and Club Makokola is the *Mpwepwe Fisheries Training Institute,* a joint venture of the Malawi, British, and Danish governments assisted by the U.N. Development Program.

Club Makokola

Km 96: Turnoff (R) 2 km to *Club Makokola,* Box 59, Mangochi, tel. 28; or Box 447, Blantyre, tel. 2268; cable CLUBMAK. 25 dbl rondavels incl 1 suite, all w/bath, a-c. Rates: FB: sgl—K10; dbl—K16. Credit: DC. Named after the chief of a nearby fishing village, Club Makokola is a modern, privately owned hotel that opened June 1970. Brightly furnished rondavels have locally woven straw rugs and baskets. Central building includes outdoor and indoor bars, and airy dining room, all overlooking large lawn and lakeshore. Club has own vegetable garden and serves à la carte (e.g., grilled lake *chambo,* "monkey gland" steak, each K1–2) and table d'hôte (breakfast—K1; lunch—K1.50; tea—25t; dinner—K2). Facilities: wide beach with bar, 3 tennis courts, 9-hole golf course, croquet, badminton. Boat hire per hour: sailing—K1.25; fishing—K1.25; small speed—K8; large speed—K10; 10 minutes of water skiing—K1.50. Boat trips to bird-populated Boadzulu Island. Also fishing and snorkeling equipment. Rating: 2d-class international, very well planned. Definitely deserves ★.

Km 118: Turnoff to *Nkhudzi Bay* 2 km, where Later Stone Age flakes, Early Iron Age "Muwudzu ware," and a Later Iron Age cemetery have been found. The Muwudzu ware dates from A.D. 1100 to 1500, and it is thought that it was done by new immigrants. Associated with it are trade beads, iron and copper, and some worked ivory.

Monkey Bay

Km 125: Turnoff to Monkey Bay 12 km and Cape Maclear 23 km. *Monkey Bay* is a sheltered, deep-water port, with holiday cottages, a hotel, and the floating dock operations of the Malawi Railways for the *Ilala II*, the *Chauncy Maples* (see p. 635), and the *Nkhwazi*, a 295-ton general cargo boat built in 1955. Also on Monkey Bay is the *Monkey Bay Fisheries Research Unit*, a small government-sponsored group of experts studying and classifying the lake's more than 240 varieties of fish. **Accommodations:** *Monkey Bay Hotel*, Box 30, Monkey Bay; tel. 15; cable MOTEL. 11 dbls, 4 trpls in rooms and chalets; 4 rms w/bath. Rates: B&B: sgl w/bath—K4.50; dbl w/bath—K7.50. A private home in the 1940s, later the Marina Beach Hotel, the homey and cheerful Monkey Bay Hotel has bar-lounge with an exotic lake-fish aquarium, local weapons and masks, stuffed animals. Dining room features à la carte lake fish: *chambo* à la Portuguese—90t. Facilities: gently sloping beach, diving raft, badminton, tennis. Boat rental per hour: sail—55t; motor—K2; kayak—55t. Rating: 1st-class local, and for its geniality we give it ★. . . . **Camping** is allowed on the hotel grounds for 50t with use of most facilities.

Cape Maclear

Cape Maclear is a hilly promontory thrusting itself north in the southern end of the lake. At the M15 junction, go north toward Monkey Bay for 6 km, turn left at signposted dirt road, follow up and down for 19 km to the Cape. Cape Maclear was so named by Livingstone, in his 1861 explorations of the lake by boat, after his "excellent friend Sir Thomas Maclear the Astronomer Royal at the Cape of Good Hope." The oldest relic of interest on the Cape is *Mwalawamphini,* a large boulder which is a national monument. The rock is signposted at Km 13 along the twisty, hilly road, and a 100-yard walk will take you to it. The boulder is 25 feet high, 30 feet wide, with an interesting series of vertical diagonal grooves on its face. It was formed millions of years ago, first by granite and then by aplite pushing up in a molten state, cooling, solidifying, and contracting along intersection shrinkage cracks. A boulder of this material rolled down the hill and half of it fell away, leaving the aplite dike showing; further weathering enlarged the shrinkage cracks, making the rock look carved. The rock is called Mwalawamphini by the local people, and means "rock of tribal marks" because its markings are similar to tribal marks once cut on people's bodies.

The oldest recorded dwellers of Cape Maclear are the Nyanja, noted in the Livingstone brothers' (David and Charles) journals in 1861. The Nyanja were probably responsible for legends around *Nkhunguni Hill,* which rises behind *Otter Point* (the jut of land on the west side of the Cape), and which was thought to be the habitat of spirits, who were approached when rain was wanted.

After Livingstone's death in 1873, the United Free Church of Scotland and the Church of Scotland sent a mission party to establish a mission called Livingstonia and carry on the doctor's dreams of defeating the slave trade and civilizing the interior. In the *Ilala,* the lake's first motorized boat, the mission party steamed onto the waters, stopping at Mponda's village for settlement permission, then arriving at Cape Maclear on October 17, 1875. Sixteen buildings, including the first two-story house in Malawi, were erected lying along the slight ridge about 100 yards from the shore and parallel to it. The mission party worked at Cape Maclear (the first school in the country was here) until moving to Bandawe in 1881 and to the final site of Livingstonia in 1894. The *remains of the mission buildings* and the small *graveyard* along with Otter Point are national monuments. The old mission site is to the right at Km 18, then a short walk to the beach.

During the 20th century Cape Maclear was briefly the location of a luxury hotel and the landing spot for a BOAC/South African Airways flying boat service; both hotel and flying service failed from lack of business. Now you can spend some pleasant, restful days on the clear Cape, enjoying the sunsets from one of the few places on the western shore where they can be seen. Nearby is *Chambe village,* known for its Gule Wamkulu dancers. If you're lucky, you might catch a glimpse of one of the 10 to 20 leopards in the area. **Accommodations:** *Golden Sands Holiday Camp,* Box 393, Blantyre, tel. 2254. At the end of road S39, Km 19 from the turnoff by Monkey Bay. 32 unfurnished rooms; beds and mattresses for hire; all share ablution block. Rates: rms—K1; bed and mattress—50t more, plus K1 daily for use of facilities. Day visitors, adults—25t; child—15t. Barbecue pits by beach, bar, boat and swimming equipment rental, nice beach. . . . **Camping** costs K1 for adult, 50t for 13–17-year-olds.

Back on the Lakeshore Road, at Km 150 is the turnoff to *Ntakataka,* near which on the north bank of the Nadzipulu River is a small thicket known as *"Malawi,"* the main rain shrine of the Karonga, a subgroup of the original Malawi or Maravi people.

Km 175: Turnoff (R) to *Chipoka* 1 km, the harbor used by Malawi Railways to connect the rail line with the boat service. Cargo and passengers transfer here to ride the *Ilala* or *Chauncy Maples* around the lake, or reversely to catch the train south to Blantyre.

Salima

Km 202: Junction: (L) to Lilongwe 105 km on M5; (R) to Salima and lakeshore; turn right. Km 203: Turnoff (L) to *Salima* 1 km, district town and the northernmost railway terminus in Malawi.

Km 218: Turnoff (R) to *Fish Eagle Inn* 8 km. The turnoff earlier at Km 205 is not recommended—it is deeply rutted. Box 16, Salima; tel. 01312; cable FISHIN. 29 rms incl 4 suites in block, chalets, or rondavels; about half w/bath. Rates: FB: sgl—K6.25; dbl—K11.50. Credit: DC. Inn started as a rest house-fishing lodge 45 years ago. The simple buildings spreading over a wide bluff include a thatch-roofed bar and large table d'hôte dining room: breakfast—95t; lunch—K1.35; dinner—K1.50. Nice long beach. Boat rental, per hour: canoe—50t; rowboat—75t; motor—K5. Rating: 2d-class local, pleasant enough, but there are better places to stay.

Km 222: Turnoff (R) to *ivory carver,* an old gentleman working in his hut up the road ½ km on the right; and to *Senga Bay* 2 km, headquarters of an important agricultural project in the Salima district, the $6.6-million German-aided Lakeshore Development Project. Started in 1968, the 1,500-square-mile project's purpose is to increase the lakeshore farmers' income by teaching them modern techniques, especially crop rotation and use of fertilizers, for growing the cash crops of cotton, rice, maize, groundnuts, and tobacco.

Km 224: *Grand Beach Hotel,* Box 11, Salima, tel. 03421; cable TOURVEST, Blantyre. 13 sgls, 17 dbls, 13 trpls in chalet blocks, beach apartments, and rondavels; about half w/bath. Rates: FB: sgl—K5.75 to K7; dbl—K10.50 to K12. Credit: DC. Built in 1920 with apartments added in 1967, the hotel is a favorite of Europeans in Zambia. The best rooms are the newish beach apartments. Main building has bar, billiard room, patio, lounge, table d'hôte dining room: breakfast—K1.25; lunch—K1.75; dinner—K2.25. Facilities: grand beach (with high surf when windy), mini-golf course, badminton. Boats per hour: sail—K1; dabchick (flat, 1-man sail)—K1; motor—K1.50. Rating: 1st-class local, with lots of happy bustle, good for families. . . . **Camping** is above the beach, with running water, ablution block, shade trees. Fee: 50t per person, pay at hotel desk. Be careful of getting stuck in the sand when you park.

Route Q-4: Salima–Nkhotakota

This is the middle extension of what in time will be the long Lakeshore Road going from Mangochi in the south to Karonga in the north. This section is not often traveled by tourists because Nkhotakota is not a major lake destination unless you happen to be riding the *Ilala,* in which case it's a port of call.

The route starts at the turnoff into Salima, and at Km 1 is the turnoff (L) to the Lakeshore Road going south to Monkey Bay 89 km. Km 21: Junction: M5 continues straight to Lilongwe 81 km; this route turns right and until eventually paved the road is dirt. Km 58: Chirua Bridge, which is liable to flooding. Km 79: Lipsyozi Bridge, and Km 82: Nazikoko Bridge—both for light traffic only, owing to possible washaways. Km 105: Chia Ferry, which operates 6 A.M.–6 P.M. daily. By 1975 there will be a 14-foot, 2-span bridge replacing the ferry. Km 105: Junction: M10 goes west (L) to Kasungu 122 km; the Lakeshore Road continues north to Nkhata Bay; M10 goes east (R) into Nkhotakota 1 km; turn right.

Nkhotakota

Km 131: *Nkhotakota,* much of whose history was wrapped up in the slave trade, since it was the principal port on the west side of the lake, controlled for years by Jumbe ("chief"), a coast Arab who

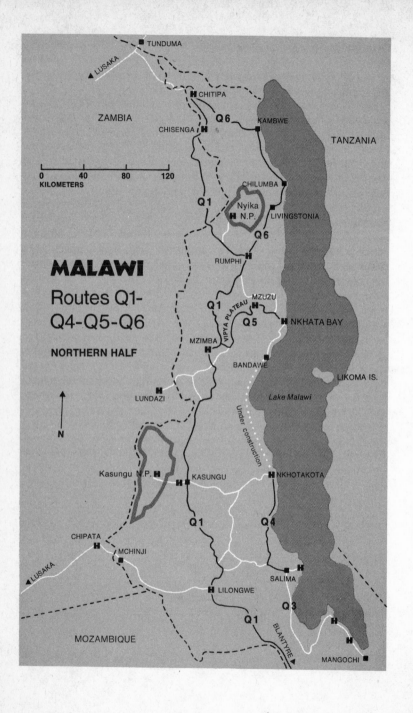

represented the Sultan of Zanzibar. Thousands of captives were shipped in dhows from Nkhotakota to Losefa on the east shore, from there brutally marched to the seacoast, and those that survived were sold on the slave block on Zanzibar. Livingstone called twice at Nkhotakota, the second time coming by foot over the Kirk Range in 1863. Reputedly on this visit he sat under a "magnificent *wild fig tree*" in town (two signposted trees compete for this distinction now), while grimly watching the slaves being herded into stockades, and while waiting, ironically, for the hospitality of Jumbe, the slaver. Jumbe's slaving ceased only when Commissioner Johnston bought the, by then, old man's allegiance around 1889 with a guaranteed yearly subsidy of £300. Jumbe is supposedly buried near the *mosque,* which has carved Arab doors dating from about 1750. Like Mangochi, Nkhotakota has many Yao Moslems. Another historic spot is the *UMCA Mission Church,* finished in 1902. In its chancel is the grave of Bishop Chauncy Maples, who drowned in September 1895 on his way to Likoma Island in the mission's boat *Sheriff.* The town market area is lined with kapok trees, some planted by Arabs and dating to 1895. The central *Freedom Square* is where Dr. Banda held his first major political rally after his release from Gwelo Prison (Rhodesia) in 1960. Ask in town for directions to the handicraft sellers, the ivory carver, and the hot springs. The long beach, dotted with dugout canoes, is where much of the action is when the *Ilala* and *Chauncy Maples* call.

Accommodations

Government Rest House, P.O. Nkhotakota, tel. 1. By the airfield. 4 beds, indoor dining room. Rates: see p. 626. . . . *District Council Rest House,* on the beach near the dock. Ionesco's *Bald Soprano* line "C'est curieux, c'est bizarre" aptly sums up this place, for it incorporates parts of giant machines, car radiators, cogwheels, etc., painted a gray-silver. And it was built by jailed tax evaders. It has several stark singles, doubles, and dorm rooms, and also features a bar sculpted from concrete—but no bartender, glasses, or bottles—just the bar. Rates: 75t for bed and bedding in dorm-style room; dbl—K1.50 each; "special" dbl—K2 each. . . . **Camping** on the grounds, 50t each; K1.50 each to have food cooked and camp. . . . Just up the beach is another, similarly kitschy but smaller rest house, constructed in 1968–69, officially opened by President Banda, but now condemned. . . . **Camping** outside this one is free, and a caretaker will allow you use of the indoor toilet.

Route Q-5: Mzimba–Vipya Plateau–Mzuzu–Nkhata Bay

This route goes from the small town of Mzimba in northern Malawi up and through the lovely highland Vipya Plateau and down to the medium-sized town of Mzuzu via a wide one-lane dirt road with some very steep stretches. From Mzuzu there is an unexpected one-lane paved strip road for 14 km and then more dirt to picturesque Nkhata Bay on Lake Malawi.

As you leave Mzimba and go north on M1, at Km 13 is a junction: M1 (1) continues north to Rumphi 143 km (our Route Q-1); M12 (R) goes northeast to Mzuzu; turn right.

Vipya Plateau

Km 35–85: The *Vipya Plateau* is the lovely high region (5,000 to 6,000 feet altitude) you drive up, across, and down between Mzimba and Mzuzu. Spread over the grassy plains are lush forest plantations, the main one being the Vipya Pulpwood Scheme. It now has 52,000 acres of pine and 4,000 acres of eucalyptus; planting is expanding by 15,000 acres per year until 1978. That will be sufficient for a pulp mill to produce an annual 180,000 tons of pulp and paper products. Near *Chikangawa,* Km 35, a few well-preserved iron smelting furnaces from the Iron Age were found. At Km 53 you pass several rocky outcrops or inselbergs, the largest called *Elephant Rock,* which can be approached via a signposted path on the right.

Km 106: Turnoff (L) to Mzuzu Airport 1 km and to *Ekwendeni* 23 km, site of the large Central African Presbyterian Church (CCAP) Mission, built in the 1880s and now a national monument. This road also goes to Rumphi 70 km.

Mzuzu

Km 107: *Mzuzu* (pop. 8,500) owes its origin to the high price of tung oil at the end of World War II. Tung oil is a pale, yellow, pungent drying oil from the seeds of tung trees, used in quick-drying varnishes and paints, and as a waterproofing agent. In the mid-1940s Charles Boardman, the Nyasaland tung development officer, searched for land at 3,000–5,000 feet altitude, enough to plant 20,000 acres of tung trees. Investigating the Northern Region, he came upon a place where the old, disused Timbiri mission track (which had provided the link between Ekwendeni and Nkhata Bay) crossed a stream—here

Mzuzu was founded in 1947. The price of tung oil has fluctuated greatly since then, mostly downward, being dependent upon the competitive quantity of oil marketed by China and Argentina. Mzuzu is the headquarters for the Northern Region, and is an attractive, tree-lined town with most facilities. **Accommodations:** *Government Rest House,* Box 10, Mzuzu; tel. 391. On Laws Ave. off M12 going toward Nkhata Bay. 19 beds. Rates: see p. 626.

Km 107–149: This is an extensive, irrigated, tea-growing district, with Chombe Tea Estate the largest development. The Smallholders' Tea Authority has about 80 acres owned by small farmers. A Young Pioneer settlement called Limpasa has planted irrigated rice in the Limpasa Dambo. At Km 136 is a turnoff (L) to Chikwina 20 km, an alternate dirt road through the hills.

Km 149: Turnoff (R) to Chinteche 40 km, and Bandawe 50 km. On the dirt road down (to become part of the long Lakeshore Road), you drive through rubber plantations and dense rain forests before reaching *Chinteche,* ancient canoe-crossing point, and in ᐧ1878 the battlefield of the Tonga and Ngoni. The Tonga repulsed the Ngoni invaders, and now are spread over about 50 miles of this coastline. *New Bandawe* (Thipula) has a CCAP mission established in the 1920s, while Bandawe Point or *Old Bandawe* (Makuzi) was the second site of the CCAP Livingstonia Mission, between Cape Maclear in 1881 and Livingstonia in 1894. The original *church* still stands, and nearby is the cemetery containing whole missionary families struck down by malaria, and British soldiers killed in World War I. The Lakeshore Road continues south to Nkhotakota and Salima. Across from Bandawe Point is *Likoma Island,* a small, rocky, barren piece of land 4 miles by 2 miles, off the Mozambique side of Lake Malawi. The Universities Mission to Central Africa (UMCA) established a mission in 1885, but when the east shore came under Portuguese rule, the mission became secluded from events on the western mainland. Nevertheless, an extraordinary 320-foot-long *cathedral* was built in 1902 out of local stone, with a carved soapstone choir and chancel, covering 37,000 square feet on the tiny island. **Accommodations:** *Government Rest House,* Box 1, Nkhata Bay; tel. 7. 4 beds. On the beach near the cathedral. Rates: see p. 626.

Nkhata Bay

Back on the road, at Km 153 *Nkhata Bay* is reached. This is a peaceful, pretty lake port—small fishing boats bob in the sparkling blue harbor, people gather at the local market and play soccer on Sundays, children romp on the golden sand at nearby Chikale Beach. Looking at this idyllic setting it is hard to imagine that it was the scene of much bloodshed, both in Livingstone's time and again as recently as 1959. When Livingstone and his party visited in 1861, the area was like an inferno, with decaying corpses, shriveled crops, and burned-out villages, destruction caused by Ngoni raiders. Nkhata Bay was the farthest land point on the lake that Livingstone journeyed to, and to his death he believed that the lake was 100 miles shorter than it actually is.

Nkhata Bay was the scene of a riot in 1959. Then it was a stronghold of the African Congress (the pre-independence party opposed to federation with the Rhodesias), whose annual general meeting was held here in 1958. On March 3, 1959, in a country-wide coup labeled Operation Sunrise, the colonial government arrested hundreds of Congress members, including Dr. Banda. Nine Congress members were arrested by the Nkhata Bay district commissioner and put on the boat *Mpasa*, guarded by 12 soldiers and a sergeant from the Royal Rhodesia Regiment. When the townspeople found out, they angrily stormed to the wharf and stood their ground for several hours, harassing the soldiers. Finally they advanced beyond the sergeant's patience, and he ordered his men to fire. Minutes later 40 bodies lay sprawled. Seventeen of the 20 dead from this equivalent of the Boston Massacre now lie in the overgrown *cemetery* in town. March 3 is remembered as Martyrs Day, a national holiday.

But today in Nkhata Bay the loudest sounds heard are the toots on the *Ilala*'s whistle as it makes its twice-weekly call. About 2 km from town is *Chikale Beach,* perfect for swimming, boating, and camping. **Accommodations:** *Government Rest House,* Box 1, Nkhata Bay; tel. 7. About ½ km up the steep hill from the village square. 16 beds, screened terrace, and dining room. Rates: see p. 626. . . . **Camping** is really fine on Chikale Beach. No facilities except a pit latrine, but a beautiful, free site. Watch your belongings, though.

Route Q-6: Rumphi–Livingstonia–Karonga–Chitipa–Nyala, Zambia

Scenically this route is superb, especially the first 82 km from Rumphi down the precipitous Livingstonia Escarpment to Lake Malawi. From there the road is paved, as part of the projected Lakeshore Road, north to Karonga. Then our route heads west over hill and dale on twisty, wide, one-lane dirt to Chitipa and the Zambia border.

Beginning in Rumphi and going south on M1, at Km 4 go straight on M11 east toward Livingstonia. Km 4–68: The drive through this area is really gorgeous. The road first parallels the South Rukuru River, then winds up and down through the Nchenachean-Livingstonia Hills. The Nyika Plateau grandly towers to the west, and its streams drop through narrow gorges on their way to Lake Malawi. Km 45: Turnoff (R) on D9 to Chiweta 15 km, Chitimba 30 km (alternative route to lakeshore). At Km 57 is *Muzinga Falls*, where a small rushing stream falls into the North Rukuru River. All along this mountainous region crops of maize and bananas terrace the slopes, and small huts cling to the hillsides.

Livingstonia

Km 68: Turnoff (R) to *Livingstonia*, the Church of Central Africa Presbyterian mission perched on the 4,500-foot Mumbwe Plateau. This was the third and final site of the Free Church of Scotland mission, and was chosen by Dr. Robert Laws in 1894 after the sites at Cape Maclear and Bandawe both proved unhealthful. Most of the original buildings are protected as national monuments. The oldest is the *technical block*, which is still used as part of the technical school; there are also primary and secondary schools. The mission has long been an education center, training many of Malawi's leaders. In the center of the village is the clock tower, built in 1905 as one of the earliest illuminated clocks in Africa. Under the tower was the old *post office*, which now houses the administrative offices of the church. The *stone house*, up the road to the right of the clock tower, was built in 1903, modeled on a Scottish manse with a bay window and long porch, and was Dr. Laws's home for 25 years; the mission's present minister and his family still live in the house. The largest building is the *church*, whose foundation stone was laid in 1916, and which has a large stained glass window depicting David Livingstone with his faithful helpers, Susi and Chuma, all at Livingstonia (where they actually never visited) speaking to a family group whose likenesses were copied from patients at the mission's hospital.

The *David Gordon Memorial Hospital* was built in 1910 with £5,000 given by two sisters in Montrose, Scotland, in memory of their brother. Beyond the hospital, with the 6,600-foot *Mount Nam-*

khowa in the background, is the homestead, which now houses the primary school and food store. Built into the four floors of its tower is flour mill equipment bought for $250 in 1900 in Wisconsin by Dr. Laws. Livingstonia commands some sweeping views. To the west hovers the Nyika Plateau. Below, on the lake's west shore the *Luromo* peninsula juts into the lake, and on Sunday afternoons the *Ilala* approaches *Chilumba Bay,* hidden behind the northern arm of *Mount Chombe* (formerly Mount Waller). On the east shore, to the north, the *Livingstone Mountains,* 10,000 feet high in places, plunge down to the Tanzanian shore. **Camping** is permitted (free) at the small picnic ground near the gasoline pumps. There are no facilities, other than a table and trash basket, but a latrine and a rest house may be built later.

Back on the main road, at Km 71 are *Manchewa Falls* on the north side (L) of the road. A short walk brings you to the edge of one of the two falls—this view is dizzying and dangerous. About 50 yards farther down the path is the fuller view of the first, and to the right second, cataract in which the Chitimba River plunges nearly 1,000 feet before joining Lake Malawi below. Under the falls were found several Later Stone Age and Iron Age rock shelters and caves, and Iron Age pottery was found on the slopes above the falls.

Km 72–82: The *Livingstonia Escarpment* (also called the *Gorode*) is exciting. In 10 km you descend via 20 hairpin bends more than 2,500 feet to the lakeshore below the mission. The road was an early engineering feat, built by the missionaries in order to get from the mission to the lake for supplies brought by boat. It is advisable to have a four-wheel-drive vehicle for this stretch, especially if you are going up it (an alternative route is to turn off at Km 45 and take D9 to Chiweta and then Chilumba). In a long-wheel-base vehicle be prepared to back up to maneuver around about six of the bends. Between times there are good views of Chitimba and Young's bays below. Eventually the new Lakeshore Road will pass around the bottom of Mount Chombe, making the Gorode a strictly local road for the mission, but one hopes it will be maintained for its scenic beauty and historic value.

Km 82: *Chitimba Bay* (formerly Florence Bay) was the scene of a major marine disaster when the diesel steamer *Vipya* sank July 30, 1946. The ill-fated boat, owned by the Nyasaland Railways, had its maiden voyage on June 28, 1946. On its fourth weekly trip around the lake it encountered a fierce squall (part of a lake-long storm), capsized, and sank in a few minutes a few miles from Florence Bay below Livingstonia. Of the 194 passengers and crew, 145 were lost, including the captain. Km 102: Turnoff (R) to Chilumba 3 km.

Km 121: *Carved baobab tree,* on the west side (L) of the road. Inscribed 6 inches high in it about 12 feet from the ground: "No. 49 CNF J. HEIBERG," the regimental number and name of a German soldier thought to have been a reconnaissance scout for the German forces that invaded Karonga from Tanganyika in September 1914. Km 128: Under a large shade tree on the east side (R) of the road is a *straw market;* the workmanship is very good, and if you bargain, so are the prices.

Karonga

Km 160: Turnoff (R) to *Karonga,* district headquarters and an area with a long past. In what are called the *Chiwondo Beds* were discovered the only Lower Pleistocene fossil fauna in Malawi, dating back 2 million years. The fossils show that the lakeshore was once more open than today, supporting elephants, rhinos, giraffes, giant pigs, many bovids, gazelles, three-toed horses, ostriches, large and pygmy hippos, crocodiles, water tortoises, and fish. The University of California excavating team also turned up an Early Stone Age *elephant butchery,* yielding a complete tool kit—choppers, scrapers, and knives—used between 50,000 and 100,000 years ago.

More recently the infamous Arab slave trader Mlozi established a stockade as his headquarters at Karonga, terrorizing the Nkonde villages around him and establishing forts on the British-built Stevenson Road. The African Lakes Company man called for reinforcements from Blantyre to help him deal with Mlozi and his men, and a vicious little war went on for eight years. In 1889 Harry Johnston made a peace treaty with Mlozi which was to be renewed in 1894, but Mlozi rejected the offer and promised big trouble. Johnston speedily commandeered all the British ships on the lake, and the Germans even loaned their *Hermann von Wissman.* By the first week in December 1895, 400 Sikh and African troops marched in darkness toward Mlozi's stockades around Karonga and at daybreak began firing. Three days later Mlozi was captured hiding in his cellar, and was tried the next day by a panel of Nkonde chiefs summoned by Johnston. He was convicted, sentenced to death, and hanged from a tree. Karonga and Lake Malawi were free at last from slavery. *Mlozi's stockade* is about 16 km along the Chendo Track toward Chitipa, and the site is unmarked. The *African Lakes Company stockade,* built in 1887, is in Karonga, but not much is left.

Karonga had Malawi's only World War I land battle, September 9, 1914. In a *cemetery* in Karonga are buried some of the German and British casualties, and nearby is a large *baobab tree* which the British troops fortified and used as an observation and gun post.

About 5 km north of Karonga is *Kambwe,* the *Ilala*'s northernmost port of call. Another 18 km up the coast is *Kaporo,* around which an experimental Taiwanese rice project, started in 1965, proved so successful that the World Bank granted a $9.9-million loan for 1,700 acres of irrigated rice along the northern lakeshore. **Accommodations:** *Government Rest House,* P.O. Karonga, tel. 14. Relatively modern with 12 beds. Rates: see p. 626.

Km 160–255: The *Chendo Track* (formerly the Stevenson Road), partially built by the African Lakes Company in 1883 to link missions and extract trade between Lakes Malawi and Tanganyika, but owing to a money shortage was left unfinished, extending 70 miles west from Karonga. It was completed to Lake Tanganyika after 1898 under Robert Codrington, the BSA administrator in Northeastern Rhodesia.

At *Chitipa,* Km 255, is a junction: M1 south (L) goes to Rumphi 232 km; M1 north (R) goes to the border. Turn right to get to the Malawi border post at Km 256, the Zambia post at Km 266.

ACKNOWLEDGMENTS

This book could not have been written without the assistance of a multitude of people in a variety of places in Eastern Africa and elsewhere over a long period before and after our 16 months of traveling and writing. We cannot thank everybody by name, but we wish to give particular mention to the following:

Tourism authorities: Ethiopian Tourist Organization and Hon. Hapte Selassie Taffesse, Minister of State; Woizerit (Miss) Heriti Woldemariam; Woizero (Mrs.) Elizabeth Yemane Berhan; Ato (Mr.) Girma Bekele; Ms. Ellen Drake; and Mrs. Hazel Relton. Ethiopian Airlines and Ato Abebe Kebede.

Kenya Ministry of Tourism and Wildlife and Miss Ceila Curtis, Mr. Francis Ngenya, Mr. G. N. Macharia, Mr. Samuel S. Ruoro, and Mr. James O. Ochoki. Also Hon. L. O. Kibinge, Ambassador of Kenya in Washington, D.C.

Zambia National Tourist Bureau and Mr. A. K. Mwanamwambwa, Chief Tourist Officer; Mr. Partick McCoy, Mr. Ian Kazembe, Mr. Xen Vlahakis and Mrs. Jeanne Harris.

Tanzania Tourist Corporation and Mr. Lui Sebo. Ministry of Natural Resources and Mr. G. A. Kilipamwambu.

Malawi Department of Tourism and Mr. T. Jake Muwamba, Director of Tourism; and Mr. J. R. Phiri.

Our expedition sponsors: GAF Corporation, New York City, and Messrs. Charles Manley, Jeff Wagner, Jack Sand, James L. Bikoff, and Paul Weiner. Primus-Sievert, North Haven, Conn., and Mr. Arne Erickson, President. Eureka Tent & Awning Co., Inc., Binghamton, N.Y., and Mr. Robert DeMartine, President. Levi Strauss & Co., San Francisco, and Mr. Bud Johns. Cutter Laboratories, Berkeley, Calif., and Mr. R. L. Fay. Telescope Folding Furniture Co., Inc., Granville, N.Y., and Mr. Henry Vanderminden, President, and Mr. Thomas C.

Mahoney. Mobil Oil Kenya Ltd., Nairobi, and Mr. M. J. Queen, Sales Manager.

The following are also to be acknowledged: Mr. Webb Garling-house, Short Hills, N.J.; Mr. Bob Harwell, Fresno, Calif.; Mr. Edward B. Connolly, attorney, New York City; Mr. Patrick Heininger, Washington, D.C.; Mr. and Mrs. David Gerard, Addis Ababa, Ethiopia; Mr. Robert D. Sloane, STAR Service, West Hartford, Conn.; Mr. Stephen Kellogg, Barclays Bank, New York City; Ato Brhane Meskel Zelelew, Axum, Ethiopia; Ato Haddis Weldegiorgsi, Asmara, Ethiopia; Sr. Sontanella, Addis Ababa, Ethiopia; Mr. John Carver, Capital City Development Corp., Lilongwe, Malawi; Mr. P. A. Cole-King, Department of Antiquities, Blantyre, Malawi; Mr. P. M. Berry, Department of Wildlife, Fisheries, and National Parks, Chilanga, Zambia; Mr. D. W. Phillipson, British Institute of East Africa, Nairobi; Mr. and Mrs. Joe Cheffings, Bateleur Safaris, Nairobi; Mr. John Storm Roberts, *Africa Report*, New York City; Mr. Hal Jacob, Granada Hills, Calif.; Mr. Arthur Houghton, Cairo; Mrs. Virginia Roth, Cahill-Laughlin Tours, New York City; Ms. Dorothea F. Watkins, State Department, Washington, D.C.; Mr. Charles Miller, New York City; Mr. and Mrs. Derek Hazelton, Johannesburg; Mr. and Mrs. John Yost, Nairobi; Mr. Harry Andersen, Andersen Tours, Berkeley, Calif.

We owe special debts of gratitude to Mrs. Laura Magary, New York City; Mr. and Mrs. Peter Fraser, Oakland, Calif.; Mr. and Mrs. Erik Fraser, San Francisco, Calif.; Mr. and Mrs. James Fraser, Bloomfield, Conn.; Mr. and Mrs. Richard Mills, Thornwood, N.Y.; Mr. Frank A. Magary, Miami, Fla.; Mr. and Mrs. Peter LePelley and Mr. and Mrs. Howard Crooks, Nairobi.

We thank, generally, all hotel managers and staff who conducted us around, and all people who answered our questions and our letters.

Mrs. Rena Fennessy, Nairobi, contributed the wildlife drawings.

Our editor at Harper & Row, Mr. M. S. Wyeth, Jr., we thank for commissioning this book and giving us the time to finish it. We also thank Ms. Victoria Schochet for her editorial guidance.

Finally, these acknowledgments would not be complete without thanks to our agent, Mr. Max Gartenberg, New York City. He is more responsible for the creation of this book than his modesty would ever admit.

INDEX

A. A. & Bunson Travel, 86–7, 99
aardvark, 237, 526
aardwolf, 257, 526, 602
abbreviations used, xix–xxi
Abercrombie & Kent, 111
Aberdare Country Club, 239
Aberdare Natl. Park, 241–4
Abraha Castle Hotel, 507
Acharya Travel Agency, 100
accommodations (*see also* place
    names; names of accommoda-
    tions), 5
  booking, 86–7, 315, 447
  campsites, *see* Camping and
    campsites
  Ethiopia, 447; low budget, 482,
    520–1, 525, 528, 531
  game and wildlife parks, *see*
    names
  Kenya, 85–7; low budget, 159–60,
    184–5, 219, 351
  low-budget, 49 (*see also* countries
    under accommodations)
  Malawi, 625–6
  rates, 86
  rating systems, xviii–xix, 86
  self-service, *see* Lodgings, self-
    service
  service charges, 74, 86
  Tanzania, 314–15; low budget,
    351
  tipping for services, 74–5
  Zambia, 542–3

Acropol Hotel, 408
Across Africa Safaris, 113
activities, *see* What to see and do;
    subjects
Addis Ababa, 446, 474–7
  accommodations, 480–2
  car rental, 458
  cinemas, 487
  driving tour, 477–80
  getting around, 486
  information sources, 486–7
  libraries, 487
  maps, 448–9
  museums, 487–8
  nightlife, entertainment, 488
  religious services, 488
  restaurants, eating places, 482–6
  shops and services, 469–70, 488
  taxis, 486
  tours, package, and tour opera-
    tors, 459–64
  travel agencies in, 455
Addis Ababa Hilton, 480, 483, 485
Adowa (Adua), 447, 515–16
Adulis Ruins, 447, 525
Adulis Travel, 435, 459
Adventures Unlimited, 16
Africa House Hotel, 362
African
  & Alpine Safaris, 111
  Explorers, 16
  Lakes Corp., 633
  Safari Club, 16, 53

African (*cont'd*)
 Safari Lodges, 87
 Tours & Hotels, 87
 Travel Advisors, 111
Africana Hotel Vacation Village,
 341, 354, 416–17
Africana Tours, 330
Afrique Hotel, 350–1
Afro Tours/Kearline Tours, 330
Agip Motel: Dar es Salaam, 349,
 353; Nairobi, 157
Ahamed Bros., 109–10, 113
Ahamed's Elephant Camp, 237
Air & Marine Travel Service, 54
Air Kenya, 100
air travel, xviii, 51–2
 African Safari Club, 53
 airports, 96–7, 323–4, 453–4,
 548–9
 charters: affinity group, 51; in
 East Africa, 101–2; in
 Ethiopia, 456; illegal, 52;
 inclusive tour (ITCs), 51; in
 Kenya, 101–2; London–
 Nairobi, 52; in Malawi, 634; in
 Tanzania, 327; tour group
 (TGCs), 52; in Zambia, 551–2
 economy, ordinary, 50
 Ethiopia: in, 455–6; to, 452–4
 excursion from: Europe, 52; U.S.,
 50
 group inclusive tours (GITs), 50
 Kenya: in, 100–2; to, 95–7
 jet lag, 58
 Malawi: in, 633–4; to, 630–1
 non-IATA airlines, 50
 Skytrain, 51
 Tanzania: in, 326–7; to, 322–4
 youth and student fares, 51
 Zambia: in, 551–2; to, 547–9
Aircraft Co. of Ethiopia, 456
Airlines Hotel, 351, 354
Airtour & Travel, 633
AITS, Inc., 17
Albergo Italia, 520, 521
Alexander (John) Safaris, 111
Alexander's (John) Karantina
 Tented Camp, 258
Amalgamated Safaris, 562

Ambassadeur Hotel, 153–4, 163
Ambo (Hagere Hiwot), 446
Amboni Sisal Estates, 403
Amboseli
 Natl. Park and Game Reserve, 83
 85, 192, 226–9
 New Lodge, 228
 Safari Camp, 228
 Serena Lodge, 228–9
American Express, 17, 71
American Institute for Foreign
 Study, 17
Andrews Motel, 568
Angling Soc. of Malawi, 644
animals (*see also* Game and wildlife
 parks; species, names), xviii
 import regulations, U.S., 70
 orphanage for, 299
 photography, 66–7, 225, 303
 problems, 39
ant-bear, 237
antelope
 Kenya, 135, 221–2, 232, 242, 257,
 278, 300–1
 Malawi, 625, 654, 657, 667–8
 Tanzania, 394, 409, 414, 425, 431,
 433
 Zambia, 542, 578, 593, 599, 601,
 602, 617
Arba Minch Bekele Molla Hotel,
 535
Archer's Tours, 17, 112, 113
Ark, The, 83, 241, 243–4
Aruba Lodge, 198–9
Arusha
 Gymkhana Club, 385
 Inn, 382
 Natl. Park, 387–90
 tribe, 381
Arusha, city of, 312, 314, 381–2
 accommodations, 382–3
 car rental, 329
 information source, 383
 maps, 316
 restaurants, eating places, 383
 routes to and from, 384–95,
 403–6, 420–8
 shops and services, 383
 taxis, 383

Arusha, city of (*cont'd*)
    tours, package, and tour opera-
        tors, 330–3
Asmara, 446–7, 518–19
    accommodations, 519–21
    car rental, 458
    cinemas, 522
    information source, 522
    map, 449
    museums, 523
    nightlife, 522
    restaurants, eating places, 521–2
    shops and services, 470, 471, 523
    tours, package, and tour opera-
        tors, 460, 464
Assem Wenz Hotel, 516
At-Your-Service (Ethiopian Tourist
        Trading Co.), 459
Austrian Hut, 250
auto club, 107, 329, 459, 554
Automobile Association of East
        Africa, 107
Automobile Club Eritrea, 459
autos, *see* Cars and campers;
        Driving
Avenue Motors Tours & Safaris, 114
Awash Natl. Park, 446, 449, 472,
        525–7
Awassa Bekele Molla Hotel, 535
Axum
    Air Service, 459
    Hotel, 520
    Travel Agency, 460
Axum, city of, 446, 447, 449, 470,
        471, 509–15
A'Zambezi River Lodge, 581

baboon
    Ethiopia, 473, 507, 508, 533
    Kenya, 224, 254, 300, 302
    Malawi, 668
    Tanzania, 364, 375, 379, 388, 425
    Zambia, 593, 599
Bagamoyo, 313, 314, 419–20
Baggage International, 69
Bahar Dar, 446, 449, 490–1
Bahari Beach Hotel, 341, 354, 417
Bale Mountains, 473, 527
Bamburi, 203–4

Bamburi Beach Hotel, 204
banks, 127, 334–5, 468, 557, 640
baobab trees, 191, 222
Barabaig, 422
Barn Motel, 568
Bateleur Safaris, 111
Batoka, 615
Behobeho Lodge, 395
Belle Vue du Lac, 535
Bestway Tours & Safaris, 113
Bet Emanuel, 503
Bet Giorgis, 503
Bet Mariam, 501–2
Bet Maskal, 502
Bet Medhane Alem, 501
bibliography, *see* Books and pub-
        lications
Big Five Tours & Safaris, 113
Bigways Tours & Safaris, 114
Biharamulo Game Reserve, 432–3
binoculars, 55
birds and birdwatching, 8
    Ethiopia, 473, 493, 508, 525, 526,
        531, 532–4
    Kenya, 84, 137–8, 191, 196, 198,
        213, 221–2, 227, 237, 242, 254,
        257, 261, 267, 272, 276–7, 280,
        281, 288, 289, 291, 300, 303,
        305
    Malawi, 643, 655, 657, 661
    Tanzania, 340, 364, 366, 369, 375,
        379, 388, 394, 409, 414, 433
    Zambia, 561, 578, 590, 599, 603,
        619
Blantyre, 625, 644–9
    accommodations, 649–50
    cinemas, 651
    libraries, 652
    restaurants, eating places, 650–1
    routes to and from, 652–69
    shops and services, 641–2, 652
    taxis, 651
Blantyre Rest House, 650
Blixen, Karen (Isak Dinesen), 296
Blue Lagoon, 542, 601
Blue Marlin Hotel, 213
Blue Nile (Abbai), 490
    Gorge, 441, 489–90
    Tissisat Falls, 441, 490, 491

Blue Nile Spring Hotel, 494
Blue Posts Hotel, 237
boat travel, 8
    East Africa, to, 53–4
    Kenya, to, 97
    Malawi, in, 635–6, 672
    Tanzania, to, 324
    Zambia, in, 552, 578; to, 549
bongo, 142, 241, 242, 246
Bonnett, Len, 110, 111
books and publications, 10–11
    on driving, 3–4
    on Ethiopia, 449–50
    on expedition planning, 44–5
    on health, 59
    on Kenya and East Africa, 90–2,
        136
    on Malawi, 628, 629
    on Tanzania, 317–18, 375
    on Zambia, 544–5, 561–2
Boran, 258
Boulevard Hotel, 154
Brendan Tours, 17
British American Club, 52
Bruce Safaris, 111
Brunners Hotel, 158
budget travel (*see also* Camping and
        campsites; Tours, individual;
        subjects), 3–13, 634
    accommodations, 49; Ethiopia,
        482, 520–1, 525, 528, 531;
        Kenya, 59–60, 184–5, 219;
        Tanzania, 351
    documents, 63
    hitchhiking, 48–9
buffalo
    Ethiopia, 531
    Kenya, 222, 224, 227, 232, 237,
        241, 246, 254, 290, 300
    Malawi, 668
    Tanzania, 374, 379, 388, 389, 392,
        395, 414, 425, 433
    Zambia, 593, 599, 601, 602, 617
Buffalo Springs, 255, 256
Buffet de la Gare, 526–7
Bumi Hills Safari Lodge, 616–7
Bunson Travel Service, 99
buses, 48
    Ethiopia, in, 457, 486, 522

buses (*cont'd*)
    Kenya: in, 103–4, 168, 187; to,
        98
    Malawi: in, 635; to, 632
    Tanzania: in, 328; to, 325
    Zambia: in, 533; to, 549–50
bushbuck
    Ethiopia, 526
    Kenya, 241, 246, 290, 300, 301
    Malawi, 654, 667, 668
    Tanzania, 375
    Zambia, 617
Bushmen, 422
bushpig, 578, 617, 668
Bushwhacker's Safari Camp, 191
business hours, 127, 334, 468, 557,
    640
butterflies, 289
Bwacha Rest House, 590

cables, 129, 336
calendar, Ethiopian, 467
cameras and film, 66–7
camping and campsites, 3, 38–9
    animals and insects, 39
    costs, 13, 39–43
    equipment and supplies, 38–9, 44,
        109
    Ethiopia, 447; Awash, 527; Bale,
        527; Lalibela, 505; Rift Valley
        Lakes, 534, 535; Semyen
        Mountains, 507–9
    game and wildlife parks (*see also*
        names), 137, 198–9, 228, 229,
        233
    Kenya, 108–10; Aberdare, 244;
        Amboseli, 228, 229; Bamburi,
        204; Eldoret, 284; English
        Point, 203; Kerio Valley, 291;
        Kibwezi, 191; Kikambala, 206;
        Kisumu, 288; Kitale, 289; Lake
        Baringo, 281; Lake Naivasha,
        274; Lake Nakuru, 278–9; Lake
        Rudolf, 269; Malindi, 214;
        Maralal, 264; Marsabit, 258;
        Masai Mara, 233; Merille
        River, 257; Meru, 263; Molo,
        286; Mombasa, 185; Mt. Elgon,
        290; Mt. Kenya, 250; Mtwapa,

camping and campsites (*cont'd*)
205; Murang'a, 259; Nairobi,
160; Nanyuki, 252; Naro Moru,
245; Nyeri, 240; Saiwa Swamp,
291; Samburu, 256; Shelly
Beach (Timbwana), 221;
Shimba Hills (Tiwi), 222; Tana
River, 237; -Tanzania, self-drive
safari, 39–43; Thego, 245;
Thomson's Falls, 264; Tsavo,
198–9; Watamu, 211
Malawi: Blantyre, 650; Lake
Malawi area, 673, 674, 676,
677, 682, 684; Nkhotakota, 679;
Nyika, 655; Zomba Plateau,
663
safaris, *see* Safaris
Tanzania: Arusha, 382–3, 390;
Dar es Salaam, 351–2, 418;
Iringa, 425; -Kenya, self-drive
safari, 39–43; Kilimanjaro, 403;
Korogwe, 393; Lake Duluti,
385; Lake Manyara, 380;
Lushoto, 393; Mbeya, 413;
Mikumi, 410; Moshi, 391;
Ngorongoro, 377; Ruaha, 428;
Serengeti, 370; Tanga, 405;
Tarangire, 422
vehicles, *see* Cars and campers;
Driving
Zambia: Chipata, 597; Chipoma
Falls, 584; Choma Dam, 600;
Kafue, 604; Kariba, 617;
Kundalila Falls, 588; Luangwa,
594–5; Lusaka, 568; Ndola,
610; Victoria Falls, 580, 581
canoeing, 8
Cape Maclear, 674–6
caracal, 364, 526, 654
Carnelley's Fisherman's Camp, 273
carnet, 61–2, 94, 547
cars and campers (*see also* Driving)
buying and selling, 45–6, 108
camping (*see also* Camping and
campsites), 3, 30–43
carnet or triptyque, 61–2, 94, 547
chauffeurs, hiring, 33
choosing, 31, 44

cars and campers (*cont'd*)
documents, 61–2, 94, 321–2, 452,
547, 630
Ethiopia regulations, 452
insurance, 32, 60–1, 94, 322, 547,
630
Kenya regulations, 94
Malawi regulations, 630
outfitting, 45
renting, 13, 14, 31–3, 46;
Ethiopia, 457–8; Kenya, 104–7;
Malawi, 636; Tanzania, 322,
328–9; Zambia, 553–4
servicing, 108, 329–30, 459, 554,
637
Tanzania regulations, 321–2
Zambia regulations, 547
Caspair, 100
Castle Hotel, 183, 186, 187
Casuarina Hotel, 205
Chagga, 397–8
Chalets Hotel, 580
cheetah
Ethiopia, 531
Kenya, 227, 254, 261
Tanzania, 368–9, 374, 375, 409,
425
Zambia, 578, 599, 603
Chelinda Camp, 655
Cherangani Hills, 84, 141, 291
Chichele Lodge, 595
Chifubwa Stream Rock Engravings,
542, 613
Chilanga, 590–1
children, traveling with, 5–6
chimpanzee, 433, 435
Chingola, 613
Chipata, 596–7
Chipepo Rest Camp, 600
Chiromo-Swiss Grill Hotel, 158,
163, 170
Chisenga Govt. Rest House, 652
Chitipa Govt. Rest House, 652
church services, 172–3, 188, 488,
570–1, 652
CIAAO Hotel, 520, 521
cinemas, 171–2, 187–8, 355, 487,
522, 570, 651
City Park Campground, 160

civet, 364
clothing, 48, 54–5, 627
Club Makakola, 673–4
Club Tours, Inc., 17–18
Club Universe (Unitours), 18
CMB Line, 53–4
Coffee Tree Hostel, 391
Coffee Tree Inn, 433
Cohaito (Coloe) Ruins, 447, 517–8
College Inn, 154–5
conservation (*see also* Game and
    wildlife parks), 135–6, 142,
    339, 561
Contact (E. A.), 110, 111
Continental Express, 18
Continental Hotel, 650
conversion
    currency, xxi–xxii, 72–3
    metric, xxi
Copperbelt, 542, 606–8
Coppersmith Arms, 609
Coral Beach Hotel, 204–5
Coraldene Beach Hotel, 204
Corallo Hotel, 525
Cory Mann George (Malawi), 633
costs (*see also* specific subjects,
    places), 3, 13
    Kenya-Tanzania self-drive safari,
        39–43
    living, 73
    low-budget, daily, 49
credit cards, 73–4
Crested Crane Hotel, 586–7
crocodile
    Ethiopia, 526, 531, 534
    Kenya, 194–5, 224, 237, 255, 267,
        288
    Tanzania, 414
    Zambia, 578
cruises, 8
Crystal Springs Hotel, 597
cuisine (*see also* Restaurants, eating
    places; names of hotels, etc.),
    65
currency
    black market, 72, 83, 312
    conversion, xxi–xxii, 72–3, 82–3
    Ethiopia, 445–6, 451
    Kenya, 72, 82–3, 93–4

currency (*cont'd*)
    Malawi, 624, 630
    security precautions, 73–4
    Tanzania, 72, 312, 321
    traveler's checks, 72, 94
    Zambia, 540–1, 547
customs regulations
    Ethiopia, 451
    Kenya, 69, 93
    Malawi, 629–30
    Tanzania, 320–1
    United States, 69–70
    vehicles, 61–2
    Zambia, 546–7
Cutty Sark Hotel, 616

D'Afrique Hotel, 481, 484
Dahlak Islands, 525
Dallol Depression, 527–8
Danakil Desert (Depression), 448,
    527–8
Dar es Salaam, 313, 314, 342–5
    accommodations, 349–51
    buses, 354
    camping, 351–2
    car rental, 329
    cinemas, 355
    getting around, 354
    information, 354
    libraries, 355
    maps, 316
    nightlife, entertainment, 354–5
    religious services, 335
    restaurants, eating places, 352–4
    routes to and from, 402–20
    shops and services, 355–6
    taxis, 354
    tours, package, and tour opera-
        tors, 330, 332–3
    walking tours, 345–9
    transport, 328
Debre Berhan Selassie, 497–8, 499
Debre Damo, 447, 516
Debre Libanos, 446, 489
Debre Zeit, 446, 528
Dedza, 659–60
Dedza Govt. Rest House, 659–60
Deluxe Hotel, 431–2
Devon Hotel, 157

Diani, 84, 222–4
diarrhea, 57
dik-dik, 193, 254, 367
Dik Dik Safaris, 113
diplomatic missions
   Ethiopia: in, 468; of, 451
   Kenya: in, 127–8; of, 93
   Malawi: in, 640–1; of, 629
   Tanzania: in, 335; of, 320
   Zambia: in, 557–8; of, 546
Diwa Hill Rock Paintings, 660
documents, *see* Entry requirements
Dodoma, 423–4
Dodoma Hotel, 424
Dolphin Hotel, 204
Don's Inn, 205
dress and appearance, 48, 54–5, 627
Driftwood Club, 213–14
driving (*see also* Cars and campers),
    xviii, 3, 30–3
   auto clubs, 107, 329, 459, 554
   camping, *see* Camping and camp-
    sites
   distances, 34–5
   Ethiopia: in, 452, 458–9; to,
    454–5
   gasoline, 31, 75, 84–5, 326
   Kenya: in, 104, 107–8; to, 98–9
   literature on, 34, 107
   Malawi: in, 630, 636–7; to, 632–3
   permit, international, 63, 322, 630
   road conditions, 31, 34
   routes, *see* countries
   Tanzania: in, 321–2, 329–30; to,
    325–6
   tips on, 33–4
   visas, 62
   Zambia: in, 547, 554; to, 550
duiker
   Kenya, 222, 246, 290
   Malawi, 654, 667, 668
   Zambia, 60, 602, 617

East Africa (*see also* countries, sub-
    jects)
   itinerary, individual, 28–30
   tours from Kenya, package, 120–2
East Africa Natl. Shipping Line, 53

East African
   Airways, 97, 100–1, 326–7, 634
   Community, 381–2
   Holidays, 52–3
   Natural History Soc., 138
   Railway Marine Services, 324
   Railways, 102–3, 288, 325, 328
   Road Services, 98, 103, 325, 328
   Safari Rally, 261
   Sun Sea & Safari, 112, 113
   Travel Consultants, 18–19, 52
   Wild Life Soc., 136, 317
East Rudolf Natl. Park, 266, 267
Eastern Travel & Tourist Agency,
   460
Eboo's Tours & Safaris, 112, 113
Eden Roc Hotel, 213
Edinburgh Hotel, 612
eland
   Ethiopia, 531
   Kenya, 300–1
   Malawi, 654, 657, 667
   Tanzania, 374, 394, 414, 425, 426,
    433
   Zambia, 593, 599, 601, 602
Eldoret, 283–4
electricity, 126, 334, 466, 557, 640
elephant
   Ethiopia, 473, 531
   Kenya, 77, 84, 135, 142, 192–3,
    195, 196, 197, 222, 224, 227,
    241, 242, 246, 254, 257, 261,
    290
   Malawi, 667
   Tanzania, 313, 304, 374, 375,
    379, 388, 389, 392, 394, 409,
    412, 414, 424, 426, 433
   Zambia, 593–4, 617
Elephant's Head Hotel, 590
Elgeyo, 291
Eliye Springs Lodge, 268
Ellerman Lines Safaris, 111
El Molo, 266
Embu (town and tribe), 259
Emslies Ltd., 326
Encounter Overland, 46
entertainment, *see* Nightlife, enter-
   tainment

entry requirements, 60–3
  Ethiopia, 450–2
  Kenya, 62, 92–5
  Malawi, 629–30
  Tanzania, 62, 93, 318–22
  Zambia, 545–7
Equator Hotel, 382, 383
Equator Inn, 157–8
Equatorial Travels, 113
ETCO Ltd., 99
Ethiopia, Kingdom of (*see also* names, places, subjects), 1–2, 441–535
  accommodations, 447
  air travel: in, 455–6; to, 452–3
  airports, 453–4
  banks, 468
  birds, *see* Birds and birdwatching
  books to read, 449–50
  buses, 457, 486, 522
  business hours, 467
  calendar, 467
  camping (*see also* Camping and campsites), 447
  car rental, 457–8
  cuisine, 65
  currency, 445–6, 451
  customs regulations, 451
  diplomatic missions: in, 468; of, 451
  driving: in, 452, 458–9; to, 454–5
  electricity, 466
  entry requirements, 450–2
  firearms, 452
  fishing, 473, 527, 534
  getting around, 455–64
  getting to, 452–5
  health, 468–9
  historic, prehistoric sites, 474
  history, 441–5
  holidays, 467
  hunting, 474, 531
  identity card, 451
  information sources, 449–50, 486–7, 522
  itinerary, individual, 28–30
  language, 465–6
  length of stays, 446
  mail, telegrams, 469

Ethiopia, Kingdom of (*cont'd*)
  game and wildlife parks, 446, 449, 472–3
  newspapers, 450
  maps, 9, 448–9
  routes: Historic, 446, 447, 489–518; Kenya connector, 9, 258–9
  shopping, 67–8, 469–72, 488–9, 523
  sports, 473
  taxis, 480, 522
  telephones, 469
  time, 466
  tipping, 75
  tourism authorities, 448
  tours, package, and tour operators, 459–64
  trains: in, 456–7; to, 454
  travel agents in, 455
  vehicle documents, 452
  visa, 62, 450–1
  vital statistics, 445
  water sports, 473, 533
  weather, 447–8
  weights and measures, 466
  what to see and do, 446–7
  when to go, 447–8, 493, 498, 504, 507, 508, 515, 524, 526, 530, 532, 534
Ethiopia Hotel: Addis Ababa, 481, 483; Adigrat, 517
Ethiopian
  Airlines, 448, 454, 455–6
  Tourist Organization, 448
  Tourist Trading Co. (At-Your-Service), 459
events (*see also* Holidays; What to see and do), 6
Excellent Hotel, 184
expeditions, organized group overland (*see also* Tours, package)
  air fares, 47, 52
  operators, 46–7
expeditions, organizing own
  costs, 43
  Nairobi as origin, 45–6
  information sources, 44–5
  itinerary planning, 44
  members, 43–4

expeditions, organizing own (*cont'd*)
trans-African, 43
vehicles and equipment, 44, 45–6

Fairview Hotel, 156
Falasha, 472
Falcon Hotel, 609–10
Farrell Lines, 53
Fasil Hotel, 499
Feira Rest House, 592
firearms, 95, 322, 452, 547, 630
fishing, 8
charter firms, 141
Ethiopia, 473, 527, 534
Kenya, 140–2, 223, 244–5, 259, 266, 272
Malawi, 643–4, 662
Tanzania, 341–2, 412, 434, 438
Zambia, 541–2, 562, 616, 617, 618
Flamingo Tours, 112, 113
food (*see also* Cuisine; Restaurants, eating places), 57, 65
Foreign Individual Tour (FIT), 2–3, 13
Foreign Tours, 19
Forest & Frontier Lodges, 87
Forodhani Hotel, 351, 354
Forship Travel Agency, 460
Fort Jesus, 84, 138, 179–80
Fort Ikoma, 428–30
Fort Johnston (Mangochi), 672–3
Four Winds Travel, 19
Fourways Travel Service (T), 326
fox, 364, 473, 507, 508, 526, 527
Franco-Ethiopian Railway, 454, 457
freight forwarders, 69
Freighter Travel Service, 54
freighters to East Africa (*see also* Boat travel), 53–4
Furaha lodging house, 219

Gabbra, 258
Galila Palace Hotel, 531
Gambela Reserve, 473
game and wildlife parks (*see also* names of animals, parks), 39, 192–3
accommodations, *see* names
birds, *see* Birds and birdwatching

game and wildlife parks (*cont'd*)
camping, *see* Camping and campsites; names of parks
entry fees, 136–7, 339–40, 473, 527, 594, 603–4, 618
Ethiopia, 446, 449, 472–3
Kenya, 83–4, 89–90, 135–8, 192–9, 209–11, 221–2, 225–33, 241–4, 254–8, 259–63, 276–9, 287–90, 298–305
Malawi, 625, 642–3, 654–5, 657, 667–9
maps, 89–90, 316–17
marine parks, 84, 135, 137, 209–11
photography, 135, 137, 225, 226, 254–5, 276, 303
ranger, hiring, 32
Tanzania, 312–14, 338–40, 362–70, 387–90, 392–5, 408–10, 414, 420–2, 425–8, 431–3, 435
rules, 75–6
when to visit, *see* names
Zambia, 541, 542, 560–1, 578, 592–5, 599, 601–4, 617–19, 654–5
Game Department (Kenya), 87
Gateway Holidays/Globus Tours, 19
gazelle
Ethiopia, 526, 531, 533, 534
Kenya, 197, 231, 254, 300
Tanzania, 364, 366, 367, 368, 374, 375
Gedi, 84, 138, 207–9
Gelada baboon, 473, 507, 508
General Ethiopian International Travel Agency, 460
General Ethiopian Transport, 457
General Tours, 19
genet, 364, 654
gerenuk, 193, 254, 261, 392
getting to . . . (*see also* specific mode of travel; place names)
East Africa, 49–54
Ethiopia, 452–5
Kenya, 95–9
Malawi, 630–3
Tanzania, 322–6
Zambia, 547–50

Ghion Imperial Hotel, 480–1, 483
giant forest hog, 241, 242
giraffe
  Ethiopia, 531
  Kenya, 84, 136, 142, 225, 227,
    281, 254, 257, 261, 267, 300
  Tanzania, 388, 392, 409, 412, 414,
    425, 426
  Zambia, 578
Globe Star, 19–20
Globetrotters Club, 48
Gold Lion (hotel), 435
Golden Sands Holiday Camp, 676
golf, 8, 139
Gombe Stream Natl. Park, 313, 435
Gondar, 446, 449, 494–9
gorilla, 433
Governor's Camp, 223
Grand Beach Hotel, 677
Grand Hotel, 528
Grasshopper Inn, 619
Great African Adventure, 47
Great Uhuru Railway, 325, 549
Green Hotel, 507
group package tours (*see also* Tours,
    package), 2, 14–28, 50
  overland expeditions, 46–9
Grosvenor Hotel, 156–7
Grumeti Luxury Tented Camp, 370
grysbok, 432, 602, 617, 668

Hadza, 422
Hansmax Tours & Travel, 113
Harambee Hotel, 481, 483, 485
Harrar, 446, 449, 471, 528–31
  Elephant Sanctuary, 473
hartebeest
  Ethiopia, 531
  Kenya, 300
  Malawi, 654, 657, 668
  Tanzania, 366, 374, 375, 394, 409,
    425, 531, 433
  Zambia, 593, 602, 617
health
  books and publications, 59
  checkups, 58
  diarrhea, 57
  Ethiopia, 468–9
  food and, 57

health (*cont'd*)
  insurance, 60, 61
  Kenya, 128
  jet lag, 58
  malaria, 57
  medical: facilities, 58; history, 59;
    kits, 58–9
  mountain illnesses, 58, 401
  sleeping sickness, 57–8
  Tanzania, 335
  vaccinations, inoculations, 55–6
  water: drinking, 56–7; swimming,
    56, 57
Hehe, 424–5
Hellenic Lines, 53
Hemphill World Air Cruises (Hemp-
    hill Travel Service), 20
Henderson Travel Service, 20
Henkle (J. W.) Presents (Africa
    Unlimited), 20–1
Highlands Hotel, 286
Highways Ltd., 114
Hilton Hotels, 87; Addis Ababa,
    480; Nairobi, 152, 161–2, 164,
    167, 170
Hilton Lodges: Axum, 515; Bahar
    Dar, 494; Gondar, 499;
    Lalibela, 505; Salt Lick, 224–5;
    Taita Hills, 224–5
hippo
  Ethiopia, 526, 531, 533, 534
  Kenya, 194–5, 237, 261, 277, 288
  Tanzania, 364, 374, 375, 388, 414
  Zambia, 593, 599, 617
hitchhiking, 48–9, 634
holidays, 126–7, 334, 467, 557, 640
Home Farm, 252
Horombo Hut, 403
hotels, *see* Accommodations; names
    (by proper name, not word
    hotel)
hours of business, 127, 334, 468,
    557, 640
Hughes Overland, 47
Hunter's Lodge, 190–1
Hunter (Thomas) & Co., 550
hunting, 7, 13, 30
  conservation and, 135–6, 142
  Ethiopia, 474, 531

hunting (*cont'd*)
  firearms, 95, 322, 452, 547, 630
  Kenya, 142
  Malawi, 644
  Zambia, 542, 562
hunting dog, 364, 373–4
Hurlingham Hotel, 157
hyena
  Ethiopia, 526, 530, 533
  Kenya, 241, 254, 257
  Malawi, 654
  Tanzania, 364, 366, 374, 375, 376, 394
  Zambia, 593, 599, 602
hyrax, 246, 366, 367, 425, 526
Hyrax Hill, 84, 138, 275

ibex, 473, 507–8
Ideal Tours, 21
impala
  Kenya, 197, 224, 254, 278, 300
  Malawi, 668
  Tanzania, 409
  Zambia, 593, 599, 602
Imperial Hotel, 519–20, 521
information sources, 8–9
  bibliography, general, 10–11
  customs regulations, 70
  driving, 34
  Ethiopia, 449–50, 486–7, 522
  expeditions, organizing own, 44–5
  freighter travel, 54
  health, 59
  hitchhiking, 48–9
  Kenya, 88–92, 136, 169, 187, 188, 250
  low-budget travel, 48–9
  Malawi, 627–9
  maps, *see* Maps
  mountain climbing, 250
  neighboring countries, 11–13
  Tanzania, 317–19, 354, 375, 383
  Zambia, 544–5, 561–2, 570, 575, 583
inoculations, vaccinations, 55–6
insects, 39
insurance
  health, 60, 61
  property, 60

insurance (*cont'd*)
  vehicle, 32, 60–1, 94, 322, 547, 630
Inter-Continental Hotels: Lusaka, 567–9; Nairobi, 153, 161, 165, 170; Victoria Falls, 579
International Sea & Air Shipping, 69
International Travel & Tour, 633
Ipusukelo Hotel, 610
Iringa, 424–5
Isanzu, 422
Isimila, 411–12
Isoka Rest House, 588
ITCO Tourist & Travel Agency, 460
Itegue Hotel, Addis Ababa, 482
Itegue Menen Hotel, 499, 531
itinerary, planning, 1–2, 28–30, 44
Ivory Safaris, 113
Izaak Walton Inn, 259

jackal
  Ethiopia, 533, 534
  Kenya, 302
  Malawi, 654
  Tanzania, 364, 366, 374, 375, 425
  Zambia, 599, 601
Jadini Beach Hotel, 223
Jaffries Hotel, 432
Jambo Safaris, 112, 113
jobs, availability, 43
Jubilee Tours & Safaris, 114
Jumba-la-Mtwana, 138
Jumbo Tours, 14

Kabwe, 589–90
Kachalola Hotel, 592
Kafue Natl. Park, 541, 602–4
Kakamega Forest, 288–9
Kalambo Falls, 541, 619–20
Kalundu Mound, 542, 600
Kalundu Motel, 600
Kamba, 191
Kami Hut, 250
Kanamai Conference & Holiday Centre (Kanamai Youth Hostel), 206
Kanduchi Beach Hotel, 341, 417
Kaoma Rest House, 605

Kapata Rest House, 597
Karege Ujamaa Village, 418
Karen, 296
Kareyu Lodge, 526
Kariandusi, 84, 138, 275
Kariba Dam and Lake, 542, 614–17
Kariba Heights Hotel, 616
Karl Pollman & Gordon Harvey
    Wildlife Safaris, 111
Karonga, 685–6
Kasaba Bay, 541, 617–18
Kasaba Bay Lodge, 618
Kassam's Travel Agencies, 326
Kasungu, 656–7
    Govt. Rest House, 657
    Inn, 656–7
    Natl. Park, 625, 657
Katavi Game Reserve, 414
Katete Rest House, 595
Katolola Rock Paintings, 598
Kearline Tours, 112, 113, 330
Kearlines, 99
Kearsley Travel, 326
Kentmere Club, 156
Keekorok Lodge, 233
Kenya
    Beach Hotel, 204
    Bus Service, 103
    Flying Safaris, 114
    Mystery Tours, 112, 113
    Safari Lodges & Hotels, 87
Kenya, Republic of (*see also* names,
    places, subjects), 1, 77–305
    accommodations, 85–7
    air travel: in, 100–2; to, 95–6
    airports, 96–7, 190
    banks, 127
    beach resorts, 201–24
    birdwatching, *see* Birds and bird-
        watching
    boats to, 97
    books to read, 90–1
    buses: in, 103–4, 168, 187; to, 98
    business hours, 127
    camping (*see also* Camping and
        campsites), 108–10
    car rentals, 104–7
    cuisine, 65
    currency, 72, 82–3, 93–4

Kenya, Republic of (*cont'd*)
    customs regulations, 69, 93
    diplomatic missions: in, 127–8; of,
        93
    driving: in, 104, 107; to, 98–9
    electricity, 126
    entry requirements, 92–5
    firearms, 95
    fishing, 140–2, 223
    game and wildlife parks, 83–4,
        89–90
    game viewing lodges, 83
    getting around in, 99–122
    getting to, 95–9
    health, 128
    historic, prehistoric sites, 138
    history, 78–82
    holidays, 126–7
    hunting, 142
    information sources, 88–92, 136,
        169, 187, 188, 250
    itinerary, individual, 28–30
    language, 123–6
    length of stays, 123–6
    mail, telegrams, 128–9
    maps, 9–10, 89–90
    newspapers, 91
    photography, 67
    pronunciation of name, 63
    routes: K-1: Nairobi–Mombasa,
        188–201; K-2: Mombasa–North
        Coast–Malindi–Lamu, 201–19;
        K-3: Mombasa–South Coast,
        219–24; K-4: Taveta–Taita
        Hills–Voi, 224–5; K-5:
        Namanga–Amboseli–Kajiado–
        Nairobi, 225–9; K-6: Nairobi–
        Masai Mara, 229–34; K-7:
        Nairobi–Nyeri–Nanyuki–
        Isiolo–Marsabit–Ethiopia, 234–
        59; K-8: Murang'a–Embu–
        Meru–Isiolo, 259–63; K-9:
        Nanyuki–Nyahururu (Thom-
        son's Falls)–Nakuru, 263–9;
        K-10: Nairobi–Naivasha–
        Nakuru–Eldoret–Uganda, 269–
        84; K-11: Western Kenya cir-
        cuit from Nakuru, 284–92;
        K-12: Limuru High Country–

Kenya, Republic of (*cont'd*)
Kikuyu Escarpment from
Nairobi, 292–5; K-13: Karen–
Ngong Hills from Nairobi,
295–8; K-14: Nairobi Natl.
Park–Olorgesailie–Lake Magadi
from Nairobi, 298–305
safaris and safari operators, 110–
12
shipping purchases from, 69
shopping, 67, 68–9, 130–5, 173–4
sports, 138–42
taxis, 104, 168, 187
telephones, 129–30
time, 126
tourism authorities, 88–9
tours, package, and tour operators,
112–22
trains: in, 102–3; to, 97–8
travel agents in, 99–100
vehicle documents, 94
visa, 62, 92–3
visitor's pass, 92
vital statistics, 82
water sports, 138, 139–40
weather, 88
weights and measures, 126
what to see and do, 83–5
when to go, 88, 197, 210, 227, 232,
242, 249, 255, 258, 262, 268,
272, 278, 303
Ker, Downey & Selby Safaris, 111,
330, 342
Kericho, 84, 286–8
Kerio Valley, 84, 291–2
Kibo
crater, 396–7
Hotel, 401, 403
Hut, 403
Safaris, 113
Kigombe, 405, 406
Kikambala, 205–6
Kikuyu, 81, 240–1
Kilaguni Lodge, 197
Kilifi, 206–7
Kilimanjaro, 312, 313, 317, 342,
395–403
guides and tours, 401, 422

Kilimanjaro (*cont'd*)
Hotel, 349, 352, 353, 354
Mountain Club, 397
Kilwa Ruins, 313, 314, 436–8
Kimbla Travel (U.K.), 21, 47
Kim Safaris, 111
Kingfisher Safaris, 111
Kisumu, 288–9
Kisumu Hotel, 288
Kipsigis, 283
Kirsten Air & Steamship Agency, 54
Kitale, 289
Club, 289
Hotel, 289
Youth Hostel, 289
Kitani Lodge & Shelter Camp, 198
Kitwe, 611–12
klipspringer, 193, 364, 526, 533, 617,
654–5, 667
Koka Dam and Lake, 446, 531
Koka Hotel, 531
Kolo rock paintings, 423
Kongoni, 300
KTDC Hotel Management, 87
Ku Chawe Inn, 663
kudu
Ethiopia, 526, 531, 533, 534
Kenya, 142, 193, 257, 261
Malawi, 667, 668
Tanzania, 392, 394, 409, 425, 426,
427
Zambia, 593, 599, 602
Kudu (Africa) Ltd., 111
Kundalila Falls, 587–8
Kunduchi Ruins, 313, 418
Kuoni Travel, 21
K.U.T. Tours (Pan Universal), 21

La Hacienda Hotel, 602
Lake Abaya, 534
Lake Abiata, 533
Lake Awassa, 533–4
Lake Baringo, 84, 280–1
Lodge, 281
Self-Service Lodge, 281
Tenters Camp, 281
Lake Chilwa, 660–1
Lake Elmenteita, 274
Lake Hannington, 280

Lake Hotel: Bukoba, 433; Mwanza, 431
Lake Kariba, 542
Lake Langano, 533
Lake Magadi, 305
Lake Malawi (*see also* area town names), 625, 627, 643, 670–2
Lake Manyara Hotel, 378
Lake Manyara Natl. Park, 312, 313, 316–17, 378
Lake Naivasha, 84, 142, 271–4
Hotel, 272–3
Lake Nakuru, 83, 85, 137, 276–9
Lake Rudolf, 84, 85, 88, 141, 264–9
Lake Rudolf Angling Lodge, 268
Lake Rukwa, 313
Lake Shalla, 533
Lake Shamo, 534
Lake Tana, 446, 449, 490–3
Lake Tanganyika, 342, 433–5, 617–19
Lake Victoria, 288, 430–1
Lake View Inn, 616
Lake Zwai (Zuai), 532–3
Lalibela, 446, 449, 471, 499–505
Lambwe Valley Game Reserve, 135, 287–8
Lamu, 84, 85, 215–19
Lamu Leisure Lodge, 219
Langano Bekele Molla Hotel, 535
language
    Briticisms, 64
    Ethiopia, 465–6
    Kenya, 123–6
    Malawi, 638–9
    pronouncing country names, 63
    Tanzania, 334
    Zambia, 556
Lawford's Hotel, 213
Lawns Hotel, 393
lechwe, 542, 599, 601, 602
Leisure Bay Motel, 616
length of stays
    Ethiopia, 446
    individual itineraries, 28–9
    Kenya, 85
    Malawi, 625
    package tours, 13

length of stays (*cont'd*)
    Tanzania, 313–14
    Zambia, 541–2
Lengwe Game Camp, 668
Lengwe Natl. Park, 625, 667–8
Leopold Walford, 550
leopard
    Ethiopia, 126, 531
    Kenya, 83, 142, 222, 231, 241–2, 246, 254, 261, 290
    Malawi, 654, 657, 667
    Tanzania, 364, 366, 374, 375, 392, 394, 409, 414, 425, 433
    Zambia, 593, 603
Leopard Rock Safari Lodge, 262–3
libraries, 172, 355, 487, 570, 652
Lifupa Game Camp, 657
Lighttours, 113
Lilongwe Hotel, 659
Lilongwe, 625, 658–9
Limbe Rest House, 650
Lindblad Travel, 21–2
Lindblad Travel & Tony Irwin, 114
lion
    Ethiopia, 526, 531, 534
    Kenya, 193, 199–200, 224, 225, 227, 231, 241, 254, 261–2, 300, 302–3
    Malawi, 654, 657, 667
    Tanzania, 364, 366, 374, 375, 379, 392, 394, 409, 414, 425, 433
    Zambia, 593, 599, 603
Lion of Judah Tour Agency, 460
Lion Travel & Tourist Agency, 460
Lislind International, 22
literature, *see* Books and publications; Information sources
Livingstone, city of (*see also* Victoria Falls), 541, 576–7, 601
    accommodations, 579–81
    drive around area of, 578–9
    shopping, 560
Livingstone Hotel, 390–1
Livingstone Memorial, 588
Livingstonia, 683–4
Lloyd Triestino, 53
Lobo Wildlife Lodge, 369–70
Lochinvar Natl. Park, 542, 599
Lochinvar Lodge, 599

lodgings, self-service
  Kenya: Buffalo Springs, 256;
     Kibwezi, 191; Lake Baringo,
     281; Mt. Kenya, 250; Murang'a,
     258; Naro Moru, 244–5;
     Olorgesailie, 305; Shimba Hills,
     222; Thego, 244; Tsavo, 198
  Tanzania: Serengeti, 370
  Zambia: Kafue, 604; Kariba, 616;
     Lochinvar, 599; Luangwa, 594;
     Victoria Falls, 579–80
Lotus Hotel, 184
Lozi, 605
Luambe Natl. Park, 592
Luamfwa Lodge, 595
Luangwa Natl. Park, 541, 592–5
Luanshya, 611
Lugard's Falls, 196
Luna (New Ghedem) Hotel, 524–5
Luo, 288
Lusaka, 542, 562
  accommodations, 567–8
  airport, 548
  cinemas, 570
  information sources, 570
  libraries, 570
  religious services, 570–1
  restaurants, eating places, 568–9
  routes to and from, 584–617
  shops and services, 559, 571
  taxis, 570
Lusaka Hotel, 568
Lyambai Hotel, 605–6
Lykes Line, 53

Mackenzie Dalgety Travel Services,
     99
Mackinder's Camp, 249–50
Mafia Island, 313, 314, 438–9
Mafia Island Lodge, 341, 439
mail, 14, 71–2
  Ethiopia, 469
  Kenya, 128–9
  Malawi, 641
  shipping purchases home, 69
  Tanzania, 336
  Zambia, 558
Makalle, 447, 505–7
Maki Bekele Molla Hotel, 534

Makokola Club, 673–4
Malaika Safaris, 113
malaria, 57
Malawi Dept. of Tourism, 627
Malawi Railways, 635
Malawi, Republic of (*see also*
     names, places, subjects), 2,
     621–86
  accommodations, 625–6
  air travel: in, 633–4; to, 630–1
  airline offices, 633–4
  airports, 631
  banks, 640
  birdwatching (*see also* Birds and
     birdwatching), 643
  boats, 635–6, 672
  books to read, 628
  buses: in, 635; to, 632
  business hours, 640
  car rental, 636
  currency, 624, 630
  customs regulations, 629–30
  diplomatic missions: in, 640–1; of,
     629
  dress and appearance, 627
  driving: in, 630, 636–7; to, 632–3
  electricity, 640
  entry requirements, 629–30
  firearms, 630
  fishing, 643–4
  game and wildlife parks, 625,
     642–3
  getting around, 633–8
  getting to, 630–3
  historic, prehistoric sites, 643
  history, 621–4
  holidays, 640
  hunting, 644
  information sources, 627–9
  language, 638–9
  length of stays, 625
  mail, telegrams, 641
  maps, 627–8
  newspapers, 628
  pronunciation of name, 63
  routes: Q-1: Nyala, Zambia–
     Rumphi–Lilongwe–Zomba–
     Limbe (Blantyre)–Thyolo–
     Mulanje–Mozambique, 652–66;

Malawi, Republic of (*cont'd*)
Q-2: Blantyre–Lengwe Natl.
Park–Chiromo–Tholo, 666–9;
Q-3: Liwonde Barrage–
Mangochi–Monkey Bay–
Salima, 669–77; Q-4: Salima–
Nkhotakota, 677–9; Q-5:
Mzimba–Vipya Plateau–
Mzuzu–Nkhata Bay, 680–2;
Q-6: Rumphi–Livingstonia–
Karonga–Chitipa–Nyala,
Zambia, 682–6
shopping, 68, 641–2, 652
taxis, 651
telephones, 641
time, 639
tourism authority, 627
tours, package, 637–8
trains: in, 635; to, 631–2
travel agents in, 633
vehicle documents, 630
vital statistics, 624
weather, 626
weights and measures, 639
what to see and do, 625
when to go, 626
Malindi, 85, 139, 211–13
accommodations, 213–14
tour operators, 122–3
routes to and from, 201–19
Malindi Bustani (hotel), 214
Mandara Hut, 403
Maneaters Motel, 199
Mangochi, 672–3
Manor Hotel, 183, 186
maps, 9–10
Ethiopia, 9, 448–9
Kenya, 9–10, 89–90
Malawi, 627–8
Tanzania, 9–10, 316–17
Zambia, 544
Mara Serena Lodge, 233
Marakwet, 291
Maralal Safari Lodge, 265
Maramba Govt. Rest House, 580
Marangu Hotel, 401, 402–3
Marsabit
Lodge, 258

Marsabit (*cont'd*)
Natl. Reserve, 84, 85, 88, 137,
257–8
Tented Lodge, 258
Masai, 67, 225–6, 231, 375, 380–1
Masai Lodge, 155, 163–4, 242
Masai Mara, 84, 85, 88, 231–3
Massawa, 446–7, 448, 523–5
Matara Ruins, 447, 515
Mathews Safaris Tanzania, 342
Mau Mau, 81, 240–1
Maupintour, 22
Mawenzi Hotel, 350
Mayfair Hotel, 156, 165, 170
Mbala, 619
Mbeya, 413
Guest House, 413
Hotel, 413
Range, 313, 413
measures, *see* Weights and measures
medical facilities (*see also* Health),
58
meeting people, 6–7
Menegai Crater, 276
Merali Bus Services, 98, 325
Merriman & Finnerty Assoc. (Brien
Merriman's Africa), 22
Meru, 84, 260
Mulika Lodge, 262
Natl. Park, 260–3
tribe, 381
metric conversion, xxi
Mfuwe Lodge, 595
Midland Hotel, 279
Mikolongwe Cave Paintings, 664
Mikumi Natl. Park, 313, 314, 317,
408–10
Wildlife Camp, 410
Wildlife Lodge, 409–10
Millimani Hotel, 154, 163, 170
Mini-Cabs & Tours, 113
Mitchell Cotts & Co. (EA), 99
Mkoma Rock Paintings, 595
Mkomazi Game Reserve, 392
Mkushi Rest House, 589
Mnarani Club, 206–7
Molo, 286
Mombasa, 84, 85, 88, 174–8
accommodations, 183–5

Mombasa (*cont'd*)
  camping, 185
  car rental, 104–6
  fishing, 140–1
  getting around, 187
  information sources, 187, 188
  nightlife, entertainment, 187–8
  places of interest, 178–83
  religious services, 188
  restaurants, eating places, 186–7
  routes to and from, 188–224
  shops and services, 130–4, 188
  tours, package, and tour operators,
    114, 120, 122–3
  walking tour, 178–82
Mombasa Beach Hotel, 203
Mombasa Marina, 185
Mombo Hotel, 393
Momela Game Lodge, 390
money, *see* Currency
Mongu, 605–6
Mongu Rest House, 606
Monkey Bay, 674
Monkey Bay Hotel, 674
monkeys
  Ethiopia, 526, 533, 534
  Kenya, 142, 194, 241, 291
  Malawi, 668
  Tanzania, 364, 375, 379, 388, 389,
    433
  Zambia, 593, 599
Monze Hotel, 599
Moore McCormack Lines, 54
Morogoro, 408
Moshi, 316, 390–2, 395
Motel, The, 580
motels, *see* Accommodations; proper
    names
Mt. Elgon, 84, 141, 389–90
Mt. Elgon Lodge & Youth Hostel,
    290
Mt. Kenya, 83, 84, 85, 141, 245–52
Mt. Kenya Safari Club, 251–2
Mt. Meru, 342, 388–9
Mt. Meru Game Sanctuary, 385–7
Mt. Mulanje, 625
Mt. Soche Hotel, 649, 650
Mountain
    Lodge, 83, 244

Mountain (*cont'd*)
  Safaris, 111
  Travel, 22–3
mountain climbing, 8, 58
  Ethiopia, 473
  health, 58, 400–1
  information sources, 250
  Kenya, 245, 248–9, 250, 290
  Malawi, 625, 666
  Tanzania, 384–5, 389, 396, 399–
    402
mountain nyala, 473, 527, 534
Mozambique Railways, 632
Mpulungu Rest House, 617
Msembe Camp, 428
Muchinga Motel, 590
Mufulira, 610
Mulanje Mountains, 665–6
mule trips, 8, 447, 507–9
Munda Wanga Park, Gardens, 590–1
Murang'a (Fort Hall), 259
Musi-o-Tunya Inter-Continental
    Hotel, 579
Musi-o-Tunya Zoological Park, 578
Musoma Hotel, 430
Mwanza, 431–2
Mwasungia Scenery Guest House,
    225
Mzima Springs, 194
Mzimba Govt. Rest House, 656
Mzuzu, 680–1
Mzuzu Govt. Rest House, 681

Naaz Hotel, 382, 383
Ndabaka Gate Self-Service Cottages,
    370
Ndola, 548, 608–10
Ndutu Safaris Lodge, 370
Nairobi
  Hilton, 152, 161–2, 164, 167, 170
  Natl. Park, 135, 136–7, 242, 299–
    304
Nairobi, city of, 85, 88, 142–6
  accommodations, 151–60
  art galleries, 172
  buses, 168
  campsites, 160
  car rental, 104–6
  cinemas, 171–2

Nairobi, city of (*cont'd*)
  culture, entertainment, 170–2
  getting around, 168–9
  information sources, 169
  libraries, 172
  maps, 89–90
  nightlife, 169–70
  as origin of own expedition, 45–6
  places of interest, 146–51
  religious services, 172–3
  restaurants, eating places, 160–8
  routes to and from, 188–201, 225–
    34, 292–305
  safaris, safari operators, 110–12
  shops and services, 130–5, 173–4
  street names, 168–9
  taxis, 168
  theater, 170–1
  tours, package, and tour opera-
    tors, 112–19, 122–3
  walking tour, 146–50
Nakuru, 279–80
Nakuru Lake, 83, 85, 137, 276–9
Naivasha, 274
  Inn, 274
  Lake, 84, 142, 271–4
  Marina Club, 273
  Youth Hostel, 273–4
Namanga, 225
Namanga Hotel, 229
Nandi
  Bear, 283
  Hills, 282–3
  tribe, 282
Nanyuki, 251–2
Nanyuki Youth Hostel, 252
Naro Moru River Lodge, 244–5
Narok Club, 231
Nash's Hotel, 650
National Fauna Preservation Soc.,
    643
National Tourist & Travel Agency,
    460
Nazareth, 531
Ndorobo, 282–3
New Africa Hotel, 341, 349, 352,
    353
New Ainsworth Hotel, 158
New Arusha Hotel, 382, 383

New Avenue Hotel, 154, 164
New Carlton Hotel, 183–4, 186
New Continental Hotel, 158
New Fairmount Hotel, 580
New Ghedem (Luna) Hotel, 524–5
New Kisumu Hotel, 288
New Lincoln Hotel, 284
New Mahrus Hotel, 219
New Mwanza Hotel, 431
New Safari Hotel, 382, 383
New Sea Breezes Hotel, 219
New Soni Falls Hotel, 393
New Stanley Hotel, 153, 161, 163,
    170
New Wagon Wheel Hotel, 284
newspapers, 91, 318, 450, 561, 628
Ngobit Fishing Lodge, 245
Ngong Hills, 297–8
Ngorongoro
  Crater, 312, 313, 317, 374–8
  Crater Farm, 378
  Crater House, 377
  Crater Lodge, 377
  Forest Resort Lodge, 377
  Wildlife Lodge, 377
Ngulia Safari Camp, 198
Ngulia Safari Lodge, 197–8
Ngurdoto Crater, 387–8
nightlife, entertainment
  Ethiopia, 487, 522, 525
  Kenya, 169–72, 187–8, 190
  Tanzania, 354–5
Nilestar Tours (Africa), 23
Nilestar Tours (Intl.), 113
Njiru Country Club, 156
Nkamba Bay, 541, 617–19
Nkamba Bay Lodge, 618–19
Nkana Hotel, 612
Nkhata Bay, 681–2
Nkhotakota, 677–9
Nkhotakota Govt. Rest House, 679
Nkopola Campsite, 673
Nkopola Lodge, 673
Norfolk Hotel, 152, 161, 165
North Bank Rest Camp, 579–80
North Western Hotel, 580
Northern Ethiopia Railways, 456
Northern Frontier Dist. (NFD),
    252–4

Nsalu Hill Cave, 542, 587
Nyahururu, 263–5
nyala, 473, 527, 534, 625, 667–8
Nyala Hotel, 519, 521
Nyali, 201–3
Nyali Beach Hotel, 203
Nyamwezi, 432
Nyati Tours, 113
Nyeri, 238–41
Nyika Natl. Park, 625, 654–5

Oaklands, 393
Oasis Lodge, 268–9
Ocean Sports, 211
Ocean View Beach Hotel, 204
Oceanic Hotel, 183, 186, 187
Oceanic Motel, 351
Oceans Magazine, 23
Odd Jobs, 99–100, 112
okapi, 433
Ol Tukai Lodge, 229
Oldeani Residential Club, 378
Olduvai Gorge, 312, 313, 317, 371–4
Olorgesailie, 138, 304–5
Omar Khayyam Hotel, 158
Omo Natl. Park, 449, 531–2
oribi, 290, 533, 599, 601, 602
oryx
    Ethiopia, 526
    Kenya, 142, 193, 254, 261, 265
    Tanzania, 392
Osirwa Safari Cottages, 384
Outrigger Club, 183
Outspan Hotel, 239
overland tours (*see also* Camping
    and campsites)
    group, organized, 46–9
    organizing own, 43–6
Oyster Bay Hotel, 349–50

package tours, *see* Tours, package
Palm Beach Hotel, 350
Palm Court Hotel: Mombasa, 184;
    Tanga, 405
Palm Tours, 114
Palmtree Tours & Safaris, 114
Pan American, 71
Panafric Hotel, 153, 161, 162–3, 170
Pangani, 405, 406

pangolin, 602
Park East Tours, 23
Park Tours & Safaris, 113
passport, 61
Paw-Line Tours & Travel, 113
Pemba Channel Fishing Club, 223
Penn Overland, 23–4, 46
people
    meeting, 6–7
    photographing, 67
Peponi Hotel, 219
Percival Tours Inc., 24, 87
Petauke Rest House, 592
Peter's Holiday Motel, 581
Petley's Inn, 218–19
pets, 60, 70
photography, 65–7
    game and wildlife parks, 135, 137,
        225, 226, 254–5, 276, 303
    safari, 13, 30, 342, 542
Pitt & Scott Ltd., 54
Pierre C. T. Verheye's Adventure-
    land Safaris, 24
Pig & Whistle Hotel, 260
places to go, *see* What to see and do;
    names
planning (*see also* specific countries,
    subjects), 1–13
    accommodations, 5
    bibliography, general, 10–11
    children, 5–6
    costs, 3, 13, 14
    clothing, 54–5
    documents, 61–3
    driving, 3, 30–43
    events, calendar of, 6
    expeditions, organizing own, 43–6
    general information, 63–76
    health, 55–9
    individual tours, 28–43
    information sources, 8–9
    insurance, 60–1
    maps, 9–10
    meeting people, 6–7
    money, 72–4
    neighboring countries, visiting,
        11–13
    package tours, *see* Tours, package
    passports and visas, 61, 62–3

planning (*cont'd*)
  pets, 60, 70
  purchases, 67–72
  safety, security, 4, 73–4
  things to do, 7–8
  tips on, 13–14
  tour operators, 14–28
  travel arrangements, 2–4
  vaccinations, inoculations, 55–6
  weather conditions, 6
  when to go, 6
  where to go, 1–2
Planter's Hotel, 405
Plaza Hotel, 482
Plums Hotel, 159
Point Pleasure (hotel), 616
Polish Ocean Lines, 53
Pollman (Karl) & Harvey (Gordon)
  Wildlife Safaris, 111
President Hotel, 610
Prestonair, 551
Prospair, 552
Prince Makonnen Hotel, 499
publications, *see* Books and publications
puku, 593, 617

Questers Tours and Travels, 24

Ras Hotel: Addis Ababa, 481–2,
  484; Debre Zeit, 528; Harrar,
  530–1; Lake Tana, 493–4
Ras Kitau Beach Hotel, 215
Ras Mengasha Hotel, 515
Red Sea Hotel, 524
reedbuck
  Ethiopia, 526, 533
  Kenya, 278
  Malawi, 625, 654, 657
  Tanzania, 409, 414, 432
  Zambia, 601, 617
Reef Hotel, 203
religious services, 172–3, 188, 488,
  570–1, 652
Rendille, 257–8
reptiles (*see also* Crocodile), 367,
  578
rest houses, *see* place or proper
  names

restaurants, eating places (*see also*
  Accommodations; names of
  hotels, etc.), 74
  Addis Ababa, 482–6
  Arusha, 383
  Asmara, 521–2
  Blantyre, 650–1
  Dar es Salaam, 352–4
  Kitwe, 612
  Lusaka, 568–9
  Massawa, 525
  Mombasa, 185–7
  Nairobi, 160–8
  Ndola, 610
  Tanga, 405
Rex Hotel, 184
rhino
  Ethiopia, 531
  Kenya, 142, 192, 193, 224, 225,
    227, 241, 254, 261, 290, 300
  Tanzania, 364, 374, 375, 388, 392,
    394, 409, 425, 426, 433
  Zambia, 578, 593, 603
Rhino Safaris, 113
Rhodesia, *see* Victoria Falls, Kariba
  Dam and Lake
Rhodesia Railways, 549
Ridgeway Hotel, 567–8, 569
Rift Valley, 292–5
  lakes, 446, 532–5
Rima Island Lodge, 273
Root & Leakey's Photographic
  Safaris, 111
routes (*see also* names of countries,
  places)
  distances, xvii
  identification system, xvii–xviii
Rowallan Camp, 160
Ruaha Natl. Park, 313, 314, 315,
  425–8
Rubondo Island Game Reserve, 433
Rumanyika Orugundu Game Re-
  serve, 433
Rumphi Govt. Rest House, 656
Rutland Hotel, 610
Ryall's Hotel, 649, 650–1

Saa Nane Island Game Reserve, 431
Sadani Game Reserve, 394

Safari
  Air Services Tours, 114
  Camp Services, 111
  Desk, 111
  Park Hotel, 155
Safariland Hotel, 157
Safariland Lodge, 273
safaris (*see also* Tours, individual;
    Tours, package)
  air, 114
  camping packages, 109–10
  costs, 3, 13, 14, 39–43, 110–11
  Kenya, 110–12
  luxury, 3, 13, 30, 110–12
  operators, 110–12, 330
  photo, 13, 30, 342
  self-drive (*see also* Camping and
    campsites), 30–46
  walking, 4, 8
Safaris Unlimited, 111
safety, security, 73–4
Saiwa Swamp, 84, 290–1
Salima, 677–8
Salt Lick Lodge, 83, 224–5
Samburu
  Game Lodge, 256
  Game Reserve, 84, 85, 136, 242,
    254–6
  tribe, 67, 256
Sankuri-Tana River Tented Camp,
    237
Savannah Travel & Tours, 114
Savoy Hotel: Morogoro, 408; Ndola,
    609
Seafarers, 211
Seafaris, 341
Seaview Hotel: Dar es Salaam, 351;
    Tanga, 405
Secret Valley Game Lodge, 83, 241,
    252
Selous Game Reserve, 313, 314,
    394–5
Semyen fox, 473, 507, 508, 527
Semyen Mountains, 447, 449, 473,
    507–9
Serena Beach Hotel, 205
Serena Lodges and Hotels, 87
Serengeti, 312, 313, 316–17, 362–
    70, 428

Seronera, 428
Seronera Wildlife Lodge, 370
serval, 526, 654
Seven Olives Hotel, 505
Severin Sea Lodge, 204
Shanzu, 204–5
Shashamane Bekele Molla Hotel,
    555
Shelly Beach Hotel, 219
Shimba Hills, 84, 221–2
shipping purchases home, 69
Shire Highlands Hotel, 649–50
Shire River, 643
shopping, 4, 67–9
  customs, *see* Customs regulations
  Ethiopia, 67–8, 469–72, 488–9,
    523
  Kenya, 67, 68–9, 130–5, 173–4,
    188
  Malawi, 68, 641–2, 652
  shipping purchases, 69
  Tanzania, 336–8, 355–6, 359, 383
  Zambia, 68, 559–60, 571
Siafu Expeditions Ltd., 46
Siavonga Rest Camp, 616
Sierra Club, 25
Sigala Lodge, 199
Silver Spear Tours, 112, 113
Silverbeck Hotel, 252
Silversands Hotel, 352, 417–18
Simba Safaris, 25
Sinazongwe Rest House, 600
Sindbad Hotel, 213
Sirikwa, 291
Sirikwa Safaris, 111–12
SITA World Travel, 25
sitatunga, 84, 290–1, 433, 602, 618
Six-Eighty Hotel, 154, 166–7
Skytrain, 51
Skyway Hotel, 350
sleeping sickness, 57–8
Small World Country Club, 190
Snowline Safaris, 112
Solwezi Hotel, 613
Somali (shiftas), 253
South African Airways, 634
South African Railways, 549
South Beach Leisure Lodge, 222–3
South Luangwa Natl. Park, 593–5

South Pare Mountains, 392–3
Special Tours & Travel, 25
Splendid Hotel, 184, 186
sports (*see also* Hunting; Fishing;
    Mountain climbing; Water
    sports), 8
  Ethiopia, 473
  Kenya, 138–9
Sportsman's Arms Hotel, 252
Stag's Head Hotel, 229
State Travel Service, 326
steinbuck (steinbok), 432, 602
Subzali Tours & Safaris, 330
Sukuma, 431
Sumbu Natl. Park, 541, 617–19
Sun 'n Sand Hotel, 205–6
Sun Sea & Safari, 52, 100
Sundowner Tours, 25
suni, 668
Sunny Safaris, 113
Sunshine Holidays, 100
Swan (W.F. & R.K.) (Hellenic),
    25–6
swimming, 56, 57
Sykes Travel Agents, 326

Taita Hills, 224–5
Taita Hills Game Lodge, 224, 225
Takim's Agencies, 326
Tana River Camps, 237–8
Tanga, 330, 333, 404–5
Tanga Hotel, 405
Tanga Touring Service, 330
Tanzanair, 327
Tanzania
    Friendship Tourist Bureau, 330,
        361
    Tours Ltd., 330, 331
    Wildlife Safaris, 342
    Zambia Railway, 325, 549
Tanzania, Republic of (*see also*
    names, places, subjects), 1,
    306–439
  accommodations, 314–15
  air travel: in, 326–7; to, 322–3
  airports, 323–4
  banks, 334–5
  beach resorts, 313, 416–18
  birdwatching, *see* Birds and bird-
    watching

Tanzania, Republic of (*cont'd*)
  boats to, 324
  books to read, 317–18
  buses: in, 328; to, 325
  business hours, 334
  camping, *see* Camping and camp-
    sites
  car rental, 322, 328–9
  currency, 72, 312, 321
  customs regulations, 320–1
  diplomatic missions: in, 335; of,
    320
  driving: in, 321–2, 329–30; to,
    325–6
  electricity, 334
  entry requirements, 319–22
  firearms, 322
  fishing, 341–2
  game and wildlife parks, 312–14,
    338–40
  getting around, 326–33
  getting to, 322–6
  hunting ban, 142, 342
  health, 335
  historic, prehistoric sites, 340
  history, 305–11
  holidays, 334
  information sources, 317–19, 354,
    375, 383
  itinerary, individual, 28–30
  language, 334
  length of stays, 313–14
  mail, telegrams, 336
  maps, 9–10, 316–17
  newspapers, 318
  photo safaris, 342
  pronunciation of name, 63
  routes: T-1: Serengeti–
    Ngorongoro–Lake Manyara–
    Arusha, 362–83; T-2: Arusha–
    Namanga, Kenya, 384–5; T-3:
    Arusha–Moshi–Dar es Salaam,
    385–95; T-4: Moshi–Kiliman-
    jaro (Marangu)–Taveta, Kenya,
    395–403; T-5: Lunga Lunga,
    Kenya–Tanga–junction with
    Arusha–Dar es Salaam high-
    way, 403–6; T-6: Dar es
    Salaam–Mikumi–Iringa–
    Mbeya–Tunduna–Zambia, 406–

Tanzania, Republic of (*cont'd*)
14; T-7: Dar es Salaam–beach
hotels–Bagamoyo, 414–20; T-8:
Arusha–Tarangire–Dodoma–
Iringa, 420–8; T-9: Seronera,
Serengeti–Fort Ikoma–Lake
Victoria–Lake Tanganyika–
Gombe Stream, 428–35
shopping, 67, 68–9, 336–8, 355–6,
359, 383
taxis, 354, 383
telephones, 336
time, 334
tour and safari operators and
package tours, 330–3
tourism offices, 315–16
trains: in, 328; to, 325
vehicle documents, 321–2
visa, 62, 93, 319–20
visitor's pass, 319–20
vital statistics, 311–12
water sports, 341–2
weather, 315
weights and measures, 334
what to see and do, 312–13
when to go, 315, 361, 369, 376,
380, 389, 395, 402, 409, 422,
427
Tanzanite Hotel, 387
Tarangire Natl. Park, 312, 313,
420–2
Tarangire Safari Camp, 422
Taveta, 224
taxis
Ethiopia, 486, 522
Kenya, 104, 168, 187
Malawi, 651
Tanzania, 354, 383
Zambia, 570
tipping, 74–5
tea growing, 84, 286–7
Tea Hotel, 287
TEJ Processing Center, 49
telegrams, 129, 336, 469, 558, 641
Teleki Hut, 250
telephones, 129–30, 336, 469, 558–9,
641
Tembo Tours & Safaris, 113–14
theater, *see* Cinemas; Nightlife,
entertainment

Thiba Fishing Camp, 259
Thika, 236–7
Thomas Hunter & Co., 550
Thomson's Falls, 84, 263–5
Thomson's Falls Lodge, 264
Thorn Tree Safaris, 112, 114, 330
Thru the Lens Tours, 26
Thyolo, 664–5
tiang, 531
Tic-Air, 100
Tim Air Charters, 327
Timbwani Camping Site, 185
time, 126, 334, 466, 556, 639
tipping, 74–5
Tissisat Falls, 446, 490, 491
Tonga, 615
Tongoni, 405–6
Topi, 232, 267, 366, 414
tortoise, 526
Tot Rest House, 292
Touring Hotel: Axum, 515; Makelle,
507
tours, individual
drive yourself, 30–4
itinerary, planning, 28–30
package (FIT), 2–3
safaris, luxury, 30
agencies and operators, 14–28, 46–
53, 112–14, 330, 459–60, 554
tours, package
booking, 13
camping, 109–10
clothing and sundries, 55
costs, 3, 13, 14–28, 46–54
East Africa, 120–2
Ethiopia, 459–64
group, 2, 14–28, 46–52
group inclusive (GITs), 50
individual, foreign (FITs), 2–3
insurance, 60
Kenya, 112–22, 333
length, *see* Length of stays
local, 13
Malawi, 637–8
"meet the people," 7
overland expeditions, 46–52
safari, 3–4, 7–8
Tanzania, 330–3
three continents, 15
tipping, 75

tours, package (*cont'd*)
  unusual, 13: from U.S., 14–28
  walking safari, 3, 8
  Zambia, 554–6
Trade Winds Hotel, 223
Trail Finders Ltd., 48
train travel, 8
  Ethiopia: in, 456–7; to, 454
  Kenya: in, 102–3; to, 97–8
  Malawi: in, 635; to, 631–2
  Tanzania: in, 328; to, 59, 325
  Zambia: in, 552; to, 549
Trans-Africa Guides, 112
transportation, *see* Getting to . . . ;
  specific mode of transportation
Travcoa, 26–7
travel agents (*see also* Safaris; Tour,
  package; names)
  in Ethiopia, 455
  in Kenya, 99–100
  in Malawi, 633
  in Tanzania, 326
  in Zambia, 550
travel arrangements (*see also* spe-
  cific forms of transportation),
  2–4, 13
Travel Bureau, 114
traveler's checks, 72, 94
Travelers Inn, 393
Travellers Ltd., 550
Travelworld, 27
Treetops, 83, 85, 241, 243
Tsavo
  Inn, 199
  Natl. Park (Tsavo East; Tsavo
    West), 83, 85, 135, 137, 192–9
  Tsafaris (Cottars Camp), 198
Tudor House Hotel, 184
Turkana, 266
Turnbull Gibson & Co., 550
Turtle Bay Hotel, 210
Twiga Hotel, 350, 353
Twiga Lodge, 222
Two Fishes Hotel, 223

Ufficio Viaggi, 461
Uganda
  itinerary, individual, 28–30
  maps, 9–10
  visas, 93

United Bus Co., 325
United Bus Co. of Zambia, 553
United European American Club,
  51–2
United Kenya Club, 158–9
United States Customs regulations,
  69–70
United Touring, 104, 112, 114, 460,
  633
  International, 27–8
United Transport (Malawi), 632,
  635
Usambara Mountains, 313, 393
Uwanda Game Reserve, 414
Uwanjani Hotel, 362

vaccinations, 55–6
Verheye's (Pierre C.T.)
  Adventureland Safaris, 24
Victoria Falls
  Casino-Hotel, 580
  Hotel, 580–1
  Travel Bureau, 550
Victoria Falls region, 541, 542, 560,
  570–6, 581–3
  Field Museum, 575
Victoria House, 362
Village Dancers Hotel, 240
Vipya Plateau, 680
visas, 62–3
  Ethiopia, 62, 450
  Kenya, 62, 92–3
  Tanzania, 93, 319–20
  Uganda, 93
  Zambia, 545–6
volcanic areas
  Ethiopia, 527
  Kenya, 194, 195, 196, 266, 274,
    276
  Tanzania, 373, 374–6, 387–9,
    396–402

Wabe Shebelle Hotel, 481, 484, 485
walking safari, 3, 8
Waitos, 490–1
Walia ibex, 473, 507–8
Wambwera, 438
warthog
  Ethiopia, 526, 533
  Kenya, 241, 300, 301–2

warthog (*cont'd*)
  Malawi, 625, 668
  Tanzania, 388, 409, 425
  Zambia, 578, 593, 617
Watamu Beach Club Center, 210–11
Watamu Marine Natl. Park, 84, 85,
    139, 209–11
water, drinking, 56–7
water sports, 8
  Ethiopia, 473, 533
  Kenya, 138, 139–40
  swimming, 56, 57
  Tanzania, 340–1
waterbuck
  Ethiopia, 531
  Kenya, 222, 224, 241, 277–8,
    290, 300
  Malawi, 667
  Tanzania, 374, 375, 388, 409, 425,
    431
  Zambia, 593, 602, 617
weather (*see also* When to visit), 6
  Ethiopia, 447–8
  Kenya, 88
  Malawi, 626
  Tanzania, 315
  Zambia, 543
weights and measures, 126, 334, 466,
    556, 639
  metric conversion, 126
Welwello Hotel, 517
Westwood Park Country Club,
    155–6, 160, 170
what to see and do (*see also* names,
    places, subjects), 6, 7–8
  how long to stay, *see* Length of
    stays
  Ethiopia, 446–7
  Kenya, 83–5
  Malawi, 625
  Tanzania, 312–13
  Zambia, 541–2
when to go, 6, 14
  Ethiopia, 447–8, 493, 498, 504,
    507, 508, 515, 524, 526, 530,
    532, 534
  Kenya, 88, 197, 210, 227, 232,
    242, 249, 255, 258, 262, 268,
    272, 278, 303

when to go (*cont'd*)
  Malawi, 626
  Tanzania, 315, 361, 369, 376, 380,
    389, 395, 402, 409, 422, 427
  Zambia, 543, 583, 594, 603, 618
where to stay, *see* Accommodations;
    place names; names of hotels,
    etc.
Whispering Palms Hotel, 205
White Horse Inn, 425
White Hotel, 520
White Rhino Hotel, 239–40
Whitesands Hotel & Lido, 204
wild dog, 374, 593, 601
wild pig, 534
wildebeest
  Kenya, 231, 300
  Tanzania, 364, 367, 374, 375,
    394, 409, 431
  Zambia, 593, 599, 602
Wilderness Expeditions, 28
Wilderness Trails, 112
wildlife, *see* Birds and birdwatching;
    Game and wildlife parks; names
    of animals
Wildlife Lodges/Kenya Hotels, 87
Wollisso (Ghion), 446
World Travel Consultants, 28

Ya Bwawani, Hoteli, 361–2
Yatta Plateau, 196
Yeha, 447, 516
Yellow Bird Safaris, 112, 114
YMCA: Dar es Salaam, 351; Moshi,
    391, 401–2; Nairobi, 159
youth
  documents, 63
  fares, 51
  hitchhiking, 48–9
  hostels, 252, 273–4, 289, 290, 391
YWCA: Kisumu, 288; Nairobi, 159

Zamair, 552
Zambesi
  Motel, 269
  Travel Bureau, 550
  River Transport, 552
Zambia Airways, 548, 551, 634
Zambia Natl. Tourist Bureau, 543

Zambia, Republic of (*see also*
names, places, subjects), 2,
536–620
accommodations, 542–3
air travel: in, 551–2; to, 547–9
airline offices, 551
airports, 548–9
banks, 557
birdwatching (*see also* Birds and
birdwatching), 561
boats: in, 552, 578; to, 549
books to read, 544–5
buses: in, 553; to, 549–50
business hours, 557
car rentals, 553–4
currency, 540–1, 547
customs regulations, 546–7
diplomatic missions: in, 557–8; of,
546
driving: in, 547, 554; to, 550
electricity, 557
entry requirements, 545–7
firearms, 547
fishing, 562
game and wildlife parks, 541, 542,
560–1
getting around, 550–6
getting to, 547–50
historic, prehistoric sites, 561–2
history, 536–40
holidays, 557
hunting, 542, 562
information sources, 544–5, 561–
2, 570, 575, 583
itinerary, individual, 28–30
language, 556
length of stays, 541–2
mail, telegrams, 558
maps, 544
newspapers, 545
pronunciation of name, 63
routes: Z-1: (Great North Road)
Tunduma, Tanzania–Mkike–
Kapiri Mposhi–Kabwe–Lusaka–
Chirundu, Rhodesia, 584–91;
Z-2: (Great East Road)
Lusaka–Luangwa Valley–
Chipata–Malawi, 591–8; Z-3:
Lusaka–Livingstone–Victoria

Zambia, Republic of (*cont'd*)
Falls, 598–601; Z-4: Lusaka–
Blue Lagoon–Kafue Natl.
Park–Mongu, 601–6; Z-5:
Lusaka–Copperbelt–Zaire, 606–
14; Z-6: Lusaka–Siavonga–
Kariba Dam–Rhodesia, 614–17;
Z-7: Tunduma, Tanzania–
Mbala–Lake Tanganyika–
Kalambo Falls, 617–20
shopping, 68, 559–60, 571
taxis, 570
telephones, 558
time, 556
tourism authority, 543–4
tours, package, 554–6
trains: in, 552; to, 549
travel agents in, 550
vehicle documents, 547
visa, 545–6
vital statistics, 540
weather, 543
weights and measures, 556
what to see and do, 541–2
when to go, 543, 583, 594, 603,
618
Zanji Safaris, 112
Zanzibar, 313, 314, 330, 356–8
accommodations, 361–2
Island, 359–61
Town, 359
transportation, 361
when to go, 361
Zanzibar Hotel, 362
Zawi Hill Rock Paintings, 596
zebra
Ethiopia, 526, 531, 534
Kenya, 84, 136, 142, 193, 197,
231, 246, 254, 261, 265, 267,
300
Malawi, 625, 654, 657
Tanzania, 364, 367–8, 374, 375,
392, 394, 409, 412, 414, 425,
431
Zambia, 578, 593, 599, 601, 603
Zomba, 625, 661
Govt. Hostel, 663
Plateau, 625, 662–3
Zwai Bekele Molla Hotel, 534–5

75 76 77 78 10 9 8 7 6 5 4 3 2 1

MILES KILOMETERS TABLE

1 Kilometer equals ⅝ mile

1	2	3	4	5	6	7	8	9	10
1.6	3.2	4.8	6.4	8.1	9.7	11.3	12.9	14.5	16.1
11	12	13	14	15	16	17	18	19	20
17.7	19.3	20.9	22.5	24.1	25.8	27.4	29.0	30.6	32.2
21	22	23	24	25	26	27	28	29	30
33.8	35.4	37.0	38.6	40.2	41.8	43.5	45.1	46.7	48.3
31	32	33	34	35	36	37	38	39	40
49.9	51.5	53.1	54.7	56.3	57.9	59.6	61.2	62.8	64.4
41	42	43	44	45	46	47	48	49	50
66.0	67.6	69.2	70.8	72.4	74.0	75.6	77.3	78.9	80.5
51	52	53	54	55	56	57	58	59	60
82.1	83.7	85.3	86.9	88.5	90.1	91.7	93.3	95.0	96.6
61	62	63	64	65	66	67	68	69	70
98.2	99.8	101.4	103.0	104.6	106.2	107.8	109.4	111.1	111.7
71	72	73	74	75	76	77	78	79	80
114.3	115.9	117.5	119.1	120.7	122.3	123.9	125.5	127.1	128.8
81	82	83	84	85	86	87	88	89	90
130.4	132.0	133.6	135.2	136.8	138.4	140.0	141.6	143.2	144.9
91	92	93	94	95	96	97	98	99	100
146.4	148.1	149.7	151.3	152.9	154.5	156.1	157.7	159.3	160.9
200	300	400	500	600	700	800	900	1000	2000
322	483	644	804	965	1,126	1,287	1,448	1,609	3,218

Miles
Kilometers

CURRENCY CONVERSION TABLE

U.S. dollars to East African shillings (separate, officially equal shilling currencies of Kenya, Tanzania, and Uganda)

7c −/50	14c 1/−	28c 2/−	42c 3/−	56c 4/−
70c 5/−	84c 6/−	98c 7/−	$1.12 8/−	$1.26 9/−
$1.40 10/−	$2.10 15/−	$2.80 20/−	$3.50 25/−	$4.20 30/−
$4.90 35/−	$5.60 40/−	$6.30 45/−	$7.00 50/−	$8.40 60/−
$9.80 70/−	$11.20 80/−	$12.60 90/−	$14.00 100/−	$17.50 125/−
$21.00 150/−	$28.00 200/−	$35.00 250/−	$70.00 500/−	$140.00 1,000/−

$1.00 equals 7.14 shillings
20 shillings equal 1/−

Shillings Dollars